Converting Content for Web Publishing:
Time-Saving Tools and Techniques

Janine Warner
Ken Milburn
Jessica Burdman

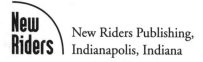
New Riders Publishing,
Indianapolis, Indiana

Converting Content for Web Publishing

By Janine Warner, Ken Milburn, and Jessica Burdman

Published by:
New Riders Publishing
201 West 103rd Street
Indianapolis, IN 46290 USA

Copyright © 1996 by New Riders Publishing

Printed in the United States of America 1 2 3 4 5 6 7 8 9 0

Images and text reprinted with permission from the *Point Reyes Light* newpaper: http://www.ptreyeslight.com

Library of Congress Cataloging-in-Publication Data

```
Burdman, Jessica R.
   Conversion techniques for Web publishing/Jessica
Burdman, Ken Milburn, Janine Warner.
      p.   cm.
   Includes index.
   ISBN 1-56205-685-9
   1. File conversion (Computer science) 2. Web
publishing.
   I. Milburn, Ken, 1935-    . II. Warner, Janine,
   1967-    .
   III. Title.
QA76.9.F48B86   1996
005.74--dc20                              96-38616
                                              CIP
```

Warning and Disclaimer

Publisher Don Fowley

Publishing Manager Julie Fairweather

Marketing Manager Mary Foote

Managing Editor Carla Hall

Acquisitions Editor
Sean Angus

Development Editor
Christopher Cleveland

Project Editor
Sarah Kearns

Copy Editors
Gina Brown
Malinda McCain

Technical Editors
Jessica Burdman
Randall Potts

Associate Marketing Manager
Tamara Apple

Acquisitions Coordinator
Tracy Turgeson

Administrative Coordinator
Karen Opal

Cover Designers
Karen Ruggles
Sandra Schroeder

Cover Production
Aren Howell

Book Designers
Gary Adair
Sandra Schroeder

Production Manager
Kelly Dobbs

Production Team Supervisor
Laurie Casey

Graphics Image Specialists
Stephen Adams
Debra Bolhuis
Kevin Cliburn

Production Analyst
Jason Hand

Production Team
Heather Butler, Cindy Fields,
Christopher Morris,
Eric Puckett, Beth Rago,
Daniela Raderstorf,
Elizabeth San Miguel

Indexer
Christopher Cleveland

About the Authors

Janine Warner is a freelance writer, author, and the owner of Vision Communication Technologies, an Internet Design company in Northern California. She has developed more than a dozen Web sites, often coordinating teams of graphic designers, programmers, editors, and HTML developers. Janine's company's Web projects have involved setting up secure commerce servers, animated graphics, interactive forms, and other advanced features. Clients include Doonesbury, Century Theaters, Investor's Edge, The Microprocessor Report, ConnectMedia, The Oracle Review, the *Coastal Traveler*, and the Pulitzer Prize-winning *Point Reyes Light* newspaper. She has also taught HTML and other computer-related courses at several private companies.

Janine earned a degree in Journalism and Spanish at the University of Massachusetts and worked for more than eight years as a reporter and managing editor at several California newspapers. Her articles and reviews of HTML authoring tools have appeared in *Publish* and *Digital Video* magazines. Janine is also the co-author of *Hybrid HTML Design: A Multibrowser HTML Reference*, New Riders, May 1996. For more about Vision Communication Technologies, direct your browser to http://www.visiontec.com/.

Ken Milburn's passions are computer graphics and photography. He started his post-college career as a freelance photographer, specializing in glamour and travel. Since 1981, he has been consulting on, writing about, and doing creative work with personal computer based graphics, design, and multimedia. Ken's writing experience includes two feature-length screenplays, a stint as contributing editor for *Whole Earth Software Review*, and several years as lead graphics reviewer for *InfoWorld*.

Since then, over 250 of Ken's articles and reviews on computer graphics and multimedia have appeared in such nationally renowned publications as *InfoWorld*, *PC World*, *MacWeek*, *Mac User*, *Popular Computing*, *PCComputing*, *Computer Graphics World*, *Publish Magazine*, and *Windows Magazine*. He's also written columns for *Microtimes* and *Computer Currents*.

In the meantime, Ken has maintained his interest in photography and art. A second career in photodigital illustration work has been developing for the past three years. His illustrations have been sold to such clients as *Multimedia Live!*, *Computer Artist Magazine*, and *Me!dia Magazine*. Examples of his work have been selected to be shown on the CD-ROMs for Fractal Design's Painter 4.0 and Movie Works 2.0. The Ventana Press desktop publishing design guide "Looking Good in Color" by Gary Preister also features his work in its gallery section. Seven one-man shows have exhibited at The Anon Salon in San Francisco, The Mill Valley Film Festival Multimedia Fest, the NBMA Electronic Picnic, and at several Bay-area restaurants and coffee houses.

Jessica Burdman is a Web site designer, business analyst, and technical editor. As lead production manager at Aslan Computing, she has created complex interactive sites for leading technology clients such as Netscape, NetFRAME Systems, and Whitetree Inc. Prior to joining Aslan Computing, she worked as a technical editor for Genentech Inc., where she edited several pharmaceutical books and papers, including *Vaccine Design*, published by Plenum Publishing in 1994.

Jessica has a Master's degree in creative writing and has taught both creative and technical writing at San Francisco State University. Her own work has been published in numerous literary magazines for which she has won several awards, including the Sara DeFord Prize for Creative Writing, The Anne Fields Poetry Prize, and the Lizzette Woodworth Reese Award for Excellence in Writing.

Trademark Acknowledgments

Acknowledgments

Janine's Acknowledgments

I want to start by thanking both of my co-authors for their humor, hard work, and dedication to this project. Thanks for making me laugh when I wanted to scream and for helping me keep my sanity when I needed someone to talk to at 2 a.m. I can't tell you how fortunate I feel that you both helped me write this book (even if you didn't know what you were getting yourselves into).

To Ken, thanks for being one of my closest and dearest friends, for sharing your insights and wisdom, and for all the great hugs!

To Jessica, thanks for making me laugh at the ridiculousness of life and of the techy world we have come to live in, for inspiring me to take better care of my body, and for juggling all your clients and still making your deadlines on this book.

I want to thank my first co-author, Kevin Ready, with whom I wrote *Hybrid HTML Design*, for helping me get my start in the publishing world and encouraging me to go on to write another book.

Thanks to my incredible mother, Malinda McCain, who finally "officially" copyedited my work after contributing to my writing "unofficially" for so many years. I feel very fortunate to have a mother who is not only my great friend, but also a talented colleague. Everyone at the publishing company raves about you and thanks me for bringing you to New Riders. I also want to thank her partner, Janice Webster, for being supportive of both of us and so interested in what I'm doing.

Thanks to my dad, Robin Warner, for encouraging me to start my own business and bragging about me at the office. I hope you get to use this book in your work now that you are helping people set up servers and Web sites. Thanks to Helen Welford, his delightful wife, for all her love and support. And thanks to my Grandfather Warner, who helped me have confidence in my intelligence and ability to succeed.

Thanks to Kim Ladin, Web designer extraordinaire, for her contributions to this book in the BeyondPress and BBEdit sections. After using those programs heavily for so many conversions for LAN Times, she had much to offer to those chapters. Thanks also to Sheila Castelli for being such a great colleague, adding her favorite URLs to the Web resources appendix, and having such great dinner parties.

A special thanks to Francisco Rivera, my colleague and friend who brings such hot graphics and animations to my Web sites and is always so calm and mellow under pressure. Thanks for working extra hard to help me keep all our clients happy while I was writing this book.

Thanks to my favorite journalism professors, Norm Sims and Karen List, who continue to be supportive instructors and great resources in my life. Rest assured, I still want to go to graduate school—it's just that my business and books are getting in the way these days. Thanks again to David Mitchell, the publisher of the *Point Reyes Light* newspaper, one of my closest friends and greatest mentors.

And finally, thanks to Brett Phaneuf, one of my dearest friends from college, for taking me away to Spain and Morocco for a few weeks after I finished this book.

Contents at a Glance

Table of Contents

2 Design Considerations for the Web   17

7 FrameMaker Conversion   237

8 PageMaker Conversion   267

9 PDF (Portable Document Format) Files   285

10 Graphics Basics   319

13 Tailoring Converted Files 461

14: HTML Tutorial and Reference   529

CHAPTER 1

Introduction

In the days of print, production schedules revolved around the time it took for layout and paste up, the time constraints of getting information to a printer, and finally the delays of physically delivering newspapers or magazines to readers. On the Web, you don't have those delays, so people think information should be available immediately. Now, all the pressure falls on the Web designer—you can't blame the printer or the delivery truck; you are always expected get information online quickly. But much of the content you're expected to get on the Web was designed for print, so it comes to you as word processing files, spreadsheets, desktop publishing files, and large, high-resolution images. This book is designed to help you do the impossible—convert those files quickly and get them on the Web before your clients or boss complain that you're taking too long.

Who Should Read This Book

This book is for anyone working on the World Wide Web who is challenged with the task of converting information designed for print into HTML pages and graphics that will look good on a Web site.

Most Web designers, whether they work on the Internet or an internal intranet, are challenged with the task of converting text and graphics from a myriad of programs. Whether you work for a publication or a large corporation, or serve small business clients, this book is designed to meet your needs. You'll find solutions to your problems if you work with any of the following software:

- Microsoft Office
- ClarisWorks
- WordPerfect
- Most other word processing programs
- Spreadsheets such as Excel and Lotus
- QuarkXPress
- PageMaker
- FrameMaker

- Photoshop
- Illustrator
- Many other graphics programs

This book will teach you the most effective and efficient ways of transforming content from all these programs into a format that will work on the Web—and it won't stop there. The goal is to take the time and tedium out of conversion so you'll have time to focus on beautiful designs.

Taking the Tedium Out of HTML Conversion

Many books can teach you the HyperText Markup Language (HTML), but they are all designed with the expectation that you are creating the content and then placing the HTML code around it. This book is written with the understanding that most people who do Web development are creating Web pages based on words and graphics created and formatted in another program first.

Converting Content for Web Publishing was developed by three experienced HTML designers who have faced these problems and spent considerable time learning to handle the issues of content and graphics conversion. As we go through the source programs and formats, we use real case studies, demonstrating techniques and workarounds we have developed for the actual files submitted to us by clients. We never use documents created by a software company to show how easy their conversion program is to use. Instead, we have intentionally selected files that include the most difficult design issues—sidebars, columnar text, and large, high-resolution graphics—to help you learn the best ways to tackle the problems faced by HTML designers.

Case Studies: Three Web Design Companies Featured

To illustrate the techniques in this book, we've chosen three Web design companies to provide case studies. Each company submitted files from programs such as QuarkXPress and Microsoft Word that were difficult to convert. You will find these documents on the book's accompanying CD-ROM, so you can follow along with the tutorials while using the same materials. We selected these companies because they do so much content conversion and receive documents created in a variety of word processing, spreadsheet, desktop publishing, and graphics programs.

Aslan Computing, http://www.aslaninc.com/

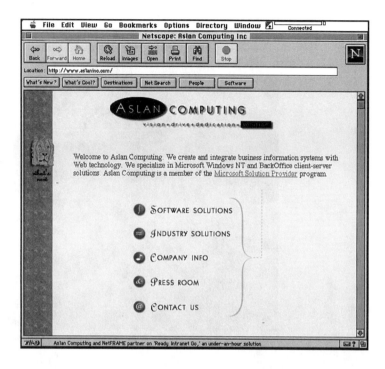

Aslan Computing creates and integrates business information systems with the World Wide Web, specializing in Microsoft Windows NT and Microsoft BackOffice client-server technology. Aslan is a member of the Microsoft Solution Provider program. The company offers a customized package of Internet, intranet, and client/server information systems services that integrate Web technology with BackOffice functions to enable a new generation of proactive business processes. Clients of Aslan include Netscape Communications, Whitetree, Inc., Netframe Systems, Intel Corporation, Microsoft Consulting Services, Tri-Valley Growers of Northern California, Nicholas Applegate Capital Management, Syntex Corporation, and Genentech, Inc. Jessica Burdman, who is a co-author of this book, is a partner in Aslan.

Investor's Edge, http://www.irnet.com/

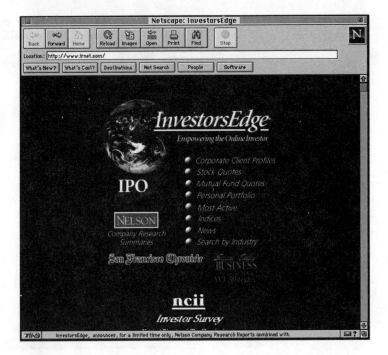

Investor's Edge was created by Ethos Corporation in April, 1995. Their vision was to create a site on the World Wide Web that would not only offer up-to-the-minute financial information, but would also act as a forum where publicly traded companies could present their corporate financial information. Today the Web site attracts more than one million hits each week and features information on every publicly traded company in America. Corporate partners include Microsoft, Hewlett Packard, Nelson Publications, and Data Broadcasting Corp.

Vision Communication Technologies, http://www.visiontec.com/

Vision Communication Technologies has contributed to more than a dozen commercial Web sites, including the Doonesbury Web site, the Pulitzer prize-winning *Point Reyes Light* newspaper, and the Microdesign Resources Microprocessor Report. Working for a variety of clients has required Vision Communication Technologies to handle content from a myriad of programs on both the Mac and PC, and to create Web sites for Mac, Windows, and Unix Web servers. Vision Communication Technologies was founded by author Janine Warner.

To Convert or Not to Convert

There has been considerable controversy in the industry about whether existing content should be converted for the Web or whether designers should start over from scratch. Many argue that print and the Internet are radically different and require distinct design approaches and philosophies. While this is unquestionably true, it is important to find efficient ways to use existing information. And realistically, most of us don't have time to start over. This book does not suggest simply throwing brochures and newsletters up on the Web. The goal is to teach you how to get the content you need out of its original format quickly and efficiently, so you can focus your energy and creativity on making that content look great on the Web, transforming the converted information into something that does work well in this new medium.

Beyond HTML

This book recognizes that good Web design requires more than simply converting files designed for print into HTML. It goes well beyond the best conversion methods to demonstrate how to tailor converted files and put them together to create intuitive and dynamic Web sites. You'll learn how to handle content in a wide variety of formats, from word processing files to spreadsheets to desktop publishing programs. You'll examine how to use the latest tools, such as BeyondPress from Astrobyte, a QuarkXPress converter that takes the tedium out of XPress conversion, and DeBabelizer, which can batch-convert images and make them load as fast as possible without losing too much quality. You'll learn the best ways to handle tricky formatting issues such as sidebars and columnar data. Finally, you'll explore alternatives to HTML, such as Portable Document Formats (PDFs) and Microsoft Office viewers (especially useful on intranets).

HTML Review

At the end of this book, you'll find an HTML reference and tutorial, covering all the HTML 2.0 and 3.2 tags, as well as the Netscape and Microsoft extensions commonly used on the Web. This is included as a reference for those who are familiar with HTML, and serves as an introduction for those who may be new to Web design. If you've never done HTML before, you may want to read that chapter first. If you're familiar with the language already, you'll find it an excellent reference for any unfamiliar tags or a good place to double-check your knowledge as you go through the lessons in the rest of the book.

Why I Wanted to Write This Book

When I began doing Web site design, one of my first clients was Investor's Edge, a Web site company that provided stock market information and gained early attention for setting up a database-generated Web site with a live stockfeed, updated every 15 minutes. They were on the cutting edge, attracting hundreds of thousands of hits every day, and I was excited to land the job. Unfortunately, my work with them was not so glamorous. I was charged with converting corporate annual reports from QuarkXPress into HTML. It was valuable information for an investor, but tedious work for a starry-eyed newbie Web designer.

The annual reports were huge files designed for print, so the first thing I did was buy a Zip drive for copying the files to take home to work on. I'd stop by the Investor's Edge office, copy an 80 megabyte file (complete with high-resolution graphics) onto a Zip disk, and take it back to my PowerMac. There I would painstakingly clip the text out of QuarkXPress, paste it into my favorite HTML editor (World Wide Web Weaver), and reformat it with HTML tags. After hours of manual coding, I still had to convert all the graphics, first opening them in Photoshop to reduce the size and number of colors, and then taking them into GIFConverter to interlace them so they would load more smoothly.

The worst part—the absolutely worst part—was formatting the pages of financial data that came in each report. This consisted of pages and pages of columnar data—numbers that had to be carefully aligned in <PRE> text in HTML because it was the only option at the time (this was before HTML tables were common on the Web). This meant setting the <PRE> and close </PRE> tags on each side of the table and manually typing a tab next to each item in each column. Hundreds and hundreds—make that thousands—of times I hit that tab key. I got very fast, but it was still a mind-numbing process and was generally best done with good music and any other distractions I could find that didn't impact my dexterity too much.

When I was finished, I had turned that 80 megabyte QuarkXPress file into something that fit on a floppy disk and worked on the Windows NT server they used (you have to love the Mac for taking things cross-platform). Each of those annual report conversions took about eight hours. It was, and still is, the most boring thing I have ever done on the Web. But it was a long time ago in Web years, and if one dog year equals seven human years, one Web year equals 10.

Thank the Electronic Gods and Goddesses of the world, things have changed. If you're still doing anything remotely like what I just described, you're going to love this book. Never again will you have to clip text out of XPress and convert graphics one at time. And I promise you won't be hitting that tab key thousands of times, either.

I wanted to write this book to save other Web designers the grief I suffered in those early days. I'm fortunate to come from a background as a journalist, so I figured out early on how to get paid to write software reviews and at the same time stay up to date on the latest tools of the trade. The hours of research I had to do to keep up with the best technology became the other part of my fledgling business, as I split my time between freelance writing and Web design. I was fortunate to attract increasingly interesting clients, and I discovered many tricks for converting content as efficiently as possible so I could focus my time on making Web sites look good. I found I could tailor the results of conversion programs, and use these new tools to work quickly and efficiently so I'd still have time for good design.

In this book, with the help of my co-authors Ken Milburn and Jessica Burdman, I'll show you the coolest tricks, how to use the best and newest programs, and how to take the tedium out of Web site conversion and design.

File Format Conversion: The Challenges Facing Web Designers

When I write Web design proposals, I always include an assumption section in which I tell my clients that I expect to get their information in digital format. I don't like to type—and I tell my clients that they don't want to pay my rates for typing. But to avoid that tedious task, I must be ready to receive content in any digital format they throw at me.

Those of us in the computer industry spend considerable time arguing that there should be standards, but in reality, people are using many different programs to create materials for print. As a result, you are going to receive material in a variety of formats. As a Web designer, you can expect to get files in any of a half dozen or so word processing programs, in at least three different desktop publishing programs, and in a variety of graphics programs, such as Photoshop—and then there's the spreadsheet category. Oh, and don't forget that not everyone uses a PC (or a Mac).

If you can't handle this variety, you'll be limited in your work. You can always take the printed copy and retype it and then design it in HTML, but you'll be wasting your time, and you'll have trouble making it in this increasingly competitive market. Ideally, you should have a Mac and a PC and all the programs you might get files in, but that isn't practical, or affordable, for everyone. In addition, therefore, to looking at all these programs individually, we'll introduce you to software solutions such as Adobe's File Utilities, explained in Chapter 5, which can help you convert files from a myriad of word processing formats into a format you can read with whatever software you already have. Because almost no one can afford all the software and hardware they want (there's always another program or gadget on the list), this book also includes alternatives to make that unnecessary.

Cross-Platform Issues with Conversion

After you've figured out how to convert files, you still may run into problems if you have to take them from one platform to another. Thus, we'll also teach you about naming structures and conversion issues that have to do with moving Web sites from the Mac to the PC or Unix, or vice versa. One of the greatest features of HTML is its universality, and if they're designed properly, the same HTML files can work on all these platforms. Because the goal is always to make things fast on the Web, HTML files and graphics are small and easy to move around. It's the original content designed for print that causes the biggest problems in terms of compatibility and large file sizes, but we'll give you some tips there, as well.

Limitations of the Web: How HTML Differs from Print

I hate to break this to you, but you just can't do in HTML much of what you can do in print. You can't use big, high-resolution images, and you can't have complete control over fonts and spacing (although that's improving). On the positive side, there are wonderful new features possible only on the Web—hyperlinked text, interaction, video, sound, and animations, to name a few. You need to understand up front, however, that print and the Web are radically different mediums.

Despite significant advances in the HTML authoring tools covered in this book, you do need at least a basic knowledge of HTML to practice good Web design and to understand many of the features and limitations of the available HTML authoring tools. That's why we've included an HTML tutorial and reference at the end of this book. HTML editors and converters are getting better and better at hiding code from you, but the conversion techniques described in this book will make a great deal more sense if you understand the basic features, limitations, and rules of HTML.

Planning Ahead and Working with Graphic Designers

If you have the luxury of working with the graphic designers who are creating the original content, or if you are so talented you are doing both creation and conversion yourself, you have a distinct advantage. Although this book is designed to help you deal with any form of content from any source, working with the original designers can help you make the entire process more efficient.

Many of the conversion programs treated in this book work best if you use consistent styles in programs such as XPress or FrameMaker. Similarly, if most of your content comes to you in a word processing format, consistency can again save you time in conversion. Good graphic designers usually follow consistent styles, but some of the most difficult content to handle was poorly designed for its original purpose, making it even harder to convert for the Web.

If you work for a magazine or other publication that produces similar kinds of content over and over, working with the graphic designers can help you develop systems to make conversion easier. Many of the new conversion programs will let you save the settings for future conversions, but this only works if things remain consistent. Similarly, if you spend time creating a macro for a word processing or spreadsheet conversion, you'll want to be able to use it for future work. If possible, talk through the potential problems with the original designers of the content—it could save hours of time later.

Conversion Utilities: What You'll Need

If you want to be able to efficiently convert content from many different programs and formats, you need a variety of software. A good conversion program will go a long way toward transforming your content, but you should still have an HTML editor to tailor the design after you finish converting.

> **Note** HTML conversion programs, such as BeyondPress or HTML Transit, are designed to batch process content from its original program (such as QuarkXPress, FrameMaker, or a word processor) into HTML and graphics formats for the Web. HTML Editors are designed to place HTML tags around content as it is being created, and can also be used to add tags to existing content or to change the format and design of pages that have been converted.

Similarly, you can convert all your graphics in Photoshop, but to get the best image quality at the best speed, you'll do better in a program such as DeBabelizer. This program is also great for converting many graphics at once. If you can't afford high-end graphics programs such as these, consider the helpful shareware and freeware utilities discussed in this book. They may be a little more cumbersome and tedious, but if price is your limitation, you'll appreciate the tips on great free software, shareware, and other programs included in Appendix B.

What This Book Covers

This book is designed to teach you how to handle content in every format you are likely to receive it in. Drawing on the combined experience of the three authors of this book, each chapter covers a different aspect of conversion for the Web, and goes on to include chapters on Web site management, tailoring converted files, and an HTML tutorial and reference.

Chapter 2, "Design Considerations for the Web"

In Chapter 2, you'll learn about design considerations and how to get your mind set for working on the Web. This chapter is for those who have experience with print design, as well as those who are new to graphic design issues in general. We'll talk about what you can do in print that you can't do on the Web, and we'll get you started thinking about the great new features made possible by the Web.

The biggest difference between print and the Web is *hypertext*. The ability to hyperlink related information calls for an entirely new approach to design. Hyperlinks are a great way to include related information, such as a glossary, in a readily available manner, but hyperlinks can also be misused. This book will teach you about creating intuitive designs and giving users a variety of navigational options.

The book will look at how print issues relate to the Web; for example, text that is a great sidebar in print works well as a hyperlink to another page in HTML. We'll also talk about planning ahead and storyboarding (a process borrowed from the film world that involves outlining the flow of information before you design it) to help you organize content and ensure structure and systems to facilitate growth.

Chapter 3, "Microsoft Office Document Conversion"

Chapter 3 covers the Microsoft Office suite, a very popular program and one of the ways you're most likely to receive content. You'll learn how to use the Microsoft Internet Assistants for Word, Excel, and PowerPoint. These little add-ons are free to anyone who has these Microsoft products, and they work as both converters and simple HTML editors. As we teach you about the Office products, we'll also show you how to take advantage of the features included in the programs, such as sophisticated search and replace options. You'll also learn about special viewers for Word, Excel, and PowerPoint that enable you to put such files on a Web site without converting them to HTML. This is a particularly useful option on an intranet, where you have greater control over the kinds of helper applications your users will have available.

Chapter 4, "ClarisWorks and Corel WordPerfect Suite Document Conversion"

Chapter 4 discusses word processing programs in general, such as WordPerfect and ClarisWorks, and includes conversion tips for spreadsheet programs, such as Quattro Pro and ClarisWorks. You'll also learn about conversion utilities for spreadsheets and how to use a spreadsheet program to automate the conversion of the columnar text you might find in other programs, such as XPress.

Chapter 5, "Batch Conversion Utilities"

Chapter 5 covers batch converters for word processors and teaches you how to convert many files at once. This chapter also covers multiple file types, using programs such as Adobe File Utilities to convert documents from one word processing program to another. This is a great program for all those less popular programs, such as MacWrite or XYWrite, in which your clients may send you files. Using Adobe File Utilities, you can convert those files from more than 250 Mac, DOS, Windows, and Unix formats.

Chapter 5 also compares high-end and low-end batch converters, and teaches you how to set up custom templates for batch conversion. This chapter includes a great program called HTML Transit, designed to batch-convert huge word processing files from a number of programs. It also covers Web Publisher Pro.

Chapter 6, "QuarkXPress Conversion"

Chapter 6 gets into detail about the best ways to convert QuarkXPress documents. You'll learn a few tricks and shortcuts for manual conversion, but much of the chapter is dedicated to teaching you the ins and outs of BeyondPress, by far the best HTML conversion program found for any desktop publishing program. BeyondPress lets you map style sheets to HTML code, making quick and effective global changes possible. It converts text formatting (such as alignment, bold, and italics), enables you to create new pages to break up long documents, handles complex formatting issues such as sidebars, and even turns columnar text into HTML tables. But that's not all: the latest version offers advanced image-conversion options, turning high-resolution graphics into GIFs or JPEGs, setting transparency and interlacing, and scaling image size. Best of all, any of these features can be handled one at a time or set globally to convert all your images and text at once.

Chapter 7, "FrameMaker Conversion"

Chapter 7 covers converting FrameMaker documents with a focus on how to work with extremely large files. Again, in addition to looking at the manual conversion process and features built into FrameMaker, you'll learn how to use third-party programs, such as WebWorks Publisher and HTML Transit, designed to make FrameMaker conversion faster and easier. One advantage of using these programs is that when you set up a conversion, you can save it. Then, if you make further changes to the original FrameMaker document, you can simply run the conversion again to update the Web site.

Chapter 8, "PageMaker Conversion"

In Chapter 8, you'll learn about converting PageMaker documents. Unfortunately, Adobe's conversion program for PageMaker 6.0 is still limited, but you'll learn how to get the most out of it. You'll then learn the most efficient ways to do manual conversion, handle complex formatting issues in PageMaker, and use other programs, such as word processing converters, to supplement your efforts. .

Chapter 9, "PDF (Portable Document Format) Files"

Chapter 9 covers alternatives to HTML, with a look at how to create PDF documents. This chapter covers Adobe's Acrobat and demonstrates how using it is almost as easy as sending the file to print. This chapter also covers other portable document formats, such as Common Ground and Novell's Envoy. The problem with PDF files in the past was that they had to be completely downloaded before they could be viewed, and the user had to have a special viewer to see them. Now that Netscape Navigator and Microsoft's Internet Explorer offer better viewing options for PDF files, they have become an even better solution for preparing files for Internet/intranet use, especially for documents that must maintain exact formatting and are likely to be printed as well as viewed on a computer screen. PDF files are easier to create than HTML conversions and maintain complex formatting. Thus, they are especially useful for documents that must have precise design features or files you want to get on the Web quickly.

Chapters 10 and 11, "Graphics Basics" and "Graphics Creation"

Chapters 10 and 11 cover one of the most colorful aspects of Web design—graphics. These chapters will teach you to create GIFs and JPEGs, the two most widely supported image formats on the Web, and are full of great tips on how to make your images fast-loading and attractive. These chapters cover complex issues such as transparency and how to avoid the "halo" effect that results from dithering. You'll even get into some advanced Web techniques, such as creating animated GIFs. These chapters also provide some great tips for using complicated graphics programs in addition to coverage of Adobe's latest Photoshop 4.0 and an inside look at that wonderful, but complex, program, DeBabelizer.

Chapter 12, "Web Site Organization and Management"

Chapter 12 covers Web site organization and management. This is especially important as Web sites grow to include hundreds of files and other content from a variety of formats and designers. In this chapter, you'll learn how to set up multiple directories, organizing files to ensure that your Web site is easily expandable. You'll learn how to build Web sites conducive to growth and how early organization can save hours of frustrating reorganization later. You'll also learn how to use Web site management tools found in Adobe's SiteMill and Microsoft's FrontPage. With programs such as these, you can view an entire site in a graphic environment, correcting and changing links with drag-and-drop ease. For those of you who have already gotten well into a project before thinking about Web site management, you'll find a special section on creating order out of chaos—how to build in structure without breaking all your links.

In Chapter 12, you'll also learn about cross-platform issues. Web designers often receive content created for a specific platform and must (in addition to converting it to HTML) ensure it will work on a server on a different platform. Cross-platform issues include naming conventions and the file-name limitations of PC and Unix servers. You'll also get the first view of a great new utility called Rename! The File Name Enforcer, which can be used to change file names and ensure that they conform to the requirements of the server you use.

Chapter 13, "Tailoring Converted Files"

Chapter 13 is where you get into creating good designs and tailoring converted documents. Many conversion programs still lack the most sophisticated HTML features, such as tables and frames. These converters also offer limited control over image placement and other design options. In Chapter 13, you'll learn about HTML editors and how to use them to add advanced HTML tags and make up for other limitations of conversion programs. Also covered in this chapter are the attributes of good Web design, how to make links and other features intuitive for your users, and a few other little touches to make your Web sites shimmer.

Chapter 14, "HTML Tutorial and Reference"

Chapter 14 is an HTML tutorial and reference designed to provide everything you need to know about the current implementation of HTML, even if this is the first book you've ever bought on the subject. This step-by-step tutorial, complete with examples and illustrations, teaches you how to write HTML so you can better understand the programs and concepts in the rest of the book. This chapter also serves as a handy reference, listing all the HTML 2.0 and 3.2 tags and attributes, as well as common Netscape and Microsoft extensions. If you have questions about HTML tags or attributes as you go through the rest of the book, Chapter 14 provides an excellent reference on all the HTML tags you need to create beautiful and dynamic Web sites.

Appendices

This book also includes four appendices:

Appendix A, "Special Character Tags," is a helpful table that shows you how to insert special characters in your Web pages.

Appendix B, "Software Reference," provides a long list of software programs and utilities that can make Web work easier and more efficient. In this appendix, you'll find a description of each program, where you can find it on the Web, and why you'll want to use it.

Appendix C, "Online Resources for Web Developers," includes some of our favorite Web resources, including where to find other HTML design references and a list of places to download pre-made graphics and background images, Java applets, and Shockwave files. You'll also find references to CGI scripts and other programming resources.

Appendix D, "Putting a Web Site Online: FTP Software," includes valuable and necessary information on how to upload your HTML files to a Web server with FTP after you've finished all of your conversion and cleanup. This appendix includes the essentials on using Fetch 3.0 for Macintosh users and WS_FTP for Windows users.

CD-ROM

And finally, tucked into the back cover, you'll find a CD-ROM full of software samples and other resources. The CD-ROM includes sample documents from the book so you can follow along with the conversion lessons, using the original files for practice. You'll also find sample or trial versions of nearly all the conversion and authoring programs covered in the book, such as the following:

- Adobe's new file translator
- DeBabelizer Lite and a demo of the full version

- HTML conversion programs
  - BeyondPress for QuarkXPress
  - Adobe's HTML Author for PageMaker
  - WebWorks Light for FrameMaker
  - WebMaker 2 for FrameMaker
- HTML Editors
  - World Wide Web Weaver
  - BBEdit Lite
  - SiteMill 2.0 (for the Macintosh)
  - FrontPage
  - HTML Assistant Pro 2
  - Hot Dog (for Windows)
- Conversion utilities
  - ColorIt! (Macintosh)
  - PaintShop Pro (Windows)

A Book Worth Waiting For

As Ken, Jessica, and I were working on this book, we talked to many HTML designers about the problems they faced and the techniques they had learned so we could include those things in our chapters. The response we got was incredible. "When can I get that book?" people asked. "I need that now," people said. It was clear we had come across problems that almost every Web designer in the world faces in their work.

We've all learned from each other in the process of writing this book. Jessica and I anxiously awaited the graphics chapter from Ken so we could learn some good image tricks (he knows so much about graphics!), and we all poured over each of the conversion chapters to learn about the best software and techniques for getting content on the Web. We wrote this book because we have faced all of these problems in our own work, and have spent way too much time trying to figure out the solutions. Anyone working on the Web will save time and grief with the lessons and tips they'll learn in *Converting Content for Web Publishing*.

CHAPTER 2
Design Considerations for the Web

The very nature of the Web makes its content significantly different from the conventional data typically found in printed materials. The objective of this book is to show you how to easily convert printed materials for display on a World Wide Web site. At the same time, this book wouldn't be serving you well if it didn't make you aware that this conversion process will serve little purpose if it doesn't also involve redesigning. Don't be nervous. If you can follow a recipe in a cookbook or the instructions in a computer manual, you are quite capable of creating a useful and viewable Web site.

This chapter isn't meant to be a "how-to" chapter for specific HTML coding techniques, many of which are covered elsewhere in this book. If you don't find exactly what you are looking for within the pages of this book, there are hundreds of books on the subject, and many of the best published by New Riders. HTML tags, especially some of the newer ones most specifically concerned with design, are evolving at a stupendous rate. Keeping up to date is a difficult task. The best places to discover new tags and services are on the Web sites for the W3 Consortium (the organization in charge of setting HTML standards) and the sites for the two most widely used browsers, Netscape Navigator and Microsoft Internet Explorer.

> **Note**
>
> If you are determined to stay up-to-the minute on changes in the HTML code specifications, check out the following Web sites:
>
> Microsoft Internet Explorer
> http://www.microsoft.com/workshop/design/
>
> Netscape Navigator
> http://www.netscape.com
>
> World Wide Web Consortium
> http://www.w3.org/pub/WWW/

The first step toward designing a successful site, especially if that site consists mainly of content converted from print, is realizing the fundamental differences between the print experience and the Web experience. You should learn these differences so well that they become a part of your every waking moment. Okay, maybe that's overdoing it just a bit, but not much. Here are the six characteristics of the Web that set it apart from a print medium:

1. You are not the author, the viewer is.

2. The Web is a multimedia experience.

3. The Web is a hypermedia experience.

4. The Web is a landscape view (paper is portrait).

5. People get tired of reading sooner faster on a computer screen.

6. You have restricted control over type and layout.

The Viewer Is the Author

You may have written all the copy yourself (unlikely for readers of this book, but possible). You may have even created all the graphics and multimedia elements and done all the site design and implementation. Because so many different types of content are involved, a Web site is more likely to be created by a team than by an individual; however, even if you are the sole creator of the entire site, you can't be the *author* unless you're the only person who ever uses the site. Why? Because if the site is designed properly, every viewer will have a different experience.

Most people read a book or magazine article from front-to-back, left-to-right, and top-to-bottom. The writer creates the experience for the reader. In the process of "surfing" the Web, your readers or viewers create their own experience. In other words, they are the authors. This is so because of all the other differences between print and the Web described in the following sections.

The Web Is a Nonlinear Hypermedia Experience

The most distinctive characteristic of the World Wide Web is hyperlinks—we've come to simply call them links. *Links* enable the reader to skip around to only those parts of a site of immediate interest or importance (or to the entire World Wide Web). If you design these links so it's easy and fun to gather a wealth of disparate information, you're well on your way to having a successful site. Part of the secret to accomplishing this is to make sure it's easy both to "get there" and to get back. Another part of the secret is to keep informational segments as short as possible without leaving out important information. Make sure your readers know what an informational segment is all about, the second they see it. You want readers to be able to move on quickly if material doesn't interest them. Furthermore, it is the tendency of readers to skip anything that doesn't immediately grab their interest. This is due to the overwhelming amount of information on the Web and the fact that Web pages still load slower than most people can turn a page in a book.

The Web Is a Multimedia Experience

The World Wide Web was invented as a vehicle for providing multimedia on the Internet. It was the intent of its inventors to provide a context for visually and aurally stimulating content. The fact that early browsers, such as Netscape 1.1 and Mosaic, recognized only the most primitive HTML code and weren't compatible with many of today's most popular multimedia plug-ins almost seemed to belie that purpose. Today's browsers are much more advanced. Netscape Navigator 3.0 has a built-in Internet phone, VRML browser, QuickTime and QuickTime VR player, Adobe Acrobat 3.0, and Shockwave. There are also more than 200 third-party Netscape Navigator and Microsoft Internet Explorer-compatible plug-ins that make it possible to play virtually any type of content possible over the Web. Microsoft Internet Explorer 3.0 claims to be compatible with Netscape Navigator plug-ins and features a new technology called ActiveX. Both Netscape Navigator 3.0 and Microsoft Internet Explorer 3.0 also feature advance formatting and layout capabilities that will be discussed in more detail later in this chapter.

Design Considerations for the Web

Narrowcast Web Sites

As someone who is converting existing content to the Web, how does this wealth of multimedia potential affect the way you will design your site? First, some of these technologies are best suited to site applications that are "narrowcast" to specific viewers. That means you can assume your viewers have identical browser and hardware configurations and high-speed connections to handle the impractically huge files created by many of these media types. This situation is most likely to exist if the site you are creating is designed for a corporate intranet. Even on an intranet, the company may use bandwidth for many other things and not want to spare it for multimedia on a Web site.

Broadcast Web Sites

If you are "broadcasting" your site to the general World Wide Web audience, use motion and sound with caution and use it sparingly. Most viewers use 28.8 modems and many still use 14.4 models. These connections are ten times slower than ISDN connections and a hundred times slower than T1 connections. Chapter 11, "Graphics

Creation," will provide you with hints and help for making Web-efficient movies (this includes computer-generated animation) and analog sound files (AIFF on Mac or WAV for Windows).

Other types of multimedia may actually speed things up. These include multimedia graphics files based on vector information and MIDI (Musical Instrument Device Interface) sound files. These media types download faster because the data for these files is text in the form of written instructions to the computer, often taking less space than a paragraph or two of HTML code and body text.

The Web Is a Landscape View (Paper Is Portrait)

It's the oddest thing. Printed pages are usually printed so the layout will be seen in an upright or portrait position, just like the pages in this book. Computer monitors, on the other hand, are wider than they are tall. One reason browser default window sizes are about a third narrower than the screen is that, otherwise, each line of text is too long for quick scanning. Remember, unless text is confined to a fixed-width column in a table, the browser will wrap text to fit inside the window. Also, the landscape orientation of the computer screen usually means the top and bottom of a page's content will be invisible most of the time. People don't seem to mind doing some scrolling to read text, but you want to make sure they don't have to scroll to get the point of the page.

Finally, the fact that a computer screen's proportions are different from paper's means you will have to create a new layout for your content. In the process, you will probably want to add some graphics to accomplish the following:

- Hold the reader's interest by avoiding too many solid expanses of text.

- Keep the reader oriented to the type of information or the article being read by using graphics that are related to the information.

Keep It Short and Add Links

When you hold a book in your hands, it's easy to move about when you feel stiff or restless. A computer monitor tends to hold you much more rigidly in place. Also, the screen is backlit, which makes looking at it a bit like staring into oncoming headlights. No wonder people get restless and want to move on. Keep your text short and break up long pieces into short chunks. Give people plenty of links so they can move about within your site when they get restless. Otherwise, they'll just leave or (worse) turn off the computer.

You Have Limited Control Over Type and Layout

For the first time in their 3.0 versions, Netscape Navigator and Microsoft Internet Explorer introduced tags that enable you to specify real fonts. Microsoft Internet Explorer 3.0 even has a feature called "Cascading Style Sheets", which the company claims will give you full typographic layout control. In other words, you can have the same kind of control over design as you have in print—except the "paper" is always someone else's screen, and no two screens are exactly the same color. As with many other leading-edge Web technologies, there's little chance your readers will be able to reap the benefits of this design control unless you can dictate that they all use Microsoft Internet Explorer 3.0. Also, none of the conversion tools mentioned in this book support Cascading Style Sheets. Because of this design restriction, you can never ensure how a page may look in different browser windows. The following two figures show how Web pages appear in different window sizes.

At the moment, one of the best characteristics of Cascading Style Sheets is that Web pages that use them will look like any other Web page in a browser that doesn't support them.

Meanwhile, most browsers enable you to control text size only by relative size. Heading 1 may be larger than Heading 2, but exactly how large it is depends on the browser and platform on which it is viewed.

You don't get many choices of fonts, either. It's a little like Henry Ford saying, "You can have any color Model T you like…as long as it's black."

There's a good reason for these limitations. They give you a broader potential audience than you would have otherwise. The goal of the Internet is to provide information in a way that is viewable on nearly every computer in the world. By keeping design elements relative to one another instead of specific to space, you allow for differences among computer screens and other unpredictable variables. Even when such innovations as specifiable fonts and Cascading Style Sheets become *de rigueur*, this will be true. Why? Because the system that's reading your Web pages may have a completely different set of fonts than the system with which you designed your pages. So then what happens? Simple—the receiving system simply "decides" which fonts to substitute for those that are specified.

Figure 2.1a

The same Web page in two different window sizes.

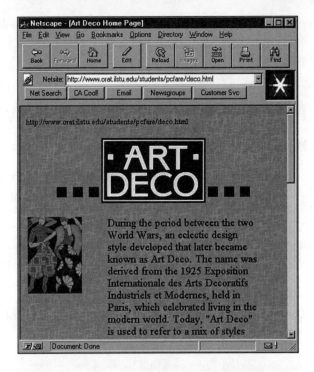

Figure 2.1b

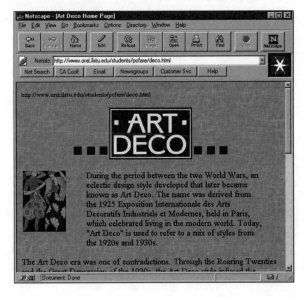

Of course, there is a workaround technology called *Portable Documents* that can be used on the Web. This technology will give you exactly the control over type and layout you have on paper. The best way to learn that such rigid control isn't particularly suited to the Web is to convert some of your content to Acrobat 3.0 PDF files and then, without rearranging the content, view them in a browser that supports (or has built-in) the Acrobat 3.0 plug-in. Your designs will be the same as they were in print, but they won't take into consideration all the variables among computers and the differences between the printed page and the computer screen. To learn more about creating PDF files, read Chapter 9, "PDF (Portable Document Format) Files."

The Rules of the Information Highway

Most design rules are made to be broken. If you want your Web pages to be appealing and intelligible, here are a few rules you should never break:

- Keep it under 640×480.
- Keep it concise.
- Make it easy to navigate.
- Make it quick to download.
- Pay attention to details.

Keep It Under 640×480

A minority of the monitors in existence are larger than 15 inches. Although it is possible to set small monitors to higher resolutions, the great majority of Windows and Mac machines are set at 640×480. Even when a viewer has a larger screen, the browser window defaults to a smaller size. Viewers will get annoyed if they have to spend time resizing the window before they can read its contents. If you design for a larger window size, you are cutting out about 75 percent of your potential audience.

Keep It Concise

Reading on-screen is more tiring than reading on paper. Besides, it's a more kinetic medium by nature. Cut everything you don't really need. If you have detailed explanations or descriptions, try moving them to another page and providing a link to them. Then the reader can skim more efficiently and still find details when they're needed.

Design Considerations for the Web

Make It Easy to Navigate

Ask yourself the following questions about your site and its individual pages:

- Are strangers likely to understand what the links mean?

- Are the purpose and destination of navigational graphics clear?

- Does everyone understand where the links go and why they might want to go there?

- Can the viewer return to previous pages or sections easily?

You also want to make sure there are text navigation menus that duplicate graphical navigation tools. You can create these using the Alt attribute in the image tag or as a separate line of linked text. (To learn more about the Alt tag, see the image tag section under HTML 2.0 in Chapter 14.) If you don't provide a text alternative, some of your viewers won't be able to tell where graphic links go on your site. Believe it or not, many Web surfers still use Lynx, a text-only browser primarily utilized at universities or by viewers with older computers. Even those surfing with graphical browsers, such as Navigator, have the option to surf with graphics turned off. If graphics don't load or the viewer doesn't understand their purpose, the text will still make it easy to get around in the site.

Here are two more worthwhile "tricks" you can add to your site to make navigation easier:

- A search engine

- A site map

Both are especially useful if the site is complex and involves dozens (or hundreds) of pages.

Search Engines

Adding a search engine may mean finding (or having written) a CGI or JavaScript script. A program called Simple Search, by Matt Wright, is available for free downloading from the following URL:

```
http://worldwidemart.com/scripts/search.shtml
```

Complete instructions on how to embed (insert) this search engine on your Web page and install the necessary CGI script on the server are included with the program. Before you bother to download, check with your site provider to make sure they will accommodate CGI scripts from outside sources.

Site Maps

Site maps are much easier to use than search engines. Create a hierarchical outline of all the pages on your site by using bulleted list tags in HTML, and then just link each heading to the appropriate page.

If your ISP supports client-side image maps, your site map can be much more attractive without the programming hassle. Make a flowchart in a drawing program and save or export it as a bitmap; then use a WYSIWYG HTML editor that supports image maps, such as Adobe PageMill or Microsoft FrontPage, to make the image map. If you don't have one of these programs, there are some shareware utilities expressly for making image maps from GIF files. A list of these types of programs and where to find them is included in Appendix B. Figure 2.2 shows a Web page that uses an image map.

Figure 2.2

A Web page that uses image maps.

Make It Quick to Download

Scattered throughout this book are numerous tips for making Web pages load as quickly as possible. I'll restate one of these tricks here because it's useful on such an overall level. Whenever possible, recycle the same graphics in different locations throughout your site. Most browsers store what they've already loaded in a cache on the client hard drive, so when you call an image for the second time, it loads from a local hard drive rather than over a modem connection.

Oversized graphics and an overabundance of multimedia are the most prevalent causes of slow-loading Web pages. Chapters 10 and 11 of this book are devoted to dozens of tricks for making graphics load faster (and, incidentally, look better).

A good resource for other tips on how to conserve bandwidth is the Bandwidth Conservation Society:

```
http://www.infohiway.com/way/faster/index.html
```

Pay Attention to Details

You need to include numerous details on most sites. Knowing what these are in advance can save you time when you do the final detail checking and correcting before posting pages to your server.

Here's a list of details usually worth inserting after you have converted the original document:

- **Make sure all pages have a title that matches the page contents.** Be sure these title bars are good indicators of the page's content. When readers *bookmark* the page (save the location in their browser for easy access later), it is this title that goes in the bookmark list.

- **Make sure all pages have a navigation bar.** If it's likely the viewer will have to scroll through the page, there should be a navigation bar at both ends. Remember, images don't load in all browsers. Also, not all browsers recognize frames. This means you should provide an alternative way of navigating if your design calls for permanent navigation from inside a frame.

- **Make sure all image tags have Alt=descriptive text in them.** You can check this by browsing with images off. If an image doesn't load, Alt="descriptive text" provides a way for the viewer to know what to expect to see in that particular location.

- **Check the spelling.** Nothing looks more unprofessional than misspellings. Most HTML editors have a spell checker that will check everything on a page. Some even have spell checkers that will check every page on a site (Hot Dog Pro for Windows and BBEdit for the Macintosh, for instance). These days, almost all WYSIWYG HTML editors have a built-in spell checker. Many of the conversion programs covered in this book also check spelling.

- **Check for consistency between elements.** This is especially important if you have style sheets. Also check the consistency of meaning; in other words, does the same symbol or icon always mean the same thing? Do you have more than one icon or symbol for the same function?

- **Check alignment of elements.** Does text start at the top right of the image and wrap around the bottom as you intended? Does a row of images align consistently, or are they unintentionally staggered? It's easy to forget alignment tags in the haste of putting elements onto a page. If items are out of alignment, you can use the Search capability in your HTML editor to find `align=` until you come to the items that are out of alignment. Then enter the correct codes. If you neglected to add the align attribute in the first place, you'll need to fix these manually.

- **Make sure there are plenty of contact links.** Because contact links are seldom part of the content you have converted, it's easy to forget to make it easy for visitors to your site to contact you. It's a good idea to put a "contact us" (call it what you like) link on every page. It could link to your personal e-mail address, to a mail form, or to a page with a directory of e-mail addresses for key company contacts.

- **Make sure your dates are up to date.** Don't leave out the year. Don't date items unless there's a reason to, because they eventually make your site look old and tired unless the item is updated and re-dated.

The Design Guru Point of View

Crystal Waters, David Siegel, Laura LeMay, Clement Mok, and Lynda Weinman are only a few examples of best-selling authors whose careers as designers have also contributed to giving them the aura of religious leaders. These reputations are well deserved, too. All have made major contributions to the progression of state-of-the-Web-design-art. It is inevitable that in the course of establishing these reputations, all have formed strong personal "rules" about what does and doesn't represent good Web design. It pays to listen to these rules and to try making them your own—especially if they seem to work for you. Here's the rub. Often these authors disagree violently over such questions as whether a good designer designs for a specific browser or for all browsers. They even disagree about whether you should or shouldn't ever use a horizontal bar tag in your HTML code.

So what do you do? Listen to all of them and then find your own way. To put it another way, follow the path that seems best suited to the task at hand, to your own style, and to your audience. Also, remember this: if you ever hope to join the ranks of these exalted designers, you too must dare to be different.

Designing for the Widest Audience

Some Web pages are meant to be narrowcast to a specific audience, but most Web sites are meant to be intelligible for anyone who reaches them. Many sites are there for sales, advertising, or publicity reasons and must reach as many viewers as possible. One way to reach more viewers is to design for the widest range of client platforms and software.

Do these three things if you want to reach as many viewers as possible:

1. Minimize download time by managing bandwidth.

2. Design pages that can be read intelligibly (if not uniformly) by multiple browsers.

3. Design pages that look good and perform well on any platform.

Managing Bandwidth

Although there are numerous tricks and techniques for making pages load faster, it all boils down to remembering three facts:

- Graphics eat bandwidth.

- Multimedia gobbles bandwidth.

- Text uses very little bandwidth.

You need to use all the tricks in Chapters 10 and 11 to make sure graphics files are as small as possible. If they're small, a whole page full of graphics can load within a fairly reasonable time. Having said that, use graphics sparingly and tastefully. Your pages will load faster and be more widely appreciated. When it comes to multimedia, new technologies that allow for faster streaming movie and sound files make at least some multimedia practical. Even if you create files that are as small as possible when you use these technologies, you are well advised to use them sparingly. When you do need to show multimedia files or large graphics, put them on a separate page and let the reader know—before the download is activated—how long it will take to download the file.

Cross-Browser Design Considerations

Browsers are getting more versatile by the second. Considering that the two most versatile and popular browsers are either literally or nearly free, it is surprising that cross-browser authoring is even an issue—but it is an issue, for several reasons. First, many people don't upgrade, because they're reluctant to "fix what ain't broke." Then there's the (mostly unfounded) fear that it will take time to learn to use the new browser. Corporations tend to be slow to upgrade because they don't want to spend money retraining more often than necessary or upgrading an entire network frequently. Finally, many readers access the Web through such online services as CompuServe and America Online. At the moment, these services use proprietary browsers that are less than state-of-the-art. Figures 2.3a and 2.3b provide examples of browser differences.

Figure 2.3a

The same Web page in two different browsers.

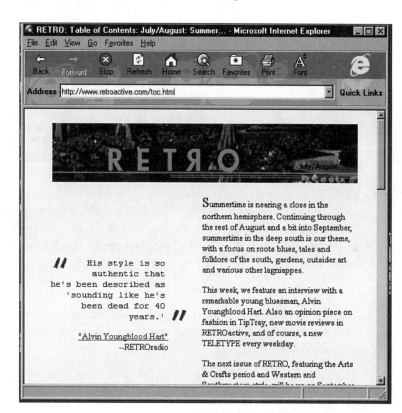

Figure 2.3b

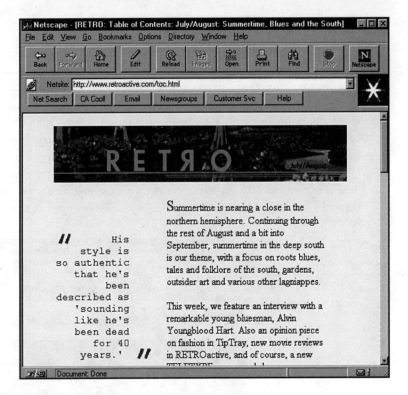

The trick is to design Web pages that look as good as can be in an antique browser while they look as good (or nearly as good) as possible in Netscape Navigator 3.0 or Microsoft Internet Explorer 3.0. The easy way to do this is to create both a state-of-the-art site and a basic (I call it "historically correct") site. It's not really twice as much work—just carry out the following steps:

1. Create the fully featured site first.

2. Then, without changing the names of any files, copy the whole site into a directory called "text," and take out the image references and any embedded multimedia files.

3. Next, create a link to the text site from the home page and fix any links that may be broken in this process. If you have set relative links among the pages, you shouldn't have too much to fix.

4. You can stop at step 3, but if you are technically set up for it, you can go on to create what is known as a virtual server so that the link from the home page goes to the text site directory, and from there, the text site is the "virtual" Web site.

Creating a virtual server and a virtual path to a directory is something that whoever is the technical Webmaster should know how to do. It is very easy to do with Netscape, Purveyor, and Microsoft server products. If you are not sure about this, or are not running your own server, simply setting the link to the directory called "text" and following steps 1–3 will suffice.

The alternative is to make sure you don't use tags or embed media that can't be seen by lower-capability browsers without incorporating other tags that provide alternatives. For example, if you use the <EMBED> tag to link a multimedia file, you can use the <NOEMBED> tag and link a GIF or JPEG alternative that will be displayed by browsers that don't support multimedia file types. There are so many tricks for doing this it takes a whole book to describe them all. That book is *Hybrid HTML: A Multiple Browser Reference* by Kevin Ready and Janine Warner (who also co-authored this book). The publisher, as you might guess, is New Riders. Far as I can tell, it's the only one on the market dedicated to this purpose.

Multiple-Platform Considerations

The World Wide Web was designed to be a multi-platform medium. Given this fact, why should you have concerns about designing for multiple platforms? Well, there aren't many concerns, but turning your attention to a few things will pay off in the long run.

- Use browser-safe colors.
- Keep your images on the light side.
- Windows windows are smaller.

Use Browser-Safe Colors

Both Netscape Navigator and Microsoft Internet Explorer use 216-color palettes on systems that can view only 256 colors (standard VGA). The colors in these palettes are virtually the same, so you're safe using the same palette. Use browser-safe colors only when you have control over which colors will be used in a graphic and only when the graphic is more suited to GIF format than JPEG. In other words, don't try to use browser-safe colors on fully shaded artwork or photos. You can find browser-safe palettes for several programs on the CD that comes with this book. There's also a detailed explanation on how to use these palettes in the graphics-related chapters, Chapters 10 and 11.

Keep Your Images on the Light Side

This caveat doesn't really apply to those who are creating their images on Windows computers. Macintoshes are reputed to create slightly brighter graphics than Windows machines. I haven't found this to be the case, but because the rumor persists, it can't hurt to cater to it. This dark(er) reputation seems to come from the fact that more Windows users set their screens (usually for no good reason) at a puny 256 colors, which makes photos and other graphics not designed with browser-safe colors look like "petri dish contents." So if you're creating your graphics on a Mac, lighten up (just a little).

Windows Windows are Smaller

The browser windows for most Windows browsers (Microsoft Internet Explorer excluded) are smaller, by a couple of lines of 12-point text, than their Macintosh counterparts. This is just enough of a difference to cut off the captions under a photo or hide the bottom navigation bar. So, if you're composing pages on a Mac, make your pages a couple of lines shorter than they really need to be.

Maintaining Corporate Identity

The fact that you have less layout control on the Web than in print may make it a bit harder (or impossible) to maintain all the document specifications dictated by company policy (or by the firm who designed your corporate identity). After all, you can't count on using specific fonts (or even sans serif fonts) for body text, accurate margins and spacing between elements, or exact color reproduction on the viewer's computer. Figure 2.4 shows how Macromedia makes it obvious that it's their page.

Making your Web pages an obvious product of your organization is an important advertising and public relations tool.

So what do you do about it? Make sure you use the other, more controllable elements of corporate identity as often as possible—without being totally obnoxious. These include the company logo, mascots, icons, and other standard corporate graphics. You can also create headlines and text banners in a vector design program such as CorelDRAW! or Illustrator, using all the PostScript corporate identity specifications (exact typeface and point size, for example) for these elements. Then send them to Photoshop (or whatever bitmap image editor you use) to be turned into GIF-format Web graphics. Another thing you can do is come as close as possible to approximating company colors within the confines of the browser-safe palette.

Figure 2.4

No doubt whose Web page this is.

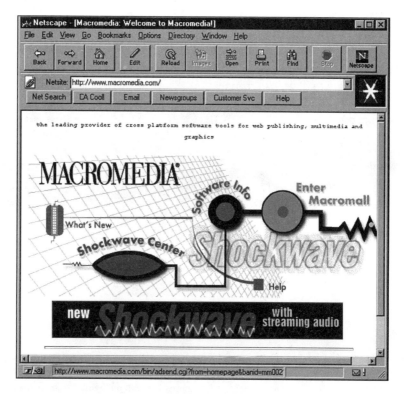

Tricks for Controlling Layout

If I were to rewrite the rules of good Web design, rule number one would be "Cheat" and rule number two would be "Wait." It's another way of saying no matter how restrictive current HTML capabilities may be, there's usually a workaround, and if you wait a short while, the capabilities will improve. This section will cover workarounds and some of the latest design-oriented HTML tags.

These workarounds and tags fall into the following categories:

- Graphic type
- Clear GIFs
- Tables
- Frames
- Font tags
- Space tags
- Style sheet tags

Graphic Type

If you are determined to keep exact control over text, you can use graphics in place of text, as shown in figure 2.5. But you should use this trick sparingly, — graphics take longer to download than text.

Figure 2.5

A Web page that uses graphic type for headlines.

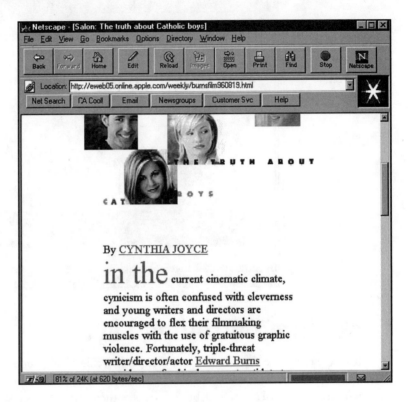

You can get around the lack of specific typefaces for headlines, drop caps, logos, illustrations, and ad banners by including the real typeface as part of a graphic. The use of align=right and align=left attributes in an <IMG> tag make it possible to wrap text around the left or right side of a graphic, as shown in figure 2.6. You may need the next couple of workarounds to help you place graphic type exactly where you want it.

Clear GIFs

Recently, some browsers (notably Netscape Navigator 3.0 and Microsoft Internet Explorer 4.0) and the W3 Consortium have begun to incorporate margin and spacing tags that enable you to place text exactly where you want it (although the text block still changes shape when you resize the window). Unfortunately, most of your viewers' browsers won't be updated enough to support these tags.

Figure 2.6

Text wrapped around a graphic with the ALIGN=LEFT tag.

The use of what have come to be known as clear GIFs can overcome these limitations. Clear GIFs are used to create exact spacing on a page. Clear GIFs and transparent GIFs aren't synonymous. A transparent GIF (a.k.a. tGIF) is an apparently free-form graphic that "floats" over the background because the image's background is transparent. A clear GIF is simply invisible. It can be any size, but is usually only a single pixel. To make "white space" on a page, you simply insert a single pixel clear image onto the page and make the height= and width= attributes reflect the amount of desired "white space." Use the `align=right` or `align=left` attributes within the image tag to make the text line up on one side or the other of the clear GIF.

For instructions on how to make a clear GIF, refer to Chapter 10, "Graphics Basics."

Tables

HTML tables also provide greater design control. Used without a border, they enable you to better align images and text on a page, and are often the only way to approximate the kind of design control you can achieve using multiple text boxes in a desktop publishing program.

Suppose you have a page layout requirement that looks like figure 2.7.

Figure 2.7

Page layout that requires tables on the Web.

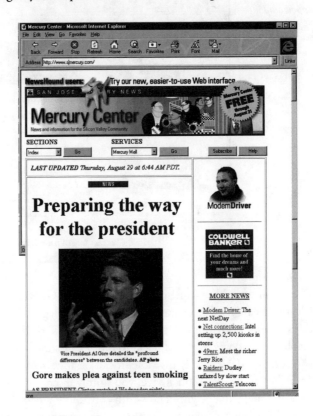

This figure shows a complex page design. The headings are graphical text; each has to be centered above an image. Immediately to the right of the graphical heading is a block of related text. This text block also spans the area occupied by the photo. Such layouts are commonplace in PageMaker or FrameMaker. To do this kind of layout in HTML, however, you have to employ tables.

Tables are now understood by nearly all current-issue browsers (yes, even AOL's). In addition to making traditional "spreadsheet" tables possible, tables provide an excellent workaround for making blocks of text appear where you want them. The table in figure 2.9 was not created for a table the way they are traditionally used in a spreadsheet program. Instead, this table is used for careful alignment of graphic and text elements on a Web page. By making the Border=0 (the default for HTML tables), the table itself is invisible, but the table tags provide better formatting control.

Table Appearance and Layout Issues

Tables enable you to divide your pages into any number of sections. These sections are defined in rows and columns, just as in an ordinary statistical table or spreadsheet.

The difference is that cells can be any size and adjacent cells can be joined. WYSIWYG editors such as Adobe PageMill, Microsoft FrontPage, and Claris Home Page are wonderful paste-up boards for laying out pages in tables. You can insert a table anywhere, bring up a dialog box to enter the properties of the table, and type in the specifications you want. The exact properties recognized by competing WYSIWYG editors vary slightly. All will let you specify column width in either pixels or a percentage of the screen, table height, and border and cell padding. Most will also let you specify background colors for individual cells and provide some way of merging cells together. If you don't want to use a WYSIWYG editor to make tables, you can get complete instructions in Chapter 14, "HTML Tutorial and Reference," in the HTML 3.2 section on tables.

Usually, if you're using tables for layout, you will want to turn off the borders by inserting the `table border = "0"` attribute. You can use the cell padding attribute to establish margins inside frames. Just remember that these margins will be uniform on all four sides of the cell. If you want margins that are not uniform on all sides, you can insert a clear GIF, as described earlier in this chapter, and set the desired height or width to control exact spacing within a table cell. For example, to force the width to a specific dimension, place a clear GIF in the cell and specify a height of one pixel and a width of as many pixels as you want for spacing.

Unless they're told to do otherwise, tables will expand and contract to fit within the browser window. This is good news and bad news. Reshaping the table could easily mess with your layout. But forcing a table to be too wide will leave many of your viewers having to scroll to see the entire table. You have two options when specifying table width: a percentage, which will change according to the window size, or a fixed pixel width, which will remain constant, even if the user has to scroll to see it. Use a fixed width only if you have a compelling reason or if the table is narrow enough that few, if any, viewers would have to scroll to see all of it. If you do use a percentage or don't specify the width, it's a good idea to change the size of the window on your own screen to and test it to ensure that the design looks good, even if its width is altered. Another trick with tables is to use the Center tag to center-align the entire table. Then, even if the window changes, at least the table will be in the center of the screen.

Browser Support for Tables

Tables have proven so useful that only a few old browsers still refuse to support them. Unfortunately, many people still use those browsers. If they look at one of your table-formatted pages, they're likely to see only a disorganized jumble of text and graphics. It's easy for you to prevent this, though, by inserting the <BR> tag at the end of each table cell, just before the </TD> tag. This causes table-impaired browsers to show the cell contents "stacked" in order of appearance. Because the contents are in logical order, the page will still be readable. You can also use <P> tags to provide greater variation of spacing, but they will affect the layout in browsers that support tables.

Of course, there is one catch. Older versions of Mosaic will not show the contents of a nested table (a table within a table). If people who use those browsers are important to you, you will simply have to give them an alternative page or refrain from using nested tables. Personally, I think it's time they grew into a better browser. Costs nothing. Makes your life richer.

Font Tags

Until recently, there has been no way to specify type by conventional finite measurements such as points, picas, or inches. Even now that the latest Navigator and Internet Explorer browsers support font size, most of your viewers will probably be using browsers that don't support this kind of font control. HTML traditionally specifies font sizes relative to a given browser's default font size. The actual size of this default font varies from browser to browser and from platform to platform. For instance, Netscape Navigator defaults to a Times Roman 12 point type, but the user can specify any font and size they choose in browser preferences. Incidentally, on the Macintosh, Times Roman 12 appears smaller than on the Windows operating system. (Times 12 on the Mac is about the equivalent of Times 10 on the PC.)

There are two ways to vary font size in HTML code prior to the W3C 3.2 specification: you had to use a header tag (<H1>–<H6>). Netscape then introduced the <FONT SIZE=1>–<FONT SIZE 7> tag. The header tags cause a hard return at the end of the tag, so you can't put larger type within a paragraph.

Netscape's solution, now supported by many browsers, is to use the Font Size tag (browsers that don't support font size will ignore it). You can begin and end the Font Size tag anywhere in your text. No hard return is placed after it. This makes it possible to change font sizes at any place within a paragraph. The default font size in most browsers is the equivalent of Font Size=3; unlike header tags where H1 is the largest, Font Size 7 is the largest, and Font Size 1 is the smallest. Now Netscape has taken this a step further and the font size tag can be used to specify exact point sizes. As you have probably already guessed, only Netscape Navigator 3.0 and Microsoft Internet Explorer 3.0 currently support point-specific font size tags. For more on font size, read the font sections in Chapter 14, "HTML Tutorial and Reference."

When to Use Frames

Frames are subdivisions of the browser window that can show static information, such as a navigation chart, or dynamic information, such as another Web page or even another Web site. Frames can be fixed in size or adjustable according to overall window size. They can appear with or without scroll bars. Frames are a fairly new innovation on the Web, having been introduced by Netscape for Navigator 2.0. Although they are not part of the HTML 3.2 specification, frames are increasingly supported by other browsers, including Internet Explorer 2.0+.

Frames add innovative design control as they enable you to display multiple HTML pages in one browser window and to control the contents of each framed area individually. A common use of frames is to create a page with two or more sections and place links in one section that, when selected, display in another section on the same page. Using the Target attribute of the frames tag, you can specify if a link opens a file in another frame on the same page, opens a new browser window, or replaces the page completely. In figure 2.8, you see an example of a page created with frames.

Figure 2.8

A Web site that uses frames.

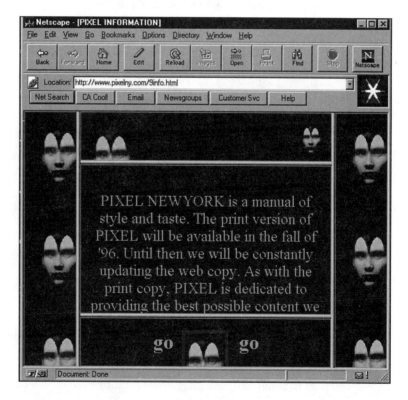

There is nothing in print to compare to frames, so you won't find them being implemented by your conversion program. If you want to use frames, you will have to create them after you have made your conversion. Remember, however, that more than half the browsers out there still don't recognize frames. If you decide to use them, create alternate pages that can be read by viewers who can't see frames. This can be done using the Noframes tag to display a separate page for browsers that can't display the main HTML page. For more on how to do this, see the section in Chapter 14 on the Noframes tag.

Design Considerations for the Web

Frames pose another problem: it is possible to create any number of frames within a page window. Unfortunately, because frames are new, people tend to overdo them. Putting too many frames in a given location makes the site harder to read (because the individual windows are too small) and too hard to navigate. This has led many viewers to passionately hate frames, and many sites that rushed to implement frames when they were first introduced have either abandoned them or minimized their use.

Before you consider using frames, here's a list of things you shouldn't do with them:

- **Don't use frames on pages where they're not absolutely needed.** Using them for the sake of gimmickry is just plain annoying.

- **Limit your use of scroll bars.** In fact, avoid scrolling altogether wherever possible. If you have a long text article in one fairly large window, making your users scroll to see all of it makes sense. Don't make them scroll through pages full of graphics, however—it will take forever for that frame to load.

- **Keep the size of most frames rigid.** By default, frames can be resized by dragging their borders. Usually this means important information gets partially hidden within such frames as those that hold navigation icons. The Noresize attribute keeps such frames sized so they reveal all their contents. For more on Noresize and other Frame attributes, see the frames section under Netscape in Chapter 14.

- **Never substitute frames for tables.** Tables are easier to code and debug and far easier to change or update when content changes. Furthermore, they look better and don't add unnecessary detail to the user interface.

- **Don't place frames within frames.** The windows just get too darned small to be useful for much of anything, and the screen looks terrifyingly complicated.

Although frames should be used sparingly, some conditions definitely benefit from their use. Here's a list of good uses for frames:

- **For keeping users grounded in your site.** Suppose you want to show your readers other sites that reference the copy and images on your pages. It's easy enough to implement external links, but how does the reader get back to your page after they've spent ten minutes exploring the other site? Keep the navigation bar or table of contents for your site in a narrow frame at one edge of your site, as shown in figure 2.9. Then have the main frame be the target frame for the links.

Figure 2.9

A permanent navigation bar occupies the left frame.

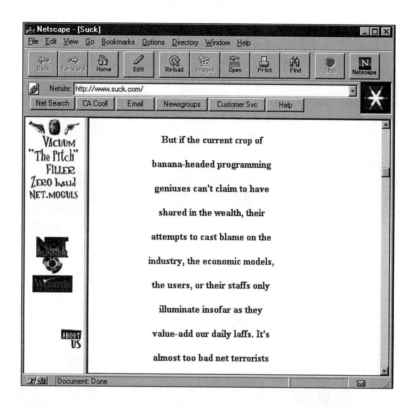

- **For a picture gallery or catalog.** Thumbnails are displayed in the small sideframe. If you click on a thumbnail, the large main window shows the enlarged image.

- **For advertising banners and logos.** You can use one frame to keep logos or advertising banners constantly in view, while navigable, changing information is shown in the main frame.

New Tricks for Making the Web Look More Like Print

The very latest generations of browsers, especially as evidenced by Microsoft Internet Explorer 3.0 and Netscape Navigator 3.0, support something closely approximating true typographical layout control. Both browsers support multiple columns, vertical control, white space control (limiting the need for clear GIFs), PostScript and TrueType fonts in exact point sizes, and wrapped text within tables.

Internet Explorer also jumps ahead with a feature called style sheets. *Style sheets* enable you to make formatting changes for a whole page from one location. This will be a huge boon to designers, who will be able to show clients alternate designs quickly. Style sheets behave in much the same way as style templates in word processing and page layout programs. At the beginning of a Web page, you can insert a styles tag that specifies how other tags are to be laid out, typeset, and formatted. Style sheets can control margin indents, leading, typefaces, and colors. Style sheets can also be used to specify styles for an entire Web site. For more on style sheets, see the Microsoft section of Chapter 14.

Fonts, margins, leading, multiple columns, vertical control, white space control, and style sheets are all included in the W3 Consortium's HTML 3.2 specification. This means that all browsers will support these features eventually. Netscape Navigator 3.0 already supports all but style sheets, and promises to support them in version 4.0. By the time you read this, you will probably see a beta version of 4.0 with cascading style sheets.

You might as well start including typographical layout control in your HTML code now, even though not everyone will be able to appreciate it. A considerable number of people (a million a day for the first few days of introduction) have downloaded Microsoft Internet Explorer 3.0 or Netscape Navigator 3.0 and are avidly looking for enhanced pages.

> **Note**
>
> You won't have to do a thing to these enhanced pages to make them perfectly legible in browsers that don't support the features in this section. These browsers will ignore tags they don't recognize, and display those tags they do recognize. However, until all browsers support these features, it is important to test your pages on your lowest common denominator browser to make sure that these browsers will receive a decent-looking page.

When to Add Material to Enhance the Site

There's quite a bit you can do on a Web site to hold a reader's attention that you can't do in print—or can't do as well. Also, because the Web is a more dynamic medium, you will probably be well served to make your material look more dynamic (and less long-winded) than it did in print. You already know you should do this by cutting your text down to essential information written as concisely as possible. You also know to break long sequences of text into smaller documents and to link pages of detailed information to text that contains basic information. Once you have added this interactivity, you will probably find it desirable to add more graphics—especially charts and illustrations that are visual examples of what the text is describing.

What else can you add to enhance your site? Here's a list:

- Backgrounds
- Multimedia
    - Animated GIFs
    - QuickTime
    - Shockwave
    - Acrobat 3.0 Presentations
    - VRML
    - RealAudio

Backgrounds

You can make the background a solid color, an image, or a textured pattern. Make sure you can read the foreground images and text clearly when they're superimposed on this background. Use a color that contrasts strongly with the text. If the background is a pattern, make sure the pattern doesn't contain flecks too close in color to the color of the text. If you like a particular texture pattern that seems to interfere with the text, use your image editor's contrast and gamma curve controls to remove the more pronounced shadows and highlights. You may also want to lighten or darken the image overall so that it contrasts more with the text.

Another way to make text contrast with a background pattern is to put the text into table cells, and then color the background of the cells. This will place the text on a block of solid color that overlays the textured background pattern. Currently, only Netscape Navigator 3.0 and Microsoft Internet Explorer 3.0 support colored cell backgrounds.

Multimedia

Multimedia in this context means video sequences, animation, sound (either as background or synchronized to a video or animation), and vector illustrations. Multimedia content can be played inside the browser window, in line with the other content on a page, provided the content is compatible with Netscape 3.0 built-in plug-ins. All this material can be played in older browsers if these browsers are compatible with Netscape plug-ins or have a supporting plug-in architecture of their own. Don't use materials that your reader won't have the patience or disk space to download. The following table displays download time to give you an idea of what you can expect when you use multimedia files on the Web.

Download Times

Content	Size	14.4 Kbps	28.8 Kbps	64 Kbps	1.5 Kbps
Small graphics and animation	30 KB	30 sec.	10 sec.	6 sec.	1 sec.
Small complete movie	100–200 KB	100–200 sec.	50–100 sec.	20–40 sec.	1 sec.
Short video clip	500 KB	500 sec.	120–240 sec.	90 sec.	3 sec.
Full-size movie	1 MB	N.A.	N.A.	180 sec.	6 sec.
MPEG video stream	—	N.A.	N.A.	N.A.	Continuous

Streaming Technology

The latest innovation in multimedia-playing plug-ins is *streaming* audio and video. Until very recently, you had to download an entire movie or sound file before you could see or hear it. This doesn't seem so bad until you look at the download chart and realize how long this can take. Streaming technology changes all that. When a file that uses streaming technology is downloaded, it starts playing as soon as enough material has arrived at the client computer that the rest will download before the movie finishes playing. This typically means that a movie will download and start playing in about one-third the time it would otherwise take. Both QuickTime and Shockwave now have players that feature streaming.

Alternatives for Non-Multimedia-Supported Browsers

First-generation browsers won't be able to see any of this material. This won't be a problem if you use the Noembed and Image tags in conjunction with the Embed tag to substitute a still graphic where the multimedia "event" would have occurred in a more advanced browser.

For example, if you want to embed a .mov file in a Web site and provide a still GIF as an alternative for viewers who can display a movie file, here's how such a code would look:

```
<EMBED SRC=video.mov>
<NOEMBED>
<IMG SRC="still.gif">
</NOEMBED>
```

These same instructions can be used for embedding VRML, RealAudio, or any other material enabled by plug-ins.

Plug-In Accessibility

The fact that the incorporation of multimedia relies on plug-ins creates a problem. There are well over 100 Netscape-compatible plug-ins, and not much chance your audience will have the more exotic ones. Even if you tell them they need the plug-in and give them a download link for it, chances are readers won't take the time to download and install it. Some plug-ins are exceedingly popular, partly because they're versatile in the types of materials they can show, partly because they're cleaner and more efficient than competing plug-ins that show the same media types, and mostly because Netscape Navigator 3.0 has them built in.

If you want to download Netscape plug-ins, 83 of them (as of August 1996) are available for free download at the following URL:

```
http://www.netscape.com/comprod/products/navigator/version_2.0/
↪plug-ins/index.html
```

Microsoft claims that any plug-in you install in Navigator (any version) will work automatically in Microsoft Internet Explorer if you install or reinstall it.

Animated GIFs

Animated GIFs are the only way to show animation on a Web page without requiring a plug-in for viewing. Netscape Navigator 2.0+ and Internet Explorer 3.0+ support animated GIFs. Other browsers will simply display the first or last frame of the animation as a still image. Animated GIFs work best when they consist of a few looping frames or a series of timed still images used as a slide show. Animated GIFs tend to load more quickly than plug-in animations, but that's at least partially because their files are usually made to be smaller in the first place. You can link an animated GIF to any URL, but you can't program in any interactivity, such as showing another animation or playing a sound. There's no way to synchronize sound to an animated GIF, either. To learn more about animated GIFs, see Chapters 10 and 11.

QuickTime

QuickTime is a cross-platform multimedia format originated by Apple Computer. It has been around for some time and has been playable in plug-ins from third-party vendors and as a MIME type. However, site developers tended to restrict its use because most QuickTime movies run several megabytes and can consume many minutes or hours of download time. The latest version of the QuickTime player is built into Netscape Navigator 3.0.

The best reasons for considering QuickTime as your multimedia vehicle are as follows:

● **Download speed.** The QuickTime player plug-in that's built into Netscape Navigator 3.0 and available for Microsoft Internet Explorer 3.0 uses streaming technology. It also has a new feature called *fast start*, which puts the first frame of the movie inline with your Web page almost as soon as it loads. To play the movie, you just click on the image. Several vendors have introduced utility software that makes it possible to compress QuickTime movies to amazingly small sizes (see Chapter 11).

● **Media versatility.** QuickTime movies don't have to be movies. To put it another way, a QuickTime movie can be a single frame or sound file. Sound files can be MIDI (synthesizer) files so small they can download nearly instantaneously and provide background music for your Web page. A QuickTime movie can also be a vector drawing file saved in the Macintosh PICT format. You can't zoom and pan the drawing when using the current state of the QuickTime plug-in; however, Shockwave for Freehand or Adobe Acrobat supports this kind of application. In short, virtually any kind of media file you can create on a Macintosh can be put into a QuickTime movie.

QuickTime also includes QuickTime VR. The VR stands for Virtual Reality, which is a somewhat overblown description of what the technology does for you. There are actually two separate kinds of QuickTime VR "experiences": Scenes and Objects.

● Scenes are still frames taken in panoramic sequence. Special software welds these stills together seamlessly, with the result that you can pan to see everything within a 360° arc (or even sphere) of where the camera is placed. You can also tilt up and down and pan in and out. It's wonderful technology for showing what a location looks like in first person—such as a trade show floor, shopping mall, or vacation spot. Figure 2.10 provides an example of a QuickTime VR panorama.

Figure 2.10

*A QuickTime VR
panorama seen
in a Web page.*

- Objects are still frames taken equidistantly around the perimeter of an
  isolated subject, such as a computer or fashion model. When these stills
  are welded together and shown within a QuickTime player or plug-in, the
  viewer can spin and rotate the object to view it from any side or angle.
  This is especially valuable technology for scientific, medical, or catalog
  sites.

QuickTime VR Scenes and Objects load quite quickly compared to most
movies, but these file formats don't yet implement streaming. Because the data is
in the form of a single graphics file, streaming technology may not even be
applicable here.

- **High-quality movie playback.** QuickTime has been generally considered a
  more advanced technology for inline video than Microsoft's Video for Windows
  (AVI) format. Microsoft is improving on this technology with their introduction
  of ActiveMovie, but this technology is too new to have yet achieved widespread
  acceptance, and the jury is still out as to which will win in the long run.

● **Availability of the largest amount of premade material.** Because so much multimedia and graphics material has originated on Macintosh computers, and because of QuickTime's cross-platform playback quality, there is more stock material available in this format than in others. This isn't meant to imply, however, that there isn't a large selection of materials available in AVI format.

QuickTime files will play on both Macintosh and Windows computers, but must be authored on a Macintosh. This is not quite as severe a limitation as it seems, because you can use a conversion program (such as DeBabelizer) to convert Windows-made movies (such as AVI files) to QuickTime. In fact, this is probably the most universal way to play AVI files on the Web, although it is certainly not the only choice.

To find out nearly everything you ever wanted to know about QuickTime for the Web, visit the following site:

```
http://www.quicktime.apple.com
```

Shockwave

Macromedia's Shockwave is the name for a series of plug-ins and authoring tools for playing Director 4 and 5 movies, displaying Freehand graphics files, playing Authorware titles, and playing background sounds. Shockwave has the following advantages over QuickTime: you can include many (not yet all) of the interactive features of Director and Authorware, and you can author from either the Macintosh or Windows platform. In addition, Shockwave has recently been "stream"-lined; in other words, it now incorporates streaming technology, and can be used to play sound files to match QuickTime's capabilities.

Shockwave is 32-bit native on Windows 95, NT, and Power Macintosh, and consists of the following features:

● Compression utilities and Xtras for Macromedia authoring tools—Authorware, Director, and Freehand.

● Plug-ins and controllers for Netscape Navigator, Internet Explorer, and other popular browsers that usher in a new era of interactive multimedia, sound, and graphics to the World Wide Web and intranets.

Shockwave has many overlapping capabilities with QuickTime. The biggest difference is that Director and Authorware are development programs for creating interactive multi-media. Shockwave for Freehand is a better vehicle than QuickTime for showing detailed line drawings (vector files) such as maps and etchings because it allows for infinite zooming and panning around the drawing. It also enables the author to place links at specific locations on the drawing. Figures 2.11a and 2.11b show two views of a city map.

Figure 2.11a

Two views of a city map.

Figure 2.11b

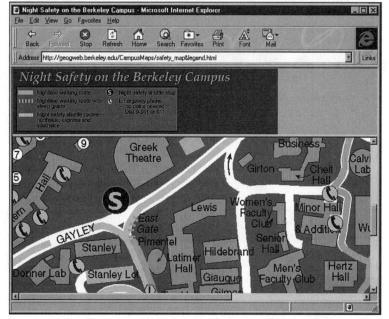

For comprehensive information on Shockwave, visit the Macromedia Web site at the following:

```
http://www.macromedia.com
```

The Macromedia site also links to many other sites that feature Shockwave examples and contain information on creating and publishing materials for Shockwave.

Acrobat 3.0

Acrobat is Adobe System's Portable Document Format (PDF). A portable document carries all font and layout specifications with it, regardless of the platform on which it is viewed. It is the best solution for putting print documents on the Web when those print documents must be as close as possible to their paper counterparts. Because this book contains a whole chapter—Chapter 9, "PDF (Portable Document Format) Files"—on portable documents, I won't go into detail here.

It is important to note that Acrobat 3.0 is much more capable than earlier versions. Streaming technology causes the first page to load nearly instantaneously, even over slow modems. It is now possible to place any kind of hyperlink in a document.

When it comes to showing detailed technical drawings and other vector files, Acrobat has an edge over all the other technologies because the drawings can be created in any drawing program that can output to PostScript (in other words, most drawing programs). Acrobat also enables you to link locations on a drawing and to zoom and pan the drawing for details.

Finally, Acrobat is an excellent medium for creating Web presentations. These presentations can be authored in Adobe's Web Presenter, and then simply embedded as Acrobat files. Virtually every feature of Adobe Persuasion is available for your slide show, including transitions between slides and animated bullet text. The best part is that the graphics description files for the slides are vector-based and consequently load very quickly.

For more details on Acrobat, see Chapter 9. Also, visit the Adobe site at the following:

```
http://www.adobe.com
```

VRML

VRML (Virtual Reality Modeling Language) enables you to visit a three-dimensional model and walk through it as though it were a real-life experience. Graphics can be mapped to the surfaces of the 3D model, and links can be attached to surfaces. Links can display a media type, take you to another model or another part of the model you're in, or perform any of the functions you'd expect from any Web hyperlink.

VRML is especially suited for sites that are meant to tour a location, for game sites, and for exhibits, shopping malls, and galleries, as shown in figure 2.12.

Figure 2.12

A VRML gallery.

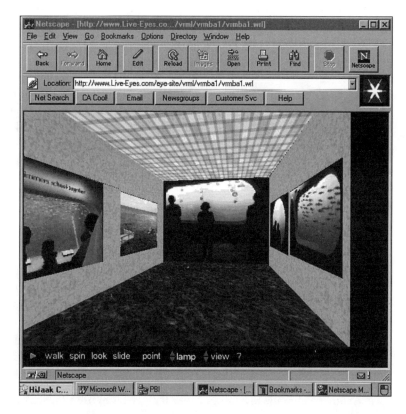

Numerous programs and methods are available for creating VRML worlds. Among these are almost all popular 3D modeling programs, such as 3D Studio MAX (Autodesk), TrueSpace2 (Caligari), and Extreme 3D (Macromedia). Players and plug-ins abound. You will probably get the broadest range of compatibility from the Live 3D plug-in now built into Netscape Navigator 3.0.

RealAudio

RealAudio is a plug-in for playing very highly compressed (read fast-loading) audio files. The quality of RealAudio sound has recently improved by a quantum leap, but it's still no competition for Dolby THX. If you want background music, you're much better off with a QuickTime MIDI file that can be synthesized to the best quality output from the soundboard in your computer. RealAudio is ideally suited for narration, analog (AIFF, WAV) sound effects, and ambient (atmospheric) sound recordings, such as an audience clapping or the sounds of Broadway traffic.

Basic Design Rules

There are some principles of design that apply to all media. If you're not a professional designer whose training and experience have already taught you these rules, don't fret. These basic rules are just common sense. You can learn them quickly—and you may already know them instinctively. Use them and your work won't look shabby in the eyes of a layperson.

Storyboarding

I know. I just told you not to be intimidated and now it sounds as if I'm telling you to become an instant artist. Relax. You don't need to show this storyboard to anyone besides yourself (if you do need the approval of a committee, just hire a real artist to interpret your storyboard). The best newbie storyboarding technique I've found is simply to sketch pages on 3×5 index cards, and then lay them out on the floor and figure out where the links go. If the links don't work or you're not comfortable with the organization of the pages, rearrange the layout of the cards and redraw the links (I use colored twine so I can move it easily). For more on storyboarding and other Web site planning issues, see Chapter 12, "Web Site Organization and Management."

Another technique that works better for some is to use a flowchart program. Outline the basic page context in each organizational box, and then connect the links. Some people will find this technique less satisfactory, however, because you can't sketch placement of non-text elements and because internal links are difficult to show.

Don't worry about how much time you're spending at this stage of design. Every ten minutes you spend working out your storyboard will save you three hours of site development time.

Form Follows Function

The best site is the one that gives viewers what they are looking for in a way that is intuitive to use. Make sure all the elements in your design have a purpose. Don't reinvent the car without making it easier to get from point A to point B in the process. If you put the clutch in the trunk because it isn't so "unsightly" there, nobody's going to be able to drive the car. If you take out the clutch altogether because you design an automatic transmission, that's a different story.

Your Web page isn't necessarily going to follow the same organization as the original print document. The design of a Web page needs to be inspired by its functional objectives.

Defining Site Purpose

Before you start designing pages, make sure you have defined the purpose of your Web site. Write it down if you have to and refer to it frequently to ensure that all your designs reflect your overall goals and objectives.

List the answers to the following questions:

- Who is your audience?

    Create a good demographic profile of your target audience. What is their sex, median age, and average income? Are they likely to be liberal or conservative? Are they business people, kids, or nerds? The more demographic questions you can answer, the clearer it will become what your site should look like and how it should be organized.

- What do you want the site to do for you? Do you want it to get you a job? Build your ego? Sell your products? Teach your students? Attract paid subscribers?

- Is fun appropriate?

    The answers to the other questions in this list will dictate whether the look of the site should be elegant, conservative, or whacky. Obviously, a game site aimed at 14-year-olds will have a brighter, more hand-made feel than a site targeting investment brokers.

Space Is Good

Often one of the best design features you can add to a page is nothing at all—often known as "white space." Why add white space? There are many reasons, such as the following:

- Space gives the eye a rest.
- Space is useful for isolating one group (type) of information from another.
- Space focuses the viewer's attention.

Space isn't always good. If there's a lot of information to navigate to, start by putting it in front of the viewer—even if it means crowding the first scene. There's an exception to this rule: if your site is meant to be a discovery adventure, you may want to make information accessible only after a "treasure hunt." Do this, however, only if you have carefully determined that this approach is appropriate to your site and only if you can make the discovery a truly rewarding (as opposed to frustrating) experience. I can't tell you how to do this. It takes testing and experimentation—which is why we seldom see it done well.

Less Is More

Make sure the point isn't hidden in verbosity or graphical excess. Keeping content and structure simple makes information quicker and easier to read.

Keep It Grouped

Keep related items physically close to one another. You want your viewer to understand instantly which pieces of information are related.

Keep Groups Aligned

Make it easy to track the flow of information visually. Never put related information on opposite sides of something (unless it's a chart with arrows pointing to the parent of the relationship).

Keep Styles Consistent

Make sure all elements of like type follow the same design parameters, such as type style, banner size, and page background color. If you use too many different elements on a page, you will quickly have a very busy design. Defining a set of colors that you will use consistently throughout the site is a good way to ensure a consistent style.

Make Sure Everything Is Readable

Don't use type that's too small to read. If text has become fuzzy, jagged, or mushy in the course of creating a graphic, redo it. Don't use background patterns that interfere with your text. Make sure the alternative color of links doesn't make them disappear against the background. Make sure that your visited link color is also distinguishable against the background, and make sure it contrasts enough with the link color to make it obvious which links have been selected.

Change Is Constant

The best way to ensure that your site attracts a large and growing audience is to keep it fresh and dynamic. Redesign it as often as possible, but don't make changes so drastic that repeat visitors will feel they've surfed to the wrong wave. The sites on the Internet that report the most hits are those that are changed most frequently.

Violate the Rules Whenever It Doesn't Look Ugly

This is not to say you should violate the rules at every opportunity, thus defeating their purpose. This would make the pages look ugly and become the exception that proves the rule.

Violating a rule occasionally, on the other hand, can draw favorable attention by giving things a fresh look. Don't be afraid to experiment. You can always put things back the way you found them.

Figure 2.13 shows a rule violation—a full-page graphic. But in this case it works, because it was carefully constructed to load quickly.

Design Considerations for the Web

Figure 2.13

There's no HTML text in this full-page graphic.

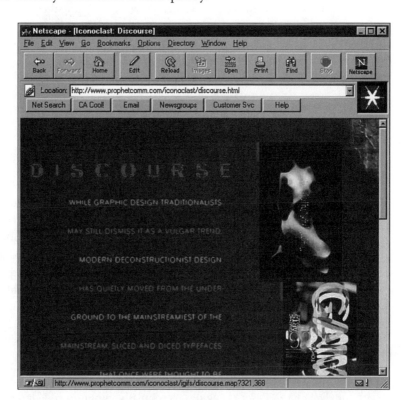

Viewer Turn-Offs and Other Design No-Nos

Like your parents used to say, there are some things you'd be better off without. The following sections point out things your Web pages would be better off without.

Horizontal Bars

Avoid solid horizontal bars like the plague. They were originated to separate the content on one portion of the page from the content on another. If you need to do this, it is more visually interesting to insert a graphic or to give the reader a visual break by simply inserting some unfilled space. If you do want to use a more space-saving separator bar, consider using a graphic. There are examples of broken bars in Chapter 11, "Graphics Creation," which encourage the eye to sneak through the cracks and keep moving down the page.

Long Sign-Up Forms

If you must have them, give the reader a reward for filling them out. Don't make people waste their time before they even know whether or not your site is worth seeing. They will either give up and go elsewhere before they've filled out the form or be so annoyed they'll never return.

Gratuitous Special Effects

Chapter 11 takes great care to show you how to add depth to type and buttons, and points out a great many plug-ins and utilities that will create a specific look for a button or icon. This is the place to warn you that there is a problem with these tools: they're too easy to use. This ease of use leads to overuse until drop shadowed text and beveled buttons have become a cliché. Like most clichés, there is good reason for their popularity. A Web page that has depth is more involving. Depth in graphics also visually conveys the three-dimensional nature of hypertext information. These techniques, however, are no longer impressive for their own sake, so don't overuse them. Also, be consistent in placing them so they aid in understanding the function of a graphic. For instance, a 3D beveled button is useful because it looks as though it should be pushed.

Under Construction Signs

If the site is well designed, it is always under construction. It is the nature of the Web to be dynamic and ever-changing. As soon as you put up an "Under Construction" sign, you have told your audience the site isn't well designed. If you must put up a notice that a page is a placeholder, just say so—something like this:

This page is a substitute for the real thing.

The real thing will be a surprise to us all.

Come back and check it out later.

Overcrowding

Don't overwhelm your pages with graphics, banners, frames, or other gimmicks. Some complex sites such as C-Net and HotWired have found having lots of information densely packed on introductory pages helps users orient themselves to what they can expect to find. This is a legitimate reason for crowding, but some "tricks" make these pages seem far less crowded than they are (such as careful organization and grouping of like elements or sans serif type for small menus).

Too Much Scrolling

Make sure that any given graphic, paragraph, or principal design groups can be seen within a 450×300 pixel window. This will ensure that most people won't have to scroll or resize their windows to capture the whole meaning of any important content element.

It is especially annoying to have to scroll or resize to see a whole picture. If you're an artist who can't stand to see your work presented in low resolution, the best advice is to refrain from putting it on the Web. As a practical matter, the Web will never be more than 72 dpi. Forcing people to scroll to see an image won't make them think more of you as an artist.

It's almost never a good idea to make viewers scroll an image map or a graphics-filled table. Here's the litmus test: have a stranger navigate to the page and see if they react with pleasure or confusion.

The one instance in which scrolling is okay is text. It's better to let people scroll down text in a long article than to make them jump, which interrupts continuity.

Download "My Favorite Browser" First!

Sometimes graphically oriented sites will have to require a specific browser because there's no other way to see what the designer had in mind. If that's the case, provide a preview page that explains the situation and gives the viewer the choice of not going there. Better yet, add an alternative page that provides the information without showing the design.

Be tender about suggesting what browser users should use. It's a personal choice, not a commandment. Alternate browsers are not always possible for viewers from many Internet Service Providers, such as the estimated six million users of AOL. You could say something like: "This site's best personality comes through when viewed with MyFavoriteBrowser." Then place a download icon the user can click on to download a (preferably free) copy.

No Contact Address for the Person/Department You Want to Contact

When a company doesn't have mail links to key departments and personnel, I start to wonder why they have a Web site. Are they too good to talk to ordinary people? Why would a company want to hide their marketing or public relations people? Are they not ready to sell their products and services? Do they not want publicity for fear it will bring them too much business? I suspect the real reason they do this is to keep key personnel from being swamped with e-mail. A much better answer is to link this connection to a separate mail box and use a mail reader that sorts received mail by sender or key subject word. If the viewer has to fill out a form in order to send their mail, the mail can be sorted by field before being read. It is up to you to make your site useful to your viewers. Otherwise, don't be surprised if you give a party and no one comes.

Dead-End Navigation

Don't force people to use the browser's Back or Forward buttons to do their navigating. Some of the more ancient browsers don't even have these buttons. A common error is letting people navigate to a dead end by creating a page without access to the site map, a navigation bar, or the previous page. I don't know anyone who hasn't made this design error at least once, so be sure to check your site for this possibility before you upload it to your Web server.

Run-On, Rambling, Oversized Text

Among designers, it's considered a mortal sin to crowd pages with dense type. Computer screens are significantly harder to read than the printed page. Keep your paragraphs short and your sentence construction simple, and leave eye-resting white space between concepts.

Too Many Frames

Use frames sparingly. Actually, don't use them at all unless you really need them. There are three reasons for this advice:

1. About half the designers I know hate frames. I suspect the general public is even more intolerant, because most sites that started using them have dropped them.

2. Frames chop the viewing area into small pieces, making it much harder to fit content without requiring excessive scrolling.

3. Frames can make navigation more confusing.

Inaccessible Information

Make it clear, right on the front page, how the site is structured. Be sure to include an obvious link to a table of contents, map of the site, or both. Also include a search engine. No one wants to waste time looking for information they know very well is somewhere on the site.

Checking the Site

When you have finished composing your content, make a list of things to check, as follows, and go through each page. When potential clients are looking at a site, they judge you by these details in evaluating your ability to create a site for them.

- **Spelling.** Use a spell checker on all pages.

- **Titles.** Make sure each element has a text title.

- **Matching content.** Make sure title bars match page contents. The title bar is used to describe bookmarks that viewers set in their browsers.

- **Alignment.** Make sure like elements align at the same point.

- **Link checking.** Make sure all links go to their expected destination and that there are no broken links.

- **Window resizing.** Resize the windows to make sure your layout doesn't get jumbled.

- **Test with repeated viewing.** Are any elements starting to bug you? Should you reorganize your content?

- **Include contact information.** Can the viewer contact everyone? Principals in the company? Public relations? Technical support?

Summary

The topic of Web site design is far too broad to be covered completely in one chapter. Entire books have been devoted to just that subject. In fact, a great book on this topic is *Web Concept and Design* by Crystal Waters (New Riders, 1996).

This chapter provides basic Web design concepts to help you create an effective, attractive Web site. The goal is to highlight the differences between print and the Web, and prepare you for the concepts and conversion techniques in the rest of this book. Now that you have a general sense of the design differences, you should be ready to convert your content.

CHAPTER 3
Microsoft Office Document Conversion

Microsoft's Office Suite is a powerful set of integrated applications designed for increasing productivity in the workplace. Two of the four programs shipped as part of Office—Word and Excel—are the most widely used word processing and spreadsheet programs in the business community. It makes sense that Microsoft is now offering free Internet Assistants for all the applications in Office: Word, Excel, PowerPoint, and Access (Windows only). With increasing focus on intranet applications, a tool to convert the many documents created in Office applications is highly desirable if you want to get existing Office documents up on an internal Web quickly.

The intranet is similar to a LAN, or local area network, which you may or may not have in your office. The difference is that an intranet makes it possible to share documents regardless of computer platform because most documents available on an intranet are formatted as HTML (HyperText Markup Language), which is understood by all computer systems. The importance of this kind of universality among business documents is just beginning to be understood by business managers and employees. Documents of all kinds can be put on an intranet, with all relevant references available by a single click. Collaborative reports, such as in medical research, can be easily accessed by all members of the research team simultaneously. As an example, the Pharmaceutical R&D team at a leading biotechnology company shares a Web site for each research effort. The project leader and her assistant maintain the site; scientists and research associates contribute papers, images, diagrams, reference searches, and any other type of document pertaining to the project. They convert most of their documents into HTML by using Internet Assistants for MS Office Suite. In this way, everyone on the research team shares the information and adds to it easily.

So imagine not being required to learn anything about HTML to publish your documents on the Internet or within a corporate intranet. Imagine being able to access an HTML document over the Web that references an Excel pivot table. Imagine, in addition to viewing the table in Excel, being able to manipulate it so you are viewing the data values you need at the time—all without quitting your browser. Internet Assistants (IAs) and Viewers for Office make such powerful document sharing possible.

Where Can I Get Internet Assistants?

Internet Assistants for Word, Excel, and PowerPoint are available for free download at Microsoft's Web site, as follows:

```
http://www.microsoft.com/workshop/author/default.htm
```

Note

Make sure that you download version 2.0 of Internet Assistants. It is significantly better than version 1.0.

Internet Assistants are also on the CD that accompanies this book. Keep a browser bookmark (by selecting Bookmark, Add Bookmark from the toolbar in your browser window) at the Microsoft site so that you are kept aware of updates and improvements to Internet Assistants.

Internet Assistant vs. Viewers

Internet Assistants for Word, Excel, and PowerPoint convert existing documents into HTML. Viewers for these Office programs enable your users to view Office documents over the Internet in their native form without converting them to HTML. There are pros and cons for using either Internet Assistants or Viewers. In general, if you have static Office documents that you want to put on a Web site, using the IAs is your best bet. If, however, you have Excel workbooks with pivot tables that provide changing views of data, it's best to use the Excel Viewer, because Viewers offer a toolbar similar to the toolbars in Excel, Word, and PowerPoint.

The following table shows some hypothetical situations to help you figure out when you might want to use Internet Assistants and when you might want to rely on your users having Viewers.

Using Internet Assistant vs. Viewers

Situation	Use Internet Assistant	Use Viewers
You want documents to be in HTML format.	×	
You want to let people open and edit a document over the Web.		×
You want to add hyperlinks to a document.	×	
You don't know if your user has the Viewers.	×	

Situation	Use Internet Assistant	Use Viewers
You want people to be able to see your pivot tables.	×	
You want your users to see your PowerPoint slides.	×	×
You want your users to see your PowerPoint animations.		×
You are publishing documents primarily for an Internet Web site.	×	
You are publishing documents primarily for an intranet Web site.	×	×

You will notice that in some situations, both IA and Viewer is checked. This is because in these situations, you need to decide for yourself in which format you would like the document published: Native or HTML.

Note

In general, I use the Viewers for Office documents that go up on our intranet, and the IAs for documents that go up on our Web site. When I convert a PowerPoint presentation, I usually use the IA if the document has no animation, and the Animation Publisher (an additional PowerPoint conversion tool) if it does. The Viewer is available over our network, but that Viewer is the least used in our company, probably because the PowerPoint IA is so good. For more information about PowerPoint Animation Publisher and Player, see the section in this chapter titled "Animating PowerPoint Presentations."

Windows vs. Macintosh

This chapter covers the following Internet Assistants:

● IA for Word—Windows

● IA for Word—Macintosh

● IA for Excel—Windows

● IA for Excel—Macintosh

● IA for PowerPoint 95—Windows only

The commands for converting documents into HTML are essentially the same for both Windows and Macintosh. The Macintosh version is slightly slower in performance; however, the current release, 2.0, is a significant improvement over the 1.0 release. Make sure you download the current version.

Microsoft Office
Document Conversion

As yet, there is no Internet Assistant for PowerPoint on the Macintosh. As of this writing, there is no easy workaround for converting Macintosh presentations into HTML.

Word Document Conversion

This section focuses on converting documents you have already created in Word into HTML; however, this chapter is recommended for anyone who wants to create documents specifically for the Web, as it covers the problems associated with the conversion process, including the gap between Word's features and the features supported in Internet Assistant (IA) for Word, version 2.0. Anyone who wants to use Microsoft Word and Internet Assistant for creating Web documents needs to be aware of which functions convert and which don't. This section also makes recommendations on editing your existing Word document so that the document converts as cleanly as possible.

A brief summary of Word elements that will be covered in this chapter are as follows:

- Basic formatting elements, such as bold and italic
- Bulleted lists, numbered lists, and bibliographic (or definition) lists
- Tables
- Handling multiple-column documents
- Handling embedded images
- Handling sound
- Forms documents

Installing Internet Assistant for Word

To install Internet Assistant for Word, Mac users should follow these setup instructions:

1. Exit from Word, if it is running.

2. Double click on MacIAb2.sea from the folder where it is located on your hard disk.

3. Open the Setup Disk folder that was created in the previous step.

4. Double-click on the Internet Assistant Setup application.

5. Follow the instructions on your screen.

6. After setup completes successfully, launch Word.

Basic Document Conversion

When you install Internet Assistant for Word, it becomes part of Word's interface. You don't need to switch between Word and Internet Assistant for Word; indeed, you won't know that Internet Assistant is running. When you convert an existing document into an HTML document, you are basically choosing a different file format (.htm or .html) than the usual file formats (.doc, .txt, .rtf).

In the following sections, you will learn how Internet Assistant for Word handles simple documents, with little formatting, and more complex documents, such as documents with images, tables, multiple columns, and forms.

Saving Word Files as HTML Documents

Once Internet Assistant for Word is installed on your machine, open a Word document and select the File menu. Select Save As, and you will see that the option to save your document as an HTML document appears in the list of file formats (see fig. 3.1).

Figure 3.1

Save as an HTML document.

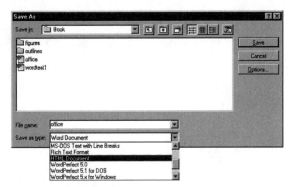

Internet Assistant will save your document as an HTML file with an .htm or .html (if on a Mac) extension. In addition, Internet Assistant will convert basic formatting commands into their respective HTML equivalents. Table 3.2 shows which commands available on the Word toolbar and Format menu are supported by Internet Assistant for Word.

> **N o t e**
> Some Word commands will only become available after you have saved a document as HTML.

This table is meant to be read as a list of formatting types provided in Word (either by simply typing them out or by making a menu selection) that have an HTML tag and that Internet Assistant recognizes. For example, there is no Word equivalent for a Directory list <DIR>, but if you type a list of short items, Internet Assistant for Word will insert a <DIR> tag. If you are not familiar with HTML tags, you might want to check out Chapter 14, "HTML Tutorial and Reference."

HTML Tags and Word Commands Supported by Internet Assistant

HTML Tag	Menu Selection	Action Performed
<A HREF=...>	Insert menu, HyperLink	Creates an anchor that jumps to another document or file—called a hyperlink.
<A HREF="#...>	Insert menu, HyperLink	Creates a hyperlink that jumps to another Bookmark Location in File or location within the same document.
<B>	Toolbar	Formats text in bold type.
<BASE>	File menu, HTML Document Info; Advanced	Provides a base URL so hyperlinks can be referenced relative to this URL when they are not on the current document.
<BGSOUND>	Format menu, Background Sound	Plays a sound when a reader opens your document.
<BLOCKQUOTE>	Occurs when typed	Sets off a block of text quoted from another source.
<BGCOLOR>	Format menu, Background the	Adds a background color to BODY tag.
 	SHIFT+ENTER	Forces a line break without the extra space.
<CENTER>	Format menu, Center Align	Centers graphics or paragraphs.

HTML Tag	Menu Selection	Action Performed
<DIR>	Occurs when typed	Creates a list of short items.
<DL>	Styles	Creates a list of terms and definitions.
<DL COMPACT>	Styles	Creates a two-column list of terms and definitions (a definition list) with no vertical space between entries.
<DT>...<DD>	Definition Term/ Definition	These styles are automatically applied when you create a definition list.
<EM>	Emphasis	Emphasizes text, usually by italicizing.
<FONT>	Format menu, Font	Changes size and typeface of text.
<FORM>	Insert menu, Form Field	Inserts an interactive data entry form that will be displayed as part of the current HTML document.
<H1>–<H6>	Styles	Sets up a hierarchy of headings.
<HR>	Toolbar, icon	Inserts a horizontal line between text.
<I>	Format, Font	Italicizes text.
<IMG>	Insert, Picture	Inserts an image.
<ISINDEX>	File menu, HTML Document Info	Indicates to browsers that your document is an index document, which can be searched by using keywords.
<LI>	Toolbar, icon (part of bulleted or numbered list)	Identifies an item in a list. This style is automatically applied with the <UL> or <OL> style; you do not create it directly.

continues

Microsoft Office
Document Conversion

HTML Tags and Word Commands Supported by Internet Assistant (continued)

HTML Tag	Menu Selection	Action Performed
<MARQUEE>	Insert menu, Marquee	Inserts a scrolling text marquee. For information on the attributes of this tag, click on the Marquee command in the Insert menu.
<MENU>	Menu	Creates a list of items, usually with one line per item.
<OL>	Toolbar, icon	Creates a numbered list.
<STRIKE>	Strikethrough	Identifies "strike-out" text.
<STRONG>	Strong, drop-down menu in toolbar	Identifies words you want to make even more important than words with the <EM> tag. Typically displayed in bold type. In most browsers, looks the same as when using <B>.
<SUB>	Format menu, Font	Formats subscript text.
<SUP>	Format menu, Font	Formats superscript text.
<TABLE>	Table menu, Insert Table	Inserts a table into your document.
<TT>	Typewriter, drop-down menu in toolbar	Formats text in Courier.
<U>	Underline, icon	Underlines text.
<UL>	Toolbar, icon	Creates a list of items whose order is not important. Displayed as a bulleted list.

Creating Hyperlinks

If you are using IA for word on the Windows platform, you can insert hyperlinks into a converted Word document even before you save it as an HTML document. If you are on the Mac platform, you can add them after you convert your document into HTML. *Hyperlinks* are clickable text or icons that enable you to "jump" to other

documents on your Web site or on the Internet. To create hyperlinks, follow these
steps:

1. Highlight the text you would like to use as your link.

2. Choose Hyperlink from the Insert menu (see fig. 3.2).

3. The dialog box shown in figure 3.3 will appear.

Figure 3.2

Inserting a hyperlink.

In the box that says File or URL, type the URL or file name of the document to
which you want to link. An URL (Uniform Resource Locator) is the path name
(address) of a file on your computer, your local network, or the Internet (see fig.
3.3).

If the file is located on your computer or your local network, you can press the
Browse button to locate it the way you locate any file on your computer or
network.

If the file is on another Web site on the Internet, you need to use an absolute
path, meaning you need to type the full URL as you see it on your Web browser
(http://www.name.etc/). Choose Link Path, click on the Use Fixed Link Path
option, and then type over the text that appears. This is slightly confusing,
because the text that appears is an absolute path from your own hard drive, but
it is not the path name of the file or Web site to which you will be linking.

Figure 3.3

Specifying an URL.

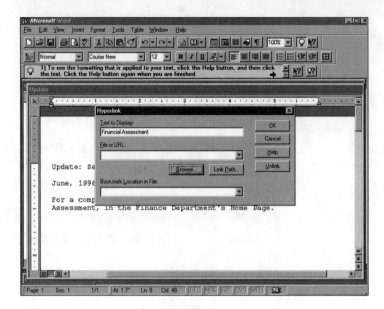

4. Click on OK.

To delete a hyperlink, follow steps 1 and 2, and then choose Unlink. This will delete the link, but not the text.

Converting a Word File that Contains Images

If you have a Word document (file) that contains images, Internet Assistant for Word will automatically convert these images into GIF files. GIF files are one of the two most widely used graphics file formats on the Web. (To learn more about GIFs, see Chapter 10, "Graphics Basics.") Before the program begins converting your document, it will alert you to the images in the document and ask if you want to convert the images as well, or ignore them. *Be careful.* Although this may sound like a great feature, it has two serious drawbacks, as follows:

● The program does not prompt you to name these images. This means that you will not be able to create links to these images without first looking at the source code of your document to figure out what their names are. If you don't know HTML, this can be confusing.

● The program does not let you specify where these image files are being placed.

IA will name the images sequentially; that is, if you have five images in a document, IA will name them IMG0001-IMG0005. If you want to rename them, you need to edit the actual HTML source code to reflect the change of name.

Not being able to specify where you want your images to be placed is a slightly more problematic issue. In general, it is not a good idea to keep your images in the same file as your HTML files. This is because eventually your Web site will grow to be many files and images, and you will need to create some order from your chaotic directory of files and images. One way of creating order is to keep "like" files together, such as image files. But when you change the location of a file, you also must change the URL of that file in any hyperlink that references it. This is a lot of work because it involves opening and editing the source code in any document that links to the image file that has been moved. You can learn more aboout editing source code in Chapter 13, "Tailoring Converted Documents," and also later in this chapter.

> **Note**
>
> A useful way to manage images is to keep them in a central directory. A good rule of thumb is to keep an Images directory at the root-level directory of your Web site that contains those images used throughout your Web site. For images used only for a specific directory (such as a Company Products banner used only for documents located in the Company Products directory), it's best to have an Images directory within that directory; in this case, the Company Products directory.

Although editing the source code of your converted file is sometimes necessary, it certainly should not be your usual process for working with images. In general, save your images with file names that you create yourself. That way, if you need to reuse them in another Web document, you can easily reference them.

> **Note**
>
> Luckily, there is a shareware utility available that will not only rename files in a batch process, but will also update any links to these files. The utility is called Rename, and it is available on the CD that comes with this book.

Complex Document Conversion

Basic documents consist of plain text, character formatting options such as bold, italic, and underline, and list formats. The following sections will show how Internet Assistant handles more complex formatting options, such as tables, forms, and multiple columns.

Converting Tables in Word

If you've ever tried to hard-code a complex table in HTML, you will appreciate how well Internet Assistant converts a table. All the native formatting functionality of

Microsoft Office
Document Conversion

Word's table feature converts cleanly into HTML, with the exception of putting a border around certain table cells. Figures 3.4a and 3.4b show the differences between a table in a Word document and the same table once it's converted into an HTML document.

Figure 3.4a

A table as it appears in Word.

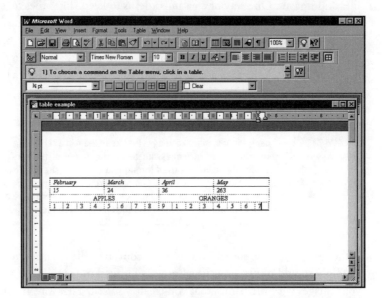

Figure 3.4b

The same table converted into HTML.

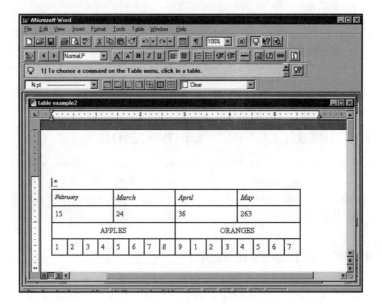

Converting a Multicolumnar Layout

IA for Word does not yet support Word's multicolumn tool, so any document that has columns will be converted into a single-column document. HTML also doesn't truly support multicolumn formatting, but Web designers get around this by putting text and graphics into a table with borders set to zero, which functions as a layout grid. With Internet Assistant, any graphics within a multicolumn document will be converted into the document, with text wrapping around the graphic.

In general, if you are going to be authoring multicolumn documents, such as newsletters, for both print and the Web, you would be better off using a standard desktop publishing application such as QuarkXPress or PageMaker. QuarkXPress is a more viable option because the HTML conversion utilities created for Quark are better than the ones for PageMaker (see Chapter 6, "QuarkXPress Conversion," and Chapter 8, "PageMaker Conversion," for more information).

If, however, you have a few multicolumn documents that you need to convert, here is a workaround:

1. Save the document under a different name to use as a backup in case you make a mistake.

2. Highlight the multicolumn text and select the Column tool from the toolbar.

3. Select one column. The document becomes a single-column document.

4. Next, you will need to replace all your paragraph marks with hard line returns. Go to the Edit menu and click on Replace. To have Word search for paragraph marks, you need to input the character for paragraph mark. Using the "special" button at the bottom of the dialog box, locate the "paragraph" character from the drop-down menu and select it. The paragraph character will appear in the Find box.

   You now want to input a manual line break into the "replace" box. Again, use the "special" button at the bottom of the dialog box, and choose "manual line break" from the drop-down menu.

5. While the text is still highlighted, go into the Table menu and select Convert Text to Table.

6. A dialog box will appear. Choose the following options:

   ● Set the number of columns to 2

   ● Set the number of rows to 1

   ● Set "separate text at:" to "Paragraph"

7. Without leaving the dialog box, click on AutoFormat. Choose the following options:

- Under Formats, click on "none."

- Uncheck all formatting options. By doing this, you will eliminate table borders and any other table formatting option, so that your converted document appears as a simple two-column document, without borders or any other special formatting style that is usually applied to tables. Because you don't want your users to see a table, this is the best set of options to choose. Click on OK to begin conversion.

8. Word will put your document into a table. You can then save it as an HTML document. You will need to go through the document and replace your hard line returns with paragraph marks if you want to set off your paragraphs with more space than what the hard line returns provide. To do this, go back and repeat step 4, this time reversing the find and replace options.

It's a hack, but it works.

> **Note**
>
> After you convert your text to a table, you might want to move some text around to make your two columns look more even. You can do this by simply cutting and pasting text, even though the document is in HTML format.

Converting and Creating Forms in Word

Forms are the most interactive element of the Web today. With forms, you can collect important information about users of your Web site. You can also offer online registration to training courses, seminars, customer service programs, and much more. Forms are usually made "interactive" when combined with a CGI script or Java or ActiveX program. Although CGI, Java, and ActiveX are beyond the scope of this chapter, it is important to know that they are necessary to process the information that is captured in a form. If you plan on using forms, you will need to work with a programmer to create a script or program to process your information. Depending on what kind of Web server you have (the software that makes it possible for your Web pages to be viewed over the Internet or your intranet), there may be some "stock" CGI scripts that came with your server to process certain kinds of forms information, such as a registration form. Programs like Microsoft FrontPage come with these kinds of CGI scripts.

Although still in its early development stages, Internet Assistant's form conversion tool has almost all the form design elements you need to design basic forms for the Web.

The Text field, Drop Down Item field, Radio Button field, and Checkbox field all convert well. Figure 3.5a shows a form created in Word. Figure 3.5b shows the same form converted into an HTML document. This form is placed in a table so that the form fields line up neatly.

Figure 3.5a

A form created in Word.

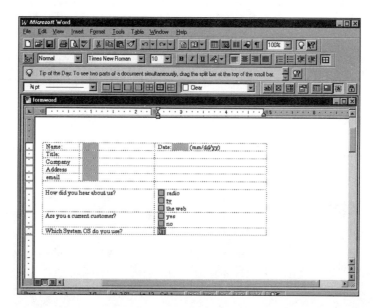

Figure 3.5b

The same form converted into HTML.

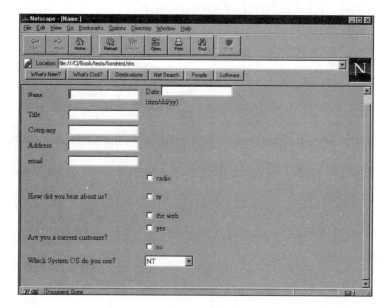

Notice where the text lines up in the HTML form. It is not vertically aligned to the top of the data cell, as it is in the Word document. Although Word's default is to vertically align text at the top of a table cell, when Internet Assistant for Word converts a document, it does not specify where to align the text. The result is text aligned to the bottom of the data cell, which is the default option for HTML. To rectify this, hard-code your table data cells with the <VALIGN> tag. The <VALIGN> tag aligns the text in a table cell to the Top, Center, or Bottom of a table cell. Hard-coding, and how to do it when using Internet Assistant, is explained later in the chapter.

It will help if the forms feature in the next release of Internet Assistant includes some stock CGI scripts and the option to choose an event (a programming command that makes the form actually DO something, such as input the collected data into a database or mail the data in a flat file to the person who needs it). The current version of Internet Assistant does not include the <FORM ACTION> tag, which tells the browser that the form is going to call a CGI script. This, too, needs to be hard-coded (but in addition, you must know where to find a CGI script that will process the information you need to get from the form).

> **Note**
> You can find some basic CGI scripts written in Perl (one of the most common script-ing languages because it is cross-platform) at perlWWW:
>
> ```
> http://www.oac.uci.edu/indiv/ehood/perlWWW
> ```
>
> Perl CGI scripts will run on any kind of Web server.

Ensuring a Clean Conversion

Before you convert your Word file to HTML, it is a good idea to go through the document, using Word's Search and Replace utility to get rid of any symbols and marks that do not convert cleanly. If Internet Assistant fails to convert a character to HTML, it adds textual bleeps and squiggly characters to the document in place of the appropriate symbols and marks. The following table is a summary of all symbols and marks that don't convert to HTML. It's best to delete these characters before you convert your document, or use Replace in Word to replace them with text equivalents.

A Summary of Word Symbols That Convert to HTML

Symbol	Text Equivalent	HTML Support
@	at sign	YES
#	number sign	YES
$	dollar sign	YES

Symbol	Text Equivalent	HTML Support
%	percent sign	YES
&	ampersand	YES
★	star	YES
--	double dash	YES
'	apostrophe	NO
	sum	NO
α	alpha	NO
β	beta	NO
	infinity	NO
°	degree	NO
±	plus or minus	NO
"	smart quotes	NO
	greater than or equal to	NO
	approximately	NO
®	registered name	YES
©	copyright	YES
™	trademark	NO
—	em dash	NO
–	en dash	NO

Microsoft Office
Document Conversion

Author Note

Some valuable macros available on the Web delete and replace characters not supported in HTML. One I've used before is located at the following:

```
http://arirang.snu.ac.kr/www-archive/tools/editing
macros/ms-winword/
```

If you are accustomed to using macros to handle repetitive tasks, you will appreciate this macro.

Post-Conversion Cleanup: Editing Your Source Code

Often you will want to add some formatting to your converted document that Internet Assistant does not support. For example, when we converted the table in the previous example, the data in the table cell did not align itself where we wanted it to. What we need to do is to insert the <VALIGN=TOP> tag within the data cells, to tell the browser that we want to align the text to the top of the data cell. To add such formatting, you will want to edit the source code of the converted document.

The source code is the HTML code that makes your document look the way it does. Internet Assistant shields you from having to work with the source code by providing an interface that mimics Word, but you will probably need to edit your source code to add formatting features Internet Assistant does not currently support.

> **Note**
>
> Editing source code requires that you know something about HTML. If you have never looked at HTML code before, this is not a job you should be undertaking. If you are going to be converting lots of documents into Web documents, however, investigate Chapter 14, "HTML Tutorial and Reference," or some of the many HTML tutorials available on the Web. This will teach you what kind of tags to add to your document and where to add them. An HTML document's source code can look like pure pandemonium if you are not familiar with HTML structure and tags. Chapter 14 also provides an exhaustive list of HTML resources on the Web.
>
> Just to clarify: you do not need to know every HTML tag or be an HTML expert to effectively edit your source code. You just need enough familiarity with HTML so that you aren't confused by what you see.

Now you can take the earlier form example and edit the source code to align the text to the top of the data cell. Go back and look at figures 3.5a and 3.5b. Did you notice that the answers to the question "How did you hear about us?" do not line up the same way in the two figures? Assume that the first choice, radio, should line up with the question, with the other choices listed underneath. This can be accomplished by editing the source code with the <VALIGN> attribute.

> **Note**
>
> An *attribute* is a modification to a tag. A tag can have many attributes; each attribute specifies a different formatting result. For example, the ‹TABLE› tag has several attributes—BORDER, ALIGN, WIDTH, HEIGHT—just to name a few. These attributes extend the control a designer has over how the table should look. ‹TABLE BORDER=0› specifies that the table should have a border of 0, meaning no borders around cells.

The <VALIGN> tag specifies the alignment of text within a table cell. The "V" stands for vertical, as in vertical alignment. The default setting (if none is specified) aligns the text in the center of the cell. Hence, in this example, the words "How did you hear about us" and "radio" are not aligned; instead, "How did you hear about us" is aligned to "tv," the center of the table cell.

The code should be edited so "How did you hear about us" is aligned to the top of the next data cell. To do this, first switch from HTML Edit mode into Edit Source mode, as follows:

1. From the View menu, select HTML Source (see fig. 3.6).

Figure 3.6

Switching from HTML Edit mode to View Source mode.

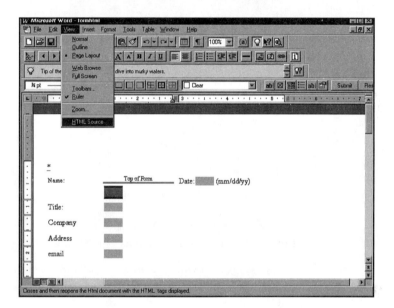

Microsoft Office
Document Conversion

2. A document will appear on your screen. This is the HTML source document. It is usually named Document1 (see fig. 3.7).

   Scroll down to where the <TABLE> tag appears. You are now inside the table. Tables are coded horizontally; first a row is created <TR>, and then each table data cell <TD>.

3. Scroll down to the row that contains the "How did you hear about us?" text. The code that precedes this text is the code you want to edit. The code looks like this:

```
<TR><TD COLSPAN=2 WIDTH=240>How did you hear about us?</TD>
<TD WIDTH=240><INPUT TYPE="CHECKBOX" NAME="Check1"> radio
```

The <TR> tag specifies the row. The <TR> tag is followed by a <TD> tag. There can be many <TD> tags per row; in this case, two: one for the question "How did you hear about us" and one for the answers. The <TD> tag is the one to which you want to add the attribute.

Figure 3.7

Viewing the source code.

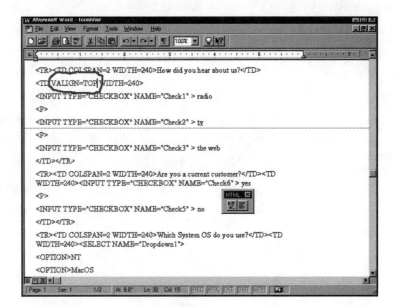

4. Place your cursor before the WIDTH=240 attribute, and type **VALIGN=TOP**. Make sure you do this in *both* <TD> tags in that row.

5. When you have finished typing, *don't press save*! You need to go back to HTML edit mode. A small icon will appear on your screen that looks like the one in figure 3.8.

Figure 3.8

The HTML Edit icon.

6. Click on the Pencil icon. A dialog box will ask if you would like to save your changes. Now you can save your document.

Warning

It is very important to save your document *only* when you are in HTML Edit mode, not View Source mode. If you save your document in View Source mode, you will save your source code as your HTML document. Then, when you view your document in your browser, you will be seeing your source code converted into HTML. In other words, Internet Assistant will put HTML tags around your HTML tags. You will then need a stiff drink and some Tums.

Despite some bugs, IA for Word is very easy to use. It works best with simple documents that need to go up on the Web or an intranet fairly quickly. Internet Assistant for Windows far exceeds the one for the Macintosh, which is unfortunate. The next chapter discusses the other, and better, choices for word processing conversion on the Mac.

Excel Spreadsheet Conversion

The process for converting Excel spreadsheets by using Internet Assistant is slightly more sophisticated than the process for converting Word documents. A *wizard* guides the process, asking formatting questions as you proceed. Internet Assistant Wizard gives the option of saving the spreadsheet as a stand-alone HTML document or into an existing HTML template. The example here converts a quarterly report spreadsheet into an existing Quarterly Report HTML template posted on Aslan Computing's Web site. Later in the chapter, the same spreadsheet will be displayed as it is posted on Aslan's intranet in its native format. By using Microsoft's Excel Viewer, senior management executives can edit the document they are viewing over the intranet.

Installing Internet Assistant for Excel

After you download IA for Excel from the Microsoft site, or copy it from this disk, you will need to save the add-in file, HTML.XLA, into the Microsoft Excel Library directory. The path to this directory is different depending on which version of Excel you are running.

For stand-alone Excel 5.0, you will find the Library directory directly under the Excel directory (for example, C:\Excel\Library on a Microsoft Windows system and My Computer: Microsoft Office: Microsoft Excel: Macro Library on an Apple Macintosh system).

For MS Office and Excel 7.0, you will find the Library directory under the MSOffice and Excel directories (for example, C:\MSOffice\Excel\Library).

After you have copied the HTML.XLA file to the proper library directory, start Excel and click on the Tools menu and choose Add-ins. There will be a box for Internet Assistant Wizard. Check the box and click on OK.

Converting Excel Spreadsheets with Internet Assistant Wizard

The following example will convert an Excel spreadsheet that contains quarterly receivables for all employees of Aslan Computing. The example assumes Internet Assistant is already loaded on your computer.

Before you convert your Excel spreadsheet, highlight the area you want to convert, then proceed as follows:

1. In the Tools menu, select Internet Assistant Wizard. The Wizard dialog box appears.

2. The first step of the wizard will ask you to select or enter the range of data you want to convert. If you selected the range before you started the wizard, the range should appear. Click on Next.

3. The wizard gives you two options: convert the data into an independent HTML document or convert the data into HTML and place it into an existing template. In this example, the latter option will be implemented (see fig. 3.9).

Figure 3.9

Saving the table into an existing template.

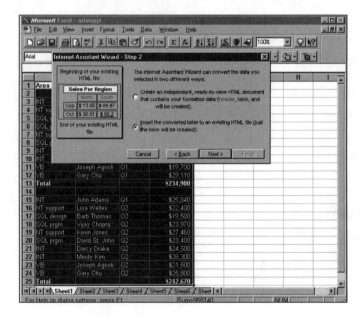

Microsoft Office
Document Conversion

> **Note**
>
> An existing template can be any HTML page that you reuse when data changes. For example, a sales report form generally has the same structure each time it is put up on a Web site, but the figures change per quarter. If you wanted to put the converted spreadsheet into the place in the template where you want the table to appear, you would type the following where you want the table to appear (see fig. 3.10):
>
> ```
> <!--##Table##-->
> ```

Figure 3.10

The source code for inserting an Excel table into a template.

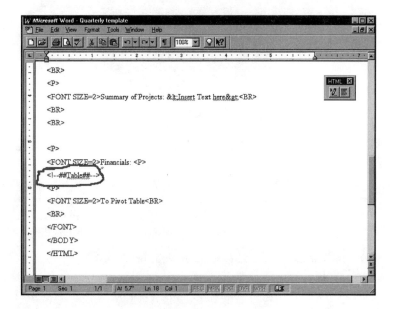

5. Internet Assistant then asks for the path name to the template. You can type it in, or browse for it (see fig. 3.11). Our template is called quartemp.htm. Click on Next.

6. The next step in the Internet Wizard gives two options: convert as much of the formatting as possible or convert the data only. In general, it is best to convert as much of the formatting as possible. If you choose to select the data only, IA does not put borders around your table cells, and blank cells are ignored. If you have used blank cells as a formatting feature (to give more space to the table, for example), these blank cells will not be converted, and you might not retain the formatting of the table that you want. Click on Next.

Figure 3.11

Browsing for the template.

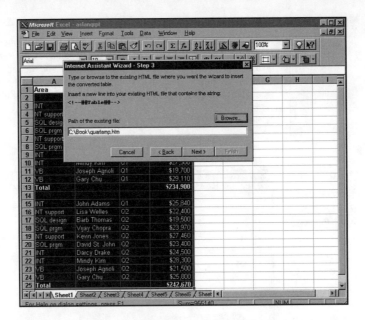

7. Internet Assistant now asks you to name the new file. This new file is your template file with your converted spreadsheet imported into it. This is a great feature, because it enables you to preserve your template for future use. In this example, the file is named quarpt.htm. Click on Finish.

8. You can now open the file in your browser.

Figure 3.12

The converted data within a document template.

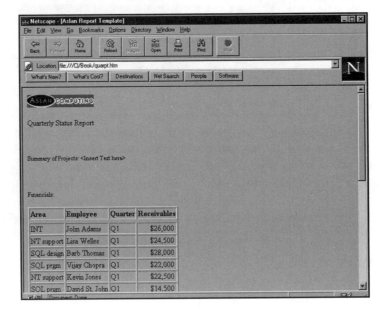

Saving a Spreadsheet as an Independent HTML Document

In the last exercise, the quarterly report was saved into an existing spreadsheet. Internet Assistant also provides the option to save your spreadsheet as an independent HTML document. The steps of the wizard are the same, until you get to step 4, where you save the document as an HTML document. The process is the same again, starting with step 6. Again, save as much of the formatting as possible, as this creates a more readable table. You can see the resulting HTML table in figure 3.13.

Figure 3.13

The quarterly report saved as an independent HTML file.

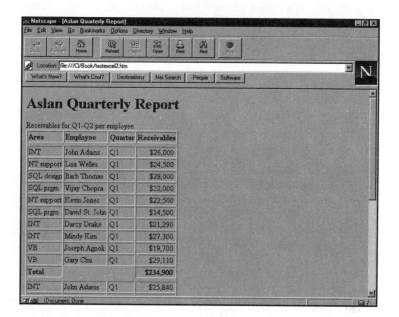

In general, you would choose the option to save an Excel spreadsheet into an existing template if you had a predefined "look" for a document. For example, you might save a blank HTML document that contained only a header graphic and a footer graphic. This would be your "template" for a page. You could then reuse this page whenever you wanted to convert your Excel spreadsheet into an HTML table with those particular graphics. Using templates comes in handy if you have a Web site with a consistent look and feel.

On the other hand, if you have a random Excel document that you need to get up quickly, and for which you don't have a template, then choose the option to convert the spreadsheet into an independent HTML document. Using this option is especially good for putting up documents on an intranet, where "more matter with less art" should certainly be the rule of thumb.

The Excel Viewer: An Intranet Power Tool

Earlier in the chapter, I said I would make a case for not converting certain documents into HTML at all. Excel is a powerful data presentation program that derives its power from features such as pivot tables, which enable you to change the presentation of the data. The Excel Viewer makes it possible for people viewing documents over the Internet or their corporate intranet to apply Excel's native functionality without having Excel installed on their computer.

Intranet Design Concerns

If you are designing pages for the Internet, then you won't know if your users have the Excel Viewer. Some designers make the Viewer available to download from their own Web site. Others don't want to burden users with downloading and configuring software. That's a choice you will need to make. If you are designing pages for a corporate intranet, however, you can make the Excel viewer available on your local network (it's free!). With that in mind, why not keep your Excel documents in their native format? The following example shows how Aslan Computing shares its quarterly financial data on its intranet.

The Excel Viewer is available on the CD that accompanies this book, and is also downloadable from the Microsoft Web site, as follows:

```
http://www.microsoft.com/msexcel/it_xl.htm
```

Microsoft Excel for Windows 95 is built to automatically configure itself as a helper application for Netscape Navigator and Microsoft Internet Explorer. This means that when you click on the setup/install icon after downloading, it will do everything you need it to do to view Excel spreadsheets over the Web.

The Excel Viewer and an Intranet Application

Aslan posts its quarterly earnings with emphasis on an individual consultant's receivables and area of expertise. This means that business development executives can see which areas of expertise are bringing in the most in receivables, accounting specialists can keep track of a consultant's income, financial specialists can track quarterly growth, and project managers can match projected budgets with actual figures.

The quarterly earnings document was created in Excel, and then the creator used the Pivot Table wizard (see Excel's Help if you have never used the wizard) to organize the various ways data could be viewed within Excel.

The document looks like figure 3.14.

Figure 3.14

A quarterly report in Excel.

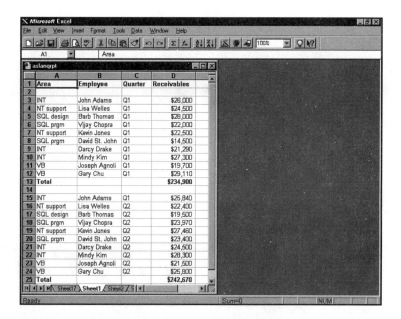

It also contains a pivot table that enables receivables to be tracked by Employee (see fig. 3.16) and Area (see fig. 3.17).

On the Aslan Web site, users link to the table in the Financials section. Because the document is saved with the .xls extension, and because the Viewer is installed on each employee's computer, the Excel Viewer automatically starts up.

The Excel Viewer has a toolbar similar to the one in Excel. When in the Viewer, if you click on the Pencil icon, you can edit and move the data in the table. You are not actually changing the document on the Web site. The document you are editing is a document copied to your temp file in your Windows directory or to your cache file in your system folder (Macintosh). You will probably have to hunt for it, as both operating systems give the files obscure numerical names.

To see the total of Mindy Kim's receivables (for example), you can switch to a pivot table by clicking on the next sheet in the Workbook. This brings up the pivot table. To edit or change the views of the pivot table, click on the Pencil icon on the toolbar (see fig. 3.17). This opens the document for editing.

Figure 3.15

The pivot table showing receivables tracked by Employee.

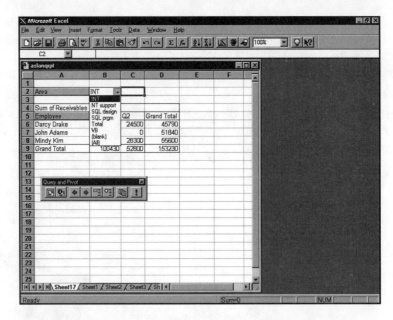

Figure 3.16

The pivot table showing receivables tracked by Area.

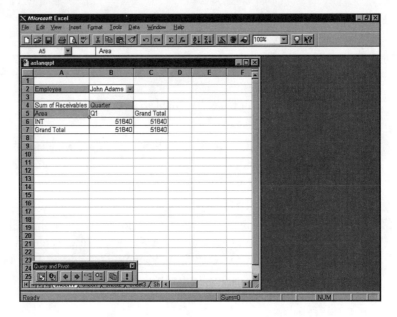

You can also view total receivables for each area: Internet, NT, and Visual Basic Programming (VB). This enables comparisons of which areas are growing in the business, compared to the year—or even the quarter—before.

Figure 3.17

Manipulating a pivot table in Excel Viewer.

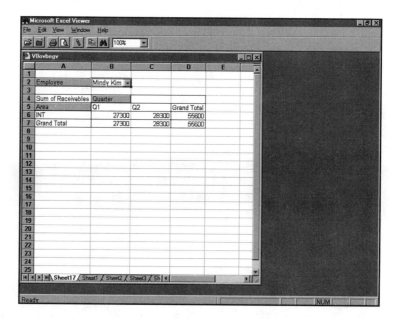

Microsoft Office
Document Conversion

The Excel Viewer adds a lot of value to intranet and Internet applications if deployed well. As suggested earlier, the Excel Viewer is better suited for intranet applications; however, because it downloads quickly, you may want to provide a link to it from your Web site so users can manipulate data.

Tips for Converting Word and Excel Tables

As you have seen, both Word and Excel's Internet Assistants convert tables into HTML. In some instances, it would be more desirable to import a spreadsheet into a Word document and then convert it, rather than converting it in Excel. Generally, if you want to have more control in formatting the table, or if you want to include images in your document, importing the table into Word and then converting it is the best choice.

In deciding whether to import a document into Word, base your decision on whether it will be an Internet or an intranet document. If the table is going to appear on a Web site, import it into Word and then convert it. If the table is going to be put on an intranet, convert it directly in Excel. The reasons are cosmetic. By default, tables converted by Word don't have borders and, for the most part, just look better. Figures 3.18a and 3.18b illustrate this. Later on in this chapter, a case will be made for not converting the document at all, but instead using the Microsoft Excel Viewer to both view and manipulate the data in the table. Doing this with Excel documents that contain financial comparisons and pivot tables is recommended because users can manipulate the data with the help of the Excel Viewer, a very valuable application for corporate intranets.

Figure 3.18a shows an Excel spreadsheet that was imported into Word, and then converted into HTML with Word's Internet Assistant. Figure 3.18b is the same Excel spreadsheet converted by the IA for Excel and saved as an independent HTML document.

Figure 3.18a

An Excel table imported into Word, then saved as HTML.

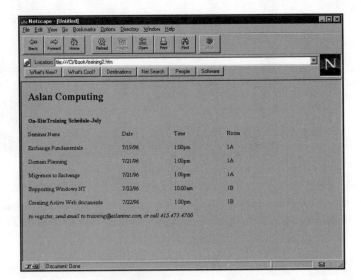

Figure 3.18b

An Excel table converted by Internet Assistant.

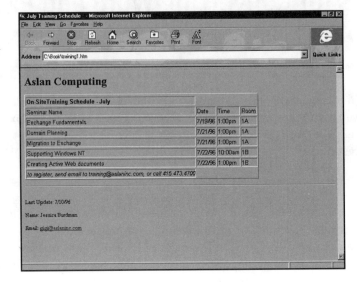

Converting PowerPoint Presentations

The winner of the prize for Best Internet Assistant for the Office Suite is definitely the PowerPoint Internet Assistant. This assistant is the smartest of the three discussed in this chapter. With the PowerPoint IA, you can convert your presentations in one easy command, Export As HTML, but that is just where the beauty of the converter begins. In addition to creating exact graphical representations of your presentation slides, the IA also makes a text-only version with hyperlinks intact. This gives you the option of making a text-only version available to people who have nongraphical browsers or who have turned off graphics in their browsers. If you know something about HTML, you'll understand that PowerPoint Internet Assistant creates client-side image maps of the original slides, thereby making the resulting HTML page a clickable image map with hyperlinks to the other pages in the presentation.

With the IA for PowerPoint, you can do the following:

- Create graphically advanced Web pages with one single command

- Incorporate sound and animation by using the PowerPoint Animation Player

- Create text-only equivalents of your slides for users with non-graphical, low-bandwith Internet connections

PowerPoint is one of the leading presentation software packages on the market today. Many business people use PowerPoint to create sales, research, marketing, and many other kinds of presentations, which they then might file away into notebooks or keep on disk. If a colleague wanted to obtain copies of the presentation, he would need to borrow the notebook or obtain a copy on disk. This method of sharing research was often used in businesses and academia before the corporate intranet. Now you can create a directory for presentations and make your valuable information available to anyone who has access to your corporate intranet. You don't need to be responsible for making copies on paper or on disk; you can simply send someone an URL for your presentation, and they can look it up and copy it themselves.

> **Note**
>
> On our intranet site, we have a directory called ppt, which contains all the presentations our business development people create. When writing online reports, we often link to the text-only versions of these slides.

The following example is a presentation on migrating to Exchange, Microsoft's new e-mail/groupware application.

Microsoft Office
Document Conversion

If you want to follow along with the examples provided on the book's CD, use the exchange.ppt file:

1. Open the PowerPoint presentation you want to convert; in this case, exchange.ppt.

2. On the File menu, click on Export as HTML (see fig. 3.19).

Figure 3.19

Export as HTML command.

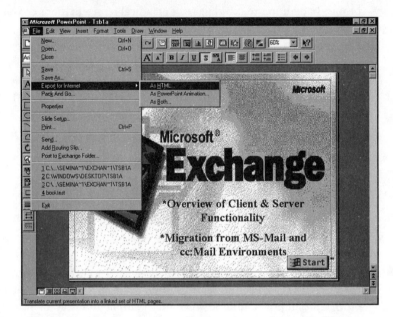

3. Set the following options in the HTML Export Options dialog box (see fig. 3.20):

    ● Output style: Select either Grayscale or Color, depending on how you want your slides to appear. The usual choice would be Color if you have slides that use several colors.

    ● Output format: Select either JPEG or GIF to indicate the file format you want for your slides. GIF files are bigger files and take longer to download, but their resolution is clearer. JPEG files are smaller than GIF files, but not as clearly rendered. Photographs, however, usually make good JPEG files.

    ● JPEG compression quality: You can move the slide control to set the quality level for JPEG format. A lower setting will result in a smaller file, but text and lines may appear blurred or streaked. If you use a lot of photographic images in your slides, JPEG files can save space and increase speed when you download your Web documents.

● Folder for HTML Export: Specify the name of the drive and folder in which you want to save the files created for your Web pages. Note that PowerPoint IA will save each presentation in its own folder. To select a different directory, click on Browse.

Figure 3.20

HTML Options when converting PowerPoint presentations.

4. Click on OK.

After a few moments, you'll see a slide show appear in a window. Internet Assistant uses this window to convert the images of your slides. You'll also notice that the more slides you have in your presentation and the more interactive settings you've set, the longer this process will take.

Microsoft Office
Document Conversion

Note

Interactive settings are actions that can occur within a presentation when you click your mouse. The Interactive Settings options are available under the Tools menu and consist of the following:

● Going to the next slide

● Playing a sound

● Running a program

● Calling up an object to appear (such as an image created in Excel)

When the conversion is finished, open up the directory that contains your converted presentation. Remember, this is the folder you specified in the HTML Options dialog box.

You will see a list of files similar to the ones in figure 3.21.

Figure 3.21

Slide files created by Internet Assistant.

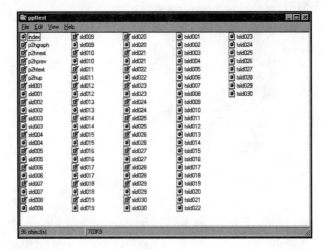

The index.htm file is a list of all the slides in the presentation. The slide names are presented as hyperlinks to the slides, and your name and the name of the presentation appear at the top (see fig. 3.22). It is a convention of HTML developers to name the first file of any directory "index.htm" or "index.html," so the IA for PowerPoint follows this convention.

Figure 3.22

The index file.

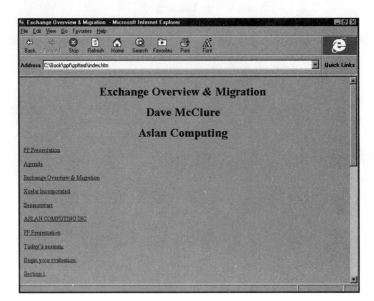

The files with the Sld prefix, such as Sld001.htm, are the graphical slide files. In the example, we have 30 slides, so we will have 30 Sld files.

The files with the Tsld prefix, such as Tsld001.htm, are the text representations of the slides. On each graphical slide, there is a button with an "A" on it, which links to the textual version of that slide (see figs. 3.23a and 3.23b).

Note

You might be wondering why anyone would want to provide text-only versions of their slides when the IA for PowerPoint provides such a rich alternative to text. One reason for doing so is to provide an alternative for people who have graphics turned off on their browsers, or who might have a low-bandwidth connection (if they are viewing your presentation over the Internet instead of within an intranet). Another advantage of providing text-only versions of slides is that it enables people who might be using parts of your presentation to prepare papers or reports to literally copy and paste the text that they need.

Figure 3.23a

Link to the text version.

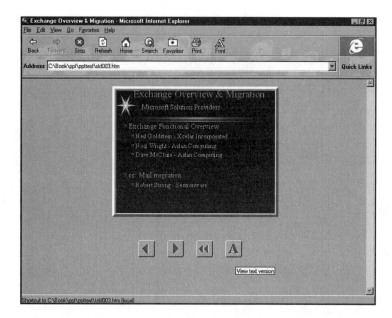

Figure 3.23b

The text version.

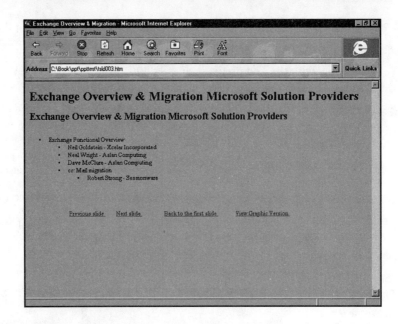

Changing Image Size

Because the IA for PowerPoint creates graphical slides from screen shots of the PowerPoint presentation, you can control the size of the images somewhat by controlling the size of your monitor's display settings. For example, if you have an 1124×768 display, your images are going to be much bigger than if your display is set to 640×480. What does this mean in terms of your HTML presentation? Bigger images create bigger files, which take longer to download over the Internet. If you are going to put these presentations up on an external Web site, set your monitor display to 640×480 before you convert your presentation. The following steps will do this in Windows 95:

1. In the Start menu, point to Settings, and then click on Control Panel.

2. Double-click on Display, and then click on the Settings tab.

3. Move the slide control to 640×480, and then click on OK.

Using Interactive Settings to Create Image Maps

PowerPoint has many features that enable you to build sophisticated Web presentations. Because Internet Assistant creates client-side image maps from PowerPoint slides, you can take advantage of this built-in function by creating your own buttons and clickable banners. To do so, use any of the Shape tools and assign an interactive setting to it.

Note

An *image map* is a graphic that has different clickable regions on it. You see this a lot in Web sites that appear to have one large graphic as a home page, but when you click on different parts of it, you go to different places within the Web site. Image maps are created by programs that let you divide an image into coordinates (such as WebMap or MapEdit). Then, you assign different URLs to the the different sets of coordinates. With IA for PowerPoint, you create an image map that enables you to click on an image in the slide, and then go to the next slide, thereby simulating a slide show.

For example, in figure 3.24, I created the oval shape, wrote **Next** in it, and then used interactive settings to hyperlink it to the next slide. Following are the instructions on how to do this:

1. Click on any Shape tool in the toolbar, and draw a shape on the slide.

2. Using the Text tool, (the tool with the "A"), write **Next** on the shape.

3. Select the shape by clicking on it.

4. Go up to the Tools menu and select Interactive Settings (see fig. 3.24).

5. The Interactive Settings option enables you to assign an action to an object. Click on the Next Slide radio button. This assigns the action of linking to the next slide when someone clicks on the oval object.

Figure 3.24

Using interactive settings to create image maps.

Another great feature of the Interactive Settings command is that it enables you to type any of the Internet-supported protocols (mailto, ftp, http) into the Run Program box. This means that you can assign a protocol to an object. In figure 3.25, the Web address of Aslan, Inc., is assigned to the banner that contains the address www.aslaninc.com.

Figure 3.25

Assigning interactive settings.

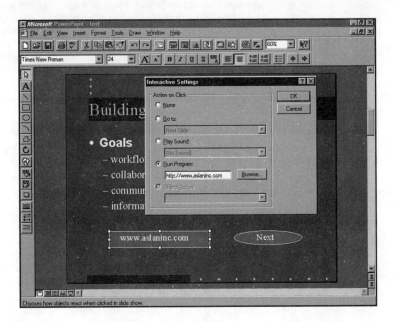

When this presentation is exported into an HTML document, that rectangular box will become a hyperlink to Aslan, Inc.'s Web site.

You can also assign a sound to a mouse click; however, you need to be using PowerPoint Animation Publisher (instead of IA for PowerPoint) to convert the sound into a sound file that can be heard over the Internet. In the next section, "Animating PowerPoint Presentations," you will see how sound and other animation elements are converted into Web documents.

Animating PowerPoint Presentations

The PowerPoint Animation Player and Animation Publisher are additional add-ons to PowerPoint, like the IA and Viewer. The Animation Publisher makes it possible for you to publish PowerPoint animations on the Web. For people to view these animations, they must have the PowerPoint Animation Player, a plug-in much like the Shockwave for Director plug-in. The Animation Player can be downloaded from http://www.microsoft.com/ia/ppt/index.htm, and is also available on the CD that accompanies this book. The good news is that the Player is very small and takes much less time to download than the Shockwave plug-in.

The PowerPoint Animation Player and Publisher is available at the following:

```
http://www.microsoft.com/mspowerpoint/internet/player/
installing.htm
```

After you download the PowerPoint Animation Player and Publisher, you will need to set up your browser to recognize the Player as a helper application:

- If using Microsoft Internet Explorer, click on Open in the Internet Explorer dialog box.

- If using Netscape Navigator, save to a folder and run axpub.exe.

If you are familiar with PowerPoint, you already know it offers powerful animation effects. These effects can now be converted into a format that can be viewed over the Internet or within an intranet. If you aren't familiar with PowerPoint, try playing around with the Animation Effects command in the Toolbar menu to see what it can do as a stand-alone application. When you become familiar with PowerPoint, you will soon understand how it can help you build exciting, interactive Web pages.

Here is a brief summary of animation effects that PowerPoint offers (these options are located on the PowerPoint toolbar):

- Animate Title—title drops in from top.
- Build Slide Text—draws slide text one line at a time.
- Drive-n Effect—text "slides" in and stops short on page.
- Flying Effect—text flies in (doesn't convert well).
- Flash Once—text or object flashes once.
- Laser Text Effect—text "shoots" in (doesn't convert well).
- Typewriter Text Effect—text "types" in (doesn't convert well).
- Reverse Text Build—text builds on the page from the middle of the words out.
- Drop-in Text Effect—text drops in from the top of the screen (or wherever you tell it to using Animations Settings from the Tools menu).

When you select an effect, you can further customize it by choosing Animation Settings from the Tools menu. Animation Settings enables you to choose from which direction the text flies in.

Microsoft Office Document Conversion

The rest of this section assumes that you know a little bit about PowerPoint, and that you have a presentation you would like to convert or are using the examples provided here. This section also assumes that you have downloaded and installed the PowerPoint Animation Player and Animation Publisher.

Converting Existing PowerPoint Presentations

To convert an existing presentation to a PowerPoint Animation file, follow these steps:

1. Open exchange.ppt or your own presentation (or start a new one!).

2. In the PowerPoint File menu, click on Export as PowerPoint Animation. If you have the PowerPoint Assistant installed, click on Export for Internet instead and select As PowerPoint Animation.

3. The PowerPoint Publisher will prompt you to select a folder and enter a file name. Remember that each PowerPoint presentation needs to be saved into its own folder. Select or create a folder and enter a file name.

4. Click on OK.

Note

> The PowerPoint Animation (PPZ) file is compressed and optimized for the Internet. You will not be able to open this file through PowerPoint. You can only view it by using a browser or the PowerPoint Viewer.

PowerPoint creates a PowerPoint Animation (PPZ) file and also an HTML file that you can use to access your PowerPoint Animation file from a Web browser.

Viewing your PowerPoint Animation Through a Browser

To view your PowerPoint Animation through a browser, follow these steps:

1. Start your Internet browser.

2. Select Open File and locate the folder in which you saved the Animation file.

3. Double-click on the HTML file for your PowerPoint Animation file.

If you're using Microsoft Internet Explorer 2.0 or Netscape Navigator 1.22, you'll see a link to your PowerPoint Animation file. Click on the link and the Animation Player will open the file in full screen. If you're using Microsoft Internet Explorer 3.0 or Netscape Navigator 2.0, the Animation file will play in your browser.

Embedding a PowerPoint Animation in an Existing HTML Page

The PowerPoint Animation Publisher automatically creates an HTML page for you that contains the tag for embedding the corresponding PowerPoint Animation file. This is the <OBJECT> </OBJECT> tag. If you want to add animations to existing pages, copy this paired tag into an existing HTML file. The PowerPoint Animation tag is everything between, and including, the <OBJECT> and </OBJECT> tags.

You can open the HTML file created by the PowerPoint Animation Publisher in Internet Assistant for Word. Then you can edit the file in Internet Assistant for Word, just as you can any other HTML file. Or, you can copy the HTML code into an existing HTML file.

Figure 3.26 shows the code that you would cut out to embed the PowerPoint Animation into an existing HTML page. For more information about editing source code, refer back to the section of the chapter titled "Editing Source Code." Additionally, you can also refer to Chapter 13, "Tailoring Converted Documents."

Figure 3.26

The HTML code behind a PowerPoint Animation.

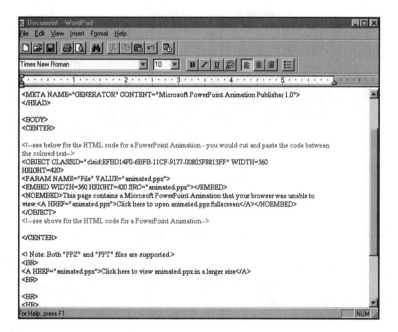

Microsoft Office
Document Conversion

Advanced Options

You can further customize your converted PowerPoint presentation for animation by adding sound or changing image size.

Inserting Sound into Animation Files

In RealAudio, you can add voice narration to slides, or a musical accompaniment, and then provide a hyperlink from PowerPoint presentations to the sound file. The advantage is that RealAudio streams the sound to make it available on a low-bandwidth connection (for example, a 28.8 Kbps modem) at acceptable download times. Users need the RealAudio Player to hear the narration. You will need RealAudio encoder to create RealAudio sound files.

The RealAudio system allows playback of audio in real-time over Internet connections of 14.4 Kbps and faster. For more information about RealAudio, check out the following:

```
http:www.realaudio.com
```

You will need to open the PowerPoint Presentation by using Internet Assistant for Word, and then hard code the tag for the sound file. The sound file is specified by a SOUND parameter added to the <EMBED> tag (shown in bold in the following example):

```
<OBJECT CLASSID="clsid:EFBD14F0-6BFB-11CF-9177-00805F8813FF">
<PARAM NAME="File" VALUE="exchange.ppz">
<PARAM NAME="Sound" VALUE="/intranet.aslan.com/media/bach.ram">
<EMBED WIDTH=400 HEIGHT=200 SRC="exchange.ppt"
SOUND="/intranet.aslan.com/media/bach.ram"></EMBED>
<NOEMBED>
<A HREF="exchange.ppz">Exchange Animation</A>
</NOEMBED>
</OBJECT>
```

Don't be alarmed by all those numbers. That part of the tag will be created by the PowerPoint Animation Publisher. All you need to type is the following:

```
SOUND="/intranet.aslan.com/media/bach.ram"
within the <EMBED> </EMBED> tags.
```

For those of you who want to know a little more about the HTML generated by the Powerpoint Animation Publisher, the following table contains a brief summary.

Summary of HTML Code Generated by the Powerpoint Animation Publisher

HTML Tag or Attribute	Characteristics
<OBJECT>	Used by Microsoft Internet Explorer 3.0.
CLASSID	Tells Internet Explorer the unique ID of the PowerPoint Animation Player so it can start the Player.
HEIGHT and WIDTH	Specifies the dimensions of the animation.
PARAM	Specifies the path to the PowerPoint Animation file.
<EMBED>	Used by Netscape Navigator 2.0.
SRC	Specifies the path to the PowerPoint Animation file.
<NOEMBED>	Used by other browsers.
HREF	Specifies a link to the PowerPoint Animation file.

Changing Image Size

The PowerPoint Animation Publisher uses the current size of your animation in PowerPoint to create the HTML file. If you want to change the size of your animation, you need to change the way the presentation appears on your screen. To do this, try one of the following:

● Choose a different scale. From the Draw menu, select Scale. Enter a percentage in the Scale To box.

● Change the size of the slides in your file before exporting as a PowerPoint Animation. In the File menu, click on Slide Setup. Enter the height and width you want to use.

● Open the HTML file created by PowerPoint Animation Publisher in Notepad or your favorite editor, and then change the default height and width settings. Remember to keep the ratio between height and width the same or you'll get unwanted black space around your image.

Microsoft Office Document Conversion

When to Use Powerpoint Add-In Applications

There's a rather easy way to decide when to use these applications, as follows:

Add On	When to Use
Internet Assistant	If your presentation contains no animations or if you don't want to convert animations.
Animation Publisher	If you want to convert your animations and if you can provide users with the Animation Player to view them.
Animation Player	To view presentations that have animations and that have been converted by the PowerPoint Animation Publisher.
PowerPoint Viewer	To view presentations that have not been converted or if you want your users to be able to edit and add to your presentation.

It is a good idea to make the PowerPoint Viewer and the PowerPoint Animation Publisher available for download from your Web site if the presentation is posted there, or from your local network if it is posted on your intranet.

Configuring Your Web Server to Acknowledge Non-Web Files

If you are going to be posting documents that require Viewers, it is important to make sure your Web server knows how to handle the request for a document with the file extensions .ppt, .xls, and .doc. If you have ever configured your browser to handle MIME types such as Shockwave files, PDF files, and other non-htm files, the process will look similar. You will need to do this for both an Internet and intranet site, because the server "serves" requests for both.

The process is slightly different for non-Microsoft Internet Information Servers.

If you're using Netscape Navigator 2.0, the Web server must send the PowerPoint Animation files as a special type of file to avoid the error message: Netscape was unable to find a plug-in for application/octet-stream.

You can resolve the problem by adding or asking your Web server administrator to add the following MIME mapping to the server:

```
.PPT -> application/mspowerpoint
.PPZ -> application/mspowerpoint
.PPS -> application/mspowerpoint
.POT -> application/mspowerpoint
.XLS-> application/msexcel
.DOC-> application/msword
```

If you're using the Microsoft Internet Information Server, add (or ask your Web server administrator to add) the following registry entries on your server:

```
[HKEY_LOCAL_MACHINE\SYSTEM\CurrentControlSet\Services\InetInfo\
➥Parameters\MimeMap]
"application/ms-powerpoint,ppt,,5"=""
"application/ms-powerpoint,ppz,,5"=""
"application/ms-powerpoint,pps,,5"=""
"application/ms-powerpoint,pot,,5"=""
"application/ms-excel,xls,,5"=""
"application/ms-word,doc,,5"=""
```

Be sure to read about MIME mapping in the documentation for your Web server. If you are using an Internet Service Provider, contact their technical support department and ask if their servers support the preceding MIME types—chances are they do. If they don't, insist that they start.

Summary

Microsoft's Internet Assistants offer an easy solution to getting your existing Office documents up on your Web site or your intranet. Although some tricks and workarounds are necessary, the ease with which you can create these HTML documents makes Office a desirable Web publishing medium. From a business standpoint, using the Office Suite of Internet Assistants makes sense because the software is free, and users can easily leverage their existing knowledge of Office applications. From a user's standpoint, using Internet Assistants is a fast and easy way to get documents up on the Web with relatively little hassle.

Microsoft Office
Document Conversion

CHAPTER 4

ClarisWorks and Corel WordPerfect Suite Document Conversion

In the previous chapter on converting Microsoft Office documents, you saw that Microsoft has developed several software add-ins that enable you to convert word processing, spreadsheet, and presentation documents into HTML. Not to be outdone, Claris Corporation and Corel, Inc., the makers of ClarisWorks and Corel WordPerfect Suite, have created similar features to enable you to convert existing documents and create Web documents within their applications. Unlike Microsoft's Office Assistants, the Web publishing feature is built right into the latest versions of ClarisWorks (4.0) and WordPerfect Suite (7). As could be expected, Claris (a subsidiary of Apple Computer) has developed an application slightly more comprehensive for the MacOS than for Windows in that it provides HTML primer documentation and more extensive templates and examples; however, both the Windows and Macintosh versions of the software are evaluated here. Corel WordPerfect Suite 7 is a strong competitor to Microsoft Office, matching not only Office's conversion capabilities, but also its interface and ease of use. The Windows version of Corel's software offers users more features than the Mac version, but if you are using WordPerfect for the Macintosh, you can still take advantage of the conversion techniques for the WordPerfect Suite offered in this chapter.

The Scope of This Chapter

This chapter will cover the conversion of simple word processing documents; complex word processing documents containing tables, images, and embedded objects; spreadsheets; and presentations into Web-ready documents. This chapter also provides a brief evaluation of several shareware products that convert word processing, spreadsheet, and Rich Text Format (RTF) documents. These shareware applications are available on the Web, and the Web address (URL) of each program evaluated is listed in its section.

Converting ClarisWorks 4.0 Documents

The focus of this section will be on converting ClarisWorks 4.0 documents (word processing and spreadsheet) into HTML documents. Although ClarisWorks 4.0 has a drawing program as part of the Suite, it does not have an HTML converter add-in to accommodate preparing these images for the Web. If you have a graphic created in

ClarisWorks, refer to Chapter 10, "Graphics Basics," and Chapter 11, "Graphics Creation," for more information.

ClarisWorks has a conversion tool built into it that enables you to save your documents as HTML. While this may sound like a simple task, you will see that this option doesn't always format your documents the way you want them formatted for publication on the Web. This being so, this section will show you some good tricks and workarounds for refining ClarisWorks documents to look great on the Web.

Converting a Simple Word Processing Document

Figure 4.1 is a press release that was created in ClarisWorks. To convert it into an HTML document, choose Save As from the File menu and then choose HTML as the file type (in ClarisWorks 4.0, HTML is among the usual file types that you can save as CWS, RTF, TEXT, and so on). ClarisWorks will convert the document into HTML and prompt you to save the file with an .HTM extension.

Figure 4.1

A simple document before conversion.

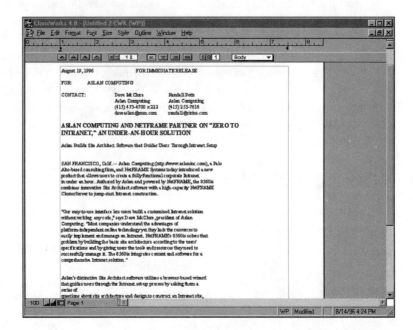

As you can see, a simple document such as this press release converts fairly well. In general, simple text documents convert quite cleanly, with no need for editing any of the HTML source code. This is a good thing, because editing the source code of a converted ClarisWorks document is almost impossible, as you will see in the next section.

Converting a Complex Document

The next example is the same press release, but modified to include more complex formatting and an image (see fig. 4.2). (The images are not standard press release media; they were included for this example to show you how ClarisWorks handles images.) We will convert this document by selecting Save As from the File menu, and then selecting HTML.

Figure 4.2

A more complex document before conversion.

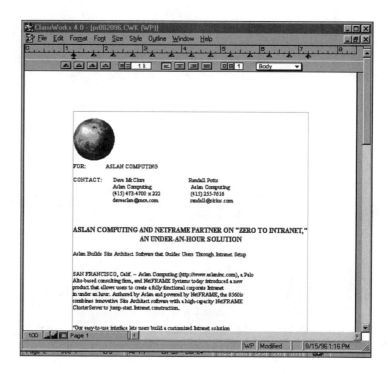

If you look at your document in a browser, you will notice that it doesn't look the same as it did in word processing format. This is because ClarisWorks 4.0 doesn't yet support many of the HTML tags widely used on the Web today, including the <CENTER> tag. Figure 4.3 shows the press release when viewed in a browser.

Notice that the headline is no longer centered, some of the text has moved around on the page, and there is a broken graphic icon. As stated earlier, Claris does not support the <CENTER> tag, and it turns images (and other embedded objects) into PICT files (if you are using a Mac or the MacOS) or WMF files (if you are using Windows). Unfortunately, PICT and WMF files cannot be viewed through a browser. To fix this, you will need to edit the HTML source code, and you will need to convert the graphic into a GIF or JPEG file. This chapter will discuss ways to edit the source code of your

Figure 4.3

The converted complex document when viewed in a browser.

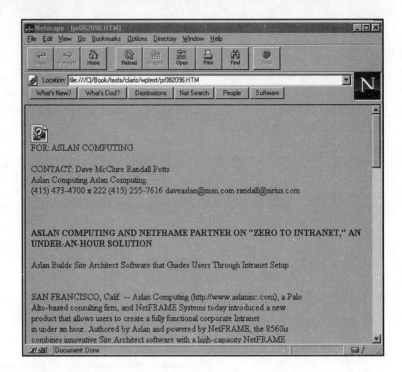

Claris document. To learn about converting PICT or WMF files into GIFs or JPEG files, refer to Chapter 10.

First of all, if you have never seen HTML source code, you might want to scan Chapter 14, "HTML Tutorial and Reference." However, this chapter will give enough explanation of the HTML editing process so you will be able to make minor editorial changes to your document without reading an entire tutorial.

Now that the document has been converted into HTML, you need to realign the heading so it is centered, get rid of the broken graphic or convert it, and realign the text for the two press contacts. Surprisingly, ClarisWorks does not provide you with the option of editing source code. This presents a problem. How do you fix what you have converted? There are some workarounds, and I do mean "workarounds." Inelegant though they are, if you have a Claris document to convert, you will need to use one of the three solutions listed here and detailed in the sections that follow.

● Solution 1: View the source in your browser, and then copy and paste it to a plaintext editor such as NotePad, WordPad, SimpleText, or BBEdit, where you can edit the source code.

> **Tip**
>
> It's best to use a plaintext editor that has search and replace capability. Often you can get rid of unwanted formatting by doing a global search and replace, instead of manually deleting individual occurrences of text. BBEdit 4.0 is one of the most desirable text editors because of its capability to do global search and replace within subdirectories; however, if you don't have the resources to buy expensive software, use WordPad (a Windows accessory) or World Wide Web Weaver (Mac-Shareware).

- Solution 2: Use Claris Home Page, a WYSIWYG HTML authoring tool, to open and edit the document in its HTML format.

- Solution 3: Save the original document in RTF (Rich Text Format) and use RTFtoHTML, a third-party shareware converter.

Stealing the Source Code from Your Browser

This solution is challenging, even if you do know HTML. It requires that you understand the concepts of HTML so that you don't accidentally delete important code characters. Before you attempt to do this, have a look at Chapter 14. After you know a little about how HTML tags are constructed, you should be able to handle stealing source code from your browser without worry.

1. While you are in your browser, select View, Document Source.
   You will see the source code of your document. This code is basically a page description code. The letters in brackets are descriptors of text-formatting options.

2. Select the text of your HTML document.

3. Choose Edit, Copy.

4. Open your favorite plaintext editor. (WordPad for Windows is shown in the example.)

5. Paste the document into the window of the text editor.

The first thing to notice about the code of this document is the <BR> or break tag at every line end. This is the equivalent to having a hard return at the end of each line in your word processing document. The break at the end of every line makes it impossible for text to realign itself as the browser window is resized. This means that the first thing you need to do is remove the <BR> tags. You can do a global search and replace, replacing each occurrence of the <BR> tag with a space, but you will be left with one

ClarisWorks and Corel
WordPerfect Suite
Document Conversion

big block of text. In this case, because the document is a single page, it is feasible (and best) to delete all <BR> tags manually within the document and place a <P> (paragraph) tag at the end of each paragraph. Figure 4.4 shows the document in the text editor before deleting the <BR> tags.

> **Note**
>
> If the document is more than a single page, it is not feasible to delete all the <BR> tags manually. A good solution here would be to add a unique set of characters to each place where you would like the paragraph to break (such as XXX). Then, with the XXXs between each paragraph, do a global search and replace for the <BR> tag, replacing it with a space. Then, do a global search and replace for the XXXs, replacing them with a <P>. You will end up with no <BR> tags at the end of the lines, and <P> (paragraph) tags between your paragraphs.

Figure 4.4

The source code of a converted ClarisWorks document.

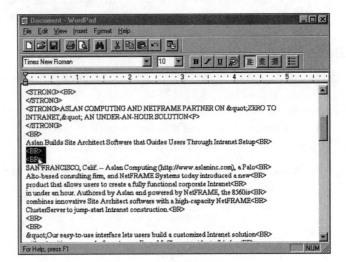

To center the headline text, put a <CENTER> (open center) tag above or below the headline, and a </CENTER> (close center) tag after or before the headline.

The last thing to fix on this page is the alignment of the press names. The press contact names and phone numbers were originally lined up in text tables created by using tabs. Because there is no HTML tag equivalent to a tab, the conversion process grouped the text together. You have two options:

1. Place the text into an HTML table to emulate the two-column look of the list.

2. Place one press contact under the other.

Figure 4.5 shows the latter option, and figure 4.6 shows how the changes display in the browser.

Figure 4.5

Editing the source code by using a plaintext editor.

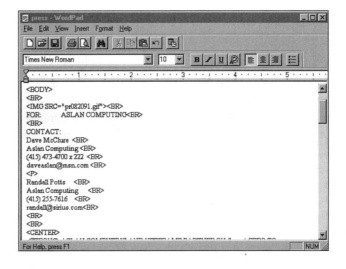

Figure 4.6

The changes to source code as displayed in a browser.

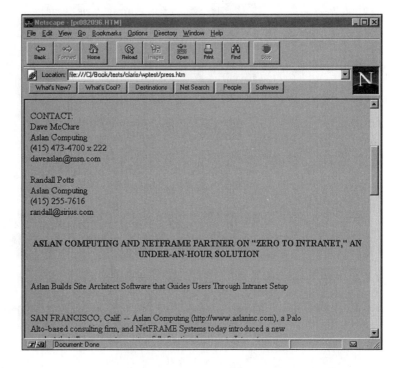

ClarisWorks and Corel
WordPerfect Suite
Document Conversion

To learn more tricks and tips about editing your document after you convert it to HTML, see Chapter 13, "Tailoring Converted Files."

Using Claris HomePage to Open and Edit the Converted Document's Source Code

Claris recently released an excellent WYSIWYG HTML authoring tool called HomePage. It is available in beta format for a free evaluation, and you can download it from Claris' Web site at http://www.claris.com. This is an excellent HTML authoring tool that works wonderfully with ClarisWorks. When you save your ClarisWorks document as HTML, open it in HomePage. You will see a view of your document that is completely editable even if you don't know any HTML. You can reposition mis-aligned text, import the graphic into a Web-acceptable format, create tables, change background color, and more. HomePage is available for both the MacOS and Windows, and it is excellent on both platforms. For more information about Claris HomePage, see Chapter 13.

Figure 4.7 shows the document as it appears in HomePage on the Macintosh.

Figure 4.7

The document as it appears in HomePage.

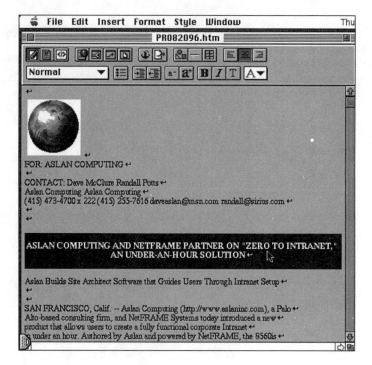

Using an RTF-to-HTML Converter

The third option for converting complex ClarisWorks documents, especially if you don't have Claris HomePage, is to use an RTF-to-HTML converter, such as RTFtoHTML. This shareware program is easy to use and is available at chris@sunpack.com. It is quick to download and only costs $25.00.

With this option, first save your document as RTF (Rich Text Format) instead of HTML. You do this by choosing Save As and then RTF (Rich Text Format) from the list of file types. Then follow these steps to convert the document into HTML:

1. Start RTFtoHTML and choose Open from the File menu.

2. Locate the RTF file you want to convert. When you click on it to open it, RTFtoHTML will convert it. You won't see the file in the RTFtoHTML window; instead, you will see a report log of the conversion process. When the process has finished, start your browser and view the file through your browser.

To learn more about RTFtoHTML, see the last section of this chapter, which covers shareware and freeware applications to enable conversion of word processing and spreadsheet documents into HTML.

HTML Tags Supported by ClarisWorks

ClarisWorks supports disappointingly few HTML tags. If you are using ClarisWorks to create documents explicitly for the Web, it would be smart to create a specific style sheet that only enables you to use the styles supported by the ClarisWorks translator. Figure 4.8 is a ClarisWorks document using a wide range of formatting types. Most of the formatting types in figure 4.8 have HTML 2.0 or 3.2 equivalents, but ClarisWorks' translation feature does not support them all, as figure 4.9 illustrates.

ClarisWorks and Corel
WordPerfect Suite
Document Conversion

Note

ClarisWorks translator only supports bold and italic. It does not support lists and centering, and as you saw in the earlier examples, it does not support paragraph tags and image conversion into Web-ready graphics.

Figure 4.8

A ClarisWorks document that uses a range of formatting styles

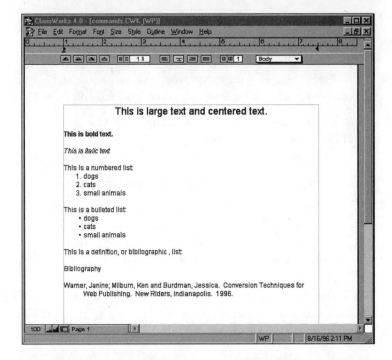

Figure 4.9

The same document converted into HTML by using the Claris translator.

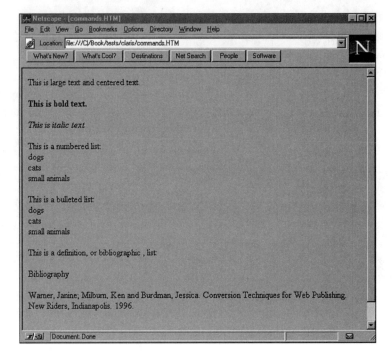

Converting ClarisWorks Spreadsheets

Converting a ClarisWorks spreadsheet into HTML is a bit tricky. Claris does not yet have a translator utility for converting spreadsheets into HTML, so converting your spreadsheet requires a bit of maneuvering between file formats and shareware programs.

The best workaround out there is an application called TwoClicks Tables, a browser application located at the following:

```
http://www.twoclicks.com/cgi-bin/tabdemo.pl
```

With TwoClicks Tables, you paste your spreadsheet data into a window in a browser, select your formatting preferences, and—voila!—a new HTML table appears in your browser with your spreadsheet information in it. Best of all, it works great on both Windows and Macintosh platforms.

Figure 4.10 shows a ClarisWorks spreadsheet in native format. The text was selected, copied, and pasted into the TwoClicks Tables window (see fig. 4.11).

Here is a more thorough explanation of this process:

1. Copy your spreadsheet data to your computer's clipboard. Launch your browser and go to the TwoClicks Tables URL>.

2. Paste your data into the large window of the Web page.

3. After you have pasted your table data, scroll through the list of options under the window where you have pasted your data, and select such formatting options as background color, text color, table border size, and hard return size.

4. At the end of the formatting selections, click on "Create Table." TwoClicks Tables then creates a table based on your spreadsheet data and your selections, displaying the table in a new browser window.

Figure 4.12 shows the output of TwoClicks Tables.

Now that you have your spreadsheet table converted into an HTML document on the Web, how do you get it into an HTML document on your own computer? After all, what you have essentially done is input your table data into a form on the Web, which then processed the data and made a table for you. But the table now is located on the TwoClicks Tables Web site. You need to copy the table for your own use. The only way to do this is to choose Document Source from the View menu of your browser; select the HTML code you see there; copy and paste it into a plaintext editor such as NotePad, SimpleText, or BBEdit; and save it with an .htm file extension.

ClarisWorks and Corel
WordPerfect Suite
Document Conversion

Figure 4.10

A ClarisWorks spreadsheet.

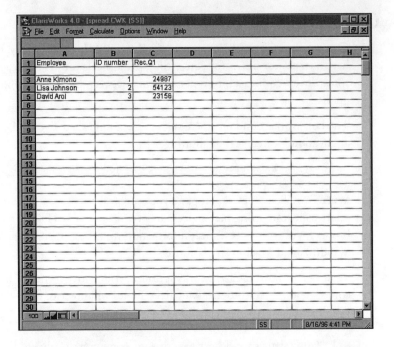

Figure 4.11

TwoClicks Tables: a spreadsheet converter.

Figure 4.12

The output of TwoClicks Tables.

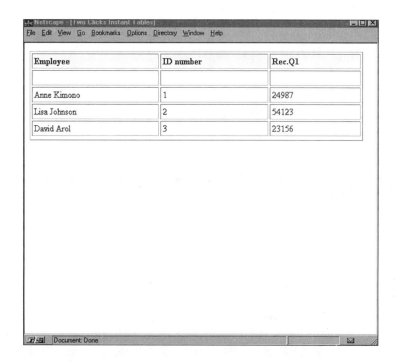

TwoClicks Tables writes nice, neat code, which you will appreciate if you are developing a Web site. Figure 4.13 shows how the code looks when viewed in a browser window.

Figure 4.13

The source code of TwoClicks Tables.

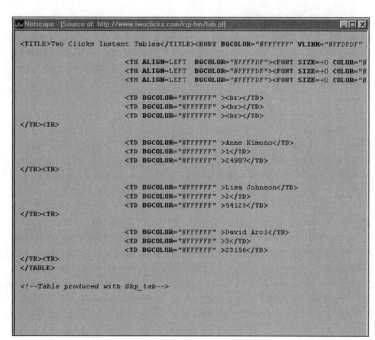

Workarounds for Mac and Windows Users Who Don't Own ClarisWorks 4.0

For Mac users and Windows users who don't have ClarisWorks 4.0, but need to convert ClarisWorks files given to them by clients, a number of shareware utilities will convert a ClarisWorks file into HTML fairly well. For more information, see the last section of this chapter, titled "Shareware."

Converting Corel WordPerfect Suite 7 Documents

Corel's WordPerfect Suite 7 is a feature-rich application for creating both standard print documents and Web documents. Like Claris, WordPerfect Suite 7 has conversion functionality built into its latest release. Unlike ClarisWorks, Corel WordPerfect Suite supports all HTML 2.0 tags, and many HTML 3.2 tags as well. This makes Corel WordPerfect Suite 7 desirable not only to hobbyist Web publishers, but also to Web developers and designers who receive WordPerfect Suite files from their clients and are looking for the best way to convert these files to HTML. With Corel WordPerfect Suite 7, you can convert files to HTML and then use its WYSIWYG HTML editor to fine tune the converted document.

> **Note**
>
> Macintosh users still need to wait for the latest release of Corel WordPerfect Suite to take advantage of built-in Web publishing features, but if you are using a Mac and are looking for ways to convert WordPerfect or Quattro Pro Files to HTML, see the section titled "Shareware." Several of the tools reviewed there do a good job of translating these files to HTML, even without Corel WordPerfect or Quattro Pro running on your computer.

Converting WordPerfect Documents

The HTML conversion feature of WordPerfect Suite is easy to use, is truly WYSIWYG, and requires little knowledge of HTML to obtain great-looking documents. The following sections will cover converting both simple documents with little formatting and complex documents with tables and images.

Converting Simple WordPerfect Documents

For comparison purposes, we will convert the same documents converted in the ClarisWorks section of this chapter. As you read here, refer to the ClarisWorks section for perspective.

First, open the document you want to convert and choose Internet Publisher from the File menu. In this case, the press release displayed earlier as a ClarisWorks document will be converted from WordPerfect format to HTML. When you choose Internet Publisher, you are given four options (see fig. 4.14). These options will be explained in the following bulleted list, because their functions are not adequately explained by the dialog box:

Figure 4.14

Options for saving your Corel WordPerfect file as HTML.

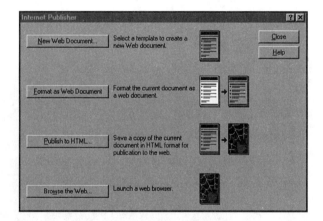

- New Web Document: This option gives you the choice of either using a blank Web page template or using a Web page "expert" to guide you through a content-generating process. This last option is similar to assistants or wizards in software programs such as Excel.

- Format as Web Document: This option enables you to format your document by using Web-specific styles only. When you choose this option, you are editing a WordPerfect document that looks like a Web document; however, it does not have the .htm file extension. You need to choose the next option to actually create a Web-ready document.

- Publish to HTML: This option makes a copy of the current document, formats the copy into HTML, and gives it an .htm file extension. The HTML file is placed into the same directory as the file you are converting. In other words, the document that remains in front of you is your WordPerfect document. To view the HTML document, you need to open it in WordPerfect or your browser. When you open the document in WordPerfect, you can edit it and then save it.

● Browse the Web: This option calls up your browser. If you have two browsers and one of them is Netscape, the browser called up when this option is selected is Netscape. Even if Internet Explorer is running at the time this option is selected, Netscape will still be called up.

You can change this default setting. To do so, click on the QuickConnect icon on the Corel WordPerfect Suite toolbar. Choose Providers and choose the browser you want. When you install WordPerfect Suite, the setup application detects any Internet Service software loaded on your machine, so if you have AOL or CompuServe, for example, you will also see these services listed. In addition, the setup application will import your bookmark files, so you will see them there too.

In this example, Publish to HTML was selected. The file was saved with an .htm file extension. Figure 4.15 shows how it looks when viewed in a browser window.

Figure 4.15

A converted document when "Publish to HTML" was selected.

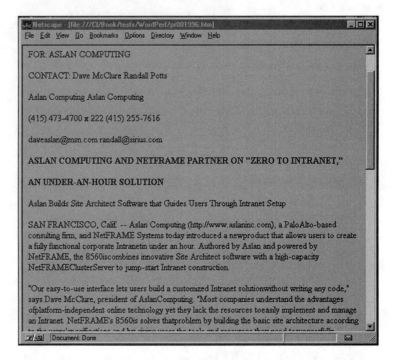

As you saw with the ClarisWorks example, the tab-delimited text does not translate into HTML, largely because the only HTML equivalent for tabbed text is converting tab-delimited text into a table—and WordPerfect isn't smart enough to do that yet.

The next thing to do is edit the document. Luckily, the WYSIWYG editor in Corel WordPerfect Suite is quite good—you can open up the HTML document within Word Perfect and edit it right there. When you open up an HTML document in WordPerfect, you get a toolbar that provides you with HTML-only formatting styles—in English, not HTML. This means that you will be able to choose HTML-only formatting styles without knowing HTML. You can apply styles that can be interpreted by Web browsers and that you can also understand. Figure 4.16 shows the HTML version of the press release when it is opened in WordPerfect.

Figure 4.16

The HTML version of the press release viewed in WordPerfect.

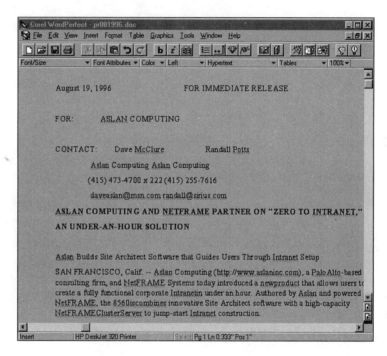

While in WordPerfect, you can edit the document as easily as you would a regular WordPerfect document.

Converting Complex WordPerfect Documents

Now we will look at how WordPerfect converts the more complex press release we used earlier in the ClarisWorks section. If you didn't read that section, it's okay. You only need to know that this document contains a table, an image, and some centered text (see fig. 4.17). "Complex" is used loosely here; the document is complex because it contains elements that are part of the latest HTML specification, which many converters still do not support. The following section, "Multiple-Column Documents," will discuss still more complex document conversion.

Figure 4.17

A complex WordPerfect document.

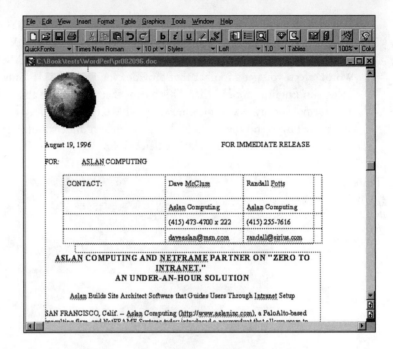

For this example, choose File, Internet Publisher, Publish to HTML. As stated before, this option saves a copy of the WordPerfect document as an HTML document with the same name, but with the .htm file extension. When you open the file in a browser—voila!—perfection. The image has been successfully converted, the table has also been successfully converted, and all text is centered where it should be. Figure 4.18 shows how the file looks in a browser.

WordPerfect HTML Support

As you can see, WordPerfect supports some of the more recent HTML tags, such as <CENTER> and <TABLE>. Table 4.1 is a list of most of the formatting options available in WordPerfect, along with the HTML equivalent tags.

WordPerfect Formatting Options with HTML Equivalents

WordPerfect Formatting Style	*HTML Equivalent*
Address	<ADDRESS>
Background color	<BG COLOR>
Bibliography	<DL>, </DL>
Bold text	<B>, </B>; <STRONG>, </STRONG>
Bullet list	<UL>, </UL>
Centered text	<P Align=Center>
Font	<FONT>, </FONT>
Font size	<FONT SIZE>,</FONT SIZE>
Insert image	<IMG SRC> (also supports the ALIGN and VALIGN attributes)
Insert sound	<A HREF="filename.wav"> file
Insert table	<TABLE>, </TABLE>
Insert hyperlink	<A HREF="filename.htm">
Indented quotation	<BLOCKQUOTE>
Italic text	<I>, </I>; <EMP>, </EMP>
Left justified text	<P Align=Left>
Line break	<HR>
Monospaced font	<PRE>
Normal	<BODY>
Numbered list	<OL>, </OL>
Right justification	<P Align=right>
Text color	<FONT COLOR>, </FONT COLOR>

ClarisWorks and Corel WordPerfect Suite Document Conversion

Figure 4.18

The complex WordPerfect document converted to HTML.

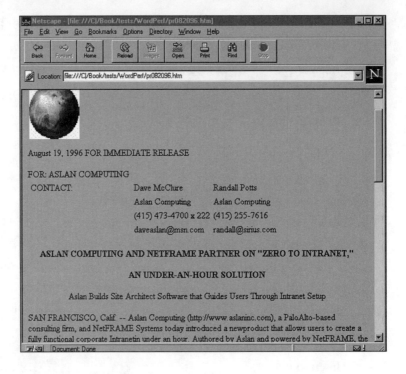

Multiple-Column WordPerfect Documents

WordPerfect is good, but it's not perfect. You cannot simply publish a multiple-column document to HTML without playing around with it first. There are two workarounds to this problem, as follows:

1. Create a two-column (or more) table and divide your text within the columns. You can do this either in regular WordPerfect mode or HTML mode (after saving the document as an HTML document).

2. Export the document as an RTF file and use RTFtoHTML, a shareware converter available on the CD that comes with this book.

Editing Your Converted WordPerfect Documents

WordPerfect does a good job of converting most documents, but in some instances you may want to edit the converted document. For example, suppose you convert a document that contains a table. Then after you convert it, you find you would like to align the text in the table data cells to the bottom of the cell, instead of to the top. You might be inclined to go back to your original document, edit the table there, and reconvert it, but you don't have to do this. You don't even have to figure out a way to edit the source code. WordPerfect is capable of efficiently and accurately editing an HTML document without your having to work with source code. When you open an HTML document in WordPerfect, the program enables you to use its HTML-specific toolbars only. The other WordPerfect toolbars disappear. Contrary to what you may think, these toolbars are rich with functionality—so much so you rarely need to insert custom HTML tags.

WordPerfect Bullet Boxes

If you are familiar with WordPerfect, you know that for every element on a page, WordPerfect creates a *bullet box* that enables you to format that element without affecting the formatting for the rest of the document. This bullet box looks like a small box the size of a large bullet item and appears to the right of the element (such as a paragraph or an image) when you run your cursor on or near that element. When you click on it, the bullet box displays the attributes of the element for you to edit. If you are unfamiliar with WordPerfect and have purchased it only to deal with your clients' files, you are going to be glad you spent the money, because this bullet box makes editing the attributes of your HTML document a breeze.

Editing Images

Figure 4.19 shows the two edit boxes associated with editing an image. By using the tools available in the boxes, you can assign a map to an image (you can't create the map file, only the code that tells the browser which map file to use). You can also type alternate text for the image for nongraphical browsers, reposition the image on the page, and set Height and Width attributes for it. Additionally, you can use the Image Tools bar to rotate the image, as well as to manipulate brightness, contrast, and fill. WordPerfect does not come close to the capabilities of Photoshop or even PaintShop Pro, but it will do in a pinch if these programs are not available to you.

The one significant function missing from the Image Editing Box is the option to make a transparent GIF. There is no way to do this with the current version of Corel WordPerfect Suite 7. In this instance, with the background color of the image being white, you can make the background color of the whole document white so that the image appears to be transparent.

If you would like to make a GIF transparent, you can do so fairly easily. See Chapter 10, "Graphics Basics," for more information about obtaining the necessary software to make a transparent GIF.

ClarisWorks and Corel
WordPerfect Suite
Document Conversion

Figure 4.19

WordPerfect's edit boxes.

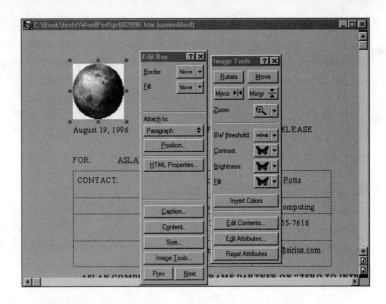

Adding Background Color and Text

Adding background color and text is as easy as choosing Text, Background Colors from the Format menu. When you do this, you can change not only background color and text color, but hypertext link color, active link color, and visited link color, as well. You can also import an image to use as a background tile or full-screen background. (For more on background options, see Chapter 10.)

Creating Hypertext Links

You can easily create a hypertext link within your converted document by choosing Hypertext, Web Links from the Tools menu. When you do this, a new toolbar appears at the top of your document. Choose Create; the Create Hyperlink dialog box appears. Then choose Document. You can type a full URL, browse your hard disk by clicking on the small icon to the right of the text box, or browse the Web by clicking on Browse. You can also choose to have your hypertext link appear as text (by clicking the "text" radio button) or as a button (by choosing Button at the bottom of the dialog box). Unfortunately, the "button" selection is an unattractive gray color, and there is no way to modify the button.

Editing Tables

The edit, or button, boxes that enable you to edit the attributes of each table cell appear in the upper-right corner of the table cell as you pass your cursor over it. To change the alignment of text in one or more of the table cells, select the edit box and click on Format. This brings up the Properties for Table Format dialog box featured in figure 4.20.

Figure 4.20

The Properties for Table Format dialog box.

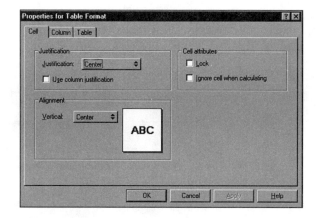

Three options appear in the dialog box: Cell, Column, and Table. If you know HTML, you know that editing these three options is the same as adding or changing attributes to the <TD> and <TABLE> tags. (If you view your source code while viewing the document in a browser, you can see the changes in code.) If you don't know HTML, all the better—simply play around with the formatting of the table cell, column, or entire table until you are satisfied by how the table looks.

Note

There is one drawback for designers who want to manipulate table size: WordPerfect does not enable you to set measurements in pixels, only inches. If you are familiar with HTML and accustomed to working with pixels and percentages to control table and table data cell size, this is a problem. Time to get out the old designer's ruler so you can recall how many pixels there are per inch.

Shareware Solutions for Mac and Windows Users

For Mac users and Windows users who don't have Corel WordPerfect Suite 7 and still need to convert files, there are a number of shareware utilities that will convert a WordPerfect file into HTML fairly well. See the last section of this chapter, titled "Shareware," for more information.

Converting Corel Quattro Pro Spreadsheets

You can easily convert a Corel Quattro Pro spreadsheet into HTML by choosing Save As, HTML from the File menu. Quattro Pro will then save a copy of the file with an .htm extension.

A simple Quattro Pro spreadsheet converts well. Figure 4.21 shows the Aslan Computing Quarterly Receivables spreadsheet converted into an HTML table.

Figure 4.21

A simple spreadsheet converted from Quattro Pro.

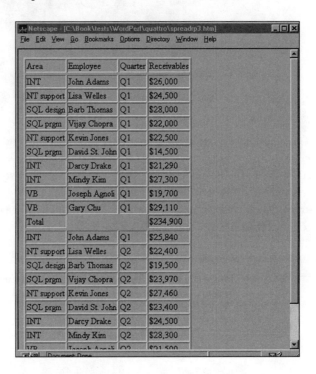

If you view the HTML source code of a converted table in your browser, you will see that the Quattro Pro converter adds a BORDER attribute to the <TABLE> tag. HTML enthusiasts will notice that in this example, the Quattro Pro converter adds the attributes VALIGN and NOWRAP to the table data cells, which is a nice touch because it looks great and you don't need to edit source code to get it to look that way (see fig. 4.22). Many converters stick to the basic "white bread" tags and do not include attributes.

> **Note**
>
> Attributes extend a tag's formatting capacity. By including them in this process, Corel eliminates the hassle of having to add attributes manually.

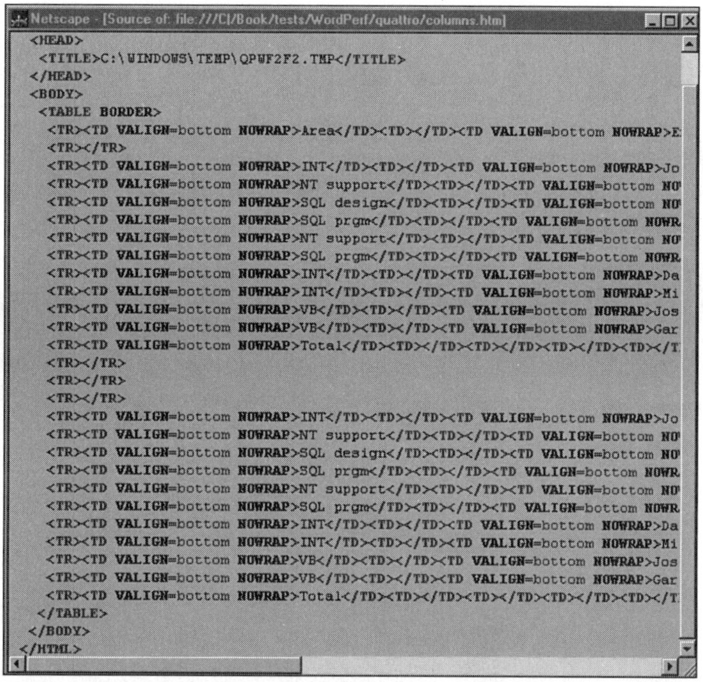

Figure 4.22

*The source code
of the converted
spreadsheet.*

```
Netscape - [Source of: file:///C|/Book/tests/WordPerf/quattro/columns.htm]    _ □ ×
 <HEAD>
  <TITLE>C:\WINDOWS\TEMP\QPWF2F2.TMP</TITLE>
 </HEAD>
 <BODY>
  <TABLE BORDER>
   <TR><TD VALIGN=bottom NOWRAP>Area</TD><TD></TD><TD VALIGN=bottom NOWRAP>E
   <TR></TR>
   <TR><TD VALIGN=bottom NOWRAP>INT</TD><TD></TD><TD VALIGN=bottom NOWRAP>Jo
   <TR><TD VALIGN=bottom NOWRAP>NT support</TD><TD></TD><TD VALIGN=bottom NO
   <TR><TD VALIGN=bottom NOWRAP>SQL design</TD><TD></TD><TD VALIGN=bottom NO
   <TR><TD VALIGN=bottom NOWRAP>SQL prgm</TD><TD></TD><TD VALIGN=bottom NOWR
   <TR><TD VALIGN=bottom NOWRAP>NT support</TD><TD></TD><TD VALIGN=bottom NO
   <TR><TD VALIGN=bottom NOWRAP>SQL prgm</TD><TD></TD><TD VALIGN=bottom NOWR
   <TR><TD VALIGN=bottom NOWRAP>INT</TD><TD></TD><TD VALIGN=bottom NOWRAP>Da
   <TR><TD VALIGN=bottom NOWRAP>INT</TD><TD></TD><TD VALIGN=bottom NOWRAP>Mi
   <TR><TD VALIGN=bottom NOWRAP>VB</TD><TD></TD><TD VALIGN=bottom NOWRAP>Jos
   <TR><TD VALIGN=bottom NOWRAP>VB</TD><TD></TD><TD VALIGN=bottom NOWRAP>Gar
   <TR><TD VALIGN=bottom NOWRAP>Total</TD><TD></TD><TD></TD><TD></T
   <TR></TR>
   <TR></TR>
   <TR></TR>
   <TR><TD VALIGN=bottom NOWRAP>INT</TD><TD></TD><TD VALIGN=bottom NOWRAP>Jo
   <TR><TD VALIGN=bottom NOWRAP>NT support</TD><TD></TD><TD VALIGN=bottom NO
   <TR><TD VALIGN=bottom NOWRAP>SQL design</TD><TD></TD><TD VALIGN=bottom NO
   <TR><TD VALIGN=bottom NOWRAP>SQL prgm</TD><TD></TD><TD VALIGN=bottom NOWR
   <TR><TD VALIGN=bottom NOWRAP>NT support</TD><TD></TD><TD VALIGN=bottom NO
   <TR><TD VALIGN=bottom NOWRAP>SQL prgm</TD><TD></TD><TD VALIGN=bottom NOWR
   <TR><TD VALIGN=bottom NOWRAP>INT</TD><TD></TD><TD VALIGN=bottom NOWRAP>Da
   <TR><TD VALIGN=bottom NOWRAP>INT</TD><TD></TD><TD VALIGN=bottom NOWRAP>Mi
   <TR><TD VALIGN=bottom NOWRAP>VB</TD><TD></TD><TD VALIGN=bottom NOWRAP>Jos
   <TR><TD VALIGN=bottom NOWRAP>VB</TD><TD></TD><TD VALIGN=bottom NOWRAP>Gar
   <TR><TD VALIGN=bottom NOWRAP>Total</TD><TD></TD><TD></TD><TD></T
  </TABLE>
 </BODY>
</HTML>
```

Limitations to Exporting your Converted Document

Unlike the Internet Assistant Wizard that works in tandem with Microsoft Excel (refer
to Chapter 3, "Microsoft Office Document Conversion," if you haven't already), the
Quattro Pro conversion process takes just one step. This makes formatting simple
spreadsheet tables fast; however, your display or export options are limited. For
example, you cannot save your Quattro Pro table into an existing HTML template the
way you can with Excel. If you have a report template in HTML that you would like
to update frequently with your latest sales reports, this is a problem, but you can
combat this limitation with several different methods:

1. If you have Excel, you might consider exporting the Quattro Pro spreadsheet
   into an Excel spreadsheet and using the Internet Assistant for Excel.

2. You can copy and paste the source code manually into your report template.

Converting Quattro Pro Documents with Blank Rows or Columns

Converting a simple spreadsheet is a fairly easy process, but what about a spreadsheet that contains blank columns and rows? Often, blank columns and rows are inserted to make a spreadsheet easier to read. If your job is to convert these spreadsheets into readable HTML documents, you will want to ensure that the spreadsheet is as readable in HTML format as in its native Quattro Pro format. In the next example, several blank rows and columns have been added to the simple spreadsheet used in the previous example (see fig. 4.23).

Figure 4.23

A spreadsheet with blank columns and rows.

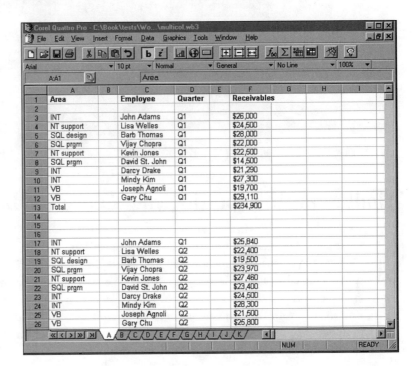

When the spreadsheet is converted to HTML, a blank row gets converted into a single blank table row and a blank column gets converted into a single blank data cell. The problem is that the width of the blank row or column is not specified in the conversion. The <TD> and <TR> tags inserted to create the blank row and column do not have the WIDTH attribute appended to them, so the converted document does not look like the original, as you can see in figure 4.24.

The best workaround to this problem is to open the converted HTML document in WordPerfect and edit the table there. If you haven't read the section on converting word processing documents, flip through it until you come to the section "Editing Tables."

Figure 4.24

The same spreadsheet converted to HTML.

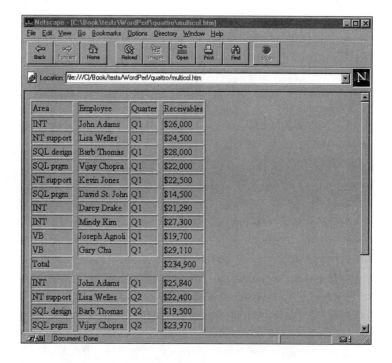

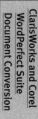

If you are familiar with HTML, another workaround is to open the document in a plaintext editor such as NotePad or in an HTML editor such as Hot Dog or HTML Pro, and then add the WIDTH attribute to the blank <TD></TD> tag. Specify the width in pixels (rather than by percentage), so you can be sure of a fixed size. For example, if you want the column to be 30 pixels wide, amend the tag to read:

```
<TD WIDTH="30"></TD>
```

To learn more about table attributes, refer to Chapter 14, "HTML Tutorial and Reference."

Converting Quattro Pro Spreadsheets that Contain Images or Objects

If your spreadsheets contain embedded charts, objects, maps, or images, you need to export these objects and convert them separately. If you leave them in, the converter will alert you that it is not possible to convert the chart, image, or object. If you are a Web designer trying to convert a spreadsheet for a client, consider cutting the images from the document and converting them separately. The images will be in bitmapped format. (Refer to Chapters 10 and 11 for tips and tricks for converting images.)

ClarisWorks and Corel
WordPerfect Suite
Document Conversion

If you have spreadsheets with charts or images and you own a copy of Corel WordPerfect Suite, consider saving them as Envoy documents. See the next section for a more in-depth description of this process.

Using Envoy to Publish Spreadsheets with Charts and Images

Envoy is a publishing tool (part of Corel WordPerfect Suite) that enables you to keep all your document's formatting intact, because documents created in Envoy are published in electronic form, not print form. Therefore, what you see on-screen when you publish your document to Envoy will be exactly what your viewers will see on the Web site.

Under the File menu in all WordPerfect Suite applications is an option to Publish to Envoy. Selecting this option changes your spreadsheet document into an Envoy document, giving it an .evy extension.

The drawback to publishing documents in Envoy is that your users need an Envoy Viewer to read the document. The Viewer is freely distributable, meaning you can make it available to download from your Web site, but users will often lose interest rather than download additional software to view a file. A great alternative to this is to create an executable (runtime) file. A *runtime* file is a file that has been converted into an application. When a user downloads the file and clicks on it, it will "run" the way an application runs.

To create a runtime file, follow these steps (you first need to save your document as an Envoy file):

1. In Envoy, open the document you want to convert to a runtime file.

2. Choose File, Save As from the Save File as Type drop-down list box.

3. Select Envoy Runtime Files (*.exe).

4. Type a file name, but be sure to keep the .exe file extension. Click on OK.

After you create this runtime file, open your HTML document in WordPerfect (if you have it) or in a text editor if you're using one, and create a link to this file. When users click on this link, the browser will prompt them to save the file to their hard disk, where they can then run the file. As a gesture of *netiquette* (the manners of the Web), provide a brief description of this process for your users to read before they begin downloading the file.

Shareware Solutions for MacOS and Windows Users

Several fairly good shareware programs are available for Mac and Windows users who don't have access to Corel WordPerfect Suite 7. For Mac users, the MacOS version of Corel WordPerfect Suite could very well be on the market by the time this book is published. A complete evaluation of these programs is discussed in the shareware section of this chapter.

Converting Corel Presentations Documents

Converting a presentation from Corel Presentations into HTML is easy, creative, fun, and fast. A wizard guides you through the process, during which you choose your background color, hyperlink color, preferred image file type (GIF or JPEG), and layout style. You can choose from four layout styles, covered in depth later in this chapter in the Export Options section. The most impressive layout style is Frames, which converts your presentation into a frame set. A *frame set*, for those of you who are new to HTML, is a formatting type that enables you to divide a Web browser screen into sections, each of which can have its own page load within it. Using Frames enables you to keep one part of your Web browser screen static, while the other part changes with user interaction (scrolling).

The Conversion Process

This section provides an overview of the steps you will go through to convert a Corel Presentations document into HTML. Be sure to read this section and the following sections on export options and formatting options before you begin converting your presentation. The many useful tips included in these sections will enable you to take full advantage of the functions the conversion tool offers. When you have read these sections (they're short!), you will be able to return to this section and swiftly and capably convert your Presentations document into a sophisticated series of Web pages. Here are the steps:

1. While in Presentations, open the document you want to convert.

2. From the File menu, choose Publish, To Internet.

3. A list of four options appears: Frame-Enhanced Page, Multiple Pages, Single Page, and Single Gallery-Style Page. Each of these options is described in depth in the next section, "Export Options."

4. When you have selected an export option, the program will prompt you to title the presentation and save it to a folder. This folder is the directory for this presentation alone. *This is an important step!* All Corel presentations must be saved in their own folders (directories), because Corel names the first slide of every presentation index.htm and names the following ones slide1.htm, slide2.htm, and so on. If you export another presentation to the same folder, you will overwrite your previous presentation.

> **Warning**
>
> Each presentation must be saved into its own directory because Corel's conversion tool does not have a unique naming method, nor does it enable you to name the slides yourself. The first slide of each presentation is named "index.htm." The rest of the slides are named "slide1.htm," "slide2.htm," and so on. If you export more than one presentation to the same directory, you will overwrite the previous presentation.

5. In the Export Options dialog box are two buttons, Color Options and More Options. Color Options enables you to choose a color scheme for your Web page (background color and link color). More Options enables you to specify the image type you prefer to use (GIF or JPEG). You can also type in any information you want to appear as a footer, including your e-mail address and latest update date. Color Options and More Options are more fully explained in the sections "Choosing Background and Link Colors," "Choosing Footer and Comments Information," "Choosing Image File Type," and "Making the Presentation Available for Downloading," which appear later in this chapter.

Publishing Options

After you choose Publish, To Internet from the File menu, you are prompted to choose a format for your converted presentation. This section will help you decide which format is best for your needs. Keep in mind that you can go back and reconvert your presentation if you think you would prefer another layout.

Publishing as a Frames-Enhanced Document

The Frame-Enhanced Page option publishes your document as a frame set. As stated before, a frame set divides a browser page into sections, each of which loads a different URL (Web page). A frame set makes it possible to keep one section of your browser static, while making the other section variable. When you convert your Presentations document into an HTML frame set, one section of the frame contains a hyperlinked list of the slides that comprise the presentation, and the other section loads each slide as it is selected by clicking on the hyperlinked list. Figure 4.25 shows how the document looks as a frames-enhanced Web page.

Figure 4.25

Publishing as a frames-enhanced page.

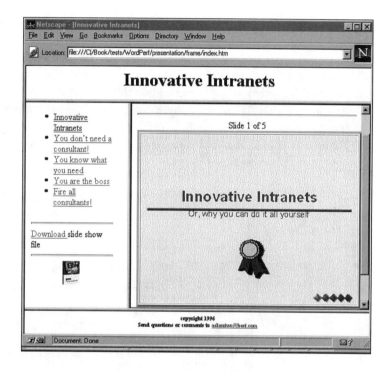

Using a frames-enhanced page means users can see all the slides of a presentation at once, making it easy for them to view the slides in the order that interests them. Frames are the current "hot" tag on the Web, and using them is an indication of your Web savvy, so to speak. Savvy, however, is hardly the reason to use frames. In general, frames provide a compact way to present a lot of information in a small space.

Before you decide to use the frames-enhanced publishing option, you need to know a few drawbacks to using frames:

- The major drawback is that many browsers do not yet support frames. As of this writing, Netscape Navigator 2.0 and later, Internet Explorer 3.0 and later, and Oracle's PowerBrowser are the only browsers that support frames.

- Many people find frame sets distracting and unattractive. Netscape Navigator's frames have scroll bars and borders that can detract from the layout of the presentation. Internet Explorer supports borderless frames, but in the Corel Presentations converter, the default layout is to create frames with borders.

ClarisWorks and Corel WordPerfect Suite Document Conversion

Note

If this section seems to downplay the good aspects of frames, it doesn't mean to. The point is to convince you to think about when and why to use frames, and not just to use them because they're the current rage.

The <FRAMESET> tag has a complementary <NOFRAMES> tag that enables Web designers to place alternative Web pages to be viewed by someone not using a frames-enabled browser. Corel Presentations supports this tag! This is a two-thumbs-up for Corel for providing a wonderful solution to the problem of browser-specific tags. If you don't know HTML, rest assured that if you select this option, Corel Presentations will provide a <NOFRAMES> alternative in case some of your viewers are using non-frames browsers. Web designers familiar with HTML will love the code Corel outputs. Figure 4.26 shows the source code for the frames-enabled document in figure 4.25, as viewed in a plaintext editor.

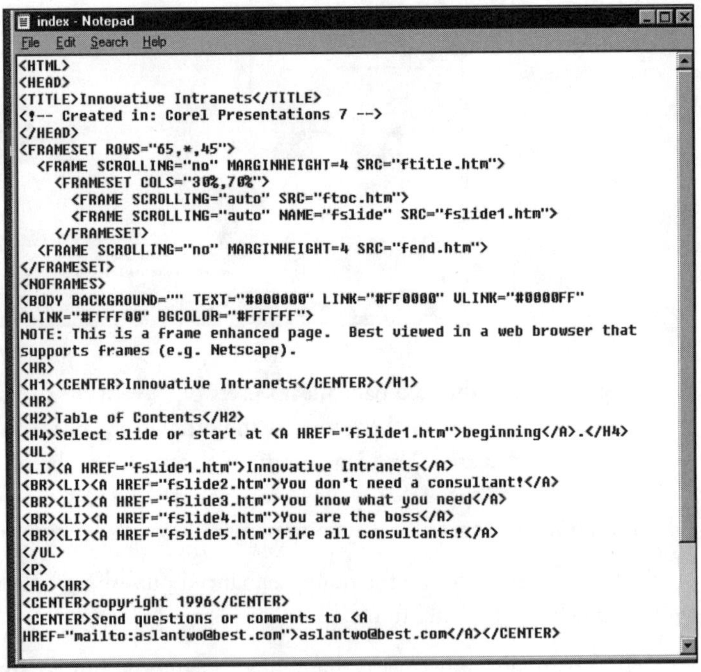

Figure 4.26

The source code for the frames-enhanced document.

```
index - Notepad
File  Edit  Search  Help
<HTML>
<HEAD>
<TITLE>Innovative Intranets</TITLE>
<!-- Created in: Corel Presentations 7 -->
</HEAD>
<FRAMESET ROWS="65,*,45">
  <FRAME SCROLLING="no" MARGINHEIGHT=4 SRC="ftitle.htm">
    <FRAMESET COLS="30%,70%">
      <FRAME SCROLLING="auto" SRC="ftoc.htm">
      <FRAME SCROLLING="auto" NAME="fslide" SRC="fslide1.htm">
    </FRAMESET>
  <FRAME SCROLLING="no" MARGINHEIGHT=4 SRC="fend.htm">
</FRAMESET>
<NOFRAMES>
<BODY BACKGROUND="" TEXT="#000000" LINK="#FF0000" ULINK="#0000FF"
ALINK="#FFFF00" BGCOLOR="#FFFFFF">
NOTE: This is a frame enhanced page.  Best viewed in a web browser that
supports frames (e.g. Netscape).
<HR>
<H1><CENTER>Innovative Intranets</CENTER></H1>
<HR>
<H2>Table of Contents</H2>
<H4>Select slide or start at <A HREF="fslide1.htm">beginning</A>.</H4>
<UL>
<LI><A HREF="fslide1.htm">Innovative Intranets</A>
<BR><LI><A HREF="fslide2.htm">You don't need a consultant!</A>
<BR><LI><A HREF="fslide3.htm">You know what you need</A>
<BR><LI><A HREF="fslide4.htm">You are the boss</A>
<BR><LI><A HREF="fslide5.htm">Fire all consultants!</A>
</UL>
<P>
<H6><HR>
<CENTER>copyright 1996</CENTER>
<CENTER>Send questions or comments to <A
HREF="mailto:aslantwo@best.com">aslantwo@best.com</A></CENTER>
```

Publishing as a Multiple-Page Document

The Multiple Pages option publishes your presentations document as a series of Web pages, with each page being a slide from your presentation. If you have a 25-page presentation, you will generate 25 pages of HTML when you convert it. Figure 4.27 shows you how the first page of this presentation will look in your browser.

Figure 4.27

Publishing as a multiple-page document.

When you choose this option, Corel Presentations adds navigational icons on the bottom of each page for ease of navigation between slides. The navigational icons are arrows and a button that says TOC, which directs the user to the Table of Contents for the slide presentation. Unfortunately, you cannot (easily) change these navigation icons, but there is a workaround for substituting your own icons for the default ones.

Tip

When Corel Presentations converts your document into HTML, it automatically adds graphic files that it uses as navigational icons. These icons are a left arrow to go back to the previous slide, a right arrow to go forward to the next slide, and a TOC button to take you to the first slide. These graphics are named larrow.gif, rarrow.gif, and toc.gif. To substitute your own icons for these, simply remove these files from the folder and replace them with ones you create—the key to success is to name them the same names.

This Multiple Page publishing option is a good one if you prefer your viewers not to have to scroll or do a lot of clicking and maneuvering. This option best simulates an actual slide presentation and is the best way to go if you want to download the presentation and print it out. It will print single pages with one slide per page.

ClarisWorks and Corel
WordPerfect Suite
Document Conversion

Publishing as a Single-Page Document

The Single Page option publishes your document as one very long document with anchor links connecting the slides.

> **Note**
>
> The anchor link <A NAME> is a hyperlink that goes from one place in a Web document to another place in the same Web document. (To learn more about this and other tags, see Chapter 14.)

This option is good if you have fewer than ten slides. With more than ten, you have a hefty-sized file that takes a long time to load, because each slide is saved as a GIF file (average size about 10 KB). Each HTML page is then about 14 KB altogether. This may not sound like much, but multiply 14 KB times ten pages, and you have one big file with over 100 KB of images. This is why you should only choose this option for small presentations. Figure 4.28 shows how your Presentations document looks as a single-page document.

Figure 4.28

Publishing as a single-page document.

Publishing as a Gallery Document

The Gallery Document option publishes your Corel Presentations document as a single-page document, but instead of having sequential navigation through the various slides, Corel publishes thumbnail images of the slides that link to larger versions in the same document. The same drawback applies to this option as to the single-page option, in that it should only be used for short presentations. One reason for using this publishing option is ease of access to tables or comparisons made in the presentation. Users of your Web site (either Internet or intranet) can quickly locate a given slide by scanning the thumbnails in the comparison chart. A possible drawback is that there is no left arrow, or "back" icon, with this publishing option, so users will rely heavily on their browser's Back button. Figure 4.29 shows how your Corel Presentations document will look as a gallery document.

Figure 4.29

Publishing as a gallery document.

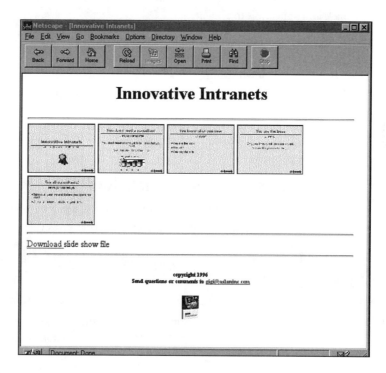

Formatting Options

In addition to being able to control the layout of your Corel Presentations document, you can control such other elements on the resulting Web documents as background color, footer information, image file type, and more. This enables you to integrate your presentations document files with any existing Web style you might be using. For example, suppose you are converting a presentation for a client whose Web site has a black background with white type. If you don't have control of background and text color, you must convert the document and then manually update the background and link colors on every page by editing the source code.

Making the Presentation Available for Downloading

After you choose your layout option, the Formatting option dialog box appears. This dialog box asks you to title your presentation (this is the title that will appear in the title bar of your browser window) and to save it to a folder (directory) on your hard drive. Additionally, there is an option to make your presentation available for downloading. Selecting this option causes a link to be created on the converted document(s) that links to the original presentation in its native format. When users click on this link, they are prompted by their browser to either save the file to their hard drive or pick an application to view it.

A drawback to this feature is that the dialog box does not enable you to input any kind of text to tell your readers what file format the presentation is in. The browser, when it begins downloading, does let the user know the MIME type (essentially the file format) of the document and usually asks the user to choose an application to view the file. Still, it would be ideal to let users know what to do with the file before they begin downloading it. Putting a note of instruction on your Web site is a courteous and helpful way around this drawback.

Choosing Background and Link Colors

In addition to background and link colors, there is a button called Color Options. If you click on it, you activate another dialog box that gives the option to choose a text color; colors for hyperlink, active link, and visited link; and background color or wallpaper. Additionally, you can check a box to use the Default Settings (the box says "Use the Default Settings").

Note
Active link and visited link are the colors that hypertext links become as they are being clicked on (active link) and after they have been viewed (visited link).

As stated earlier, being able to control these various options before the conversion takes place is a significant time saver. To manually edit the source code of a 25-slide presentation is tedious for a Web developer, and a major project for someone just getting acquainted with converting documents to HTML.

Choosing Footer Information

Beneath the Color Options button is a More Options button. If you click on this button, you will see an option to Change Footer Information. Have you seen a Web site with a line of copyright information or an e-mail address for a Webmaster (for example: Please send all comments to Webmaster@website.com)? If so, you have seen a footer. If you leave this option on the default setting, your Web files will have Corel's copyright information and Web site link as their footer. It's a good idea to put your own footer there instead, or at least click on None so nothing appears in the footer.

A footer is a good way to make it easy for viewers of your Web site to report bugs, broken links, and other feedback about your Web site to you or the Webmaster. In the text box that says "Include E-mail Address," put the address of the person you want viewers to write to. If you are responsible only for your presentations document, and would like to receive feedback about your presentation but not the entire Web site, specify this by clicking on the "Show Custom Information" button and then typing the information in the lines provided. Your footer information will appear in small text at the bottom of each page in your presentations Web documents.

Choosing Image File Type and Size

Also available in the More Options dialog box is the option to convert and size the slides as either JPEG or GIF files. The default option is to convert the image into a GIF, with Width=400 and Height=300. These are good standards, because the GIF file format is recommended for most Web art, and the image size fits well in a monitor 640×480 pixels wide, the default standard size browser. Additionally, as you can see in figure 4.29, this image size fits well in all the Export Options.

You should also read Chapter 10 if you want to make a truly educated decision on what kind of image file type is right for the kind of artwork you have in your presentations.

Shareware for Macintosh and Windows Users

For Web developers who receive Corel or ClarisWorks documents from clients to convert, but who do not own the programs themselves, there are several shareware programs to help get the job done.

Word Processing Document Converters

Out of all the document converters, the word processing ones are the best. Also, there are more word processing document converters than spreadsheet converters, and more spreadsheet converters than presentation converters. The law of supply and demand definitely applies; most of the documents created by these programs are word processing documents.

ClarisWorks and Corel
WordPerfect Suite
Document Conversion

XTML+ (Macintosh)

URL: http://www.hotfiles.com/swbrowse/mc14/4/4/mac-MC14445.html

For: ClarisWorks

HTML+ is an XTND filter. It converts the formatting of any document created with a word processor that supports XTND exports (which ClarisWorks does). It then assigns HTML tags based on that formatting. It also works with the freeware program clip2gif to translate graphics into GIF images, creating the necessary links to these images as it converts the document.

See also the RTFtoHTML converter, a wonderful cross-platform utility that converts RTF (Rich Text Format) files to HTML swiftly and effectively.

WordPerfect HTML Macros (Macintosh)

URL: http://www.tiac.net/users/mdw/imap/wpmacro.html

For: WordPerfect

WordPerfect HTML Macros adds several HTML macros to your Macro menu. When you select one of these macros, you are prompted to enter information. After you enter this information, the macro runs, replacing the regular formatting of your document with HTML code. Some of the HTML macros available from this pull-down menu are HTML Forms, HTML Headers, HTML Image, HTML Links, and HTML Lists. Using this macro program does require some knowledge of HTML tags.

WPTOHTML (Windows)

URL: http://www.lib.ox.ac.uk/~hunter

FOR: WordPerfect

WPTOHTML 2.0 converts WordPerfect files to HTML and also provides a set of HTML editing tools. The conversion tools make it easy for someone who knows very little HTML to convert a document successfully. It also provides a nice set of HTML authoring and editing tools for users who do know HTML. In this sense, WPTOHTML 2.0 scales to the ability of its users. If your WordPerfect document contains cross-references, indexes, endnotes, or a table of contents, they will not convert when you use WPTOHTML 2.0.

RTFtoHTML (Macintosh or Windows)

URL: http://www.sunpack.com/RTF/

For: ClarisWorks, WordPerfect, Microsoft Word, and all major word processing programs

RTFtoHTML is a fantastic utility that converts documents saved in RTF (Rich Text Format) to HTML. *RTF* is a file format developed by Microsoft and now widely used by most major word processing programs on the MacOS, Windows, and Unix platforms.

In addition to being a superior utility, the documentation and guidelines for its use are also very good. You can check out the RTFtoHTML manual at the following:

```
http://www.sunpack.com/RTF/guide.htm
```

Spreadsheet Converters

Of all the spreadsheet converters tested (and there aren't too many of them), TableCloth Pro is by far the best. If you are looking for a stand-alone spreadsheet converter application for Quattro Pro and ClarisWorks, this is really the only one available.

TableCloth Pro (Macintosh)

URL: http://pinky.istore.com/tc/index.html

For: ClarisWorks, Quattro Pro, Excel, Lotus 1-2-3, FileMaker Pro, and any spreadsheet or database program that can output tab-delimited, ASCII text

TableCloth is an AppleScript applet that converts tab-delimited text to HTML table format. Because it converts simple ASCII text, it can convert files from a multitude of spreadsheet and database applications. Users of Microsoft Excel, ClarisWorks, Lotus 1-2-3, and Claris FileMaker Pro can all benefit from the easy table generation provided in TableCloth.

TwoClicks Tables (Cross-Platform)

URL: http://www.twoclicks.com/cgi-bin/tabdemo.pl

For: All spreadsheet data

This online application enables you to paste your spreadsheet data into a window in a browser, select your formatting preferences, and press a button to generate an HTML table. You can then download the source code and use the table yourself. This application is described in this chapter in the section called "Converted ClarisWorks Spreadsheets."

Summary

Following Microsoft's lead in developing conversion utilities for its Office Suite, Claris Corporation and Corel, Inc., have built-in functions to convert Works and Office Suite documents into HTML. Comparing the two, Corel certainly comes out ahead; however, Corel does not yet have a Macintosh version of its product with the same functionality as its Windows version. Claris, on the other hand, while not as comprehensive a converter, does provide a Macintosh and Windows version of its product that is roughly equivalent in functionality, with the Macintosh version being slightly more comprehensive.

In general, there are many options for converting documents in both programs. Third-party developers continue to create shareware utilities to meet the needs of users looking for quick, inexpensive methods of document conversion. A good habit is to choose utilities that are updated frequently—check the dates on the versions when you go to the Web site to download the software. You could come to love a utility, only to find its student author has abandoned the development effort in favor of a trip to India.

With the growing focus on intranets, Office and Works documents are becoming the most desirable documents for converting and publishing onto the corporate intranet. The obvious reason for this is that many, if not most, business documents are created in Office or Works Suites. Business managers should keep track of conversion add-ins and utilities and provide upgrades to their office suite or works suite software applications as often as possible, thus ensuring that employees converting existing documents into HTML can benefit from the latest technologies. A corporate intranet is, after all, only as useful as the documents that exist there—be aware of the advances in conversion technologies and get ready to take advantage of them as soon as possible.

Batch Conversion Utilities

This chapter is designed to relieve the workload of all the people out there who have been given the task of getting a pile of documents up onto a Web site or corporate intranet quickly. Especially in the case of the corporate intranets, there are reams of documents—human resource policies, procedures manuals, forms, and reports—that need to go online to truly make a useful productivity resource. But who is going to take the time to convert these documents to HTML? The tools reviewed in this chapter make this job a lot easier. Two of these tools, HTML Transit and Web Publisher Pro, are high-end conversion utilities that enable you to customize the output of the conversion by creating a custom template for the "look" of the document. The third utility discussed in this chapter, Adobe File Utilities, is a suite of utilities that have many useful features, one of which is the capability to convert a large number of files at the same time.

The term for converting two or more documents at the same time is called "batch" conversion, because you are converting "batches" of files.

HTML Transit and Web Publisher Pro are available for the Windows platform only; however, Adobe File Utilities is cross-platform and works well with both Windows and the MacOS.

Although both HTML Transit and Web Publisher Pro purport to be able to convert documents for someone who knows no HTML, the real power of both these tools comes from being able to customize the templates that are critical to converting documents to HTML. To be able to customize these templates, it is a good idea to know a little about HTML tags—it makes the process less confusing. This book contains a tutorial about HTML tags in Chapter 14; use it as a reference when customizing your templates.

This chapter will describe the features of each tool. It will also help you through the template-creation process with HTML Transit and Web Publisher Pro, because this is the most crucial (and most difficult) process when using a batch converter.

Converting Documents by Using HTML Transit

HTML Transit by InfoAccess, Inc., is a multiple-file conversion program that converts Microsoft Word, WordPerfect, and RTF (rich text format) files into HTML. Whether you need to convert just one file or 50 files, the conversion process is the same. HTML Transit is a template-based conversion tool. This means it converts multiple files by using a template created from one of your source documents.

> **Note**
>
> A *source document* is the document or documents you want to convert. HTML Transit "borrows" the styles in one of your source documents and creates an HTML template based on the structural elements of your file. A *structural element* is an element that determines how your document looks; for example, a heading is a structural element, but plain text is not. HTML Transit creates an HTML template that uses the same or similar structural elements as the original document.

HTML Transit's power lies in its capability to incorporate styles from existing word processing documents, and use these styles to create templates. After HTML Transit incorporates styles from these documents, you can use HTML Transit's many features to customize the template.

> **Note**
>
> The most important thing to realize is that you can import many different documents with many different styles, and will still be able to create a custom template that will unify the looks of these imported documents. The way you do this is by assigning HTML tags to certain structural elements. For example, if you imported one document with heading 1 levels, and another document with Roman numeral headings, you can assign an ‹H1› tag to both these elements. Then, when you translate the document into HTML, you will see that both the heading 1 style and the Roman numeral style will have ‹H1› level headings. You will learn more about this in the "Further Customizing Your Template" section, which comes later in this chapter.

The next section will give you a general overview of the batch conversion process. The following sections will then help you create and customize your templates—one of the most powerful aspects of HTML Transit.

The Conversion Procedure

When you open HTML Transit, it automatically opens a default template (default.hmp). The .hmp file extension denotes it as a template file. To begin each publishing project, you open a new or existing template. Create a new template for new projects or for projects that have a different look and feel than the existing templates.

1. If you want to create a new template, choose Save As from the File menu and save default.hmp under a new name.

2. With your template open, click on Set Up Files on the main screen. Click on the Select Files property page. The property page is where you associate the files you want to convert with this template (see fig. 5.1).

   When you are associating a file with a template, you are telling HTML Transit that you will be translating the file using the specified template. You will see that you will begin to develop and use certain templates for certain files. For example, your press release files, which probably have a certain style, will be associated with your press.hmp template (or whatever you choose to name it).

Figure 5.1

Selecting files to convert.

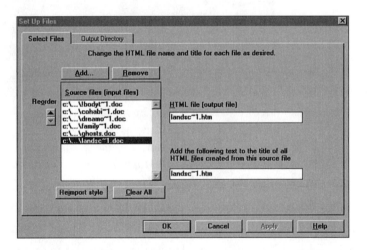

3. Click on Add to open the Select Input Files dialog box and select the source files you want to convert. You will be able to browse your hard disk to look for them.

4. Click on Insert to import styles from your source files, and then click on OK to return to the Select Files property page. The files you selected for conversion are now listed in the Source Files list.

Batch Conversion Utilities

Note

This process is slightly different if you open a template you have used before in HTML Transit. Once you have used a template to do a translation, HTML Transit lists the converted files associated with that template in the Source Files list.

5. After you've selected your source files, click on the Output Directory tab (see fig. 5.2). Here you can identify directories where you want to store the HTML documents and graphics files HTML Transit creates during conversion.

Figure 5.2

Identifying where to store your converted files.

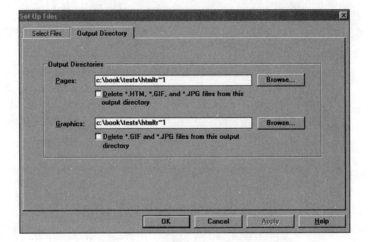

You can place HTML documents in one directory and graphics in another or store both in the same directory, though this is not recommended (see Chapter 12, "Web Site Organization and Management," for reasons to separate image files from HTML files). You can also delete any unwanted or unused files so you can start with a clean directory.

6. Click on OK to exit the Output Directory page and return to HTML Transit's main screen.

7. Click on Translate Publication on the main screen to convert your source files into HTML.

For the most part, HTML Transit does a good job of converting files to HTML; however, you might want to add a graphic later, or move some text around, change text to bold, and so on. If you want to modify the translated document, check out Chapter 13, "Tailoring Converted Files."

> **Note**
>
> In case you were wondering what happens to word processing text features such as index items, cross references, and hidden text, these features are also imported as styles, and you can then customize your template to handle these features as you like. For example, if you have some hidden text in your word processing document, you could choose to assign a custom HTML tag to that text, such as a ‹FONT COLOR› tag. This would make all your hidden text appear in a different font color.

Creating Custom Templates in HTML Transit

This is probably the most important section of the chapter, because in this section you can customize your template so that all your documents come out looking exactly the way you want them to. This is what makes template conversion so desirable—you can fiddle with the template, testing on only one document, until you get it right. Then you can convert all your documents confidently, knowing that they will look exactly how you want them to look. (No more source code editing!) This also means that if something needs to change on all these documents, such as a new graphic added or a horizontal line deleted, you need only edit one document (the template document) and then reconvert the batch. It is immeasurably faster than hand-editing all your documents.

Using the Template Wizard

The template wizard guides you through a set of steps to begin creating a new template. It is a good place to start, because it helps you set up your output directory and walks you through setting up the major structural elements of your Web page. The major structural elements include heading levels, background color, text color, and separator bars, called "translator elements" by HTML Transit. After using the template wizard, you can further customize your template as detailed in the next section.

Using a word processing file of your own, follow along with this process. The file used for this example is shown in figure 5.3.

It is a good idea to create a directory to store all your templates, so before you begin this process, create a "templates" directory. You might also want to create a destination directory for your translated file. If none is specified, HTML Transit will place them in a directory called "output" in the HTML Transit directory.

Figure 5.3

The file before conversion.

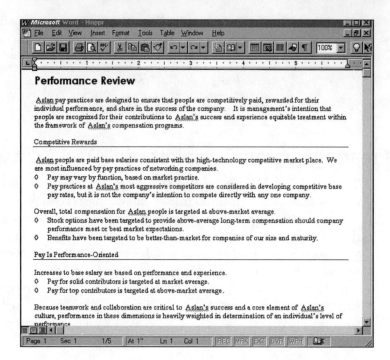

1. Start HTML Transit. The default.hmp template will be open. The document converted here is a standard Performance Review policy. This document contains basic formatting and has a table in it.

2. Click on the button for the template wizard. A welcome screen appears. This screen provides an overview of the template creation process. Click on Next.

3. The wizard asks you to locate the file you want to convert (see fig. 5.4). If you are planning to convert a batch of files with different levels of formatting, choose the file with the most structural elements. For example, if you are converting a series of procedures documents, and one of them has tables and diagrams in addition to text and headings, that's the file to use here. Click on Next.

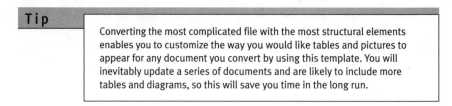

Tip

Converting the most complicated file with the most structural elements enables you to customize the way you would like tables and pictures to appear for any document you convert by using this template. You will inevitably update a series of documents and are likely to include more tables and diagrams, so this will save you time in the long run.

4. HTML Transit will begin the conversion process, which takes about five seconds.

Figure 5.4

The template wizard.

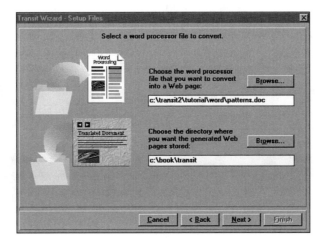

The next few screens will guide you through choosing the look of the major structural elements on your page. Click on Next.

5. The next screen asks you to choose a background. You can choose a texture from HTML Transit's gallery or a simple background color. One drawback here is that you can't choose your own background image; however, there is a workaround to this (see the following tip). Click on Next.

> **Tip**
>
> The HTML Transit gallery is a collection of Web art objects that you can use to add graphical elements such as navigation buttons, background images, and separator bars to your documents. Add your own background images, icons, and separator bars to this collection, which is located in the Transit directory in a folder called "Gallery" on your hard drive. When you add images here, you can easily choose them when going through the template wizard.

6. On the next screen, choose your highest heading level and the kind of separator bars you would like to associate with your heading, as well as the alignment of these elements on your page. By choosing your highest heading level, you are telling HTML transit what size you would like your highest heading level to be. All subheadings under this will be smaller. If, when HTML Transit imports your document, it does not detect a heading level, the text box on the screen will read "No highest heading level." You can change this choice to Normal, which should make your highest heading level a header 1 (the largest) or you can change it to whatever heading size you would like for your highest level (see fig. 5.5). When you have made your selections, click on Next.

Batch Conversion
Utilities

Figure 5.5

The template wizard's formatting options.

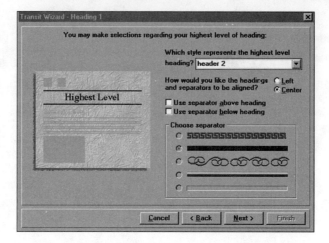

7. The next screen asks you to repeat step 6 for your second level headings. When you have made your selections, click on Next.

8. The next screen asks if you would like to split the imported file into two or more files. It is a good idea to select this option if you have a long document and you don't want your viewers to have to scroll through it. HTML Transit will create the necessary links to these pages when it converts the document.

9. The next screen enables you to create a footer that could contain the Webmaster's e-mail address, copyright information, or any other information you want to include on the bottom of each page. When you have finished typing your information, click on Next.

10. Figure 5.6 shows the last screen of the template wizard. When you have finished, you have a new template to use for converting files you want to have the same format.

After finishing the wizard, you can go on to customize your new template. The next section will show you how to test your converted document; then, after viewing the results of this conversion, you can go on to "Further Customizing Your Template." There, you will learn how to insert custom HTML in your template, further tailoring your template to create Web pages that match your desired specifications.

Testing Your Converted Document

At this point, you have the option to choose "Translate Publication" to see if you need to further customize your template. Click on "Translate Publication" and a process screen will appear. You will be able to see HTML Transit's translation monitor, which is basically a dialog box showing levels of progress. When HTML Transit has finished, you can click on "Browse Publication" from the main menu to see your converted document. The document converted in this exercise can be seen in figure 5.7.

Figure 5.6

The "Finished" screen of the template wizard.

Figure 5.7

The document after a simple conversion.

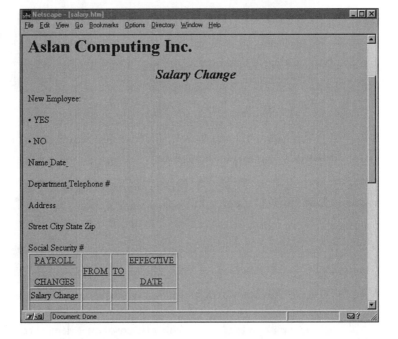

There are several things to note about the document:

⬤ Form check boxes were converted into bullets.

- Table data cell boxes did not retain their original sizes.

- Elements that were aligned with tabs in the original document did not retain their alignment.

Form elements are currently not supported in HTML Transit 2.0 beta, which is why the check boxes have been converted to bullets.

The release version of HTML Transit 2.0 should be able to convert the appropriate table data cells' sizes. Unfortunately, the release version was not available at the time of this writing.

Because tabs do not yet have an HTML tag, you can do one of two things:

1. Read Chapter 13, "Tailoring Converted Files," for tips on cleaning up converted documents.

2. Further customize your template so that you can assign an element to handle tabs. We will do that in the next section.

Further Customizing Your Template

When the wizard is done, you will once again be at the main menu screen. The template you created is still open; you can see it in the title bar of the HTML Transit window. You have four choices for further customizing your template, as follows:

- **Assign Elements.** This option enables you to assign custom HTML tags to certain text patterns in your source documents. You can also assign custom HTML tags to the translator elements created based on the styles of the document used to create the template.

> **Note**
>
> HTML Transit calls all structural elements such as headers and separator bars *translator elements*, because HTML Transit uses these elements to *translate* the structure of a document into HTML. The terms "structural elements" and "translator elements" are synonymous throughout the chapter.

- **Format.** This option enables you to modify paragraph alignment, font face and size, separator or hard return size, and image file type (GIF or JPEG). It also enables you to input custom HTML tags either before or after elements on the page.

- **Navigate.** This option enables you to select buttons or icons to use as navigation tools throughout the converted files. It lets you create button bars, as well as corresponding text menu bars.

● **Globals.** This option enables you to select global elements such as background color, text color, table attributes, frame attributes, and the order of certain elements at the top and bottom of your HTML page. (*Global* means the elements will appear throughout your converted Web files as you select them here.)

These four options used to further customize your template are described in greater detail in the sections that follow.

Assigning Elements to Your Template

This section will discuss how to assign some structural elements to the salary review template previously created.

It is important to know that HTML Transit imports styles from your original document. If there are no styles associated with your document, there are no elements to modify, because the contents of your entire document will have been interpreted as the Normal style.

> **N o t e**
>
> When HTML Transit imports styles, it is importing the standard word processing styles of the document. Many people create word processing documents without using styles or style sheets, and you may find yourself importing and converting many documents that do not have styles. HTML Transit will not recognize headers that are not defined as headers in the original document, and will translate them as plain text.

You can, however, assign a style to a *pattern* of text within your document. For example, if you have tabbed text within your document and you would like it to appear bold, you can associate a bold <B> tag with that tabbed text. You will see how to do that in the section called "Using Text Patterns for Style Identification."

In this next exercise, you will assign a custom tag to one of the translator elements:

1. From the main screen, click on Assign Elements.

2. Click on the Assign Tags menu option.

3. In the list of translator elements, select the translator element to which you want to assign a tag. Note that if there are no styles in your document, your options are Default and Normal. You will be assigning the <FONT COLOR> tag to the Heading 1 Translator Element.

    The HTML tag assigned by default to that translator element appears in the Standard Tag drop-down list. Again, if your document does not contain styles, only the Default and Normal styles are listed. Normal style usually means a paragraph tag will separate paragraphs, so the only tag you see is the paragraph tag.

4. Under the Associated Tag option, select the tag you want to assign to that translator element. Select either a standard tag from the drop-down list or enter a custom tag. A custom tag is an HTML tag you input yourself.

In this example, we will add the custom tag <FONT COLOR>, so click on the "Custom Tag" radio button. Notice that there are two check boxes. In the first check box, "Place before element," type **<FONT COLOR="#219CA0">**. In the second check box, "Place after element," type **</FONT COLOR>**. If you are unfamiliar with HTML, we are specifying a font color to the heading 1 element, using the font color tag. HTML tags are "open" and "close" tags; thus, we need a tag both before and after the element. The number that we specify is a hexadecimal code for a teal color. You can learn more about hexadecimal colors and HTML in Chapter 14, "HTML Tutorial and Reference." See figure 5.8 to see how you would fill in the Assign Tags property page.

Figure 5.8

Adding a custom HTML tag.

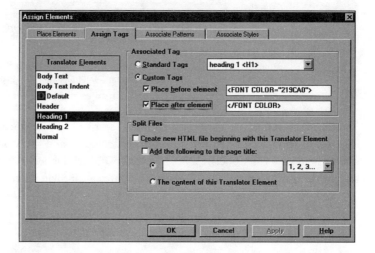

5. Repeat steps 3 and 4 to change the default assignment of any other HTML tags you want to change.

6. Click on OK when you have completed your changes.

7. Choose File, Save to save your changes to the template file.

You can also split your file into several smaller files by clicking on the "Create new HTML file beginning with this Translator Element" check box in the Split Files section of the Assign Tags dialog box. Why would you want to do this? Suppose you are converting a 50-page document. This would be one long Web page. Clicking on the check box enables you to split the file at the occurrence of a designated translator element; thus, you can have HTML Transit split the file at every section heading. This will split your Web page so it has a single page per section heading.

> **Note**
>
> Does this sound confusing? If you are new to using styles, or to HTML in general, customizing a template may seem incredibly confusing. Go through the process a few times, checking the results of the conversion by using your browser. Once you have converted several documents, you will begin to understand how to use the functions described here to create documents the way you want them to look. It takes some time to become proficient at this, but the tool is worth the effort.

Using Text Patterns for Style Identification

If your source files don't have assigned style names other than the default or Normal style, you can define patterns for the content of your source files and associate these patterns with translator elements. The patterns can then be added to your template file instead of styles.

You use one or more formatting characters to create a pattern "string"—a series of related text or formatting characters—associated with particular formatting in the content of your source files. If the content contains text that has no style, but is differentiated by font size, for example, you can associate pattern attributes with this particular formatting in the content of the files.

The first step in using patterns is to define them as translator elements (headings, in this case). This process is detailed in the following step-by-step procedure:

1. Click on Assign Elements on the main screen and then click on the Associate Patterns tab.

2. Click on Add. A new dialog box will pop up. This is where you define your pattern.

3. From the Specifying Pattern Strings list, select the format characters you want to use to create a pattern string that identifies a specific paragraph format. You can click on each selection, in turn, to automatically place the format characters (\t for tab, \d for digit, and so on) in the Pattern String text box. The format characters are given to you in the Pattern String text box, so don't worry—you don't have to learn them!

   For example, if you have a heading at a particular level set off in a paragraph by itself that follows the pattern "1. Heading One" (that is, a single numeral

Batch Conversion Utilities

followed by a period and a tab, and then the heading itself beginning with an initial capital letter), type \d\t\A in the Pattern text box, as shown in figure 5.9.

In your example, you will center the tabbed text, because there is no HTML equivalent to tabbed text.

Figure 5.9

Specifying pattern strings.

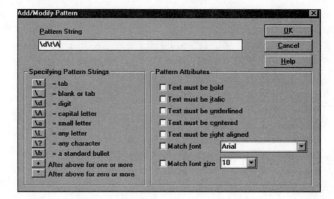

Add/Modify Pattern

Pattern String

\d\t\A

OK

Cancel

Help

Specifying Pattern Strings

\t   = tab
_   = blank or tab
\d   = digit
\A   = capital letter
\a   = small letter
\L   = any letter
\?   = any character
\b   = a standard bullet
+   After above for one or more
*   After above for zero or more

Pattern Attributes

☐ Text must be bold
☐ Text must be italic
☐ Text must be underlined
☐ Text must be centered
☐ Text must be right aligned
☐ Match font   Arial
☐ Match font size 10

Note

It would be ideal if you could add HTML tags in this property page, so that you could add a line break ‹BR› or paragraph tag ‹P› to a pattern string. This would enable you to break up lines of tabbed text so that they could at least appear on their own line.

4. Click on OK to return to the Associate Patterns dialog box.

   The pattern you just entered is now listed in the Pattern Strings list box.

5. From the Associated Translator Element list, select the translator element you want to associate the pattern with. If you know HTML and you don't see the element you want (such as the italic tag), you can add it by clicking on Add above the Associated Translator Element box, and then typing the HTML code for the tag in the text box.

Using the Format Option

The Format option enables you to select the major formatting attributes of your converted document. These attributes are Font Face, Paragraph Alignment, Image File type (the kind of image types you would like your images converted into), and any kind of custom HTML you would like to insert either above the body of the docu-ment or after the body of the document.

The format options are very straightforward, and you should be able to make your choices easily by clicking your way through each option.

As an example, you will add an icon to appear before the heading. Because you are formatting a heading 1, click on "Heading 1" in the Translator Elements box, and then click on "Icons." You will be placing the icon before the content, and then searching the gallery to find the icon. See figure 5.10 to see how you have filled out the property page.

Figure 5.10

Using the Format option to insert an icon.

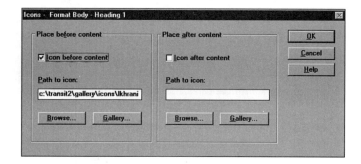

Using the Navigate Option

The Navigate option enables you to choose graphical buttons to use as navigation icons so you can link graphically to your converted files. In addition to choosing buttons, you can also choose to have a button bar created to appear on the page. HTML Transit will also provide a text bar if you specify it in the element text bar option. Like the Format option, the Navigate option is easy to set up, and the gallery of buttons and icons is better than you would expect from a program whose focus is on batch conversion and not design.

If you are converting multiple pages from a print publication, you will need a way to bring all these pages together to make Web browsing them easy. The best way to do this is to create a table of contents and an index. Fortunately, HTML Transit does this for you automatically. Unless you choose navigational icons, HTML Transit will insert text links on the Table of Contents page, which will serve as your navigation between pages. However, for your users to be able to click sequentially through your documents, as well as back to previous documents, or back to your table of contents, you will need to assign navigational tools.

Click on the Navigate option. You have four property pages: page button bar, element button bar, page text bar, and element text bar. Generally, you would choose one of these methods of creating navigation, although you could choose to have both a page button and page text bar, placed at different locations on the page. You would do this out of consideration for people with nongraphical browsers, or who are surfing with graphics turned off. In this example, you will be choosing the page button bar.

Batch Conversion Utilities

First, you need to decide what you will be linking to. The choices are previous page, next page, top of page, TOC, index, or specific page. You will link to the previous page, the next page, and the TOC.

1. Check the options that you want to link to from your page or pages.

2. Click on Gallery to choose from HTML Transit's gallery of buttons, or Browse to use your own.

3. At the bottom of the property page, you will see a box called "Placement." Click on where you would like these icons to appear. You can choose both "Top" and "Bottom" of the page, so your users won't have to scroll to be able to navigate through your publication. Click on OK when you are finished.

Now is a good time to save your template, too.

Using the Globals Option

The Globals option enables you to select global options throughout the Web files you convert. These options include the following:

- Background color and text
- Separator or hard return graphics
- Address (text that appears at the bottom of the pages with copyright information and Webmaster e-mail link)
- Table preferences
- Frame preferences

When you click on the Globals button, you will see tabbed buttons for all the Global settings. Each option is very straightforward: simply click on the options you want. For example, in the Background and Text Color option, click on the colors you want for background color, text color, hyperlink color, active link color, and visited link color. You can also choose the font you would like, but remember that font face is still a browser-specific option, and the font face you choose may not show up in all browsers that view your page.

The most advanced option in the Globals section is the Frames option. This option enables you to create a frame that lists the index of your converted document's headings in one frame, leaving the other frame to display the documents. Frames are a browser-specific feature, and you may not want to choose a frames layout because not all browsers support them. However, if you are converting documents for your corporate intranet, and you know your browser supports frames and all employees of your company use the same browser, then you can use frames without wondering if your viewers will be able to see your documents.

HTML Transit makes good frame documents. Because it enables you to create a table of contents, as well as an index, you can choose to use a frame to display your converted documents, while keeping the table of contents and the index available at all times.

Figure 5.11

The converted document after further customization.

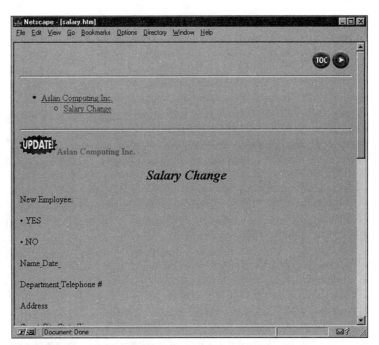

Converting Documents by Using Web Publisher Professional

Web Publisher Professional (developed by SkiSoft) is a batch-conversion utility that enables you to do a large variety of tasks, such as the following:

- Design a template
- Import and convert word processing files in most major applications

- View Web files
- Archive Web files

Web Publisher Pro will support the following applications:

- Microsoft Word
- WordPerfect
- FrameMaker
- Lotus Ami Pro
- Lotus WordPro
- Microsoft Works
- Microsoft Excel

In addition, Web Publisher Pro features a drag-and-drop interface onto which you can drag a file, drop it onto the window, and—presto!—your file has been converted to HTML. One of Web Publisher Pro's best features is its capability to convert tables and even nested tables. There are, however, some minor bugs when converting non-RTF (Rich Text Format) files, but if you want to take the time to convert your files into RTF, you won't be disappointed with Web Publisher Pro.

The Conversion Procedure

There are two ways to convert documents when using Web Publisher Pro. The first, and easiest, is to drag and drop the files you want to convert onto the Web Publisher window. Figure 5.12 shows the Web Publisher window as it appears when you start up Web Publisher Pro.

Figure 5.12

Drag and drop files onto the Web Publisher window.

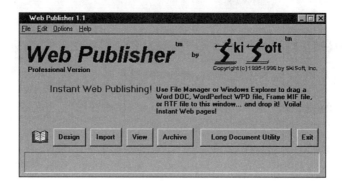

From File Manager or Windows Explorer, simply drag the file over to the Web Publisher window. Web Publisher uses its Normal template to create a Web page based on your document.

The second way to convert documents is to go through the Import Files process, which is accessible from a button on the drag-and-drop window. A brief description of all the functions of Web Publisher Pro follows, because these functions aren't entirely clear when you start the program. Also, after you click on a function, the Help menu mysteriously disappears. It is only accessible from the main menu. Keep this book handy when you go through the conversion process!

When the program starts, the following options are available from the main menu screen:

- **Design:** This option enables you to design a custom template for the Web pages you want to convert. Use this option if you have a document to convert that must look a certain way, with certain graphics, such as a banner graphic or button bar.

- **Import:** This option enables you to choose the files you want to import and to specify the directory to which you would like to output the converted files.

- **View:** This option enables you to view your converted file in your browser of choice (as long as it's installed on your system). You would use this option to test how your document looks after conversion.

- **Archive:** This option creates a zipped archive of your converted files. A *zipped archive* is a file that consists of many compressed files. Archiving (zipping) files enables you to store and e-mail files easily, without taking up disk drive space or download time. You might use this option to store older versions of Web pages, just for reference.

- **Long Document Utility:** This option enables you to take a large file, such as a FrameMaker document, and convert it into several smaller files. With this option, you can specify where you want Web Publisher to split the document. If you have a five-section document, for example, you can split it into five separate Web pages by specifying the section head as the place where you want to break the document. This utility is only available to people who have purchased Web Publisher Professional, which is different from the standard version of Web Publisher. This chapter reviews Web Publisher Professional.

In the next example, you will import a file using Web Publisher Pro:

1. Click on the Import button to import a document or documents to be converted.

Batch Conversion Utilities

2. The Import Utility dialog box pops up (see fig. 5.13). This box asks you to choose a template and an output directory for this document.

Figure 5.13

The Import Utility dialog box.

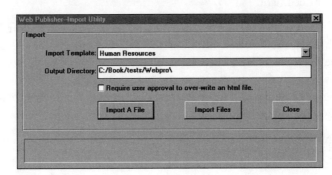

The default template is called Normal. This template simply changes word processing style headings into HTML headings and separates paragraphs with paragraph tags. It is always best to use the Normal template when you are working with word processing documents that use standard style sheets, because the Normal template is based on standard style sheets. It is also good to work with the Normal template if there are no styles imported, because it will only insert paragraph tags to your document if no other style has been defined. In other words, you really can't go wrong with Normal—you just won't get fancy formatting.

3. To choose a directory, type in a path name. Web Publisher Pro does not let you browse for a directory, but it will create any directory you type, as long as you start the path name from your root directory (usually C:\).

4. Web Publisher will ask you to locate the file you want to convert. You can now use the Browse button to find the file. When you double-click on the file name, Web Publisher begins the conversion.

Web Publisher's conversion process can be slow. First it takes your word processing document and converts it into an RTF file. Then, it converts the RTF file into an HTML file. If the file has large images (such as a full-color screen shot), this process can take up to several minutes and might even crash your machine. However, if your document is already in RTF before you start converting it with Web Publisher Pro, the process is quick.

Note

Web Publisher Pro converts RTF files much more quickly and with less toil and trouble than it does regular word processing files. To save a document in Rich Text Format in your word processing application, choose Save As from the File menu and choose RTF as the file type.

After your file has been converted, you can click on View on the main menu screen to view your document. When you install Web Publisher Pro, it scans your hard drive for browsers and creates buttons for these browsers, which appear in the View window for you. It's a nice feature.

Using the Design Utility to Create Custom Templates

Using the Normal template is okay if you have plain word processing files you need to get up on the Web quickly, but what if you are converting a large manual and you need to put a banner and footer on every page? With the Design utility, you can create a template specifically for any pages that go in a specific section of your Web site.

The following example shows the process of creating a template specifically for a human resources department, and then converts several files, using the template for the original document.

1. From the main menu screen, click on Design. A dialog box with several tab-style property pages will show up. The first property page is called About. This is where you name your template and write any information about it. It is usually a good idea to provide a description of your templates so you don't forget what they were created for. Figure 5.14 shows a description entered for a custom template.

Figure 5.14

Providing a description for your custom template.

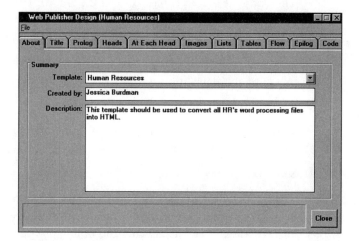

Batch Conversion Utilities

2. Click on the Title property page. This page will use the information you input to create a title for your Web pages. Your options are described in the following list:

● Set Title from First HEADING in the file.

   This option is the default and works well on most documents. This option tells Web Publisher to make the HTML Title the same as the first heading it finds in the source document.

   If Web Publisher does not find any headings in the source document, it will not create an HTML title for the document.

● Set Title from First Text with any TITLE Style.

   This option is recommended if your documents use standard style sheets. This option tells Web Publisher to set the HTML Title from the first text it finds that has a "Title" style.

● Set Title from First Text with THIS Style.

   This option is recommended if your documents use unusual style sheets. With this option, Web Publisher will create the HTML Title from the first text it finds that has a style you select.

● Set Title from First Paragraph.

   This option tells Web Publisher to set the HTML Title from the first paragraph it finds in the source document.

   If you use this, be sure the title is the first paragraph. Don't use this option when you publish documents that have a date, author name, or some other text above the title.

● Set Title from First Text with This FONT.

   This option enables you to instruct Web Publisher to recognize the title of a document from its font face and point size.

● Set Title to THIS.

   This option enables you to type a title for the document you are converting. If you are just publishing one document, this option is okay. If you are converting several documents, this option probably isn't the best option because all the document titles will be the same.

3. Click on the Prolog property page. This is where you can input a banner graphic that is not part of your original source files. Check the Banner box and click on Files to browse for your banner graphic. When you have found it, click on the next property page, Heads.

A banner is a useful navigational tool. If you convert a manual for the human resources department, and you have a human resources banner, you can choose to have this banner display on all the pages of your manual. This way, your users will know they are in the human resources section of your Web site at all times.

4. The Heads property page is where you can set Web Publisher Pro to create anchor links (within a document or among several documents) based on the heading. In short, it will make your heading hyperlinks. In this example, because the document doesn't have a specific style, you will choose to have heading links based on font size (see fig. 5.15).

An anchor link is a hyperlink. It is most often referred to as an anchor when the link moves you to a different "anchor" or place, within a document. However, any link is an anchor. That's what the <A> in the <A HREF> tag means. (If you don't know HTML, this last sentence won't make too much sense to you. To find out more about HTML, see Chapter 14.)

Figure 5.15

Choosing a heading based on font size.

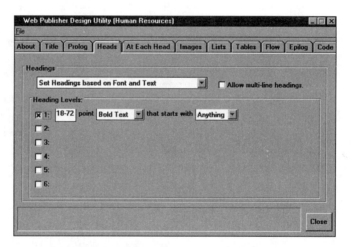

5. The At Each Head property page enables you to select navigational icons to appear at each heading, if you want them there. If you don't want them, leave them blank.

6. The Images property page enables you to specify whether you want to include images in your converted document. In addition, it enables you to specify monochrome, 16-bit color, or 256-bit color. If you don't know a lot about graphic conversion, choose 256-bit color—it's the default. If you want to find out more about 256- vs. 16-bit color, and Web graphics in general, please check out Chapters 10 and 11.

Batch Conversion Utilities

7. The Lists property page enables you to specify what kind of lists can appear in your Web page. You can even specify to add a bullet to begin paragraphs starting with specific characters. For example, if your original document has a bulleted list that begins with asterisks (*), you can instruct Web Publisher Pro to replace these asterisks with bullets. Specifying a special character such as an asterisk is not that intuitive, so look at figure 5.16 to see how it's done.

Figure 5.16

Specifying a bulleted list.

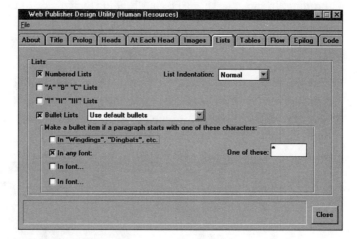

8. The Tables property box enables you to specify table width, borders and size of borders, and alignment of text and images within cells. Web Publisher creates beautiful tables; an enhancement to this property page would be to show a user what the table would look like after choosing these options.

9. The Flow property page enables you control the fonts' layout, and "flow" of your Web pages. For example, you can choose to suppress text that has the words "continued" or "cont." or "continued on next page"—because you are no longer dealing with paper documents, you don't need to tell your reader that the page is "continued." You can also specify to end each paragraph with a hard paragraph break—this would cause visible gaps between your paragraphs.

10. The Epilog property page enables you to specify certain elements to add at the end of your Web page. Your options are an index of pages, a return link to a specific Web page (such as the main home page of your Web site), or a "signature," such as a mail-to link or a quote.

11. The Code property tag enables you to insert custom HTML code at the beginning and end of your Web document. This is an advanced option; if you don't know HTML, don't worry about it.

However, if you DO know HTML, this is the place to add custom tags at the top and bottom of each Web page. One reason for doing this would be to include what is commonly known as server-parsed HTML—an HTML file that appears on every page, such as a navigational bar, an e-mail address, and a last-updated date. Then, when one of these elements change, only one file needs to be updated—the one that is referenced by the custom HTML code.

At this point, the process of creating a custom template is almost done. Click on Close, and you will return to the Web Publisher main menu. From here, you can drag the human resource files onto the main menu window and convert them to HTML, using the Human Resources template you just created.

> **Note**
>
> When you create a template, it's best to test the template by converting just one of the files first; then view it in your browser and see if you like the way Web Publisher converted your file. If you don't, you can use the Design utility to edit your template.

The Long Document Utility

The Long Document utility is a function that takes long documents already converted into HTML and splits them into smaller Web files. Long in this case can mean anything from five pages to a 500-page FrameMaker manual. You can specify the heading level at which you would like Web Publisher Professional to split the document. This produces a set of small HTML files, each representing a logical unit of the original document. Using this utility enables you to easily navigate through a large amount of material.

Web Publisher Pro will insert visual navigational icons into each of these small files to enable the user to jump to any heading in the file, or to the next file or the previous file. You can choose the visual icons by clicking the buttons Prev (previous) and Next on the Long Document utility property page.

In addition to creating a set of smaller Web pages, Web Publisher Professional also creates a master table of contents that displays all the headings in the document. Links in the table of contents enable the user to jump to any desired section of the document, just by clicking.

An obvious drawback to this utility is the need to convert the document into HTML *before* you use the utility.

The next example will demonstrate using the Long Document utility for converting a long HTML file into several smaller Web pages:

Batch Conversion
Utilities

1. Starting from the main menu, click on Long Document Utility. The Long Document Utility property page comes up. Figure 5.17 shows the property page for using the Long Document utility.

Figure 5.17

The Long Document Utility dialog box.

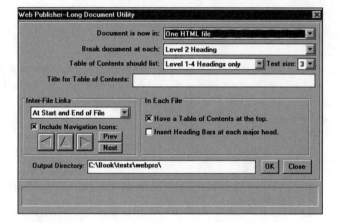

Note

The Long Document utility is limited in that it doesn't enable you to specify special text characters as places to break files. In short, if your document has not been converted into a document using standard HTML headings, the Long Document utility will not work. In the example used here, the original headings were manually changed from Roman numeral headings in a large font size and in bold (I. Scope of the Chapter) to HTML Level 1 headings (‹H1›). This is a lot of manual effort, so the Long Document utility may not be worth the effort for you. Cheer up—this saves you money, because you can buy the standard version of Web Publisher (which does not include the Long Document utility) for much less than the Professional version. Aside from the existence of this utility, not much else is different in the two versions.

2. When the Long Document Utility property page comes up, specify where you would like Web Publisher Pro to break the document. In this case, because each section is formatted in Level 2 headings, the selection here is Level 2 Heading. You can also specify a title for the table of contents in the text box provided. The table of contents will consist of an HTML page with this title and links to the section levels, which will now be broken into separate pages.

3. When you are finished with this property page, click on OK. Web Publisher Pro will separate your document into individual files that will appear in a new window. You can now view these files in your Web browser. Start with the file name that ends in TOC—this is the table of contents for the files you have split.

Warning
This program—specifically, the capability to convert non-RTF files—still has some bugs. It is still in its early stages of development and does have a lot of promise; however, you might want to wait until the next release before you make the purchase.

Adobe File Utilities

Adobe File Utilities is an inexpensive program that includes the following three applications:

DocuComp

Word for Word

Viewer95

When used together, Word for Word and Viewer95 make it possible to read almost any file type, view it, and then save it as any other file type. In addition to being able to read all kinds of file types, Adobe File Utilities can convert multiple files at a time.

Here are just a few of the file types Adobe File Utilities can read and convert to the following:

- Word (doc)
- WordPerfect (doc)
- MacWrite
- FrameMaker (mif)
- Ami Pro
- ASCII (all operating systems)
- Excel (xls)
- Quattro Pro (wq)
- XEROX
- WordStar
- HTML
- RTF

Batch Conversion
Utilities

Unlike HTML Transit and Web Publisher Pro, Adobe File Utilities does not have the capability to customize templates, nor does it provide the kind of design elements the other two provide. Its primary function is to convert files from one format to another in a no-frills way, and it performs this task well, with little need for tailoring the document after conversion. Use Adobe File Utilities if you don't want to create a unified "look" for the documents you are converting.

This section will review Viewer95 and Word for Word, and will show how to use one or both to convert multiple files.

Adobe File Utilities will easily convert the following elements:

- Tables

- Lists

- Bulleted lists

- Numbered lists

- Images (into JPEGs only)

Adobe File Utilities will NOT support the following:

- Form fields

- Multiple columns

Using Viewer95 to View and Convert Files

If you are running the Windows version of Adobe File Utilities, you can use Viewer95 to look at files whose native applications are not on your local system. If you have multiple documents to convert, you might want to take a look at them to see how they look in their native format.

> **Note**
>
> Viewer95 is a Windows-only application. The Macintosh version of Adobe File Utilities comes with DocuComp and Word for Word. Viewer95 is similar to the Windows Explorer in that it enables you to see the hierarchical structure of your drive and directories and lets you open, view, and save documents in other file formats, all in its main window.

You will use Viewer95 to convert single files from one file format to another. You use Word for Word to convert multiple files.

Follow these instructions to convert a document into HTML (or another type) using Viewer95:

1. After starting Viewer95, navigate to one of the files you want to convert. When you locate it, click on it to highlight it (see fig. 5.18).

Figure 5.18

Opening a file in Viewer95.

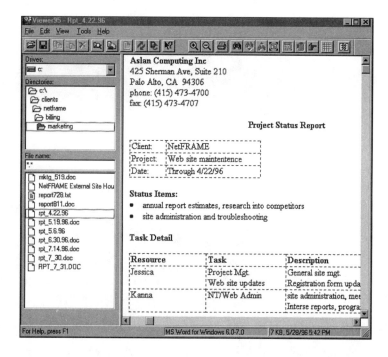

2. From the File menu, select View filename, with "filename" being the name of the file you have highlighted.

3. The file will appear in the large window. At this point, if you have many files to look at, repeat steps 1–3 to view all the files. If you want to convert any of these files to HTML, click on Save As in the File menu.

4. Scroll through the file types. You will see that you can save the file in any version of HTML, from 1 to 3, and that you can save the file with or without Netscape extensions.

Note

While Viewer95 boasts that it can save documents in HTML 3.0 with Netscape extensions, it does not support form fields, which are an earlier version of HTML. It does, however, support tables, which are probably the most important tags of the HTML 3.0 specification.

Batch Conversion Utilities

If you choose to convert the file into HTML, you can open your browser window to see the result. Figure 5.19 shows the file saved as HTML 3.0, with Netscape extensions.

Figure 5.19

A Word file converted with Adobe Viewer95.

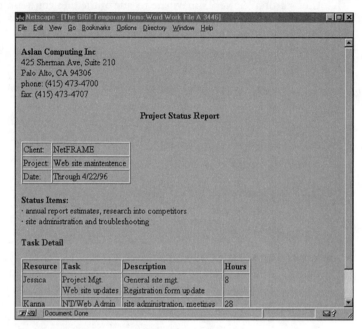

Using Word for Word to Convert Multiple Files

Macintosh and Windows users can use Word for Word to convert multiple files of almost any file type into HTML. The user interface is not slick (it looks like an old Windows 3.1 application and isn't very aesthetically appealing); however, it is very straightforward and easy to set up:

1. Start Word for Word. The window shown in figure 5.20 will appear.

    This window is divided into two major sections: Source and Target. *Source* means the files that exist on your hard drive, which you can choose to convert. Below the word Source is a button called Format. Make sure the option for Format is <AUTOMATIC RECOGNITION>. This option will enable Word for Word to recognize the files in their native format. Target means the file formats that these files will become, as well as the path to the output directory. (The output directory is the directory where you want the converted files stored.)

2. Navigate to the directory that contains the files you want to convert. When you find the files, you can click on Select to choose one at a time or Select All to select all the files in the directory. Clicking on Select will move the file from the Source window to the To Do window at the bottom of the screen. The To Do window is a "holding pen" for documents waiting to be converted. Do this for all the files you want to convert.

Figure 5.20

The Word for Word window.

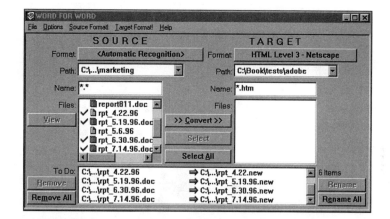

Tip

You don't need to have all your files in the same directory to convert them simultaneously. Navigate to the directory that contains one of the files you want to convert, and then click on Select. The document's name will appear in the To Do window at the bottom of the screen. It will not be converted...yet. You can go on to select more files in different directories, clicking on Select to move them to the To Do window.

3. When you have finished selecting files and moving them from the Source window to the To Do window, you can choose the file format to which you would like to convert the documents. Click on the Format button and select HTML 3.0 (or whatever version of HTML you prefer).

4. In the Path box, navigate to the directory where you would like to store the converted files.

5. In the Name box, type *.**htm**. This tells Word for Word to store the converted documents with the .htm file extension. If you don't do this, Word for Word will save the document with a .new file extension.

Batch Conversion
Utilities

Tip

If at any time you want to quickly view a file you are converting, highlight the file name in the Source listing and click on the View button. This brings up another window with a preview of the document in its native state. (An Excel spreadsheet, for example, will look exactly as it does in Excel.) This is a good thing to know if you are converting a number of files and want to double-check that you are converting the files you want to convert. Instead of opening up the native application, you can simple click on the View button.

6. When all the files you want to convert are in the To Do window, click on Convert. The files will be converted, and you will see a progress screen, as shown in figure 5.21.

Figure 5.21

The conversion progress screen.

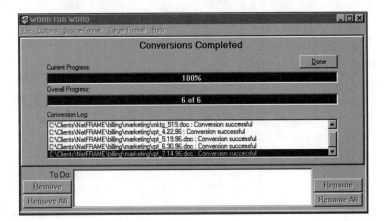

7. Click on the Done button, and you will return to the Word for Word window. Under the Target window, you will now see a listing of the files you have just converted. To view a file as it will appear on the Web, open the file while in your browser. (By selecting File, Open file, while in Netscape Navigator, or your browser of choice.)

Note

In case you were wondering, Viewer95 cannot convert spreadsheets into HTML—only word processing documents of all kinds.

One drawback to Adobe File Utilities is that it does not convert spreadsheets into tables. Instead, it converts spreadsheets into rows, putting a break after each row of text. If you need to convert a spreadsheet quickly, check out Chapter 4, under the section "Shareware." There is a fast and easy application called TwoClicks Tables that you can run over the Web.

Figure 5.22 shows a spreadsheet before it is converted to HTML with Word for Word, and figure 5.23 shows the same spreadsheet after conversion, as seen in a browser.

Figure 5.22

A spreadsheet before conversion to HTML with Word for Word.

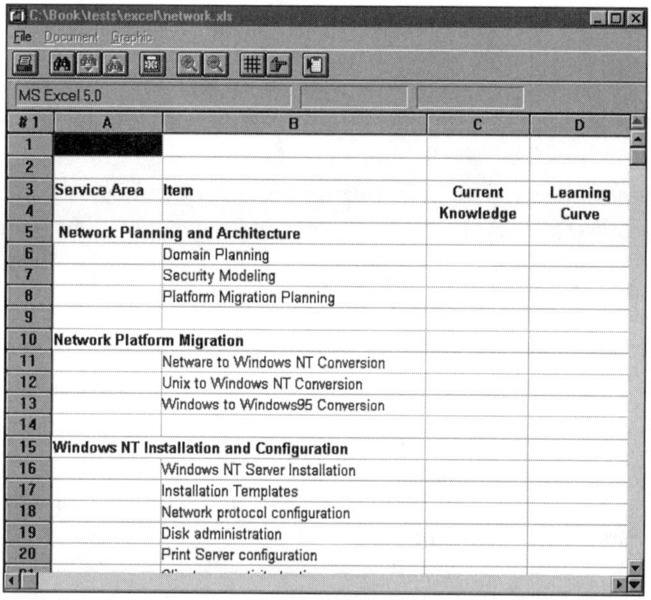

Figure 5.23

A spreadsheet after conversion to HTML with Word for Word.

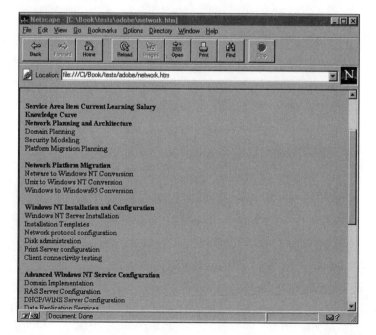

Summary

As the race to get existing business documents onto the Web progresses, the need for tools that will convert multiple files at the same time grows exponentially. All the tools discussed in this chapter will convert multiple files into HTML. Choose your conversion program according to your Web site needs and your audience. You can choose a high-end converter that provides design options and customizable templates, such as HTML Transit or Web Publisher Pro. Or you can go with an inexpensive utility such as Adobe File Utilities, if reformatting your documents isn't important to you or if you are familiar with HTML and want to hand-tailor your converted documents.

If you are repeatedly converting documents for various departments within an organization where each department has a different "look and feel," you should definitely choose either HTML Transit or Web Publisher Pro and invest the time in learning how to customize templates. In the long run, setting up a template for each type of document you convert can save you lots of time.

If you are a Web developer who finds yourself doing repeat jobs for clients, templates will save you time spent in conversion, freeing you to focus on design and the more creative aspects of content development.

CHAPTER 6

QuarkXPress Conversion

More Web designers receive documents in QuarkXPress than in any other desktop publishing program. Although FrameMaker and PageMaker contribute much information that ultimately ends up on the Web, QuarkXPress is the clear leader in producing files destined for HTML. There is a good side and a bad side to this fact. The bad side is that XPress documents are likely to be the most complex files you will ever need to convert, prone to complex formatting issues such as the following:

- Multiple columns of text

- Tables

- Sidebars

- Stories that continue on subsequent pages

- High-resolution, full-color images

The good side is that the best HTML conversion program on the market was designed for QuarkXPress documents. BeyondPress 2.0 by Astrobyte is a robust, versatile conversion program capable of handling sophisticated design features in XPress and turning them into advanced HTML options on a Web page. With the capability to map XPress style sheets to HTML code and convert images to GIF or JPEG formats, BeyondPress can save you hours when converting long, complex XPress documents. It's also highly tailorable, meaning you can override global settings to change any individual elements separately, and you can add your own HTML tags or combinations of tags to the program's list of styles. Best of all, Astrobyte has worked out a lot of the bugs in version 2.0, so you won't need to do as much clean-up after conversion as with many other programs.

Unfortunately, there is bad news for Windows users. If you are on a Windows system, you don't have this great converter at your disposal. In fact, there are no good XPress-to-HTML converters for Windows. This is one of those rare exceptions in a software industry that increasingly targets Windows 95 users. Because most graphic designers using XPress are working on Macintosh operating systems, the developers of both of the most common HTML conversion programs for XPress have no current plans to make their programs cross-platform. If you're a diehard Windows fan, you may not like this advice, but if you have lots of XPress conversions ahead of you, you should consider buying a Macintosh. Manually converting complex XPress documents can take hours of tedious work. In the "Manual Conversions" section at the end of this chapter, you will learn the basic steps required to do a manual conversion on a Windows or Macintosh system, but if you can use BeyondPress on a Mac, you are much better off.

If you have a Macintosh, the biggest obstacle to working with BeyondPress is the price tag. $595 for an XTension that fits on one floppy disk may seem steep, but if you are converting lots of complex files, it's still less than you would have to pay a good HTML designer to do the conversion manually. The alternative, HexWeb XT by HexMac International, is a little cheaper at $349, but its interface is more confusing, setting up a conversion takes longer, and you will need to do much more clean-up after you export the files. You'll find a basic description of HexWeb and a couple of other programs at the end of this chapter. BeyondPress, clearly the best of the programs available, is described in detail in this chapter.

BeyondPress Features

Some of the useful features of BeyondPress include the following:

- Maps XPress style sheets to HTML styles for global conversion settings.
- Has the capability to add HTML tags or combinations of tags to HTML Style options.
- Converts images to GIF or JPEG and supports interlacing, transparency, and the creation of image maps.
- Itemizes contents of a document, enabling you to break long files into multiple HTML pages and control the order in which elements will be displayed on Web pages.
- Has the capability to create links between elements of the XPress document or to URLs on another Web site.
- Can set background images and colors.
- Overrides global settings to change any individual elements separately.

BeyondPress Limitations

BeyondPress does have some limitations, as described in the following list:

- Not available for the Windows operating system.
- High price tag—retails for $595.

● Requires some tailoring for sophisticated design features such as HTML frames and complex tables.

One other program that may help you in the future is the soon-to-be released Cyber-Press by Extensis. CyberPress is essentially a "lite" version of BeyondPress with a much lighter price tag. It's expected to retail at $149, and will include a copy of Adobe's PageMill, a WYSIWYG HTML editor that was much improved in the 2.0 release. The bundle should be a pretty good deal if you're doing only simple conversions. For $449.95, you'll be able to upgrade from CyberPress to the full version of BeyondPress later.

The QuarkXPress Document

This chapter assumes that you are familiar with QuarkXPress; however, even if you haven't used XPress much, you should be able to follow the exercises in this chapter and do HTML conversion without getting into the complex features of XPress. Most conversion of this kind only involves extracting information from a formatted document, so don't worry too much about manipulating images or text in the original XPress file.

Before you begin the actual conversion process, it's a good idea to study the original XPress document and consider how you will want to redesign elements that don't lend themselves to the Web. As Chapter 2, "Design Considerations for the Web," explains, the approach you take with a desktop publishing program such as QuarkXPress is very different from design considerations for the Web. Thus, the first thing you should do is study the elements in the XPress document and consider how you will handle them in the Web page. There are a number of questions you should consider before you begin to convert your documents. The following sections will help you determine how best to turn your XPress files into Web pages.

How Many HTML Pages Should be Created from the Original Document?

This is an important consideration, as a large XPress file will be unwieldy on the Web if you turn it into one mammoth HTML page. A good guideline here is to turn each distinct article into its own page. If you don't have a hard copy of the original document, it's a good idea to print it out before you get started, so you have a reference you can study to get the overall picture.

QuarkXPress
Conversion

What Kind of Front Page Will You Create for the Web Version?

If the XPress file is a newsletter, it will likely start with a front page featuring two or more stories that continue inside. If it is a magazine or annual report, one large graphic may serve as a cover design. Neither design is likely to work well in an HTML file without alteration, but good options exist. Perhaps by using an HTML table, you could get both main stories on the front page and still have room for links to other stories. Perhaps that one large cover image could serve as a background tile. You might consider reducing the cover image to half its original size and listing the table of contents and links beside it on the main page. Study the file carefully and consider how best to transform it into something that works well on the Web. An image this large will be difficult for a program such as BeyondPress to handle and is best converted separately using the techniques described in Chapters 10 and 11.

How Will the Pages Link Together?

The table of contents of a QuarkXPress document is often inside, usually on page two or three. If there is no table of contents, you may need to create one. If you want people to follow the document in a linear fashion, you can link each story to the bottom of a previous story so readers must go through them one after the other (not recommended, however, as it would be a boring setup in the world of nonlinear hyperlinks). A combination of options is ideal, providing users with a variety of navigational paths that lead them to the information most interesting to them. This could include a table of contents on a main page, linking to each inside article and from each article to the next and previous articles, and a navigational bar on each page that links to all the main sections.

How Will You Handle Sidebars and Other Separate Text Boxes?

The most common option for this design dilemma is to put sidebars on separate pages and link them to the main story. If you want to keep them on the same page, you can use an HTML table to handle this design, but you'll have to do it in an HTML editor after you have finished the initial conversion. This is one trick BeyondPress is not quite up to yet. BeyondPress will convert basic tables, such as columnar rows of text or numbers, but sophisticated table use for putting multiple articles on the same page still has to be done in an HTML editor or by manually creating the code.

How Should You Handle Image Conversion and Arrangement?

The first thing you need to do is eliminate some of the images in the original file. It simply may not be worth the download time to present in your Web pages all the images from the original XPress print document. As a general rule, don't use more than two images per HTML page unless they are very small. All images should have the smallest file size possible, but limiting the number is also good practice. Another option is to provide a thumbnail version of an image with the main story, linking it to a larger image users can choose to view. This is a great compromise, because you can create a main page that loads quickly and still provide your users the option of taking the time to download a detailed image. For more information on images, see Chapters 10 and 11.

What Overall Design and Navigation Features Will Work Best for This Document?

You may want to create a simple sketch on paper, outlining how the original document will be laid out on HTML pages. Think about how each page should be linked in relation to the others, and how information flows through the original XPress file and ultimately through the new HTML pages. Also consider how this information will be integrated into the rest of the Web site. If this document is to become its own complete Web site, you need a strong front page. If it is to be built into a larger Web site, you want a design that fits with the overall design of the site, navigational features that follow the same patterns, and links from new pages back to other pages in the Web site so users don't get lost.

> **Note**
>
> If you need to do only simple conversions, or just can't afford the price of BeyondPress (or a Macintosh computer), go directly to "Manual Conversions" at the end of this chapter to learn techniques that will work for you.

BeyondPress: The Best Way to Convert QuarkXPress

BeyondPress is a QuarkXPress XTension that converts XPress files into HTML and converts graphics into JPEGs and GIFs. BeyondPress adds a Document Content palette under the View menu where it lists all the elements of an XPress document so you can specify what to export and what not to export (you'll probably want to

QuarkXPress Conversion

suppress page numbers, for example). You can also move elements into new folders, much as you do in the Finder on the Macintosh, to turn the XPress file into multiple pages and designate which elements will appear on each page.

One of the most useful features of this program is the capability to map XPress styles to HTML styles. This can be set globally and can be overridden, enabling you to alter the style of any individual element while leaving other elements in the global style. This is useful for text and graphics. For example, setting images to be reduced to 50 percent of original size and converted into GIFs may work for most of the images in your XPress file, but if you want a few images at 80 percent and converted into JPEGs, you can set them individually.

Using the XTension's Preferences, you can customize each article you export. In addition to a list of HTML options included in BeyondPress 2.0, you can create and add your own HTML styles. You can also include a header, footer, and background image on any or every page.

> **Note**
>
> Astrobyte's directions for installing BeyondPress tell you to put the BeyondPress folder in the XTension's folder inside the Quark folder. If, however, you can't get XPress to recognize the new XTension, try taking the BeyondPress XTension out of its folder and placing it at the top level of the Quark XPress Xtensions folder. You will have to restart QuarkXPress for it to recognize a new XTension.

Setting BeyondPress Preferences

Before you get started, you should understand some basic things about setting Preferences in BeyondPress. If you change Preferences with an XPress document open, those Preferences will be saved with that document. This is a useful feature in case you want to Export the same document again later, especially if changes are made to the original file. By saving these Preferences with the original document, BeyondPress saves you the trouble of resetting all the Preferences each time you set up an export. If, however, you want to set Preferences that are available for any document you convert (for example, if you want to add your own HTML code to the list of HTML options), make these changes when no XPress document is open—BeyondPress will save them as default settings for all future documents.

Another nice feature of BeyondPress is the capability to import or append Preferences. This is great, especially if you are working with a team of developers, because you can ensure that everyone is starting with the same settings. You can import or append Preferences from another document you have prepared with BeyondPress, from the default settings you selected when no document was open, or from the Factory Preferences that ship with BeyondPress.

There are two ways to open the BeyondPress Preferences dialog box, as follows:

1. In XPress, choose Edit, Preferences, BeyondPress.

2. From the top row of the Document Content palette, select the Preferences icon (see fig. 6.1).

Figure 6.1

Selecting BeyondPress Preferences.

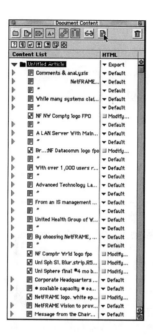

The Preferences icon is indicated by the cursor in figure 6.1. Select this icon from the top row of the Document Content palette to open the Preferences dialog box.

The Preferences dialog box in BeyondPress offers a range of options for specifying how conversions will be done. The following series of figures and descriptions explains each of the Preferences dialog boxes.

Application Preferences

Application Preferences specify general settings for BeyondPress, such as the browser you want to use to preview conversions and how the XTension will handle some of the elements in the original XPress document (see fig. 6.2). The Application Preference options are listed in the following table.

QuarkXPress Conversion

Application Preferences Option	Action Performed
Show Hidden Text	Displays document anchors.
Ignore Empty Boxes	Suppresses empty text boxes in Document Content palette.
Ignore Unchanged Master Items	Suppresses original Master XPress page items in Document Content palette.
Use Scripts Menu	Records BeyondPress actions.
HTML Browser	Selects browser for converted document preview.

Figure 6.2

The Application Preferences dialog box.

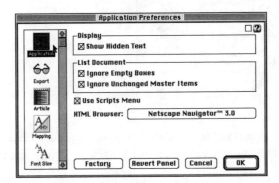

A more detailed description of each of these options follows:

1. The *Show Hidden Text* option enables you to view anchors in a document.

2. Checking the *Ignore Empty Boxes* option prevents empty pictures or text boxes in the original XPress document from being listed in the Document Content palette.

3. *Ignore Unchanged Master Items* prevents items that originated in a Master XPress page from being listed in the Document Content palette unless they have been changed manually.

4. *Use Scripts Menu* enables you to record BeyondPress actions with the AppleScript script editor. (Note: you must create a Scripts folder and place it in the XPress folder on your hard drive before you can use this feature. To make this active, restart XPress.)

5. The *HTML Browser* option enables you to select any Web browser on your hard drive to view Exported or Previewed files.

Export Preferences

Export Preferences specify many conversion options, such as the file name extension used, type of links created, and where converted images will be stored (see fig. 6.3). The Export Preferences options are listed in the following table.

Export Preferences Option	Action Performed
Destination Platform	Specifies file names and extensions.
Limit Tags to HTML 1.0	Limits the use of HTML tags to only those approved as part of the HTML 1.0 standard.
Convert Bold and Italic Fonts	If unchecked, prevents BeyondPress from converting bold and italic font styles.
Create Relative URLs	Specifies the kind of link path. If checked, creates relative links; if unchecked, creates absolute links.
Convert Text Color	If checked, BeyondPress will assign a hexadecimal color code to colored text as it is converted.
Readable HTML	Creates HTML code with spacing that makes is easier to read the raw code.
Date and Time	Specifies the way date and time will be displayed.

continues

(continued)

Export Preferences Option	Action Performed
Shared Images	Identifies images that will be used more than once in the converted document.
Unshared Images	Specifies the directory where converted images will be stored.

Figure 6.3

The Export Preferences dialog box.

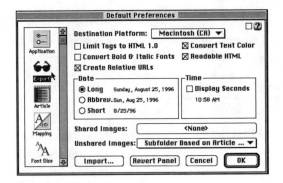

A more detailed description of each of these options follows:

1. The *Destination Platform* ensures that file names and extensions created during export comply with the requirements of the designated platform. The options are Macintosh, DOS/Windows, and Unix. Make this selection based on the server you will be using for your Web site.

2. *Limit Tags to HTML 1.0* is provided in an effort to help ensure your HTML pages will work in low-end browsers, but it's a bit misleading, as HTML 1.0 was so short-lived as to rarely be specified by any program. Now that HTML 3.2 tags are supported by BeyondPress 2.0, be sure your pages will look good in all the browsers your audience will be using. (To learn more about this, see Chapter 13, "Tailoring Converted Files," and Chapter 14, "HTML Tutorial and Reference.")

3. *Convert Bold and Italic Fonts* enables you to decide whether bold and italics are converted. Unfortunately, you cannot set the program to convert only one or the other. Also note that this setting only affects formatting set by the use of a specific font. If you are using manual bold and italics rather than the unique font style, this conversion feature cannot be turned off, even by unchecking this box.

4. *Create Relative URLs* should almost always be checked, as this enables the program to set relative links (those that are set in relation to the location of another file in the Web site's directory structure) as opposed to absolute links (those that must include the full Web address, such as http://www.domain _name.com/file_name.html).

5. *Convert Text Color* enables you to convert colored text in the original file to text that is colored by a corresponding hexadecimal color in the HTML file.

6. *Readable HTML* inserts spaces and returns in the HTML code, making it easier to read and edit manually. Always check this one. Even if you don't plan to edit the HTML code, someone else may have to do it someday, and you have nothing to lose by creating clean code.

7. The *Date and Time* sections specify the format of the date or time Master Elements. The three options for adding date and time elements to an exported document are to set them as headers or footers in Article Preferences, use the icons in the Document Content palette to drag them into any article, or embed them in another Master or Custom Element and add them to the Content list.

8. Checking *Shared Images* lets you designate images you will want to use in more than one place in the exported HTML files.

9. Checking *Unshared Images* enables you to designate one of three options for storing all other images. Choose Article Folder to save images in the same folder as the HTML page. Choose Common Article Subfolder to create one primary images folder where all converted images will be stored. Choose Subfolder Based on Article File Name to save the converted images in a subfolder with the accompanying HTML page. The name of the image subfolder is based on the name of the primary folder that holds the article and images folder.

Article Preferences

Article Preferences specify background options and text and link colors, as well as headers and footers for every page that is converted (see fig. 6.4). The Article Preferences options are listed in the following table.

Article Preferences Option	Action Performed
Background	Sets a hexadecimal background color or background image.

continues

QuarkXPress
Conversion

(continued)

Article Preferences Option	Action Performed
Format	Specifies if the background image is in GIF or JPEG format.
Name	Assigns a special name to the background image so that it can be referenced in Shared Images and used on multiple pages.
Text and Link Colors	Assigns hexadecimal colors for text and links in HTML files.
Meta Tags	Specifies information to be included for the Meta tag in the head section.
Header and Footer options	Enable you to set header and footers that will be placed on every HTML page.

Figure 6.4

The Article Preferences dialog box.

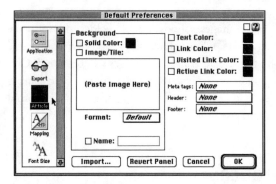

A more detailed description of each of these options follows:

1. *Background* options enable you to set a solid color or a background image. If you select Solid Color, click on the black box next to the option; a color wheel appears where you can choose a color that BeyondPress will approximate with a hexadecimal color code. You can use any image as a background by pasting it into the box. Note that background images should be kept small.

2. The *Format* option enables you to select GIF or JPEG as the format for the background image.

3. The *Name* option is for naming the background image, only necessary if you want the file stored in the Shared Images folder you set in Export Preferences. If the background will be used only once, you do not need to name it in Preferences.

4. In the top-right section of the Article Preferences dialog box, you can specify text and link colors. If you check Convert Text Color in Export Preferences, the text color you specify here is applied to black text in the XPress document. Colored text in the XPress document is converted to a similar hexadecimal color in the HTML document. The Link Color will be set to the color of all linked text; Visited Link Color specifies the color a link will appear in after it has been selected by a user; Active Link Color specifies the color a link will appear in as it's being selected by the user.

5. *Meta tags* are used to embed information within the <HEAD> tags of an HTML document. This information will not be displayed in the browser window. Meta tags are commonly used to provide information for search engines. You will find a list of options under this pop-up menu for the Meta tag, but you can add anything you want to this option in the Master Elements panel described later in this section.

6. *Header* and *Footer* options enable you to place information at the top or bottom of every page you convert during Export. This is a common way to add the time and date stamp, as well as a convenient way to build in a Web site menu bar or other navigational option. The only caution here is to ensure that all relative links work. Because the header and footer are placed on every page, be sure they all have the same relative location to the linked options in a menu bar, or you may have to alter them after the conversion. (For more on such alterations, see Chapter 13.)

Mapping Preferences

Mapping Preferences enable you to match style sheets to HTML tags (see fig 6.5).

The *Style Sheet Mapping* list is used to match XPress styles to HTML styles to make global conversion settings in your document. Because no XPress document was loaded for these sample screen shots, no styles are listed. In the next section, when you go through the actual conversion of a case study document, you will see these preferences in action.

QuarkXPress
Conversion

Figure 6.5

The Mapping Preferences dialog box.

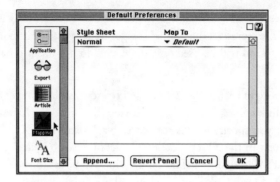

Font Size Preferences

Font Size Preferences are used to match HTML styles to point sizes in XPress for converting headlines (see fig. 6.6).

Figure 6.6

The Font Size Preferences dialog box.

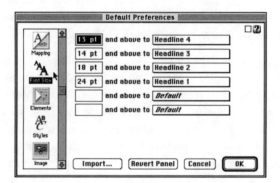

Font Size Preferences enable you to assign header styles based on the size of the font in the original document, a supplementary mapping system not requiring the use of XPress style sheets. If the document you are working on has headlines set only by size and not by a specified XPress style, this provides an alternate setting for conversion.

Master Elements Preferences

Master Elements, represented by icons at the top of the Document Content palette, enable you to add spacing and other options to your Web pages (see fig. 6.7).

Figure 6.7

The Master Elements Preferences dialog box.

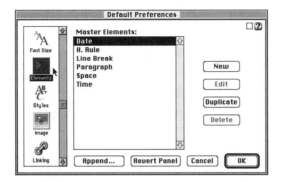

Master Elements can be inserted anywhere in the XPress document you are converting. These elements are dragged into place in the Document Content palette to provide additional spacing based on the Line Break or Paragraph options, to create a horizontal rule, or (because you can add Master Elements) to add any feature to your document.

Adding Master Elements

The capability to add Master Elements makes it easy to build in commonly used HTML code or text so that it can be inserted into any page you convert (see fig. 6.8).

Figure 6.8

Adding Master Elements.

You can add any HTML code or text as a Master Element, making it easy and efficient to build in commonly used features as you convert an XPress document. In figure 6.8, a navigation bar is added to the Master Elements. A navigation bar is a common feature for enabling users to move easily to any of the main pages on a Web site. To add this as a feature, create a new text file that contains only the words and HTML

QuarkXPress
Conversion

code you want as the Master Element. In this case, the navigation bar was copied out of an existing page in a Web site and saved as a text file. Then, using the browse function of BeyondPress, it was located on the hard drive, and the code and words were automatically copied into the dialog box for the new Master Element.

Master Elements can contain up to 32,000 characters of text and HTML code. In the section on the Document Content palette that follows, you will see how this new Master Element can be built into any page during the conversion process. Anything you commonly use on your Web pages can make a good Master Style. Master Elements included with BeyondPress are as follows:

- Date
- Time and Date
- Horizontal Rule
- Line Break
- Paragraph
- Space
- Time

Master Styles Preferences

BeyondPress includes a list of HTML tags as Master Styles, and makes it possible to create your own HTML styles as well (see fig. 6.9).

Figure 6.9

The Master Styles Preferences dialog box.

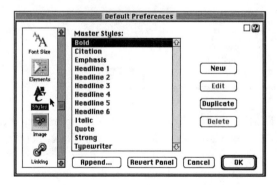

Master Styles are all of the HTML styles available for your conversion. This list includes the most common HTML 2.0 tags (Bold, Citation, Emphasis, Headers 1 through 6, Italic, Quote, Strong, and Typewriter). HTML Tables and Lists are also options in BeyondPress, but are handled differently, as you'll learn in the Preferences section of Tables and Lists that follow. If these were the only options you could use, this would be a limited program, but Astrobyte made the program highly expandable by making it possible to add HTML styles to the list. You cannot alter or delete the default Master Styles, but you can add your own tags, as has been done in figure 6.10.

Adding Master Styles

The capability to add Master Styles makes BeyondPress a very versatile program (see fig. 6.10). You can add any HTML tag not included with the program or add combinations of tags to further automate conversion.

Figure 6.10

The Edit Master Style dialog box.

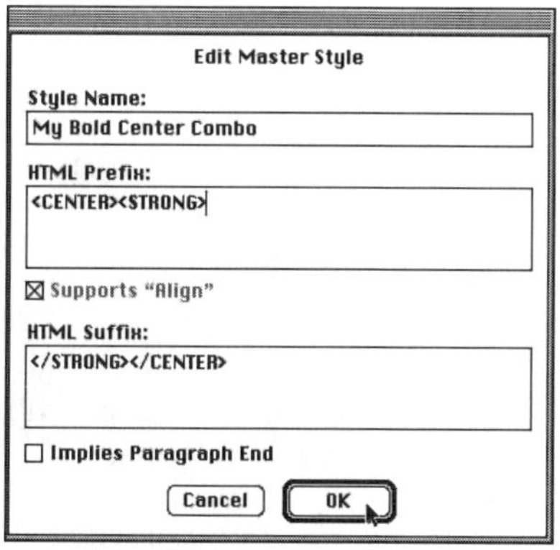

To add a Master Style, select New from the Master Styles Preferences. In the Edit Master Style dialog box that appears, enter a name for your new style and type the HTML prefix and suffix in their respective boxes. You have to know HTML code to add a style (see Chapter 14 if you need help). You can create a style by using one HTML tag or a combination, as in figure 6.10. Notice that you must enter all the opening tags in the HTML Prefix box and all the closing tags in the HTML Suffix box. Remember, too, that HTML tags must be created in the proper order and the open and close tags of each HTML option must be complete. Also, any nested tags must be surrounded by the first tag as in the example, where the <CENTER> tag is the first in the Prefix section and the last in the Suffix section, ensuring that it surrounds the <STRONG> and </STRONG> tags.

QuarkXPress
Conversion

This is a great way to speed the conversion process because you can add custom HTML styles that you use frequently in your documents. If, for example, all your headlines will be formatted with Header 1 and centered, you could create a Master Style using those tags. The prefix would look like this: <CENTER><H1>. The suffix would be: </H1></CENTER>. You can add as many Master Styles as you want and use them to make global settings or assign the styles to individual elements.

Image Preferences

Many of the most dramatic improvements to BeyondPress 2.0 are found in Image Preferences (see fig. 6.11). The capability to control size, convert to GIF or JPEG, and specify the number of colors in a GIF or the compression level for a JPEG make this a much better program for image conversion. The Image Preferences options are listed in the following table.

Image Preferences Option	*Action Performed*
Scale Basis	Specifies if image scaling should be based on the original image or its size in XPress.
Alignment	Sets image alignment to Top, Middle, Bottom, Left, Center, or Right.
Format	Controls if images will be converted to GIF or JPEG.
JPEG Quality	Sets the compression level.
GIF Palette	Enables you to choose the color palette for your GIFs.
Scale	Sets image scaling during conversion to a percentage between 1 and 400.
HSPACE and VSPACE	Specifies the amount of horizontal and vertical space around an image.
Border	Specifies the number of pixels of the border around an image.
Image	Can be set to create client-side image maps or server-side image maps for NCSA and CERN.

Image Preferences Option	Action Performed
Reimport High Res Images	Instructs BeyondPress to use the original images for conversion instead of the low-resolution images in the XPress document.
Revert After Export	Restores the low-resolution previews after conversion.
Output WIDTH/HEIGHT	Automatically includes the height and width of the converted image in the HTML code.
Shrink Solid Images	Turns solid color areas into pixel GIFs with height and width tags that correspond to the original size.
Anti-Alias	Controls anti-aliasing. Options are: Off, Low, Medium, and High.

Figure 6.11

The Image Preferences dialog box.

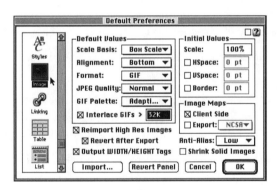

A more detailed description of each of these options follows:

1. The *Scale Basis* preference enables you to designate which image size will be used when the conversion is set. There are two options under this preference, as follows:

    ● *Box Scale* sets BeyondPress to convert the image based on the size the image is scaled to in the XPress document.

    ● *Unscaled Image* tells BeyondPress to use the original image size for the conversion.

2. *Alignment* provides the most common HTML image alignment options. You can choose Top, Middle, Bottom, Left, Center, or Right. Remember that the Preferences dialog box will set a global alignment option that will be applied to all your images, but you can override these settings to change the alignment of any individual image. (You'll learn more about that as you go through the case study conversion in the next section, "Converting a Document with BeyondPress.")

3. *Format* enables you to select GIF or JPEG as the default option for image conversion. Again, you can override this on any individual image during the conversion setup. For more information on which format is best for your images, see Chapter 10, "Graphics Basics."

4. *JPEG Quality* lets you set the compression level for JPEG images. The pop-up menu provides the same five compression levels you would find in Photoshop (very low, low, normal, high, and very high). The higher the JPEG quality, the less it will be compressed. This results in better-looking images, but much larger file sizes that take longer to download. If you want the best image quality during conversion, you may be better off using a program such as Photoshop or DeBabelizer to convert your images. To learn how to convert your images by using one of these programs, refer to Chapter 11, "Graphics Creation."

5. The *GIF Palette* option enables you to choose the best color palette for your GIFs:

   - *Apple System 256* provides the fastest conversion and a consistent palette, but is not the best color palette for images on the Web, where they will generally be viewed on other platforms as well.

   - *Adaptive color palette* adjusts to the best palette, using the number of colors you specify (any number between 2 and 256). Astrobyte warns that the program requires more RAM if you choose this option.

   - *Load from GIF* enables you to select the palette of any one GIF to be used for all your images. This may be the best option if you select a GIF you created by using the Netscape color palette, a palette designed for optimal color use on all platforms. For more information on color palettes, see Chapter 10.

6. In the top right of this dialog box, the *Scale* option enables you to set a percentage between 1 and 400 for scaling all images. This option can also be set on an image-by-image basis, as you will see in "Converting a Document with BeyondPress."

7. *HSPACE* and *VSPACE* enable you to set the horizontal and vertical space that will surround each image. Employing the image attributes, this option uses a pixel value to set spacing.

8. The *Border* option enables you to specify a pixel size for the border around the image. Note that if an image is linked, it automatically has a border the color of the link text specified in Article Preferences. Often the best option here is to set the border to equal 0 pixels so the image has no border created by HTML code. If you want a border around an image, you will have greater control if you create it in a program such as Photoshop. Colored link borders often detract from the image. Setting the border to 0 will prevent the colored link borders created in the HTML code and displayed by the browser.

9. The *Image Maps* section of this Preferences dialog box enables you to specify if you will be using a client-side image map—executed by the browser—or a server-side image map—executed by a CGI script on the server. If you choose Export, you get two options for the server-side map, NCSA and CERN, the two most common servers among Unix systems. BeyondPress includes a utility for creating image map coordinates. For more on image maps, see "Creating an Image Map with BeyondPress" later in this chapter.

10. The *Reimport High Res Images* option enables you to use the original images for conversion instead of the low-resolution images displayed in the QuarkXPress document. If you use the low-resolution images, you are likely to have poor-quality images after conversion. Using the original high-resolution images, however, will take longer to convert, require more RAM during conversion, and result in larger file sizes. BeyondPress offers good image conversion capabilities, but you have greater control and can produce better-looking images with smaller file sizes if you convert your original images by using programs such as Photoshop or DeBabelizer.

11. The *Revert After Export* option restores the low-resolution previews to the original QuarkXPress document after conversion.

12. The *Output WIDTH/HEIGHT Tags* option adds the Height and Width attributes to all the image tags in the HTML code. This is always a good idea. Including the height and width of the image enables the browser to load the page efficiently. Because the browser does not have to wait for the entire image to load before determining how much space it will need, the rest of the page loads more quickly.

13. The *Shrink Solid Images* option corresponds with the Height and Width option. This feature enables BeyondPress to produce a great trick. If the image you are converting consists of one solid color and nothing else, BeyondPress will convert

QuarkXPress
Conversion

it to a single pixel image, and then use the Height and Width attributes to reproduce it at the size you have selected for conversion. This creates a very small image size that loads quickly and is redrawn to fill the space indicated by the Height and Width attributes.

14. The *Anti-Alias* option includes a pop-up menu with four choices: Off, Low, Medium, and High. Antialiasing produces smoother lines in images as they are converted, but the higher the antialiasing, the larger the file size of the converted image and the more time it takes to convert and ultimately to load in the browser.

Linking Preferences

Linking Preferences enables you to associate a list of frequently used URLs (see fig. 6.12).

Figure 6.12

The Linking Preferences dialog box.

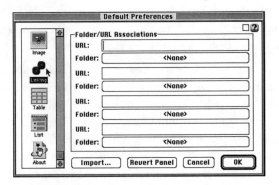

The *Folder/URL Associations* option enables you to list URLs you will frequently use in your converted file and associate them with a folder on your hard drive. When you set an external link in your XPress file, you can then use the URLs listed in this Preferences dialog box without typing them each time.

Table Preferences

Table Preferences control the characteristics of tables, including width, alignment, and row and column attributes (see fig. 6.13). The Table Preferences options are included in the following table.

Table Preference Option	Action Performed
Border Width	Sets the size of the table border.
Cell Padding	Controls the space surrounding the data in a table cell.
Cell Spacing	Controls the space between table cells.
Header Rows	Specifies the number of header rows created.
Header Columns	Specifies the number of header columns.
Table Width	Specifies table width in pixels and percentages.
Alignment	Controls alignment of the table.

Figure 6.13

The Table Preferences dialog box.

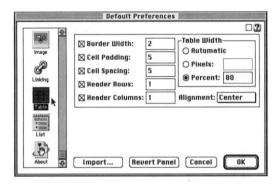

A more detailed description of each of these options follows:

1. Border Width enables you to set the width of the border that will surround the table and also affects the width of the lines between table cells. This can be set to any pixel value, but should generally be limited to less than five pixels, because anything more will produce too heavy a border for a table on a Web page. Remember that HTML tables are displayed with three-dimensional borders that appear even larger than the pixel size specified.

2. *Cell Padding* controls the amount of space surrounding the data in a table cell and is specified with a pixel value.

3. *Cell Spacing* controls the amount of space between table cells and is also set as a pixel value.

4. The *Header Rows* option specifies the number of rows to be created, using the <TH> tag for a table heading instead of the <TD> tag for table data cells. Table headers are displayed in bold type and centered within the cell.

5. The *Header Columns* option specifies the number of columns to be created, using the <TH> tag. Header Columns are also displayed in bold type and centered within the cell.

6. The *Table Width* settings enable you to specify the overall width of the table.

   ● Choosing *Automatic* lets the browser size the table according to the size of the browser window and preferences.

   ● Specifying the size by *Pixels* sets a fixed width that will not change even if the browser window is not wide enough to display the entire table. This is a good way to control the width, but can be problematic on smaller monitors because the user may have to scroll horizontally to view the entire table.

   ● Specifying the size by the Percent option lets the browser display the table as a percentage of the display area available. Using this option, the table will be resized to fit the specified percentage of the total viewing area of your user.

7. The *Alignment* option specifies the alignment of the table in relation to other elements on the Web page. Options are Standard (which aligns the table according to the browser's preferences), Left, Center, and Right.

List Preferences

List Preferences control the type of list used, including bullet style and type of numbering or lettering system (see fig. 6.14). The List Preferences options are included in the following table.

List Preferences Option	Action Performed
List Type	Specifies the kind of HTML list used: Ordered, Unordered, Definition, Menu, or Directory.
Level	Controls the indentation of Ordered or Unordered lists.
Dingbat	Specifies the type of bullet for an Unordered list, and the use of numbers, Roman numerals, or letters for Ordered lists.
Strip Leading Characters	Removes the bullets or numbers from the list in the original XPress file.

Figure 6.14

The List Preferences dialog box.

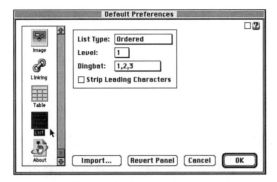

A more detailed description of each of these options follows:

1. *List Type* enables you to choose the kind of HTML list you want your XPress list converted into. Options are as follows:

   - *Ordered* numbers the list items.

   - *Unordered* uses bullets to set off list items.

   - *Definition Term* creates subheads from the Definition Body text.

   - *Definition Body* indents multiple paragraphs.

   - *Menu* condenses the space between list items, and uses bullets to set off items.

   - *Directory* condenses the space between paragraphs.

   The descriptions of list options given here are based on the display in Netscape Navigator. Other browsers may produce slightly different displays.

2. The *Level* option may be used with Ordered or Unordered lists to designate how far the list will be indented. The larger the level number, the further it will be indented.

3. The *Dingbat* options change for Ordered and Unordered lists. If you have selected an Ordered list, you may choose from numbers, letters, or Roman numerals in the Dingbat options. For an Unordered list, the options are various types of bullet symbols.

4. The *Strip Leading Characters* option lets BeyondPress remove the numbers or bullets that may already appear in the lists in the original XPress document. If there are no such characters in the original document, do not check the Strip Leading Characters option, because by doing so you may lose the initial characters in each of the list items. Note that this will only affect elements you set to be converted as lists.

QuarkXPress
Conversion

About

About, the final option in the Preferences dialog box, provides a shortcut to the Astrobyte Web site. Another useful feature in this options dialog box controls the *splash screen*. Unchecking the Show Splash Screen option will prevent the BeyondPress screen from appearing every time you launch QuarkXPress.

Importing BeyondPress Preferences

A great feature of BeyondPress is the capability to import preferences from other documents you have converted. This enables you to reuse settings on similar files, further automating the conversion process, especially if you are working on many similar documents. A magazine or newspaper, for example, is likely to have consistent styles and formatting from issue to issue. Using the Preferences import features of BeyondPress, you can reuse all the settings from one issue when you start on the next. The following explains the three ways that preferences can be imported:

- To import preferences to a specific Preferences area for the Export, Article, Image, Linking, and Table Preferences, simply select the *Import* button while you are in that dialog box, navigate to the document that has the preferences you want, and when you select it, the preferences you saved with the selected file will replace the preferences in the new file you are working on. Remember that any preferences you set while an XPress document is open are saved with that document, and can be imported into other documents later.

- To add preferences, you can use the Append button in the Mapping, Elements, and Styles dialog areas. This enables you to keep any new settings you have created and add settings from another document. Again, to do this, simply select the Append button in any of these three dialog areas and navigate to the document you want to append preferences from; those settings will be added to the document you are currently working on.

- You can also import or append all preferences at once by holding down the Option key and selecting any Import or Append button in any of the Preferences dialog boxes. This will replace or append all the preferences in the current document with those in the previous document.

Case Study: Converting a Document with BeyondPress

Now that you are familiar with the preferences in BeyondPress and have set the standard defaults without any document open, you are ready to tackle a conversion and learn more of the details of using BeyondPress.

This case study comes from NetFRAME, a client of Aslan Computing, Inc. This is not a long document, only six pages, but it includes all the difficult elements common in an XPress document—large, high-resolution images; complex text formatting; and a table with text and numbers in columns. The first thing to do is study the original document.

Large Cover Images

In figure 6.15, you see the cover art on this file—a large, high-resolution image not likely, in its present state, to work well on the Web.

Figure 6.15

Large cover images.

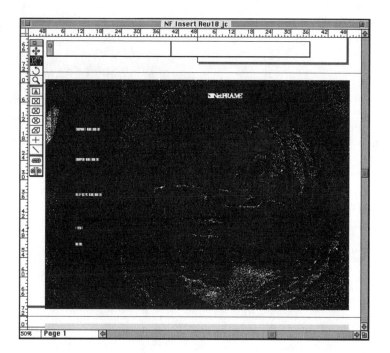

A large cover image, such as the one on this NetFRAME document, will not work well on the Web, where images take much longer to load than text. As you study the original document, consider alternative designs. This cover image might work well, for example, if it is reduced dramatically (to perhaps a tenth of its original size) and used as a background tile.

In figure 6.16, you see the other big challenges in this document. At the top of figure 6.16 are a number of small images on a colored background, each with related text. At the bottom left is a table with text and numbers in columns. Again, think about how these elements will work on the Web. The images at the top are small, so they may not need to be reduced in size when they are converted, but how will you position them in an HTML document? BeyondPress, which will be used to convert this file in the next section, will convert the table at the bottom left of this page quite nicely. BeyondPress can also convert the small images with their accompanying text and can arrange them by using left, right, and center alignment; however, it can't arrange them exactly as they are displayed in the original document.

Figure 6.16

*Tables and other
complex formatting.*

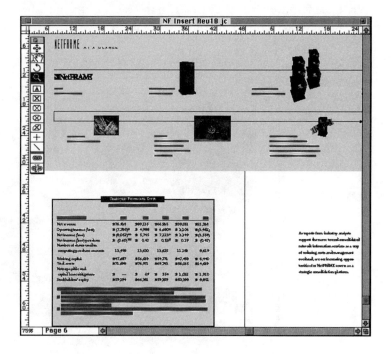

The only way the corresponding Web page can have a layout similar to the print document would be by using an HTML table with no borders. As with most other HTML authoring tools on the market, BeyondPress can't handle that for you. Nonetheless, you can use the tips and exercises in Chapter 13, "Tailoring Converted Files," to arrange these elements almost exactly as they appear in the original document, after you do the conversion with BeyondPress. Another consideration for this section of the original document (although you cannot see it in the black-and-white images that accompany this chapter), is a yellow background behind these images and behind the table. This can also be handled by BeyondPress 2.0, as you'll see in the following sections.

Complex Formatting Elements

On this page of the original document, tables and small graphics arranged in separate text boxes make this a difficult conversion.

The table in the bottom left corner of figure 6.16 can be converted with BeyondPress 2.0. The images and accompanying text in the top of this image will have to be converted by using left, right, or center alignment.

In figure 6.17, you see another page from the original XPress document, called Comments and Analysis. A series of quotes, two of which include small graphics, are spread around the page. Again, this type of layout requires an HTML table with no borders, but might be re-created on the Web page by using the list tags.

Figure 6.17

Comments and Analysis.

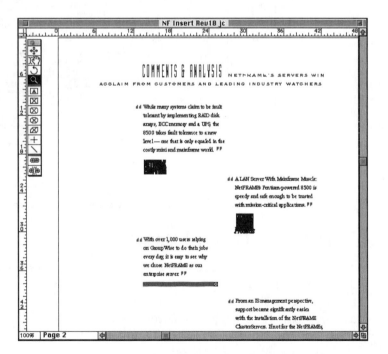

Basic Plaintext Elements

XPress pages, such as the Message from the Chairman, are the easiest to convert. When all you have to handle is basic text with a simple headline, you don't need much set up in BeyondPress, and you'll need little, if any, tailoring after conversion.

Figure 6.18 shows a Message from the Chairman. This is one of the simplest sections to convert, as it is primarily text. The only difficult decision involves the pull-out sentence in the bottom-left corner of the page. The simplest thing to do with this is place it at the top or bottom of the HTML page.

This will be one of the simplest pages to convert, as it is just text.

Figure 6.18

A Message from the Chairman.

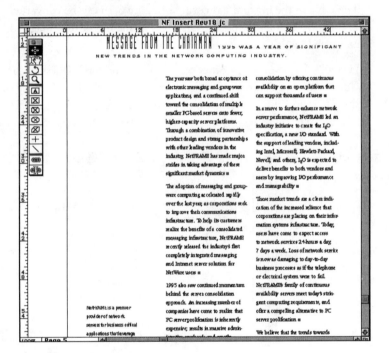

Evaluating the Overall Design

Now that you have identified all the individual elements in the original XPress file, think about the overall design of the Web pages you will be creating. The file used in this case study will not become its own Web site, but will be a relatively small addition to a large commercial Web site done for NetFRAME by Aslan Computing. Thus, as you consider how to redesign this document for the Web, you must also consider how to build it into an existing Web site.

This report will become its own section on the NetFRAME site, so it can have a distinct front page with links to the other elements in the file. Because this Web site is worked on by a number of developers, it is important to consult with members of the team about how the page will link to other areas of the Web site and what is needed to keep the design consistent with the rest of the HTML pages. For now, assume that these considerations are taken care of, and approach this as a unique section.

There are six distinct pages: the front and back covers, filled by a single large graphic; a page of quotes and small icons called Comments and Analysis; a page of text that is a Message from the Chairman; and the most complex pages to convert, two pages with small pictures that tell the history of the company and include brief descriptions with accompanying text. At the bottom left of those two pages is a table showing financial data from 1991 to 1995. Now you must decide what to do with all these images and text on Web pages.

As mentioned earlier, the large graphic on the front and back covers could be turned into a small image and used as a background for the main page. There is some text there already—the company's vision statement on the front cover and address information on the back. On the Web, you cannot simply ask users to turn pages, so you need to come up with a navigational system for this document. No table of contents exists for this short document, but the clear headings on each section could be listed on the front page and linked to the other sections as separate pages.

Thus, the front page could have a background tile created from the main image, the company logo and vision that are already there, and then a list of the contents of the rest of the document. This list should include a link to a page with the three addresses listed on the back of the original document. Putting these addresses on the front page would clutter the design and seems unnecessary on the Web, where physical addresses are not so important. A separate file linked from the front page will still make it easy for users to find the company locations if they need to. The front page will then have links to the internal sections, listed as follows:

- Comments and Analysis
- Message from the Chairman
- NetFRAME at a Glance
- Selected Financial Data
- Company Contact Information and Addresses

You've worked out the structure and organization of the document, and it's time to set up the conversion. First, you'll see how to convert this document by using

BeyondPress. In the "Manual Conversions" section at the end of this chapter, you'll also learn how to do the conversion without the helpful assistance of such a program.

BeyondPress Step by Step

Now that you have completed the preliminary work of assessing the XPress file and determining how to present it on the Web, you are ready to set up the BeyondPress conversion. This time, pay attention to the details of this program, using it to organize the elements in your XPress file and convert according to your preferences. Remember, the conversion settings can be set globally as you saw in the Preferences section, or they can be set individually for any item in the document.

Loading the XPress File

The first thing to do is open the original document in QuarkXPress. This may seem obvious, but you can't use BeyondPress to convert a document if you don't have XPress to open it with in the first place. After the file is open in XPress, choose the Document Content palette under the View menu. This will open an empty Document Content palette. To load the elements of the original document into BeyondPress, choose the List Document icon in the palette (indicated by the cursor in figure 6.19).

Open the Document Content palette available under the View menu. Select the List Document icon to load the elements from the original document into BeyondPress. (Note that the cursor is pointing to the List Document icon in the top row of the Content palette in figure 6.19.)

Previewing Exports with BeyondPress Default Settings

Before setting the individual Preferences options in BeyondPress, it's not a bad idea to preview the file as it is initially set by BeyondPress. To do this, after completing the preliminary steps just described, select Preview (indicated by the Sunglasses icon in the Document Content palette). The file will be previewed in the browser you select, using the default options in BeyondPress.

Figure 6.19

The Document Content palette.

Previewing the XPress file without adjusting any of the preferences results in a Web page not as well organized and formatted as it would be if you took time to arrange it before conversion. Even though this quick conversion isn't laid out exactly the way you want, it provides a great deal of information about the original file and usually only takes a few seconds and almost no effort to generate.

Advantages of Previewing

The advantage of this initial preview is what it tells you about the file text and images and how they will look in a Web page. Study the preview in your favorite browser to get an overview of the elements in this document. This is especially helpful if you are not the graphic designer who created the original file, because it helps you determine which elements of the file are graphics rather than simply text over a background color. This also helps you see how the text boxes are linked. This preview, combined with a printed version of the document, goes a long way toward helping you organize and set up the final XPress conversion.

QuarkXPress Conversion

Previewing the Case Study

Using the NetFRAME case study document as an example, take a look at what BeyondPress did without any adjustments to the default settings. Without changing the organization of the file, BeyondPress converted the entire document into one page. In figures 6.20 and 6.21, you see a couple of sample screens of that page as viewed in Netscape Navigator 3.0.

Figure 6.20

A sample preview.

In this preview, viewed in Navigator 3.0, you can see that BeyondPress has simply listed the small images and accompanying text. This preview is done only to get a general idea of what to expect. The next step is to arrange the preferences in BeyondPress to produce a well-designed Web page.

When you don't specify how BeyondPress should convert the table in this document, it turns it into lines of text and loses the formatting necessary to create columns.

Clearly the preview that results from simply loading the document into BeyondPress is not the way you want your final document to look; however, you have learned some valuable things from reviewing it. For example, it's now evident that the yellow background behind those small images was just that, a background, and not one large image. If you want the same look, you must set a background color in BeyondPress. From the preview, you also realize that you'll have to set the table in the XPress document to be converted into an HTML table by BeyondPress if you want it to display with the proper spacing and alignment. The next thing to do is set the preferences for this document and arrange elements in the Document Content palette.

Figure 6.21

The table.

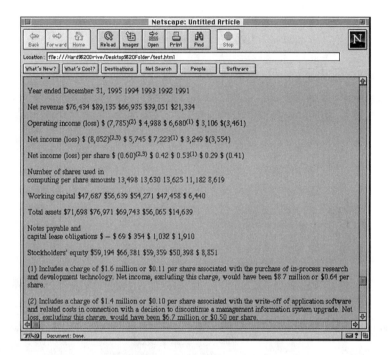

The Document Content Palette Icons

The Document Content palette is where BeyondPress lists all the elements of your XPress document and enables you to arrange their order for export. You can resize the palette by dragging the corner to make it larger and can arrange the spacing of the two columns by dragging the dotted vertical line. Take a look at the options in the Document Content palette displayed in figure 6.22. Across the top is a series of icons.

Refer to figure 6.22 to see the icons described in the following list. The icons are listed from left to right as they appear in the palette.

1. The *Folder* icon enables you to create a new folder in the Document Content palette, into which you can then drag other elements. Use this feature to break up long XPress documents. Each folder will be converted as a separate HTML page.

2. The icon that looks like a file with a small arrow off to the right is the *List Document* icon. Selecting this icon lists all the elements in the original XPress document in the palette.

QuarkXPress Conversion

3. The square with an X and an arrow is the *Add Items* icon. Use this to add selected text boxes from the original document to a folder in the palette.

4. The A with an arrow is the *Add Text* icon. Use this to add highlighted text to a folder or to create a text range.

5. The icon that looks like two links in a chain is for setting *Links.* To use this feature, highlight the text in the original document, select the Link icon, and then select the area in the XPress file that is to be the destination for the link.

6. The icon that looks like two split columns with an arrow and dotted line down the middle is the *Segment Text Chain* icon. This feature enables you to divide a text chain so you can export its contents to separate HTML pages.

7. The *Sunglasses* icon represents the Preview option. Select this to see a preview with the Web browser you selected in Preferences. This option will do a preliminary export of the XPress document without creating the HTML files that result from the Export option. If you have not selected a browser in Preferences, BeyondPress will prompt you to do so when you select the Preview option.

8. The icon that looks like a file image with circles and lines on it is a short cut to the BeyondPress Preferences dialog box.

9. The *trash can*, as you might guess, can be used to delete elements from the Document Content list.

Figure 6.22

*The Document
Content palette icons.*

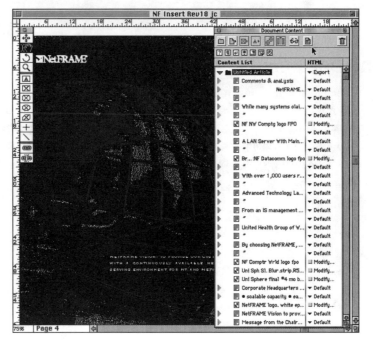

Just below the top row of icons is a second row of icons representing the Master Elements. These icons can be used to insert Master Elements into the Document Content palette list of elements. To do so, simply select the icon and then drag-and-drop it into place in the list of elements in the location where you want it to appear in the converted document. Again, refer to figure 6.22 as you read the following descriptions of the second row of icons, listed as they appear from left to right.

1. The *Question Mark* icon represents any custom Master Elements you may have added in the Master Elements preferences section.

2. The *Paragraph Mark* icon represents the HTML <P> tag and can be inserted to add space in your pages as you arrange the conversion.

3. The *Arrow* icon represents a line break and inserts a <BR> tag.

4. The icon with a pound sign on it represents a single space and can be used to add a space between elements in the document list.

5. The icon that looks like a small paragraph mark with a line under it can be used to insert a Horizontal Rule tag, the <HR> HTML tag that places a line across the screen.

6. The icon with the number 12 on it will insert the date the file is converted. The format of the date is set in Export Preferences.

7. The last icon in the row looks like a small clock and can be used to insert the time the file is converted.

Arranging Elements in the Document Content Palette

Okay, enough testing and studying of this program and document. It's time to start arranging elements in the Document Content palette and preparing this NetFRAME file for final conversion. Assuming that you've already opened the file in QuarkXPress and loaded it into the Document Content palette by using the List Document icon, you should now be looking at a list of elements presented in the order they appear in the original XPress file.

Note

A copy of the original NetFRAME file and graphics is included on the CD-ROM that accompanies this book. Use it if you want to follow along with the same file.

QuarkXPress Conversion

Reviewing the list of elements, notice that each item is named as it appears in the original document. If it is an image, it will have the same name as the original image file. If it is a text block, the name will be the first few words in the text block.

Finding Document Elements in the Document Content Palette

To identify where an element is in the original document, simply double-click on the listing in the Content palette. BeyondPress navigates to the location of the original element in the XPress file and causes it to flash, making it easy to identify. The inverse of this is also true: double-clicking on a text box or graphic in the XPress file reveals its location and representation in the Document Content palette list. This is especially helpful when working on a document you did not create. An example of this is displayed in figure 6.23.

Figure 6.23

You can locate an element in BeyondPress by double-clicking on the Content palette icon.

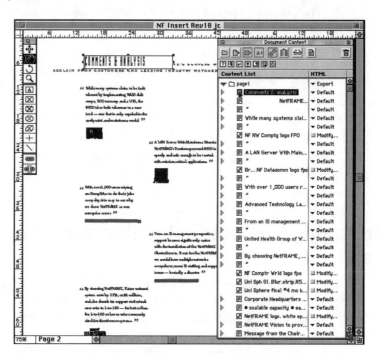

Renaming Document Elements in the Document Content Palette

You can rename any element in the Document Content palette by selecting the item and typing a new name, the same way you would in the Finder on your Macintosh. This is important to do for folders, which will have a file name based on the folder name when converted into an HTML page. It is also important for graphics, which will be named based on their names in the Content palette. You can also move elements around with the same drag-and-drop techniques any good Mac user is familiar with. BeyondPress will convert the items in this list and arrange them in the same order as in the Content palette.

Creating Multiple HTML Pages from One Document

To arrange elements on distinct HTML pages, create a new folder and drag items into that folder. Each folder will be converted into a unique HTML page with all the elements in that folder in the same order as in the Content palette. To create a new folder, select the New Article icon, the one that looks like a folder in the top row of icons in the Content palette.

The goal here is to turn the NetFRAME document into six pages, as assessed earlier in this chapter, so the first thing to do is create five new folders in addition to the one already at the top of the Document Content list. This XPress file will be built into a large Web site, with a directory name that distinguishes it in the site. Thus a simple naming structure, such as page1, page2, and so on, is probably the best choice for this file. When you have six folders created, you can start moving things around.

> **Note**
>
> One of the most frustrating aspects of BeyondPress is that it always places new folders at the end of the list of items in the Content palette. Although you can move any other element to a new location in this list, folders are stuck at the bottom. This means that you must scroll up and down the list when you want to move elements from higher up the list down into a new folder.

The first folder (which has been named page1) contains all the elements when you load the document. To organize elements into separate pages, drag all the elements you will want on the second HTML page to the second folder, those you want on the third page to the third folder, and so on. By process of elimination, after you have moved everything else into the other folders, what's left in the first folder should be what you want on the main HTML page. If there are elements, such as page numbers, that you don't want displayed on any page, you can suppress them using the setting arrow to the right of the element name or delete them using the trash can icon.

According to the earlier assessment made after studying the entire XPress file, Comments and Analysis is to be on a separate page. This was the page with the quotes and small logos. Thus, all the text boxes and graphics that appear on this page are dragged into the page2 folder. Because all the quotation marks were created in separate text boxes using colored text, each quotation mark appears as a separate element in the Document Content palette. Leave them as they are and drag them along with the other elements; they will be converted as colored text and placed in the proper locations. Before preparing the final export, you can do another preview of the document to make sure they appear the way you want them in the HTML page. In figure 6.24, all the elements from the Comments and Analysis page have been moved to the page2 folder.

Figure 6.24

Moving the elements from the Comments and Analysis page into the page2 folder.

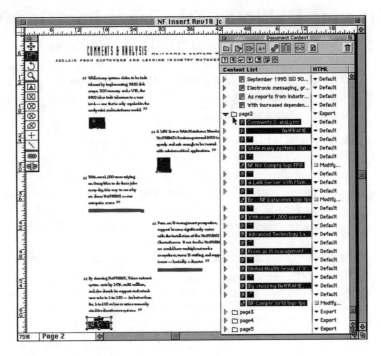

Second, identify the text and headline for the Message from the Chairman page and drag these into the page3 folder (see fig. 6.25).

Next, move the NetFRAME-at-a-glance elements into the page4 folder, the Selected Financial Data into the page5 folder, and the company contact and address information from the back cover into the page6 folder. Now take a look at what's left in the page1 folder. In figure 6.26, you can see that after moving all the other elements, the only ones left in the page1 folder are those from the main page.

Figure 6.25

Moving the elements from the Message from the Chairman page into the page3 folder.

Figure 6.26

The elements for the first HTML page remain in the page1 folder.

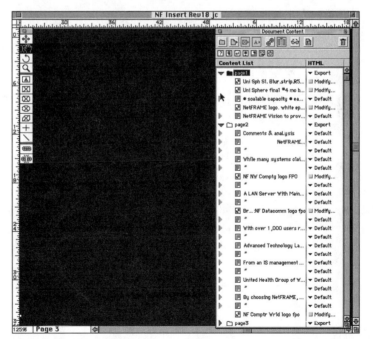

Assigning Preferences for Document Conversion

Now that all elements are in their respective locations, it's time to set preferences. Begin by setting global preferences and then tailor individual elements as needed. You've seen BeyondPress's preferences explained in detail, so only the highlights will be covered with respect to this case study.

Start by setting the Image Preferences to GIF with an adaptive palette, scaling images at 100 percent—most of them are small already.

Continue by setting Horizontal and Vertical space to 5 pixels and image Borders to 0.

Next, map the XPress style sheets to HTML styles in the Mapping Preferences dialog box. Note that the Default option in Mapping Preferences results in regular text in the HTML code. For a look at Mapping Preferences in action on this file, see figure 6.27.

Figure 6.27

Mapping XPress style sheets to HTML styles.

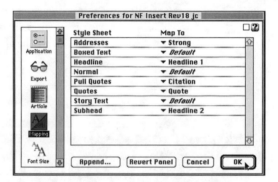

Changing Individual Element Settings

After making global preference settings such as Style Sheet Mapping and Image Preferences, you'll now want to go through the list of elements individually and make alterations as required. As you go through the list, it's also a good time to add paragraph and line breaks to your pages.

> **Tip**
>
> If you want spaces to separate elements, drag the Master Element icons into place in the Document Content palette between the elements you want spaced apart. You can use single spaces, line breaks, paragraph breaks, and horizontal rules to add space between elements.

Modifying Text Box Settings

To alter the setting of a text box, select the description next to the list item, such as Default, and a pop-up menu appears, listing all available HTML styles. To change the setting, select any option from the list. If you have set all the quotes to the regular default text, for example, and want to make one of them stand out more than the others, change its setting to the Strong tag.

Modifying Image Settings

Images can be altered by selecting the word Modify that appears to the right of the image icon and list item. Selecting Modify opens the Image Settings dialog box, revealing a host of image conversion options, not all of which are available in the global Image Preferences dialog box. For example, the Image Settings dialog box includes a place for Alternative text, using the ALT attribute to insert text in the HTML code that will display if a browser does not display the image. Such settings must be specified on an image-by-image basis because they should be unique to each image. Other settings unique to this dialog box include the capability to specify a transparent color by using the Eyedropper tool, and the capability to create an image map by using the Linking tool (for more on this option, see "Creating an Image Map with BeyondPress," later in this chapter). Other settings can be changed in this dialog box to override the global settings specified in Image Preferences. For example, you can change the scaling percentage, select a different alignment option, or convert an image to a JPEG instead of a GIF. Figure 6.28 shows the Awards image from the NetFRAME file displayed in the Image Settings dialog box.

Converting the Financial Data Table

Another element that needs to be set individually is the table in the Financial Data section. This would be a tedious and difficult process if you had to copy the text out of XPress and reformat it. With the table conversion capabilities, however, it is a relatively simple page in this file. The following are the steps used to convert the table in this case study:

1. Select the icon to the right of the table listing in the Document Content palette and choose Table from the pop-up menu.

2. In the Table preferences dialog box that appears, set the border to 2, and also set cell padding and spacing to 2.

3. In this case, there is no need to change the number of rows and columns. The number of table columns and rows should automatically reflect the table you are

adjusting, but always double check. You can change these numbers to override the automatic settings.

4. Specify two header rows and one header column to make the headers bold for this table.

Figure 6.28

The Awards image from the NetFRAME file, as displayed in the Image Settings dialog box.

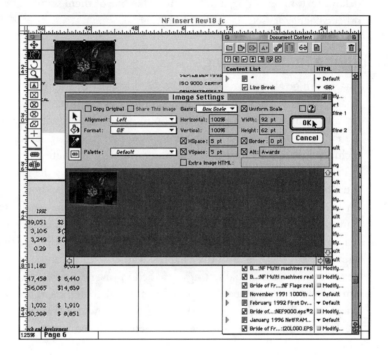

Once you have completed the preferences, close the dialog box and you are ready to convert the page. It's a good idea to select the Preview option at this point to ensure that the table will be properly converted before you do your final export. The Table Preferences dialog box described earlier in this chapter always opens with the default settings. Because each table you convert is likely to be different, BeyondPress gives you the chance to change those settings to better represent each unique table. Figure 6.29 shows the options selected for this table, while figure 6.30 shows a preview of how the table will be displayed in Netscape after conversion.

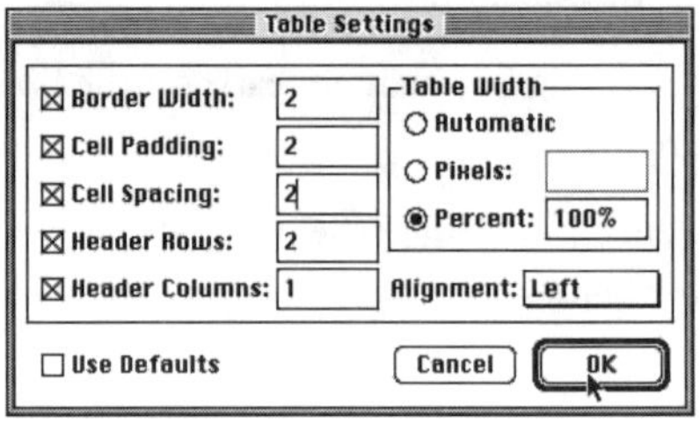

Figure 6.29

The Table Settings dialog box.

Figure 6.30

Previewing the table as it will appear in Netscape after conversion.

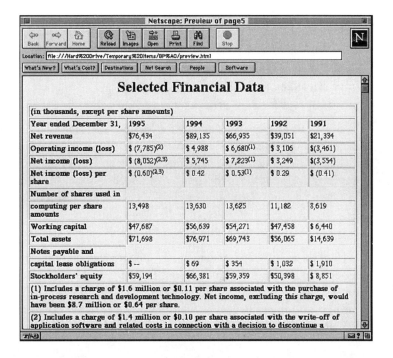

Overall, BeyondPress does a great job of automating one of the most tedious aspects of QuarkXPress conversion, but there are a few minor flaws you may want to correct in this table. Notice the two places where the column text on the left wraps to a second line. BeyondPress placed it in two different rows instead of combining it as was intended in the original table. Some designers may not be unhappy with this, because it is clear which column headings go with which row of numbers. If you want to correct this, however, you have two options:

1. Alter the table in the original XPress file, making the table wider and fitting all the text on one line.

2. Alter the HTML code after conversion by deleting the extra table row and moving the text into the cell with the rest of the line that wrapped.

To learn more about altering HTML pages after export, read Chapter 13, "Tailoring Converted Files."

Exporting the Document

After arranging all the conversion settings and previewing any pages you wanted to check before exporting, it's time for the final conversion. You should understand up front that although BeyondPress is a great tool and does much to automate this process, it's still far from perfect.

Figure 6.31 provides a look at how the Message from the Chairman appears in Netscape after exporting. Here you can see another of BeyondPress's limitations. In the highlighted area, notice the hard returns in the middle of the sentence, formatted that way in the original XPress document. Although this may have worked for the spacing in XPress, it doesn't look good on the Web, where the text scrolls all the way across the page. Again, either alter the text in the original document before exporting, or fix this in the HTML code by deleting the <BR> tags that cause the line breaks.

Each of the exported pages contains a number of similar problems, making this an ideal document to revisit in Chapter 13, where you'll learn how to put the finishing touches on this type of conversion by using HTML text and WYSIWYG editors. In the next section of this chapter, you'll learn about some very common and annoying limitations of BeyondPress and what you can do about them.

Figure 6.31

A preview of the Message from the Chairman as it will appear in Netscape after conversion.

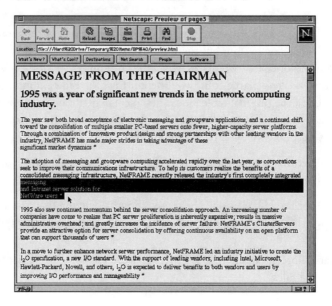

Creating an Image Map with BeyondPress

Although the case study in this chapter doesn't require an image map, you should know how to create one with BeyondPress. Image maps are commonly used on the Web, and this is a nice built-in feature not found in most conversion programs. Image maps enable you to link sections of an image to different URLs so that a user reaches different destinations by selecting different sections of the image.

Before you create an image map in BeyondPress, you should specify whether you want a client-side image map (one that is interpreted by the browser) or a server-side image map (one that uses a CGI script on the server). BeyondPress will export the necessary files for NCSA or CERN server CGI scripts. In this example, you'll be creating a client-side image map, an increasingly popular option because they are now supported by both the Netscape Navigator and Microsoft Internet Explorer browsers. For more information on client-side and server-side image maps, see Chapter 14, "HTML Tutorial and Reference."

Use the following steps to create an image map in BeyondPress:

1. Select an image in the Document Content palette and click on the Modify icon in the right column to open the Image Settings dialog box.

2. Select the Linking tool (the last icon at the bottom of the toolbar on the left side of the dialog box). You must select the Image Map option in Image Preferences for this tool to be available.

3. Once you've selected the Linking tool, drag the cursor to create a box around any section of the image. Figure 6.32 shows how the Link tool is used to specify a section of the image.

4. In the dialog box that appears at the top of figure 6.32, type the URL the boxed section will link to.

5. After you click on OK in the Link Destination dialog box, the link will be outlined, numbered, and named according to the URL.

6. Repeat steps 3–5 to designate as many hot sections in the image as you want.

You can edit the image map by dragging the handle of a link box to resize it, dragging the entire box to a different position, or double-clicking on a link to change the URL. If you set a regular link for the entire image, this becomes the default link, which is triggered if a user selects an area of the image not specified in the image map.

A big limitation of creating image maps in BeyondPress is not being able to set internal links from this dialog box. You can, however, change the links in the HTML code after you export the file. To learn more about how to make these kinds of changes, read Chapter 13, "Tailoring Converted Files."

Figure 6.32

BeyondPress support for client-side or server-side image maps for NCSA or CERN servers.

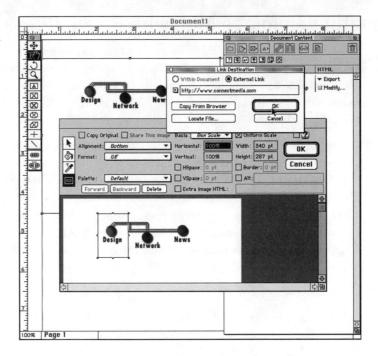

Note

More is not always better with image maps. Be careful not to make linked areas so small they become difficult for users to distinguish and select properly. As you create hot spots in an image, also try to make sure they correspond with sections of the image that make it clear what they will link to.

Overcoming the Limitations of BeyondPress: Tips for Conversion

Some designers might call the following list of problems "bugs." Others might refer to them as understandable limitations of a program that does a good job overall of converting a document designed for print into a file that will work in a completely new medium. Whatever your assessment is, you should be aware of the following problems, quirks, or glitches you may face when using BeyondPress to convert QuarkXPress documents.

Headline Conversion

When BeyondPress exports Headlines, it gives them <B> (Bold) or <I> (Italic) tags if the original XPress text includes this formatting—even if the formatting results from use of a font that is bold, heavy, black, oblique, italic, or whatever. Although it is not technically incorrect to use both an <H1> tag and a <B> tag, it is considered bad form because it is redundant. All Header tags automatically make the text bold.

If this problem occurs frequently in your conversion, it may be worthwhile to make global changes to your XPress document before exporting the stories with Beyond-Press. Where possible, save time by changing the style sheet definitions in XPress so bold or italic fonts are replaced with plain 'ole Roman ones. You can also use the Font Usage dialog box in QuarkXPress to replace fonts and styles directly. Be careful not to override bold or italic settings you want to keep—for example, in the body text of the document. If the problem of unnecessary format tags is infrequent, it's easier to deal with on a case-by-case basis. Manually select the text and change it to a plain typeface before conversion.

Hyphenation

BeyondPress will export hyphens from auto-hyphenation. The easiest solution to this problem is to change the Hyphenation and Justification definitions to deselect auto-hyphenation before exporting.

Line Breaks

As you saw in the Message from the Chairman example, designers frequently use line breaks to balance lines in print. BeyondPress has no way to distinguish such line breaks and exports them as the <BR> tag to your HTML documents. One solution is to do a Find and Replace of the entire document before conversion. If you search for the special character \n (= line break) in XPress and replace it with nothing or a single white space, you should solve this problem.

Multiple Links to the Same Place

BeyondPress will not enable you to create two internal links to the same piece of text. This is a problem when a document contains multiple internal references to one item such as a heading, contact information, or a definition. To get around this, create links to different parts of the same text block. The code for this is a little messy, but it works. Essentially, you set multiple Anchor tags to the same section of text, anchoring different words each time. Anchor tags do not affect the text the way links do, but do provide a target for a link that is set from somewhere else within the document. Of course, you can set more links in an HTML editor after conversion if you prefer. Following is an example of a heading with two Anchor tags for links:

```
<H3><A NAME="link1">This is<A NAME="link2">a heading</H3>
```

Multiple Uses of Text

BeyondPress will not allow the same piece of text to be exported twice, which means that you can't take one item from the XPress document and use it in more than one of the exported HTML pages. To get around this, duplicate the item as many times as you need to reuse it. You can also save it in a separate text file and use it to create a Master Element in BeyondPress, which you can then drag-and-drop into as many places as you like.

Removing the BeyondPress Credit Line

BeyondPress automatically inserts its own credit line at the bottom of every exported document. If this annoys you, use BBEdit (described in detail in Chapter 13) to do a global search and destroy. The programmers at Astrobyte deserve a lot of credit for creating this program, but you may not want their tag line on every one of your pages.

Creating Style-Naming Schemes

This tip is particularly useful if you are working with a team of developers. Because you can create your own HTML styles in BeyondPress, you may find it helpful to generate a list of HTML style names that make sense in terms of the documents you're converting. For example: if your standard subhead style is <H4>, create a new style in BeyondPress's Preferences and call it "Subhead." Define it, using the open <H4> and close </H4> tags. The "Subhead" style will then be available in the pop-up menu of HTML styles, and no one should be confused about which format to use for subheads.

Exporting Monaco Text

QuarkXPress text that is formatted with the Monaco font will be exported with <TT> tags (typewriter text). This can be very useful. For example, if your printed materials list computer code in a particular typeface, you can replace that typeface with Monaco before exporting to HTML, thus forcing the appropriate HTML text into <TT> style.

Restricting Conversion to HTML 1.0

BeyondPress gives you the option of limiting its conversion to HTML 1.0 tags. This option doesn't function strictly (it will still export tables if you set them up that way), but it can be useful strategy if you want to keep the exported code simple. For example, if you select this option, BeyondPress will export <P> tags without alignment attributes.

Manual Conversions

If you are doing QuarkXPress conversions on a PC or do not have BeyondPress for the Mac, you are in for a much more difficult and tedious conversion process than the one described in the first part of this chapter. Unfortunately, there are no conversion programs for the PC available for XPress in Windows, and neither of the two major conversion developers have any plans to create a Windows version. This leaves you with the following two less-than-ideal options.

The Copy and Paste Method

The first is the tried-and-true copy and paste method. Choose the Text tool in XPress, select all the text in a text box, and copy. Then move to a word processing program, text editor, or HTML editor, and paste the text. Repeat this action until you have all the elements you want on the new page. Because accompanying text, such as a headline, is often placed in a distinct text box in XPress, you'll be forced to do the copy and paste for each text block individually. A workaround worth considering is to alter the original file by moving related text elements into one text box. With this done, you only have to copy and paste once between programs.

The Save Text Option Method

Unlike PageMaker, XPress does not have a Text Export option, but the Save Text option located under the File menu serves a similar purpose. You can use this feature to save the contents of any text box in a variety of other formats.

> **Note**
>
> On the Mac, your options are ASCII Text, MacWrite, Microsoft Word, WordPerfect, WriteNow, or XPress Tags.
>
> On a Windows system, your options are ASCII, RTF (Rich Text Format), XPress Tags, Word for DOS, Word for Windows, WordPerfect, and XYWrite III Plus.

QuarkXPress
Conversion

The advantage of using the Save Text option instead of copy and paste is that it preserves basic formatting such as font size, bold, and italic. This means that you can complete the conversion in a conversion program designed for word processing. You can then automate part of the process by using a program such as HTML Transit (described in detail in Chapter 5, "Batch Conversion Utilities"), thus saving yourself some time. Again, to take best advantage of this feature, you may want to alter the original document by placing all related text elements in one text box before using the Save Text option. Otherwise, you must save the contents of each text box as a separate file and copy and paste them into one file afterward. Rearranging elements in the original document can enable you to export the contents of an entire page at once, saving you time in the next step as you take those files through a conversion program designed for a word processor. Word processing and spreadsheet conversion programs are covered in Chapters 3, 4, and 5. Check the index to find the specific section for the program you prefer.

Other XPress Conversion Programs

There are some other QuarkXPress conversion programs available. HexWeb XT, by HexMac International, is similar to BeyondPress, although not nearly as robust. e-Gate, by the French company Rosebud Technologies, boasts a customizable solution for high-end users. A new program, CyberPress, will soon provide a low-end solution. This is a "lite" version of BeyondPress that will be bundled with Adobe PageMill. All of these programs are described briefly in the following sections.

HexWeb XT

HexWeb XT is similar to BeyondPress in that it is a Mac-only XTension for XPress conversion. Unlike BeyondPress, however, HexWeb XT does not map style sheets to HTML code and lacks many of the other more sophisticated features of BeyondPress. The program is limited to matching point sizes to header tags and converting basic formatting such as bold and italic.

Instead of using a Document Content palette to list XPress elements where they can be rearranged and organized as separate pages, HexWeb XT lets you select text boxes in a sequence and then export the boxes selected as one page. This might be a more intuitive approach at first glance, but the program offers no feedback in terms of which boxes have been selected. Also, you cannot go back and change your mind about order, but must start over with a new page.

HexWeb XT does provide basic image conversion and can be used to set links by specifying elements in the original document. Header and footer elements repeated on every page can be defined in settings. One feature BeyondPress lacks is the HexWeb Index, which automatically generates a table of contents file after all HTML articles have been exported.

HexWeb International states that most of their product's users are newspaper and magazine publishers. One of the most popular features, according to the company, is the capability to keep images and caption text together during the conversion process. *The Detroit News* is one of their clients.

HexWeb XT, by HexMac International, retails for $345. For more information on the program, visit their Web site at the following:

```
http://www.hexmac.de/
```

e-Gate: A Custom XPress Conversion Program

Rosebud Technologies, a consulting company in Paris that services the European publishing market, offers a custom XPress conversion tool for high-end users. The program was a bit beyond the scope of this book, partially because it has to be customized and partially because it costs a minimum of $950 (that's 4,800 francs).

Note Rosebud Technologies offered a free demonstration, but although New Riders Publishing is generally very good to its writers, a trip to Paris was a little more than they were willing to cover for this book. The following is a description of the product sent via e-mail from the company. If anyone wants to send me to Paris, I'll be happy to write a more personal review of the program.

According to Rosebud Technologies, the goal of e-Gate is to export Quark articles by using "meta-information," such as publication name, section name, date of publication, page number, source file name, and so on. The program was designed to enable publishers to build editorial or document databases (in structured ASCII or HTML) as part of the conversion process. For this to be possible, the company needs at least one day to customize the system for each publication. Although it is possible for an end user to alter the program after this initial customization, Rosebud states they like to do the initial set-up themselves. The customization takes into account the identification of meta information, as well as common editorial elements. e-Gate is designed for the publishing market with the idea that every publication has a defined graphical chart (that is, titles are in Helvetica 32 bold, subtitles in Helvetica 24 italics, and so on).

e-Gate does not rely on style sheets, but rather on the structure of the QuarkXPress elements. According to the company, the strength of the product comes from the fact that they recognize structure and extract meta information. There is currently no evaluation product available, because each system must be tailored to the unique features of the publication. Several European publications are already using the product. Their Web sites are available through the company's Web site listed at the end of this section.

e-Gate comes into its own when you have a publication that needs to be extracted into other formats on a regular basis, or when the publication you want to extract has a lot of pages. If you have lots of ad-hoc documents in Quark, you're probably better off with BeyondPress or HexWeb, according to the company.

You can find Rosebud Technologies at the following:

```
http://www.rosebud.fr/
```

CyberPress

CyberPress, by Extensis, is scheduled to ship by the fall of 1996. Developed in cooperation with Astrobyte, CyberPress is a "lite" version of BeyondPress that will be bundled with Adobe PageMill. The package will retail for $149.95. Registered CyberPress users may upgrade to BeyondPress from Astrobyte for $449.95.

For more information on CyberPress, visit the Extensis Web site at the following:

```
http://www.extensis.com/
```

Summary

If you have to do large or frequent QuarkXPress conversions and have access to Macintosh, you should buy BeyondPress to automate your HTML development process. If you are on a Windows machine, consider the word processing conversion programs available and select a tool that will help automate the process after you move the text out of XPress and into a word processing format.

If you do nothing but XPress conversion (for example, if you work at a magazine or other publication that produces many similar XPress files on a regular basis), you might consider a custom option such as e-Gate. Hiring a programmer to create a conversion script unique to your original publication may also be cheaper than keeping a stable of HTML designers to manually convert all your documents.

Overall, if you have the option (and a Mac), your best bet is clearly BeyondPress. Although HexWeb XT offers some nice features, at $345 it's not a much better deal and is an inferior product. Keep your eyes out for CyberPress. A "lite" version of BeyondPress may be enough for you. Bundled with PageMill (vastly improved in the 2.0 upgrade), this may be a great way to get started.

QuarkXPress Conversion

CHAPTER 7

FrameMaker Conversion

FrameMaker is a desktop publishing tool designed to be particularly useful for the publication of long documents, such as books, instruction manuals, and theses. FrameMaker also supports hyperlinking, making it a serious contender as application-of-choice for publishing CD-ROM documents, especially for such purposes as reference, education, and training. Finally, because third-party developers are creating programs to convert long FrameMaker files into a series of smaller Web files, FrameMaker files such as manuals and employee handbooks are becoming useful intranet files.

FrameMaker is designed so it is easy to set up "style sheets" or "master pages" for an entire document. Thereafter, as you place text on a page, it is automatically formatted when assigned a particular style, such as heading levels, columns, headers, footers, and page numbers. Because these elements tend to be more consistent in FrameMaker, the documents are somewhat easier to convert to predictable-looking Web pages than documents made in more design-oriented desktop publishing programs such as PageMaker or QuarkXPress.

FrameMaker conversion programs exist for PC, Macintosh, and Unix platforms, making FrameMaker documents very good candidates for accessibility and clean conversion to the Web.

Finally, there are four commercial FrameMaker-to-HTML conversion programs, so you have more options for FrameMaker than for QuarkXPress or PageMaker. This chapter will concentrate on the most popular of the FrameMaker conversion programs, WebWorks Publisher 3.0, and will also describe Harlequin's WebMaker conversion program. Two other programs that convert FrameMaker files, Web Publisher Pro and HTML Transit, are covered in Chapter 5, "Batch Conversion Utilities," because they are well suited for converting multiple word processing files. All four of the programs for converting FrameMaker documents also convert the text formats that can be imported by FrameMaker. The importable text formats are plain text, WordPerfect, Word, and RTF (Rich Text Format). Because most word processing applications output to either text or RTF format, the reality is that you can import text from almost all applications.

If you don't have one of these conversion programs, you can manually convert a FrameMaker file by using copy-and-paste to remove the content and reformat it in a text editor. Similar to PageMaker and XPress, FrameMaker enables you to export text by using the Save As option to convert content to text, RTF (Rich Text Format), or MIF (Maker Interchange Format, similar to RTF) files. After you have taken the content out of FrameMaker, you can complete the process with a conversion program that supports text or RTF. Alternatively, you can open the files in an HTML text editor such as BBEdit or Hot Dog; or a WYSIWYG HTML editor, such as Claris HomePage 1.0 (all of which are covered in Chapter 13, "Tailoring Converted Files"). These HTML editors enable you to create complex HTML elements, such as frames and tables.

How FrameMaker Differs from Other Page-Makeup Programs

FrameMaker documents are structured somewhat like Web pages in that the structure is imposed by style "tags." These tags are a bit like the styles in most word processing programs. They define what each paragraph will look like when it's printed (and don't forget, this includes headers, headlines, footnotes, and so forth). In other words, they define the type face, type style, leading, kerning (the space between individual letters), margins, and spacing. This kind of structure has two significant advantages:

1. It is very easy to change the appearance of all paragraphs that relate to a specific style.

2. It is easier (and probably more predictable) to apply a set of rules for converting these FrameMaker tags to HTML tags.

The disadvantage is that the tags have to relate to one another or to the document as a whole.

Another characteristic of FrameMaker documents is that a publication can consist of many separate files, all gathered into something FrameMaker calls a *book*. A book file is simply an index of all the files in the publication. When converting FrameMaker to HTML, both Quadralay WebWorks Publisher and Harlequin WebMaker enable you to convert all the separate files that make up a book at once by simply telling the programs you want to convert a book.

Creating a book is easy. You open a "book window" and simply list all the files you want to include in the book. The only trick is that the files must be listed in the order in which you want them to appear in the book. You then can specify a numbering system for each document. For instance, you can specify lowercase Roman numerals for the table of contents and decimal number for each file that is a chapter. Decimal numbering is the numbering system used in this book.

Editing the FrameMaker Document Before Conversion

This chapter assumes you already have a working knowledge of the FrameMaker program itself, so the focus of the following sections will be on how to use WebWorks Publisher 3.0—a powerful conversion program from Quadralay, designed to turn FrameMaker documents into Web pages.

Editing for brevity is almost always part of the process of converting conventional print documents into Web publications. Unless you are working on an intranet or must reproduce all the content of a file for the Web, it's a good idea to shorten the original file. Most users of the Web won't read long documents online. Because FrameMaker's reputation is based largely on its capabilities for handling long documents, editing is especially likely to be a requirement of the conversion process for FrameMaker documents. Remember, you can convert FrameMaker documents into PDF (as described in Chapter 9, "PDF (Portable Document Format) Files") and encourage users to download them in their entirety to print or read offline.

With the need to edit in mind, it's almost always a good idea to study the FrameMaker document so you can decide what to do about content that won't translate well to the Web. Before you do this, be sure to read Chapter 2 on Web design and Chapters 10 and 11 on graphics for the Web. If you work with a printed copy of the document, you can mark it up, making notes on which material to cut and which material to reconstruct into a different format from the original. For instance, your document may have a number of full-page, high-resolution photos or illustrations. These will need to be reduced considerably in size and resolution. You will probably also want to reduce their number so pages can load more quickly. It is much easier to make edits in the original FrameMaker document than to manually scan the converted HTML code, sort the text and graphics from the tags, and manually edit content after the conversion. You may want to do this for final refinements, but the closer the document is to the final converted result, the more time you will save. This also saves you time and energy for making the subtle refinements that result in award-winning Web pages.

Questions to Consider Before Conversion

It's always a good idea to plan ahead before you begin converting a document, especially one that is as complicated and long as some FrameMaker documents. The following questions will help you organize your objectives so that the conversion process does not seem daunting. Some of these questions are based on the conversion processes of the programs discussed here; others will help you figure out how you want to handle elements like graphics and sidebars that appear in the original document.

1. How many pages are in the original document and how many HTML pages will you turn it into?

   A book chapter is usually too unwieldy in length to make a manageable Web page. With so many print pages (and their accompanying graphics) to load, it could take nearly a minute before the first screen loads. Your audience will shortly grow impatient and move on to some other site, so try not to make any given Web page more than a few printed pages long. Also, be sure to create anchors and a table of contents for each of these "sections," so users won't have to scroll endlessly before finding the material they are looking for.

2. What kind of front pages will you create for the Web version?

   Seldom will the front page of a print document be rich enough, either in content or color, to serve well as the home page of a Web document. The home page should command the user's attention, make it easy for the user to under-stand what the Web site is all about, and make it obvious how to navigate the site. Fail to do all that on an opening Web page, and you will lose all but your most dedicated audience.

3. How will the pages link together?

   Most FrameMaker document sets (books) include a table of contents. If the document is a CD-ROM or network publication, the TOC may already have convertible links to each major page. If you subdivide and edit the publication after conversion, however, you will need to re-establish most (probably all) of those links. In addition, you will almost certainly want to add new links that make it easier to navigate between the screen-size chunks of information viewable in a browser.

   Also, take advantage of the Web's hypermedia capabilities. Don't just stick to links that keep the user moving along a linear path—let your viewers jump to any and all information related to the topic they are currently reading. Also, don't forget to put navigation bars on each page.

4. How will you handle sidebars and other text boxes?

   Think about how you will handle warnings, notes, footnotes, sidebars, and diagrams. Dropped into the middle of the text, they interrupt the flow of the story. Once again, remember that the Web is hypermedia—anything can be linked to anything. It's usually best to put supplementary materials on their own pages, then link these pages to the main body of material. You may want to use small icons (such as a radiation symbol for a warning or a check mark for a note) when linking to these materials. You can also link miniaturized representations (thumbnails) of large graphics such as organizational charts or full-screen photos.

To keep some of these elements in context with the main copy, consider the use of HTML tables. A WYSIWYG HTML editor that handles tables is the easiest way to deal with this. Open the converted HTML document containing the sidebars in the WYSIWYG editor, insert a table, and then cut and paste content to fit so it appears to wrap around the sidebar.

5. How will you handle image conversion and placement?

This is really a subject for extended study. Unless you're already a graphics pro who thoroughly understands the limitations imposed by the fact that most Web surfers use 14.4 or 28.8 modems, read Chapters 10 and 11. You will also do well to get hold of a copy of Lynda Weinman's *Designing Web Graphics.*

At the moment, the main thing to remember is that it's seldom wise to show more than a couple of illustrations (any graphic more than 75 pixels square) on a single Web page. If you need to show large graphics, consider showing them on a separate page and linking them to a thumbnail in context with the material to which it relates. This also gives you the option of associating a more detailed caption with the larger image.

An unfortunate weakness of Quadralay WebWorks Publisher is that it doesn't handle all graphics as comprehensively as some of the other conversion programs covered in this book. You will have to convert some images separately and manually place them into the converted text. Consider using a WYSIWYG HTML editor for this purpose, such as FrontPage, HomePage, PageMill 2.0, or NetObjects Fusion. Such products give you immediate visual feedback on the effect your graphics have in context with the text and other elements surrounding them.

6. What overall navigation features will work best for this document?

Consider doing a storyboard or flowchart showing how the HTML version of your FrameMaker document will be organized and linked. Once again, remember to take advantage of the hypermedia nature of the Web.

Preparing Your FrameMaker Document for HTML

The most alluring concept of automating conversion of print documents to HTML is "prepare once, publish many." It is theoretically possible to prepare and format creative content only once, in a manner that will enable it to be simultaneously published on paper, on a CD-ROM, on a network, or on the Web (both Internet and intranet). It's more a pleasant dream than an absolute reality, as each medium has special characteristics you will want to take advantage of if it is to be used to its fullest capacity. Nevertheless, "prepare once" should be your goal. The closer you come to the ideal (without making counterproductive compromises), the more time and money you will save.

Keeping time and money in mind, here are some rules to follow when composing your FrameMaker documents:

- Use paragraph and character tags consistently.

  This makes it much easier to apply global changes to the entire document. You can then make the conversion, preview it in a browser, and quickly make any needed adjustments. Also, many converters work by having you apply a given translating rule to a given document style. If you have been consistent in applying styles, you can globally search-and-replace the rules and reapply them to all those tags at once.

- Use heading levels consistently.

  This relates to the preceding rule. If your heading levels are consistent, it's easy to make global document changes.

- Use cross-references liberally to link related textual or visual information throughout the document.

  Of course, you can place more links in a document after it's been converted, but what you really want is to be able to automatically update all the document links if you make a change. You can do this best inside FrameMaker. You will have to make another conversion after updating the links. Besides, once again, it's less work to do it once.

- Make cross-references work for both print and electronic media.

  Referencing page numbers, for instance, works well for printed pages, but page numbers are nearly meaningless in the context of the Web. References indicated by subject, rather than cross-page, work equally well for both print and Web.

● Use FrameMaker's styles for bulleted or numbered text.

If text needs to be numbered or bulleted, be sure to use FrameMaker's styles (such as autonumbering) for doing that, rather than doing it manually. This is important because the conversion programs rely on styles to both map the appropriate HTML tag to the converted document and to create a reusable template in case you want to reconvert the document. It's also easier to autonumber than to do it manually.

● Ensure text flow order.

Make sure the text flows in the order your conversion program expects—smaller page number to larger page number, left to right, top to bottom. If you don't use such logical text flow (for instance, if you continue an article on a preceding page), text will be in the wrong position in the HTML code and, therefore, on your Web site.

● Attach anchored frames to their own paragraphs.

A graphic in an anchored frame will be attached to the preceding paragraph when it is converted and aligned to the bottom (at least this is so in Harlequin WebMaker). The result will be a misaligned graphic. Solve this problem by attaching the graphic to an empty paragraph.

● Place all graphics in anchored frames.

Some conversion programs, such as Harlequin WebMaker, won't convert graphics unless they're in anchored frames. HTML can't place a graphic without some information about where to put it. The converter can't provide the information if the frame isn't anchored. In other words, no anchored frame—no graphic.

● Consider the resolution of imported graphics.

This is a good rule to follow when converting any kind of document in any kind of converter, so you may have seen the same warning (probably phrased differently) elsewhere in this book. This bears repeating because graphics intended for printer resolution are usually specified at 150–300 dpi (dots per inch). The ideal resolution for the Web is 72 dpi, one-quarter the size of a 150-dpi file. The difference in download times is major. Worse, the higher-resolution file will flow well beyond the borders of most browser screens.

Quadralay WebWorks Publisher

WebWorks Publisher is the easiest and most popular program for converting a FrameMaker document. WebWorks Publisher translates both standard FrameMaker and FrameMaker's MIF (Media Interchange Format) files. It has a clean and nonintimidating interface (as seen in fig. 7.1) and a preconfigured set of tag-interpretation defaults. This gives you the ability to put a publication into HTML code—complete with graphics (if you have followed the suggestions in the preceding sections) and tables—with the push of three or four buttons.

Figure 7.1

The WebWorks Publisher user interface.

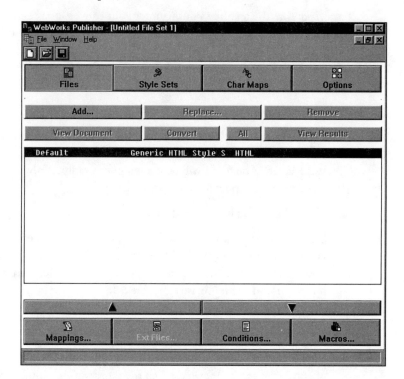

Note

A version of Quadralay WebWorks Publisher, called HTML Lite, is bundled with Adobe FrameMaker 5.0. HTML Lite is extremely user friendly, but is much less versatile than Quadralay WebWorks Publisher, which sports about four times as many features. Actually, if you want easy, HTML Lite will be hard to beat. Like a lot of other "easy" software, it doesn't do a lot; for instance, it doesn't convert graphics or tables, and it won't convert an entire FrameMaker book. On the other hand, if you just want to get the basic layout up on the screen pronto, HTML Lite is certainly accessible and can be learned in minutes. The other advantage of HTML Lite is that it can act as "training wheels" for Quadralay WebWorks Publisher.

WebWorks Publisher Features

Perhaps WebWorks Publisher's greatest strengths are its flexible graphics conversion options and its elegant, no-pain translation of tables. Graphics can be scaled or rotated on output and can be converted to either GIF or JPEG format. GIFs can be transparent. You can automatically adjust bit depth and create both a thumbnail and a larger, linked graphic. The other outstanding characteristic is a capability to do equations, including Greek and Latin symbols and special character sets.

Quadralay WebWorks Publisher is in version 3.0 for Windows, but has stayed at version 2.4 for the Macintosh. If you're already familiar with Quadralay WebWorks Publisher, but have a Macintosh or haven't yet upgraded, you may want to know what features you're missing. The following list shows what you get in version 3.0:

- HTML 3.0 tables

- Support for SGI-IRIX and IBM-AIX flavors of Unix

- Better performance

- Conversion of graphics that are not in anchored frames

- New system macros for creating custom navigation bars that automatically hyperlink all pages and documents

- Nested macros

Any hyperlinks already in your FrameMaker document are automatically translated and linked in HTML.

WebWorks Publisher is intended to be used by those who know little or nothing about HTML, although it produces highly editable code any expert can easily customize. The program is also highly configurable, so you have the freedom to automatically interpret FrameMaker styles in many creative ways. For example, you could try specifying all the first-level heads as heading1, take a look at the result, and re-specify heading2 in the same macro.

Quadralay WebWorks Publisher can be configured for arbitrary file splitting, giving you the option of shortening your pages just for the Web version of your publication, while keeping the print version undisturbed. WebWorks Publisher automatically adjusts the table of contents and index files when you do this.

How WebWorks Publisher Works

When you open WebWorks Publisher, you will see menus and control bars surrounding a blank gray window. When you choose File, Open, New, the window color changes to white to let you know the program is ready to start creating a file set. *File sets* are Web site structures created in WebWorks Publisher when you add files to the File Set. These structures are stored in a file recognizable by the .wdt extension name.

Before you start the exercise that follows, there are some things you need to know about preparing for a trouble-free conversion. First, make sure FrameMaker (preferably version 5.0.1) is already loaded on the same system as Quadralay WebWorks Publisher—otherwise, Publisher won't run at all. Also, make sure you have the latest version of Quadralay WebWorks Publisher, because there were some glitches in version 6.0.4. The version mentioned here is version 6.0.8. If you have a version of FrameMaker earlier than 5.0.1 for Windows, you will not be able to employ long file names. This means if you try to save your translated files to New Folder, the conversion will mysteriously fail.

This first simple exercise will show you how to batch-convert a series of files, using the default configuration for FrameMaker style tags.

Exercise 7.1

1. Open Windows Explorer and create a new folder called ECO (the example used is a file on ecology). To create a new folder, first select the drive or directory where you want to place the new folder as a subdirectory. Choose File, New, Folder. A New Folder icon will appear in the file directory window. Highlight this name to change it to eight characters or less.

2. Double-click on the Quadralay WebWorks Publisher icon to open the program. From the Main menu, choose File, Open, New.

3. Click on the Add button in the new window. A file navigation window opens. Navigate to the directory where you saved the book you want to convert to HTML. For this example, the folder will be c:\Maker5\Samples\Overview\ Book\.

4. You can either add individual files or a whole FrameMaker book. To load an entire book, find the file with the .BK extension (for this exercise, select the file called ECOLOGY.BK) and double-click. All the files in the book will appear listed in the File Set window.

5. You can convert an individual file in the set by simply highlighting it and clicking on the Convert button (see fig. 7.2). To convert an entire book and preserve any existing hyperlinks between these files, click on the All button.

Figure 7.2

*Selecting the book
(.BK) file.*

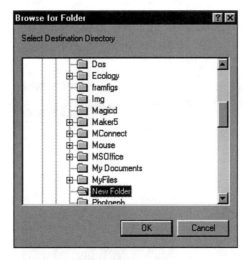

6. A Warning dialog box appears. It states, in part, "The operation requires that a valid destination directory be specified." Click on OK.

7. A file-browsing window opens. Navigate to the folder you previously created to hold your translated publication. Double-click on the folder.

8. Several progress-thermometer windows appear in sequence, each reporting the conversion of a file or graphic. When the thermometers stop, the conversion process is complete. You will see all the files in the book folder listed in the File Set window. If the translation has been successful, the View Results button will no longer be grayed. Click on the View Results button.

9. Netscape Navigator opens and loads your converted file. This assumes you have installed Netscape Navigator on the same system on which you are converting your files. If you have a different browser preference, you can set that browser as the default for WebWorks Publisher.

Figures 7.3 and 7.4 show the "before and after" of the results of Exercise 7.1.

Note that the main headings are the same size and style as the body text and that Quadralay WebWorks Publisher did not translate all the graphics.

Figure 7.3

FrameMaker view of the Ecology sample book.

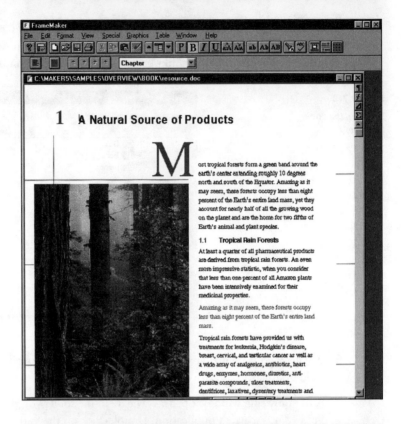

Figure 7.4

Navigator view of the Ecology sample book.

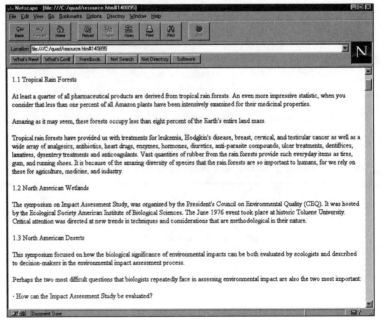

Graphics Troubleshooting

Quadralay WebWorks Publisher won't convert graphics at all unless the Seiko ColorPoint PS printer is chosen as the default printer by using the Windows 95 printer settings. You must do this before starting Quadralay WebWorks Publisher. The following step-by-step procedure demonstrates how to accomplish this:

1. From the Start menu, choose Settings, Printers.

2. When the Printers Control Panel window opens, double-click on the Add Printer icon. The Add Printer dialog box opens.

3. Click on the Next button until the Add Printer Wizard window opens. Scroll down the list until you have chosen Seiko in the left column and ColorPoint PS in the right column.

4. Click on Next until you see a list of available ports. Choose LPT1 (you don't need to configure this port, because you aren't actually going to output to a real printer).

5. Click on Next until you are asked if you want to select the ColorPoint PS as the default printer. Click on Yes.

6. Click on Next until you are asked if you want to print a test page. Click on No, and then click on Finish.

From now on, the Color Point will appear as one of the printers in your Printers Control Panel. To make any printer the default printer, select its icon, press the right mouse button, and choose Set as Default from the pop-up menu. Remember, you must always have the Seiko ColorPoint PS chosen as the default printer before running Quadralay WebWorks Publisher—unless you don't want to convert any color graphics.

Frankly, you will make more efficient graphics if you convert them separately. However, you will get quicker feedback on the final changes you may want to make if you convert them automatically first.

Verifying Conversion Success

Don't let this first translation discourage you. All the links have been correctly interpreted, so it's easy to navigate around the Web publication. More important, the table has been interpreted to near perfection. Figures 7.5 and 7.6 show the table as it appears in FrameMaker 5.0 and as it appears after the default Quadralay WebWorks Publisher conversion to HTML.

Figure 7.5

FrameMaker view of the Ecology table.

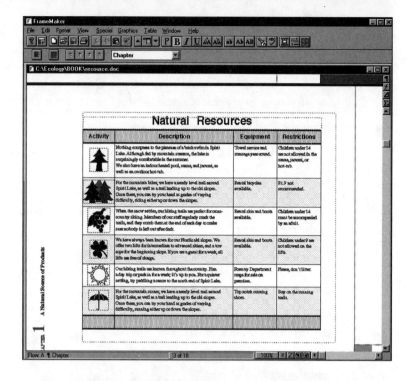

Figure 7.6

Navigator view of the Ecology table.

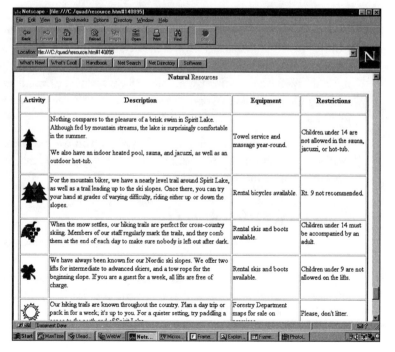

Setting Quadralay WebWorks Publisher's Defaults

If you want the results of the conversion to look more like the original FrameMaker pages, you will need to make several adjustments in the File Set window. If you look at the File Set window (refer to figure 7.1), you will see several buttons surrounding the screen. Each of these buttons controls some aspect of how Quadralay WebWorks Publisher interprets the conversion of your FrameMaker file to HTML. The buttons are as follows:

- Style Sets
- Character Maps
- Options
- Mappings
- External Files
- Conditions
- Macros

The seven sections that follow explain what each of these settings does and the basics of how you're likely (or not likely) to use them. Of course, you can find more detail in the Quadralay WebWorks Publisher manual located on the CD-ROM for this book. It is in HTML format, so you can load it into your browser and read it offline.

> **Note**
>
> After you have chosen the settings, you can apply them to all the files in the list by clicking on the All button. Alternatively, you can apply settings to a single file by selecting one file and then clicking on the Convert button.
>
> You may find a group of settings that work for you most of the time. If so, you can save these settings and use them on any file set. Doing this involves the use of the Style Sets button, described later in this chapter.

Style Sets

Style sets are the mappings that specify how various elements (such as paragraphs and text characters) will be converted to HTML. Each file has its own local style set.

Mapping FrameMaker Styles—The Mappings Button

When you performed Exercise 7.1, the style-mapping options were set to their defaults.

Mapping styles is how Quadralay WebWorks Publisher assigns HTML styles to each of the FrameMaker paragraph styles in a document. You can map any FrameMaker style to any HTML style, but sensible mapping is usually obvious from the style names. For instance, you might map the FrameMaker "Heading 1" style to the HTML "Header 1" tag. Tags with the same style name in both FrameMaker and HTML are automatically assigned to the HTML style of that name. If there's a difference, as in the preceding heading/header example, you must assign a style in the style set assigned to that particular document.

Styles can be assigned to all character, paragraph, and marker tags. A whole group of styles can be assigned to any FrameMaker document or documents. This group of styles is called a style set.

To set styles for any file in the File Set window, follow the steps in Exercise 7.2.

Exercise 7.2

1. In the File Set window, select the file you want to map; then click on the Mappings button.

2. From the Style Mappings pull-down menu, choose Paragraph Styles. Any FrameMaker styles used in the document will appear in the Style Mappings window, as shown in figure 7.7.

3. Use the scroll bar in the main window to find a FrameMaker paragraph style you want to map. Select it. Under the word From, you will see the name of the style you have chosen.

4. In the To drop-down menu, use the scrollbar to read through the list of new style types until you find the one most likely to meet your needs. Select it. The drop-down menu collapses, and the new style is shown in its window. You also see the name of the new style to the right of the old style in the main window.

5. Following the preceding steps, continue naming styles for all the FrameMaker styles you want to change.

Figure 7.7

The Style Set Mappings Dialog window.

Note

The Title style tag actually does two things at once: (1) the Title paragraph is placed in the HTML ‹TITLE› tag, which makes it appear as the title of the browser window, and (2) it is designated as ‹H1›, so it appears in the HTML document in large, bold-faced letters at approximately the same location as in the FrameMaker document.

You can map styles with seemingly endless variation. Start by making mapping assignments that seem logical. View the document in your browser and note those elements you would like to change; then repeat the process in Exercise 7.2 to make any needed changes. The process is so quick and easy, it's almost intuitive.

If you still don't get exactly the results you're after, you can make changes in the FrameMaker document without leaving Quadralay WebWorks Publisher, as follows:

1. Click on the View Document button in the File Sets window. The document will open in FrameMaker.

2. Make any editorial changes you normally would, and then save the document.

3. In the File Sets window, choose Convert to reconvert the file.

4. When conversion is completed, click on View Results.

Style-Mapping Types

It is easier to understand how to map styles if you understand how styles are categorized. The four types of styles—Paragraph, Character, Marker, and Font—are explained next:

- **Paragraph.** These styles correspond to FrameMaker's paragraph styles. They are the first styles you're likely to want to assign. The HTML equivalents to these styles include such tags as Headers H1–H6, Title, Head, Body, and Line and Paragraph Breaks. Any HTML reference, including Chapter 14 of this book, "HTML Tutorial and Reference," can give you a complete listing of these.

- **Character.** These styles affect the appearance of the style of individual letters. Typical character tags are bold, italic, and underline.

- **Marker.** These styles correspond to hyperlinks. You probably don't want to remap markers unless you become an expert at Quadralay WebWorks Publisher's macros.

- **Font.** Fonts can be mapped to either the Generic HTML Character Set or the Symbol Font Character Set. Symbol fonts are especially useful for translating mathematical equations.

The Style Sets Button

The Style Sets button is responsible for assigning and customizing style sets. When you map an HTML style to a FrameMaker tag, you are assigning a Quadralay WebWorks Publisher macro to that tag. You can edit these tags to customize them to your liking.

To modify style sets, click on the Style Sets button in the File Set window. The only style set that comes with WebWorks Publisher is the Generic HTML style set. To create new style sets, click on the New button or the Edit button (to modify the existing style set). The Style Set Designer window appears. A look at this window, shown in figure 7.8, will give you a good idea of the flexibility with which you can configure style sets to convert your documents automatically.

The following table shows the parameters you can set in the Style Set Designer window.

Parameter	Description
Style Groups	A pull-down menu listing all the style group types: Paragraphs, Characters, Markers, New Files, Tables, and Anchored Frames.

Parameter	Description
Style Name	Shows the name of the currently selected name in the open Style Group.
Macro Window	This window shows the actual macro associated with the selected style name. You can edit this macro here just as you would in any text editor. For complete instructions on how to compose and change macros, see the online documentation for Quadralay WebWorks Publisher on the CD-ROM that accompanies this book.
Options Check Boxes	These check boxes appear only for certain style groups, such as Paragraphs. To use these options, simply choose the ones you want to implement.

Figure 7.8

*The WebWorks
Publisher Style Set
Designer window.*

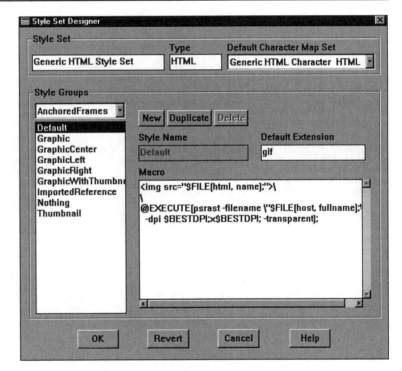

Some style groups have different options windows beyond those previously described. These extra options are rarely used. Of course, there's full documentation on the accompanying CD-ROM if you want to know more.

The Options Button

Choosing the Options button enables you to specify a destination directory for the HTML output of the conversion and to set file-naming options. You can browse for the directory you want to set, specify the file-naming conventions you want to use (one instance where you're less likely to need Rename! as a separate file-name verification utility), and set the check boxes to indicate which file types to save to that directory after conversion. These file types can be New Files, Tables, and Anchored Frames. Figure 7.9 will help you visualize the information in this section.

Figure 7.9

The options window.

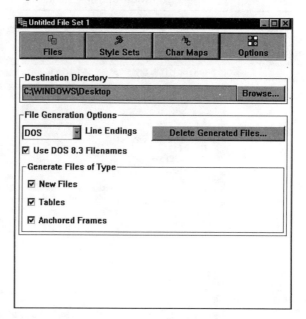

The uses for each of these file types can be found in the table that follows.

File Type	Description
New Files	All files to be translated to HTML tagged text.
Anchored Frames	Any graphics you want converted to GIF or JPEG. The procedure for doing this is in a later section, "Placing Graphics in Anchored Frames."

File Type	Description
Tables	Generates a table as a graphic for pre-HTML 3.0 browsers. This file type is not needed if the HTML 3.0 table tag is used for converting tables.

Note

You may want to set your destination directory options so all old files are deleted each time you create a new conversion. This way, you won't accidentally end up with duplicated files when you experiment with setting these parameters.

The External Files Button

Choosing the External Files button enables you to map each file in the File Set list to a different style set. Figure 7.10 shows the dialog box you see when you click on the External Files button.

Figure 7.10

*The External Files
Dialog window.*

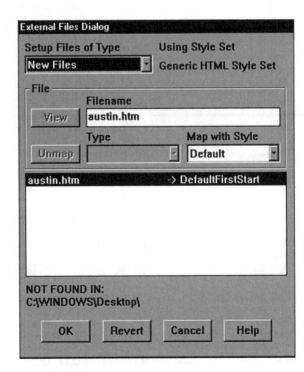

If you don't make any changes in the External Files dialog box, Quadralay WebWorks Publisher automatically maps external files (all the file names in the File Set list are external files) to the defaults shown in the following table.

Default	Description
Default	When there is only one file in a File Set.
DefaultFirstStart	Always the first file in a File Set.
DefaultSingle	All other files in a File Set except the first or last in the list.
DefaultLastEnd	Always the last file in the Set.

File Splitting

You probably want to split your original files into shorter HTML pages. If so, add navigation bars (TOC|Prev|Next|Index) to the top and bottom of the pages. Quadralay WebWorks Publisher will do this for you automatically. To divide files, map the headers at the beginning of each section you want to subdivide to Split Headers (refer to the previous section on mapping FrameMaker styles). The following table illustrates the style mappings appropriate for split files.

Style Mapping	Description
DefaultFirst Start	Always the first file in a file set.
Default	When there is only one file in a file set.
DefaultSingle	All other files in a file set except the first or last in the list.
DefaultFirst	The first file in a split document.
DefaultIntermediate	The middle file in a split document.
DefaultLast	The last file in a split document group.
DefaultLastEnd	Always the last file in the set.

Setting Up and Converting Tables

Quadralay WebWorks Publisher will convert tables to either GIF format or HTML 3.0 (which it does by default). Converting tables to GIFs means the table becomes a graphic. If it's a big table, this means that it's a big graphic and could take some time to load. On the other hand, GIF graphics can be viewed in all browsers.

Taking the default HTML 3.0 table conversion option isn't as "dangerous" as it once was, because most of today's popular browsers (even including the latest from CompuServe and AOL) can read tables. Still, you can't be sure of reaching the widest possible audience, because you can't be sure that they have the most recent browsers.

Following the steps in Exercise 7.3 will enable you to reset the default table interpretation from HTML 3.0 to GIF. This exercise assumes that you have already selected external files to be converted in WebWorks Publisher; the File Sets window is, therefore, open.

Exercise 7.3

1. At the bottom of the File Set window, click on the Ext. Files button.

2. Pull down the Setup Files of Type menu and choose Tables. WebWorks Publisher scans the document for tables, listing those it finds in the list window.

3. Select one of the tables in the box. Pull down the Type menu and choose PostScript.

4. Pull down the Map with Style menu and choose Graphic.

5. Repeat steps 1–4 for each table you want to convert as a graphic.

6. Click on OK. The window will close, and Quadralay WebWorks Publisher will automatically convert the designated tables as GIF graphics during the conversion process.

Converting Graphics

Quadralay WebWorks Publisher will convert all graphics that have been placed in anchored frames. Conversely, graphics that are in floating frames will not be converted.

Warning

If you are working with multi-page files that contain large graphics, you will need more than 16 MB of RAM for Quadralay WebWorks Publisher to convert the graphics. Otherwise, the program converts the document text and perhaps a few of the smaller graphics. This discovery was made just before going to press, which is why you don't see an example of a large, converted graphic.

Placing Graphics in Anchored Frames

If you want graphics to be converted, they must be placed in anchored frames. If you have a document that contains graphics in "floating" frames, follow the procedure in Exercise 7.4 to use FrameMaker to put them in anchored frames.

Exercise 7.4

1. Select the graphic and use the Edit, Cut command to remove it and place it on the Windows clipboard.

2. Make an anchored frame that is attached to the paragraph with which the graphic will be associated. (For more on this, see the section, "Preparing Your FrameMaker Document for HTML," earlier in this chapter, or check the FrameMaker documentation.)

3. Move the cursor inside the anchored frame. From the main menu, choose Edit, Paste. The graphic reappears inside the anchored frame.

4. Use the corner handles that appear around a selected anchored frame to size it appropriately.

Style-Mapping Options for Graphics

There are several ways to map styles for graphics. For instance, there may be certain graphics that you would always want centered on the page with no text flowing on either side, and other graphics that you would want to appear to be part of the surrounding paragraph. In the last instance, you would probably want text to flow around the graphic. The following table gives a reference for the meaning of all the style-mapping options. It also gives an idea of Quadralay WebWorks Publisher's versatility at interpreting graphics for your Web pages.

Style-Mapping Option	Description
Default and Graphic	These styles are the same. Use for PostScript, PICT (Mac only), and PPM types.
Graphic Centered	Same as Default and Graphic, except the graphic will be centered in the browser window. Text will flow above and below the graphic, but not on the sides.
Graphic Left	Graphic on left; text flows on right.

Style-Mapping Option	Description
Graphic Right	Graphic on right; text flows on left.
Graphic w/ Thumbnail	Graphic is displayed as a miniature in the browser, but is linked to a graphic of the original size.
Imported Reference	Used when you select the reference type.
Skip	Leaves graphic unconverted. Graphic won't appear in the browser.
Thumbnail	Generates only a thumbnail with no link and no larger graphic.

Graphics Imported by Reference

One type of graphic has to be handled as a special case by Quadralay WebWorks Publisher. This graphic hasn't actually been made part of a FrameMaker page, but is "imported by reference." In other words, the FrameMaker page displays the graphic by looking up the external file to which it is referenced. Actually, this is nothing new to HTML, where all graphics are displayed by an external reference placed in the IMG tag. For example:

```
<IMG SRC="images\graphic.gif">
```

...where images is the directory and graphic.gif is the name of the external file containing the image.

You will know if images in your FrameMaker document were imported by reference as soon as you open the External Files dialog box. Any graphics in the list that were imported by reference will say so. You can map these graphics to any of the styles in the preceding section. To do so, first select the file name of the graphic imported by reference. Next, pull down the Map with Style menu and select the desired style.

Dealing with User Macros

Quadralay WebWorks Publisher uses a command file called a macro to execute each of the conversions corresponding to a style in the Style Set Designer. Don't worry—this book isn't going to try to train you to become a programmer. Macro files are simply text commands that you can edit just as in any word processor. You will seldom find a need to write a whole macro—just change a word here and there in the text shown in the Style Set Macro text window.

WebWorks Publisher comes with a number of pre-written macros, defined in the table that follows.

Macro	Description
CharMapDir	Names the directory path for the chars (characters) directory. Symbol GIFs are stored here.
NavBar	Specifies the navigation bar graphic. Top, Previous, Next, and Last are the valid buttons.
NavBarEnd	Specifies the graphic for the last navigation bar in a file set—in other words, the last page on the site. Previous and Top are the only valid buttons.
NavBarStart	Specifies the graphic for the first page in a file set. Next and Last are the valid buttons.
NewFileClose	Adds the following information to the bottom of the Web page: e-mail address, copyright, version, and update information.
UserBackground	Specifies the background color for the page.
UserEmail	Specifies an e-mail address to be placed on the last page of the document.

Editing a macro is easy, but it helps to have an HTML reference handy. In the Style Set Designer window, there's a scrolling sub-window entitled "Macro." The actual text of the macro assigned to the style group highlighted in the Style Group window is shown in this Macro window. You can edit anything, just as you could if the same line of text were in Windows Notepad. However, all you're likely to want to edit are the elements that come after signs (=) in a tag. For instance, you could change the background color by changing the hexadecimal number that comes after the background tag.

You can disable macros for individual files in the File Set. To do so, first select the file for which you want to disable the macro. Click on the Macros button. Select the macro you want to disable, and check the box next to "Uses Original." Do any text editing to revise the macro, and click on OK. The macro for that one file is now different than the same macro for all the other files in the set.

The Char(acter) Maps Button

Quadralay WebWorks Publisher enables you to specify character mapping for File Sets. *Character mapping* refers to whether characters will appear as their HTML equivalent, as a graphic, or will use symbol characters. To access the Character Mappings Dialog window, as shown in figure 7.11, click on the Char Maps button in the File Set window. In the next window, click on the Edit button.

Figure 7.11

The Character Mappings Dialog window.

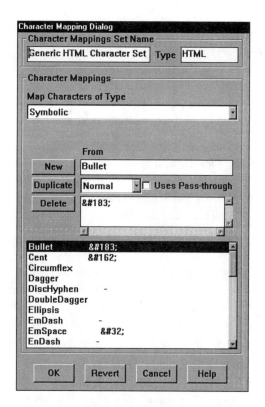

Two character sets are packaged with WebWorks Publisher, Generic and Symbolic. The Generic character set translates standard text into HTML, including such special characters as bullets, cent signs, and em dashes. Such special characters are given their ISO Latin 1 codes so browsers can interpret the HTML code properly. You will seldom want to fiddle with these codes, but should you want to customize them, you can do so by editing the text for the code in the Character Mapping dialog box. This will be especially useful because codes are approved for such characters as ©. At this point, you can simply type in the code alongside the name of the character.

The Symbolic Character Set maps the original symbol characters to HTML or, if there is no HTML equivalent, to a graphic character that will be seen inline with the text.

The Conditions Button

FrameMaker documents can contain something called conditional text. *Conditional text* is actually part of the document that is seen only if certain conditions are met. The condition is met when the reader of the FrameMaker document expresses a preference by pressing a hyperlink button. Thus, if supervisors reading an online maintenance manual want to see the material directed at them, they push the button labeled "Supervisor," rather than buttons labeled "Management" or "Line Worker."

Quadralay WebWorks Publisher can convert these conditions to HTML, thus making it practical to have several versions of a Web publication for different audiences (or those equipped with different browsers).

Harlequin WebMaker

The easy runner-up in the FrameMaker conversion race is Britain's Harlequin WebMaker. This is a substantial company that develops, sells, and supports products for the publications industry. WebMaker is available in same-version form for Windows, Macintosh, and Unix. The retail price is $99, and you can download the program from the Harlequin Web site at the following:

```
http://www.harlequin.com
```

The two reasons for WebWorks Publisher's popularity over WebMaker's are (1) it has a somewhat more inviting interface and (2) it is published by a U.S. company. The Made in USA label may translate to potential buyers as more readily available support, although I have received enthusiastic and prompt support from both companies, and both have local (San Francisco Bay area, at least) offices.

The features of WebMaker versus Quadralay WebWorks Publisher are quite comparable. WebMaker seems to have a slight advantage when it comes to the ease of programming style markers. WebWorks Publisher can convert graphics to both JPEG and GIF formats. WebMaker only converts to GIF.

WebMaker does have some important and unique strengths, however—RapidRules and a Java Applet Navigation Panel. If these sound important to your way of doing things, check into the product more carefully. You can even download your own free evaluation copy and the complete user manual from the Web site listed previously.

RapidRules

RapidRules is a new WebMaker feature that enables you to automate the creation of a conversion template. Even after this template is created, you can still customize the complete conversion process.

RapidRules seems a bit like magic. It scans a FrameMaker document for tag information, and then assigns the styles considered by its artificial intelligence engine to most closely match the look of the original FrameMaker document. If speed is of the essence, RapidRules may make WebMaker the FrameMaker converter for you.

Java Applet Navigation Panel

The Java Applet Navigation Panel is a WebMaker navigation panel programmed in Java. This panel can be placed automatically by WebMaker in context on any HTML Web page. It includes features such as a scrollable table of contents.

Summary

This chapter has given you an overview and some exercises that cover the most widely used options for converting FrameMaker documents for the Web. We concentrate on Quadralay's WebWorks Publisher, because it has been the best-selling FrameMaker converter. We've balanced that with some reasons why you might want to consider Harlequin's WebMaker as an alternative FrameMaker conversion utility.

For Quadralay WebWorks Publisher, the chapter covers the purpose of each of the program's functions separately, as follows:

- Features
- How it works
- Graphics conversion
- Style sets
- Character maps
- Options
- Mappings
- Settings
- Conditions
- Macros

The next chapter, "PageMaker Conversion," examines the available PageMaker programs, teaches you various conversion techniques, and includes tips on how to use a combination of programs to make simple or complex PageMaker documents look great on the Web.

CHAPTER 8

PageMaker Conversion

If you are working with PageMaker documents, you'll find there are few obvious solutions for your conversion needs. Unfortunately, programs for PageMaker conversion aren't as numerous as for QuarkXPress and FrameMaker, and the ones that are available lack many of the useful features described in other chapters in this book. In this chapter, you'll learn what programs are available and how to compensate for their limitations by using other software products.

Adobe showed great foresight when it bundled a plug-in for PageMaker-to-HTML conversion with version 6.0. Unfortunately, this plug-in is so limited and so buggy you shouldn't bother with it unless you are working with a very simple document. In the 6.5 upgrade, Adobe promises to fix the bugs, but it's still not as robust a converter as you'll find for other desktop programs. Because it's about the only option for converting PageMaker to HTML, you will learn how to use it in this chapter, and you will also learn a few other techniques for manual PageMaker conversion.

Because PageMaker-to-HTML conversion is still more tedious than many of the other conversion processes, you should give the Portable Document Format option more consideration here than you might with other programs. PDF files are an alternative to HTML that enable you to create hyperlinked, digital documents from files created for print. PDF conversion is covered in great detail in Chapter 9, "PDF (Portable Document Format) Files." In that chapter, you will learn how portable documents work, how easy they are to create (almost as easy as sending a document to print), and how best to create them. Now that PDF files are supported by Netscape Navigator 3.0, they provide a viable option for displaying information on the Web. If you are on an intranet, you should have greater control of the software your audience is using and may find PDF files even more valuable for putting your PageMaker files online.

If you have to convert your documents into HTML, this chapter will teach you how to get the most out of Adobe's PageMaker conversion program and whether there are other converters on the market worth using (sorry to tell you up front the selection is slim). Most important, this chapter will teach you techniques that will work for you and potential problems to watch out for. It will also include tips on how to use a combination of programs to make simple or complex PageMaker documents look good on the Web.

Evaluating a PageMaker Document Before Conversion

As seen with other desktop publishing programs, many design features you are likely to find in a PageMaker document don't lend themselves easily to HTML conversion. Large, high-resolution graphics, sidebars, and stories that continue from one page to another work well in print, but are not easily replicated on the Web. The first thing you should do when you receive a PageMaker file is study the elements and consider how best to present them in the world of hypertext.

Sidebars, for example, should usually be hyperlinked from the main article to a separate HTML page. Images must be converted to GIF or JPEG and reduced to the smallest possible file size, and continuations must be brought back together in one large HTML document or placed on multiple pages and hyperlinked to one another. For more information on general conversion issues, see Chapter 2, "Design Considerations for the Web."

PageMaker Conversion Options

Before getting into specifics on any of the PageMaker conversion options, take a look at the following list and consider what may work best for you. Each option described here will be explained in greater detail in subsequent sections of this chapter.

1. Use Adobe's HTML Author. This plug-in, which ships with PageMaker 6.0, is extremely limited in its functions and is only suited to very simple conversions. You can, however, use it to convert basic PageMaker files and then use an HTML editor to make your pages more interesting. The program does not convert graphics, so you'll have to do those in another chapter, but it will convert basic text, providing the formatting is simple. That means that all the headlines and text flow all the way across the page (the program can't handle columns), and do not continue on a later page. With some documents, you may find that altering the original PageMaker file to a simpler layout will make it possible to use this conversion program.

2. Copy the content out of each text box and paste it into a word processor, text editor, or HTML editor to perform the HTML markup manually. This may be one of the most obvious options, but not necessarily the most efficient because you will lose all formatting—even basic design features such as bold and italic text.

3. Use one of PageMaker's export options to export the content to text, RTF (Rich Text Format), or any of a number of word processing formats Adobe provides, and then perform the HTML markup manually. This is generally a little better than the copy-and-paste method described in the previous option, as it retains any formatting used in PageMaker and provides some reference for you as you manually insert bold, italic, and other formatting tags.

4. Export the content to a word processing program or RTF, and then use a conversion program that works on that format to automate at least part of the conversion process. In many cases, this is the most efficient option available, especially if you have Microsoft Word, explained in Chapter 3, or other HTML conversion programs for word processors, explained in Chapters 4 and 5. Many of the programs described in these chapters will convert word processing or RTF files and can be used to help automate the PageMaker conversion process.

> **Note**
>
> **Image Conversion**
>
> Unfortunately, none of the PageMaker conversion programs on the market today are sophisticated enough to include image conversion. As a result, the first thing you should do is collect all the images from the PageMaker file and prepare them for conversion separately. Chapter 13 will provide you with many great ways to convert your image files efficiently.

A Case Study: Manual Conversion

The PageMaker file converted in this section is a newsletter designed by a nonprofit agency in San Rafael, California, that was submitted to Vision Communication Technologies. The first thing you'll learn in this chapter is how to use the export features of PageMaker to get the text out of a file in preparation for conversion to HTML. Given the limitations of Adobe's HTML Author, this should be the best option for almost any file you want to convert. Because none of the options available will convert graphics, the images are removed for this example (see Chapter 10, "Graphics Basics," for more information).

The conversion method you'll learn about here is not an ideal solution, but given the limitations, it's the most efficient and practical way to handle files such as this. PageMaker was designed to import content, not export it, but at least Adobe had the foresight to build in a few options for retrieving text from PageMaker. If you are working directly with graphic designers, or are a designer yourself, you may be fortunate enough to have access to the original files. If you have the content in a word processing program already, you may find it more efficient to go back to the original files than to take the text out of PageMaker. However, because many people make edits after importing text into a desktop publishing program, you may still prefer to export the text rather than reconcile any edits that have already been made.

Exporting PageMaker Text

You can always use the copy-and-paste method to get your content out of PageMaker. Simply select the Text tool, select all the text by highlighting the story you want, choose Copy, and then open a word processing program or HTML editor and paste the text into a new page. This is a quick way to get one story or segment of text out of PageMaker, but for larger files, you'll be better off using the Export option. Export has the advantage of preserving basic formatting. When you simply copy and paste, you lose any formatting from the original document. When you export into a program that supports formatting options, such as Microsoft Word, you can preserve the boldface, italics, alignment, and—although they won't do you much good—fonts in the exported document.

Exported Text Options

PageMaker 6.0 provides a range of text-export options enabling you to convert content into the following formats:

- ASCII text
- RTF (Rich Text Format)
- Microsoft Word 3.0 or 4.0
- DCA/RTF (Document Content Architecture) RTF
- MacWrite II
- Tagged text
- WriteNow 2.0 or 3.0
- XyWrite 3

Select the option you find easiest to convert into HTML. Base this decision on the other software available to you and the nature of the formatting in the PageMaker file.

Best Bet Formats

The format into which you export your PageMaker file will make a big difference in the next step to converting it. If you choose a format such as RTF, for example, you'll be able to salvage much of the formatting in the original document and open it in almost any other program. You'll even be able to open it in an HTML editor if you want to do the markup manually.

ASCII text is useful because you can open it in any text editor, but exporting to Microsoft Word, if you have it available, will enable you to take advantage of programs that can convert formatting from Word. Conversion programs such as HTML Transit by Info Access (explained in Chapter 5, "Batch Conversion Utilities") are much more versatile and robust than the built-in PageMaker converter from Adobe. RTF, or the Rich Text Format, is supported by most programs that convert word processing or FrameMaker documents.

> **Note**
>
> If you don't find all the PageMaker export options listed in this chapter, you may need to reinstall PageMaker. If you chose Custom Install when you first installed PageMaker, you may not have selected all the export options as you went through the installation process. During a custom installation from the PageMaker CD-ROM or disks, the export features are optional. At that time, you may not have anticipated needing these features to get content back out of PageMaker.

The Export Process in PageMaker

PageMaker built in the Export feature under the File menu, making this a relatively simple process, as described here:

1. Open the file in PageMaker.

2. Select the Text tool from the Tool palette and highlight all the text in the section you want to extract. This is best done with the Select All option under Edit. (This will only select as much text as you have in linked text boxes.)

3. Choose File, Export. A dialog box will appear.

4. Choose the format you want to export to, such as MS Word or RTF.

Figure 8.1 shows Microsoft Word as the format option; however, you should choose the option that works best for you based on the word processing programs and HTML converters you prefer and have available.

Figure 8.1

Microsoft Word is selected as the Export option.

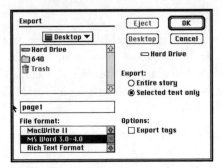

Reducing Export Piecework

Although the Export option is better than the copy-and-paste method, you will still have to export one story at a time (to be more specific, one set of linked text boxes at a time). Most designers put headlines in a separate text box; if this is the case, you will also have to export each headline separately. One workaround for this is to alter the PageMaker document by inserting each headline into the text box of the related story before exporting. Related elements will then stay together in the exported files and save you more copy-and-paste work later. It's always a good idea to save a copy of your original PageMaker document before you start rearranging it. For the conversion, you don't have to worry about what the document looks like in PageMaker as long as related items are in the same text boxes. You may also want to delete continuations and other superfluous features you may not want in the exported file, such as page numbers or continuation references.

Font Problems: Ligatures and Little Boxes

If you export text or copy and paste it, and then open the file in word processors and text editors, you may find some disturbing changes to some characters. For example, certain combined characters known as "ligatures"—such as fi and fl—are sometimes misread by the program and turned into little boxes like this: □

Figure 8.2 shows an example of these irregular characters in SimpleText. What's happening is that the ligatures are not being read properly. If you look at the heading above the highlighted section, you'll notice that this doesn't happen to a capital F. When it does happen, it is incredibly frustrating! Fixing it manually is extremely tedious, and you can't use search and replace because at least two different character combinations turn into the same little box.

To fix this, simply change the font in the exported document, and you should find that the characters return to their more legible form. Another fix to this problem is to use MS Word 6.0.1, which is able to differentiate between these characters in any font.

Figure 8.2

The strange little box phenomenon.

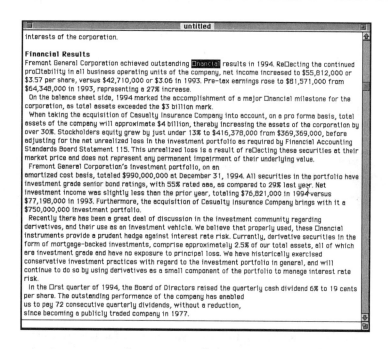

untitled

interests of the corporation.

Financial Results

Fremont General Corporation achieved outstanding ☐nancial results in 1994. Re☐ecting the continued pro☐tability in all business operating units of the company, net income increased to $55,812,000 or $3.57 per share, versus $42,710,000 or $3.06 in 1993. Pre-tax earnings rose to $81,571,000 from $64,348,000 in 1993, representing a 27% increase.

On the balance sheet side, 1994 marked the accomplishment of a major ☐nancial milestone for the corporation, as total assets exceeded the $3 billion mark.

When taking the acquisition of Casualty Insurance Company into account, on a pro forma basis, total assets of the company will approximate $4 billion, thereby increasing the assets of the corporation by over 30%. Stockholders equity grew by just under 13% to $416,378,000 from $369,369,000, before adjusting for the net unrealized loss in the investment portfolio as required by Financial Accounting Standards Board Statement 115. This unrealized loss is a result of re☐ecting these securities at their market price and does not represent any permanent impairment of their underlying value.

Fremont General Corporation's investment portfolio, on an amortized cost basis, totaled $990,000,000 at December 31, 1994. All securities in the portfolio have investment grade senior bond ratings, with 55% rated aaa, as compared to 29% last year. Net investment income was slightly less than the prior year, totaling $76,821,000 in 1994 versus $77,198,000 in 1993. Furthermore, the acquisition of Casualty Insurance Company brings with it a $750,000,000 investment portfolio.

Recently there has been a great deal of discussion in the investment community regarding derivatives, and their use as an investment vehicle. We believe that properly used, these ☐nancial instruments provide a prudent hedge against interest rate risk. Currently, derivative securities in the form of mortgage-backed investments, comprise approximately 2.5% of our total assets, all of which are investment grade and have no exposure to principal loss. We have historically exercised conservative investment practices with regard to the investment portfolio in general, and will continue to do so by using derivatives as a small component of the portfolio to manage interest rate risk.

In the ☐rst quarter of 1994, the Board of Directors raised the quarterly cash dividend 6% to 19 cents per share. The outstanding performance of the company has enabled us to pay 72 consecutive quarterly dividends, without a reduction, since becoming a publicly traded company in 1977.

> **Note**
>
> If you don't have enough RAM to have both PageMaker and MS Word 6.0.1 open at once (they're both memory hogs), remember that you can use the export function without having Microsoft Word open. Simply export all your files from PageMaker, then quit PageMaker and open them in Word later. It's not as convenient as using both programs simultaneously, but if you don't have the RAM, it will work.

Converting the Exported Text

Now that you've exported all the text from your PageMaker file to a word processor, HTML editor, or whatever you chose, you'll want to refer to other chapters in this book to learn how best to take it from here. If you are using Microsoft Word, read Chapter 3, "Microsoft Office Document Conversion." If you are using MS Word on a Macintosh or are using another word processing program, Chapter 4, "ClarisWorks and Corel WordPerfect Suite Document Conversion," and Chapter 5, "Batch Conversion Utilities," will help you. If you exported to RTF, you will find that Chapter 7, "FrameMaker Conversion," covers programs that convert RTF files. Finally, if you've saved as text and want to move directly to working in an HTML editor, Chapter 13, "Tailoring Converted Files," will help you with using these programs.

Organizing Converted PageMaker Files

It's a good idea to export each text section of a PageMaker document into a distinct file and keep the files in one directory so you can manage them easily with other conversion or editing programs. If you're converting a large PageMaker file, you'll need to create many HTML files and then link them together. To help users move between these various files, which now represent individual Web pages, you may want to create a front page. This front page, commonly called an index page and titled index.htm, should have links to each of the separate text documents you exported into separate files. To further aid navigation between pages, consider using other navigational links such as Next Page and Previous Page.

The process of converting documents into HTML may itself create navigational issues. For example, sidebars often require separate pages in an HTML document, so it is useful to link them to both the story that refers to them and the index page.

Graphics Handling in PageMaker

As for all those graphics you've ignored while you were exporting the text, you'll now want to gather them into their own directory and refer to Chapter 10, "Graphics Basics," to turn them into GIFs or JPEGs. Then use an HTML editor to link these image files to specific locations on your Web pages. Chapter 13 will teach you how best to place your images in your HTML pages.

You don't have to remove the images from your PageMaker document to use the conversion techniques in this book, but you may find it less confusing if you can focus only on the text as you go through conversion. If you didn't get the original image files when you got the PageMaker file, one of your only options will be to take a screen capture of the image and then convert the screen capture. This is a less than ideal solution as you will lose image quality, but because graphics on the Web should only be 72 dpi resolution anyway, you may find that the quality is good enough. Whenever possible, get the original image files from the graphic designer—this gives you much greater control over final image quality on the Web.

Adobe's HTML Author Plug-In

If you don't like the idea of exporting your text one story at a time, you may want to try Adobe's HTML Author. For all practical purposes, it is the only option available for automated PageMaker conversion. Unfortunately, it's so limited in its capability to handle complex formatting, you can only use it for very simple PageMaker files. HTML Author is only designed to handle files that are linear—don't use multiple columns or continuations, and don't wrap text around images or other formatting elements. If your document is too complex, you may find that it's worth altering the original PageMaker file so you can use HTML Author.

Limitations of HTML Author

HTML Author is limited primarily because Adobe chose only to provide a subset of the HTML 2.0 standard. If you're still new to HTML or unfamiliar with the differences, you can learn more about this in Chapter 14, "HTML Tutorial and Reference." Although HTML 2.0 is widely supported by browsers on the Web, it provides only the most basic HTML tags. HTML Author doesn't support alignment and can't handle HTML tables, background colors, images, or many other features you're likely to want in your Web pages. (Don't despair—you'll learn how to add these features if you read Chapter 13.)

Adobe's documentation isn't much help, either. Although it does a reasonable job of explaining what you can't do in HTML 2.0, the manual offers no advice about how to work around these limitations. Instead, it suggests making your PageMaker document simple and linear before you even try converting it. In fact, Adobe tells you to design your PageMaker document "with the limitations of HTML in mind." This is not practical advice for most Web designers, who are not the ones who created the document in the first place. Even if you design the file, HTML 2.0 restricts you to such basic design options in PageMaker that you are not likely to want to use the same document for print. (To explain briefly, anything you can't do in a very simple word processor, you can't convert with HTML Author.) Although Adobe suggests it is possible to create a Web page by using PageMaker because you can use HTML Author to convert it to HTML, this is terribly inefficient and not worth your time and effort. If you are starting from scratch, you're much better off using one of the HTML editors described in Chapter 13 than designing a page for the Web in PageMaker.

On the other hand, perhaps what you have is a relatively simple PageMaker document that is still too complex for HTML Author. It may be easy enough to alter the document in PageMaker so you can use the conversion program, thus saving time overall because you don't have to export files one at a time.

Tailoring PageMaker Documents for HTML Author Conversion

The newsletter discussed in the previous section is much too complicated for HTML Author. It has multiple columns of text and stories that continue on subsequent pages—both of which are more than Adobe's conversion program can handle. HTML Author doesn't provide any native image conversion capabilities; however, if you convert the images to GIF or JPEG and then replace them in the PageMaker file, HTML Author will export them with the text. If you want more control over image placement, remove the images from the original document and then insert them in the Web page later by using an HTML editor, such as Adobe's PageMill.

Testing PageMaker Documents for HTML Compatibility

Before you alter the original document, it's not a bad idea to test HTML Author and see what it can and can't handle in the file. To begin, open the document in PageMaker and select HTML Author from the plug-ins list under Utilities in the menu. As you can see in figure 8.3, the first thing HTML Author does is scan your document for "HTML compatibility." You can always cancel this, but at least the first time through it's not a bad idea to see what Author considers "incompatible."

Figure 8.3

Scanning your document for HTML compatibility.

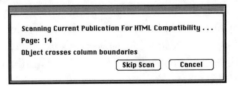

When it's done, HTML Author displays a list of all of the formatting that is "not supported by HTML." Don't panic if it displays a long list, such as the one you see in figure 8.4.

You can expect incompatible elements to be present in all but the simplest PageMaker documents. Keep in mind that anything not possible in HTML 2.0 will be displayed as a potential problem. Also be aware that even though PageMaker's conversion program can't handle these elements very well, Adobe claims you can still use the converter on the file. Unfortunately, the program is quite unstable in PageMaker 6.0. If you try to convert a complex document, it is likely to crash your computer. Complex formatting, according to HTML Author, is just about anything you couldn't do in a simple word processor. You can't use multiple columns of text, you can't wrap words around graphics or other elements, and you can't convert stories that continue on subsequent pages (HTML Author will convert them in their location in the PageMaker file and they will be mixed in with the text on that page, not with the beginning of the file it is linked to).

Take a look at the list of errors to get a sense of formatting issues that may be problematic as you go through conversion. Adobe recommends going back and changing these elements to simpler formatting options before conversion. If you want to use this program, you should follow this suggestion or, as you've just been warned, you're in for a crash. The next logical step in this process is to reformat your file in PageMaker so HTML Author can convert it.

Figure 8.4

Formatting in PageMaker that is not supported by HTML 2.0 will be displayed as an error.

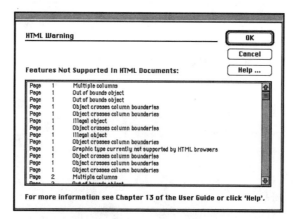

Reformatting a PageMaker File for Conversion

To use HTML Author effectively, you first need to make changes to the PageMaker file. You should always make a copy, so your original file will still be the way it was designed for print. If you are working with a very complex file, HTML Author is probably not worth the effort, and the export options explained earlier in this chapter are a better option. If you are doing a relatively simple conversion such as the one described here, altering the PageMaker file by using HTML Author may be worthwhile.

After studying the incompatibilities list, you should have a good idea of what won't work. You can't leave the text in multiple columns, so reformat all the text boxes to larger boxes that flow all the way across the page and fit the text within them. At the same time, collect any continuations from later pages and move them back into position with the beginning of the story, so each article is in one text box on the same page. (You should also remove all images, as explained earlier.) Moving boxes around like this doesn't take long, because you don't have to worry about how your changes look in PageMaker. Just follow the rules of HTML Author. If there are styles applied in the PageMaker document, you'll want to read about converting styles in step 6 of Exercise 8.1 before you finish your modifications.

To illustrate reformatting a document, take a look at figure 8.5, the original front page of the newsletter that serves as a case study in this chapter. Notice that there are two stories on this page that continue later in the document. There are also three columns across the page and text that wraps around the image box. Fortunately, creating this page took much longer than it will take to reformat and simplify.

Figure 8.5

Multiple columns of text and continuations have to be reformatted.

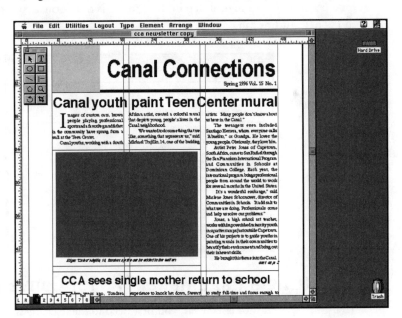

The first step is to add a page to this file after the first page so you can move the second story to its own page. Reducing the page size in PageMaker makes it easier to drag the pieces of the second story to this new page. Once you have cleared space, drag the first column of the main story out so that it fills the entire page. Stretch it all the way around the page and all the continued text will move in to fill the new, enlarged box. At the same time, you should delete any elements on the page that you don't need, removing the text box, image caption, and the continuation line that refers readers to the rest of the story. In figure 8.6, you see that the story now fills the box and the columns have disappeared as the first column is enlarged. Dragging the box down as far as it will go will also collect the end of the story linked to a later page.

Figure 8.6

Drag the text box in the first column across the page until it fills the entire screen.

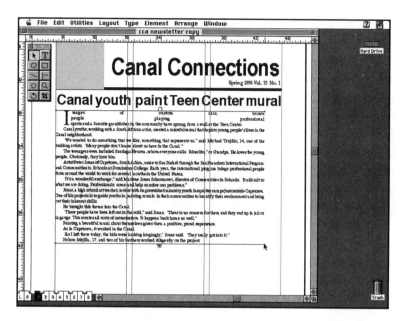

Repeat this step with each story until you have a file that is designed in a very simple, linear fashion. Each headline flows all the way across the page and is immediately followed by the story that goes with it, each story is set to fill the entire page and no longer wraps around multiple columns or images, and there are no images. With a file such as this newsletter, this should be a quick process as you simply delete what you don't need and drag the boxes across the page to get rid of columns and text wraps. Don't worry about what the altered document looks like. It will be completely reformatted using HTML before you're done.

This newsletter had to be reduced to the simplest formatting options in PageMaker before HTML Author would work. If you start with a relatively simple document in PageMaker, such as this newsletter, this may be worth the effort.

Setting Up a Conversion in HTML Author

Now that you have simplified the PageMaker file, you're ready to tackle it with HTML Author. Again, let HTML Author scan your document for "errors" (anything Author considers an HTML incompatibility). After scanning, the HTML Author dialog box automatically opens. You won't want to close this dialog box until you have the entire conversion set up and have converted the document. Otherwise, you'll have to go through the scanning process again.

The following exercise will demonstrate how to set up the PageMaker-to-HTML conversion, using HTML Author (see figure 8.7 for an illustration of the HTML Author dialog box).

Exercise 8.1

1. Choose the Contents tab from the folder-like options in the dialog box.

2. Choose New.

Figure 8.7

To begin a conversion, choose Contents and then choose New.

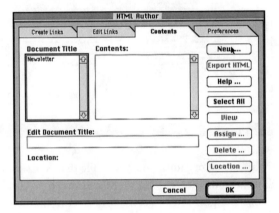

3. In the next dialog box that appears, name the document. The name you provide here is what will be used as the title of the HTML page. Then, from the radio button options, choose PageMaker Pages if you want to designate what will be converted by page, or Stories if you want to designate the elements to be converted by each text in the document. Keep in mind there seems to be a bug in 6.0 that makes the Stories option unpredictable. Choosing Pages is your best option here. Click on Next to move to the next dialog box (see fig. 8.8).

Figure 8.8

Name the document, choose PageMaker Pages, and then choose Next.

4. The next dialog box provides a list of all the pages in the document in a box on the left (see fig. 8.9). Choose Add All to move them to the box on the right, labeled Assigned to Document. This will enable you to convert all the pages as one, the only efficient option in this program. If you are going convert one page or story at a time, you will probably be better off using the Text Export options described in the previous section in this chapter. Selecting all the pages will create one long HTML document, but the program is too buggy to be good for much else. You can cut and paste later to create multiple documents, using an HTML editor.

Figure 8.9

Choose Add All to move the numbered pages to the Assigned to Document box.

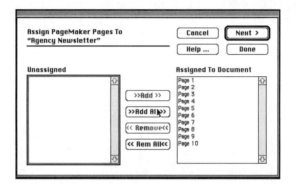

5. In the next dialog box, shown in figure 8.10, name the HTML file (document). In this case, the name shouldn't matter, because you are going to turn this page into multiple files later. To be as efficient as possible here, name this file whatever you plan to call the first HTML file in this series. You then can leave the first story in this file and just cut and paste the subsequent stories into new HTML files. When you are ready to convert the document, check the Export HTML Now box. When you click on OK, HTML Author will convert the file immediately. For now, leave that box blank and click on OK to return to the main HTML Author dialog box to set preferences.

Figure 8.10

Name the HTML document and click on OK.

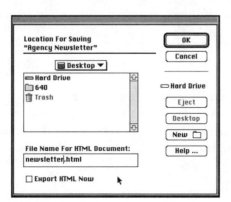

6. When you have returned to the main HTML Author dialog box, select the folder option labeled Preferences. This is where you map HTML Styles to PageMaker styles (see fig. 8.11). There are two limitations you should be aware of before you start. First, you must select the HTML Style option on the left before you select the PageMaker style on the right. Second—and the biggest limitation here—you can only map each HTML Style once. Thus, if you have two different PageMaker styles for headlines and you will want both to be H1 HTML styles, your only option is to change them all to one style as you modify the original PageMaker document. If you didn't do that, go back and do it now. When you have mapped your styles, you are ready to do the conversion. You could now select the Links option in HTML Author to set up hyperlinks in the PageMaker document, but this is tedious, requiring you to close out of HTML Author and return to it for each link, so you are better off setting your links later in an HTML editor. (You'll learn all about setting links in Chapter 13.)

Figure 8.11

In this dialog box, you can map HTML Styles to PageMaker Styles.

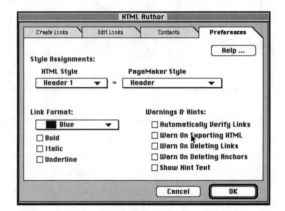

7. Finally, return to the Contents folder option in the main HTML Author dialog box and choose Export HTML. This will export the document to a new HTML file with the name and location you specified in step 5.

If you have followed these instructions carefully and limited your document to only those formatting options supported by HTML Author, you should now have one large HTML file with all your pages and headlines formatted in HTML with paragraph marks, header tags, and the few other options supported by this program. You probably won't be happy with the way this looks in a browser, so you should now go to Chapter 13, "Tailoring Converted Files," and use an HTML editor to turn this file into multiple HTML pages, set links, place your graphics, and add any other, more sophisticated HTML style options you want.

Other PageMaker Conversion Programs

A big hole exists in this area of software that has yet to be addressed by Adobe or any third-party developers. Although HTML Author is very limited, it still seems to be a little better than anything else out there designed for PageMaker. To save you the trouble of searching out these programs for yourself, this section describes the other PageMaker conversion utilities. After carefully reviewing these utilities, we are sorry to report that they are probably not very useful for converting typical PageMaker files. However, because they are all free, you don't have much to lose. Keep your eye out for future versions—they may get better.

WebSucker 2.8

WebSucker 2.8 is a HyperCard stack for the Macintosh, originally designed for the *Clark University Scarlet* student newspaper. The best part about this program is that it's free; however, even at that price, it may not be worth the download time. As the program's creator, Mitchell S. Cohen, readily admits, "This really is a hack. The programming is an absolute mess, really to the point of embarrassment."

Although the 2.8 upgrade is supposed to support PageMaker 6.0 as well as 5.0, it's buggy and even more limited than HTML Author. But again, it is free, so you may want to try it out on your projects and all you have to lose is the download time (the program is about 1.3 MB). WebSucker 2.8 was tested on the same document described earlier in this chapter and couldn't even recognize PageMaker 6.0. You may have better luck if you're using PageMaker 5.0, because the program was originally designed for that version. You can find WebSucker at http://www.iii.net/users/mcohen.html/.

Dave

If you query most online search engines with the words "PageMaker to HTML," the first program that appears on the list is *Dave*, another Macintosh program created for a student newspaper. Unfortunately, Dave's not first on the list because it's one of the best—it's first because it seems to have been the first program ever developed for PageMaker conversion, and it hasn't changed since then. According to the program's creator, Jeff Boulter, the program hasn't been updated since Sept 11, 1995. Boulter recommends WebSucker (described previously) and states that he hopes the upgrade to PageMaker 6.0 will make it unnecessary to improve his program, Dave. If you're still determined to try this program, you can find it at http://www.bucknell.edu/bucknellian/dave/.

pm2html

This is yet another limited HTML converter for PageMaker, but pm2hmtl works on Windows. If you want to try it out, you'll find it at http://www.w3.org/pub/WWW/Tools/PM2html.html/.

Summary

Regretfully, there aren't many viable solutions for converting PageMaker documents, but until Adobe sends out an upgrade to HTML Author, or some third-party company creates a better alternative, you have limited options for converting this desktop publishing program. Exporting to a word processing format or RTF, and then using another conversion program, is your best bet for almost every conversion you'll face in PageMaker.

HTML Author can be used for quick, simple conversions, but you'll definitely want to use an HTML editor to clean up the exported file and add links and graphics. Unfortunately, there are no programs that support image conversion directly from PageMaker.

Overall, use this chapter for the preliminary work in your PageMaker document and then refer to other sections of this book (as noted throughout the chapter) to finish the conversion, convert graphics, and add sophisticated formatting options.

PDF (Portable Document Format) Files

If you just can't get the look, feel, or function you expect from your conventional document by converting it to HTML, there's an alternative. Generically, the alternative is known as a "portable document." First, this chapter will talk about the qualities, pros, and cons of portable documents in general. Then, the focus will turn to "tips and tricks" for using the latest version of the most popular portable document system, Adobe Acrobat 3.0. Finally, there will be a short discussion of the strengths and weaknesses of the two major competitors to Adobe Acrobat: Common Ground and Corel Envoy.

What Are Portable Documents?

Portable documents are documents saved to a format that can be displayed and printed on virtually any type of popular computer system, regardless of operating system, display, or printing capabilities, with fidelity to the original. It is possible to create portable documents from any application that can print. Furthermore, the process of creating a portable document for your existing document (regardless of what application created it) is as easy as printing that document. No coding is ever required for anything you will do in this chapter. Think about this for a minute: whether you want to distribute a multimedia presentation, highly formatted spreadsheet and database data, or illustrated Japanese poems written in both Kanji and English, you can create a portable document.

Publish-Once Portable Documents

The beauty of portable documents is their "publish-once" nature. *Publish-once* means you don't need to re-create your content for each medium of distribution—paper, CD-ROM, computer network, or the Internet. You may, however, want to edit, rearrange, and enhance that content for different media, which you can do in any program that creates portable documents. It is also be possible to create hyperlinks between various sections of the document.

PDFs Are Environmentally Conscious

Converting your company's publication and data content to portable document format is something everyone should do, regardless of whether you ever use a Web site. We now create mountains of paper. Even if that weren't environmentally dangerous, it's unmanageable. We can't easily access the information we store on (way too much) paper. Furthermore, all that paper is expensive. You can put 90,000 pages of paper on one CD-ROM that costs as little as a dollar to duplicate. At four cents a page (dirt cheap for the first copy), it would cost you $3,600 to put the same amount of information on paper.

Here comes the good part: when you have put those 90,000 pages of information in a PDF file (or many PDF files in separate places, as long as they are electronically accessible, as in a network or the Internet), you can instantly find any keyword in that whole 90,000 pages! At least one portable-document-making program, Adobe Acrobat 3.0, enables you to create hyperlinks between any word, graphic element, or page to any other. In other words, most portable documents can be made highly interactive.

Portable Documents and the Web

So far, portable documents have been used on the Web primarily to give remote viewers the means to download and locally print a document that looks the same in Tokyo or Moscow as it did in the Alice, Texas, *Daily Herald* (if there were such a paper). That capability alone is reason enough to include the subject of portable documents in this book. Up until now, however, portable documents have been an extraordinarily poor substitute for Web site content in HTML. Why? First, they were too much trouble to see and navigate through online. Second, the PDF files for publications were much too big to be practical on the Web. File sizes of several megabytes are not unknown.

Even given these limitations, there are at least three good reasons to include portable documents in your Web site, as described in the following list:

- **Forms.** If you want your viewers to fill out a paper form by hand, sign it, and fax or mail it back, portable documents are ideal. Forms are shorter than most other types of documents. Because they're usually only a page or two, they load quickly into a browser. In addition, the small type and ruled lines on most forms don't work very well in HTML markup.

- **Detailed drawings.** Wall-sized organizational charts, blueprints of turbine engine mechanics or circuit board design, and pencil etchings don't show up on the Web in enough detail, but portable documents use vectors and Béziers to describe shapes, rather than dots. If you zoom in to 800 percent, you see finer detail—not chunky pixels. Also, because these files are described in mathematical formulas, the file size is a fraction of that for a comparable size GIF or JPEG bitmap, so the file will load within seconds—not minutes.

● **Presentations.** You can print presentation slides via a PostScript printer driver, then read them into Acrobat, Common Ground, or Envoy and turn the slides into pages in a portable document. Because presentation slides are usually composed mainly of sparse, large text, the files load with much greater efficiency than if the slides were turned into bitmapped graphics and embedded into an HTML document with an image tag.

Portable document technology, as you will see later in this chapter, is improving to the point where it will be practical to consider publishing the full range of documents on the Web as portable documents.

Portable Documents vs. HTML

HTML takes on more sophisticated publishing capabilities with each passing day. It is becoming more and more practical to specify typefaces and styles, to control page layout, and to make more sophisticated use of graphics and graphic design. So are PDF and HTML going to merge? In this author's opinion, no. They will each come closer to doing what a designer intends, but there are fundamental differences that make either PDF or HTML more suited to certain areas of endeavor.

Portable documents are based on a page description language. HTML is based on a markup language. The markup language describes how a variety of browsers and computers will compromise to show data in a fashion that's relatively close to the designer's intent. The emphasis is on *relative* size and positioning of visual elements. A page description language describes every aspect of a page's content (such as specific fonts, leading, spacing, and Pantone colors) with micron-level precision.

If you collect content with "office applications" (word processing, spreadsheets, databases), design it in a desktop publishing program (Quark, PageMaker, FrameMaker), and then convert it to HTML and print to a portable document, you will be close to a "publish-once" solution. What remains is "tailoring" the publication in each medium (paper, HTML, portable document on CD-ROM, portable document presentation, and portable Web document) so it works well in that medium. It's a lot of extra work. It's also a lot *less* work than creating new content and designs for each medium separately.

Leading the push for publish-once processes is Adobe Acrobat 3.0. Web-specific commands and features in Adobe Acrobat 3.0 make it possible to view portable documents from within the browser (currently Netscape Navigator 2+ and MS Internet Explorer), compress portable documents to much smaller file sizes, and load pages individually so even a large document appears almost as quickly as an HTML page. You can speed things up even further by loading text first, then graphics, then multimedia. Multimedia? In a portable document? Yes, and interactive hyperlinks, too. You can point and click to make links between words, pages, or hot spots. You can link to these objects between documents, and you can link to any Web address (URL).

Disadvantages of Portable Documents?

You will have to balance your use of portable documents with your use of HTML. Use portable documents as a supplement and an alternative. Here are some reasons why portable documents won't be taking over the Net:

- Portable documents only work inline for browsers that have a plug-in Reader. Currently, the only portable document format with an inline plug-in is Acrobat 3.0. All the others use helper applications that call up the Reader application in a separate window after the entire file has downloaded.

- Some popular browsers may not have access to either a plug-in or a helper app. Viewers using such browsers won't have access to the portable documents on your site.

- Portable documents don't load or print as quickly as Web documents (although Acrobat 3.0 is much faster than earlier versions).

- Several portable document formats are available, each with different features.

- Viewers must be willing to install the Reader. Although Readers are freely downloadable and distributable, people aren't always willing to take the time to acquire and install them. Give them an incentive. The best incentive is to provide a portable document so valuable viewers will be compelled to download the Reader. This could be the entry form for a contest, an income tax form…or whatever your creative imagination can come up with. From then on, the Reader will be available, regardless of where the next compatible portable document is found.

- The audience has to be trained to use the Reader. One way to lower this audience barrier would be to put an interactive Reader lesson on your Web site.

PDF (Portable Document Format) Files

> **Note**
>
> As this chapter was being written, Adobe announced Acrobat Exchange 3.0 for Internet Explorer 3.0. This would indicate that *Acrobat 3.0 files are now compatible with Microsoft Internet Explorer 3.0, as well as Netscape Navigator 3.0.*

Requirements for Creating Portable Documents

Creating portable documents is as easy as printing, but much cheaper. You don't need a printer and you don't need paper. When you install the software (for example, Acrobat Exchange, Common Ground, or Envoy), you have installed a printer driver. If that printer driver is installed in a graphical operating system such as Mac OS or Windows (any flavor), an application running under that operating system can create a portable document. Select the software as the active printer, execute the command to print, and check the option to Print to a File. The resulting file is a portable document—simple as that. Of course, there will be options (quite a few in the case of Acrobat 3.0) for how and to what degree to compress such elements as text, line drawings, monochrome bitmaps, and color bitmaps. You will also be asked whether you want to embed fonts, which makes file sizes larger, but ensures that specific fonts will be shown and not "substituted" by the destination computer system. There are also ways to create portable documents from documents that have already been printed. For instance, Acrobat 3.0 includes an application called Distiller, which is discussed in more detail later in this chapter.

Using Adobe Acrobat 3.0

This chapter focuses on the capabilities of Adobe Acrobat 3.0 for several reasons. For one thing, Adobe is the leading manufacturer of software that contributes to both page and Web design.

Photoshop, Illustrator, PageMaker, FrameMaker, Page/SiteMill, and the PostScript page description language are all Adobe products. It's unlikely that even Macromedia's site has Web pages that don't contain at least some content originated from an Adobe product. This is not said to promote Adobe. The point is, they have the power; therefore, they're the company most likely to win the battle of who sets the portable document standards.

In addition, Adobe has been around longer than the competition and has sold far more copies of Acrobat. A copy of Acrobat Reader and several PDF documents are on the CD-ROM of every product Adobe makes—and even accompanies a number of other software publishers' products.

Acrobat's integration with the Web is also far better than the competition's. Version 3.0 enables you to actually embed a PDF page in an HTML page with the use of the <EMBED> tag. When the browser comes to the tag, the first PDF page is loaded. Clicking on that page loads the inline Acrobat Reader, but only if there are multiple pages. The <EMBED> tag can also use WIDTH and HEIGHT to scale the page, so you can insert a technical drawing and then use the browser's scroll bars to scroll around it.

What Acrobat 3.0 Can Do for Your Web Site

In addition to all the benefits of portable documents cited at the beginning of this chapter, Acrobat 3.0 has numerous enhancements especially useful to Web site developers.

PDF-Browser Compatibility

Viewing portable documents (Adobe calls them PDF documents—for Portable Document Format) no longer takes place in an external helper app window. Instead, the document appears right inside your browser and occupies the same space as an HTML page. The Acrobat (either Reader or Exchange—depending on which you've installed) toolbar even appears just below the Navigator or Explorer toolbar.

Speed Loading with PDF

It's startling how much faster PDF pages load from the Web, provided, that is, those pages have been "Web-optimized" for Acrobat 3.0. Optimization specifically for the Internet is now built into Exchange 3.0. Most important, pages and objects are reordered for page-on-demand access. In other words, your browser need only load one page before you are able to see the file. Another benefit of the new Web optimization is the compression of files to a significantly higher level, because duplicate text, line art, and images are combined and referenced from a single location. Pages now load much faster because of something Adobe calls "progressive rendering," meaning that now, as in HTML, text loads first, followed by hyperlinks, then images, and then multimedia. Thus the viewer is likely to see informational content first. Add up all the effects of Web-optimization, and viewing PDF files on the Web becomes nearly as quick as viewing HTML pages. For more detail on the process of optimizing Adobe PDF files, see the section entitled "Optimizing (Byteserving) PDF Files for the Web," later in this chapter.

> **Note**
>
> Unfortunately, not all PDF files on the Web are optimized by 3.0. It is reasonable to expect competition for viewership to change that over time. Existing files are likely to catch up in a hurry with the new Batch Optimize capability, which makes it quick and easy to optimize all the old files on a site. You can even choose to delete or create thumbnails during the process, so you can add navigational finesse to the site in the process.

Relative Link Support

Another terrific enhancement in 3.0 is improved linking. You can now link anything in a PDF document to anything else in that or any other PDF document or to any HTML document—provided those documents reside on the same computer, network, or Inter/intranet. You could do some of this in earlier versions, but because relative links went unrecognized, the capability wasn't implemented much. Relative links now work, a major boon to the publish-once process. A single collection of hypertext-linked files can be published simultaneously on local drives, network drives, CD-ROM, or a Web server. All the links will work automatically on all those devices.

Advantages of the PDF Writer

Acrobat 3.0 sports a much improved printer driver (PDF Writer). The improvements fall into several categories. First, some applications get a new File menu selection called PDF Writer, so you don't have to change printers in order to create a PDF document. Next, compression options include ZIP compression, which can make smaller, faster-loading Web files. You can create subsets of the fonts within the document, and fewer fonts mean significantly smaller file sizes (keep this in mind when you're designing the document). Page size setup is more flexible, so it's easier to fit pages to video displays. Finally, PDF Writer automatically downsamples (resizes) color images to 72 dpi. Mysteriously, monochrome images stay at 300 dpi, but there's a hidden advantage, because you can zoom in on a monochrome image to several degrees of magnification before it starts falling apart. Color calibration is also improved. For more information on the PDF Writer, please see the section titled, "PDF Writer," later in this chapter.

PDF (Portable Document Format) Files

The Acrobat 3.0 Products

The number of products that make up the Acrobat Suite has narrowed with the Acrobat 3.0 release. Several products that used to be sold separately, such as Distiller and Capture, are now included in Acrobat Exchange. The following sections provide more detailed information on the features of Acrobat 3.0 products.

Acrobat Exchange

Acrobat Exchange 3.0 incorporates the features of what were formerly four separate products, some of which have been combined under the same interface. It still helps to think of these products as the four main functional areas of Acrobat authoring: PDF Writer, Editor, Distiller, and Capture.

PDF Writer

The PDF Writer is a printer driver that enables you to print a document from any application to a PDF file. When you install Acrobat Exchange 3.0, PDF Writer is automatically installed as a printer device in the operating system, along with any others that might be there. You can choose PDF Writer as the printer from any application that uses the operating system's printer driver. Once that's done, simply executing your application's print command from its File menu will produce a PDF file more "Web-optimized" than earlier versions. For instance, TrueType fonts are supported across platforms, and page-at-a-time and text-first loading are automatically implemented (see the section called "Optimizing (Byteserving) PDF Files for the Web"). By selecting Printer Options in the Print dialog box, other Web-optimization choices can be made, such as graphics-compression options and embedding fonts or leaving them to the destination Reader for interpretation. Embedding fonts results in larger file sizes, but leads to more accurate page reproduction. For more on font embedding, see the section titled, "Font Embedding: When Is It Appropriate?"

Exchange Editor

The Exchange Editor is used to fine tune PDF documents, once they've been created by PDF Writer, and has some very important hypermedia authoring functions, as follows:

- You can create forms with real typesetting specifications and can add HTML-like features such as radio buttons and pop-up lists.

- You can add interactivity to existing documents. The capability to hyperlink to text, pages, images, and URLs has already been mentioned. You can also import graphics for navigation buttons and link them in all the ways you can link other elements. It doesn't stop there, either. You can even create *controls* for multimedia elements that trigger sound, QuickTime movies, or AVI (Windows only) movies you've imported into any PDF file.

- You can create a keyword index so the Reader's Search Tool can find any word in the PDF document or any linked PDF document. This is done with the use of the Acrobat Catalog utility, which is included with Acrobat 3.0. Unfortunately, Catalog can't yet create a searchable keyword index that can be used on the Web, although Adobe states their intention to make this a reality in an upcoming version. At present, Catalog creates a separate index file that can't be embedded in an HTML document. There are, however, external utilities capable of creating a Web-readable index. The details of how to do this are too complex for inclusion here, however. For more information, contact Verity Software at the following:

```
http://www.verity.com
```

PDF (Portable
Document Format) Files

- Search companies, such as Yahoo, can find content within a PDF page just as easily as within an HTML document.

- Annotation (Lotus Notes).

- OLE.

- Capability to highlight text.

- Built-in capability to insert URL links.

- Image compression.

- Font embedding, capability to use TrueType fonts.

- Thumbnail editing. You can create, re-position, or delete the document navigation thumbnails.

- Color handling. PDF Writer automatically adds device-independent color information to the PDF file. PDF Writer can then automatically determine color calibration for either Macs (using Color Synch) or Windows.

Distiller

Distiller is a more sophisticated way to convert a document to a PDF file. It converts any EPS file into PDF format. Distiller can be used for drawings, illustrations, and maps, and for complex publications that contain all these. To use it, either print a file to disk by using a PostScript printer driver or print through Distiller Assistant. You can define your own default page size that will be used if your PostScript file doesn't explicitly specify a page size. Image compression can be set to either JPEG or LZW. LZW is lossless, but makes bigger file sizes better suited to print and CD-ROM distribution. You can also specify the exact resolution to which images of all types will be downsampled (re-sized for 72 dpi resolution) and whether downsampling is to be faster or more accurate. For more on Distiller, see the section entitled "Creating PDF Files with Distiller."

Capture

Acrobat Capture is no longer a plug-in, but a built-in feature of Acrobat Exchange 3.0. Capture will automatically convert any scanned document to PDF. Character, font, and page layout are automatically recognized and formatted. Capture works with TWAIN or ISIS-compatible scanners. It can also recognize documents in English, French, German, Italian, Dutch, Swedish, or Spanish and format them accordingly. Because no OCR (Optical Character Recognition) software is error-free, Capture's newfound line-at-a-time editing capability is a godsend . Numerous third-party plug-ins are available for Capture that make it even more accurate.

Catalog

Catalog is now a built-in feature of Exchange. At a single command, Catalog indexes every keyword in a document and stores this keyword index in a separate file, thus providing full high-speed text-search capabilities for PDF documents. However, these searches don't work on the Web in Acrobat version 3.0.

Interactive Features

You can also insert multimedia controls that execute menu items, help you navigate, or play movies or sounds. Supported movie formats are QuickTime (Mac and Windows) and AVI (Windows only). AIFF is the only cross-platform sound-file type supported. Check out Appendix C for further references on handling sound files within Web pages. A serious omission is the capability to play MIDI files. MIDI files are very small because they consist solely of text instructions to a music synthesizer. A file small enough to load instantly can play several minutes of background music or sound effects.

Unlike movies, which must be stored externally, sound files are stored with the PDF document and can be played on any computer system that supports sound.

Forms

User entry forms are new to Acrobat 3.0. A form created in a graphics or page-layout program for use in a publication, when shown on the Web or used in an electronic publication (such as a CD-ROM), can be made to let the user fill in multi- or single-line text fields, combo boxes, list boxes, radio buttons, and check boxes. Users can also print these forms. Acrobat also makes it possible to define what happens when the mouse button is clicked or released or the cursor is moved into a particular area on-screen.

The Acrobat Reader

The Acrobat Reader 3.0 is free. As mentioned previously, it comes with just about every new Adobe product (provided it was published since version 3.0 was released). Of course, it comes with Adobe Exchange as well. If you create PDF documents with Exchange (or any other way), you can freely distribute Reader 3.0 with them. If you (or your audience) still don't have Acrobat Reader 3.0, you can download it from http://www.adobe.com.

When you install Reader 3.0, the plug-in is automatically installed in Netscape Navigator if it's already running on your system. There's a separate version of the Reader for Microsoft Internet Explorer. It would be better to have a universal Reader that worked in all Netscape-compatible browsers, but that will have to wait.

If you have Acrobat Exchange installed on your system and are running Netscape Navigator 2.0+, you don't need to install the Reader. Exchange runs directly within your browser. Internet Explorer presently needs the Reader installed separately.

Acrobat Reader has three modes of viewing: Page, Table-of-Contents, and Thumbnail, as follows:

- In Page view, you see the main window filled with the page.

- In Table-of-Contents view, the window is split into two frames, with the narrow frame on the left listing key areas of content.

- In Thumbnail view, the left column contains miniature pictures of each page in the PDF.

When you use Reader as a Netscape or Explorer plug-in, the toolbar shows up within the browser window and is dockable (meaning that you can move the toolbar to any side of the browser window). You get continuous scrolling (once several pages of the document have loaded), and you can ask for a two-page (side-by-side) view.

In Reader, you can search for anything by clicking on the Binocular icon. A Magnifier tool lets you zoom in and out, up to 800 percent. In Acrobat Reader 3.0, text is antialiased (edge-smoothed) for smoother on-screen viewing, Reader lets you navigate transparently between HTML and PDF files.

Acrobat Web Presenter

Web Presenter is a stand-alone application based on Adobe Persuasion. Like Persuasion (I mean that operationally, too), Web Presenter makes "slide" presentations of the style that has become traditional for office-suite products such as Microsoft PowerPoint, Corel Presentations, and Lotus Freelance, and stand-alone presentation programs such as Persuasion and Harvard Graphics. Speaking of Adobe Persuasion, Web Presenter's capabilities have just been built directly into the latest version.

The advantage to Web Presenter is that you can produce a presentation very much as you would in any presentation program. You can even include the kinds of slide transitions, graphics, and multimedia that can be created in Persuasion or PowerPoint. You can also insert drawings, photos, movies, and sound from other applications with drag-and-drop ease. When you're done, simply print the presentation to a Web-optimized PDF (Adobe Portable Document Format) file. You then have the advantage of being able to play that program on any Netscape plug-in-compatible browser. Web Presenter's presentation controls include 19 different transitions and options to control what happens at the click of a mouse or the release of a mouse button (see fig. 9.1).

Figure 9.1

The Adobe Web Presenter user interface.

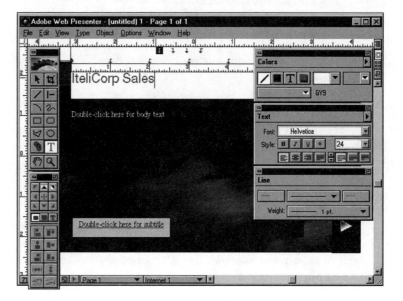

Creating PDF Files with Acrobat 3.0

Following are some practical ways to use Acrobat 3.0's new features for efficient conversion of your existing documents for your Web site. Three products can create PDF files from your existing documents—PDF Writer, Distiller, and Capture—and all three are extremely easy to use. These will be covered in the sections that follow.

Get Your File Names Web-Ready

The first thing you want to do is make sure the names of all the files you are going to convert for Web use have names that can be recognized by your server. While Apple and Unix servers will recognize more complex file names, the safest route is to give your files MS-DOS legal names. Then they can be read by any computer system anywhere.

MS-DOS file names can have eight characters and a three-character extension. The characters should be all uppercase (although DOS itself is not case-sensitive).

While you're renaming files, you might as well organize them into folders (directories) with the same names and hierarchy you will use when storing them on your Web site. Then when you add links later and send the files to your site, the links will stay valid. Acrobat 3.0 recognizes relative links. See the section entitled "Relative Link Support" for more information.

Creating PDF Files with PDF Writer

PDF Writer is the easy way to go if your documents already exist in electronic format and the software that created them is installed on your computer. All you have to do is print them. The following exercise describes how this is accomplished.

Exercise 9.1

1. Open the application that created your document. This can be any application from Photoshop to QuarkXPress, as long as it has a printer driver. Then open your document.

2. From the Main menu, choose File, Print. The Print dialog box appears. From the Name drop-down menu, choose Acrobat PDF Writer. *Do not* check the Print to File box. Click on OK. (Macintosh users will need to change printers in the Chooser. If PDF Writer is installed, it will appear among the printer selection icons.)

PDF (Portable Document Format) Files

3. Choose the Properties button. The PDF Writer on Disk dialog box opens, as shown in figure 9.2. Choose the Compression button. The Compress Text and Graphics dialog box opens. Check Compress Text and Graphics. In the Color/Grayscale Images box, check Compress Using and choose JPEG Low from the pull-down menu. In the Monochrome Images box, check Compress Using and choose CCIT Group 4. Click on OK.

Figure 9.2

The Printer Options dialog box for PDF Writer.

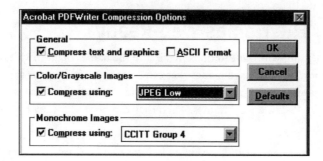

4. Choose the Fonts button in the PDF Writer on Disk dialog box. The Acrobat PDF Writer Font Embedding dialog box opens. A list of all available fonts opens. Highlight the fonts you want to be sure to embed. If you want typesetting to be completely accurate, choose all the fonts in your document. If you want to save as much file space as possible and don't mind if the browser substitutes its own fonts, don't choose any. When you're done, click on OK.

5. In the PDF Writer on Disk dialog box, choose SCREEN from the Resolution drop-down menu. Click on OK.

6. In the Print dialog box, click on OK. The Save PDF File As dialog box opens. Navigate to the folder you have created for storing this file. Click on OK. You don't need to rename the file because you've already made sure it is DOS legal.

Note

Macintosh users: PDF Writer is not compatible with QuickDraw GX. You have to turn off one or the other. Fonts that are QuickDraw GX-specific can't be used in those documents, either.

Once you've printed to a PDF, there's the business of adding links and other enhancements. You can link to sounds, link to other Web pages, link to other places in the PDF pages, and even add "mail to" options.

For a more complete discussion on linking, see the section on creating object links later in this chapter.

Creating PDF Files with Distiller

When should you use Distiller instead of PDF? Use Distiller when you have lots of graphics and fonts. Distiller reduces embedded fonts by about 40 percent over PDF Writer and does a far better job of resampling detailed drawings.

If you have the PostScript files of your documents, but not the files native to the application that created them, you can still create PDF files with Distiller. Distiller is also a good choice if you want even more control over compression and Web optimization. Distiller offers more compression control when files contain EPS artwork or super-high resolution bitmaps (such as the photos in a high-end annual report).

If you have the original document file and the application that created it, but would rather use Distiller instead of PDF Writer to create the PDF file (because you want ultimate compression control), the following exercise shows how to make the file.

PDF (Portable
Document Format) Files

Exercise 9.2

1. Macintosh: From the Apple menu, choose Chooser. Make sure AppleTalk is active and choose any PostScript printer. (You're going to save the file to disk, so you don't actually need to own the printer. The Apple LaserWriter is always available.) See figure 9.3 for a detailed view of the Add Printer Wizard for PostScript Printer selection.

Figure 9.3

The Add Printer Wizard.

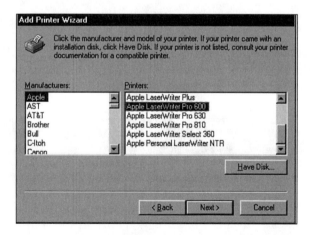

2. Windows: From the Start menu, choose Settings, Printers. If you have already configured a PostScript printer, choose it and click on OK. If you don't own a PostScript printer, choose Add Printer. Pick the Apple LaserWriter as the printer and Print to File as the port.

3. Choose File, Print. From the Print dialog box, choose Apple LaserWriter (or any other PS printer you have pre-set to print to a file). If your printer hasn't already been set to print to a file, check the Print to File box. Make sure the other settings and properties are appropriate for your document (just as if you were printing to paper). Click on OK.

4. The Print to File dialog box appears. Navigate to the folder where you want to save the file, name it (be sure to add a .PS extension), and click on OK.

The following exercise details how to use Distiller to make a PDF file. You would want to create a PDF file from Distiller, rather than PDF Writer, for the following reasons: (1) If you didn't create the document, but have access to a PostScript file version of the document in question. (2) If you elected to use Distiller instead of PDF Writer in order to exercise greater control over font embedding and graphics conversion.

Exercise 9.3

1. To start Acrobat Distiller, choose its icon. From the Main menu, choose Distiller, Job Options. Make any changes needed to the Job Options dialog box; however, the defaults work well for converting to the Web. When finished, click on OK.

2. From the Main menu, choose File, Open. In the File Open dialog box, choose any file with a .PS or .EPS extension. For a file to open, it must have been named according to the DOS 8.3 convention (see fig. 9.4). Also, you may have to change the extension saved by the printer driver from .PRN to .PS, because Distiller will only read files with a .PS or .EPS extension

Figure 9.4

The Distiller File Open dialog box.

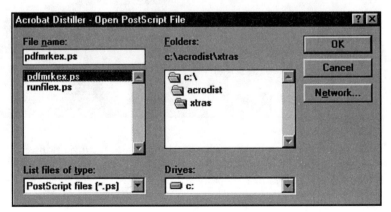

Font Embedding: When Is It Appropriate?

Font embedding is always appropriate. Distiller and PDF Writer give you the option to use substitute fonts, to use the fonts resident on the computer reading the font, or to embed fonts in the documents themselves. Because your documents are going to be read on the Web by users who have a variety of systems, embedding fonts is the only way to ensure that they will see what you posted.

The process of embedding fonts varies, depending on the platform you are using (Windows or Mac), the document you are creating, and the program you are using (PDF Writer or Distiller). Embedded fonts are usually set as the default. If not, the process is fairly intuitive and simple, and the Acrobat Exchange and Distiller manuals are clear on the subject.

TrueType fonts can be embedded, but there are some "gotchas." First, it's not a good idea to use them for Web documents because only the platform that created them will be able to interpret them as they were. If a Mac reads a document created in Windows, it will substitute fonts—even though it may have the same TT fonts in its system. Also, TrueType fonts can be embedded only when working with the PDF Writer—not in the Distiller.

Reducing PDF File Sizes

Keeping the data sizes of files as small as possible is the key to acceptable loading times for Web pages. If you've come this far in this book, that's probably no surprise to you. It's re-stated here because the "smaller is better" rule is no different for PDF files than for any other Web file type. Following is a list of hints for optimizing PDF file size. These hints apply to saving files into PDF format whether you are saving from PDF Writer or from Distiller.

1. Use the Save As command instead of Save. Save As deletes all unused pages from the document.

2. Don't use the ASCII format option. Use the default 8-bit binary option. ASCII files, in addition to being bigger, are more easily corrupted.

3. Pay attention to compression options for text and graphics. If the documents are intended primarily for Web distribution, use the highest level of compression.

4. Use Distiller instead of PDF Writer whenever possible. Distiller has more options for compressing specific kinds of graphics, including the capability to compress monochrome images (corporate logos, line drawings, blueprints) in a lossless format that is also very efficient. In addition, Distiller can automatically convert CMYK graphics to RGB.

PDF (Portable Document Format) Files

5. Convert CMYK graphics to RGB. RGB uses only three channels, not four; therefore, files are 25 percent smaller.

6. Downsize images to Web resolutions. Some PostScript printers operate at resolutions as high as 2400 dpi. Most Web graphics are viewed at 72 dpi. There can easily be a difference of several megabytes in file size. No one wants to wait to transfer such files over the Web. Even over a T1-connected intranet, it's a major waste of bandwidth.

7. Use as few fonts as possible. The more fonts you embed, the larger the file size will become.

Embedding PDF Files in an HTML Page

Typically, a PDF file takes over the entire browser window; however, you can have it load into a window within the HTML page if you like. You can also load a PDF file into a frame, but that's a subject for later discussion. See the subsection titled "Framed PDF Files" for more information.

To place a PDF file inside an HTML file, use a tag called <EMBED>. This is the same tag that enables you to insert any kind of plug-in document into a page, such as Shockwave or QuickTime.

At the moment, you can embed only one PDF file per HTML page. This may have changed by the time you read this. Because clicking on an embedded PDF file at the browser end expands it to fill the browser window, you can't use an embedded PDF file as a link. Embedding a PDF file also kills any of the PDF file's hyperlinks.

The <EMBED> tag creates a window of a size you specify and places a PDF file within that window. The <EMBED> tag has three switches (attributes), as follows:

- Src= "filename" is the name of the PDF file you want to embed. Make sure quotation marks enclose the file name.
- Width=XXX is the width of the embed window, measured in pixels.
- Height=### is the height of the embed window, measured in pixels.

If the window's width and height are different from the size of the page you are embedding, the browser will resize the original page to fit the window. This works best when you give the window and the file image the same proportions. If you're using Photoshop, you can get these measurements quickly; otherwise the browser will distort the page to make it fit the dimensions called for by the tag. The best idea, if you want to embed a file such as a drawing into an HTML page, is to make the page the right size in the first place, and then leave out the dimension tags altogether. The browser will simply load the file at its actual size.

Optimizing (Byteserving) PDF Files for the Web

Byteserving (Adobespeak for Web-optimizing) allows partial transfers of complex or lengthy documents. The following list illustrates what happens when a PDF file has been so optimized. The list assumes that the user's browser is configured with the Adobe 3.0 plug-in (now available for both Netscape Navigator 3.0 and Microsoft Internet Explorer 3.0).

1. A browser encounters a byteserved PDF file and automatically launches the 3.0 Reader plug-in.

2. The first component the server sends back to the Reader is an index of the PDF document. The Acrobat Reader uses this index to send a request back to the server for just those parts of the file needed for displaying that page. This process is invisible to the user and nearly instantaneous.

3. The byteserver script has no paging information yet and begins to deliver the whole PDF file to the user.

4. The Acrobat Reader, on the user's end, starts processing the file as it is transferred. As soon as the Reader has enough information, it builds the very first page.

5. If the person looking at the page just sits there and doesn't do anything, the server transfers the rest of the file to the Reader. If, on the other hand, the user selects an item on the first page or moves to another page, the transfer stops, and Acrobat sends a byte request to the server, starting the upon-request serving process.

Serving PDF Pages on the Web

To serve PDF one page at a time, you need the following three things:

1. Byteserving on your server.

2. Optimized PDF files. There are three ways that PDF files are optimized: (a) Any document printed from PDF Writer 3.0 will be automatically optimized.

(b) Legacy (pre-Acrobat 3.0) documents can be read into Exchange or Distiller, and then optimized from a single command on the File menu. (c) You may also use a single command on the File menu of either Exchange or Distiller to batch optimize several legacy files in one operation.

3. A link in your HTML document that calls a byteserved document.

CGI Scripts and PDF Pages

For Web-optimized pages to work, you have to place a CGI script on your server. The script is downloadable from Adobe's site and doesn't have to be written. Just send it to the Web administrator for your server or provider and have them load it into their CGI directory—that's all there is to it. By the way, the chances are good the script is already there—make a call and find out. If the CGI script is not on your computer or you just want to find out more about it, you can check the Adobe site at the following URL:

```
http://www.adobe.com/acrobat/3beta/byteserve.html
```

Byteserving technology is being incorporated into some of the new Web server technology from Netscape, but it's not here yet. Until then, use the CGI script previously described.

Configuring Your Server for PDF Files

Two common Web servers you may need to configure for PDF delivery are the NCSA HTTPD and the CERN HTTPD servers. You or your system administrator may need to make the changes described in the following text.

For HCSA HTTPD servers, check the file conf/mime.types and make sure it contains the following:

```
entry: application/pdf          pdf
```

For CERN HTTPD servers, check the file CONFIG and make sure it contains the following entry:

```
AddType      .pdf    application/pdf      8bit          1
```

The list of servers supporting Acrobat is growing daily. For the most up-to-date list, check the Adobe site at the following:

```
http://www.adobe.com/acrobat/acroweb.html#serve
```

Once you have your MIME (Multimedia Internet Mail Exchange—the map your browser uses to know which viewer to load when it encounters an embedded file) types set, you can deliver PDF just like any other files on the Web. You may also want to link to the free Adobe Acrobat Reader software for those people visiting your Web site who may not have it.

Writing a Link for Byteserved PDF Files

An ordinary link to a non-byteserved PDF document would look like this:

```
http://www.yoursite.com/subdir/pdf/document.pdf
```

To make this link work for byteserving, just squeeze the link into the appropriate place in the URL, as follows:

```
http://www.yoursite.com/cgi-bin/byteserver/subdir/pdf/document.pdf
```

Enhancing PDF Files for the Web

Once you have a PDF file, you can do several things to make your documents easier to read and navigate when they're seen in the context of the World Wide Web. These include creating links, combining PDF documents with other documents, using Article Flow, setting the default zoom level, cropping pages, and adding bookmarks and thumbnails.

Creating Object Links

You can create links between any word, graphic, or page in a PDF file to any other word, graphic, or page anywhere else in the file or, for that matter, anywhere in any other PDF file that's stored in the same folder. By using the same methods, you can also link to any URL; however, you must include the full URL. Relative addresses for URLs don't work in Acrobat 3.0 PDFs.

Because you can link between graphics, you can create graphic navigation buttons and add them to any document. Figure 9.5 shows the dialog box that appears when you press Exchange's Link tool icon.

Figure 9.5

*The Weblink Edit URL
dialog box.*

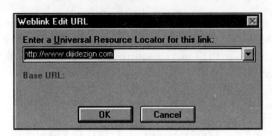

Activating a link is easy. The following steps demonstrate how to create a link to another part of the document.

Exercise 9.4

1. Choose the Link tool (the one that looks like chain links) in the Acrobat Exchange toolbar. The cursor becomes a crosshair.

2. Drag a rectangle around the item (text phrase or graphic) you want to make active. The Create Links dialog box appears.

3. Choose Go to View from the Action drop-down menu.

4. In the Magnification box, choose the magnification level you'd like to see at the link's destination (your viewers will be able to change this magnification to their own liking, but you want to start them out at the level that is likely to be most attractive or informative). Which level that is will depend on the page design. You want the viewer to see as much of the page as possible (that helps in orienting the user as to the page's contents), but you also want the page's body text to be of a readable size.

5. With the dialog box still active, navigate to the destination for your link and click on it. Back in the Create Link dialog box, click on Set Link.

Note

This procedure is slightly different on the Mac. As done previously, draw the rectangle around the text or image you want to link, adjust the settings as in step 4, and then click on Set Link. The cursor then becomes a hand, and you have to navigate to the place in the document you want to link, and then click. The hand does a little "grabbing" thing, and then the link is set.

If you want to create a link to a specific article, to another document, or to an URL, simply choose one of those actions instead of Go To View in the Action box. You will be prompted to enter any additional necessary information, such as the URL address.

Linking Documents

Linking documents varies only slightly (with little more difficulty) from linking objects within the same document. Follow the steps in Exercise 9.4 until it's time to make a choice in the Action pull-down menu. Choose Open File. In the File dialog box, choose the Select File button. The Select File to Open browser opens (it is exactly like any other File Open dialog box). Navigate to the document you want to link to and double-click on it. That's it.

If you want to, you can create a button in the linked-to PDF that takes you back to the original document. Just import a pre-made button (there are instructions for making buttons in Chapter 11, "Graphics Creation") and make it a link by following the instructions in Exercise 9.4.

Mapping PDF Files with Bookmarks

Bookmarks view is yet another way of navigating through PDF documents (whether on the Web or not). If you select the second icon from the left in the Exchange (or Reader) toolbar, you'll be in Bookmarks view. *Bookmarks*—words and phrases you have marked, as explained later in this section—appear in a "table of contents" in the left frame of the Acrobat Reader/Exchange Window (see fig. 9.6). Page numbers become superfluous because clicking on a bookmark takes you directly to that page— or to a view of that page preselected for that bookmark. In other words, you can have a bookmark for a zoomed-in view of a graphic, a sidebar, or even a footnote that would be too hard to read at normal size.

Bookmarks can also jump to other documents. To do so, follow these steps:

1. Initiate a new bookmark.

2. Edit its properties.

3. Edit Destination.

4. Open the page to be linked and click on OK.

Figure 9.6

Acrobat's navigational bookmarks.

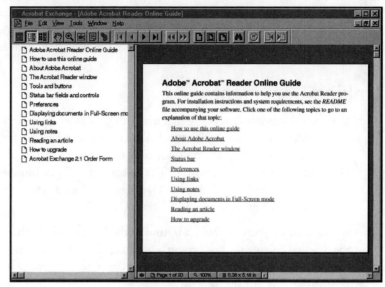

Remember, bookmarks, thumbnails, and links can always be set to jump to other sections of the same document, to another document, or to an URL. Which type of jump is determined by the Action Type pull-down in the Create Link dialog box or in the Properties dialog boxes for bookmarks and thumbnails.

Making bookmarks is even easier than any of the other exercises you've read about (or done) so far. You can make a bookmark from any text on a page, typically a subject heading, a section title, or a sidebar title. To make a bookmark, choose the Highlight Text tool, highlight the text you want to make into a bookmark, and press Ctrl+B. The name of the bookmark will appear in the Bookmark Frame. The name will be highlighted, so if you want to change the name, just type over it. That's all it takes.

Finally, you can control the view in which the viewer will see the page when the bookmark is selected. To do this, set the view to Fixed, Fit View, Fit Page, Fit Width, Fit Height, Fit Visible, or Inherit Zoom. Inherit Zoom means when the bookmark is clicked, the bookmarked item will appear at the zoom level you were using when it was bookmarked.

Combining or Extracting Documents

There will be plenty of times when you'll find it more appropriate to give a Web viewer several reference pages culled from multiple documents. As time goes by, you'll probably learn that putting too much information on a Web site is a waste of everyone's resources, as your audience simply won't take the time to make use of it. Thus the capability to combine and extract PDF documents may be more useful than it at first seems.

If you combine or extract documents already made interactive (perhaps for other purposes), the links are all retained. Usually, this is a good thing; however, you may want to change some to fit the context of the new collection.

Combining documents simply gathers collections of documents so they can be navigated with internal links and so they can be found or printed at a single address or bookmark. Extracting documents is useful if you want to keep individual documents to a size more manageable on the Web.

Article Flow: Making Documents Easier to Read on the Web

In conventional documents, articles often start on one page and continue on a later page. Or, they jump from the center of a column on the left to the top of a column on the right. Although the Acrobat Reader provides a Hand tool that enables you to drag the viewing window around the page, Article Flow makes it much easier for viewers to move through your content by letting them jump instantly to the place where the text resumes.

Article Flow is even more useful than it first appears. Even if you have your article in a continuum, it probably spans columns and pages. It might also be broken up by large spans of white space. Article Flow lets you draw sequential boxes to indicate the sequence of the article. When the reader clicks on the Hand tool, the text is automatically zoomed to fit the window width. Each click of the Hand pointer drops you to the next screen full of text—regardless of where that might be. Because you're zoomed in, the text is much easier to read on-screen.

Creating Article Flow is almost too easy for words. The following exercise will show you how.

Exercise 9.5

1. Open the PDF document to which you want to add Article Flow. From the Main menu, choose Tools, Article. The cursor changes to a Corner Frame.

2. Navigate to the beginning of the article and drag a frame around just the text you want the reader to see on-screen.

3. Move to the place where you want the reader to continue; then repeat steps 1 and 2.

4. Continue drawing frames until you reach the end of the article. At that point, double-click inside the frame (in Windows, you can also press the right mouse button). The Article Properties dialog box appears (see fig. 9.7).

Figure 9.7

The Article Properties dialog box.

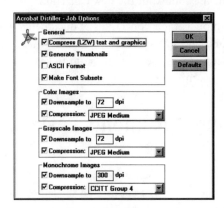

5. Fill in the information for the article (optional), and then click on OK.

Cropping Pages

White space is often used to emphasize the words and pictures on a printed page by isolating them. This technique would probably be just as effective on the Web, except text and graphics are liable to be teensy and hard to read. The easy solution is page cropping: throw out what you don't need and can't use. It's just good housekeeping.

Cropping pages also makes file sizes smaller. By now, you should know how important small file sizes are to good Web engineering. Cropping pages is easy, maybe even easier than Article Flow.

From the Main menu, choose Edit, Page, Crop. The Crop Pages dialog box appears, as shown in figure 9.8. You can adjust the page margins by pressing the margin arrows that surround the Margin Box, but it's much easier to just type them. Click on the radio button for All or Range of Pages to be cropped. If you want to crop several pages in a row the same way, choose the From radio button and type in the numbers of the first and last pages you want to include. Then click on OK.

Figure 9.8

*The Crop Pages
dialog box.*

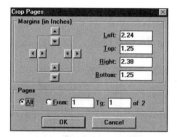

Displaying PDF Files as Thumbnails

Another way to navigate through PDF documents is Thumbnails view. To see Thumbnails view, choose the third tool icon from the left in the toolbar.

Thumbnails are miniature representations of PDF pages. Thumbnails can be used for more than just navigation. They can also be used for moving, copying, deleting, and replacing pages in one or more Acrobat documents. For instance, to move the sequence in which a page appears, drag its thumbnail to a new position between two other pages. Want to insert a page from another document? Open the other document and drag the thumbnail of the page you want to move to the Thumbnail column of the document you want to move it into.

Thumbnails also enable you to adjust the view of a page according to where the Hand tool moves the cropping box (see fig. 9.9).

Creating PDF Thumbnails

To make thumbnails, just Choose Edit, Thumbnails, Create All. You can place thumbnails for other documents in the thumbnail view of the document you're working on.

Copying PDF Thumbnails

To copy thumbnails from one document to another, split the screen so you can see both documents (Window, Tile Vertically). Put both documents in Thumbnail view (choose the Thumbnail icon in the toolbar), and then drag the thumbnail of a page from one document to the Thumbnail view in the other document.

Sequencing PDF Thumbnails

You can change the sequence of thumbnails, just by dragging pages. This also changes the sequence of pages in the document. You can also change the sequence of bookmarks by dragging their page icons, but the page to which they refer stays in place.

Figure 9.9

A thumbnail view.

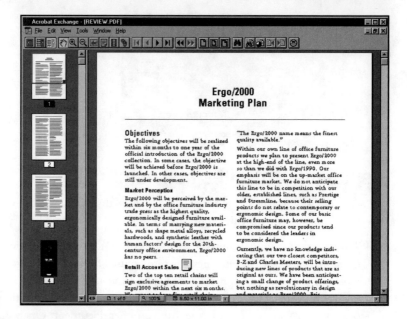

Acrobat Presentations

In addition to their usefulness for displaying pages on the Web as they would appear in print, PDF files are also useful for presentations. Presentations have a range of uses, including employee training on intranets and Internet sales pitches.

Creating Acrobat Presentations

There are two ways to make Acrobat Player viewable presentations:

- **Acrobat Exchange's built-in presentation capabilities.** The built-in presentation tool provides an easy way to turn existing print documents into presentations. It also makes it easier to link a presentation to a "standard" PDF document.

- **Adobe Web Presenter.** The Web Presenter works with Acrobat Distiller to create a PDF presentation directly from any presentation program that can print to a PostScript printer. You can drag-and-drop Web links from the Netscape Navigator 3.0 or Microsoft Internet Explorer 3.0+ browser to any part of the presentation. You can also drag-and-drop files directly from Photoshop, Illustrator, QuickTime movies, EPS graphics, and TIFF images.

In either case, creating a presentation as a PDF file has the advantage of creating a presentation that will look equally good over the Internet, over an intranet, or on disk—no matter what platform you play it on. This means you can make one presentation, once, and use it for meetings, hand-outs, or remote presentation.

Warning

Keeping the Number of Plug-Ins to a Minimum

Limit yourself to plug-ins that do more than one thing. For instance, there are numerous plug-ins that will play presentations from specific presentation packages. A better solution is to use the Acrobat Reader to play presentations created in just about any presentation program. Refer to the initial section on Web Presenter as a product of Adobe Acrobat 3.0.

Retooling Documents as Acrobat Presentations

You can also make your print documents more readable on the Web by turning them into presentations. Instead of using a presentation program to do this, use Acrobat Exchange—the capability is built in.

Making presentations enables you to simplify documents in the following ways:

- Cuts them down to essential information.

- Focuses on illustrations, charts, and sidebars.

- Formats content so scrolling isn't required (or is required less often).

If you plan to cull the highlights of existing documents for use in a presentation, a list of suggested procedures is presented in the following exercise.

PDF (Portable Document Format) Files

Exercise 9.6

1. Make a copy of the original, non-PDF document. It is this copy you are going to chop into smaller pieces, so don't risk losing information by using the original.

2. Edit out all material you will not keep in the presentation.

3. Use the Originating application to edit the document down to presentation-size pages with a horizontal aspect. To do this, change the page size to the size of a typical Web-browser's viewing window (8.2×4.2 @ 72 dpi). (If you want to use the same techniques for making presentations that will be printed on overheads, use standard letter size.) From the Main menu, choose File, Page Setup. Click on

the Landscape radio button. From the Page Setup dialog box, pull down the page size list and choose Custom. Type **8.2** in the first size box and **4.2** in the second. Click on OK.

4. Print the file to the PDF driver. Choose File, Print. From the Print dialog box, pull down the Name menu and choose Acrobat PDF Writer. Click on OK. The Save PDF File As dialog box appears. Navigate to the folder where you want to save the file, name it, and click on OK.

5. Open Acrobat Exchange. Edit the text so it looks good in the new layout.

6. Set the characteristics of the presentation. Choose Edit, Preferences, Full Screen. Set the parameters in the Change Pages box. Choose a Background Color. Then click on OK. Save the presentation under a new name, such as present.pdf.

7. This presentation can be linked to any point in another PDF file. Simply follow the steps in Exercise 9.4.

8. Presentations can also contain internal links, as described in the section on creating object links.

Framed PDF Files

Do you want to do something really cutting edge? How about creating a hybrid HTML/PDF Web interface? If you know how to work with frames, no problem. If not, here are some hints.

Actually, this isn't just a cheap trick—it's a very useful one. You can create an index to both types of documents in one frame and use the other to display the actual PDF pages. You can even have three frames: one for the directory, one for a PDF file, and one for an HTML file.

There are no special tricks to making PDF files appear in frames. Just put the PDF file name after the FRAME SRC attribute, as follows:

```
<frame src="mypage.pdf" name="my page" marginwidth="n"
  marginheight="n">
```

Also, when you want links in one frame to cause documents to appear in another frame, be sure to use the <BASE> tag in the original document. This keeps the contents of that document's frame from changing when you click on a link. You also need the switch called target= to tell the browser which frame should change when you click on a link. The tag is a simple one:

```
<base target=targetframe>
```

Other Portable Document Makers

There are two other portable document systems with sizeable followings: Corel Envoy and Common Ground. Neither is as promising for Web purposes as Adobe Acrobat, however. There are several reasons for this, the main one being that Adobe has used their marketing prowess to make Acrobat the de facto standard portable document system. This position is reinforced by the fact that no browser has a built-in plug-in for either Envoy or Common Ground. Plug-ins are available for both, but you will see their documents displayed in an external window.

Tumbleweed Software's Envoy

Envoy is a Macintosh and Windows portable document publishing system. Envoy has become well known largely because of its having been bundled with Novell WordPerfect Office. Corel has since purchased WorldPerfect from Novell, and it was unclear at publication time whether Envoy would be included with Macintosh versions of Corel's WordPerfect. Meanwhile, the program was independently developed by Tumbleweed Software, which also sells it as an independent product.

Like the Acrobat system, Envoy makes it possible to produce portable documents through a special printer driver or to batch convert existing documents. Like Acrobat, Envoy makes it possible to incorporate multimedia content and to employ hyperlinks. Also like Acrobat, Envoy can be used to create portable presentations. It also has an advantage over Acrobat in that the player is automatically implanted into the portable document, which is saved to disk as an executable file at conversion time. What this means is that you can read any Envoy document by simply double-clicking its icon. Because the player is in the document, you needn't worry about distribution.

The embedded player won't work on the Web, however, unless you have the required Netscape Navigator or Microsoft Internet Explorer plug-in. These are downloadable from the Tumbleweed Web site at the following URL:

```
http://www.tumbleweed.com/viewer.htm
```

Envoy has a significant competitive disadvantage against Acrobat 3.0 in terms of its usefulness as a means of distributing conventional documents on the Web. Envoy documents are not yet "Web optimized" to compete with Acrobat 3.0 "byteserving" technology.

Common Ground

Unlike Acrobat and Envoy, Common Ground's documents must be created in Windows. Two versions of the Common Ground Viewer also exist: a MiniViewer and the ProViewer. Either can be incorporated into a document file and distributed as an executable, much like Envoy. However, only the MiniViewer is freely distributable, but only the ProViewer supports Common Ground's more advanced features.

Common Ground's advanced features include many that are standard in Acrobat and Envoy. The most significant of these are bookmarks, panning and zooming, text search within a document, and hyperlinks. The ProViewer also does things its competition doesn't. For instance, you can convert the portable document back into some conventional formats.

At press time, there were no plug-ins or helper apps for viewing Common Ground documents on the Web. You can, of course, place a link to a Common Ground document for downloading over the Web.

For the latest developments in Common Ground, the Web site is at the following:

```
http://www.commonground.com
```

When You Should Use HTML Instead of PDF

Most Web content, at least for the time being, is better presented in HTML. Even when compared to optimized Acrobat 3.0, plain text pages load considerably faster. Web surfers will also feel more at home with the "look and feel" of HTML pages. Navigation is a bit faster, too. Use portable documents judiciously, but know that the choice is there when you need it.

The Bottom Line: Portable Documents vs. HTML

As you have no doubt surmised from reading this chapter, portable documents have some very attractive advantages in Web conversion and publishing. To summarize, here is a list of those qualities:

- Conventional documents are easy to convert. Just open them in their native application, choose your portable document writer as the printer, and print.

- You don't need a special authoring tool. Any application that can print will do.

- Different Web browsers and platforms won't affect the appearance of the document. The formatting, layout, and typesetting of your original will remain exactly as they were designed—unless you change them.

- Most portable documents support scalable vector graphics. If images are vector-based, files will be much smaller than HTML files that contain numerous or large bitmapped illustrations.

- Portable documents are nearly indespensible for sites that need to distribute a document that is faithful to the original, such as diagrams, tax and legal forms, or technical illustrations.

Hopefully, this chapter has given you enough information on when and how to employ PDF files on the Web to maximize the efficiency of information distribution in an online medium.

PDF (Portable
Document Format) Files

CHAPTER 10

Graphics Basics

Most of this book is about using automated tools, such as WebMaker, to convert your business documents for use on the Web. These programs may or may not do everything you have to do to translate all your content. They vary greatly as to how (or even whether) they deal with the graphics that were part of the data you converted to HTML.

Perhaps you are using a program that includes automating the conversion of embedded graphics files. BeyondPress, for example, is capable of automatically converting graphics to GIF89a or (progressive) JPEG, and even enables you to specify color reduction and resize the image. So it may seem the conversion program does all your graphics work for you. In fact, there is much you can do to optimize the look and performance of graphics, even after the page conversion programs have done their job.

Remember, few conversion programs give you as many options for converting graphics as BeyondPress. In fact, some don't give you any! However, even with the automated conversion capabilities of BeyondPress, you may be able to fine tune your graphics to both look better and speed the display of all the elements on your page. To do that, you have to know how to make graphics load as quickly as possible while preserving all the needed color and tonal range. Often, these steps will be different for each and every image.

If your converter doesn't totally automate the "webifying" of embedded pictures, don't think you've wasted your money. Many sites require massive amounts of information to be posted to them every day. Automation is the fastest route for getting your information up there, but reading this chapter will help you understand the settings to choose when your program asks how you want to handle graphics.

More importantly, this chapter can help you better understand the nature of Web graphics in the interest of your comprehension of where and how you might fine tune their performance for your Web site.

Why Your Web Pages Need Graphics

If you want your pages to hold the viewers' attention while they're on your site, you must use graphics. This is true even if there isn't a single picture on the printed page you're converting. Why? The current rules of the Web make the text on Web pages far duller than the typical printed page.

The browsers used by 95+ percent of Web surfers allow only two typefaces: monospaced Courier (typewriter) and a variable-spaced font (typically Times Roman). Furthermore, by using graphics, it is possible to do much to control the layout of text, headlines, pictures, and other content elements.

> **Note**
>
> It may soon be commonly possible to specify real typographical fonts on the World Wide Web. Microsoft and Adobe have jointly announced a new font standard called OpenType that incorporates both Adobe PostScript Type 1 and Microsoft TrueType standards. The two software makers will make the OpenType specification available to other operating system and Internet-based vendors. Naturally, OpenType will first appear in Microsoft products, but the idea is to set a standard that's freely available to all. Microsoft's Internet Explorer 3.0 already permits typefaces other than Times. If you'd like to see a site that displays a different font, use Microsoft Internet Explorer 3.0 as your browser and go to http://www.microsoft.com. If you don't have Microsoft Internet Explorer 3.0, you can download it for free from this URL. Netscape has announced support for OpenType in Navigator 3.0b5+.

If you want to design your pages for most browsers, using graphics is how you can control the typeface that is displayed on your users' screen. Otherwise, the reader's browser makes the choice. Graphics can also lend color and texture to your backgrounds, give emphasis to important points, make logical divisions for your content, call attention to advertising on your site (which could make a big difference in your company's bottom line), and (as they say in the biz) much, much more. To put it more tersely, adding graphics to your Web pages is the easiest way to make readers glad they found you—at least as long as the graphics load quickly and look good. The following two figures demonstrate the difference between a Web page with graphics and one without graphics.

Figure 10.1

A Web page without graphics text.

Figure 10.2

*A Web page using
graphics text.*

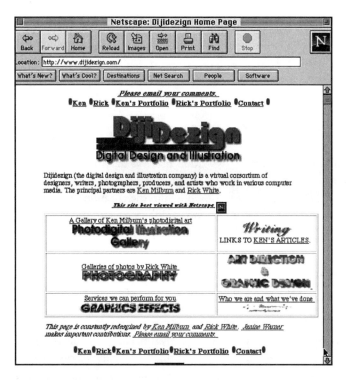

Dealing with Pictures

You've been through all the chapters that precede this one. You know how to take your existing documents from their native desktop publishing, word-processing, or office-suite applications and turn them into pages that will look good on the Internet's World Wide Web. Depending on the route you took to get here, you may or may not already have pictures on those Web pages. If you don't have pictures, you need to know how to transfer the graphics files used by your original illustrations into one of the two graphics file formats that are universally displayable on the World Wide Web—GIF (Graphics Interchange Format) and JPEG (Joint Photographic Experts Group). Before you make that transfer, you need to decide which graphics are best suited to GIF and which to JPEG. If you do have pictures embedded in your Web pages, it's because they've already been converted to one of these formats. A new graphics format just making its way onto the Web is PNG (pronounced PING). The PNG format is rich enough in features to deserve more discussion later in this chapter.

Whether your graphics have been converted or not, there are many tricks you can employ to make your graphics as Web-attractive as possible. You can also add other graphics and multimedia to make your Web pages even more appealing. Most importantly, you'll need to know the tricks for making various kinds of graphics files as small as possible. The smaller a graphic's file size, the more quickly it displays on the Web.

Nothing is more off-putting to your reader than slow-loading pages. The reader will simply go to another site where the action is. If keeping the viewer's attention is important to the goals of your Web site, this chapter and Chapter 11, "Graphics Creation," are the most important chapters in this book.

Bitmaps vs. Vector Graphics

Unless your vocation or avocation involves making or using pictures, you may not know the difference between a vector graphic and a bitmapped graphic. Vector graphics, by the way, are also known in the computer world as drawings, illllustrations, fonts, and CAD files. Bitmapped graphics are also called raster graphics and are known in computer-slang as paintings, photos, and scans.

About Bitmaps

The GIF and JPEG files that are now the standard Web picture formats are bitmapped graphics. Bitmaps are so called because the picture is made by coloring each pixel (picture element, or dot) individually. Imagine a mosaic table top. Each tile is in a particular place and is a particular color. Make the picture bigger and you still have the same number and size of tiles—they're just spread farther apart. This is why bitmapped images get rough looking (often called jaggy, blocky, or pixelated) when you zoom in on them. You can't make the picture dimensionally smaller without losing quality, either. Think about it: the only way to make the picture smaller is to throw away pixels (tiles, in our mosaic metaphor). The result is less definition in the image. Even worse, the computer doesn't know which pixels are most important to the shapes in the image. It throws out as many tiles in a pattern as necessary to achieve the target size.

The other problem with bitmaps is file size. Because pictures are made up of individual pixels, it is necessary to store several bits of data (8 bits-per-pixel for 16-million color) for each pixel in the picture. So, to make file sizes small enough for pictures to load into a Web page within a reasonable time, it becomes necessary to make as many compromises in image quality as possible in order to minimize both the number of pixels in the image (color palette reduction) and the amount of data used to describe each pixel (compression).

Note

A third bitmapped file format, designed especially for network graphics, is PNG (pronounced *ping*). PNG is a new format meant to be a patent-free replacement for GIF, but the format is not yet widely readable by browsers. It is, however, part of the HTML 3.2 specification—so you can expect it to be viewable in most widely used browsers by Q1 '97.

About Vector Graphics

Vector graphics are "resolution-independent." This technical term simply means that no matter how big or small you make the image—and no matter how many times you make it bigger or smaller—the image will always be reproduced at the maximum definition allowed by the device on which it is displayed. Furthermore, it is possible to create a highly detailed advertising illustration on a computer with marginal screen definition and very little memory, and then have that image reproduced with smooth lines and fills as a freeway billboard.

How is this possible? Vector images are stored as mathematical (more precisely, geometrical) formulae. Each shape in the image is a complete formula, known as an object. Because objects are self-contained entities, it is easy for the computer to specify changes to that object and to its relationship with other objects in the image. These changes will never have any effect on the quality of other objects in the image. The other important quality of vector images that result from their being stored as formulae is small file sizes. Remember, it makes no difference whether a circle will represent something as small as a microbe or as big as the Earth. All the information it takes to describe the shape, color, line thicknesses, and other geometrical components can likely be stored in the same space as a paragraph of text.

Why We Need Vector Graphics on the Web

The lack of an accepted vector file format is a puzzling omission by the W3 committee, but one we must live with (at least for now). Here are some of the things a vector-graphics standard file format would enable us to do:

- Load a full-page, full-color image in as little time as it takes to load an HTML page.

- Zoom-in to view any detail in the image with perfect resolution.

- Load a complex animation over a 28.8 modem and see it play instantly in place on the HTML page.

- Create interactive buttons within the drawing that contain either HTML links or cause the graphic to be displayed differently (or cause a different graphic to be displayed).

One of the best places to see all this in action on the Web is FutureWave Software's site, as follows:

```
http://www.futurewave.com
```

Graphics Basics

Employing Vector Graphics Now

There are already many ways to use and enjoy vector graphics on the Web. Unfortunately, because no standard has been set, this is a practical matter only for browsers that accept Netscape-compatible plug-ins. The built-in plug-ins in Netscape Navigator 3.0 include Shockwave (for Freehand), QuickTime (as PICT files), and Acrobat 3.0 (see Chapter 9, "PDF (Portable Document Format) Files"); all are capable of displaying vector graphics in some way. The problems with this approach are as follows:

- No built-in plug-in allows for all.

- Not all browsers are plug-in compatible.

- Many people don't want to take the time to download and install a plug-in. This situation is improving with routines that auto-download and install plug-ins when you encounter a file type for which you lack the plug-in. FutureWave's FutureSplash plug-in can work this way, even in Netscape Navigator. FutureWave makes this work by using a Java script routine that presumably could be written for any plug-in.

Graphics File Formats on the Web: When and How to Use Them

Choosing which graphics file format to use on a Web site used to be easier because there were half as many choices as you have today. The GIF format was the only format widely accepted. The demand for photographic-quality color has caused the JPEG format to be nearly as widely accepted. So now the question is: which format is best under what circumstances?

GIF

GIF (Graphics Interchange Format) is the file format to use when a graphic has the following characteristics:

- Composed of geometric shapes filled with flat colors.

- Originated with 256 colors or less.

- Small in size (fits within a 150-pixel square).

- Irregularly shaped (think of a triangular traffic sign).

- Intended as an animation not dependent on programming or special browser enhancements.

GIF is the Web's most useful and most widely used graphics file format. It comes in two flavors, GIF87a and GIF89a. For static, rectangular pictures, both flavors are fully compatible with all graphical Web browsers. In fact, the specifications for a rectangular still image are the same for both formats. All GIF files are restricted to 256 or fewer colors. They are compressed at an average ratio of about 3:1 over a noncompressed image of the same size and number of colors. GIF is better for storing images that consist mainly of flat tones because its compression technology works best on patterns made by adjacent areas of solid colors.

GIF89a

The original GIF format, 87a, was restricted to rectangular, static images. People also wanted a way to make images appear more quickly so as to spare viewers having to stare at empty place holders. GIF89a, the more recent standard, overcomes these limitations by adding three enhancements:

1. The capability to recognize a single designated color as transparent. Transparency makes it possible to create irregularly shaped graphics such as vignettes, buttons, and icons.

2. The capability to store and display multiple discrete images in the same file. This makes it possible to create auto-playing "flipbook" animations and miniature slide shows.

3. The capability to interlace images. Interlacing enables the image to load in several stages of resolution. It creates the illusion that graphics (and, therefore, whole pages) load more quickly and gives the reader a chance to see a "fuzzy" recognizable image quickly enough to know whether to wait or move on.

Saving Files as GIF

Saving your files to GIF format is easy, provided it is already in a bitmapped (also known as "raster") form. Open any image editor (such as Photoshop, Painter, PhotoPaint, or Windows Paint) and open the original file. From the Main Menu, choose File, Save As. When the File Save dialog box appears, open the drop-down list of file types and choose GIF or CompuServe GIF.

Only a few image editors are capable of saving files in GIF89a format (but the list is growing daily), and nearly none are capable of saving GIF89a animations. Photoshop 3.0.5 has an Export plug-in for GIF89a that enables you to preview color reductions, choose transparent colors by several methods, and activate interlacing. There are also numerous utilities (mentioned in the appropriate sections of this chapter) that enable you to create transparent and interlaced GIF89a files or GIF animations.

If you are planning to save to GIF format, it will pay to understand the possibilities for and ramifications of color reduction. GIF files that have fewer than 256 colors can be stored at any bit-depth from 1 to 8. The lower the bit-depth, the smaller the file size and the faster it will load. Because the Web is a low-resolution medium when compared to print, it is often possible to employ tricks to fool the human eye into seeing more colors than are really there. The most important of those tricks will be covered later in this chapter.

JPEG

JPEG is the file format in which to save your graphics if they are full-color, continuous-tone images (such as photographs) larger than approximately 150 pixels square.

The JPEG graphics file format gets its name from the committee that originated it— the Joint Photographic Experts Group. JPEG is a 24-bit, true-color file format that uses a variable lossy-compression algorithm.

When you save a file in JPEG format, you are given the choice of a range of compression levels. The higher the compression, the less faithful the image is to the original. Given the Web's (typically 72 to 90 dpi) resolution, most images will look just as nice at the highest level of compression as at the lowest. At maximum compression, a JPEG file is typically 1/100th the size of the original.

Progressive JPEG

A more recent variation on JPEG is progressive JPEG. Like interlaced GIF, progressive JPEG enables the image to load faster in stages of increasingly higher resolution. The difference between a progressive JPEG and an interlaced GIF is that the former permits a full range of color (24-bits per pixel vs. 8-bits per pixel for GIF). However, it is only now that image editors can be commonly found that enable you to save a progressive JPEG.

Note

Lossy compression is so called because not all the original image data is saved when the file is compressed. In other words, there is some "loss."

How do you save your files to JPEG? As is the case with GIF, most modern image editors or paint programs will handle the job. There are also several stand-alone utilities that will convert files from various bitmap formats to progressive JPEG. Some of these are mentioned later in this chapter. For a complete list, see Appendix B.

Warning

The Macintosh PICT file format, possibly the most common Macintosh graphics format, enables you to use JPEG compression when saving a file without actually converting the PICT file to a JPEG file. However, neither the Web nor any program expecting a JPEG file will recognize this PICT file as a JPEG file. When choosing the file type, be sure to pick JPEG, *not* PICT.

PNG

Hopefully, the PNG format will become ubiquitous, because it supports both indexed and nonindexed color (see the following section for more information on color modes) and high (but lossless) compression and transparency. PNG's transparency is vastly better than GIF's because it is accomplished through an alpha channel, which makes it possible to have partial transparency. This means that PNG can provide a way to have drop shadows and vignettes for irregularly shaped graphics, without halos— even on patterned backgrounds. If your application is designed for an intranet whose readers use a single browser that supports the format, you should be using PNG already.

PNG was not yet a safe option in Photoshop as of version 3.0.5, but may be introduced in version 4.0 when it appears. Meanwhile, there is a somewhat buggy Export plug-in called PNGForm.8BI. You can use either JASC Software's PaintShop Pro 4.0 (only $69) or Macromedia's xRes 2.0 to load files from nearly any other graphics format and then save them as PNG files. Programs that save to PNG format vary a great deal as to which PNG attributes they support. It seems pointless to describe these differences in detail in this book, because these utilities seem to be evolving rapidly and no popular browser yet supports PNG. The following Web site URL's will give you more up-to-date information on PNG's specifics, programs that it works with and developmental progress:

```
http://quest.jpl.nasa.gov/Info-ZIP/people/greg/greg_png.html
```

or

```
http://quest.jpl.nasa.gov/PNG/
```

Graphics Basics

Color Modes

There are three kinds of color "modes" in popular use for Web graphics:

- Indexed color
- High color
- True color

These modes are known by both their names and by their color depth, so if you hear one term or another, realize that they're synonymous. The *color depth* of an indexed color image can be anything from 1 to 8 bits-per-pixel. The number of colors possible in an indexed-color image is its color depth. In other words, a 256-color image is 8 bits-per-pixel, a 4-bit image contains 16 colors, a 5-bit image is 32 colors—and so forth.

The other two modes, high color and true color, are also known as either 15-bit (32,000 colors) or 16-bit (64,000 colors). True color is also known as 24-bit color and consists of 16.8 million colors, which is quite a few more than most humans are capable of perceiving in any reproduced image.

Of the three color modes, only indexed color relies on the use of a palette. Each color in a given image is indexed to a specific location in a palette attached to that image. In other words, a specific shade of green in a picture of a forest may be assigned to the third column of the fourth row in the palette. If you want to adapt an existing image to a palette other than the one that was used in creating it (usually invisibly assigned by the program that created it), you will have to use a utility that changes the index position of each color in that image to match it to the index position of the closest color in the new palette.

As you can see, these are representations of the same portrait. Below each is the assigned palette.

The palette shown below figure 10.3 is the one that was used when it was created. The palette shown below figure 10.4 Image B shows what can happen when a different palette is arbitrarily assigned to an indexed color image.

Figure 10.3

True color.

Figure 10.4

High color.

The Rules Governing Web Graphics

Web graphics have a number of unique qualities. Paying attention to these can make or break the success of your Web site. Do you want millions of viewers and lots of ad revenue? Pay attention. Here come the rules, but remember, there are exceptions to every rule!

Rule #1: File Size Is Everything

The number one motto: be frugal.

The number two motto: cheat like mad.

People looking at a Web page have a much shorter attention span than people looking at the printed page. If your graphics take any significant amount of time to load, you can bet your reader will quickly surf to another wave. The bigger the file size, the longer it takes to load. A 14.4 Kbps modem loads data from the Web at a typical rate of about .8 Kbps. This means it takes about 28 seconds to load a 20 KB file. A typical 80×100 pixel graphic will compress to an average of about 20 KB, provided you judiciously use the tricks outlined in this chapter. There are also illusions you can create to make it seem as though graphics are loading at several times the speed they really are.

There are two such illusions in common use, interlacing and alt imaging. Interlaced GIFs and progressive JPEGs both fall in the first category. These images seem to load faster because the image is progressively rendered. Each rendering uses more pixels (dots) from the file to fill the image so the picture appears quickly, but somewhat "out of focus." Then it gets sharper until all the pixels have transferred and the image is fully revealed. The advantage is that one can usually get the information needed from the image before it has fully rendered. So you know whether you want to wait for the detail or move on. The second illusion, the LOWSRC image tag, accomplishes the same end with a different technique. The LOWSRC (low-resolution source) image can be a very small black-and-white or limited-color image. The LOWSRC image loads first and stays on-screen only as long as it takes for the primary image to load. Here's what the tag looks like:

```
<IMG SRC="image.gif" LOWSRC="weeimg.gif">
```

Warning

It is possible to use code in an HTML tag to scale a graphic to a size different from the actual file size. This is a good idea or a bad idea, depending on a few variables.

It's a good idea to scale down the file if the browser has already loaded it earlier for use at a larger size. In that case, you've already stored the large file on the server and spent the time uploading the first time. The second time the file is used, it will appear almost instantaneously because all the browser has to do is scale it. Be aware, however, that the file will be a bit "fuzzier" if it's automatically scaled down. Test your file in a browser to make sure quality is acceptable. If not, scale the file down conventionally, save it to a different name, and place the new, properly resized image on your page.

It's a bad idea to scale a file to a size larger than the original if that's the size at which you want the reader to view it—unless you're after a pixelated, jagged, artistic effect. Refer to Rule #7 later in the chapter for more information on the use of Low Source for another exception to this rule. It's also a bad idea to scale an image to a size smaller than the original because the browser will have to first load the whole file, and then scale it down (which takes even longer), causing performance to suffer unnecessarily.

By the way, you should always include the height and width attributes in your ‹IMG› tag. If the browser doesn't have to make the calculation (because it's already been done in the tag attributes), the image will load faster. Okay, maybe not much faster— but these things add up in the long run.

Rule #2: The Web Is a Low-Resolution Medium

Plan on your Web pages being viewed at a typical resolution of 72 dpi (dots per inch). Although 17-inch monitors set for 800×600 pixel resolution have become quite popular, the vast majority of viewers still use 12- to 15-inch monitors set at 640×480 pixels. A 640×480×13-inch viewing area equates to 72 dpi. This compares to a resolution of over 2,000 dpi in a typical corporate annual report.

Don't even think about placing page-size (or larger) detailed technical drawings, blueprints, or even organizational charts directly on your Web page. If you reduce them so they fit into a typical window at 72 dpi, there's not enough resolution to see detail clearly. Your diagrams will look like a bad case of acne. The solution is to scan the important parts of the drawing in a 1:1 ratio at 72 dpi, and then cut and paste small "close-up" sections of the drawing into separate files. These files can then be placed directly on your Web pages, in context with the appropriate descriptive text. Someday, with a little luck, we'll get an HTML standard tag for displaying vector graphics.

Meanwhile, there is another alternative that will work for some. If you're in an intranet situation where you can control the viewer's platform, you can use Netscape Plug-Ins for inline viewing of numerous vector file formats. See the Netscape plug-ins page for a listing of these, as follows:

```
http://www.netscape.com/comprod/mirror/navcomponents_download.html
```

Rule #3: The Web Is Color-Sensitive

Make sure your graphics look okay in black and white (well, grayscale, actually). Although few still use monochrome monitors, people will often want to print out your pages on a monochrome printer. Also, if the picture looks good in grayscale, you're assured of enough contrast between important elements in the picture. Such image contrast is critical to the success of image maps and in the legibility of text superimposed on graphics.

It's even more important that graphics look good in a mere 256 colors. This is because most of your viewers leave their monitors set at 256 colors. They just aren't graphics people and may not know that they're seeing the world through dust-covered glasses. Subjects that require photorealistic shading require display in millions of colors. Otherwise, they will appear to be "banded" or posterized. Artists whose work you display in this manner will definitely be unappreciative. Besides, someone once told them that their applications would run much faster with the monitor set at 256 colors. While this may be technically true, the real-world difference to most of us is imperceptible. By the way, these comments aren't meant to pick on people who still have only SVGA display cards and monitors that are not capable of more than 256 colors. This has ceased to be a limitation since the days of the 486 processor, but quite a few offices still use the older cards, as do many laptop color computers.

Having said all that, it's not strictly true that you have to reduce all images to less than 256 colors in order to be as efficient as possible. The JPEG file format accommodates only true-color (16.7 million colors—or "millions") files, and most popular browsers, such as Netscape Navigator, will automatically adjust images (by dithering) to 256 colors on a 256-color display; however, experimentation will often prove that a file reduced to fewer colors will compress to significantly smaller sizes.

The exception to the 256-color rule is when you want to display high-quality images for photographs (browsers will do their own dithering). Even if you're showing photographs, they can often be successfully reduced to 256 colors through techniques explained further along in this chapter.

The photographs in figures 10.5 through 10.8 show the difference between different methods of color reduction, with and without dithering.

Figure 10.5

A photograph in true color (millions).

Figure 10.6

Same photo, reduced to 256 colors.

Figure 10.7

Same photo, reduced to 256 colors and dithered.

Figure 10.8

Same photo, shown in Netscape palette.

Rule #4: There Are Only Two Workable Graphics File Formats—GIF and JPEG

Both file formats can be read equally well on any type of popular computer. In addition, both are now supported by most browsers.

Unfortunately, both of these formats accommodate only bitmapped images. A bitmapped image (often called a "paint" or "photo" file in computerese) relies solely on a fixed-size mosaic of different colored pixels to paint the image. This requirement makes bitmapped images much larger than vector or "drawing" files. Furthermore, you can't enlarge or reduce a bitmapped file without the loss of image quality. This is not true of vector files.

Rule #5: Never Make a Graphic's Dimensions So Large the Reader Has to Scroll

Most of your viewers will see your pages on a screen that measures 640×480 pixels. This is roughly the size of the image on 12- to 14-inch monitors, whether Mac or PC. Although it's true that many viewers these days set their screens to higher resolutions (800×600 is quite popular) or have bigger monitors, you can't count on it. Besides, people who do that are still a small minority.

The bad news is, you can't even make your images nearly as big as 640×480 because a lot of that space is taken up by your browser. In Netscape Navigator, if the window is set at maximum, the area of a viewable page is 610×280 pixels—and most people don't even maximize the window. The best rule of thumb is to limit width to about 450 pixels.

This means the biggest graphic you should ever use is about 600 pixels wide by 260 pixels high. If you plan to have anything in addition to the graphic on the page, the graphic will have to be appropriately smaller. Thus, your portrait (vertical) aspect images will have to be smaller than 260 pixels square.

The one exception to these size limitations is backgrounds. Single-image backgrounds should be as large as the largest screen likely to view them. Also, horizontal tiles should be as wide as the largest window in which they can be viewed (1024 pixels wide is a safe bet). That way, people using large screens at a high resolution won't run out of background when these elements are used. Background elements repeat automatically if they are smaller than the viewing window. If you are making a tiled background, then, remember this: the smaller the tile, the faster it will load. For more information on backgrounds, see the section on backgrounds in this chapter.

There's another exception to this size limitation that many artists and photographers will insist on making. They feel that their images lose too much detail at such small sizes. The truth is, these images lose too much detail no matter how they are displayed on the Web. Furthermore, poor image quality relative to the original image is to your advantage in that it is one defense against the theft of your artwork.

Rule #6: Repeat the Use of the Same Image File as Often as Possible

The browser only needs to load an image once, because it caches. Caching means that the information is held in memory on the local computer. Thus, any subsequent appearance of that image will load almost instantly. This excellent trick makes the performance of your site seem miraculously fast. Keep this rule in mind when you're tempted to make a different bullet for each subject list or to use nine different kinds of page dividers within the same site. Also, sticking to rule #6 can save you considerable space on your Web server. If you're using an independent service provider, saving server space can save you money. Finally, it makes site maintenance easier because there are fewer links to track. If you want a more thorough explanation of caching (pronounced "cashing"), check the Netscape FAQ (Frequently Asked Questions) file at the following:

```
http://help.netscape.com/kb/client/960514-44.html
```

Rule #7: Don't Depend Entirely on Automated Text-to-HTML Converters

To put it another way, most converters can't do the refined steps in the Web-enhanced versions of GIF (GIF89a) or JPEG (progressive JPEG) and won't do anything to create a low source image as a substitute. Each of these qualities can contribute to making your Web site faster to load, quicker to browse, and easier on the eye.

Transparency

Transparency refers to making one color in an image invisible, enabling the image to blend smoothly with any background. The same image can thus be used on a number of pages with varying background colors and textures. Transparency is a property currently unique to the GIF89a format, so you can't make JPEG graphics transparent. Figure 10.9 shows a transparent GIF89a image.

Figure 10.9

A transparent GIF89a image.

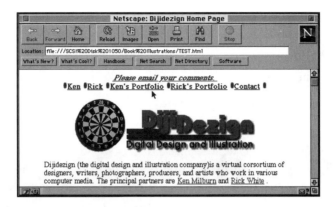

Interlacing and Progressive JPEG

One way to speed the display of graphics-enhanced Web pages is to make GIFs *interlaced* and JPEGs *progressive*. Both interlaced GIFs and progressive JPEGs appear quickly because only some of the pixels in the image are loaded first. As a result, you see a rough (out of focus) approximation of the final image while the rest of the image loads. If you think you're not interested in the detail (or you've seen it before), you can move on without waiting for the rest of the

> **Warning**
>
> **Never Interlace a Transparent Background GIF**
>
> Interlacing in conjunction with transparency causes intermittent problems with some browsers (such as Netscape Navigator). The result is a "broken GIF" icon in place of the picture. Bad idea.

file transfer. Interlaced GIFs and progressive JPEGs are both made automatically as part of the File-Save command in image editing programs, file conversion utilities, and several WYSIWYG and non-WYSIWYG HTML editors. Support for saving to progressive JPEG is significantly rarer than support for saving to interlaced GIF at this point in history. Photoshop 3.0 isn't progressive JPEG-savvy and requires that you save GIF files with the Export GIF89a filter in order to specify interlacing. Interlaced GIFs are supported by all popular browsers that support graphics. Progressive JPEGs, however, are only supported by the most advanced browsers, such as Netscape Navigator. Support for progressive JPEGs is expanding rapidly because they eliminate the need to wait for the JPEG file to decompress before becoming viewable.

Low-Sourcing

Low-sourcing can be a substitute for progressive JPEGs or interlaced GIFs. Sometimes this method is more efficient than pJPEG or iGIFs, but that depends on how you make the low-source images.

Graphics Basics

Low-sourcing gets its name from an HTML tag that substitutes a much lower-resolution version of a file until the data for a higher-resolution version has been loaded.

A low-source attribute in an image tag looks like this:

```
<IMG LOWSRC="images/pict01s.gif" SRC="images/pict01.jpg">
```

You'll want two separate files to use in an image tag with a LOWSRC attribute such as: SRC= image or LOWSRC= image. The LOWSRC= image's file size should be much smaller (less than 25 percent) than the original image. There are several techniques for making LOWSRC images. Which one you use depends on the size of the SRC image and the effect you want to achieve. The second file could be smaller because of the following reasons:

- It is a black and white version of the full-color high-source image.

- You reduced colors.

- The image dimensions are much smaller. For instance, you could simply make a copy of a 200×300 image, then scale it to 50×75 pixels, and then insert a size attribute in the image tag to force the showing of both images at the same size.

```
<IMG LOWSRC="images/pict01s.gif" SRC="images/pict01.jpg" HEIGHT=200
➥WIDTH=300>
```

Rule #8: High Bandwidth Is No Excuse for Inefficiency

Even if your site is on a corporate intranet where every viewer has a high-speed connection, there are better things to do with bandwidth (such as providing more viewers with more information and not creating bottlenecks in the network) than wasting it on unnecessarily large graphics.

Graphic Components Used on the Web and Their Characteristics

The kinds of graphics you're likely to need on your Web pages fall into categories. Understanding these categories as described in the following sections will help you understand how to create these types of graphical elements.

Text

When you use graphical text, you can use any font in your computer at any size. You can also specify any typographical attributes such as spacing, kerning, or leading. You can't do any of this with HTML text. Unlike HTML text, when you use graphics, the font style is not dependent on the destination system.

Other things you can do with graphical text are as follows:

● Freehand lettering (see fig. 10.10)

Figure 10.10

A freehand signature.

● Multi-colored letters (see fig. 10.11)

Figure 10.11

Multi-colored letters.

● Special effects such as embossing, drop shadows, glow, gradient fills, or outlining (see fig. 10.12)

Figure 10.12

Graphical text special effects.

Illustration

Illustrations are appropriate for use at some place in almost every kind of site, though they may be more important to digital magazines, catalogs, and children's sites than in heavily text-oriented sites. Illustrations differ from other types of graphics in that they are used primarily to tell the visual story alongside of (or to complement) the story you're telling in words. They are usually bigger than other types of graphics. Often they are full-color photos or gradually shaded artwork, so file sizes tend to be much larger than for other types of graphics. Illustrations can be decorative or instructional. Sometimes illustrations tell the whole story and there is little or no text on the page, as in figure 10.13. Illustrations should never be so large that the viewer has to scroll to see the whole picture. When creating or placing illustrations, take care to keep their size slightly smaller than the typical user's browser window. (See Rule #5 under the section head entitled, "The Rules Governing Web Graphics.")

Figure 10.13

A left-aligned figure with wrapping text.

Notice that in figure 10.13, the text wraps around the image. In HTML 3.2 and the Netscape extensions, text wraps when the ALIGN=left or ALIGN=right attributes are used in the <IMG> tag.

In figure 10.14, the illustration heads the page and spans two columns of the page. Although this is not always the case for decorative illustrations, it is common. In the HTML code for this page, these elements are held in place by an asymmetrical table in which the first cell spans two columns. The following is an example of how the code would look for such a table:

```
<TABLE>
<TR><TD COLSPAN=2> <IMG SRC="headtxt.gif">
</TD></TR>
<TR><TD> <IMG SRC="image.gif"> </TD>
<TD> <IMG SRC="image2.gif"> </TD> </TR>
</TABLE>
```

Figure 10.14

A graphic as a header.

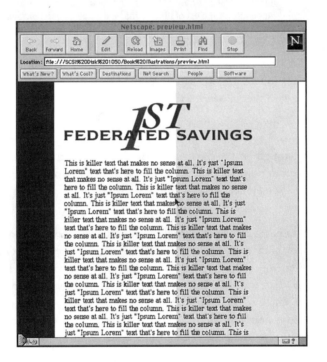

Backgrounds

Backgrounds are the "paper" on which your Web content is printed. Most browsers default to a medium gray or white background; however, you can specify any color for a background and any color for text. Any browser compliant with the HTML 3.2 specification and most current versions of currently popular browsers can properly interpret the instructions for colored backgrounds. Colored text is supported by Netscape Navigator 2+ and by Microsoft's Internet Explorer, but is not as widely supported as colored backgrounds. To be safe, keep your backgrounds light enough that black text is readable against it. Here are the HTML tags for colored backgrounds:

Graphics Basics

```
<BODY bgcolor="#000000" text="#FFFFFF">
```

Here are the HTML tags for colored text:

```
<FONT color="#FFFFFF">
```

> **Note**
>
> The "#FFFFFF" refers to the hexadecimal code for white. If you want to specify an-
> other text or background color, refer to the section on hexadecimal colors in Chap-
> ter 14, "HTML Tutorial and Reference," for a chart and guide to using them. Also, see
> Appendix B for a list of utilities that will help you use hexadecimal colors.

Suppose you want a photo or paper texture in the background. It is now possible for most browsers to read graphic backgrounds. Any image can be loaded into the background with the following HTML <BODY> tag:

```
<BODY background="bkgpatn.gif">
```

where "bkgpatn.gif" is the file name of the background image. This image will repeat itself from left to right and from top to bottom as many times as necessary to fill the entire frame. Remember, this repetition will occur more times for a full frame on a 20-inch monitor at 1024×768 pixels than on a full frame on a 640×480 12-inch monitor.

Background images can be of any type, but need to be designed so they don't interfere with the readability of text or unintentionally confuse the content of overlaying graphics. Remember: the larger the file size of the background image tile, the longer it will take that page to load. Either use every trick in the book to make the file sizes for large images small, or use very small tiles. Actually, a background tile about 20 pixels square will load nearly as fast as a 1-pixel tile and will fill the screen about twenty times faster because there are twenty times fewer repeats.

There are several types of "effects" you can expect to achieve with background images. These are discussed in the following sections.

Semi-Solid Backgrounds

Semi-solid backgrounds are created by making a background image tile that is as wide as any viewing window is likely to be (1024 pixels is a good number). The height can be as narrow as you like, as the tile simply repeats as often as necessary from top to bottom. Because this tile is so wide, its file size will be bigger unless it is very shallow. A height of one or two pixels will be the best compromise between loading time and screen-painting time. See figure 10.15 for a good example of a semi-solid background.

Figure 10.15

A background that seems to consist of more than one solid color.

Full-Screen Images

Full-screen images are those that provide all the needed information without requiring any HTML text. Usually such images contain graphic text. Usually an image map is required for some sort of negotiation. A hybrid full-screen image could be a full-screen background image tile with minimal HTML text in links (such as a navigation bar) in the foreground. These images work best if they contain very few colors and large areas of solid color so that they compress to a small enough file size to allow them to load quickly. Figure 10.16 is an example of a full-screen image.

Figure 10.16

A full-screen image that conveys all the information needed.

Textured and Patterned Backgrounds

Textured and patterned backgrounds are variations on background tiles. Textured backgrounds are simply images with no definable subject, such as sand or burlap. Patterned backgrounds are repetitions of a shape such as the drawing of an apple, flower, or company logo. Textured and patterned backgrounds are usually created as "seamless tiles" that repeat in contiguous left-to-right, top-to-bottom sequence. Figure 10.17 is an example of a patterned background.

Figure 10.17

A patterned background.

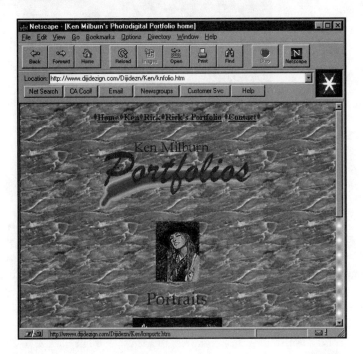

Multiple Backgrounds

Multiple backgrounds are those that use images within an image to compose a full-screen background image that appears to be several backgrounds (see fig. 10.18).

Strictly speaking, what you see in figure 10.18 isn't a background, but whole images inserted into table cells. The appearance of text over a background is "faked" by creating the text as part of the graphic image. The cell borders have been set at "0," so that they're invisible. The content has been placed within the cells so that it appears to float over the whole page. To make your design work, you'll have to spend some time experimenting with font sizes, colors, and object alignments.

Figure 10.18

The background appears to contain two photos and two textures.

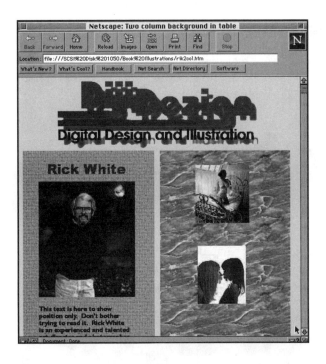

The example code for the preceding background effect is seen in the following text (to save space, the code for the table cell's foreground content, such as text and pictures, has been eliminated):

```
<TABLE BORDER="0" CELLPADDING="2"><TR><TD bgcolor="#FFFFFF">
</TD>
<TD><IMG SRC="bgtextr1.gif" >
</TD></TR>
<TR><TD><IMG SRC="bgtextr2.gif" ALIGN=left> </TD>
<TD><IMG SRC="txtwbkg.gif" BORDER="0"> </CENTER>
</TD></TR></TABLE>
```

If the border attribute is omitted, the borders will default to borders=0. What this boils down to is less typing.

Irregularly Shaped Graphics

An irregularly shaped graphic appears to have a nonrectangular border, but is in fact rectangular. This graphic appears to be irregularly shaped because its solid-color background is either clear or matches the page background's color. The name is a little misleading in another way: the shape can actually be regular (as in an oval, circle, or polygon)—it just can't be rectangular.

Irregularly shaped graphics have so many uses you will find them indispensable. First, they are the only way to make graphics text appear to be a "typeset" element of the page layout. Navigation icons (illustrated in figure 10.19) and many signature illustrations also integrate better into the layout when they don't appear to have a separate frame or background.

Figure 10.19

Irregular shapes used as navigation icons.

Bullets

Bullets are simple-shape graphics that call your attention to something. Usually, they look like tiny buttons without words and are used to set apart items in an unnumbered list. Several variations are illustrated in figure 10.20.

Figure 10.20

Examples of bullets.

Icons

Icons are small, "high-concept" images meant to give the reader a message that takes less time to read and is more universally understood than if the same message were spelled out in words. Some designers suffer from "icon mania" and use icons in places where a single word would have been more easily understood. The most universally understood icon is a circle with a diagonal line, meaning "negative, no, not." Traffic signs make good icons for the Web. Figure 10.21 shows examples of icons.

Figure 10.21

Examples of icons.

Rounded Buttons

Rounded buttons give dimension to your page and can be used for navigation (with superimposed type) or as bullets to emphasize important text. See figure 10.22 for examples of rounded buttons.

Figure 10.22

Several rounded buttons.

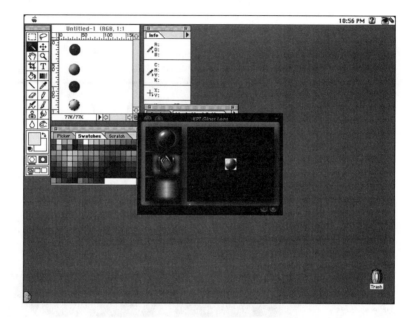

Making rounded buttons is easy if you have Kai's Power Tools (KPT) or an image editor such as Paint Shop Pro that has its own version of the KPT Glass Lens Filter. Follow the steps in Exercise 10.1 to create rounded buttons.

Exercise 10.1

1. Open a file that contains the color or texture you want to use for your button.

2. Double-click on the Rectangular Marquee tool and change it to Elliptical. Drag an ellipse around the area where you want a button. If the button has to be a particular size, make sure you have chosen Window, Palette, Show Info. If you want the button to be round rather than elliptical, press Shift as you drag.

3. Choose Edit, Copy to save your button to the Clipboard. Choose File, New and click on OK. Choose Edit, Paste. Save the selection. Choose Window, Palette, Show Layers. Double-click on the Floating Layer bar and name the layer. You

now have a floating layer and can fill the background with any color or texture you like. Your file is now cropped to exactly the size of your button. Keep the selection marquee active (or save the selection so you can bring it back).

4. Choose Selection, Load Selection and click on OK. The selection reappears on the button layer. Choose Filter, KPT Extensions, Glass Lens (Bright, Normal, or Soft for the effect you like.) Presto! You've got a button! Choose the Options Arrowhead at the upper right corner of the Layers Palette. A fly-out menu appears. Choose Flatten Image. This combines all the layers into one. Finally, save the file as CompuServe GIF.

You can also make rounded buttons in any 3D modeling program that does ray-traced rendering. Simply make a sphere, map your favorite texture to its surface, and render. Open the rendered file in your image editor, crop it, and save as GIF.

Banners

Banners are used to show and announce an advertisement (see fig. 10.23). Banners often contain image maps to link to specific sites.

Figure 10.23

Examples of small and large banners.

Standard advertising practices dictate two sizes of horizontal Web banners at 476×54 and 154×56, and a small vertical banner at 70×130 (see fig. 10.24).

Even if you don't have advertisers on your site, you may want to use banners to promote ideas, announce products your own company wants to sell, or point out features of your site.

Figure 10.24

The three sizes of Web banners.

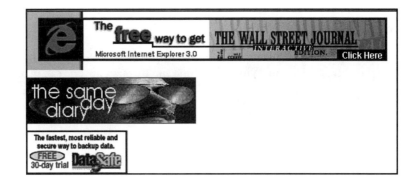

Animations

There's lots of talk these days about the Web being "everyone's" vehicle for multimedia. Although there is some truth in that statement, don't think about putting conventional animated multimedia files on your Web site unless you are working within the context of an intranet with T1 or faster connections. As cable modems and other high-speed access become more widespread, multimedia will reach its full power over the Web. In the meantime, remember that most Web access is at 28.8 Kbps or slower. That means it takes a full minute or more to download a 60 KB file, which is tiny for a motion file such as a QuickTime or Video for Windows movie. Surveys show that most Web surfers won't wait more than a minute for a page to load. You will really have to work to keep your animations as small as possible. Also, give viewers something to read or some other interesting graphics that will load first. If your viewer is busy looking or reading, pages will seem to load faster. If you need to see what actual download times are for a typical movie file size, take a look at the typical download times table available in Chapter 2, "Design Considerations for the Web."

Animations can be anything from simple "flipbook" cartoons to live-action video footage. Simple cartoon-type animations that consist of only two to ten frames are best suited for use as inline attention-getters, because their file sizes can be kept to a bare minimum for quick loading.

Animated GIFs

Animated GIFs are one of the most effective, lowest overhead ways of using animation to attract attention. With a little time and practice, anyone can make an animated GIF.

Animated GIFs are simply multiple images saved within a single GIF89a file. When the file is placed on an HTML page, using the <IMG> tag, and viewed with a supporting browser like Netscape, animation will start almost as soon as the page is loaded. No special plug-ins or helper software is required. Figure 10.25 shows an animated GIF.

Figure 10.25

An example of an animated GIF.

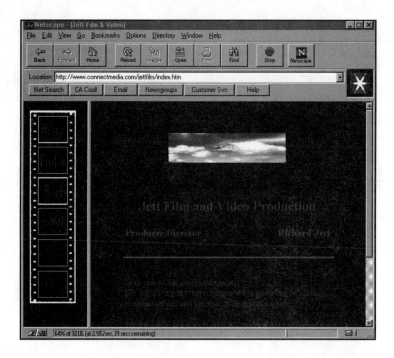

There are numerous software utilities for both the Mac and Windows that will assist in saving the individual images or "frames" of your animation as a single GIF89a file. Some also provide drawing tools, and a few even provide "tracing paper" so that you can superimpose the drawing of a new frame over the drawing of the previous frame. This helpful feature enables you to check registration (the position of objects in one frame to the position of the same objects in the next frame) as you go.

For a list of GIF89a animation utilities, check Appendix B, the software appendix in this book. The next chapter will provide a more detailed explanation of the actual process of creating animated GIFs.

Shockwave for Director

Shockwave is a trademark that applies to several browser plug-in technologies from software publisher Macromedia. Shockwave files have the extensions dir, dcr, and dxr and have a MIME type of application/x-director .The Shockwave plug-in that enables you to put interactive animation inline on a Web page is Shockwave for Director. There are Shockwave plug-ins for both Director 4.0 and 5.0 and for both Mac and PC. There are also very useful Shockwave plug-ins for Freehand and for Authorware, although Shockwave for Director 4 and 5 are definitely the most popular Shockwave plug-ins.

Although the animated diagram in figure 10.26 looks like a large file, the limited colors and small sprites make this a very efficient Director movie that plays on the Web with lightning speed. Visit Macromedia's Shockwave page to see it.

Figure 10.26

The Shockwave home page animation.

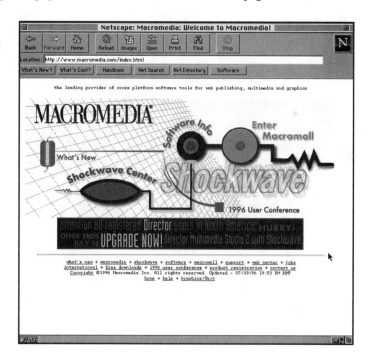

Graphics Basics

Note

Sprites consist of anything that is animated along a path, including animated objects such as walking people or flying birds.

Theoretically, Shockwave makes it possible to place almost any Director movie inline on a Web page. *Inline* means the file doesn't have to play with the aid of a separate helper application in a separate window. Typically, Director movies can run into the tens (or even hundreds) of megabytes in size. See Chapter 11, "Graphics Creation," for more information on creating Shockwave animations.

QuickTime Movies

QuickTime is Apple Computer's cross-platform format for full-motion video. QuickTime has become the most popular movie format for both Macintosh and Windows platform for several reasons, including more efficient playback, consistent synchronization regardless of hardware, and the ability to easily incorporate material from data sources other than bitmapped images. Many video and animation programs, such as Premier and Director, are capable of outputting QuickTime movies. Apple has recently enhanced QuickTime. The following list highlights the versatile features of QuickTime:

- A new Netscape plug-in enables full-motion video to play much more quickly and MIDI sound to play instantaneously.

- QuickTime is the most versatile and ubiquitous multimedia file format on the planet.

- The latest advances from Apple make it possible to start viewing even a fairly long live-action video within a fraction of the time it would usually take to load the file.

- QuickTime can display both bitmapped and vector information.

- QuickTime VR can let you pan around an entire location (called QTVR Scenes: you can look up and down, turn around, zoom in to see detail, or zoom out for a broader view) or rotate the photo of a QTVR Object (such as a piece of technical machinery) to any angle. This capability is especially valuable for sites having to do with travel, technical training, or catalog sales. The QuickTime VR environment is shown in figure 10.27.

Figure 10.27

A QuickTime VR page.

QuickTime Drawbacks

There are three major drawbacks to using QuickTime movies on your Web page, as follows:

1. You have to make the movie on a Macintosh (at least for the time being). Also, most data will have to be converted to a Macintosh file format before being placed in the movie. Image files, whether raster (paint) or vector (draw) will have to be saved to PICT format. Audio files will have to be converted to AIFF for wave sound or MID for MIDI sound.

2. The number of browsers able to view your QuickTime movies is limited to Netscape Navigator 3.0 and Microsoft Internet Explorer 3.0, as of this writing.

3. QuickTime is not interactive. In other words, you can't put interactive buttons or internal hyperlinks in a QT movie. Such interactivity features that are created in an interactivity-capable authoring environment, such as Director or AnimationWorks won't work if that title is saved or exported as a QuickTime movie, either. (Although the dedicated student can find limited workarounds, these are outside the scope of this book.)

Graphics Basics

As with animated GIFs, you can see the first frame of the movie within seconds of opening a page, provided the QuickTime movie has been pretreated for Web viewing. You can also make the movie player invisible. If there is only a sound track, the sound starts playing as soon as the page opens.

To place a QuickTime movie on your page, use the HTML <EMBED> tag (very similar to an <IMG> tag). A tag to play a MIDI background music file as soon as the page comes up, and without showing the movie controller, would look like this:

```
<EMBED SRC=Qtfile.mov HIDDEN AUTOPLAY=true CONTROLLER=false>
```

For a more detailed discussion of the uses of the <EMBED> tag, see Chapter 14, "HTML Tutorial and Reference."

There are a total of 15 optional attributes for a QuickTime file that give a Web author considerable control over the appearance and timing of the playing of a movie. For a list of these attributes, visit the following URL:

```
http://quicktime.apple.com/qt/dev/devweb.html#syntax
```

Apple has recently been working with browser makers such as Netscape and Microsoft to make Netscape-compatible plug-ins that will play QuickTime movies. It is Apple's expectation that by the time you read this, the QuickTime plug-in will be working for both Netscape Navigator 3.0 and Microsoft Internet Explorer 3.0. Chapter 11 provides a more detailed explanation of creating QuickTime movies.

Downloading QuickTime

To download the QuickTime plug-in, navigate to the following:

```
http://www.quicktime.apple.com/qt/sw/readme.html
```

You may also need the QTVR Player add-in (it modifies the QuickTime Player plug-in), as follows:

```
http://qtvr.quicktime.apple.com/
```

Microsoft ActiveMovie

Microsoft's answer to the QuickTime movie plug-in is called ActiveMovie. This is a very advanced replacement for Video for Windows, intended to be cross-platform for Windows 95 and NT and for the Power Macintosh. Microsoft has announced that ActiveMovie will be integrated into the final release of Microsoft Internet Explorer 3.0.

On the Net, ActiveMovie will play streaming MPEG1 full-motion video. Like QuickTime, ActiveMovie will be able to incorporate multiple media types, including

MPEG audio and video, AVI and QuickTime movies, and AIFF, WAV, and MID (MIDI) sound files (but not vector information stored in a metafile file format such as PICT (Mac) or WMF (Windows).

It's too soon in the development cycle to be able to cover in detail the intricacies of maximizing an ActiveMovie for Internet play. Right now, this is a job for serious developers. It also remains to be seen how successful Microsoft will be at getting ActiveMovie established as an Internet standard. At this point, they'll need Netscape's cooperation—considering the two companies are mortal enemies in the quest for browser dominance, Netscape is probably not going to be motivated to cooperate.

At the moment, ActiveMovie is most exciting as a technology for CD-ROM multimedia titles and for corporate intranets where user-platform and browser can be controlled, and infrastructure can be planned around the Microsoft Web strategy.

Java

Java is a programming language designed by Sun Microsystems to run on any kind of computer. This makes Java a programming language well suited to use on the Web. Applications written in Java can reside on the Net, instead of on a computer.

Java applications can range from very small programs, called *applets*, that perform simple tasks (such as playing an animation or running a scrolling text banner) to highly sophisticated business, graphics, and entertainment applications.

The potential for Java is so exciting that scores of books have already been written on the subject—and more are coming. Meanwhile, there are numerous Java applets available for free download from a variety of Web sites. You can place a Java applet on your Web page with an HTML tag that can be recognized by the HotJava, Netscape Navigator 2+, and Microsoft Internet Explorer 3.0+ browsers.

A typical tag for an applet looks like this:

```
<applet codebase="applets/YourApplet"
     code= YourApplet.class
     width=300
     height=50>
<param name=text value="This is my applet!">
</applet>
```

Java tags can get quite complex. A visit to Sun's Web site will give you more information than there's space for here, as follows:

```
http://java.sun.com/java.sun.com/applets/applet.html
```

Graphics Basics

Although the creation of Java applications (even if they're "applets") requires programming skills, programs that write the code for you are beginning to appear. For example, there's Kinetix HyperWire at http://www.ktx.com and AimTech's Jamba at http://www.aimtech.com.

Content Dividers (Bars)

Content dividers are best known as horizontal and vertical rules. Horizontal rules are easily placed in HTML by using the <HR> tag, but HTML imposes the following limitations:

- There are no vertical rules.

- Horizontal bars are solid and act as visual barriers to proceeding further down the page.

Both these limitations can be overcome by substituting graphics. Because you can use a graphic as a horizontal bar, there's no limitation to how you can execute it graphically. Figure 10.28 uses a piece of pre-masked clip art and repeats it across the page.

Figure 10.28

Graphics in place of a horizontal bar.

In addition to acting as subject dividers, bars (as well as banners) are a good means of letting viewers know how wide your page should be, as illustrated in figure 10.29. This improves the chances that viewers will size their viewing windows accordingly, so they can view your layout pretty much as you intended it.

Figure 10.29

Example of horizontal bar used as page-width indicator.

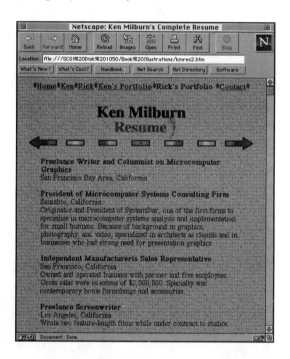

Graphics Basics

For browsers that allow tables (the big ones all do, these days), you can also make (well, simulate) vertical bars. It's a bit touchy, though. Insert a thin vertical graphic into a table cell between two cells that hold text. If you have more text than the height of the graphic, the text cell height will expand automatically. That's okay—Web pages (unlike paper) have no fixed length, but it means there's no fixed size for a vertical bar. To make this work, insert your text first, preview the result in a browser, measure the height of the page in pixels, and make your vertical bar as high as it needs to be.

Here's an example of the HTML code you'd use to make a three-cell-wide table in which the center cell holds the vertical bar:

```
<HTML>
<HEAD><TITLE>Vertical line example</TITLE></HEAD>
<BODY>
<CENTER><H1>Headline</H1></CENTER>
<TABLE BORDER=2 WIDTH=100%>
<TR>
```

```
<TD><IMG SRC=name.gif> 1</TD>
<TD ROWSPAN=3><IMG SRC=verticalline.gif VSPACE=20>Vertical line</
➥TD>
<TD><IMG SRC=name.gif> 2</TD>
</TR>
<TR>
<TD><IMG SRC=name.gif> 3</TD><TD><IMG SRC=name.gif> 4</TD>
</TR>
<TR>
<TD><IMG SRC=name.gif> 5</TD><TD><IMG SRC=name.gif> 6</TD>
</TR>
</TABLE>
</BODY>
</HTML>
```

Picture Frames

Picture frames are actually not separate graphical elements, because for them to work, they must be merged into a single graphic with the picture they frame (see fig. 10.30). Still, you can make one frame and then resize it to fit any number of pictures.

Figure 10.30

Several framed pictures.

The images in figure 10.30 show how frames can be implemented in a variety of styles. You can discover methods on creating your own frames in Chapter 11.

Alerts

Alerts are graphics meant to command the viewer's attention. You may want to announce a new feature or product, warn the viewer to avert disaster, or congratulate those who've found a treasure.

Alerts usually take the shape of irregular buttons, as exemplified by the comic strip Pow! "splash." Usually you will want to follow the procedures for making frames or buttons, and then the procedures for making graphic text. Superimpose the graphic text on the alert shape and flatten the file. Alerts are one of the best uses of inline animations.

As you can see, alerts can be photos of objects or attention-getting splashes, as illustrated in figure 10.31.

Figure 10.31

Three styles of alerts.

The New Photoshop 4.0 Features

Adobe announced Photoshop 4.0 just as this book went to press, and we were able to use a pre-release version of the software. The new features and capabilities of Photoshop are significant enhancements, both in terms of the program's overall characteristics and as regards capabilities that are specifically advantageous to creating graphics for Web pages.

The most important characteristic of the new Photoshop is that it is evolutionary, not revolutionary. You will still be able to execute the instructions in these chapters. On the other hand, had the software been in hand, it would have been possible to streamline the execution of some of the exercises.

Finally, Built-in Automation

Probably the most useful new feature is a built-in macro recording capability called the Actions Palette. It is finally possible to execute a series of often-repeated manipulations at a single click.

The Actions palette lets you record any series of actions. The recording can be saved and can be re-applied to any image or selection at any time. If you want to perform nearly the same actions, just make the changes in the edit list. You can also drag actions to a different position in the sequence, causing the sequence to be applied in a different order.

More Creative Power

Several new Photoshop 4.0 features make you a more powerful artist.

A new type of layer has been added. Called an Adjustment Layer, it is used for making adjustments in gamma curves, contrast, color balance, hue/saturation, selective color, invert, threshold, and posterize. You can have as many of these layers as you like. That may not sound too exciting, but this layer's effects can be changed at any time without changing the underlying image. If you don't like the effect, you can try it again. You can even switch underlying image areas to see the effect in combination with different elements.

The conventional Image Layers have been streamlined. Finally, you can turn a layer into a selection with a single command and floating selections now automatically become layers (this simplifies several steps in the exercises in Chapter 11).

There's a new command on the Image menu, called Free Transform, that consolidates multiple types of transform in a single tool. You can make all the adjustments to scale, rotate, skew, add perspective, then execute them all with a single click. The fact that all these operations are performed in one step results in much less image detail loss than when each of these manipulations had to be performed separately.

Other artistic enhancements include the capability to put any number of colors into a gradient fill (a fill that blends smoothly from one color to another) and the inclusion of 40 "artistic" effects filters.

Web-Specific Features

Photoshop 4.0 is able to save to PNG format, to progressive JPEG and directly to Acrobat 3.0 PDF (Portable Document Format). Gif89a is still supported as a built-in export filter, but there's still no built-in animation capability.

Photoshop also adds user-specifiable, non-printing but visible grids. The main importance of this feature to the making of Web graphics is that it makes consistent sizing of Web same-type (icons, for example) elements easier and more intuitive. You can make the grid size so that a cell is the same size (or multiple of the same size if you want divisions) as the consistent elements you want to create.

Finally, Photoshop has a new icon in the Tool palette that directly links you to Adobe's home page. This makes it much easier to keep up with late-breaking developments, downloadable updates and plug-ins, and "hot tips."

Not Quite the Same Old (Inter)Face

You'll feel right at home with the redesigned Photoshop interface, even though there are quite a few changes. Adobe has been very careful not to throw you into an unfamiliar environment. On the other hand, menus are much better organized, there are new tools and palettes for many of the features mentioned previously, and there's a more enticing 3D overall "look." You can see this firsthand in the screen shot in figure 10.32.

Figure 10.32

The Photoshop 4.0 interface.

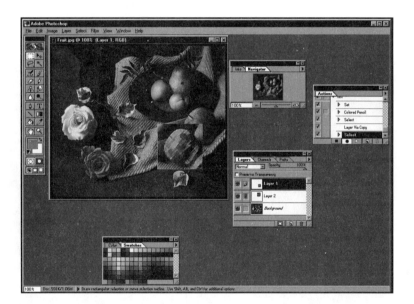

Summary

This chapter has, hopefully, given you some perspective about the use of graphics on the Web, given the present state-of-the-art. You've learned about the two basic types of graphics in use today, GIF and JPEG. You've also learned about the variations on these formats and their uses. In addition, you've glimpsed the future in our discussion of the PNG format and of the potential for vector graphics.

Next came the basic rules for using graphics on the Web. Hopefully, you'll make a copy of these rules and pin them to the wall above your monitor. The basic Web graphic types and their uses were also explained at some length.

Having read this chapter, you should be ready for some specific tips about how to make graphics that work to make your Web pages both quick-loading and visually appealing to your intended audience.

CHAPTER 11

Graphics Creation

This chapter goes into a bit more detail about how to create the types of graphics discussed in Chapter 10, "Graphics Basics." Useful alternatives for producing a certain type of graphic are provided where possible. All the primary examples are given for the procedures in the most widely used (usually cross-platform) software for a given category. Specifically, that's Adobe Photoshop 3.0.5 for bitmap image editing (Mac and Windows), Adobe Illustrator 6.0 (Mac and Windows) for Bézier-curve illustration, DeBabelizer (sorry, Windows users—this one's still for Mac only). Occasionally, I'll mention other software when it's unique in enabling you to perform specific kinds of "magic."

The following table covers some of the topics discussed in this chapter.

Using Graphics on the Web

Characteristic	Advantages	Disadvantages	Where to Use
Irregularly shaped graphics	Graphic more related to page.	Viewer's attention less focused on image.	Site page.
Soft-edged graphics	Blends with background; attention getting.	Guard against overuse.	As illustration or graphic headline.
Seamless background tiles	Quick loading textured background.	Can make text hard to read; danger of becoming cliché.	Page background in <IMG> tag.
Picture frames	Contains and categorizes graphic.	Makes image larger; slower loading.	Effect for illustration or in gallery collection.
Moving images	Command attention; instruct or entertain.	Constant movement can be annoying. May require browser plug-in.	In place of any type of static graphical element.

Of course, in a chapter focusing on Web graphics, color is a major element. Some of the isssues and procedures that you will read about in this chapter would be easier to follow if the accompanying features were in color. For your convenience, all the full color figures in this chapter have been included on the accompanying CD-ROM.

Making Irregularly Shaped Graphics

An irregularly shaped graphic is nothing more than the bitmapped image of something on a *solid* background. You can make it appear to "float" on a Web page in either of two ways:

- Match the page background color to the background color of the graphic (not quite as easy as it sounds, unless you use black or white).

- Designate the background color as transparent.

Warning

If you think the image already has a solid color background, you're probably wrong. For the background to be a solid color, all pixels must have exactly the same hexadecimal code. Any shading or texturing can result in a "diseased," speckled background. (Alternative to the following additions: discovering whether a background is actually solid can be a tedious process. You'll usually save time by following the instructions for making solid backgrounds.)

Pixels that are very slightly off are virtually impossible for the human eye to detect. Utilities are available that let you pass a cursor tool over the image and see the hex code in a window. The problem here is that you have to make sure you pass the cursor over every single pixel in order to make sure the background is solid. Here's a cheaper, easier, and quicker way.

Make sure you save everything you've done to the image up until now. Double-click on the Magic Wand tool and set its range to one pixel. Click in the background to make a selection. Pick a foreground color that is outrageously different from the existing background color. Choose Edit-Fill. When the dialog box appears, make sure Opacity is 100%, Mode is normal. Choose Foreground Color. Choose OK. Most of the background will change to the outrageous color. Zoom in. Do you see any spots or blotches in the solid background?

Unsharp edges also mean non-solid backgrounds. Any object has unsharp edges if the edges are anti-aliased, have glows, drop-shadows, or vignettes (see fig. 11.1).

There are two ways to make irregularly shaped graphics: one for use against HTML backgrounds, and the other for use against a graphics background.

Figure 11.1

The result of a "not-so-solid" background.

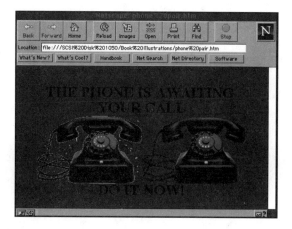

When to Use Matching Backgrounds

Use matching backgrounds whenever you want to use unsharp edges for the irregular figure. This is because GIF89a is the only currently available file format that enables transparent backgrounds. Unfortunately, because GIF89a has no provision for "alpha channel masking," only one of its 256 colors can be designated transparent.

> **Note**
>
> Alpha channel masks make it possible to have semi-transparency in an image. Such an image could fade into or "blend" with any underlying image, such as a background texture. The term "alpha channels" refers to at least some of the information in the 8 bits-per-pixels of information left over in a 32-bit image after 24 bits have been used to describe up to 16.8 million possible colors in an image. The most common use for this information is masking, since 8-bits is enough image data to describe 256 levels of gray. Any part of the mask that is less than solid black will allow some part of another image to show through.

Shades of the same color are considered different colors in computerese. Therefore, unsharp edges won't become gradually transparent and are likely to appear with blotchy halos against a textured background. Vignettes are an excellent example of images that could benefit from alpha channel masking (see fig. 11.2).

Figure 11.2

The vignette encircling this portrait is created by alpha channel masking.

Converting Non-Solid Backgrounds to Solid Backgrounds

If you're already familiar with the operations of your favorite image editor, here's the short version of how to isolate your images against a solid background. First, mask the subject from the background. In computer image editing, a *mask* is a layer that isolates parts of an image or layer from being affected by other layers or from any editing (such as brush strokes). If you will be matching backgrounds, the mask can be anti-aliased, feathered, or have semi-transparent areas. If you will be using a clear background, make sure that none of the preceding is true. Once the masking is done, invert the mask so that the background is selected. Fill the selection with a solid color. (Please, no gradients or textures!) That's it.

For those who need a more explicit tutorial, here's how to do it in Photoshop 3.0.5. On the other hand, even if you're experienced, you may find valuable procedural tips in some of the specific steps.

Exercise 11.1

1. Open the image you want to place on a clear background. Figure 11.3 is an image of a shell.

Figure 11.3

Not a solid color background.

This shell was shot on a solid white background, but the lighting and shadows give it many color values. Also, separating the whites in the shell from the whites in the background must be done manually.

2. Choose Window, Palettes, Show Channels. This opens the channels window so that you can see your mask. A mask keeps the underlying pixels from being affected by any image manipulation command, such as re-coloring or running a special-effects filter.

3. Choose the Lasso tool. This tool is used to make a freehand selection. Drawing freehand means drawing without the aid of a tool such as a ruler or compass that intentionally limits the movement of the line.

4. Double-click on the Lasso tool icon. This opens the Lasso Options Window. If you will be placing your irregular shape on an image background, click on the Lasso Options tab and make sure the Anti-Alias box is unchecked. If you will be placing your irregular shape on a matching background, you won't be using GIF89a transparency, so you may as well benefit from the smoother-looking edges produced by anti-aliasing. If this is the case, make sure the box is checked (for a complete explanation of anti-aliasing and its benefits, see the Glossary).

5. Choose Window, Zoom In to magnify the image to a ratio of 2:1.

6. Using the Lasso tool, carefully draw a marquee around the subject of the illustration. It may be easiest to start with a loose loop, then press and hold Cmd (Alt in Windows) while carving away portions of the selection, until the shape is outlined with perfect precision, as illustrated in figure 11.4.

Graphics Creation

Figure 11.4

*Selecting the shell
with the Lasso tool.*

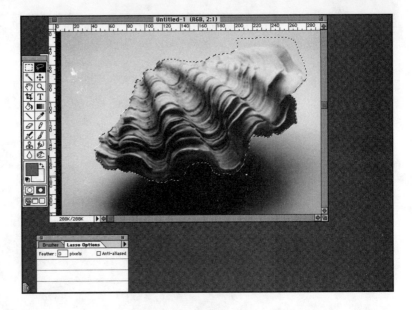

7. Choose the Quick Mask icon at the bottom of the toolbox (see fig. 11.5). Be
   sure that there are no stray background pixels around the edges of the shape that
   could cause a halo if this image is placed against a dark background. If you find
   some, fill them in with the Pencil tool, NOT the brush. All Photoshop brushes
   are anti-aliased.

Figure 11.5

*The zoomed-in shell
in Quick Mask mode.*

It is easy to see the stray white pixels at the edge of the selection. Paint them in with the Pencil tool. The Brush, Airbrush, and Clone tools are anti-aliased and will simply give you more stray pixels.

8. Choose the Standard selection mode tool (just to the left of the Quick Mask mode tool) and you'll see the selection marquee around your subject.

9. Choose Select, Save Selection. The Save Selection dialog box will appear. Click on OK.

10. In the Channels palette, double-click on the channel bar labeled #4. A Channel Options dialog box appears (see fig. 11.6). Type in a name for the selection. Someday, when you want to have several masks for an image, you'll find it much easier to identify them by name than by number. Might as well start learning good habits now. By the way, you've saved the mask so you won't have to waste time redrawing it if you decide later you want to feather, reduce, anti-alias, or use part of the mask. You must be sure, however, to save the file in a format such as .PSD (Photoshop), .TGA (Targa), or .TIF (TIFF) that can accept an alpha channel—GIF cannot.

Figure 11.6

Renaming a channel in the Channels palette.

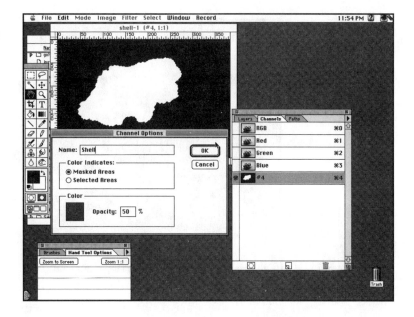

11. Click on the left column of the RGB channel. An icon of an eye appears in the RGB channel and in each of the color channels. The eye icon disappears from the mask channel, and you can see your image, with the selection marquee active.

12. Choose Select Inverse.

13. Choose the Crop tool. Drag its marquee so it just encloses your irregularly shaped object. Double-click inside the cropping marquee. You have just taken a step to ensure that the image will load as quickly as possible when it's used on a Web page. Why? Because the horizontal and vertical dimensions are no larger than they need to be. Alignment of irregular objects is also much easier when you don't have unneeded pixels. Graphics align by their actual borders, not by the irregular images within.

14. Save the file.

Matching Backgrounds to Graphics

Sometimes transparency doesn't work if you want your irregularly shaped graphics to have smooth, anti-aliased edges, drop shadows, glows, or other "semi-transparent" effects. If you set an irregularly shaped object with "semi-transparent" edges, it will have an ugly halo around the edge, as illustrated in figure 11.7.

Figure 11.7

The Ugly Halo Syndrome.

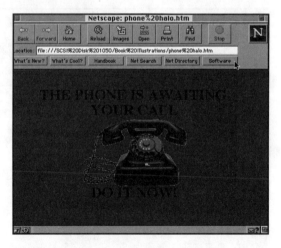

To avoid UHS (Ugly Halo Syndrome), make the background for your graphic match the background for your page, as demonstrated in Exercise 11.2.

Exercise 11.2

1. Open the HTML page that will be the background for this image. Use the browser you think will be most often used to view your page.

2. Capture this screen. To do so, press Shift+Print Scn (Windows) or Cmd+Option+3 (Mac).

3. Save the screen capture to your hard drive (this happens automatically on Macintosh).

4. Open Photoshop and open the file containing the screen capture. Also, open the file containing your irregularly shaped object.

5. If it hasn't already been done, follow the steps in Exercise 11.1 for creating an irregular object on a solid-color background.

6. Activate the Window for the irregular shape by clicking inside it. Choose Select, Load Selection; then choose Select, Float.

7. Choose Window, Palette, Show Layers. In the Layers Palette, double-click on the Layer labeled "Floating Selection." The Layer Options dialog box appears. Name the layer after the irregular shape. Make sure Mode is Normal and Opacity is 100%.

8. Click on the shape layer's eye icon to hide it. It will look as though nothing has happened, because there is still a copy of the shape on the background.

9. In Photoshop, with your irregular image still open, choose File, Open and open the screen shot you just made.

10. Choose the Eyedropper tool. Click in the background of the HTML screen. Its exact color is now your foreground color. (If the background is graphical, pick the most predominant color beneath your irregular shape.) This color now fills the Foreground Color icon in the toolbox.

11. Make your irregular shape the active window. Choose Edit, Fill. In the Fill dialog box, choose Foreground Color. Be sure Opacity is 100% (if not, type it in) and Mode is Normal. Click on OK. The entire background now fills with a solid color. If the HTML page is a solid color, the background of your graphic will match it exactly. Best of all, you haven't had to learn one thing about hexadecimal color codes (but you may want to learn this for some other purpose at some other time). See Chapter 14 for more on hex colors.

12. Crop the image as in step 13 of Exercise 11.1. Save the file.

Creating Soft-Edged Graphics Against Solid Backgrounds.

Now that you've matched the color of the background for both your graphic and the destination Web page, it's safe to give your irregularly shaped objects the illusion of having semi-transparent or "soft" edges. These fall into several general categories: vignettes, drop shadows, and special effects. The techniques for accomplishing them differ. The following exercises show how to do each one.

Vignettes

A *vignette* is a way of framing a graphic. You can use them as a substitute for frames, if it seems appropriate to the image. Vignettes were used often in Victorian photo portraiture, so using a vignette often "antiques" the image. A vignette is such a noticeable effect, you want to be sure that the use fits the look of the graphic and the page. Vignettes are also useful for making the image appear as though it were coming from a dream state. Making a vignette is easy and can give quite a bit of variation in the effect. A traditional oval vignette is shown in figure 11.8.

Figure 11.8

A traditional oval vignette.

Vignettes can be any shape, and the edges can have varying degrees of roughness. Think about the interesting variety of vignettes you could make by using multiple layers.

The basics of how to make a simple vignette are detailed in the following exercise.

Exercise 11.3

1. Open the image you want to vignette.

2. Choose the selection tool that will most easily shape the frame you want. The example in figure 11.9 demonstrates a traditional oval, created with the marquee tool. Double-click on the chosen selection tool to bring up the Tool Options dialog box. The configurations for this example were Feathering at 15 pixels, Style set to Normal, Anti-aliasing checked.

Figure 11.9

A vignette created with the oval selection tool.

3. Drag an oval selection evenly around the subject. If you need to move the selection to position it correctly over the object, press Ctrl+Alt (Win) or Cmd+Option (Mac), then click inside the selection and drag it to its new position.

4. Choose Select, Inverse.

5. Choose the Eyedropper tool to select the color of the destination background, as described in Exercise 11.2.

6. Choose Edit, Fill. In the Fill dialog box, choose Foreground Color. Make sure Mode is Normal and Opacity is 100%. You now have a feathered vignette against a solid background color.

7. Choose the Cropping tool and crop the image at the points closest to where the background becomes solid.

8. If the transition between the vignette and the background isn't totally smooth, blend the colors by using the Airbrush tool, set at 50 percent pressure with a large, feathered brush.

9. Save the file.

There is also a Photoshop-compatible plug-in filter for automating vignettes, called Photo/Graphic Edges. It's published by Auto/FX Software, where they make lots of useful plug-ins. Check their Web site at the following:

```
http://www.autofx.com/
```

Drop Shadows

Strictly speaking, a drop shadow makes an object seem to stand out from the background because of the "shadow" cast on it. The most popular use of drop shadows is for headline text and interactive buttons, but many other types of graphics can benefit from them as well (see fig. 11.10).

Figure 11.10

Images using drop shadows.

Before you create an irregular graphic with a drop shadow, be sure the background matches the background of your target Web page. Exercise 11.2 shows you how to do that.

The following exercise shows how to create drop shadows. They can be made more automatically by using any of several special effects filter packages, all mentioned in the graphics software guide in Appendix B of this book. If you don't have the budget for such filters, you can make drop shadows manually. The best way is to use Photoshop's Layers (or the layers in any other image editor that has them).

Exercise 11.4

1. It is assumed that you want to place this drop shadow in a particular Web page. Because drop shadows have soft edges, you will get UHS (Ugly Halo Syndrome) unless you create the drop shadow in a file with the same color background as the page on which you intend to use it.

2. Using your browser, navigate to the Web page on which you want to place the drop shadow. Capture the screen by using Shift+PrntScn (Windows) and saving to disk or by choosing Cmd+Option+3 (Mac). Now, in Photoshop, open the screen capture of your target Web page. Choose File, New. The New File dialog box opens. Set the file size to be approximately 25 percent larger than the element for which you want to create a drop shadow. Make sure the resolution is 72 dpi. Click on OK.

3. Choose the Eyedropper tool. Click inside the background color of the target Web page. The foreground color now matches that of the Web page.

4. Activate the New File window. Choose Select, All. Choose Edit, Fill. The Fill dialog box appears. Choose Foreground Color from the foreground window. Make sure Mode is Normal and Opacity is 100%, and click on OK. You now have a matching background.

5. Change the foreground color to one that contrasts enough with the background to make your text readable. If the text color needs to match that on another page, use the same Eyedropper technique as for matching a background.

6. Choose the Text tool and click in the new background. The text dialog box appears. Choose any font in your system from the drop-down list, being sure to set the font to the right size and style (such as bold or italic). Type the word(s) you want to use and click on OK.

7. The word(s) you typed will appear on the background, surrounded by a selection marquee. Choose Selection, Save Selection. The Save Selection dialog box appears. Click on OK. Saving the selection for text makes it easy to repeat and modify special effects later.

8. Choose Selection, Float. In the Layers palette, name the resulting layer. From the Layers palette fly-out, choose Duplicate Layer.

9. Choose the Move Object tool and press the arrow keys to offset the duplicate layer from the original by a specific number, both horizontally and vertically. Using this method makes it easier to keep the offset consistent when you make drop shadows for other objects on the same page or site.

Graphics Creation

10. In the Layers palette, drag the duplicate layer below the original layer.

11. Hide the original layer by clicking on its eye icon. Activate the duplicate layer.

12. Use Photoshop's controls to adjust the brightness of the duplicate layer. This will be your drop shadow. You can also use any of Photoshop's other image controls to affect the character of the shadow.

13. Choose Filter, Blur, Gaussian Blur. Set the blur radius to a small number such as 1.5 or 2. Look at the preview. If the blur is too little or too much, adjust the blur radius. Once you get what you like, write down the radius so that you can duplicate it for other drop-shadow text and keep the appearance of your site consistent. Click on OK.

14. Turn on the original layer.

15. From the Layers palette fly-out menu, choose Flatten Layers.

16. Crop the image as close to the letters and drop shadows as possible, so that you will be able to align text accurately.

17. Save the file.

Special Effects that Create Soft Edges

There are many other types of special effects that create soft edges. This book will not elaborate on these, because it is about efficiently converting existing content for publication on the World Wide Web. These special effects can certainly be accomplished manually, but if you want to do them quickly, buy Photoshop-compatible plug-in filters that automate the job for you.

Some of the most frequently used graphical text effects are produced automatically by third-party Photoshop-compatible plug-in filters. The most popular of these, from Alien Skin Software, come as a single set of filters on floppy disk. Alien Skin filters are available for both Macs and Windows/Intel computers. The effects produced by Alien Skin filters, except for the drop shadow, are illustrated in figure 11.11. Other third-party special effect filters produce soft edges, as well. For a more complete listing, see Appendix B.

Figure 11.11

The Alien Skin Filter effects: Glass, Glow, HSB, Noise, Swirl, and The Boss.

Those who are designing Web sites will find themselves working extensively with graphical text. These filters are especially useful for text effects, but they will work their magic on anything that's marquee-selected in Photoshop. Other types of graphics especially suited to these effects are frames, icons, banners, and interactive buttons.

Making GIF89a Backgrounds Transparent

If you want an illustration, graphical type, or other graphics element to blend with a graphic background, rather than being enclosed in a rectangular frame, you need to make the background of the graphic transparent.

So far, the only widely browser-supported file format that permits transparency is GIF89a. This is less than ideal because the format only permits one color to be transparent and does not support alpha channels. In common terminology, this means part of the graphic is either transparent or it isn't—there's no way to make gradual transparency. For the same reason, you have to be absolutely sure your background is a single color. Review the previous section on creating solid backgrounds for more information.

Warning

If you are trying to cut down file size by limiting the number of colors, and you plan to use the result with a transparent background, make sure you don't dither colors. Doing so will give your supposedly clear background a bad case of the "measles," as illustrated in figure 11.12.

Graphics Creation

Figure 11.12

An attempt to make a clear background for a dithered image.

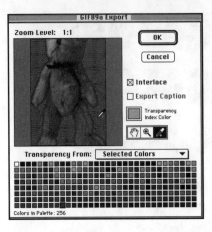

> **Note**
>
> Someday soon now, browser makers such as Netscape, Microsoft, and Oracle will support a new format that is being pushed by the W³ Consortium (the group that sets standards for the World Wide Web). It is called PNG (Portable Network Graphics) and is pronounced "ping." PNG format files can have alpha channels, so you will be able to have drop-shadowed text and other soft-edged graphics you can superimpose smoothly over any background. PNG has many other attractive qualities. PNG is discussed in more detail in Chapter 10.

The GIF89a format is just now becoming incorporated into the latest versions of all the popular image editors. If it isn't built into your image editor, there are several shareware utilities that will do the job on their own. Some additional time will be spent in this chapter talking about the usefulness of automating graphics file conversion with a Macintosh utility called DeBabelizer. DeBabelizer also enables you to save files to GIF89a format, with the option of designating a transparent color. Finally, some HTML editors, such as PageMill, enable you to designate the transparent color in an image when you place the graphic in the HTML file.

The procedures for saving files with a transparent background differ among image editors, independent utilities, and HTML editors. This is illustrated in the following sections with Photoshop for image editors, HVS WebFocus for a shareware utility, and PageMill for a WYSIWYG HTML editor.

Graphics Creation

> **Note**
>
> Most of the time when you're working with graphics, especially if you're working with photographs, you'll be working in RGB mode and "millions of colors" (or thousands, at least). Before you can save any file in GIF format, it will have to be converted to indexed color (256 or fewer colors, with each color assigned a specific place in the palette). Refer to this chapter's section on minimizing file size for more information.

Creating a Transparent GIF in Photoshop

Adobe provides a free Photoshop-compatible plug-in export filter called the GIF89a Export plug-in. It is built into Photoshop 3.0.5. If you have an earlier version, you can download the filter from Adobe's Web site:

```
http://www.adobe.com/Software.html.
```

> **Note**
>
> You can save a non-indexed RGB file by using the GIF89a export filter. The filter will automatically reduce the file to 256 colors, and you can choose fewer colors, with a preview. You cannot, however, designate a transparent color without first, in Photoshop, changing Mode to Indexed Color.

There are two ways to save a transparent background by using the GIF89a Export Filter: by choosing a transparent color or by saving from a selection. If you are isolating part of a picture that doesn't have a solid color background, saving from a selection saves you time. This procedure will be described first in the next exercise, followed by an explanation of which steps to change if you want to designate a specific color. Designating a specific color is easier if you have a truly solid color background.

Exercise 11.5

1. Make sure the GIF89a Export Filter is in your Photoshop plug-ins folder.

2. Open your image in Photoshop. Assume you have already performed the steps necessary to make it the right size. If not, refer to the section called "Scaling Graphics for the Web." Assume the image you're working with is a photo. Because you want the photo to appear at a small size, make it a GIF file so it will load quickly without having to wait for the computer to decompress it. For this reason, although larger photos are usually saved to the true-color JPEG format, save this photo to GIF.

3. Choose Mode, Indexed Color. Photoshop knows there are more than 256 colors in this image, so it opens the Indexed Color dialog box. Choose the 8-bits per pixel Radio Button in the Resolution box, Adaptive in the Palette box, and Diffusion in the Dither box. Then click on OK.

> **Note**
>
> You may wonder why we dithered this palette when we told you dithering can make it impossible to select a transparent area. The Photoshop GIF89a Export filter is unique in enabling you to do this, because you can designate the transparent area with any of the selection tools, save the selection, then designate the selection as the transparent area. The method for doing this is outlined in steps 4 and 5.

4. Choose the Lasso tool and double-click on its icon to bring up its Options dialog. Make sure "anti-aliased" is unchecked. Use the Lasso to outline the shape you want to keep as an image. This can be a loose "splash" around the subject. You could also use the Lasso to carefully silhouette your subject.

5. Choose File, Export, GIF89a Export. The GIF89a Export dialog box appears. Choose #2 from the Transparency From pull-down menu. As soon as you do this, the area outside your selection changes to medium gray, the color shown as the Transparency Index Color. Click on OK.

> **Note**
>
> The other choice in the Transparency From pull-down menu is Selected Colors. If you choose that option, you can then choose the Eyedropper icon from the group just above the pull-down menu. Use the Eyedropper to pick as many colors in the palette as you like. Each of these colors will become the same color, which can be designated as transparent when the file is exported to GIF89a. You will undoubtedly find an imaginative use for this feature.

6. The File Save As dialog box now appears. Name the file and click on OK.

Making a Clear Background Using HVS WebFocus Toolkit

Many utilities available on the Web will let you make a transparent GIF. The HVS Web Focus Toolkit has been singled out here for several reasons: it's cross-platform (Mac and Windows); it does all kinds of wonderful tricks to make your graphics files as Web-efficient as possible (more, in fact, than any other method easily accessible); it's easy-to-use.

The HVS Web Focus Toolkit will be discussed more thoroughly in the section on Minimizing File Size.

Making a Clear Background Using Adobe PageMill

If you're using an HTML editor, you may not need to go to an outside image editor, plug-in, or utility to make a transparent GIF. In fact, you may not even have to convert your files to GIF or JPEG format. Several HTML editors automatically convert any image you open, or they ask whether you want to save to JPEG or GIF. Nearly all will also let you choose a color to make transparent and give you the option of interlacing if you're saving to GIF.

Exercise 11.6 that follows demonstrates how all that works in Adobe PageMill. PageMill is better than most at this because it puts the picture in a window and lets you work visually (as illustrated in fig. 11.13), instead of having you fill in cryptic blanks in a form.

Figure 11.13

The PageMill image editing window.

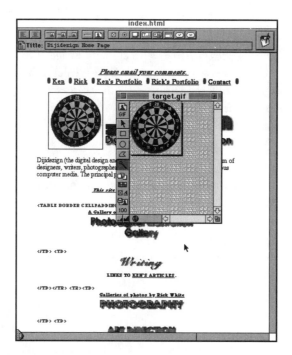

Graphics Creation

Exercise 11.6

1. While in PageMill, choose the Insert Image icon from the toolbar. A File Open dialog box appears. Open the GIF file you want to use. At this point, the image appears on your page.

2. If it isn't the right size, don't re-scale it in PageMill—even though you can do that by dragging the scale handles that appear around the image. If you scale down, the image will take too long to load. If you scale up, the image will be jagged and blurry. This happens because PageMill doesn't in fact resize the image; it just changes the HTML HSIZE and VSIZE attributes in the <IMG> tag. Go back to Photoshop, rescale to the right size, and resave.

3. When the image appears at the correct size, simply double-click on it. PageMill's Image Editor opens. From the Image Editor toolbox, choose the Palette Knife (it looks like Photoshop's Magic Wand). Click the palette knife on the color you want to make transparent. Close the Image Editor window. An Error dialog box appears, asking if you want to save changes to the image file. Click on Save. The transparency color has now been recorded in your original GIF file.

Making Seamless Background Tiles

One of the best ways to make a page look interesting is to give it a textured or image background. Any image designated as a background image in the background attribute of the <BODY> tag will automatically repeat (tile) from left to right, then top to bottom. Background tiles can be any size—they can even fill up the whole page. In order for them to look natural, background tiles have to match the edges that will touch one another. If the tile is to be a pattern consisting of images on a solid background, the tiles will abut (meet) one another seamlessly. This is illustrated in figure 11.14.

A nice trick is to place a washed-out monochrome photo or painting on an otherwise solid-color background, as shown in figures 11.15 and 11.16. The image can be saved in 3-bit color and compresses very well, due to the large area of repetition. Even so, this page will load more slowly than a background of smaller tiles, so use the technique sparingly and don't place too many large graphics in the foreground of the same page.

Figure 11.14

Techno tile back-ground.

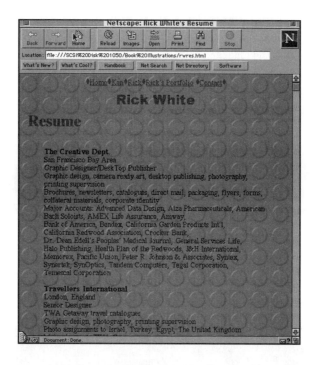

Figure 11.15

Inset of tile and page.

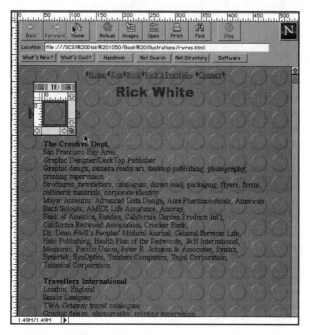

Figure 11.16

A picture background page.

A technique that gives the appearance of a full-page image, but loads quickly, is that of creating a series of colors in a wide, narrow graphic that will fill the background. This can be as simple as making a bar one-pixel high and as wide as the widest likely viewing monitor (1,024 pixels). You can change the colors in the bar as often as you like to make vertical strips on the page (see fig. 11.17). Hint: this is also a good way to make a vertical column bar.

A variation on this technique incorporates a pattern, such as the spiral notebook punch wire and line or a film strip, as part of the vertical bar. If most of the colors in the bar are the same, the file will compress to a tiny size.

The technique most commonly encountered (probably because it's so versatile) is the small textured tile. This technique can make your background look like handmade papers (as in fig. 11.18), concrete, wood—or just plain psychedelic.

Before learning how to make a seamless tile, you should know about the hundreds available in clip-art libraries. If you use these, test to make sure they've been compressed as much as possible; then place them by using the image attribute in your <BODY> tag. There are quite a few on the CD-ROM that comes with this book, and Appendix B lists numerous sources for seamless tiles on the Web.

Figure 11.17

A color column page.

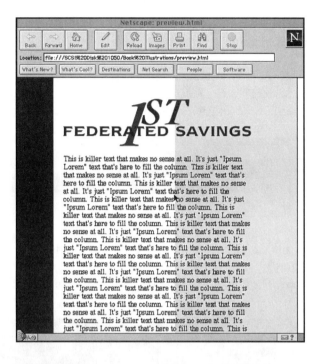

Figure 11.18

A background texture page from DijiDezign.

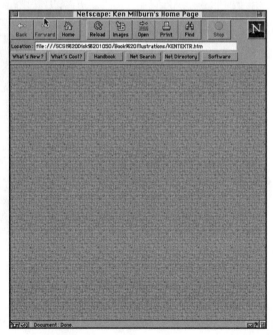

Quite a few image-editing programs have a built-in "seamless tile" filter. All you have to do is make a selection and issue the Make Seamless Tile command from the Filter menu. JASC PaintShopPro, a highly recommended low-cost (even shareware, if you don't mind being one version out-of-date) image editor for Windows (3.1 or 95) has this feature. So does Fractal Designs' Painter 4.0 (Mac and Windows). By the way, Painter is a terrific tool for painting all sorts of textures.

> **Note**
>
> The smaller the tile, the faster your background will load. The browser need only load the tile once. It then repeats the pattern from the information held in its cache. This relates to the already stated rule about repeating the same graphic as often as possible in your site.

Having said all that, the following exercise demonstrates how to make your own seamless texture tiles in Photoshop. Most image editors have an "overlap" filter similar to Photoshop's. The Photoshop windows are illustrated in figure 11.19.

Figure 11.19

Making a seamless tile in Photoshop 3.0.5.

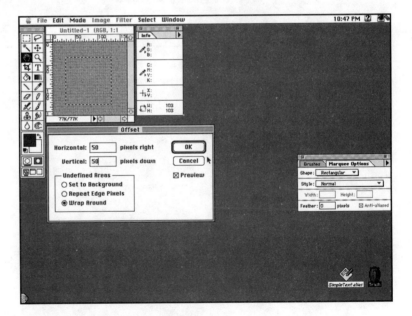

Exercise 11.7

1. With Photoshop running, open a file that has a texture you'd like to use for your background.

2. Choose the Rectangular marquee tool and drag a rectangle that's as small as possible. A 24-pixel square image is about right, because you need some space for the overlap operation in the next step.

3. Choose Edit, Copy, then File, New. Click on OK without resizing the new file, as it is already the size of your tile. When the new file window opens, Choose Edit, Paste. Then Choose Select, All.

4. Choose Filter, Other, Offset. The Offset dialog box appears. Make sure the Wrap Around radio button is checked. Make the offset about half the pixel width of your tile and click on OK.

5. Retouch the seams that are now in the center of your tile so they're not apparent. The best way to do this is with the Clone tool, with which you paint patterns over the seam to make it invisible. Other options are to simply paint over the seam with a brush, blur the entire tile with the Gaussian Blur filter, or use the Smudge tool to make the seam less obvious.

Creating Picture Frames

Picture frames help to isolate an image from its surroundings, so that the persons viewing the picture are more likely to focus their attention within the frame. They're also useful for identifying the "character" you want the image to convey. For instance, if you want to date a series of images to the 1930's, you could frame all the attendant illustrations in Art Deco frames.

There are many ways to create the basic frame, as described in the following:

- Take photos of actual picture frames.

- Create a large button with beveled edges and place the picture in the center.

- Drag a rectangular marquee around the picture and use Edit, Stroke to make a clean frame in whatever foreground color you've chosen. Remember that when you set the stroke width, half the width will be drawn on one side of the marquee and half on the other. Be sure to leave enough room around the marquee so that the stroke doesn't crop your picture.

- Texturize a basic, gray, beveled "library" frame. There are several of these on the CD-ROM accompanying this book.

Here's how to make your own picture frames in Photoshop 3.0.5. Be sure to make your frames no larger than the largest picture you can expect your viewers to see without scrolling: 610×280. As you will see in Exercise 11.8, you will be able to resize these frames to fit any smaller image. These exercises are also helpful for making buttons, bullets, and banners. Just modify the proportions and don't use components you don't need.

Creating a Stock Frame

Exercise 11.8 shows you how to make a stock frame you can resize and recolor to use for many applications. Make several of these in different shapes.

Exercise 11.8

1. Choose File, New and set the image size to approximately 800 pixels square. Later you will see how this gives you room to resize your frame to fit around its picture. When the image opens, use the foreground/background tool to select a bright contrasting foreground color.

2. Choose Edit, Fill, Foreground color (in the Contents box).

3. Choose Windows, Palettes, Show Layers. From the Layers Palette fly-out, choose Make New Layer. Do all the operations to make this stock frame on separate layers. Later, this will make it very easy to change the size of the frame, to re-shade the highlights and shadows of bevels, and to make new designs from old designs

4. Choose Windows, Palettes, Show Info. Choose the Rectangle selection marquee and drag a frame exactly 605×275 pixels.

5. Choose Select, Save Selection and click on OK when the dialog box pops up.

6. Pick a bright, just-off-white color (such as light fuchsia) for the foreground; then choose Edit, Stroke. In the dialog box, set the pixel width at 3 (just a suggestion—this is actually up to you). Click on OK. Click off the selection box. You now have a 3-pixel-wide pink frame on a lime-green background.

7. From the Layers palette fly-out, choose Duplicate Layer. Activate the new layer by clicking on it in the Layers palette. Click on Preserve Transparency in the Layers palette. Select black as the foreground color and choose Edit, Fill, Foreground Color (make sure Mode is Normal). The frame on the second layer turns black, precisely covering the frame on the first layer.

8. Double-click on the Eraser tool to bring up the Brush Options palette and set the brush size to about 20 pixels, Un-feathered. Make sure Preserve Transparency is checked in the Layers palette. Erase the top and left sides of the frame just into the corners.

9. Choose Select, Load Selection. Click on OK; then choose Select, Modify, Contrast. Enter 8 pixels in the dialog box and click on OK. You now have a new selection inside the old selection. Repeat steps 4–6 to make as many frame bevels as you like. The inside bevel should have the highlight and shadow areas reversed.

10. When you've repeated and varied these steps enough to get the frame design you like, make the Background Layer active (click on its bar in the Layers palette) and fill the layer with neutral gray. From the Layers palette fly-out, choose Flatten Image.

11. Choose the Magic Wand tool and click in the outside gray area. Then press Shift-Click inside the frame. Choose Select, Inverse and then Select, Save Selection (see fig. 11.20). Now, any time you recall the selection, you can move, recolor, or filter the frame without affecting its background or contents. You can create many new frame looks from the same original file.

Figure 11.20

Photoshop's Save Selection dialog box.

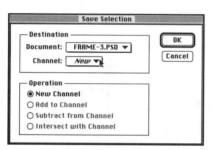

12. With the frame still selected, choose Select, and press Delete. The area inside and outside the frame become transparent. Make a new layer. It will name itself Layer 1. Rename the Background Layer to Frame. Drag the Layer 1 bar below the Frame bar. With Layer 1 active, fill it with a contrasting background color (dark gray works well because it's neutral, which means that any art put in the frame will not be adversely affected by the surrounding colors).

13. Save the file as LIBFRM01.PSD (or any file name with PSD as the extension). This saves the file to a cross-platform file name in Photoshop 3.0 format, which preserves the layers so you can easily modify and resize the frame later.

Redecorating the Frame

You can use any of the paint brushes or Photoshop filters to change the appearance of your frame.

To recolor the frame, follow the procedure outlined in Exercise 11.9.

Graphics Creation

Exercise 11.9

1. Open the library frame saved in Exercise 11.8 or one from the CD-ROM that comes with this book. Make the Frame Layer active.

2. Chose the foreground color that you would like to use to "paint" the frame. Make sure the Preserve Transparency Box is checked in the Layers palette.

3. Choose Edit, Fill, Foreground Color. Make sure Mode is set to Color in the drop-down list and click on OK.

You can also set any of the paint brushes, texture filters such as KPT Texture Explorer (shown in fig. 11.21), Adobe Texturizer, or the Xaos Terrazzo Filters—to name only a few.

Figure 11.21

The same frame redecorated with KPT Texture Explorer.

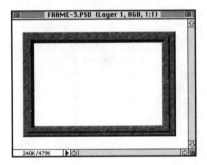

Resizing the Frame

You can resize your frame to fit any picture smaller than the frame. To do this, duplicate the frame on two layers, putting the picture on an underlying layer. Use the Move tool to adjust the frames to fit the picture border; then erase the unneeded portions of frames from the two layers (see fig. 11.22). When you do this, be sure Preserve Transparency is unchecked.

Figure 11.22

Moving the frame to fit the picture.

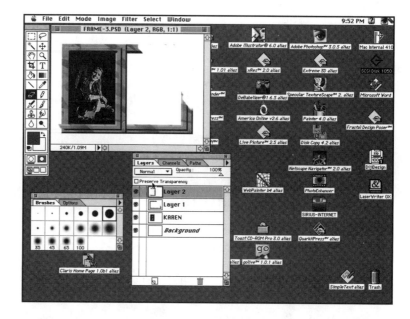

Creating Moving Graphics

Anything that moves will immediately attract more attention than a static image. That's why flashing neon and pulsating marquee lights are so popular in nighttime signage. It's also the main reason why you may want to put "movies" (video or animation) on your Web pages. The other two are education and entertainment. Watching a golfer's swing is much more informative than reading about it—and more fun, too.

The problem with Web movies is that they are composed of many "frames," and each frame is a graphic. If it takes ten frames a second to effectively animate the golfer, the moving image will be ten times larger in file size than an equivalent static one. So it will take ten times longer to appear on your screen.

One thing that helps this problem is "streaming" technology: instead of waiting for the whole "movie" to load before playing, the movie starts playing after only a few frames have loaded. Remember, however, that a longer movie will need to load more frames before it starts playing than will a shorter one. That's because enough frames have to load to ensure that most or all the movie will play smoothly as the remainder of the frames load.

So, regardless of the movie type and whether or not it "streams," use any trick you can find to make Web movies as small as possible. Also, use loops whenever you can. *Loops* are movies that repeat as soon as the last frame has played. If the last frame ends in register with the first frame, the animation will appear to go on forever. For instance, you could show a constantly flashing neon sign in only two or three frames.

Creating GIF Animations

GIF animations have two endearingly valuable characteristics: (1) They tend to be easier to make than other types of animations. (2) They don't require plug-ins in order to be visible in most post-Netscape Navigator 2.0 browsers. If your purpose in using an animation is simply to create an attention-getter, creating an animation in Java, Shockwave, or QuickTime is probably more trouble than its worth.

A GIF animation doesn't have to be the moving cartoon we traditionally call an animation. It can be a traditional slide show consisting of a series of static images (see fig. 11.23). An interesting variation on the slide show is made possible by the fact that one image in a slide show hides its predecessor rather than replacing it. You thus can make a sequence of navigation buttons that appear one at a time or create a progressive montage of overlapping photos.

Figure 11.23

An overlapping static image animation.

> **Note**
>
> It is important that all images in an animated GIF use the same palette. Otherwise, the images will shift color as they appear. An easy way to assure this is to make all the images in the same program at the same time. You can also use a program such as DeBabelizer to automate the matching of a series of image files to the same palette.

The Animated GIF Process

Making an animated GIF is a two-stage process. First, you make the frames (see fig. 11.24). Next, you import them into a utility that enables you to place them in the proper sequence. For the Macintosh, the most popular utility for this is Jacques Piguet's GIFBuilder, which is freeware and can be downloaded from:

```
http://iawww.epf1.ch/Staff/Yves.Piguet/clip2gif-home
➥ GifBuilder.html
```

You'll also find GIFBuilder on this book's accompanying CD-ROM.

If you're a Windows user, there is a versatile program worth much more than its puny $20 shareware license fee. It's called GIF Construction Set from Alchemy Mindworks. You can download it from the following:

```
http://www.mindworkshop.com
```

Figure 11.24

Individual frames in a GIF animation.

Formatting Frames in Animated GIFs

There are several ways to make the frames for your animation. First, you can place virtually any type of movie format as a clip in Adobe Premiere, then export each frame as a still image. Premiere will accept such movie formats as QuickTime, AVI (Microsoft Movie), or FLI (kinetix Animator animations).

Second, you can create animations from scratch by using such programs as Director, Gold Disk's Animation Works (for both Mac and Windows), or Kinetix Animator Pro (Windows). These programs also create movies in formats that can be used in Premiere and thus be incorporated into movies that also contain segments that originated in other file formats. Some of the programs give you the option of saving individual frames as stills. Finally, you can make animations from scratch, frame by frame, by using any paint, draw, or illustration program.

For a complete listing of animation programs, please see Appendix B.

Graphics Creation

Layering Frames for Sequencing

It is easiest to use layers for tracing paper, using a program that enables you to turn layers on and off. Photoshop, Painter, Illustrator, Freehand, xRes, and Live Picture are all capable of doing this—as are many other programs. You can then make each frame in sequence, one on top of the other. By turning layers on and off (and adjusting transparency if you're working in a program that permits it, such as Photoshop), it is easy to keep subsequent frames in register (see fig. 11.25).

Figure 11.25

Using layers for tracing paper.

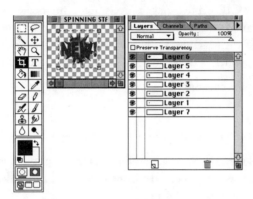

Because each layer is part of the same file, all the files are the same size and use the same palette. When you're finished, turn off all but the first layer and save (or export) the file to a single-layer bitmap format. Then turn that layer off, turn on the second layer, and save the file again. You can use the same file name, but add a number to designate the sequence of the frame (for example, Cat1, Cat2, and so forth). It's a fine way to keep track of frame sequences before placing them in your animated GIF utility.

If you want to know more about animated GIFs outside the scope of this book, here are a couple of Web sites you might find helpful. You may also find some free downloadable animations on these two sites:

```
http://member.aol.com/royalef/gifanim.htm
```

```
http://www.teleport.com/~cooler/MMMM/index.html
```

Creating Shockwave Animations

Almost anything that's been created as a Macromedia Director animation can be placed in line on a Web page, so long as the target browser is Netscape Navigator 3.0-compatible. These can include larger and more complex animations than those that are suitable for GIF animation. Shockwave animations can also incorporate Director's programmable interactivity.

Considerations for Shockwave Animations

Besides file size, there are other considerations for putting Director movies on the Web. Some new Lingo scripting commands exist that are specific to Shockwave. There are some features in Director that won't work in Shockwave. Finally, be sure that the movie you're playing will look good in the browser your viewer is using. At the time of this writing, this included only Netscape Navigator 2.1.

Macromedia has already announced its intention to make Shockwave plug-ins and technology work within more recent versions of Netscape Navigator and with Microsoft Internet Explorer 3.0. There has even been an announcement that Shockwave will be working in a future version of the America Online dial-up service. In short, by the time you read this, you can expect Shockwave to work in most popular browsers. The only way you can be sure is to test, however.

Rules for Effective Shockwave Animations

Effective and efficient Director movies for the Web should have the following characteristics:

- Smallest possible file size—preferably under 100 KB.
- Simple and looping.
- The number of colors kept to a minimum.
- Slow frame rate (as slow as you can get away with).
- If a movie has to be larger to make a point, consider linking it to a still graphic. Put in a linked line of HTML code that says, for example: "To see the full 2 MB movie, click here. It will take 20 minutes or more to come up on your screen."

Don't even bother with Shockwave movies unless your server is configured to show them. If you're not running your own server, the only way to know this will be to ask your system administrator. The foregoing precaution also pertains to Shockwave for Freehand and to Shockwave for Authorware. To get instructions on configuring your server, go to the following:

```
http://www.macromedia.com/shockwave/director/getstart.html#server
```

Graphics Creation

The Shockwave Animation Procedure

Here are the steps for creating a Shockwave animation:

1. Make a movie with data transmission rates in mind. Check out the new Web-specific Lingo commands (see New Lingo Network Extensions). Avoid Director

features not available in movies designed for the Web. For a chart of these, see the following:

```
http://www.macromedia.com/shockwave/director/
➥ create.html#unavailable
```

2. Test the movie on both Macintosh and Windows computers.

3. When the movie is finished, save it, compact it, and then save a copy of it.

4. Convert the movie into Shockwave format with the Afterburner application. Afterburner ships with Director 4, Director 5, and the Director Multimedia Studio.

Director tech notes can be found at the following URL:

```
http://www.macromedia.com/support/technotes/shockwave/tn3906.html
```

You can download Shockwave from the following URL:

```
http://www.macromedia.com/shockwave/plugin/plugin.cgi
```

Creating QuickTime Movies for the Web

Making QuickTime movies for the Web is easy if you already know how to make QuickTime movies and follow all the precautions for file size that I've already mentioned for Shockwave and for Web animation in general. Most multimedia authoring programs will save to a QuickTime movie format. If yours won't, place the materials in Adobe Premiere; then save to QuickTime format.

After you have your QuickTime movie (remember, this "movie" could be a drawing, a slideshow, or a MIDI file) you'll need to do three things, as follows:

1. Flatten the movie so it can play on both Macs and PCs. This capability is also built into some of the utilities mentioned later.

2. Make sure the movie is saved as "self contained." Otherwise, you may lose track of needed files when transferring the movie to the Web server.

3. Make the movie "fast start" for streaming video, accomplished by using a small freeware utility from Apple called Internet Movie Tool, which moves the file's "header" (identification and startup code) to the beginning of the file. This makes it possible for the movie to start playing *before* it has finished loading. Get Internet Movie Tool from the following URL:

```
http://quicktime.apple.com/qt/sw/sw.html#tool
```

Creating QuickTime Movies with MovieStar Maker

If you're not an experienced animator or multimedia author, there's a utility that will enable you to make Web-useful, simple QuickTime movies after a ten-minute familiarization with the program. It's made by Intelligence at Large and is called MovieStar Maker. You can take any QuickTime-compatible files, drag them from the finder to the MovieStar Maker icon, click on some buttons, and name the movie. That's all it takes to compose the animation and compress the result into a QuickTime movie. It's a very easy way to make a musical MIDI background, a miniature slide show, or a "flipbook" animation similar to an animated GIF (but with the option of musical accompaniment). MovieStar Maker also compresses, flattens, and puts a "fast start" header on a movie, so you won't absolutely need some of the utilities mentioned later on. To order MovieStar Maker or to find out more, surf to:

```
http://www.beingthere.com/
```

Compressing QuickTime Movies with Movie Cleaner Pro

Terran Interactive's Movie Cleaner Pro with the Web Motion plug-in is even better at compressing QuickTime movies for the Web than MovieStar Maker (see fig. 11.26). By using this program, you can experiment with compression until you get the smallest possible file size for the lowest possible level of acceptable video and sound quality. The utility even makes up your HTML EMBED tag for you. This program is highly recommended:

```
http://www.terran-int.com/
```

Figure 11.26

The Movie Cleaner Pro screen.

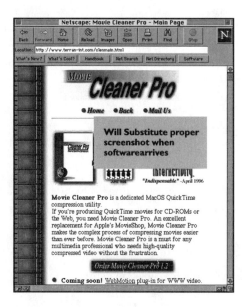

Making Graphics Fit the Web

The resolution of print media is much higher (typically 1250–2400 dpi) than the resolution of most Web viewers' computer screens (typically 72 dpi), so chances are you'll have to make your graphics much smaller to accommodate the restrictions of online publishing.

You can rescale graphics in virtually any image-editing or graphics batch-processing program. Because Web images are (so far) always bitmapped, rescaling poses problems. The original image is a fixed-size mosaic grid exactly *x* pixels across by *x* pixels deep. Any time you change the size of the mosaic, you make the program drop or add pixels. Which pixels get dropped or added determines fidelity of the resized image to the original.

Photoshop and DeBabelizer are two applications you can count on; however, programs that do a simply unacceptable job are rare these days.

Changing Image Size Using Photoshop

Most images made for reproduction on the printed page are four to eight times the resolution required of the same size image on a Web page. In order to make the file small enough to load in a reasonable time and to be fully contained within the typical browser window, you'll have to make it smaller. Making the image smaller and reducing its resolution amount to the same thing.

Rescaling is the Photoshop term for changing the size of an image. Actually, Photoshop does more than simple resizing in the process. The program "interpolates" to fill in the gaps between pixels and to smooth the jagged lines that would otherwise result by simply enlarging the existing pixels to fill the new size—or, conversely result from arbitrarily throwing out pixels in order to make an image smaller. Rescaling in Photoshop (or most any other image editor) is extremely simple; just follow the steps in Exercise 11.10.

Exercise 11.10

1. Choose Image, Image Size.

2. The Image Size dialog box appears. In the New Size box, choose pixels or pixels/inch for all three drop-down menus. Make sure Proportions is checked and File Size is unchecked.

3. Type in the longest dimension you want your graphic to be.

4. Click on OK. Save the file to a new file name.

Scaling Images to Consistent Dimensions

One requirement of graphics-to-Web conversion that often arises is that of scaling a great number of images to the same size or to fit within the same dimension. This is especially true if you have a number of images that will be used as bullets or buttons, as thumbnails, or as full-screen illustrations in a gallery or catalog.

Warning

Be sure to keep a record of any fixed or maximum dimension requirements for each category of image for each site publication you work on. Sooner or later, you will want to add another image to that category, and you don't want to have to waste time downloading and recalculating the size of an old image to get the proper number.

To scale images to a consistent size in Photoshop, follow the steps in Exercise 11.10, but make the following exceptions in Step 2: Uncheck Proportions. Type both the Height and Width dimensions. Click on OK. Be sure you really want to make all these images the same size, because doing so will often stretch them in one dimension or the other. Some images (such as plain buttons) can stand the distortion; others can't.

More often, you'll want to scale your images so they fit within a specific size; in other words, with neither the height nor the width larger than the maximum height or width.

Unsharp Masking in Photoshop

Almost always, your rescaled image will seem slightly blurry. To fix this, choose Filter, Sharpen, Unsharp Mask (it's not clear why they called it that). An Unsharp Mask dialog box appears, as illustrated in figure 11.27.

Figure 11.27

The Photoshop Unsharp Mask dialog box.

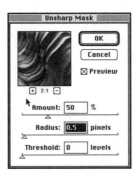

In the Unsharp Mask dialog box, the picture window shows a live preview of your image as you adjust the controls. Clicking on the buttons below the image changes the zoom level. Set your zoom level to 2:1 by clicking on the plus sign. Experiment with the controls to see what they do. When you get an effect you like, choose OK. This works; however, there's another way that permits you to see the whole image.

Before I give you the steps, I'll give you my reasoning. First, image quality is somewhat subjective and personal, so I want to make those judgments on the whole image as it will appear on-site. Second, I find this method faster when working with a whole series of images.

Set the Amount to 50%, the Radius to 0.5 pixels, the Threshold to 0 levels, and click on OK. The image is now a bit sharper. Continue to sharpen it by pressing Cmd+F (Mac) or Ctrl+F (Windows). The second the image's edges seem a bit jagged (aliased), press Cmd+Z (Mac) or Ctrl+Z (Windows) to Undo the last sharpening; then save the file.

Batch Scaling

Rescaling, resampling, or resizing (all different phrases describing the same end result) is required so often that you'll want to find a way to automate the process so that you can change the size of numerous images at once. Such an operation is called batch processing. In this instance, the processing you're doing is scaling—thus the term batch scaling.

Palettes for 256 Color Images and the Netscape Palette

As mentioned earlier, a significant percentage of Web surfers are stuck (or think they are) with viewing Web pages at a paltry 256 colors. Actually, they're not even seeing that many colors. If they're viewing the Web through Windows (it's happening to more and more people these days) and the monitor is set for 256 colors, they're only seeing 236 colors. Windows reserves 20 of the colors for itself.

Limitations of the Netscape Palette

If you're viewing Web pages in 16-bit color (high color, "thousands" of colors) or 24-bit color (true color, "millions" of colors), you can see all the colors in any full-range photo or video. (Actually, not quite all in high color, but your eye won't notice much difference unless you're preparing images for high-quality hard-copy output.) If you're viewing Web pages on a 256-color screen, you only get to see 216 colors. Why? Well, because that's the number Netscape put in their browser palette. Because the world follows Netscape's standards these days, you get the same limited palette

But wait! It gets worse. Because the Netscape palette for the Macintosh is different from the Netscape palette for Windows, if you create images on one, there's no guarantee they'll look good on the other.

Dithering the Netscape Palette

Things aren't as bad as they've been made out to be in the preceding section. Browsers also dither the Netscape palette, and it's quite surprising how well they do it. Take a look at the portrait in figure 11.28.

Figure 11.28

Portrait seen in Netscape Navigator with dithering.

Netscape Navigator does an amazing job of dithering colors. To the eye of anyone except a trained viewer, the images look surprisingly good. The surprise is, if you have photos and illustrations you want to put on the Web in JPEG format, you're in pretty good shape.

GIFs, even though they only started with 256 colors, don't do quite as well for two reasons. First, the dithering is more noticeable in what should be solid areas of color than in the smooth-shaded colors of a photo. Second, the 256 colors used to create your GIF (unless you've already taken the steps outlined next) were probably not indexed to the same palette as Netscape's.

You can do a couple of things to remedy this situation. If you're creating art to add to your Web site, you can create that art in colors Netscape Navigator won't dither or otherwise alter. Why won't it? Because you'll use colors assigned to the same index as Netscape's own palette.

Importing the Netscape Palette

The first thing you want to do is import the Netscape palette (also known as the Color Look-Up Table, or CLUT) into your image editor. Most can load the same palettes as Photoshop, so here's how to load the table into Photoshop. Just copy the N2PAL.LUT file from the CD into your Photoshop "Palettes" subdirectory ("Color Palettes" folder on the Mac). Now if you want to create new images using these colors, it's easy. Just follow the steps in Exercise 11.11.

Exercise 11.11

1. Open a new file, and choose Mode, Indexed Color. The Indexed Color dialog box pops up. Click on Custom in the Palettes box; then click on OK.

2. Another dialog box pops up, this time containing the current CLUT (probably the System Palette). Choose the Load Button. A file-loading dialog box will appear. Navigate to the Photoshop/Palettes folder and pick N2PAL.LUT from the listed palettes.

3. Choose Windows, Palette, Show Picker. The colors in the picker are the same as the colors in the Netscape palette. Choose these colors to create your art. Figure 11.29 shows the Netscape Color Lookup Table.

Figure 11.29

The Netscape Color Look-Up Table, when loaded into Photoshop.

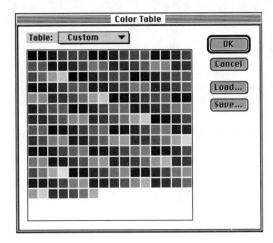

Remapping Image Colors to the Netscape Palette with DeBabelizer

If you're converting existing art, you can do it manually or you can use a palette conversion program. To do it manually, first load the image you want to convert into Photoshop. Choose Mode, Indexed Color. The Indexed Color dialog box appears. Follow the instructions in Exercise 11.12. When the Netscape palette is loaded, the colors in the active image are automatically remapped to fit.

Manually converting a hundred (or hundreds) of images would take much more time than anyone wants to spend. A better solution is a palette conversion program that automates the remapping. Usually they do a better job of remapping as well.

The best tool for remapping the colors of GIF files to the Netscape palette is DeBabelizer. DeBabelizer is a very powerful graphics file-conversion tool capable of performing numerous kinds of image manipulations on a whole series of selected files, and then saving them all to a common file format. At the same time, it's possible to save these files to a common palette.

The following exercise demonstrates how to remap your graphics to the Netscape CLUT palette in DeBabelizer.

Exercise 11.12

1. Follow the instructions in Exercise 11.11 for remapping an image to the Netscape CLUT palette in Photoshop.

2. Open the remapped Photoshop image in DeBabelizer.

3. Go to Palette, Options and choose Save. In the Save dialog box, name the palette "Netscape."

4. Open any image you want to remap to Netscape. Start recording a macro.

5. Choose Palette, Set Palette, and Remap Pixels. The Remap dialog box appears. Turn off Dithering. Click on OK. Save the file as GIF.

6. Stop recording the macro and name it RemapToNavPal.

7. Include the script RemapToNavPal in any batch-processing routine for DeBabelizer.

Graphics Creation

Note

> You could record these actions as a script, and then play the script as part of a batch operation. This would apply the Netscape palette to a whole series of images at once.

DeBabelizer is described in more detail elsewhere in this chapter in the sub-section entitled "DeBabelizer 1.6.5 (Mac)." There is no Windows alternative yet, but there will be a Windows version of DeBabelizer 2.0 about a month after we hit the shelves. It will feature a completely redesigned user interface and rewritten manual (both sorely needed). A new Macintosh version, to match the Windows version's new features, will be along a few months later. Equilibrium, which publishes DeBabelizer, hopes to synchronize future Mac and Windows versions of the software, post Spring '97.

If you want to see some good examples of Netscape-mapped colors online before you go to the trouble of converting your images, try the following sites:

● Tom Venetianer's elegant explanation of how color theory works and how it relates to the Netscape color cube. This site also has downloadable Netscape palettes for both Mac and Windows Photoshop (these same palettes are on the CD that comes with this book).

    http://mvassist.pair.com/Articles/NS2colors.html

● Victor Engel's No Dither Netscape Colors page even has an example Netscape color cube that lets you see the hexadecimal color equivalent of the color when you pass the mouse over it. You'll need a browser such as Netscape Navigator that supports client-side image maps.

    http://www.onr.com/user/lights/netcol.html

File Sizes for Different Types of Graphics

As a guide to help you keep in mind desirable file sizes, here's a table of Web page elements and the appropriate file size for each.

Graphic File Sizes

Graphic Type	File Size
Picture pages	40 KB (JPEG and HTML)
Illustrations	15–35 KB (JPEG)
Background images	1024×768, 17–35 KB

Graphic Type	File Size
Bullets	1–3 KB
Icons	2–5 KB
Banners	12–26 KB
Animations	25–500 KB
Content dividers (bars)	4 KB
Picture frames	8 KB
Alerts	2–5 KB

Minimizing File Size

You've been warned several times about how important it is to keep the file sizes of all your graphics as small as possible. What you really should do is make them as small as inhumanly possible. Programmers who have made a lifetime study of both graphics and mathematics have come up with some products that can keep a file looking amazingly good, despite it's being so small you'd think it would turn to visual garbage. None of these programs cost more than a hundred dollars. Unfortunately, they're so good, you may want them all; until you save up the money, follow these tips and tricks for keeping down file size manually.

Reducing Graphics File Sizes the Old-Fashioned Way

If you have to do it by hand, you can use the features built into your image editor to reduce file size. The following sections go into detail about the rules for keeping files to the smallest possible size.

Use as Few Colors as Needed to Make a Presentable Image

Broad areas of the same color compress more highly than tiny details and smooth-shaded (continuous tone) color. A mostly green photo of blades of grass can be reduced to far fewer than 256 colors and still look photographic. A photo of your sister wearing a patterned dress and sitting in a field of wild flowers may look strange if you try to reduce colors too much.

Use Flat Colors and Geometric Patterns

When file compression routines find repetition, they can tell the computer to repeat pixels of the given color instead of storing the data for each pixel. So the larger the areas of solid color and the more repetition in the pattern, the better the compression. This is especially true if files are stored in GIF format, which excels at repeating patterns.

Reduce Color Depth to the Lowest Number Possible

Color depth refers to the number of bits needed to describe the level of color in each pixel. Photos with a full tonal range usually require 24 bits of information per pixel, often referred to as "true color" or "millions" of colors. Because 24-bit color represents even more colors than the eye can actually see, there's no need to index colors to a specific palette. All the colors are there in all the pictures.

If you have to display quality photography or continuous-tone illustrations, you may have to save files to a 24-bit format. If so, JPEG is your only option. When saving as JPEG in almost every image editor, you get a dialog box that asks you what level of quality you want to save to. Don't be afraid to use the lowest-quality setting when you save the file. Save to a new file name so you still have the original to fall back on.

> **Note**
>
> Always save to the lowest-quality setting; then work your way up until you find the quality acceptable. This way, you'll always be sure that you've achieved minimum file size.

JPEG does a great job with smooth-toned, nongeometric subjects typically found in photos. Furthermore, it can compress files by as much as 100:1. The resultant tiny files aren't as quick to load as their number indicates, because the computer has to spend additional time decompressing the file.

Another caveat about JPEG: most clip-art, graphic text, cartoons, flat-toned poster art, or anything with sharp-edged geometrics looks horrible in JPEG because the compression tends to make random "speckles" or "artifacts" along the edges of shapes.

This brings up the fact that most Web graphics should use indexed color. This is partly because the GIF file format won't permit anything else. More importantly, the kind of images that look bad in JPEG—the kind that work best on the Web—look great in GIF.

Nominally, GIF uses 8-bit color; however, it is perfectly capable of using fewer bits-per-pixel. Exercise 11.13 explains how to reduce colors to the fewest acceptable bits-per-pixel in Photoshop. You'll want to do your image editing in RGB, because many of Photoshop's features are unavailable in indexed color.

Exercise 11.13

1. When completing your image editing in RGB, choose Indexed Color from the Mode menu.

2. A dialog box will pop up that offers numerous radio buttons. Set the Bits-per-Pixel at 3, make the Palette Adaptive, and set Dithering to None; then click on OK.

3. If the result looks bad, immediately Choose Edit, Undo. You're back to RGB color, so switch to Indexed Color again and repeat the process.

4. Leave all the settings the same, but increase the number of bits-per-pixel.

5. Repeat until you see an image you like. It doesn't have to be perfect—just acceptable.

Now you have a good start on saving this image at the smallest possible file size.

Avoid Dithering

Don't dither your colors (unless you have very good reason). Dithered colors simply don't compress very well and you can't make transparent backgrounds in dithered files. People forget that GIF files are compressed because they're lossies (unlike JPEG) and don't compress to as high a ratio. The compression algorithm used by GIF is very pattern-sensitive, so dithered colors play havoc with it.

Dithering is often used to make files appear to have smoother transitions between shades of color. If you're reducing a photograph, you'll be tempted to dither. You can reduce a photo without dithering with the aid of a program called HVS Color or a program that incorporates the HVS Color code, such as Boxtop's PhotoGIF or WebFocus. (See Appendix B for more information on these programs.)

Reduce the File to the Smallest Possible Physical Size

In other words, don't be afraid to use the cropping tool and the Image Size command. First, crop anything out of the image that doesn't contribute to its impact or, in fact, subtracts from its message. Remember, there are more pixels at the edge of a picture than in the center. A little trimming goes a long way.

Next, if the image can stand to be smaller and still be suited to its purpose, use the Image Size command. More often than not, resizing the image makes it a bit fuzzy. Use the Unsharp Mask filter at a one-pixel radius to correct this.

Use GIF Appropriately

GIF should be used for everything except photos and continuous tone illustrations larger than about 150×125 pixels. Smaller images, even photos, tend to look acceptably good in 256 colors, and any trade-off is outweighed by the fact that the files load faster in browsers because there's less decompression to calculate than for the same JPEG file.

Use JPEG Appropriately

JPEG should be used for photos and continuous tone illustrations larger than quarter screen. Both the creator and the viewer want to see these in all their glory. Use them sparingly, however. If you have a gallery or catalog that uses large numbers of large photos, for example, let the viewer start from a thumbnail page.

Link the thumbnails to the larger photos. Then a viewer can select any images that hold particular interest, and only those. The same viewers are much more likely to come back to view other images because they haven't wasted time loading images they didn't need to see.

> **Note**
>
> Thumbnails are small representations (usually about 80×100 pixels) of larger graphics, arranged in rows and columns (like a photographer's contact sheet).

File-Size Crunching Programs

The programs discussed in the following sections all do something to automate the steps previously described. How many different files can be handled at once and how many useful tricks can be performed varies from program to program. One program, DeBabelizer (now available for Macintosh and Unix), does so much that its manual is a terse 500 pages (including a few "addendums"). A Windows version is due in the fourth quarter of 1996.

DeBabelizer 1.6.5 (Mac)

DeBabelizer is a powerhouse for automated bitmapped graphics processing, manipulation, and file format translation. It gets its name from its capability to automatically convert any number of files from over 45 disparate Macintosh and Windows file formats into any single new file format. In fact, file conversion in DeBabelizer is so sophisticated, it can handle dozens of "flavors" of such file formats as JPEG and TIFF—enabling you to choose exactly which options in these formats you want to implement.

File conversion is only one of a zillion image-tweaking tasks DeBabelizer can automate. It isn't possible to describe all its features and their implementations without writing another book.

Even so, if all you ever use DeBabelizer for is to perform the tasks in the following exercise, it will pay for itself quickly. If you figure in the value of "tedium relief," it may also be worth investing in a low-end Power Mac just to run the conversions.

Exercise 11.14 demonstrates how to use DeBabelizer to transfer a list of files to a different file type, remap the palette of all those images to the Netscape palette, and crop all the images to fit within a maximum height and width—all at the same time! Furthermore, once you've set up this routine, you can reload a new set of files and repeat the whole operation with just a few mouse clicks.

Exercise 11.14

1. Use Rename (included on the CD-ROM) to rename all your files to Web-legal file names.

2. Gather the images you want to process to a given size and color scheme into a single folder.

3. Create a new folder for the destination images. This is just to help you find them more easily. You can drag and drop individual images into their appropriate folders later.

4. Now you will open DeBabelizer and do some processing on a single image, just so you can record a macro that will subsequently work on a whole batch of files.

5. First, load an image that contains the Netscape palette. Choose File, Open. The After Open Do Script dialog box appears. Check the Preview box. Navigate to your Netscape image and highlight its file name in the file box; then choose the Open button.

6. Now save the Netscape palette in DeBabelizer so you can use it again any time you want to. Choose Palette, Palette, Save. The Add Palette to List dialog box appears. Type Netscape as a new palette name. Change the Number of Colors in Palette to 216. Click on the Add button.

7. From the DeBabelizer menu bar, choose File-Open. The After Open Do Script dialog box appears. Check the Preview box. Scroll down the file list until you find a file you'd like to work on; it can be any one of the files you intend to process. Choose Open.

8. Choose Scripts, Watch Me.

9. Choose Palette, Set Palette and Remap Pixels. The Set Palette and Remap Pixels dialog box appears. Pull down the Set Palette list and choose Netscape. Check Remap pixels. Uncheck Dither when remapping (unless you're mapping subtly shaded photos, don't plan to use a transparent background, and are willing to trade image quality for loading speed). Leave everything else unchecked. Click on OK.

10. Choose Edit, Scale, Specify. The Scale dialog box appears. Choose Pixels from the Units pull-down menu. Choose the Fit to Size radio button. Type the maximum Width in the left column and maximum Height in the right column.

11. From the Method pull-down menu, choose Sine, Sharp. This choice "sharpens" the shrunken image. Click on OK.

12. Choose Script, Stop Recording. The Edit Script dialog box appears. In the Name field, type **Remap to Netscape**. Choose Save. You have recorded a script you can now incorporate into a batch-processing file. There is practically no end to the image-processing operations you can automate in this way. You can even run several image-manipulation processes before you stop recording the macro. Just make sure you stick to processes that affect the whole image (exceptions to this rule are beyond the scope of this book) and those you want to perform on the entire batch of images you plan to process.

13. From the DeBabelizer menu bar, choose File, Batch Save. A dialog box appears, asking if you want to save the current picture. Choose Discard. The Batch Save dialog box appears. Choose the New button. A new File Transfer dialog box appears. Use the drop-down list above the left file column (illustrated in fig. 11.30) to navigate to the folder you've made for the files to be processed.

Figure 11.30

DeBabelizer's Batch Save dialog box.

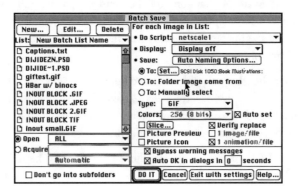

14. When the correct file list appears in the Source Directory list, choose Append All. All the file names will appear in the Batch List window. In the New Batch

List Name field, type a batch list name for this operation, and choose Save (see fig. 11.31).

Figure 11.31

Appending the batch list.

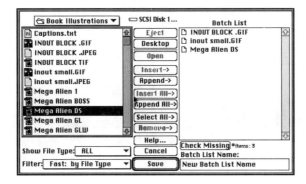

15. Now you will make several choices on the right side of the Batch Save dialog box. From the Do Script pull-down menu, choose Netscape (or whatever you called the macro script you recorded in step #12). Leave Display Off.

16. Choose Auto Naming Options. An Auto Namer dialog box appears. Choose the Original Name radio button. Check Strip Extension First. Choose the Extension for Save Type: GIF radio button. Check Don't Duplicate Extension. Click on OK.

17. Choose the To Set radio button. Then choose Set. A standard File Save As dialog box appears. Navigate to the folder you want to Save To (or make a new folder). Choose the Select "Folder Name" bar.

18. Choose GIF from the Type: pull-down menu. Check Colors: Auto Set.

19. Check the remaining boxes, as shown in figure 11.30.

20. Click on Do It.

21. Call a friend, take a shower, or check your e-mail on your other computer. In a matter of minutes, all your files will be properly processed.

Other Useful Things DeBabelizer Can Do

DeBabelizer is versatile enough to do countless other tasks, either in automated batches or one file at a time. A few of its most frequently-used capabilities are listed here:

● Change a not-so-solid background to a solid background of any color, just by marquee-selecting an area that contains all the colors you want transferred to the background (see fig. 11.32).

Graphics Creation

Figure 11.32

DeBabelizer's Background Removal dialog box.

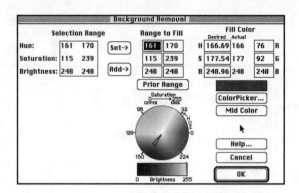

● Save all the files in a batch list to a single GIF file to make an animation.

● Run any combination of Photoshop-compatible plug-in filters for a whole batch of files. Be aware, however, that Adobe's own filters are purposely not built to Adobe's plug-in standards so that they WILL NOT work in competing applications. Because this includes such useful filters as Blur and Sharpen, you might consider using KPT Convolver or Intellihance RGB.

PaintShopPro 4.0 (Windows)

PaintShopPro 4.0 is a $69 shareware utility that will cover quite a bit of the ground discussed in this chapter. If you don't do much with graphics, are Windows-based, and need a good solid set of "training wheels" for graphics, this is the tool to get. But wait, that's not all…

Even for advanced graphics users, PaintShopPro has some very attractive features you may not even find in such sophisticated software as Photoshop. For instance, it has a good basic set of "natural media" paint brushes, a la Fractal Designs' Painter. There are very slick filters for drop shadows (you have to pay for someone else's plug-in to automate this in Photoshop). It has a built-in screen capture utility. Along with this, you get an image browser that makes thumbnails of all the images in any directory—a Godsend if you're constantly looking for graphics to use on a variety of Web pages and can't remember which file (IMAGE_13.GIF or IMAGE_14.GIF?) is the picture of the tea kettle and which is the banana.

PaintShopPro has Buttonize and Drop Shadow filters that create these effects in one step. Note that the two buttons have been painted with "natural bristle" charcoal (left) and oil (right) textures.

The following exercises show you how to use PaintShopPro 4.0 to convert an image palette (you have to do this one file at a time) and how to batch-convert files between graphic formats. PaintShopPro 4.0 can also convert files to GIF89a (with transparency support, but without animation support), progressive JPEG, and PNG (with transparency and alpha channel support) formats.

Converting to the Netscape Palette in PaintShopPro 4.0

If you're working in Windows and feel that Photoshop is overkill for your needs or budget, you may want to use JASC PaintShopPro for basic Web imaging needs. Exercise 11.15 will explain how to import the Netscape palette into PaintShopPro 4.0 for Windows 95.

Exercise 11.15

1. While in PaintShopPro, load the file called NETSCAPE.GIF.

2. From the Colors menu, choose Save Palette. The Save Palette As dialog box appears. Navigate to or create a folder in which you want to save palettes. This could be named Palettes.

3. In the File Name list box, type NETSCAPE.PAL (all PSPro palettes expect the PAL file extension). Be sure the File Type box says PAL – JASC Palette. Choose Save.

4. Load the file whose palette you want to convert to Netscape. From the Colors menu, choose Load Palette (see fig. 11.33). Navigate to your Palettes folder. Choose the file called NETSCAPE.PAL.

Figure 11.33

PaintShopPro's Load Palette dialog box.

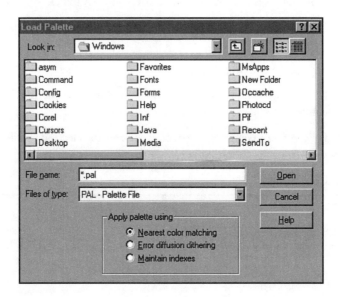

5. In the Apply Palettes Using box, choose Nearest Color Matching; then choose Open.

6. Your image's colors change slightly to reflect the new palette. Save this image to a new file name. You may also want to create a directory for images you've converted to the Netscape palette, just to make it easy to find them later.

Batch-Converting Graphics File Formats in PaintShopPro 4.0

This exercise contains instructions for converting various file formats to a GIF format with a transparent background. This will only work if all the files to be converted by the batch have the same solid background color. If not (or if you want to convert a whole variety of file types to GIF), perform that operation first by following the steps in Exercise 11.16, but leave out steps 6–9.

Exercise 11.16

1. Create a directory (folder) containing all the files you want to convert.

2. From the File menu, choose Batch Conversion. The Batch Conversion dialog box appears (see fig. 11.34).

3. Navigate to the directory you have created for the files you want to convert in this batch.

4. From the Files of type pull-down list, choose All Files.

5. In the Output Settings box, from the Type pull-down list, choose GIF.

6. Choose Options. The File Preferences dialog box appears. Choose Set the Transparency to the Background Color, and choose OK.

7. In the Output Directory box, choose Browse. Navigate to the folder into which you want to place your converted files.

8. Follow your operating system conventions for selecting files in a folder. Because you want to convert all the files in this folder, press Ctrl+A.

9. Choose Start.

Figure 11.34

Paint Shop Pro's Batch Conversion dialog box.

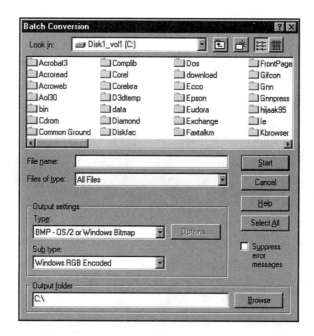

Brenda (Windows)

Brenda is a shareware utility that's the closest thing Windows has to DeBabelizer. It can do some batch image processing and palette conversion, as well as graphics file conversion.

Movie Cleaner Pro (Mac)

Movie Cleaner Pro works with one of the potentially most efficient (smallest file size) formats for putting video and animation inline on a Web site: QuickTime (which currently works only with Netscape Navigator 3.0 and Microsoft Internet Explorer 3.0, but will work with other browsers as they adopt the newest plug-in standards from Netscape as found in Navigator 3.0).

Made by Terran Interactive, Movie Cleaner Pro is designed to maximize compression of QuickTime movies for playback on CD-ROM and the Web. Once again, working with a file can be as simple as drag-and-drop.

Movie Cleaner Pro enables the user to set far more compression variables than the built-in codes in applications such as Premier or Director. Movie Cleaner Pro "interviews" the operator to set options that maximize conversion for the target playback platform. Expert users can set even more options and can even crop the movie.

Graphics Creation

Movie Cleaner Pro will recompress already compressed QuickTime movies, but works best when it can compress afresh. The program doesn't "flatten" or make the "fast start" header, but this can be done before or after compression by using the Apple Internet Movie Tool.

Terran has just introduced a new product called Web Motion that can make movies even smaller. It is a plug-in for Movie Cleaner Pro, so you'll need both products in order to run Web Motion. Movie Cleaner Pro is $189.95 and Web-Motion 1.0 is an additional $129.95.

If you want to find out more about Movie Cleaner Pro or Web Motion, check the Terran Interactive Web site at the following:

```
http://www.terran-int.com/
```

Scanning Graphics from Your Print Publications

If you are adapting content from print to Web, that content may not exist in any other form than print itself. If that is the case, the most direct way to get the graphics from those pages into print is to scan the pages on a flatbed scanner.

There are many kinds of flatbed scanners. Today's least expensive color flatbed scanners are quite adequate for scanning Web graphics.

The Rules for Scanning Web Graphics

Using a flatbed scanner makes it easy to incorporate pictures from almost any source into your Web pages. But there are good scans and bad scans. Be sure to follow the rules of good scanning, as described in the following list:

- Don't steal other people's copyrighted material. Scanners make this temptingly easy, but it is dishonest and sets you up for a well-deserved lawsuit.

- Keep your scanner's glass bed clean. Otherwise, you have to waste time retouching dust and specks.

- Set the scanner software to measure in pixels. This makes it easier to decide what the 1:1 size of your graphics will be.

- Scan at 1:1—this means 72 dpi. If you have to rescale a bitmap graphic (that's what all scanner files are), you will lose definition—by definition, as they say.

Just as important, scanning at higher resolutions takes more time, more RAM to process in Photoshop, and more space on your hard drive. Then you will have to reduce the image to Web size, which will cost you a great deal of image definition due to arbitrarily lost pixels that had to be thrown out in order to make the image smaller.

● If you must, ignore the 1:1 rule to get rid of moiré patterns or do detailed retouching. See later sections on retouching and eliminating moiré patterns for more information.

● Capture as much definition and color as possible in the original scan. Read the scanner manual carefully and practice on several images until you understand the routine. Setting color balance, white level, black level, and overall picture gamma works differently for every scanner's software and can't be explained briefly.

● If you have to do volume scanning, use software that automates the process. Some scanner software will automatically adjust for optimal gamma and color balance, eliminate moiré patterns, straighten the image(s), save multiple images on a page to different files, separate text from graphics and scan them into separate files, and convert the text to word processors such as Microsoft Word and WordPerfect. The best package I've found to do all these things is Ofoto from LightSource in Corte Madera, CA. If you haven't yet purchased a scanner, look for one that comes bundled with Ofoto. The proprietary software that comes with various scanners also does some scan automation. The software that comes with higher-end Umax scanners, such as the PowerLook series, is recommended (see fig. 11.35).

Figure 11.35

The Scanner Setup dialog box for Umax's PowerLook scanners.

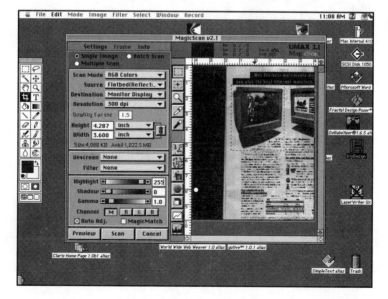

Graphics Creation

Retouching

Some artists like to work on a large image to do retouching and manipulation. Doing so makes it easier to see small details. Besides, any minor boo-boos are likely to disappear when the image is reduced for the Web. If you want to work on a large image, scanning at two or four times screen resolution should be adequate.

Eliminating Moiré Patterns

A moiré pattern is the result of the pattern made by one viewing device (for example, a monitor) being superimposed over the pattern made by another device (for example the grain inherent in film or the screening dots used to half-tone a printed page). Moiré patterns vary in appearance, but they're almost universally ugly. Most often the pattern causes banding or oil-slick-like rainbows.

A moiré pattern usually occurs when halftone images are scanned. They result from the juxtaposition of the computer's regularly spaced dot pattern (that's what bitmaps are) and the variably sized (halftone) or variably spaced and sized (stochastic screen) dots in the image.

The filters built into some scanner software are the best way to get rid of these patterns—provided they work for the image you're scanning. They usually do.

If not, or if you don't have such software, the following exercise discusses a trick to rid yourself of the ugly moiré.

Exercise 11.17

1. Scan the image at 300 dpi (or higher if your scanner has higher optical resolution in both vertical and horizontal dimensions).

2. From the Menu Bar, choose Filter, Blur, Blur. Most of the moiré pattern will disappear. Press Cmd+F (Ctrl+F for Windows) to repeat the blur until the pattern disappears.

3. This is also the best time to do any retouching that's needed. For instance, there may be type bleed-through from the reverse side of the page. Retouch this with the Clone Brush. Alternately, capture adjacent texture with the Marquee, choose Edit, Define Pattern, and then choose Edit, Fill, Pattern.

4. You may want to "paint out" unwanted background and text. Carefully select the main image; then choose Select, Inverse. Choose the foreground color you'd like to use; then choose Edit, Fill, Foreground Color.

5. From the Main Menu, choose Image, Image Size. In the New Size box, make sure Proportions is checked. Set Resolution to 72 pixels-per-inch (same as dpi). Type either the Width or Height for the new image, and click on OK. Look Ma! No moiré for moi.

6. From the Main Menu, choose Filter, Sharpen, Unsharp Mask. Set the sharpen options so that the effect is just perceptible. This means setting effect at about 20% and radius at .5 pixels. Choose OK. The image will sharpen slightly. Press Cmd+F repeatedly until the image sharpens to the point where the edges of shapes begin to become very slightly jaggy. Stop. Press Cmd+Z to undo that last Unsharp Mask operation. This is the point at which you have made the image as sharp as you can without noticeably exaggerating the effect.

> **Note**
>
> When buying a scanner, make sure you know its optical resolution. Many scanner makers claim a resolution much higher than the optical resolution, called the "interpolated resolution." In fact, it's just "salesmanship." It means the scanner software can rescale the image to a larger size before saving the file, and you can do the same thing better in Photoshop.

Summary

This chapter has shown you, cookbook style, how to perform the graphics operations most frequently needed when preparing Web graphics in Photoshop (and some other applications, when Photoshop just can't do the specific job as well). Specifically, you have learned how to make or do:

- Irregularly shaped graphics (transparent GIFs)
- Soft-edged graphics against solid backgrounds
- Seamless background tiles (for textured backgrounds)
- Picture frames
- GIF animations
- Shockwave animations
- QuickTime movies

Graphics Creation

You have also learned how to make graphics Web-efficient through color reduction and image resampling, how to use colors that most browsers will reflect accurately, and how to process images in batches (DeBabelizer, Brenda, and Movie Cleaner Pro). Finally, you have learned how to scan graphics from your print publications.

If this chapter has whetted your appetite for more knowledge about dealing with graphics, run—don't walk—to your nearest bookstore for a copy of Lynda Weinman's best-selling *Designing Web Graphics* (New Riders Publishing, 1996).

Also, don't forget: the World Wide Web is a great source for information on the latest graphics "tips and tricks." Here are a few URLs you should put in your browser's bookmarks:

MetaTools University, the resting place for Kai's Power Tips and lots of other highly useful advice:

```
http://www.metatools.com/metauniv/
```

Adobe Photoshop information:

```
http://www.adobe.com/prodindex/photoshop/main.html
```

Art Lebedev's Photoshop Original Tips and Tricks:

```
http://www.tema.ru/p/h/o/t/o/s/h/o/p/
```

DIP - Digital Pictures on the Web:

```
http://www.algonet.se/~dip/
```

Photoshop Sites Home Page:

```
http://www.fns.net/~almateus/photos.htm
```

Cool Type, Type Tricks in Photoshop:

```
http://www.bit.lv/cooltype/
```

PC Resources for Photoshop:

```
http://www.netins.net/showcase/wolf359/adobepc.htm
```

Happy surfing!

CHAPTER 12

Web Site Organization and Management

The golden rule of Web site management is Plan Ahead. If you haven't thought much about the structure of your Web site, start thinking now. I've worked for a few clients who got 30 or 40 pages into a growing Web site and then realized having all of their files in one directory was a mistake. It's more than a mistake—it's a mess.

Unfortunately, what these clients didn't realize was if they started moving things into new directories after the site grew, they'd have to change all their links. They started changing things around and then found they had broken links, but didn't remember where things were supposed to go. After that, it took hours to study the site, come up with an organizational plan, and fix all the links.

In the old days (a year ago in real time, but the equivalent of about ten years in Internet time), Web site management had to be done manually, and you had to keep track of all of the links in your head. Today there are a few programs on the market that claim to help with this kind of organization and link tracking. You'll learn about these in this chapter, but you should understand up front that they are limited and won't solve all of your potential problems. The best way to manage a Web site is still to plan ahead and start with a structure you can develop and expand upon easily.

The most important thing you'll learn in this chapter is the value of planning, storyboarding, creating directory levels and structure, and setting up systems for sites more than one person can work on efficiently. You'll also learn about coordinating content from many sources and people, with testing areas set up so you can check things before you build them into the live Web site. Finally, in case it's already too late for you, you'll find a section called "Creating Order Out of Chaos."

This chapter starts with the planning process, because Web sites have a tendency to double in size even faster than Netscape can create a new beta version of its browser.

Preliminary Web Site Planning

Before you start building, you need to make a couple of preliminary decisions: whether to register a domain name and what kind of server you'll be using. You then can settle into the planning process, and ultimately start developing your site.

Running Your Own Server vs. Using a Service Provider

Many people setting up a Web site for the first time think they need to run a Web server to put the site online. Maintaining a server, however, can be a complicated and expensive process requiring skills very different than those needed for developing HTML pages. Unless you are building a large and complex Web site, setting up a server may not be necessary, especially at first.

At the lowest end, a Web server can be set up on almost any desktop computer with a connection to the Internet. On a 14.4 or 28.8 modem, however, such a system is very slow and requires a dedicated connection. At the high end, a good Unix computer, a fast and dedicated Internet connection, and the staff to keep everything working can cost tens of thousands of dollars. The alternative is to find a service provider with an established Web server and lease a small piece of it for your own site. This can cost as little as $15 or $20 a month. Some service providers will also enable you to co-locate your own equipment at their location, so you can run your own server and share the high-speed Internet connection.

One reason it's important to decide on a server early in the planning process is that the platform of your server dictates how you should create file names. For example, you can call files just about anything-you-want.html on a Mac server; however, on a Unix server, you can't have spaces in file names and you must ensure that the case is the same in the hyperlink as in the file name. On a Windows server, you should limit yourself to the "8.3 rule," which requires that none of your file names have more than eight characters and none of the extensions more than three. (For more on file-name requirements, see the section on cross-platform issues near the end of this chapter.)

> **Note**
>
> For more thorough information on planning your connectivity options, consult *Webmaster's Guide to Internet Server Connectivity* (New Riders, 1996).

Registering Domain Names

Registering a domain name is one of the first things you should consider, no matter how you put your Web site online, because it can take up to a month to get a name approved. You may be able to put your Web site up in a temporary location for early testing, but you shouldn't start advertising until you have a domain name established. A domain name serves as a unique and permanent address on the Internet. One of its biggest advantages is that even if you move to a different Web server in the future, your users can keep coming to the same address. The mechanics of transferring the Web site to a new server can be done behind the scenes, so your public address always remains constant.

A domain name also makes your address easier to remember. If you do not register a domain name, expect your URL to be longer and more complicated, such as the following:

```
http://www.serviceprovider.com/businesses/yourname/
```

If you have your own domain name, it should look like this:

```
http://www.yourname.com/
```

The InterNIC currently charges $100 to register a domain name for two years, and $50 per year after that. Most Internet Service Providers (ISPs) will register a domain name for you for a $25 to $50 fee that includes setting up the server space for you. If you run your own server and want to register the name yourself, be aware that the InterNIC now requires you to have a second server in place as a backup before you register a domain name. If you don't have a second system you can use, you may be able to use an ISP for this purpose.

If you want to see if a particular domain name is already in use, there are several places to look them up online. One of my favorites is sponsored by a private Internet company called CarpCom. I like their list because in addition to telling you if a domain name is taken, they provide the registration information (name, address, and server information) of the person who registered it. You can use their search engine by visiting their Web site at the following:

```
http://www.primopasta.com/whois.htm/
```

When you register a domain name, be careful that you are not using another company's registered trademark. The law is still trying to catch up with the Internet and there is not a clear legal standard, but many people have lost domain names because they were the legally registered trademark of another company. Many individuals have run into trouble for intentionally grabbing the trademarked names of other companies, and then trying to sell them. On the other hand, a few have made good money with this trick. It's rumored that the 24-year-old student in Utah who registered "Windows95.com" was paid a million dollars and offered a job at Microsoft. Not all such disputes end so well, however. If you register a domain name and spend money to advertise and attract users, you risk losing that investment if you have to change the name later. As a general rule, if another company has a registered trademark, they have a distinct advantage.

The problem is that business names are generally restricted within geographic areas; for example, there could be a Sam's Diner in New York and a Sam's Diner in San Francisco and it would not cause a conflict. But the Internet transcends geographic limitations and it is still not clear how such disputes will be resolved. The best advice is that you should treat domain name registration the way you would the selection of a unique business name, searching to make sure it's not already in use by another company, and registering it early before the competition can stake a claim on it.

> **Note**
>
> InterNIC Registration Services is located at Network Solutions, Inc., Herndon, VA, and is funded by a cooperative agreement from the National Science Foundation to provide registration services for the Internet community via telephone, electronic mail, and U.S. postal mail. Registration Services works closely with domain administrators, network coordinators, Internet service providers, and other various users in its registration activities. Be aware that you must run a server to register a domain name and that most commercial service providers will do this for you.
>
> Registration Services registers domains, assigns IP network numbers and Autonomous System Numbers (ASNs), and produces the domain zone files for the community. Registration Services also provides assistance to users concerning policy and the status of their existing registration requests. You can find the InterNIC at the following:
>
> ```
> http://rs.internic.net/
> ```

Web Site Organization Methods

There are many approaches to Web site management and organization. The strategies you take as you go through this process will depend on the size and complexity of your project. If you are doing a small home page for yourself, you may not have to go through all of the steps that follow. If you are tackling a large project with a team of designers and programmers, the planning process is a crucial step that warrants considerable time and attention.

Key Points for Web Site Planning

As you delve into Web site management considerations, there are a few key points you should walk through.

Outline Your Site

Before you start building, sit down (preferably with someone you can talk things through with) and think about what you are undertaking. Good Web sites are dynamic—they are constantly being developed and added to. Before you build those first few pages, think about where you are likely to be adding content in the future, make a list of the key elements that will go into the site, and consider doing a storyboard or outline. You'll learn more about that in the "Storyboarding Techniques" section that follows.

Divide Your Site

Create logical sections of a site and always anticipate growth. You may start with one page that lists all your staff, but once they see how cool it is, every staff member may want to develop a personal page. If you are providing information for your sales team, for example, you'll probably want a separate section for each product. Make sure you ask the right questions in the planning process: What will you do when there are more products? Where will you put them? How will you find those pages again when someone wants to change the price on one of them? If you are working on a publication, you'll want to think about how to build in new issues, how to link in new stories, and where to archive old information.

Naming Schemes

Develop a consistent and logical naming structure. Keeping track of the information on the pages in your Web site will be much easier if you develop a naming structure that makes sense to everyone working on the project. Simple names such as boat.html and accident.html for your publication may make sense to you this week because you are familiar with the top stories, but six months from now if you are looking for that article on fishing, you may not remember you called it boat. Try adding dates to the end of file names, such as accident8_12.html and boat8_19.html. Another option is to create a directory for each new update and name the directory with a date. A folder named stories8_12 could contain all the stories from the August 12 issue. You then can put accident.html and any other stories in that directory, and you'll be able to find them by date as well as file name. Talk to other people who may be working on the site to be sure you create a system that makes sense to everyone and will be easy to explain if a new person joins the team. Whatever you do, don't just randomly name files and throw them all in one directory.

If you are still new to this, you may think that you don't need to worry so much about expandability in your Web site. Think again. All good Web sites grow, and the bigger they get, the harder it is to keep track of them.

Planning for Web Site Growth

After selecting your connectivity options, registering a domain name, and hashing out some preliminary issues, it's time to get organized. When you begin a Web site project, it's important to think about all the elements that will go into it before you start building. This is one of the most common mistakes among new designers—they jump right into the home page, add a few other pages, add a few more, throw it all in one directory, and before they know it, they're in chaos.

Building a Web site is not unlike building a house—you don't just start hammering boards together without a plan. Indeed, most contractors work with an architect who puts together a detailed blue print. Keep that in mind as you get started, you want to make sure you've left room for a dining room, living room, and bedrooms before you start putting up the front door.

There are two obvious analogies here:

1. **Outlines**: Most writers create an outline before they tackle a large project (if you've tried to write a long paper without an outline, you should understand this one).

2. **Storyboarding**: This analogy is borrowed from the film and video industry.

Storyboarding Techniques

Storyboarding is probably the best model for Web design because it involves more than a simple written outline. But most storyboards are still created in a linear fashion, so you have to adapt that model, too. Web sites are not linear—you don't have to read them from beginning to end the way you read a book, and you don't have to watch them from the opening music to the ending credits the way you watch a movie. This nonlinear structure is what makes the Web a dynamic environment.

There are many ways to do storyboarding. Sit down with a piece of paper and a pen; get a program designed for developing flow charts, such as MacFlow or Visio; or use a program such as Word, PageMaker, or QuarkXPress to draw boxes and arrows that represent your pages. Many people mock up page designs in Photoshop as part of this process, too. Whatever works for you is fine, but take the time to think about the Web site, what will be in it, and how and where it will grow, before you start building.

Figure 12.1 is a very simple diagram of a Web site. The first page is indicated by the large box at the top and each of the smaller boxes within it represents a button that leads to another page. Those pages are then outlined with arrows showing how pages will be linked. This kind of diagram represents the preliminary outlining of a Web site. As planning progresses, this would be expanded to show greater details, more pages, and more depth in the site.

Figure 12.1

A simple diagram of a Web site.

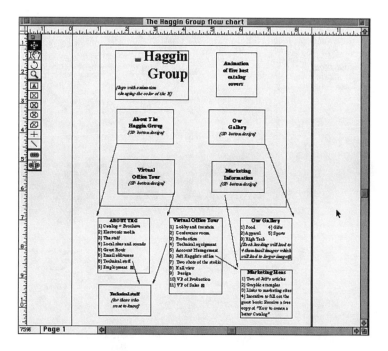

Providing Web Site Navigation Tools

A good Web site is designed so users can navigate easily and intuitively and create their own paths to find the information most relevant to them. As you plan, make sure users will be able to access key information easily, moving back and forth and returning to main pages and indexes in one step. One of the most common navigational techniques for this is the menu bar, where you create a graphic or text listing of all the main pages, such as home, contacts, products, and orders. Adding that menu bar to every page in the site provides a useful navigational tool for users. In figure 12.2, there is a navigational bar illustrated by an artist's palette. The row of icons includes headings and links to the main pages in the Web site. This row of palettes is included on every page, making it easy for users to move from one section of the site to another without having to back up to the main page to make their next selection.

Another technique is to create a table of contents or Web site map so that users can go to one page and find links to the other pages (or at least all the main pages) in the site. Search engines are also a great way to help users, but they require programming that goes well beyond HTML. Whatever you do, make sure users never get stuck on a page that leads nowhere because the link is broken or says "under construction."

Figure 12.2

The navigational bar at the bottom of this page is illustrated with an artist's palette.

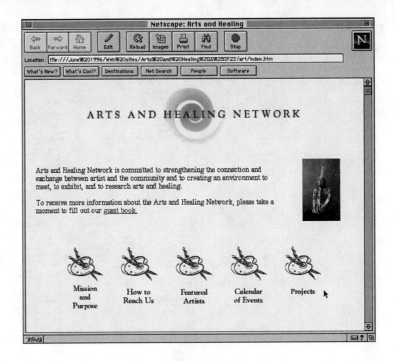

> **Note**
>
> **Never Put "Under Construction" in Your Web Site**
>
> All good Web sites are under construction. They should be built so pages can be added when they are ready to go online, not placed as empty spacers with a guy in a yellow hat saying, "You clicked on this link for no good reason—come back another day and maybe we'll have something up here." Be aware—many people will get so frustrated they'll never come back. Instead of "under construction" placeholders, create directory structures that make it easy to add in new pages later. You can let readers know new things are coming by putting notices on pages that do have content, but never make them click on a link and wait for a page to load, only to discover the information may be there someday.

Organizing Images

Before I go on, I want to make a few points about organizing images in a Web site. I've heard many HTML teachers and consultants suggest placing all your images in a single folder at the top level of the directory structure and calling it images or graphics (the name doesn't matter). You'll also find several HTML authoring tools that claim to facilitate Web site management and organization, but will only enable you to put your images in one folder. There is an advantage to this in that all your images can be linked with the same path, /images/name.gif, because the browser reads that forward slash mark and knows to go back to the top level of the directory structure to find the image folder. (For more on hyperlinks, see "Setting Links" at the end of this chapter.)

There is also a problem. If all your images are in one folder, it is likely to get too big very soon. Just as having all your HTML files in one directory gets complicated, having all your images in one folder means you're likely to lose track of them. This can be even more problematic with images than with files, because images generally take more space than HTML files. And if you ever want to update and replace your images, make sure you remove the ones you're not using. A good alternative is to store graphics in an image folder in the same directory that holds the HTML files corresponding to the images. If you have images that link throughout the site—a menu bar, for example—you may want to create an images folder at the top level for those primary images, but as you add specific images with specific pages, I recommend you keep them together. Figure 12.3 shows the view, as seen in the Finder on a Macintosh, of a directory structure where images are organized within each section of a site, and a main graphics folder is included at the top level for images that are used throughout the site. Notice that the cookies folder at the top includes cookies.html and two related graphics in an image folder. At this stage in development, this site doesn't need all these directory levels, but as these sections grow, it will be much easier to keep track of things with this kind of organization.

Figure 12.3

Images are better tracked if they are stored in folders with related html pages.

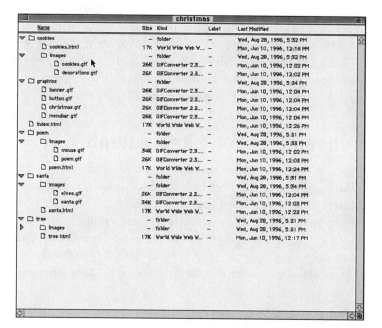

Developing a System

This chapter will look at two approaches to Web site management: one based on the work of a large Web design company that manages Web site development for a number of corporate clients, and another, more specific example, that features how a small publication went through the process of creating a system to update their site every week.

Case Study: Managing Web Site Development

Aslan Computering has been through the process of developing Web sites enough times to have developed a comprehensive system they use with each new client. On a typical project, Aslan will have seven to ten people working on a Web site. Planning falls under the responsibility of the Project Manager and the Business Analyst.

Gathering Web Site Information

The Business Analyst has a very important job—this person meets with the client to get a clear and detailed description of what the client wants in the site. Often the client has seen something he likes on the Web, but it may not be appropriate to his content and expressed goals. Thus, one of the first steps in planning is getting the client to explain all the information he wants in the site, understanding what's possible and appropriate, and agreeing on a general design.

Storyboarding Web Site Content

Next, the Business Analyst sits down to create a storyboard, often using a program as simple as MS Word to create little boxes and arrows. A navigational scheme and a directory are created and reviewed with the Project Manager. Once the structure is set, they consider the specific types of pages, headers, and footers that will be needed, logos for the various sections, and much more. They then supplement the storyboard with a few sample pages created in Photoshop to provide examples of the main pages. When all this is together, it's brought back to the client for approval.

Naming Web Site Files

After the client has signed off on the design and structure, the Project Manager and Business Analyst name every page and graphic that will be in the Web site. This may seem premature, but it helps them in a number of ways. First, they can then assign pieces of the project to a number of HTML coders and know what they will get back. Second, if they must replace a staff member in the middle of a project, this planning makes it easy to hand off to someone else. And third, while someone's creating the graphics, the HTML code can be created by another person, who has the general design of the pages and the name of each graphic to place in the code. For each large project, Aslan creates a production manual that includes all the design information, naming information, and so on, ensuring that all members of the team have an understanding of the overall project, as well as their parts of it. This may seem like a great deal of effort before they even start development, but the time spent planning a large project is more than made up in the smooth development process.

"Large corporate Web sites lend themselves to this kind of standardization and planning," says Jessica Burdman, a partner in Aslan and co-author of this book. "If someone gets pulled off the project in the middle, the structure and manual can keep it going."

Content Strategy Questionnaire

Another useful tool Aslan has created is a series of questions they ask all their clients in the early planning stages. Ultimately you must get much more specific, but the following list of questions is a great place to start for your own site or for a client. As you begin the process of planning a Web site on your own or with a client, consider the following questions:

1. What function of your business would you like your Web site to address/ enhance?

   This is a crucial question as it gets to the heart of your goals in designing the site. Consider this answer carefully and use it as the basis of all of your planning decisions. Write down the answer and refer to it throughout the planning process.

2. Is your objective in creating a Web site to inform, cut costs, entertain, showcase clients? All of the above?

   Similar to the first question, this gets at the heart of what your Web site is about. You may find that you want to satisfy a combination of goals, but keep things as focused as possible and it will help with planning and design considerations.

3. Who is the ideal "user" of your Web site? Why?

   Consider your audience. If this is a corporate intranet site designed to bring up-to-date sales information to your marketing team, you will want a very different design approach than if this is an entertainment site geared toward 12-year-olds.

Web Site Organization and Management

4. What do you want a "user" of your Web site to gain from visiting your site?

    Your users' experience will determine if they return. If the goal is to entertain, you want a dynamic site and you'll have to factor multimedia elements into your Web site management. If the goal is to provide legal resources to busy corporate executives, you may want to stick to text-based information that is easy to navigate and loads quickly.

5. Would you like to educate the general public about your product or service, or would you prefer to tailor your site to the needs of your "targeted" audience? Why?

    It is possible to accomplish both of these goals with one Web site, but you should consider dividing your project into two sections to meet dual goals. As you plan, structure the site so that the general public can find the information they want, and the target audience can navigate easily to specific elements you've prepared for them. Within the directory structure, as well as the navigational elements, you should break these two sections apart to help with organization.

6. What kind of connectivity (means of accessing the Internet) do you think your targeted audience has (14.4 or 28.8 modem, ISDN, or T1 line)?

    This is key in determining the amount of graphics and multimedia elements you should incorporate into your Web site. If you are on an intranet, you may have the advantage of a fast Internet connection, such as T1 line. But even on intranets, the demand for bandwidth for other corporate activities may limit your use of large file sizes. If your goal is to reach the general public, you should still target the 14.4 modem-speed audience. Many developers have the advantage of a fast connection and forget that most home users are still downloading pages at 14.4 or 28.8 modem speeds. If you are working on a faster connection, build in time in the testing process to check your pages on a 14.4 modem. If you don't have one, you should consider getting one (they're cheap these days).

7. Why is having a Web site important to your company?

    Again, this question gets at the heart of your goals and objectives, and is an important step in the initial planning process. Many companies are still struggling with this question and trying to justify the cost of Web site development in an unproving market. Consider this carefully. If your goal is to sell products to the general public, you may want to put lots of time and effort into marketing and creating an interesting and dynamic site. If your goal is to deliver text to your employees, you'll need a strategy that focuses on information delivery and training employees how to find it.

Web Site Development Process

Aslan also has a step-by-step planning sheet they've designed to guide the process and clarify the roles of everyone on the development team. Here's what their guidelines look like:

1. **Define Web site objectives.** Using the questionnaire described in the previous section, create a clear definition of the goals and objectives of the Web site to guide the rest of the planning process.

   Team players involved: Project Manager, Business Systems Analyst

2. **Assemble project team/define roles and responsibilities.** Gathering the staff to complete the process is an important early step. Assigning responsibilities and beginning to delegate tasks will ensure that the rest of the planning and development goes smoothly. This always requires meetings among the management team and gradually evolves to meetings with more of the development staff.

   Team players involved: Project Managers, Systems Analysts, Programmers, Integrators, Graphic Artists

3. **Define content.** This requires further meetings with the client to finalize the plans for what will comprise the Web site. This may require a series of meetings and is likely to evolve over time. It's important at this stage to assign one or two management staff to work with the client and serve as a liaison between the client and the development team.

   Team players involved: Project Manager, Systems Analyst

   A. *Define topic areas of Web site.* This gets into the more specific aspects of what will be in the Web site and how it will be organized. Defining the key areas of the site helps with developing structure.

   Team players involved: Project Managers, Graphic Artists

   B. *Define target audience.* Drawing from the results of the questionnaire, this is a key point to return to as you go through the planning process to ensure that the site will appeal to the desired user group and work on their computers and at their connections speeds. At this stage, consider the following:

   I. *Audience*—Who will be using this site? Is it designed to appeal to the target market?

   Team players involved: Project Managers, Graphic Artists

    II. *Connectivity*—How fast is their connection to the Internet? Are multimedia and graphic elements small enough to download in a reasonable time frame?

    Team players involved: Project Managers, Graphic Artists, Systems Analyst

    III. *Browser/Platform*—If you are on an intranet, you may be able to design the site for a specific browser and computer operating system. Microsoft Internet Explorer, for example, is capable of much greater functionality on a Windows 95 or Windows NT system than on a Macintosh. If you know what your audience will be using, you can optimize the site for that browser and platform. If you are trying to reach the general audience, you'll need to ensure that graphics look good on all platforms and that key features work in a variety of browsers and operating systems.

    Team players involved: Project Managers, Graphic Artists, Systems Analyst

C. **Determine media types.** The kinds of file formats you use in a Web site will have much to do with how you structure the site and arrange navigational features. Whether to include text, graphics, video, audio, or animation depends on the audience, connectivity, and budget of the project.

Team players involved: Project Managers, Graphic Artists

4. **Outline navigational model.** In this phase, you want to be thinking about how users will find information on the Web site. This is also a good time to get into more detailed storyboarding.

Team players involved: Project Managers, Graphic Artists

5. **Incorporate existing materials.** Before you get too far into the planning process, take inventory of what the company or client has already created and how it can be built into the Web site. Consider incorporating the following:

    A. Marketing campaigns

    B. Brand and brand information or art

    C. Brochures, annual reports, newsletters

    D. Advertising from print or broadcast media

6. **Draft storyboard.** Now that you have all these materials, you are ready to get into the heart of planning and storyboarding. At this stage, you should design the layout for text, graphics, and other media types in mock-up pages.

   Team players involved: Project Managers, Graphic Artists, Systems Analyst, Programmers

7. **Get sign-off on storyboard from client.** This is an important step because before you start actually doing the development work, you want to ensure that the client is happy with the design and navigational structure.

   Team players involved: Project Managers, Client Liaison

8. **Create Production and Style Guide.** Developing a written document that can be used to keep all the team players informed is an excellent way to ensure that things go smoothly, pieces fit together after creation, and that managers don't get bogged down with detailed questions about style, naming structures, and so on. The Production and Style Guide should include the following:

   A. File-naming conventions

   B. Test-to-production process steps and dates

   C. Style guide outlining general style conventions

   D. Roles and responsibilities of team members

9. **Development begins.** After all the initial planning has been taken care of, the bulk of the work is done. If the planning has been done well, things should go much more smoothly in production. This is where actual HTML development, graphics, database connectivity, and other work is completed.

10. **Test, test, test.** It can't be said or done enough on the Web. Before you put it online, make sure the site has been thoroughly tested, and preferably by more than one person.

11. **Get sign-off on test site.** Again before you put the site online, make sure everyone, especially the client, is happy with it. On a large site, you should have a staging area or beta site where development can be tested online before made available to the public. When it's ready to go, make sure the client approves it before it goes live online.

If you are bringing teams of people together to work on a variety of projects at the same time, this kind of planning and systems development can work well. If you are working on only one Web site, there are also many good ideas here. Creating a manual to explain the overall structure, set style guidelines, and include naming conventions is a great idea for any project.

Web Site Organization and Management

Policies for Web Site Revisions

When more than one person is working on a site, you also need to keep track of version control. In other words, you don't want two people working on the same file, only to find that one has inadvertently deleted the changes made by another. This becomes even more difficult to manage when people are in remote locations, pulling files off a server to work on them. There are two good solutions to this problem. One is to assign just one person to manage the final revisions and build new pieces into the site. Anyone else working on the project sends their work to the manager, who can ensure everything is okay before putting it online.

Another good strategy, particularly in an intranet environment, is to give everyone their own directory within the site and then make sure the links to that directory remain constant. For example, you have a front page with links to the sales department, technical service, and return department. Assign each department its own directory and main page. Create a file name that will remain constant and will be linked to the front page. Each department can then do whatever they want with their directory and the contents of their main page, as long as they keep the name of the page the same so the link from the front page always works.

Case Study: Weekly Newspaper Goes Online

This real-life example focuses on the development of a Web site for a small publication and gets into detail in the planning process. Before I start, I'll confess that what I'm about to teach you is not what we did—it's what we should have done. I'll start by giving you a quick recap of the mistakes we made in the early stages of the site, and then I'll show you how I would approach it now that I've had a lot more experience.

Avoiding Structural Gaffes

About a year and a half ago, I convinced the publisher of the Pulitzer Prize Winning *Point Reyes Light* newspaper to let me put his paper online. It was my first project, and I had no idea what I was doing, so I just jumped blindly into it. The first week I created a home page, marked up the week's stories and photos, and put them all in one directory because it was the easiest way to set the links. (If you don't know how to set links through multiple directory levels, be sure you read "Setting Relative Links" at the end of this chapter.)

After the second update, I realized that adding new content every week would get things messy in that single directory pretty fast. I'd been using a Mac for a long time. I was used to seeing a folder on my hard drive get full and just moving things into new folders to reorganize them, but the documents and programs on my hard drive in the past hadn't been linked to each other in a way that made their relative location important. This new folder on my computer, which contained my first (somewhat ambitious) Web site, was full of pages that were related to one another. If I started moving those around, I'd break all the links.

Fortunately, I had a friend (a 16-year-old friend) who was a very experienced HTML developer (in those days, that meant he had almost a year's experience). After I got over being intimidated by the fact that at about half my age he could figure all this out, I hired him to help me for an afternoon. Fortunately, he taught me a few things as we went along. He started by putting all my images in one folder and creating separate folders for each new batch of stories that came through. For the next few months I created a structure as I went, adding new directories and setting up systems that made updating go faster. When I first started, it took a day and half to update the site every week. With a structure and good system in place, it took about an hour. We should have planned ahead, but the advantage of hindsight is using what you learn to improve future projects. My goal here is to use the newspaper as an example so you can avoid figuring it out as you go along.

> **Note**
>
> If figure 12.4 looks at all like a Web site you are working on, you need the second part of this chapter—"Creating Structure Out of Chaos." But you should read the first half of the chapter, too. You'll need all the help you can get.

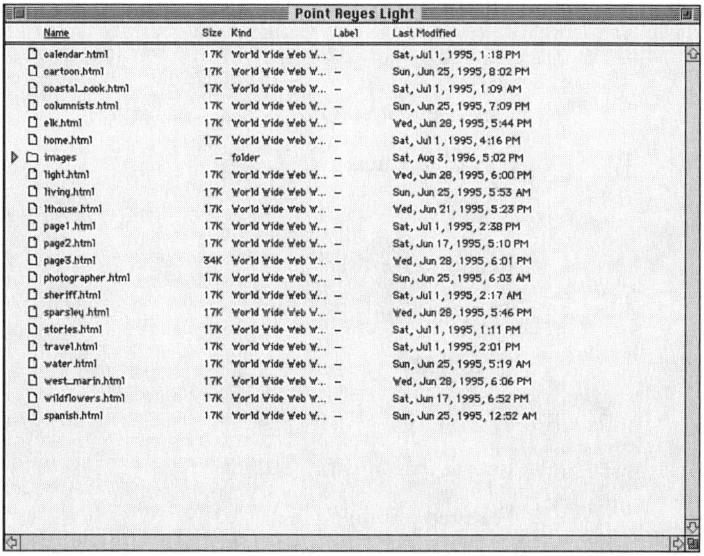

Figure 12.4

An inefficient directory structure.

Take the Project Apart: Identifying Key Elements

The *Point Reyes Light* is a weekly paper, so there is a regular and easily anticipated update routine. It also has a number of clear and distinct sections: the publisher's editorial, regular columnists, a cartoonist, featured photographer, the news, and of course, the part that keeps the whole thing going—advertising. Planning ahead means considering these logical sections and setting up a structure that makes it easy and convenient to add new material with each update.

Before you start creating an initial design, it's a good idea to make a list of all the elements of the Web site. We'll start here by listing all the regular parts of the paper, including contingencies for special sections.

1. Regular editorial content

    A. News stories

    B. Sheriff's calls

    C. Cartoons

    D. Featured photographer

    E. Regular columns

        I. Sparsely Sage and Timely

        II. Living and Loving

        III. The Coastal Cook

        IV. The Spanish column

        V. West Marin

    F. The calendar section

    G. Special features

2. Advertising

    A. Regular advertisers

    B. Travel-related ads

    C. Classifieds

3. Images

    A. Photos that illustrate stories

    B. Featured photographer

       C. Cartoonist

       D. Advertising images

    4. Special sections

       A. The Coastal Traveler

       B. Feature stories

Listing the elements is an important first step, as it gives you a chance to look at the bigger picture. With this list of the elements that make up the newspaper, we can start thinking about how to organize the Web site. It's important to recognize that many of these elements will be updated weekly. Thus, the site needs to be set up so that new items can be added and old items can be archived and still be accessible to readers.

Another good example of a Web site that has archived old stories is http://www.suck.com. The site is run by HotWired and updated daily so there is lots of material to keep track of.

Front Page Components

A good place to start with Web site planning is the front page. Ideally, you want to build a system that lets users make choices as they move through the levels of your Web site. The front page often has little content and many choices in the form of links to other pages. There are, of course, exceptions to this. If you are updating a site regularly, you may want to put breaking news on the front page and then offer other options along with it. Be careful not to put too many options on one page, however, because it can get busy and confusing.

> **N o t e**
>
> One rule of thumb of interface design is never have more than six options on a page. Otherwise, many argue, users may get overwhelmed and go somewhere else. That's not a hard and fast rule, but it is a useful guideline.

In the page for the *Point Reyes Light*, I'm about to violate the six-option suggestion because the publisher wants to give readers lots of choices. He also thinks his readers are sophisticated enough not to be intimidated by several choices. The point is, you don't have to put everything on the front page—you can put general categories at the top and get more specific as you work your way down the hierarchy of links.

The next step is to make a list of what has to go on the front page, based on the list of elements. Here's a look at what should go on the front page of the *Point Reyes Light* Web site:

Web Site Organization and Management

1. The newspaper's banner.

2. A link that provides some history about the paper and who works there.

3. A special feature story.

4. The week's news stories—the publisher chose to call that "Top of the News."

5. A link to each of the columnists, the cartoonist, and the photographer.

6. A link to a Business Directory where we can feature all the advertisers (trying to be subtle about the advertising aspect).

7. A link that goes to the *Coastal Traveler* (a travel magazine produced by the newspaper, which ultimately became its own Web site).

8. A link for the Point Reyes lighthouse, because everyone always asks about it, and the paper is named for it.

9. A link to a page to sell subscriptions.

Setting Up a Directory Structure

After the front page is in place, you need to think about how each main element will link to the rest of the site and where its corresponding HTML pages will be stored. Creating a good directory structure is one of the most important aspects of Web site management, and it's good to organize it in conjunction with organizing the links in the site. Where you store elements and how you name them is key to building new pages efficiently. How crucial this is becomes clear when, three months later, you want to change something on the 42nd page you created and need to find it in the hundreds of pages you've built since then.

To continue with our case study, we'll use what we know about the elements of the *Point Reyes Light* Web site to create a directory structure that will enable us to efficiently update the site weekly.

The Newspaper's Banner

This image will always appear on page one and is a good candidate for a general images folder at the top level of the directory structure. This could have been a static image, but we chose to link it to the page that provides history of the paper and information about who works there.

History and Staff

This links to the same place as the banner and describes how the paper won its Pulitzer Prize. Putting all the staff information on this page would be too much, so we opted to create another page that would link from this one. Planning ahead, we decided that this page could go in a general folder called Resources. Within that folder, we created a staff folder with the staff page. Later we could easily build in more staff pages when they all decided it was cool and wanted pages of their own.

A Special Feature Story

The paper regularly assigns a reporter to cover an in-depth feature story that may include several stories and photos. Thus, the Special Feature Story link should go to the first article in the feature, and that same page should include a list of supplementary stories that will be stored in the same directory. We called that directory "Features" and then created directories within it, using names with dates to distinguish each special feature section. We also created image folders in each of those subdirectories to keep the related images close to the story.

Top of the News

In this case, we have a number of stories that will be added each week. Here we must provide a list of the top news stories and set up a way to archive stories as we update. We did this with one main page that provides just a list of headlines, setting each headline to link to its story. To handle additions and archiving, we create a heading for each week with the date prominently displayed. Each week we insert the new stories above the old ones, and anyone who wants to find an old story can just scroll down the list. Each week's worth of stories goes into its own directory (again named with dates), and within each of these directories is an image directory to keep the stories and corresponding images together. When the list of headlines got too long, we created a second headline page and linked it to the bottom of the current one.

Columnists, the Cartoonist, and the Photographer

It was eventually decided that one link from the front page was not enough for all these famous contributors to the paper. We created a heading with all the columnists listed in text and linked to their weekly columns. Again, each column had to be set up so updates could be built in and older columns could be archived. In this case, we chose to have the link from the main page go directly to the current week's column. We then provided a menu list at the end of the new column that lists titles of previous columns, each linking to that column. We created a separate directory for each columnist and added the date to the name of each week's column. The cartoonist's and photographer's directories also include their own images folders so we can keep track of the graphics for their HTML pages.

> **Note**
>
> Another system we developed for managing consistent updates (such as these for columnists) is to give the current week's article a file name that doesn't include a date. For example, it could be the author's name: hamilton.html. Then each week when we add a new story, we first add a date to the one already in place and then put the new one in with the same name, hamilton.html. The older story becomes, say, hamilton8_12.html, and the newest version always has the name hamilton.html. This helps in a couple of ways. First, the link from the front page can remain constant—it always goes to hamilton.html, which means we don't have to change the front page every week. Second, we can then link the new column to hamilton8_12.html, which is already linked to the previous columns. Each week it builds because all the previous columns are linked to the bottom of the one named hamilton.html, and the column that came before it is linked to all the columns that came before that column. When we build in the new hamilton.html column, we copy all the links from the previous column to the bottom of that page and add a link to the one we are replacing. In fact, we learned that if we used the Save As feature to rename the column we are replacing, we could then just replace the body of text in the middle; all the general information at the top is already in place and the links are already at the bottom. Essentially, we move the new file in and the older file down a level, but we never have to open the old file to make any changes to it and we never have to change the front page. That saves a great deal of time.

Advertisers

In an effort to keep this a subtle part of the Web site, we created a button for the front page that said "Business Directory" and linked it to a separate page with all the advertisers listed. This listing then links to an individual page for each advertiser. To organize this, we created a business folder and created a separate directory for each advertiser, which contains that advertiser's HTML page and related graphics. This enables each advertiser to be built in as one complete and distinct directory.

The *Coastal Traveler* Magazine

We started with a special directory for the travel magazine and eventually registered a separate domain name and made it a unique Web site with a link from the newspaper's page. It was helpful that this was all in one directory, again complete with its own images folder, when we wanted to move it to the new site.

The Point Reyes Lighthouse

This is only one page and was linked with a small image of the lighthouse to catch the viewer's eye from the front page. Because it is only one page and we didn't anticipate adding a lot more here, we stored this page with the other travel information. When we moved the travel section later, it was not a big deal to duplicate these pages and build them into the resources folder.

Subscriptions

Again this is one page. Because it seems most related to the general resources, we chose to place it in the directory with the history and staff pages.

This is a relatively small Web site, but after little more than a year it has grown to hundreds of pages and graphics. Without this structure and organization in place, it would be a monster. With the structure, it's a relatively simple, approximately one-hour process for two people to convert the stories and graphics and add the new content each week. What's more, when the reporter doing the updates moved on to another job, it was easy for the new person to get up to speed and take his place. Figure 12.5 shows how the directory structure looked after two weeks of development.

Figure 12.5

The directory structure after the second week of development.

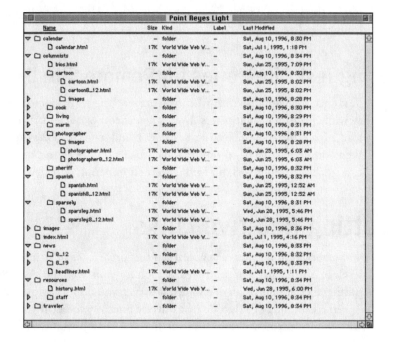

Creating a Test Directory

A test directory provides a place to check your work online before putting it into the live Web site. This is good practice, especially if more than one person is working on a Web site. If you have space on your server, the best way to do this is to keep a copy of the entire site in a test directory where you can build in new elements in relation to the entire site. If you don't have this luxury, you can create empty directories that represent the site's hierarchy and still test new additions in their relative locations.

Using Test Directories for Server-Side Functions

An online test directory is particularly useful when you are working on elements that require server-side functions, such as forms processing or server-side image maps. Before you put new additions into the live Web site, load them into the test directory to make sure they work online. It's a simple thing to set up, but many people overlook this option and run the risk of causing major problems to the site in the middle of a busy day. If you send the wrong files up or don't set the links properly, you can wreak havoc on a Web site that can take a while to fix. You don't want to do that to the live site if you can help it. Try the additions in a test directory first. Then, when you know they're flawless, send them up to the main site, and you can feel secure when you're ready to go live.

Using Test Directories for Remote Site Development

Test directories are also great when you are working with a remote team of developers or with clients in distant places. Even when clients or co-workers live nearby, I often load a "page in progress" into a test location and send them the direct URL. We can then both review the pages online while we talk on the phone, or trade e-mail about changes or additions without having to meet in person to review it.

Setting Relative Links

Throughout this chapter, you've learned the importance of creating multiple directory levels to provide structure and organization for your Web site. As soon as you start putting files in more than one folder, however, you need to know how to set hyperlinks in the HTML code that traverse directory levels. If you are already familiar with this issue, you can skip this section, but you may want to skim it for tips. If you are new to this concept, hold onto your seat. This can be a bit confusing at first, but even with tools such as SiteMill and FrontPage that provide a graphic view of links, it is important to understand how links work and how the path is set in the code.

Absolute vs. Relative Links

As you develop your HTML pages, setting links depends on keeping track of where your directories and files are in relation to one another. The first thing to learn is that local links, the ones that go to HTML documents or other files within your Web site, should be set as relative, not absolute, links. An absolute link would look something like this:

```
<A HREF="http://www.your_name.com/file_name.html">
```

The same hyperlink set as a relative link would look like this:

```
<A HREF="file_name.html">
```

Absolute links should be reserved for links to other Web sites. Do this for two reasons. First, you want to be able to test your links on your local hard drive. If you use absolute links, the links will only work if the files are on the server. Second, absolute links make the browser work harder and often take longer for your viewer to load.

If you keep all your HTML and other files in one folder, all the relative links will be as simple as the following:

```
<A HREF="file_name.html">
```

Naming Your Site's Main File

You should always use index.html as the name of the main file in your Web site, because that is what most servers are set up to deliver as the main page. When the browser gets to a domain name, it receives the index.html page first. If you don't have such a file, it will instead display a directory listing of the site that looks a bit like the list you view in an FTP program.

The main file in your site is not the only place you should use index.html. This is also a good technique in other directories, especially if you want to provide a direct address to that section of the site. For example, if you want to create a special section for a product, and your sales force will want to go directly to that page, create a directory with any name. Then, using index as the main file, all you need in the specific address is the directory name. Here's what it could look like. Assume that your domain name is www.good_deals.com, and you want the computer section to be easily accessible. If you create a directory called computers with computers.html as the main page, the address would have to be the following:

```
www.good_deals.com/computers/computers.html
```

Web Site Organization and Management

If you make index.html the main file in the computers directory, however, the address could simply be as follows:

```
www.good_deals.com/computers
```

Setting Relative Link Paths

When you start organizing pages in different directories, you must provide the path to that file in the hyperlink. Essentially, you are telling the browser where to find the file in relation to the page it is currently viewing.

Setting a path for a relative link comes easily to people who have worked in DOS or Unix, because a text-based operating system forces you to understand the structure of directories. If you have ever used "CD\" in DOS to change directories, you should have the idea.

> **Note**
>
> Remember that in DOS and Unix, the slash marks go in opposite directions. In DOS, use the backward slash mark \ as a delimiter. In Unix, use the forward slash /.

If you've only worked in Windows or Macintosh operating systems, setting relative links may seem a little confusing at first, because you have been sheltered by the graphical interface. Macintosh revolutionized computers by putting everything in folders represented by little icons you can click on. Windows followed suit, but with the Web still in its infancy, we're back to a world more like DOS than Windows. In the next sections, you'll learn how to write hyperlinks.

By this point in the book, you are probably familiar with Web site links and how they are created. But how do they really work? Essentially, the path in the link tag tells the browser where to find the page, graphic, or other file described in the HTML reference. Paths are set the same way for links to HTML pages as to graphics and other files, so after you learn this, you'll be set for everything on your site.

To describe the path, you must direct the browser up or down the hierarchy of the directory structure, indicating the name of the targeted file, as well as the names of any folders (directories) between the original file and the one that references it.

Here are the basics of how it works. If you want to set a link to a file within another folder, you need to include the directory (folder) name in the path. In other words, to go from the index.html file on the top level to a graphic in the images file, the link would look like this:

```
<A HREF="graphics/image.gif>
```

The best way to learn to set links is to see the process in action. Follow how the links are set in the examples that follow. Pay careful attention to the directory and file paths that establish the link.

If the original file is in a subdirectory, you use "../" to indicate that the path goes to a higher level. Thus, a link from the index page to the staff file located in the resources folder would look like this:

```
<A HREF="main/email.html">
```

The return link from e-mail back to index would look like this:

```
<A HREF="../index.html">
```

Set a link to who_we_are.html from index.html:

```
<A HREF="main/who_we_are.html">
```

Set a link to index.html from who_we_are.html:

```
<A HREF="../index.html">
```

Set a link to who_we_are.html from email.html:

```
<A HREF="who_we_are.html">
```

Set a link to email.html from mail_order.html:

```
<A HREF="../main/email.html">
```

To display logo.gif on the index page:

```
<IMG SRC="images/logo.gif">
```

To display button.gif on the email.html page:

```
<IMG SRC="../images/button.gif">
```

Web Site Management Tools

One of the greatest additions to the arsenal of available Web authoring programs is the advent of Web site management applications. Programs that provide a graphic display of an entire Web site and let you fix broken links with drag-and-drop ease are a welcome improvement in the lives of Web developers. Unfortunately, the best all-around program for this task, SiteMill, is only available for the Mac, and programs such as FrontPage and Spider for Windows only work on Web sites created in the HTML editor that ships with the program. Nonetheless, using these tools can save you hours of tedium and aggravation.

Adobe SiteMill: Web Site Management for Macintosh

SiteMill, Adobe's Web management tool, provides a graphic view of an entire site and corrects broken links with simple drag-and-drop functionality. PageMill, Adobe's HTML editor, is bundled with SiteMill. SiteMill will work on any Web site, regardless of the program used to author it. Although it only works on the Mac, you can move a site created on a Windows machine to the Mac and still use SiteMill to test it. You'll have to be careful of naming conventions and case issues, but you can read about that in the "Cross-Platform Issues and Testing" section later in this chapter.

Limitations

One big limitation of SiteMill (although Adobe promises an upgrade soon) is that it can't handle frames. If your Web site uses the Netscape extension (also supported by Microsoft) to display multiple HTML documents on-screen in frames, SiteMill will get very confused. Oh, and before you get too excited about this program, you should know the list price is $549 (but it's been spotted in catalogs for about $349).

Efficiency

SiteMill can check for broken links in any site that doesn't use frames. You can also display all the files in a graphic interface and then move things around while SiteMill automatically corrects the hyperlinks in the HTML code. It's impressive! Jobs that used to take hours will take minutes with SiteMill. Because one file may be linked to several other pages, remembering all the references can be a complicated task, requiring considerable searching and testing. SiteMill takes the hassle out of Web site management by displaying all your files and folders in a graphic window, where you can manipulate them and view all their incoming and outgoing links.

Tracking and Updating Links

Functional links are represented by two sets of arrows to the left of each file name. Selecting the left arrows displays the pages that link to the document; selecting the right arrows displays outgoing links. Selecting a triangle to the left of a page icon gives you a list of anchors that appear on that page. A red X indicates that a file is not linked anywhere. This is great for cleaning "strays" out of your site—you know, those graphics and pages you stopped using, but never removed. This is especially valuable if you are paying a commercial service provider by the MB for space on their server. Although you try to have your graphic file sizes as small as possible on the Web, they do take up space, and anything you can do to make the overall site smaller is worthwhile. If you update all the graphics on your main page, for example, you want to find the old images and get rid of them. When you delete old images, you risk causing a broken image link because an old file may still be in use somewhere else or you grab a new file by accident. SiteMill makes this safer. Be aware, however, that you'll have to exit SiteMill and remove unlinked files in the Finder; you can't delete files in SiteMill.

Verifying Links

To demonstrate SiteMill, I'll show you a Web site I developed for the Arts and Healing Network, a nonprofit organization in Sausalito, California. To check a site by using SiteMill, simply choose Load Site from the Site menu option, locate and select the folder on your hard drive that contains the Web site, and then watch for a few seconds while SiteMill verifies every link, checking file names against the HTML code as it prepares the graphic display of the entire site. It's quick, too—a larger site, with about 700 HTML pages and graphics, took a little over a minute to verify and load. When it's finished, the first thing SiteMill presents is an error window reporting broken links (see fig. 12.6). Here you find every page or graphic (or whatever) referred to in an HTML file, but not located where the link says it should be. Behind the error window is another window that lists every file and directory in the site.

Figure 12.6

SiteMill's error window.

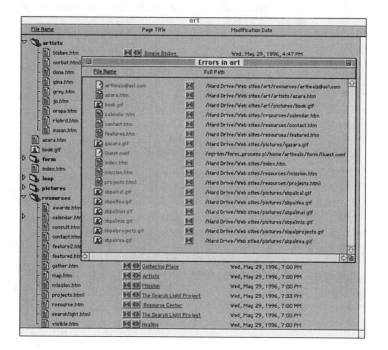

SiteMill verifies every link as it loads a site, and then displays a list of any broken links, as well as a list of all the files and directories in the site. Selecting the arrows next to a file name reveals a list of all files linked to or from that item.

Fixing Broken Links

Providing the list of broken links can save you considerable time and embarrassment, but the best part about SiteMill is its drag-and-drop link correction capabilities. It provides several options for fixing broken links.

Option A

The simplest option is to locate the file that appears in the error window. Assume it was an HTML page that was moved without all links being corrected.

Simply drag the icon that represents the original file over the item in the error window. Voila! SiteMill identifies its correct name and location and fixes the HTML tag that links to it in the referring page. It's that easy.

Option B

Another option for correcting links is to move a file in the main window to the location represented in the file structure that corresponds to the path set in the link tag (you have to know this or look at the HTML code to determine it).

Option C

A third option is to change the file name if you know that it is referred to in the HTML document by another name.

Option D

A last option is to double-click on any file, open it in PageMill, and reset the link there.

> **N o t e**
> Until the recent upgrade to PageMill, I wouldn't have recommended fixing broken links by using this HTML editor, but PageMill 2.0 is a dramatic improvement and provides a viable option for working on your site in a WYSIWYG environment. The biggest improvements are the addition of HTML table support and much cleaner raw code, complete with a built-in text editor you can use to work directly in the code. (For more on PageMill, see Chapter 13, "Tailoring Converted Files.")

SiteMill can also be used to correct links to another Web site (see fig. 12.7). It doesn't verify external links for you, but if an URL doesn't work, you can use the External References window to change it, and SiteMill will update every instance of that address throughout the Web site. You'll find the External References option under Windows in SiteMill's menu.

Figure 12.7

Correcting broken links is easy with SiteMill.

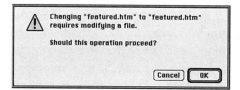

> ⚠ Changing "featured.htm" to "featured.htm" requires modifying a file.
>
> Should this operation proceed?
>
> [Cancel] [OK]

Changing Functional Links

SiteMill provides a range of options for changing functional links that enable you to reorganize a Web site and build in structure by adding new directory levels. You can also use these features to consolidate related items or move graphics into separate folders.

- To change a functional link, move or rename the file within SiteMill's graphic display. The program will alter all related links in the HTML code on every page that refers to it.

- To add organization to a site, you can add a new folder and drag any files into that folder. Again, SiteMill will correct all HTML references.

- To create a new folder at the root level, first make sure nothing is selected in the Site window. Then, under Choose Site, select Create Folder.

- To create a subdirectory, select any item inside the folder where you want the new folder to appear. Then, under Choose Site, select Create Folder.

Renaming Files and Folders

One annoying limitation you should be aware of here is that you cannot change the name of an existing folder if it already contains files. This can only be done while it is empty. You can rename any file, however, simply by selecting the file and retyping the name the way you would in the Finder. Anytime you make a change that requires SiteMill to change the HTML code, it will prompt you with a window asking if it should update the references to other files.

Case Sensitivity

If you are loading an existing Web site into SiteMill, you should be aware of limitations in identifying case differences in file names. If you are loading an existing Web site (or any pages created with a program other than PageMill or SiteMill), SiteMill will not find errors in case differences; for example, a file named ARTIST.GIF that is linked as "artist.gif." According to Adobe, this is because the Macintosh is not case sensitive and the links will work on the local hard drive. Unfortunately, this is a big problem for developers. On Windows and Mac operating systems, links work fine even if the case is different in the file name than in the hyperlink in the HTML code. But if you send the site to a Unix server (still the most common platform used by commercial service providers), your links won't work, because Unix is case sensitive. SiteMill *should* catch this problem for you because it's hard to find these errors before you put the site online. (This is another reason it's good to have a test directory to check your work before building it into the live Web site.)

SiteMill does recognize case differences in links created in PageMill and in changes made within SiteMill, so if you are working in that environment already, you shouldn't have problems. In other words, SiteMill creates links with case sensitivity about the names and will prevent these problems in sites created completely in the SiteMill/ PageMill environment, but it can't tell you if case differences are already a problem in an existing site.

Sorting Files and Folders

SiteMill works much like your desktop on the Mac. You can sort items by file name, by page title, and by modification date. You can open a folder to reveal a list of all the items contained within it, or close the folder to condense the spacing. Overall, this program is a great tool for anyone building, reorganizing, or testing a Web site. Most HTML authoring tools let you set links, but offer no way to track or view them.

FrontPage: Web Site Management for Windows

Unlike SiteMill, which is a separate but integrated part of PageMill, Microsoft's FrontPage incorporates Explorer, its Web site management tool, as a central part of the development system. When you begin to create pages in FrontPage, you use the site management program at the same time. In fact, Microsoft recommends you start in Explorer. This program is a powerful tool and offers some excellent features, especially if you are on an intranet. In addition to providing a graphical view of the site, where you can set and change HTML links, it features wizards and templates you can use to design an entire site, control the access users and authors have to the Web site, and enable multiple authors to update the same site simultaneously from remote locations.

The templates and wizards in FrontPage walk you through Web site creation with a series of options, such as a template for a sales page, order form, and many others. These are great features, but it is so difficult to incorporate existing HTML pages, pages that have been converted using other programs, or a Web site you've already put together, they don't warrant much coverage in this book or chapter. FrontPage is a great tool if you are building a new site and will be creating most of the content within the program or bringing in one page at a time using cut and paste. FrontPage is especially popular on intranets, where it can be used to build sections of a larger Web site, which can then be incorporated into the larger site manually or using other programs.

FrontPage also provides a graphical environment where you can view your entire Web site, but it has a couple of serious limitations. First, it is extremely difficult to import a site into the site management tool if it was not created in FrontPage, so it's not a great tool for testing sites created in other programs.

> **N o t e**
>
> To successfully import an existing site into the FrontPage environment, you need a strong understanding of the program and a good tech support person to walk you through the unique aspects of importing your site. The diverse contingencies possible here (depending on the features of your site) are beyond the scope of this book.

The second big drawback to FrontPage is that it limits you to two primary directories—one for images and the other for HTML pages. Microsoft seems to think that this makes it easier to keep track of things, but as I've pointed out in this chapter, trying to keep dozens, or even hundreds, of Web pages in one directory can be a mess. In fairness to FrontPage, the program does provide site management options, offering a visual display of all the pages in a site and the same kinds of drag-and-drop link correction features as you saw in SiteMill. These features help make up for the difficulty of keeping track of hundreds of files in one directory, but you will be dependent on FrontPage for doing so, and you can't use these features on a Web site created in any other program very easily.

Creating Structure Out of Chaos

If you began a Web site project without realizing the potential problems described in this chapter, you may already be lost in your site with dozens of HTML files and graphics all in one or two directories. This section is dedicated to helping you clean up this mess and restructure your site before you go any further with development.

Web Site Organization and Management

Mapping Your Site

The first thing you should do is sketch out a map or storyboard of the site on paper or in some graphics program so you can get a sense of what you have been creating and what pages link to one another. Even though you are obviously well into the process of developing the site, it's helpful to go through the exercises explained in the earlier part of this chapter. Make a list of all the elements—graphics, HTML pages, and other files—so you can look at the overall picture. Consider the front page elements and where they link, look at secondary pages, and then move down the hierarchy of links.

Creating a Directory Structure

A good way to set up directories is to put the files at each hierarchical level in the links structure into the same directory. Similarly, put each of the second-level pages into a directory, and then put the files that link to each page into its directory or into subdirectories within the same folder (directory). Look for logical divisions, such as issue updates, and distinguishable sections, such as information or product listings. And to prevent getting back into this mess in another couple of months, consider where there will be growth, leave room for it, and create new directories whenever you add a new section.

> **Note**
>
> If you are viewing the site you are trying to reorganize in Netscape or another browser, you can determine its location in the Web site structure by looking at the URL that appears in the location window in Netscape. Notice that this address will have the full location, including where the Web site is on your hard drive. All you need to worry about is the last part of this address, which will have the directory name and file name of the page you are viewing. If you can't see the entire path on your screen, place the cursor in the address and use the arrow keys to move to the right so you can view the last part of the address. For example, the following is the full address to my client list in my Web site on my hard drive in the Web sites folder. Notice that all I need to note is that this index file is located in the clients folder in the visiontec folder, which represents my Web site as it appears online:
>
> ```
> file:///Hard%20Drive/Web%20sites/visiontec/clients
> index.html
> ```

Evaluating Site Contents

If you are working on a Web site you created, you have a distinct advantage in that you should have a good idea of what's on every page, what the pages are called, and so on. If the site was created by someone else, you'll first face the arduous task of studying each page, checking where the links go, and then figuring out how to anticipate future growth. This is where Web site management tools can save your sanity, especially if there are already broken links in the Web site. Because your options are still limited on the PC, consider moving the site to a Mac temporarily so you can fix it in SiteMill before bringing it back to the Windows machine. One note of caution about SiteMill—it can't handle file name extension changes. This means that if the site has .htm extensions, you need to keep them that way. If the site has .html extensions, you need to keep those names. If you are taking a site off a Windows machine and then moving it back to a Windows machine when you're done, this shouldn't be a problem. If you're converting a site from a Mac naming structure to a PC naming structure, on the other hand, you'll want a new program called Rename! that was created specifically to handle this problem. (You'll find a description of the program at the end of the next section.)

Cross-Platform Issues and Testing

Before you send your Web site to a server, it's a good idea to test your links on your local hard drive. If you have set relative links, you can test links by simply opening any linked HTML file on your computer with any browser and selecting the hyperlinks to move through the site. (You'll learn more about links in the next section of this chapter.) Testing is almost as big a part of Web design as creating the HTML code in the first place, and you should always test your work thoroughly before you put it online. Be aware, however, that your graphics and links may work on your hard drive, but not on the server you use for putting them online. Cross-platform differences become important, because Unix, Macintosh, and Windows computers have distinct naming requirements that can cause problems when you move a site from one computer to another. Many new developers are surprised by this, because HTML files are ASCII text and can be opened by any text editor on any computer system. The links, however, may not be so universal. If you're looking for a comprehensive list of naming requirements by platform, check the references in Appendix C, "Online Resources for Web Developers."

Saving HTML Files

On a Unix, DOS, or Windows machine, HTML files will only work if the system recognizes the extension that follows the file name. For example, you have to use .htm on a PC, and many Unix systems won't recognize index.html. If you don't save your files with the proper file type indicated in the extension, a program on a Windows, DOS, or Unix system may not be able to open them. This generally isn't a problem on Macintosh computers, because compatible files are recognized by an embedded "header" rather than by a file extension created by the author. Also, for a browser to open your HTML files, you must save them as text-only. HTML editors take care of this for you, but if you are using a word processing program to create HTML pages, you may have to use the Save As function and select Text Only as the file type.

Sending Site Files to Unix Servers

The most common problems occur when you create a Web site on a Macintosh or Windows computer, and then send it to a Unix server. Because most of the servers on the Internet are Unix machines, you should be aware of one of the biggest differences right away: Unix systems are case sensitive, but Windows and Macintosh are not. This means that if you create a file called index.html and refer to it in your HTML links as INDEX.HTML, it will work on a Macintosh or Windows system, but not on a Unix server. Many HTML authors have tested and retested their work locally, only to see all their links fall apart when the site was put online. The best solution to this problem is to always be consistent in your use of case in file names. Many designers use all lowercase letters, a great option for the Mac and Unix systems. If you are using Windows, however, you will be better off using all capital letters as they are the most consistent. When you move files from a Mac to a Windows system or from Windows to DOS, the process is likely to result in changes in case, unless you are using all uppercase letters.

File Name Issues

The safest thing to do on any machine is to use ISO9660 file names, because they can be read by every computer on the planet and work on any CD-ROM cross-platform as well. The ISO9660 standard, though not commonly known, was developed to make file names more universally recognized and is supported by every operating system in known use today. ISO9660 file names follow the DOS 8.3 convention, but can't include any "special characters" (such as ~ or &) except the underline. If you are working in the Windows operating system, you will be familiar with the 8.3 rule, which limits names to no more than eight characters and a three-digit extension. This means limiting a name such as "this_is_too_long.html" to "it_works.htm." Notice the extension must be shortened to .htm instead of .html. Other extensions must also be shortened, such as .jpeg to .jpg. Although you should be able to use longer file names on Windows 95 and NT, many designers still limit themselves to the 8.3 rule—a good habit to maintain. If you want to ensure that your file names will remain consistent on any operating system, carry the 8.3 a step further and always use uppercase letters in file names and hyperlinks.

Unix File Names

Of course, every rule has its exception. In this case, Unix had to get in the way. Many Unix servers require an extension of .HTML—not .HTM— before the index file can be recognized as the main file in the Web site. (Other files can use .htm, but the main page has to be named INDEX.HTML.) Because many computers won't allow four-digit extensions, you may have to rename the index file once it's on the server. Another Unix limitation affecting Macintosh users is that file names in a Web site cannot include spaces. Many people use the underscore mark to make up for this, creating names such as "this_file.html." A file name with a space, such as "this file.html," will not work on most servers.

Windows 95 File Names

In Windows 95, where supposedly you can create any kind of file name you want, you have to be careful. If you move these files to another system, the names will be changed. Unfortunately, the real name and the cosmetic Windows 95 name are often not the same. If you leave Windows and go back to DOS to view a directory, you are likely to find this. In the following table, the left column shows how DOS views certain file names, while the right column shows what was typed into Windows 95.

DOS Names	Name as Typed in Windows 95
INDEX.HTM	index.html
FRONTBAN~JPG	Frontbanner.jpg
BUTTON.GIF	button.GIF
TEST.HTM	TEST.HTM

All the DOS names on the left are in uppercase letters and limited to 8.3; however, on the right you see how the file was named when it was created in Windows 95. The Windows 95 file name can be any mix of uppercase or lowercase and can be more than eight characters, but it's a "cosmetic" name; that is, it isn't the true file name. Now look at the last name on the list. TEST.HTM is the same in both places, so you should have no problems, illustrating the advantage of creating file names in all uppercase and limiting them to the 8.3 rule.

Sending Windows Files to Unix Servers

If you are working on a Windows system and sending the files to a Unix server, you must be careful of case. Using all uppercase letters should work as long as you don't use special characters or leave blank spaces in the name. If you are determined to use a lowercase naming structure, consider a custom solution. One Web design company developed a special "upload tool," which (among other things) changes all file names to lowercase during the upload process. This, combined with a production policy of always using lowercase within HTML links, has worked well for them. If you can't afford this kind of custom solution, consider using a new program called Rename! described in a section that follows.

Windows 95 and Windows NT

If you are only using Windows 95 and Windows NT systems, you have greater flexibility in creating file names. You can mix caps and small letters and use white spaces, long file names, and just about anything else you want (except, of course, special characters such as / and ?). Even with this variation, you should have no problems if you are working in only Windows 95 and NT.

If you are going from Windows NT or Windows 95 to Unix, case definitely matters. In this scenario, you must ensure that the name in the hyperlink is exactly the same as the file name, including case. You can, however, use long file names if there are no white spaces. For instance, you can use the following file name:

```
"first_pages_user_sees_when_he_she_hits_the_site.html".
```

Here again, you are safest with all uppercase letters, because some FTP programs change the names to all caps during the transfer process.

Rename! The File Name Enforcer

The Rename! software program will automatically convert any list of file names so they meet a specific file-naming convention. You have the option of processing the entire list automatically or typing in your own name for each file. This means you can change all the names in a Web site to fit the 8.3 naming convention of a Windows system, make them uppercase or lowercase, and ensure they will work on the operating system of your choice. As it changes the file names, the program checks all the links in your HTML pages, changing the file names as it goes, and ensuring that all names (even ones you don't change) match in case.

Suppose you have a list of long file names you want to shorten. You can set the program to use a numbered system, such as JANINE01.HTM, JANINE02.HTM, JANINE03.HTM. Alternatively, you can set the program to let you rename them individually to, for example, JANHOME1.HTM, JANBIO.HTM, JANRESU.HTM.

To learn more about Rename! or download a trial version of the program, direct your browser to the following:

```
http://www.visiontec.com/rename
```

Summary

The key to good Web site management is good planning. Taking the time in the early stages of Web design to organize the structure of the site, create systems to facilitate updates, and build in room for growth can save hours of grief and frustration later. Even with new Web site management tools available, this process is crucial to good design and a smooth development process.

One of the first issues to consider when you start into a Web site project is what kind of server you will use and what operating systems you will have to accommodate in your naming conventions. Setting up logical naming systems will help you find files and organize them in a way that makes sense to everyone on a project. Choosing the right name length and file extension for your Web pages will ensure that your links work when they get online. And setting up a test directory online where you can check your work before you build it into your live Web site will give you a good way to manage remote staff and clients and save the embarrassment of broken links in the main site.

Whether you are creating a large or small site, taking time to develop some kind of written style guide can help with overall management, provide a training guide for new members of the team, and ensure a consistent look and feel to your site. Clear and intuitive navigational features enable your users to move through the site in the most efficient and personalized way possible. Also, be sure to include such elements as a menu bar on each page and a site map or table of contents listing all, or nearly all, the pages on the site. Finally, being sure you understand how to set links, and setting relative, not absolute, links in your site will make testing easier and broken links less likely online.

All these issues should be considered as you organize and develop your Web site. Following the points outlined in this chapter will help make your Web site organization and management an easier and smoother process.

CHAPTER 13

Tailoring Converted Files

Tailoring Converted Files

The conversion techniques described in this book are only the first step to getting your files online. The goal of this book is to help you convert content quickly and efficiently so you can focus the rest of your time on creating a good design for the Web site and adding features not possible in print, such as multimedia elements and hyperlinks. The conversion programs described in this book are the best products available on the market, but none of them are perfect. After getting the most out of these programs by using the tips in this book, there will still be room for improvement.

Once you have converted your files with programs such as BeyondPress for Quark-XPress and HTML Transit for Microsoft Word or FrameMaker, you will want to use a good HTML editor to add new features and fine tune your pages. In this chapter, you will learn how to use the best HTML editors for Macintosh and Windows computers, from WYSIWYG programs that shield you from the HTML code to powerful text editors designed to make it easier to write HTML. This chapter is dedicated to helping you clean up converted files and polish your designs by using three great HTML editors, focusing on techniques and programs for tailoring your HTML pages. For more information on good design practices, read Chapter 2, "Design Considerations for the Web."

HTML Editors Covered in This Chapter

There are dozens of HTML editors on the market, and each one promises to be better than the rest. With so many programs claiming to be the best, it can be tough to decide which tool is right for you. To make matters more complicated, all of these programs are evolving rapidly.

HTML editors today are comparable to the early days of Quark and PageMaker—they provide basic layout features, but they lack many of the newest design options. Despite the claims WYSIWYG editors make about not needing HTML, you'll still need a basic understanding of the HyperText Markup Language to fully understand their features and limitations. (To learn more about HTML, read Chapter 14, "HTML Tutorial and Reference.") In the last several months, WYSIWYG programs have gotten good enough to handle sophisticated designs in a graphic environment.

Their biggest problem is that HTML is changing quickly, too, but you can always add the most advanced and newest features in a text editor when you're done.

In this chapter, you'll learn about a great WYSIWYG editor and two HTML text editors. There are so many programs with comparable feature sets that selecting an HTML editor should depend as much on the interface as on function. The WYSIWYG editor, Claris Home Page, was selected for its intuitive interface, as well as cross-platform support. Many Web design teams incorporate Macs and PCs into the development, and a program that works on both systems makes it easier to pull everything together and enables many designers to contribute to the project. Also covered in this chapter are BBEdit, a high-powered text editor for the Mac, and Hot Dog Pro, a Windows HTML text editor. These programs were selected as the best for working directly in the HTML code because they provide a good list of HTML tags and other features that make manual markup easier. Here is a brief description of each of these editors:

- Claris Home Page (Macintosh, Windows 95, and NT)

  A WYSIWYG HTML editor, Claris Home Page features a graphic design environment with drag-and-drop ease of use. Built-in options include most of the HTML 2.0 and 3.2 tags, including tables, background colors and images, and forms. In addition, the program includes Netscape and Microsoft extensions, making it possible to add attributes to tags and build Web pages using frames.

- BBEdit (Macintosh)

  An HTML text editor for the Macintosh, BBEdit enables you to write your own HTML. It features a list of HTML 2.0 and 3.2 tags that can be inserted around text, making it easy to work directly with the HTML code. This sophisticated text editor is designed for programmers as well as HTML designers, and can be used when writing CGI scripts and other high-level programming. One of BBEdit's most powerful features is multiple-page search-and-replace, which can be used for global changes to a Web site, making this an ideal tool for cleaning up converted documents.

- Hot Dog Pro (Windows 3.1 and 95)

  An HTML text editor for the Windows operating system, Hot Dog Pro features HTML 2.0 and 3.2 tags, as well as many Netscape and Microsoft extensions. This program also enables you to work directly in the HTML code and comes with built-in file transfer functions, making it easy to put your site online when you are ready.

This is a quickly changing arena—what looks like the best program this week may be outdone by someone else's upgrade next week. For the latest news on software programs, visit the Web sites of their manufacturers frequently. (You'll find a list of programs to watch and Web site addresses in Appendix B.) In addition to the programs covered in this chapter, you'll find other HTML editors on the CD-ROM that accompanies this book so you can do your own testing.

Preliminary Steps

The planning process described in Chapter 12, "Web Site Organization and Management," will help as you consider how to refine your work. If you have done the preliminary task of storyboarding or outlining your Web site, you will have an easier time tailoring your converted files and creating an overall design that works throughout the site. Before you can create a good design, however, you need a goal and a plan of action.

Expect to spend more time on a main page (whether of a Web site or one of its sections) than you will on supplementary pages. The front page is always the most important. It sets the tone for the rest of the site, and users are most likely to leave from here if they are dissatisfied. Make sure you give users options with links to multiple places in the Web site or section. With few exceptions, a front page that links to only one other page is a waste of the Web's greatest asset—hyperlinks. The exceptions are quick-loading opening pages used on some Web sites for dramatic effect. The Batman Web site, for example, opens with a well-designed graphic of the superhero and then moves to a page with links to other options. (To see this in action, check out the site at http://www.batmanforever.com/.)

Keep your target audience in mind as you design the main page. Make sure you offer enough variety so viewers with varying tastes and interests will all find something that appeals to them. At the same time, keep the focus on your main audience. Your designs should reflect the lifestyles and interests of your intended viewers. On a Web site such as Microprocessor Report—designed for engineers—graphics may have little value and users won't want to be slowed down as they seek out information. Inside the Microprocessor site are pages with many graphics (technical drawings and other relevant information best presented in images); however, these image-heavy pages are inside the site where only those viewers who choose to see them will have to wait. On the Batman Web site, however, the audience expects lots of graphics as well as animation and sounds. Putting strong images on the front page is important here.

Following the steps outlined in Chapter 12 helps ensure pages are appropriate for your audience. It also helps you determine where any new pages fit into the Web site. If your entire Web site is based on a QuarkXPress document you have converted with

BeyondPress, you will need a strong front page. If the XPress document is only a small piece of a larger Web site, you will want the final design to fit with the rest of the site and will likely use programs such as those described in this chapter to link the new pages into place. The best conversion programs let you control the styles of converted elements to create your own unique design, but they can't give you the same control you get in an HTML editor. Thus, once you've completed the conversion, you'll want to use the tools and techniques described in this chapter to add sophisticated design features. Use the information in Chapter 2 to guide you through the tailoring process.

Note

Assessing Converted Files

Before you start using the HTML editors described in this chapter, take a good look at the files you have converted and how you need to get them ready for the Web. Conversion programs are designed to move large volumes of text from traditional desktop publishing and word processing programs into basic HTML formatting, but they're not good at adding high-end HTML features or creating intricate designs. This is where the programs in this chapter come in. You have converted the text and graphics into simple HTML pages. Now you can create more complex designs by inserting tables without borders for better alignment control, adding links, creating frames, and even adding multimedia features.

All the conversion programs in this book create HTML pages that can be viewed in most standard Web browsers. Reviewing the converted pages in a browser before starting into the fine-tuning process will help you determine where you want to make changes. Consider the elements in your pages. Did the graphics convert as well as you hoped with your conversion program? If not, you can use the exercises in Chapter 11, "Graphics Creation," to convert them in a program such as Photoshop or DeBabelizer, and then link them into your pages by using an HTML editor. Study the converted files to determine where other design features may be useful and what is needed to create a cohesive design throughout the site.

Claris Home Page

Claris Home Page was selected from more than a dozen WYSIWYG HTML editors available on the market. Several of the many similar programs are included in trial or demo versions so you can compare them yourself. Claris Home Page is featured here for the reasons highlighted in the following list:

1. **User Interface.** An appealing and intuitive interface makes this program easy to use.

2. **Cross Platform.** Because this program works on both Macintosh and Windows operating systems, it is ideal for team projects where designers may be working

in different operating systems. Pages created on one platform can easily be moved to the other. The only exception to this involves the limitations of naming conventions on Windows systems. See "Cross-Platform Issues" in Chapter 12 for more on naming.

3. **High-End Features.** Many WYSIWYG programs lack high-end HTML features. Claris Home Page supports a wide range of HTML tags, including tables and frames.

4. **Drag-and-Drop.** Links can be set easily and intuitively by using drag-and-drop and copy-and-paste functions.

5. **Libraries.** A unique and valuable feature of this program enables you to save text, images, tables, and any other combination of HTML code and content in libraries for easy placement of frequently used elements.

6. **Graphics.** Claris Home Page can convert PICT and BMP images to GIF format and display GIFs and JPEGs in the WYSIWYG editing environment. It supports drag-and-drop linking of images and has a built-in utility for setting coordinates for an image map.

7. **Built-in Text Editor.** Incorporating a text editor in the program makes it easy to edit raw code without leaving the WYSIWYG editor. Changes made to the HTML code automatically affect the graphic display.

8. **Download Estimates.** You can check the estimated download time of your pages in Claris Home Page to determine how long someone will have to wait when using a 14.4 or 28.8 modem or an ISDN line. You can even check individual elements on the page to determine which graphics or text areas will take the longest to download.

Setting Home Page Preferences

As with most programs, the first thing you should do is set the preferences in Home Page to ensure that style options within the program will be tailored to your needs. The Preferences option is available under the Edit menu. At the top of the Preferences dialog box is a pull-down menu providing access to the various preferences options. Use this pull-down menu to move among the available settings. The following figures and descriptions will walk you through Home Page's preferences. These screen shots were created on a Macintosh, but with the exception of minor differences in the appearance of some of the dialog windows, the program is identical on both platforms. In fact, the same manual is shipped with both programs, and only the installation instructions differ.

General Preferences

The General Preferences in Claris Home Page enable you to set a variety of options, such as the display of toolbars, how often the program autosaves files, and the file extension used.

1. General Preferences enable you to control the display of the toolbars. Checking both boxes gives you access to shortcuts to commonly used HTML features, such as header tags, bold, and center.

2. The program features an Auto Save option. You can set the number of minutes before it is activated, or uncheck the box to disable the feature.

3. You can set the program to open in WYSIWYG edit mode, in Preview mode, or in the text editor.

4. You can specify if the program opens at a new document, at the Open dialog box, or with nothing open.

5. The last option in the General Preferences dialog box enables you to specify the extension of files as .html for Macintosh and Unix or as .htm for Windows and DOS (see fig. 13.1).

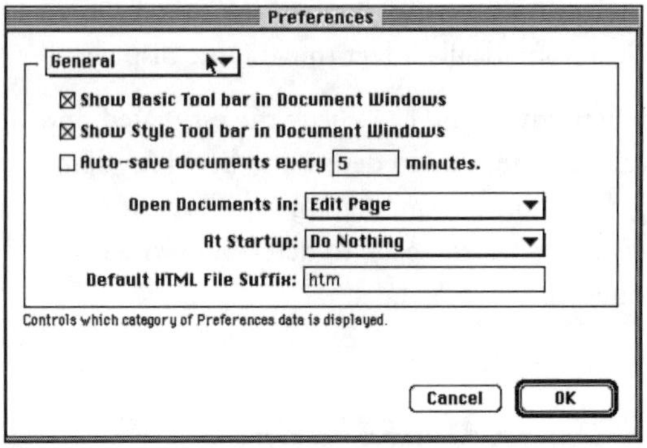

Figure 13.1

The General Preferences dialog box.

HTML Output Options

The HTML Output options let you specify preferences such as how the low breaks will be created, whether paragraph tags will include a close tag, and whether links will be created with absolute or relative paths. The following items are included in the HTML Output Preferences dialog box (see fig. 13.2):

1. **Header Comment.** Specify header elements with the option to (1) add a credit line indicating the page was created by Claris Home Page, (2) add this line and the date of creation (time-stamp), or (3) add nothing. This is a nice feature, as

many HTML authoring programs automatically insert their own credit line (whether you want it or not).

2. **Line Break Format.** This option enables Home Page to create line breaks in the HTML code appropriate for the Macintosh, Windows, or Unix operating systems. This function makes it possible to maintain spacing in the HTML code when using another text editor, such as BBEdit or Hot Dog (both described later in this chapter).

3. **Paragraph Alignment Uses.** Here you can choose either the Center tag or Alignment Parameters inserted within other tags, such as the Paragraph tag. The Center tag is the tag most commonly supported by browsers at this time and is generally your best option. Use the check boxes under the Paragraph option to do the following:

   - **Generate </P> tags.** Choose to generate Close Paragraph tags, an optional HTML element.

   - **Use Absolute Pathnames.** Unless you have a compelling reason, leave Absolute Pathnames unchecked. You are better off setting relative links, such as `<A HREF="INDEX.HTML">`, rather than absolute links, which look like `<A HREF="http://www.domain_name.com/ INDEX.HTML">`. Relative links load faster and can be tested on your local hard drive.

   - **Generate X-SAS Tags.** The third check box enables Claris Home Page to create custom tags (all of which begin with X-SAS). These are not HTML tags, but are inserted in the HTML code for use by Home Page. The program needs these tags to save information such as where the program's window will be opened on your screen and the size of the window to be displayed. These tags are completely optional, and any HTML purist will tell you not to add "extra" stuff to the code in your pages. (Be glad Claris gives you the option. Adobe's PageMill, for example, adds special code for use by the program without making it optional.) For control over window placement, check this box. If you don't care about window placement, you're better off leaving it unchecked. If you do use them, these tags should not display in any browsers as they will not be able to interpret the meaning of Home Page's X-SAS tags.

HTML Editing Option

This Preferences option enables you to specify the font and point size of the generated HTML code and controls the display of text in the text editor built into the program (see fig. 13.3). This is purely for your preferences about text appearance when working in the code, and will have no effect on the display of your pages in a browser.

Figure 13.2

The HTML Output Preferences dialog box.

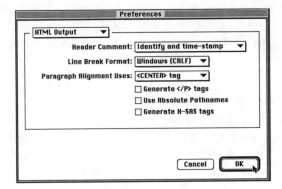

Figure 13.3

The HTML Editing Preferences dialog box.

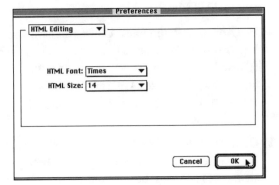

Images Options

The Images options in Claris Home Page enable you to choose whether GIFs should be interlaced, the directory where images will be stored, and whether images will be displayed in the WYSIWYG editor. The following are included in the Images Preferences dialog box, shown in figure 13.4:

1. **Make Interlaced GIF.** Specifies whether converted images are created with interlacing, a graphics feature that gives images the appearance of loading more quickly, because the entire image is loaded first at a low resolution, and then detail is added incrementally.

2. **Prompt for File Name/Location.** Brings up a dialog box each time you use the program to convert an image to GIF format. During conversion, Home Page creates a new image. If you do not check this box, the image will automatically be named by Home Page. Checking the Prompt for File Name/Location box is a

good idea, as you should use a naming convention that will make sense to you
later when trying to identify the images by file name.

3. **Display Images in Edit Mode.** Provides you with the choice of viewing images
   only in the Preview window of Home Page. This enables you to work more
   quickly in Edit Mode, because images take longer to load than text, but it
   eliminates one of the best features of a WYSIWYG editor—the capability to
   view all your page elements as you create the design. You may choose to uncheck
   this box when you are working primarily on text and don't want to be slowed
   down, but most of the time leave it checked to take full advantage of the graphic
   view of your pages while working on them.

4. **Converted Images Folder.** Enables you to specify where Home Page will store
   images you convert to GIFs. You may want to create a general images folder for
   all your graphics, or you may want one graphics folder for each section of a Web
   site, in which case you can change this as you move from section to section. The
   Set button below this option lets you browse to find the folder you want to use;
   however, you cannot create a new folder on your hard drive while using this
   program. To create a new folder, you must leave Home Page and use the Finder
   on your Mac or the Explore window on a PC to create a directory, and then
   return to Home Page to specify the new folder in this Preferences dialog box.

Figure 13.4

*The Images
Preferences
dialog box.*

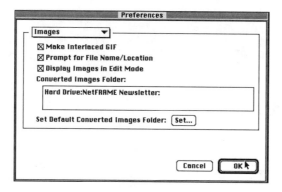

Browser Preview

The Browser Preview option lets you specify the browser in which you want to
preview your HTML pages (see fig. 13.5). Use the Set option to locate the browser on
your hard drive. Home Page will automatically set the indicated browser to load when
you select the Browser Preview option from the toolbar or menu. You should preview
your pages in the browser that you expect the majority of your viewers will use. If you
are designing for the broader Web audience, it's a good idea to preview your pages in a
variety of browsers to ensure that they look good to all of your viewers.

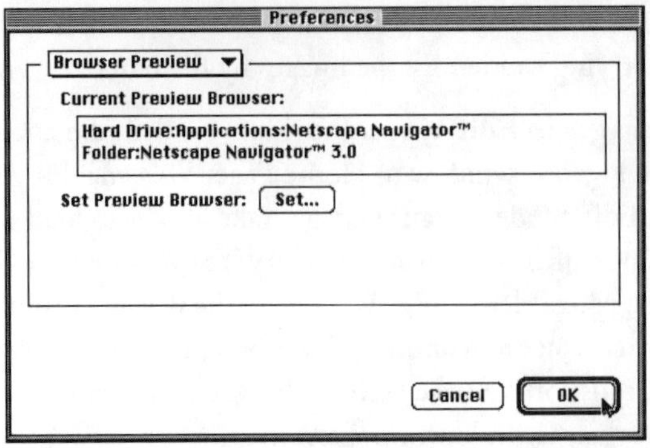

Figure 13.5

The Browser Preview Preferences dialog box.

Preferences

Browser Preview ▼

Current Preview Browser:

Hard Drive:Applications:Netscape Navigator™
Folder:Netscape Navigator™ 3.0

Set Preview Browser: [Set...]

[Cancel]   [OK]

The Toolbars

Claris Home Page features a range of HTML options in its WYSIWYG editing environment. Two toolbars offer easy access to common HTML options. More HTML tags are available under Insert, Format, and Style in the main menu. To help you identify the icons in the toolbar on the Windows operating system, the program provides small, pop-up text windows with descriptions of each icon. On the Macintosh, it displays the descriptions to the right of the toolbars. Figure 13.6 shows the toolbars.

Figure 13.6

The Claris Home Page toolbars.

The Basic Toolbar

The Basic toolbar across the top of the page includes access to a range of HTML options. The icons for this toolbar are detailed in the following list (from left to right):

- **Edit Page.** Opens the WYSIWYG editing environment.

- **Preview Page.** Opens the document in the Preview option within Home Page. You cannot edit in this environment.

- **HTML Source.** Opens the file in the built-in text editor, where you can work in the HTML code directly. Changes made in the text editor automatically affect the page when you return to the WYSIWYG editor.

- **Browser Preview.** Displays the page in the browser you specified in Browser Preferences.

- **Object Editor.** This option can be used to open a dialog box for any object on the page. Simply select an object, such as an image, table, frame, or horizontal rule, and then select the Object Editor icon. This opens a dialog box where you can alter the HTML tag, add attributes, or change attributes for the object selected.

- **Link Editor.** To use this feature, select any object or section of text on the page, and then select the Link editor icon. In the dialog window that appears, type any URL or browse your hard drive to locate a file and set the link automatically.

- **Document Options.** Opens a dialog box with three menu options: General Settings, Text and Background Colors, and HTML Extras.

  - The General Settings option enables you to change the title of the document from the default title, which is the name of the HTML file. You are likely to want to change this, because file names can't include spaces, and the length limitation on Windows machines often results in rather cryptic names. This dialog box also contains a place to set the action of a form to Get or Put (this depends on the CGI script you are using). You can also enter a base URL and a target for frames.

  - The Colors and Backgrounds dialog box provides access to a color wheel. When you select the colored box, a color wheel appears, much like the one in Photoshop. Select the color you want, and Home Page automatically determines the corresponding hexadecimal color. You can set text, link, and background colors, and set a background image.

  - HTML Extras enables you to create a Prefix Comment, text inserted within the comment tag, which does not display. This is a handy way to add the author's name or other information you want to include in the HTML code but not display in the browser. By using Tag Parameters and Head Parameters, you can add attributes or other text to the opening HTML and head tags at the beginning of the document. Unless you know HTML well, you probably won't need this option. A second HTML Extra, Text in the Head Section, enables you to add other HTML tags such as the Meta tag to the Head section. Again, you need to know HTML for this. In the Body Tag Parameters section, you can add attributes to the Body tag. Some of these attributes, such as text and links colors, are included in other areas of Home Page, but the newest Netscape and Microsoft extensions, such as Font Face, have to be set manually here. See Chapter 14, "HTML Tutorial and Reference," for more information on optional tags and attributes.

- **Insert Anchor.** Enables you to set an anchor anywhere in the Body section of a page, to which you can then set a link directly.

- **Insert Link to File.** This is a more direct way to set a link to another HTML file. The Link Editor can be used for the same purpose, but requires two steps for this function because it includes other link options as well.

- **Insert Image.** Enables you to place an image on the page by browsing the hard drive to locate the image file.

- **Insert Horizontal Rule.** Places an <HR> line across the page wherever the cursor is placed. To alter the Horizontal Rule, select the <HR> line and choose the Object Editor icon, and you can change the height and width of the rule.

- **Insert Table.** This option automatically places a basic two-row-by-two-column table on the page and opens a dialog box where you can specify height, width, number of rows and columns, cell padding, and spacing. You can also enter other HTML attributes, such as the new Netscape and Microsoft extensions, for background colors and other table features. If you select an individual cell in a table, a secondary dialog box appears where you can specify the rowspan and colspan (this lets you merge table cells), set alignment of the cell, and designate if it is a Header cell. Another text box here is for supplementary HTML tags.

- **Align Text (Left, Right, and Center).** The last three icons in the top line of the toolbar can be used to align text. Despite their names, they also work for graphics and other objects. Highlight a section of text or select an image or other object; then choose the alignment icon you want.

The Style Toolbar

The Style toolbar, the second row of icons across the top of the page, includes access to HTML style-formatting options. The icons for this toolbar are detailed in the following list (from left to right):

- **Pop-up Window.** Enables you to specify the format to be used when you enter text in the program. The default is set to Normal, which places no code around the text and text is displayed in the default size in the browser. Other options in the pop-up menu include Preformatted, Address, Headers 1 through 6, Bulleted List, Numbered List, Term, and Definition. Definition is a handy feature that enables you to set the formatting before typing the text, rather than typing the text, selecting it, and then applying the HTML style you want. As a general rule, keep this set to Normal.

- **Insert List Entry.** Enables you to create numbered or bulleted lists (known as ordered and unordered lists in HTML). The default in Home Page is an unordered (bulleted) list. When you select this icon, the pop-up window at the beginning of the line automatically changes to the Bulleted option. If you prefer an ordered list, change the pop-up option to Numbered, and the list will follow that style. When displayed in the text editor, numbered-style lists appear as the number sign #. To see the actual display, select Preview or Browser Preview in the basic toolbar. The Numbered Style option under Format in the menu enables you to designate the kind of list item used, with options of Arabic numerals, Roman numerals, and letters.

- **Indent.** Places Blockquote tags to indent the highlighted text area, image, or other selected object.

- **Outdent.** Reverses the action of the Indent option and serves as a way to remove lists as well. For example, if you create a list within a list and then want to remove the second-level list, the Outdent icon can do this automatically.

- **Smaller Text.** Uses the Font Size tag to reduce the text by one size. Note: HTML does not use point sizes, but features seven relative Font Sizes to choose from. Home Page's normal-size text is Font Size 3; thus, if you select Normal text and then choose Smaller Text, it will be reduced to Font Size 2.

- **Larger Text.** Increases the font size by one, going up to Font Size 7.

- **Bold.** Makes highlighted text bold by using the <B> tag.

- **Italic.** Makes highlighted text italic by using the <I> tag.

- **TeleType.** Use this to display computer code.

- **Text Color.** Includes five commonly used colors in a pull-down menu. Choosing Other brings up a dialog box with a color wheel so you can specify any color. Note: a funny little bug on the Macintosh displays the text in a different color while it is highlighted. To view the actual color, deselect the text.

The Tool Palette

The tool palette, available under the Window menu, adds a floating palette to the program. The floating palette includes formatting options for creating forms, such as radio buttons and check boxes. The palette also includes some of the options in the toolbars, such as the Image and Horizontal Rule icons.

Options Only Available Through the Menu

All options in the toolbar are also available through menu options. Additional options, only available through the menu, are detailed in the following list:

- Choose Insert, Applet to add Java applets. This option creates an empty colored box in the editing area where the cursor is placed. Double-click on the box, and a dialog box appears where you can specify the code, size, and spacing for the applet.

- Choose Insert, Break to create line breaks by using the <BR> tag. Pressing the Return (Enter) key while in the editing area of the program inserts a <P> tag in the HTML code.

- Choose Format, Numbered Style to designate the kind of list item to be used. Options include Arabic numerals, Roman numerals, and letters.

- The Style menu contains other HTML style tags, such as Superscript, Subscript, and Strikethrough. Under the Other option in the Style menu you can find Strong, Emphasis, Citation, Inserted, Deleted, Sample, Keyboard, Variable, and Code.

Linking and Converting Graphics

Claris Home Page can link any GIF or JPEG image to your Web pages, and can even convert PICT files on the Macintosh and BMP files on a Windows system. To convert and link a graphic to your Web page, follow the steps in Exercise 13.1.

Exercise 13.1

1. Place the cursor where you want the image to appear on the page.

2. Choose Insert, Image. Or click on the Insert Image icon in the toolbar or floating tool palette.

3. The Open dialog box appears. Locate the appropriate GIF, JPEG, BMP, or PICT file on your hard drive. Note: if the file is already a GIF or JPEG, you should first move the file to the image folder where you will want it for the Web site. This ensures the correct relative location. It is possible to link an image from anywhere on your hard drive, but you want the relative location to remain the same when you send the Web site to a server. If the graphic is a BMP or PICT file, Home Page will make a new image as it converts it and places it in the image folder you designated in Image Preferences.

4. After you locate the image, select Open. The image automatically appears on your Web page.

> **Note**
>
> The image conversion features of Claris Home Page provide a useful way to convert simple PICT or BMP files to GIFs; however, if your original images are not PICTs or BMP files, or if you want to convert them into the JPEG format, you will have to convert them in a program such as Photoshop or DeBabelizer. You can also get better results and smaller file sizes by using the tips in Chapter 11 rather than using the automatic conversion system in Claris Home Page.

WYSIWYG Editing in Home Page

Over all, creating or editing a Web page in Claris Home Page is remarkably intuitive and straightforward. Basic formatting options work much as they do in a word processing program—highlight the text, select the Toolbar icon (Bold, for example) and the formatting is applied. To deselect an option, highlight the formatted text and select the icon again. The formatting now disappears.

Setting links and inserting images is also straightforward, and items placed in the document can be moved by using drag-and-drop or copy-and-paste features. If you want to move images and text into a table, for example, simply drag the element into the table cell, and Home Page does the rest.

Case Study: Tailoring a Converted Document

The case study for this chapter is the same document converted in Chapter 6, "QuarkXPress Conversion." In this chapter, you will learn how to tailor the pages converted with BeyondPress to have better control over the final design and add a table of contents to the main page with links to the other pages. Some of the alterations made in this section could be done with BeyondPress, but will be faster and easier with Claris Home Page. BeyondPress was a great first step for this case study document. It successfully moved all the text out of XPress and into HTML pages, inserted the Paragraph tags needed after every paragraph, took care of basic formatting conversion for headlines, converted the images into GIFs and JPEGs, and converted the table of financial data into an HTML table. BeyondPress also made it easy to turn that one six-page document into six distinct HTML pages. Now you will learn how to go through each page, tailoring the design and adding links as appropriate by using Home Page.

Because most of the images in the original file were small, the GIF conversion option in BeyondPress was an easy solution for conversion. If the images were larger, the tips in Chapter 11 would produce better images and smaller file sizes. The one image in this document that could not be handled well by BeyondPress was the cover image, the full-page colored globe that served as a background for the cover of the annual report. This image was converted separately and turned into a small graphic to be used as a background tile. In the next sections, each page converted with BeyondPress will be opened in Claris Home Page for final revisions, and more text and links will be added to complete the files and create an interlinked section that can be built into the larger Web site for NetFRAME.

Fixing Backgrounds: The Cover Page Example

Figure 13.7 shows Page 1 after BeyondPress conversion. This page requires the greatest amount of tailoring. Because the image on this page is too large to convert with Beyond Press, it has been converted and reduced by using the techniques in Chapter 11. The background color on the page was set to yellow, because that was the background color in much of the original document. It was most efficient to convert all the pages globally with that background, even though this one now has a background image instead. The only text converted for this page was the vision statement and list of key points about the company. The stars that separate these points don't work as nicely on the Web, so they also need to be reformatted. In addition, in planning how to organize this document in Chapter 6, it was determined that there should be a table of contents with links from this main page to all the other pages in the document.

Figure 13.7

The Front Page after conversion with BeyondPress.

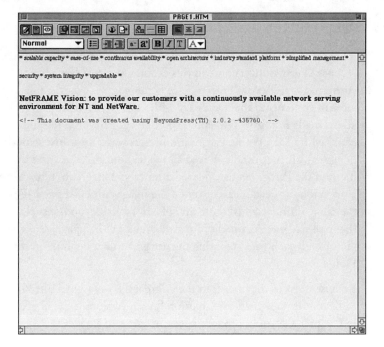

Tailoring Page 1 in Home Page

As you can see in figure 13.8, the document options dialog box, available under the Edit menu, is used to change the link and text colors and to set the reduced globe as a background image. Note that Home Page can't display the background image in the Edit or Preview options. In figure 13.9, you can see how the page looks with the background image in Netscape Navigator. An interesting thing happened here, calling attention to one of the problems caused on the Web because not all browsers support all HTML options. When the text color was set to white but the background image couldn't be displayed, the text disappeared—this can happen in browsers that support text and background colors but not background images. As a workaround, set a background color in addition to the background image. Then browsers that support background images will display the image, and browsers that only support background colors will have a dark background so users can read the white text.

Other changes to this page include using Home Page's cut-and-paste features to rearrange the text and adding a list of headlines to link to the rest of the pages. Setting the links is easy. Highlight the text, select the Link option in the toolbar, and then, in the dialog box, locate the page you want to link to.

Figure 13.8

*Using the document
options to set
background and
link colors.*

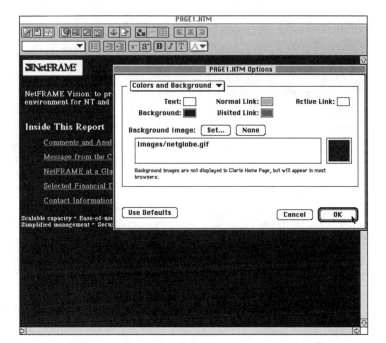

Figure 13.9

The main page displayed in Netscape Navigator, where the background image is visible.

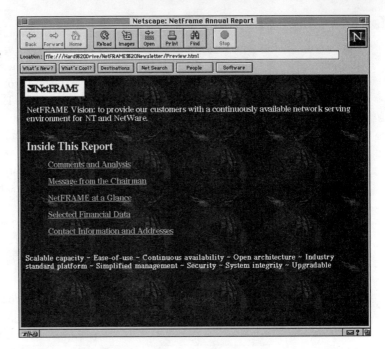

Fixing Spacing: Page 2 of the Example

Figure 13.10 shows Page 2 of the converted XPress document. In this case, the background will be made white because this was the display in the original document. The primary problems with this page involve spacing. Because the quotation marks were set off in separate text boxes in the original XPress file, paragraph marks have been created between the quotation marks and the text that should be set between them. Other spacing problems are caused by hard returns placed in the text to control the spacing in the original document, creating a narrow column in the lower part of the window.

Tailoring Page 2 in Home Page

The easiest way to fix the quotation marks is to highlight and copy one set of quotation marks and the line space that follows. Then, using the search-and-replace option, paste the quotation marks with line break into the *find* box and type a set of quotation marks without a line break in the *replace* box. Choose Replace All. The quotation marks are now flush with the quote. Repeat this step for the close quotation marks. (This problem could have been solved in XPress before conversion by using search-and-replace to do the same task.) Next, use the basic editing features of Home Page to remove any other unnecessary spaces that break up paragraphs. Finally, use Document Options to change the background to white.

Figure 13.10

*Page 2 after
conversion with
BeyondPress.*

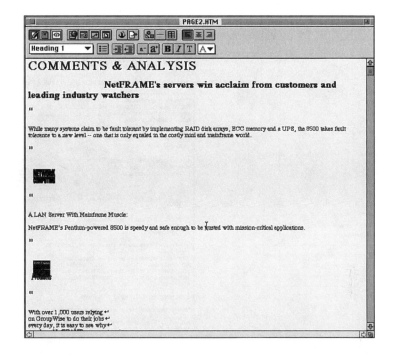

Note

When using a table for better alignment control, you will usually want to set the border size to 0 so the edges of the table are not visible. Without borders to guide you visually, however, it is difficult to cut-and-paste text and graphics into the table cells. Leave the border set at 1 until you are finished arranging the elements in the table, then return to the Table dialog box and set the border to 0 when you are finished.

To create a more narrow column of text on the page, create a table by using the Table option in the toolbar. In the dialog box that opens, set the table to one column and one row and the width to 50 percent. Then copy and paste all the text and icons into the table cell you have created. You can also use the drag-and-drop feature to highlight all the text and graphics and drag them into the table cell. Finally, open the Table dialog box again and set the border to 0 so the table's outline becomes invisible. Centering the entire table on the page creates a narrow column with white space on each side. In figure 13.11, you can see the Table dialog box and the settings required to create this column.

Figure 13.11

Using a table to create a narrow column of text.

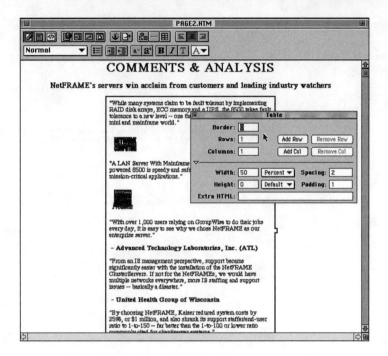

Fixing Line Breaks and Alignment: Page 3 of the Example

As you can see in figure 13.12, Page 3 also has problems with spacing and alignment. This page is quick to fix by using the editing options in Home Page the way you would in a word processor to delete the unwanted line breaks. Finally, center the headline and subhead, and this page is ready to go.

Tailoring Page 3 in Home Page

Again, the fastest way fix the spacing problems is to use search-and-replace, as the paragraph breaks you want to keep are all created with the <P> tag and the unwanted line breaks are created with the <BR> tag. This trick does not work in the WYSIWYG editing environment because Home Page can't recognize a copied line break, but it is easily accomplished in the program's built-in text editor by searching for the <BR> tags and replacing them with nothing in the Replace box. At the end of each paragraph is a star character because BeyondPress can't convert the little boxes used to end each paragraph in the original document. In this case, the search-and-replace option can be used in either the WYSIWYG mode or the text editor to replace the stars with periods. Finally, center the headline and subhead by using the alignment option in the toolbar, and set the background color to white in the document options dialog box.

Notice in figure 13.13 that the page title is also changed in the document options dialog box. This should be done with each page as you edit it, as the title is based on the file name.

Figure 13.12

Page 3 after conversion with BeyondPress.

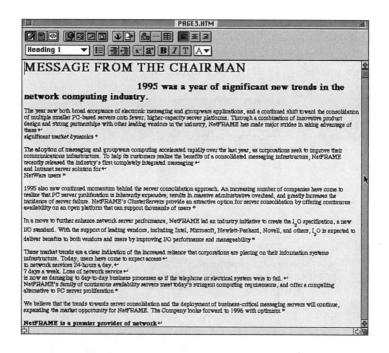

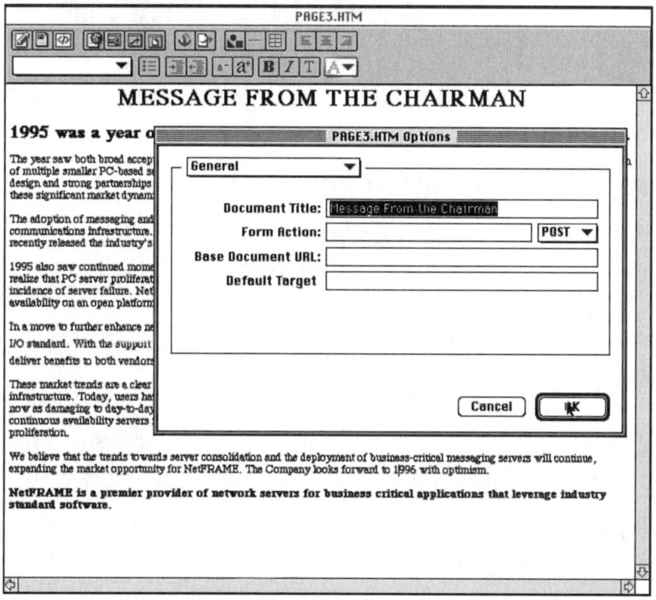

Figure 13.13

Using the document options dialog box to change the title of Page 3.

Fixing Graphic Alignment: Page 4 of the Example

In figure 13.14, you see that although BeyondPress did a good job of converting the graphics on this page into GIFs, the alignment could not be maintained, because the original file used text boxes spread across the page to create a complex design. Here again, line spacing must be corrected. To approximate the original design in XPress, a large table can be created with nested tables in each cell to control the alignment of the graphics and text that accompany them.

Figure 13.14

Page 4 after conversion with BeyondPress.

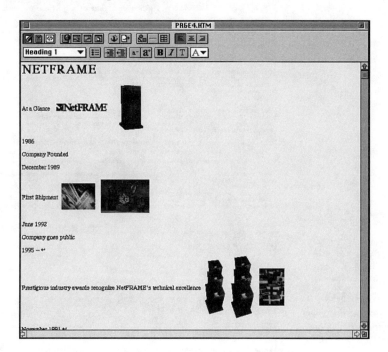

Tailoring Page 4 in Home Page

This is by far the most complex page to convert in terms of design. As you begin a conversion, be sure you have a printed copy of the original XPress page to refer to. For our example, figure 13.15 shows most of the page to remind you of the original layout. One of the problems with this design is its original creation as a two-page spread across the middle of the document. Such a design doesn't work well on the Web, where you can't predict monitor size and don't want to force people to scroll diagonally. (Remember that all documents used as case studies in this book are included on the CD-ROM. You can use these files to follow the exercises.)

This page is a time line of the history of NetFRAME and is divided into sections, each having a few lines of text and a small graphic. To best align the various text and graphic elements on this page, create a table with two columns and seven rows. Then, inside each cell in the first four rows of the main table, create a second table with two columns and one row. (If this seems confusing, hang in there—there's a method to this madness.)

Figure 13.15

Page 4 as it was designed in the original XPress document.

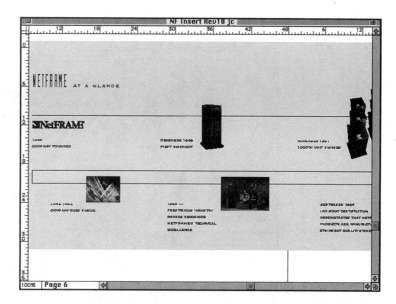

Nested tables such as these are difficult to create if you are writing the HTML code manually, but the Table Editor in Home Page makes it a relatively simple task. The nested tables—the smaller tables within the table cells of the primary table—will be used to align each section of text with the graphic that accompanies it; then you can drag-and-drop the various elements into the table cells. Select an image, for example, and drag it into one of the cells in one of the tables within the larger table. Then highlight the accompanying text and drag it into the second table cell in the same nested table. You can control the alignment by highlighting the text and using the Align Text icons in the toolbar. In figure 13.16, you can see how this will turn out. Keep all table borders turned on until you finish, and then turn off the borders on the nested tables so only the main table is visible. In figure 13.16, the nested table in the top right cell of the main table is highlighted and the dialog box is open, showing that it is set with one row, two columns, and no border. All the other nested tables are the same. Keep the border set to 1 on the main table so the division among sections is clear.

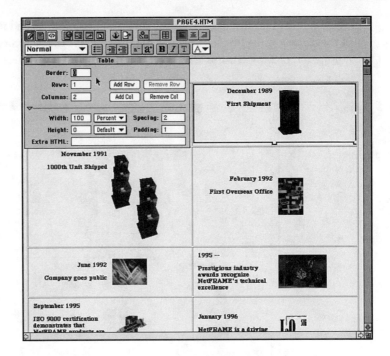

Fixing Tables: Page 5 of the Example

After the complex nested tables created for Page 4, this financial table should seem easy. BeyondPress did a good job of converting the original table, as you can see in figure 13.17. The only problem BeyondPress had was with two headings on the left side of the table that wrapped to a second line in the original document. BeyondPress created a separate row for each of these lines, easy to fix in a graphic editor such as Home Page.

Tailoring Page 5 in Home Page

Home Page makes the table on Page 5 easy to fix, as follows:

1. First, highlight the text that takes up a row by itself; in this case, *Notes payable and.* This text should be in the next row down.

2. Use the drag-and-drop feature to place the highlighted text where it belongs, taking care to place the cursor at the beginning of the text already in that cell. This ensures proper placement of the text at the beginning of the line.

3. Now there is a completely empty row where the relocated text was. To get rid of the empty row, open the Table dialog box by double-clicking anywhere in the table.

4. With the Table dialog box open, place the cursor in any cell in the row you want to delete. Figure 13.18 shows the dialog box with the cursor pointing to the Remove Row option, a handy feature for fixing this problem.

5. With the cursor in any cell in the empty row, choose the Remove Row option to delete that row. Be careful to place the cursor in a cell in the correct row. If the cursor is not placed in a cell, the Remove Row option deletes the last row of the table and all the text it contains. If you make a mistake, use the Undo feature to put the row back.

Repeat this process for the second row that has broken text, and this page is ready for the Web.

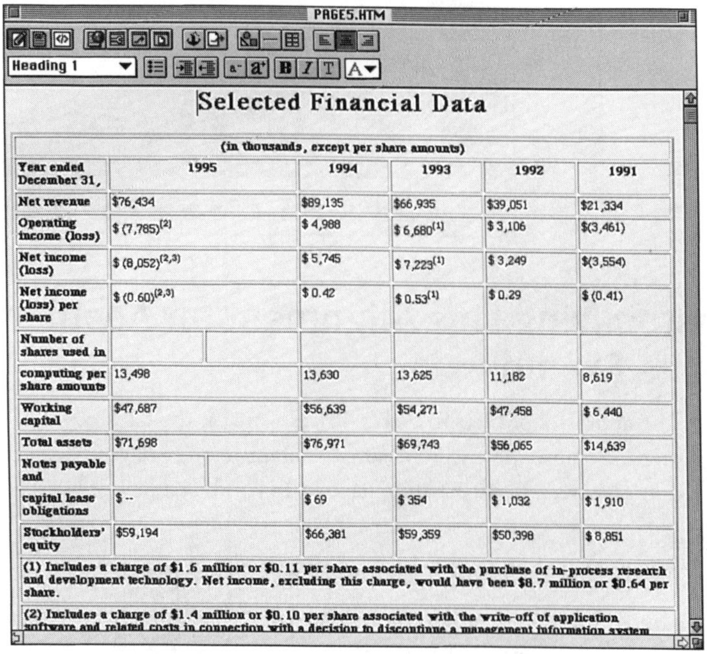

Figure 13.17

Page 5 after conversion with BeyondPress.

PAGE5.HTM

Heading 1

Selected Financial Data

(in thousands, except per share amounts)					
Year ended December 31,	1995		1994	1993	1992	1991
Net revenue	$76,434		$89,135	$66,935	$39,051	$21,334
Operating income (loss)	$ (7,785)[2]		$ 4,988	$ 6,680[1]	$ 3,106	$(3,461)
Net income (loss)	$ (8,052)[2,3]		$ 5,745	$ 7,229[1]	$ 3,249	$(3,554)
Net income (loss) per share	$ (0.60)[2,3]		$ 0.42	$ 0.53[1]	$ 0.29	$ (0.41)
Number of shares used in computing per share amounts	13,498		13,630	13,625	11,182	8,619
Working capital	$47,687		$56,639	$54,271	$47,458	$ 6,440
Total assets	$71,698		$76,971	$69,743	$56,065	$14,639
Notes payable and capital lease obligations	$ --		$ 69	$ 354	$ 1,032	$ 1,910
Stockholders' equity	$59,194		$66,381	$59,359	$50,398	$ 8,851

(1) Includes a charge of $1.6 million or $0.11 per share associated with the purchase of in-process research and development technology. Net income, excluding this charge, would have been $8.7 million or $0.64 per share.

(2) Includes a charge of $1.4 million or $0.10 per share associated with the write-off of application software and related costs in connection with a decision to discontinue a management information system

Figure 13.18

Using the Home Page Table dialog box to remove a table row.

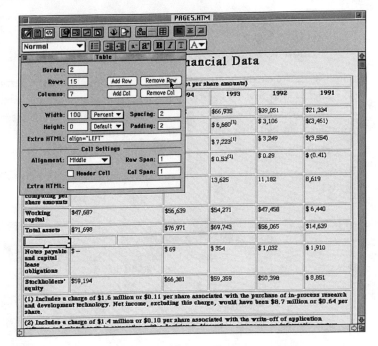

Customizing Line Alignment for Aesthetics: Page 6 of the Example

The addresses of NetFRAME's offices were on the back cover of the original document. Because there is no clear equivalent to a "back cover" on the Web, this information was created as a separate page in BeyondPress.

Tailoring Page 6 in Home Page

Minor changes are required on this page to make the between-lines spacing consistent. Centering the entire contents of the page makes the design a little more interesting. Do this by selecting all the text and clicking on the Center Text icon in the toolbar. Add horizontal rules between addresses to differentiate them and to break up the page. For this step, place the cursor between two address sections and click on the Horizontal Rule icon in the toolbar. Interest can be added to the HR lines by selecting one line and double-clicking on it to open the Horizontal Rule dialog box (or open the box by selecting the HR line and clicking on the Object Editor in the toolbar). Figure 13.19 shows the Horizontal Rule dialog box, where the size and width of the HR line can be altered—in this case to a height of 3, with a width of 70 percent.

Figure 13.19

Setting attributes for horizontal rules in Home Page.

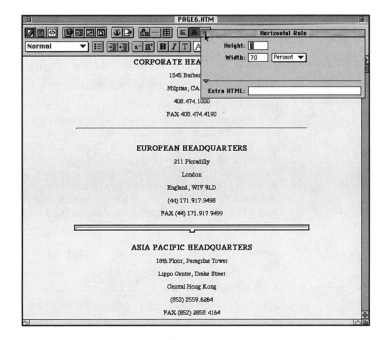

Adding Navigational Options

Now that the pages have all been cleaned up after conversion, it's time to review them and consider how a user will navigate through this section of the Web site. All the pages are linked to the main page, so a user could select any other page and then use the browser's Back button to return to the main page and move from there to another page. It's never a good idea, however, to make your users backtrack in the world of hyperlinks.

Two simple elements can be added to these pages to make them easier to navigate. The first is to add Next Page and Previous Page options, but that still leaves users in the print paradigm where they must move through a document in a linear fashion. What if someone wants to skip the Message from the Chairman? With only Next and Previous options, they must load that page to move on, or backtrack all the way to the main page to make a different selection.

A better model for the Web is the creation of a list of options featuring every page in the section. Then that list, often called a navigation bar, is linked to each page. The simplest way to do this is to open the main page, which already has links to all the pages, and copy that list with its links. Because all these pages are in the same directory, the links will be the same on every page and you can simply paste that list on page 2. Reformat the list as you see it done in figure 13.20 at the bottom of Page 2.

Note that you should delete the link for the page you are placing the navigation bar on so you don't confuse users. If you leave this link and a user selects it, the same page will reload, a rather frustrating experience.

> **Tip**
>
> Here's a tip: paste the text and links from Page 1 at the bottom of Page 2. Change the formatting and add a horizontal rule to make it clear that this is a separate section on the page. Next copy all the text, including the horizontal rule; then use the Link Editor (as seen in fig. 13.20) to remove the link for the page you're on. Save this page and move to Page 3. Paste all the copied text, and you still have all your functional links. This is nice, because all you have to do now is remove the link for Page 3, move on to the next page, paste it all again, and repeat this for each page. To test your links, switch to the Preview option in Home Page or to the Browser Preview option where you can view the pages in any browser.

Figure 13.20

A navigation bar placed at the bottom of Page 2.

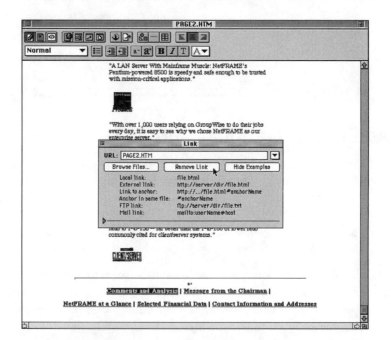

Working in the Text Editor

The text editor built into Home Page is a handy way to work in the HTML code directly, but it lacks any features designed for HTML. HTML text editors such as BBEdit and Hot Dog, described later in this chapter, include a host of HTML tags you can automatically place around selected text to make writing HTML faster and easier. The text editor in Home Page is a very limited program, similar to SimpleText on the Mac or NotePad in Windows. Nonetheless, it is a nice feature you can use for editing code directly without completely leaving the WYSIWYG program.

Warning

If you do choose to work on the code directly, be careful—it is easy to make mistakes in HTML. If you are not familiar with what you're doing, you may destroy some of the formatting and find it difficult to put back together. If you are concerned about this possibility, make a copy of your Web page as a backup before you move to the text editor and change any of the HTML code.

No Program is Perfect

Claris Home Page was selected for this book because it's one of the best WYSIWYG editors on the market today for the uses described in this chapter. As a cross-platform product capable of supporting high-end HTML features, it is an excellent choice for tailoring your converted files; however, all the programs in this new and quickly changing world of the Web have limitations, and even a few bugs, and Home Page is no exception.

Troubleshooting Lost or Misplaced Formatting

One problem you are likely to find is that Home Page (like other WYSIWYG editors) sometimes gets confused when you try to move formatted text from one section of a page to a section using different HTML formatting features. Because you can't see the HTML code in the WYSIWYG editing environment, you may inadvertently place text within other formatting tags and get unexpected results. If, for example, you try to move a headline formatted with <H1> tags and position it above an ordered or unordered list, you may instead paste it into place inside the opening List tag. If you do this in Home Page, the <H1> tag will lose its formatting and be aligned as indented text within the list. If this happens to you, move the text again, ensuring it is above the list, and then reformat it with the <H1> tags. Fortunately, this is a quick and easy fix in Home Page.

Problems with HTML Tables

One of the most sophisticated design features in Claris Home Page is the capability to create complex HTML tables, drag and drop text and images into table cells, and merge cells to create unique designs. There are some bugs still to be fixed, however. If you move formatted text into a table cell, for example, you may have to reapply formatting because Home Page removes the header tags. Home Page also has a bad habit of forcing table columns to be the same width. In a browser, you'll see that table columns generally shift to accommodate the widest contents often creating one wide column and other more narrow columns. Home Page, however, tries to spread them uniformly across the page. To compensate for this, view your tables in a browser such as Netscape as you are creating them so you get a true representation of how they will appear on the Web. Home Page may also cut off images that are too large to fit in a table with the window width displayed. This is also misleading. The image is not really cropped, but part of it may not be visible. Again, viewing the page in a browser will give you a more accurate display of your work.

You may also find problems caused by the alignment of images and other elements within a table. If you left-align an image, for example, and then follow it with text you want beneath the image, you may find that it appears below the image in Home Page, but in a browser, the text wraps up next to the image. This can then throw off the alignment of other elements on the page, causing unexpected results. This seems to happen most if you are using nested tables. If you find that the display of your pages is different in the browser than you had intended in Home Page, change the alignment attributes to change the display. For example, if you remove the align left attribute in the image, your text will properly wrap below it again. You may also find that specifying a fixed pixel width for the table instead of a percentage will help you control the display of your table.

White Space and Line Breaks

Another problem with this program, also common in other graphical HTML editors, is that it enables you to place multiple returns in your document, creating multiple <P> tags in the HTML code when you do. This is misleading, as you will see if you view your pages in a browser such as Netscape Navigator. Because the Internet was intentionally designed to use space as efficiently as possible, most browsers do not support multiple <P> or <BR> tags. Thus, adding a series of returns in the WYSIWYG editing environment in Home Page gives the appearance of producing a bunch of white space in your page, but when you preview the page in Navigator, you will find most of the space gone, because Navigator only displays one <P> or <BR> tag at a time. You can use the two tags in combination to get the equivalent of a line break and two lines of white space, but that's all you will ever get. There are other ways to control spacing, however, such as tables and horizontal rules.

Use the Built-in Text Editor

One of the reasons Home Page was selected for this book is that it includes a built-in text editor. If you are having trouble moving items around in the WYSIWYG environment, use the built-in text editor to view the code directly and get a better idea of what's happening in the background. Chapter 14 will help you decipher the code if you are new to HTML or need to look up an unfamiliar tag.

If you have trouble arranging elements or getting the format you want in the WYSIWYG section of the program, you may find it faster and easier to make your changes in the raw code. Another great feature of this program is the automatic application of changes made in the code as soon as you return to the WYSIWYG editing area.

Safeguarding Applied Formatting Options

A couple of little bugs in this program may cause you to lose applied formatting options if you switch between the WYSIWYG and text-editing environments without saving your file first. Most options are saved automatically, but if you create list items, for example, and then switch over to the text-editing area, you may find that the list disappears. This seems to be a bug in the program that will undoubtedly be fixed soon, but to play it safe, save your changes before you change editing environments.

> **Note**
>
> **Creating Space: The Clear GIF Trick**
>
> Another great trick for spacing control is to create a clear, one-pixel GIF, and then set the height and width to force space into a document. At just one pixel in size, the clear, or transparent, GIF is so tiny it takes almost no time to download. Left at its actual size it would make little difference in your layout, but you can set the height and width to anything you want, and because the transparent GIF is invisible, it forces empty space into your page.

Building the New Pages into a Larger Web Site

This conversion example represents only a small section of the NetFRAME Web site, which has grown to hundreds of pages. Thus, the final step in our case study involves building this section into the larger Web site. If you are working with a team of developers, this task may be done by a Project Coordinator and you may simply have to submit these HTML pages and graphics to someone else to incorporate into the larger Web site. On a project such as this, you may also have the site broken into sections so all developers add new elements to their sections directly. Planning and project coordination are key elements of building big Web sites such as the NetFRAME site. The information in Chapter 12 will help you organize this type of process.

Putting a Web Site Online

If this conversion represented an entire Web site, it would be ready to be put online now. You need to talk to your system administrator to learn the necessary steps for transferring pages and graphics from your computer to a Web server. Most commercial service providers offer information to developers about how to use their systems to access them by using File Transfer Protocol programs such as Fetch for the Macintosh or WS_FTP for Windows. Some HTML Editors, such as BBEdit (which you will learn about in the next section of this chapter) include built-in FTP capabilities.

BBEdit

If you work on a Macintosh, you're fortunate to have available one of the most powerful tools for customizing HTML conversions: a text-editing program called BBEdit. BBEdit is both simple and extremely powerful. It's also fast, even when dealing with large numbers of documents. Because it is designed for text-only documents (such as HTML files), BBEdit lacks the standard formatting capabilities of full-featured word processing programs. For example, it will not enable you to create bold, italic, or underlined text the way a word processor does, but it will color code your HTML tags. Using the HTML tools palette, you can easily insert HTML formatting options such as <B> tags, for bold, to create bold text in the browser display.

Sophisticated search-and-replace functions are the most powerful features this program offers for working on Web sites or batches of converted HTML files. BBEdit can do multiple-file searches to change text in every document in a directory and even within subdirectories all at once. For example, you might want to change an item in a navigational bar that appears at the bottom of every page on your 500-page Web site. In minutes, BBEdit can do automatically what would take you hours to do manually.

BBEdit was designed to work with other programs and extensions. The 4.0 CD-ROM version ships with a variety of additional features, such as Claris XTND, which adds the capability to read many word processing formats, and Internet Config, which keeps track of Internet client applications on your hard drive to ensure that your e-mail address and server information is shared by all the programs that use it.

There are other HTML text editors on the market, such as World Wide Web Weaver, a great HTML editor that you will find on the CD-ROM that accompanies this book. BBEdit was selected for coverage in this chapter because of the features in the following list:

- Performs fast and sophisticated search-and-replaces across single documents or entire sets of documents.

- Stores commonly used text in a glossary for easy access and insertion on other pages.

- Creates user-defined HTML tags and styles, making it highly extendible.

- Creates user-defined keyboard equivalents for most functions, so you can create your own shortcuts.

- Displays HTML tags in a different color from regular text to make editing easier.

- Reads and saves documents directly from or to an FTP server, so you don't need a separate FTP program.

- Converts special characters to their ASCII equivalents automatically or on demand.

- Works with AppleScript and other scripting languages so you can create your own macros and extensions.

- Maintains a palette listing all currently open documents, with the capability to save or close several files at one time.

- Runs HTML-aware spell-checking.

- Inserts open and close HTML tags around highlighted text.

- Places graphic links in documents and automatically generates size attributes.

- Drag-and-drops graphics and files from the Finder into a BBEdit document.

- Automatically turns URLs into a hot links.

- Converts tab- or comma-separated text into tables.

- Quickly creates form tags.

- Checks HTML syntax and alerts you to errors in your code.

- Creates custom HTML document templates.

When to Use BBEdit

Before jumping into the technical details, it's helpful to understand how and when to put BBEdit to work. If your work consists mainly of creating a few individual HTML pages, or if the pages you create are all very different from one another, then BBEdit's advanced capabilities may be more than you need. But you will still find that other BBEdit features, such as its HTML tools palette, FTP connection, and color-coding of HTML tags, make it a solid stand-alone HTML editor.

On the other hand, if you routinely deal with significant numbers of HTML files, or if your HTML files use the same styles and elements repeatedly, you will find BBEdit's advanced features invaluable. By automating repetitive tasks, BBEdit can save time, reduce tedium, and decrease errors.

After you have become familiar with the program, it's helpful to consider each task you regularly perform on your HTML files. Such tasks might include the following:

- Hot-linking URLs and e-mail addresses.
- Cleaning up HTML code created by an export program.
- Changing the path names of files.
- Adding a standard element, such as a navigation bar, to the end of every file.

Some of these functions can be performed by a conversion program such as Beyond-Press, but you may find that BBEdit enables you to automate these tasks more efficiently than other programs. You will also find that BBEdit runs faster than programs such as Microsoft Word and QuarkXPress.

BBEdit in the Real World

Here's an example of how BBEdit can be used to automate tasks more effectively than they can be done with other programs. Kim Ladin, who contributed much of the description and tips on how to use the programs included in this chapter, works on a Web site that requires converting about 40 stories a week from QuarkXPress to the Web. Many stories contain URLs that need to be turned into hyperlinks. When she first began doing these conversions, Kim used the linking function in BeyondPress, which worked fine. Eventually, she realized that she could partially automate the task in BBEdit and save a good deal of time. Now she simply exports the stories with BeyondPress, ignoring the Internet URLs, and then uses BBEdit to perform a global search across all the text files, searching for the string *http:*. She still manually selects each URL and creates a hypertext link, but with HTML Tools and keyboard short-cuts, the whole process is much faster than it was in BeyondPress.

BBEdit as a Clean-Up Tool

Often documents that have been converted from another application or platform contain characters that can't be read on the World Wide Web. BBEdit can take care of many of these. The Convert to ASCII extension will convert 8-bit characters such as bullets, typographers' (smart) quotes, and em dashes to their ASCII equivalents. The Zap Gremlins command in the Text menu will strip out control characters and filter line feeds. The utilities in HTML Tools also provide a "Translate" function, which not only zaps gremlins and converts to ASCII, but translates ISO-Latin characters into HTML entities also known as *special characters*.

> **Note**
> If you're not satisfied with the HTML code generated by Adobe PageMill, try the HTML Tools utility called PageMill Cleaner.

Revealing Shortcuts and Special Features

Many dialog box options have command-key equivalents. Holding down the command key for a moment or two while the dialog box is open will display these equivalents. Using the Shift and Option keys when you look at pull-down menus will reveal more advanced options. For example, when you pull down the File menu, you will find common options such as Open and Save. If you hold down Shift+Option as you open the menu, you will see these options become Open Several and Save All, enabling you to work with several files at once.

HTML Tools

The set of extensions called HTML Tools that ships with the full version of BBEdit turns the text editor into a very functional HTML editor. A variety of HTML tags are included, providing most of the HTML 2.0 and 3.2 tags. These options can be accessed through the Extensions menu, through the HTML tools palette shown in figure 13.21, or through keyboard equivalents. Note that the palette includes the most commonly used tags; additional tags can be found in the Extensions menu. Most of the HTML Tools enable you to insert HTML tags by highlighting the appropriate text and clicking on a button in the Tools palette. Preferences for these tools are set in the HTML area of BBEdit's Preferences dialog box.

HTML Tools will format text with tags for headings, character and logical formatting, font size and color specifications, lists, paragraphs, line breaks, and horizontal rules.

Figure 13.21

. *BBEdit's HTML Tools.*

Setting Attributes with the HTML Tools Palette

Most tools are associated with a dialog box with attributes such as Alignment, Heading Level, Width, and others. To open the dialog box to set attributes, hold down the option key as you select the HTML tag from the Tools palette. A great built-in shortcut enables you to use the Command key as you select the option, thus inserting the tag with the last set of attributes specified. This saves time by bypassing the dialog box, and is handy for placing similar elements on a page without the need to specify the attributes for each tag.

Advanced Markup with HTML Tools

HTML Tools will also speed creation of more complex HTML markup such as images, anchors, tables, and forms. The following sections provide more information on how to take advantage of HTML Tools to create each of these complex elements.

Linking to Local Image Files

The Image tool is particularly helpful because it provides a pop-up window when selected. In this window, you can navigate around your hard drive to locate an image, and BBEdit automatically inserts the file name and sets the link to create the correct path. This saves you the trouble of trying to remember where a file is stored, whether the name uses a capital letter, and how you wrote the extension. BBEdit takes care of all this automatically. The program also determines the pixel width and height of the graphic and inserts the attributes to specify that for you. Another dialog window lets you specify border, alignment, alternative text, and image maps. You can also use drag-and-drop to drag a graphic from the Finder onto the Image tool button. The Anchor tool works in a similar way, enabling you to specify Target and Name attributes and to drag-and-drop text files from the Finder.

Converting URLs to Hyperlinks

Turning URLs into hyperlinks is also a simple and automatic process with HTML Tools. If you need to convert URLs in a document from plain text to hypertext, select the URL and click on the Anchor button (or use Command+Ctrl+A). BBEdit automatically adds the link tags to create a hyperlink for you. It even determines the kind of address and knows when to add a prefix such as "mailto:" (for e-mail addresses).

> **Note**
>
> When you are working on documents originally created for print, be careful to assess the spacing in addresses. Print production editors often need to break long URLs over several lines. If you're creating hypertext links from URLs in exported text, keep an eye out for incorrect spaces and line breaks within the URL, which will cause the link to fail.

Creating Tables with HTML Tools

The Table tool converts tab- or comma-separated text into an HTML table and can be used to create a new table. A dialog box provides room for attributes, such as Borders, Cell Padding, Cell Spacing, Table Width (in either percent or pixels), Captions, and Headers.

Creating Form Elements with HTML Tools

The Form tool has a less-than-elegant interface but will generate tags for most form items, including text boxes, radio buttons, check boxes, scrolling lists, submit/reset buttons, and hidden fields, as well as the Get or Post form header with an associated URL. The tool does not provide any scripts for handling the forms it creates. To learn how to use a form with a script, talk to your system administrator or service provider.

Document-Level Features

HTML Tools also enable you to set document level attributes, such as background and link colors and background images. This feature conveniently includes a sample of the color combination so you can preview how your selections will look together. The available color swatches can be modified by double-clicking. Both the Apple HSL color wheel and RGB sliders are provided (but it would be nice to have hexadecimal colors available as well).

Setting Links with Anchors

The Index Document extension, located in the Extensions menu under HTML Misc, lists all the headings in a document. If you insert Name anchors in the headings, you can generate a list with links.

Checking HTML Syntax

Once your HTML documents are created and edited, HTML Tools can check your syntax. Click on the Check HTML button and check your local links by using Check Links (note that this function will not check external links). You can then preview the document in any browser specified in Preferences by selecting the Preview button on the Tools palette.

Generating HTML Headers and Footers

The New Document tool automatically generates HTML headers and footers, leaving space for various header attributes such as Title and Meta tags. This provides an easy way to set up a new HTML document. Custom document templates can be applied through this tool's dialog box by selecting the template file from the Template pop-up menu. It is also possible to reformat an existing document by using a template. First, deselect the Create New Window option in the New Document dialog box of HTML Tools. The Create button changes to Insert, enabling BBEdit to place HTML headers and footers at the beginning and end of the file.

Creating Templates

You can create custom templates and save them in BBEdit's HTML Templates folder with the extension .tmpl in the file name. Your new file will then be available in the Templates pop-up menu. A simple template might look like the following:

```
<HTML>
<HEAD>
<TITLE>#TITLE#</TITLE>
</HEAD>
<BODY>
#BODYTEXT#
</BODY>
</HTML>
```

HTML Tools Placeholders for Template Documents

HTML Tools Placeholders enable you to create templates with formatted areas where you can easily insert text that will automatically be formatted. Some of the HTML Tools placeholders are listed in the following table.

HTML Tools Placeholders

Placeholder	Function of Placeholder
#TITLE#	Document title (will appear in browser's menu bar).
#LINK#	Items drawn from the link to other documents in the New Document dialog box.
#BASE#	The base href.
#META#	Any Meta tags.
#BODYTEXT#	Indicates where existing text will be placed if a template is applied to a preexisting document.

A large number of placeholders related to the Meta tag are also available. To view this list, choose HTML Misc, under Meta tags in the Extensions menu.

File and Window Functions

BBEdit provides several handy additions to standard Macintosh file management. As you can see in figure 13.22, the Window List in the Windows menu opens a palette that lists all open files by name. A black diamond next to a file's name indicates that the file has been modified since the last save. Double-click on a file name to bring that file to the front of the list of documents listed in the window. Shift-click or command-click on a series of file names as you make your selection from the file menu to save, close, or print multiple files at once.

Figure 13.22

*The BBEdit
Window List.*

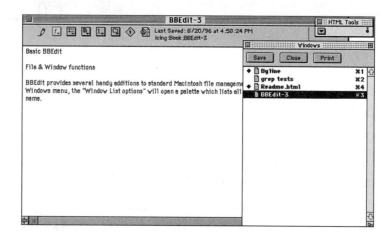

FTP Capabilities

The File menu commands Open from FTP Server and Save to FTP Server enable you to work on a remote file without having to download and upload it in a separate program. In the Open from FTP Server dialog box, the pop-up folder includes a Directory option, in which you can type the exact path name.

Note that if a file has been opened from a remote server, the standard Save command will automatically save it back to the remote server using FTP, rather than saving it locally. It's always safer to copy a file down to your hard drive and replace it on the server only after you have had a chance to test it. If you are making a quick and simple change, this is a very easy and efficient way to do so, but be careful not to overwrite the remote file on the server by mistake. If you are working on a file locally, you can use the Save to FTP Server option to automatically post the page to a remote server as you save it.

Cross-Platform Options

When saving files, BBEdit provides the option to save with Mac, Unix, or DOS line breaks, depending on the ultimate destination of the file. This choice is available both in the Save As dialog box and in the File pop-up menu on the status bar. You can also choose which file extensions to use.

In the Edit menu, BBEdit provides a number of ways to handle text wrapping and line breaks. There are three basic options:

- **No wrap.** Without wrapping, each paragraph is displayed on a single line. Long lines will disappear off the right of your screen, forcing you to scroll horizontally to see the entire line of text. Selecting no wrapping can be helpful for quickly checking the basic structure of an HTML document.

- **Soft wrap.** Soft wrapping is the form of display typical to most word processors. The program will temporarily break lines so all the text will be visible on one screen, but these line breaks are not saved with the file. Soft wrapping makes a document much easier to read.

- **Hard wrap.** Hard wrapping actually inserts a line feed character after a specified number of characters per line and saves these line breaks with the file. Saving HTML documents with hard wrapping (72 characters is a good line length) may be the best option if the documents will be read as plain ASCII text (in an e-mail program, for example). Files that are not hard wrapped may be difficult to read on other systems (in particular, if a file's line length is too long). If, after choosing the Hard Wrap command in the Text menu, you want to remove the hard wrap line feeds, simply choose Remove Line Breaks from the Text menu. Conversely, if the document has been soft wrapped, choosing Insert Line Breaks will create a hard wrap for each line.

Auto Indent

Available through the Windows Options dialog box under the Edit menu, Auto Indents adds indent spacing to each new line, placing it in the same column as the previous line. This option is useful for making HTML code more readable, particularly for tables and lists. If you are working with HTML tables, for example, the code will be easier to understand and edit if you use nesting tabs. HTML ignores white space, including tabs, at the beginning of a line, so this formatting won't affect the ultimate appearance of your table in the browser display. It does, however, make it much easier for you to read the raw HTML code.

The following is an example of code created by using the Auto Indent feature:

```
<TABLE BORDER="0">
        <TR>
                <TD>value 1</TD>
                <TD>value 2</TD>
        </TR>
        <TR>
                <TD>choice A</TD>
                <TD>choice B</TD>
        </TR>
</TABLE>
```

Color-Coded Tags

Color-coded tags enable BBEdit to display HTML tags in a different color from regular text. BBEdit can use different colors for image tags, anchor tags, and standard tags. Colors can be assigned by clicking on Text Colors in the Preferences dialog box. These options are accessible both from the Edit menu and from the Windows Options pop-up menu in the status bar. Again, this is only to make it easier for you to read the HTML code and will not affect text color in the browser display.

BBEdit's Glossary

BBEdit provides a robust glossary function that enables you to save commonly used text as well as create custom HTML styles and tags. Glossary entries can be quite complex, incorporating multiple paragraphs, HTML tags, and substitution keywords, as shown previously in figure 13.22. Each glossary entry is saved as a separate BBEdit file and should be stored in the BBEdit Glossaries folder. Keyboard equivalents can be assigned to any glossary entry.

Selecting Glossary from the Windows menu opens the Glossary window, as shown in figure 13.23. Glossary entries are organized into folders. Double-clicking on a folder displays its contents in the top half of the window. At this point, you can select a particular Glossary entry and view it in the lower half of the window. The control-key equivalents are also shown when available. To return to the main Glossary folder, select the pop-up menu in the Glossary window's status bar.

This is great for frequently used elements, such as a navigation bar or credit line that may be placed on many, or even all of the pages in a Web site. This is a great way to create custom shortcuts in the program and automate tasks that are specific to your Web site.

Figure 13.23

*The BBEdit Glossary
window.*

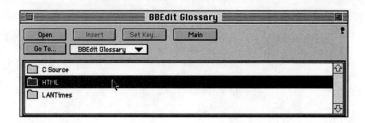

Creating Glossary Entries

To create a new glossary entry, simply create a new BBEdit document and type the appropriate text. Then save the document in a folder within the BBEdit Glossaries folder on your hard drive. The name you give the saved document will become the item's name in the Glossary window; no special file name extension is necessary. To assign a keyboard equivalent, open the Glossary window, locate the new item, and click on the Set Key button; then input the keystroke you want to use to apply the glossary code.

HTML styles and tags can be created easily through the use of substitution keywords in glossary entries. Although there are a number of keywords available (see the table that follows), the most useful for this purpose is the keyword #select#, which points to any text selection in your main document. Here is a simple example:

Say you have a standard style for bylines on your Web page, which is "Emphasis" (<EM></EM>) followed by a horizontal rule (<HR>). Define a glossary file called "Byline" as

```
<EM>#select#</EM><HR>
```

and give it the keyboard equivalent Ctrl+B.

In your text document, highlight the name you wish to change into the Byline style; for example, "Joe/Jo Reporter." Then press Ctrl+B, and BBEdit automatically reformats the selection to:

```
<EM>Joe Reporter</EM><HR>
```

Glossary Substitution Keywords

Keyword	Replaced by
#select#	The selected text.
#clipboard#	Clipboard contents.

Keyword	Replaced by
#file#	Name of the active window (this specifies that the contents of the window being viewed will replace the keyword).
#name#	User name.
#insertion#	The place where BBEdit will leave the cursor after inserting glossary item.
#date#	Current date.
#time#	Current time.

Inserting Existing Glossary Entries

Glossary entries can be inserted into text by opening the Glossary window, selecting the appropriate entry, and clicking on the Insert button. If there is a control key assigned to the glossary entry, just type that control-key sequence and the entry will be automatically inserted. This is a good idea, because using control keys means you don't have to open the Glossary window to insert glossary items.

BBEdit Extensions

A number of extensions are available that expand BBEdit's functionality. Extensions included on the 4.0 CD-ROM version of BBEdit include the following:

- **BBEdit Scripts.** This runs AppleScripts.

- **BBEdit Glossary.** This is required for the glossary functions described in the previous section.

- **BBEdit Dictionaries.** This extension is capable of adding spell-check functions that are HTML aware.

- **Claris XTND Support.** This enables BBEdit to read word processing files supported by Claris XTND.

- **ToolServer Support.** This enables BBEdit to be used with ToolServer.

For extensions to be active, they must be placed in the BBEdit Extensions folder (within the same folder as the main BBEdit application). They can also be organized hierarchically within subfolders. Extensions can be deactivated by moving them out of the BBEdit Extensions folder.

The Extensions menu allows the assignment of keyboard equivalents. Choosing Set Keys from the Extensions menu displays a list of all functions available through the active extensions. Simply click on the desired function and press the control keys you want to use. Exercise a little care here: BBEdit will not protest if you write over a command key that is already in use, including application-level sequences such as Command+C (*cut*) and Command+S (*save*).

Advanced Functions: Search-and-Replace

BBEdit's powerful search-and-replace functions make it especially useful for those who work with large numbers of HTML files. The program enables batch processing—that is, performing global search-and-replace sequences across many files at the same time. BBEdit also provides a sophisticated search language called Grep, which allows for conditional, wild-card-based pattern matches. Finally, BBEdit will store search-and-replace strings for future use—a great time saver.

Searching in BBEdit

To use the search function, select Find in BBEdit's Search menu. This opens the large dialog box shown in figure 13.24, which presents a number of options for searching and replacing.

In the upper-left area of figure 13.24 are the basic search-and-replace fields familiar to anyone who has used a word processor or page layout program. BBEdit also provides some options for modifying the search, such as case sensitivity, backwards searches,

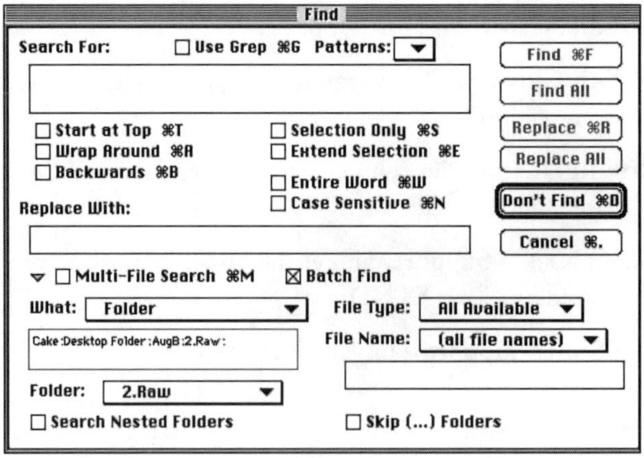

Figure 13.24

BBEdit's search-and-replace dialog box.

and so on. To perform a simple search-and-replace, enter the appropriate text, and then select the Find or Replace button on the right.

When entering search-and-replace strings, the following special characters can be used. These are great for inserting <P> tags and other coding that must be repeated throughout a document to create similar spacing in a Web page. Use the following table as a guide to these special characters.

Special Characters

Special Character	Element Character Represents
\r	Return (line break).
\n	Unix line break (line feed).
\t	Tab.
\f	Page break (form feed).

Multi-File Search-and-Replace

Here is where things get more interesting. The lower half of the Find dialog box shown in figure 13.24 presents options for searching multiple files all at once. To search through more than one file, check the box marked Multi-File Search. If you don't see anything below Multi-File Search, click on the small arrow just to the left to expand the dialog box. Then by using the What pop-up box, indicate which files you want BBEdit to search. In the Folder pop-up box, specify which folder to search. You can also choose which files to search, based on file type or file name. For example, you can search only those files in a specified folder that end in .html.

Search Options

BBEdit offers a number of options for searching, providing great control for different kinds of multiple page searches. These are all batch find options that you can specify when you do a batch search, as described in the following section.

- Search an entire folder (with the option of including sub-folders).
- Search all currently open windows.
- Search the results of a previous multi-file search.
- Search all the files in a predefined file group.

The Batch Find Option

The Batch Find option instructs BBEdit to collect all the results of the search in one window. If you do not choose Batch Find, BBEdit will search-and-replace by opening one file at a time. After each find, you will then have to instruct BBEdit to move on to the next file by choosing Find Again or Find in Next File in the Search menu. Because you can check each find before replacing, this gives you greater control, but it is much slower and you must watch the entire process.

By using Batch Find, you can let the program take care of all the searching automatically. Once you have set all the appropriate options, you can choose the Find or Replace options to search one file at a time or the Find All or Replace All options to search all selected files. When executing a Batch Replace, BBEdit provides the option to either leave the modified files open or save them to disk automatically without opening them. Again, the trade-off is control and seeing the results versus speed. The Save-to-Disk option is significantly faster, especially when searching many files at once.

The Search Results Window

If you do select Find All when in Batch mode, you will be introduced to one of BBEdit's nicest features, the Search Results window shown in figure 13.25.

Figure 13.25

BBEdit's Search Results window.

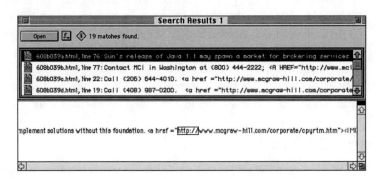

The Search Results window lists each occurrence of the search string you have specified. If you click on the listing in the top half of the window, that file will appear (with the specified text highlighted) in the lower half of the window. Files cannot be modified in this window, however. To edit the file (or execute a Replace), double-click on the listing in the top half of the window. BBEdit will then open the specified file, enabling you to make and save your changes. The Search Result window stays open until you close it. You can also choose to save or print the results as you learn about in the following section.

Before executing a batch search-and-replace on a large number of files, it's a good idea to test it on one or two files first. To do so, first set everything up for Batch mode. Instead of clicking on Replace All, click on Find. BBEdit will open the first file containing the search string. Then do a single Replace to make sure it works. When you're ready to execute the entire batch process, simply open the Find dialog box, select Multi-File and Batch Find, and click on the Replace All button. This is a powerful tool and can save you hours of work, but it can also destroy things quickly if the search is not set up properly.

Saving Search-and-Replace Patterns

The Find dialog box provides the option to save frequently used search-and-replace strings by using the Pattern pop-up menu. After you enter a search-and-replace pattern, open this menu and choose Add this Pattern. Give the pattern a name that will be easy to identify. To reuse the pattern later, select it from the list in the pop-up menu.

> **Warning**
>
> Be aware that BBEdit defaults to check the Grep search option when using a stored search-and-replace pattern. Be sure to uncheck the Grep option if it is not appropriate, or the search may fail to work properly. Grep searches will be covered in the next section.

To modify a saved search-and-replace pattern, change the entries in the Find dialog box, choose Add This Pattern, and type the existing name of the pattern. The OK button will change to Replace, and BBEdit will update the pattern. After using BBEdit's advanced find functions for a while, you will likely accumulate a long list of obsolete search patterns and folder names. To clean up these lists, go into the Preferences area in the Edit menu and choose Grep Patterns or Search Folders to delete old items.

Grep Searches

Grep is a simple language that enables you to specify complex search-and-replace strings by using wild card characters. For those who do frequent searches in BBEdit, the Grep function can be an extremely powerful tool. Be forewarned, however—Grep syntax comes from the Unix world and is not exactly user friendly. If you're familiar with Unix, you will love BBEdit's Grep capability. If you're not, you can learn Grep with just a little patience and some trial and error.

The following example gives an idea of the power of Grep. Don't try to understand the exact syntax yet; it will be discussed in more detail in a later section. For now, just consider the ways Grep searching might make your work more efficient.

For example, Grep is a great tool if you want to find every hypertext link in a document and insert the TARGET="V" attribute at the end of the link tag for frames. The links you're searching for might include the following:

```
<A HREF="http://home.netscape.com">
<A HREF="#calculator">
<A HREF="/cgi-bin/imagemap/menu.map">
```

How could you find every one of these occurrences, when the text between the quote marks varies? Grep is perfect for this. Using the wild-card characters .*, the following Grep-based search could be used:

```
Search for:    <A HREF="(.*)">
```

This Grep pattern will find all the links listed previously. Furthermore, with the wild-card character enclosed in parentheses, BBEdit is instructed to remember all the text the wild-card search finds. Then, you can instruct BBEdit to replace that wild card with itself, using the Grep pattern \1. The replace line would look like this:

```
<A HREF="\1" TARGET="V">
```

Don't worry if you don't understand this yet. The example is here to show you the power of this before you get into the details. This Grep search-and-replace will intelligently replace the lines shown previously with the following:

```
<A HREF="http://home.netscape.com" TARGET="V">
<A HREF="#calculator" TARGET="V">
<A HREF="/cgi-bin/imagemap/menu.map" TARGET="V">
```

Adding the target manually to all the links could take considerable time. The Grep search function combined with multiple-page search capabilities makes this one of the most time-saving tools found for this book.

Special Characters for Grep Searches

Now that you have seen an example of Grep, it's time to get into the technical details. The following tables provide a breakdown of some of Grep's special characters and rules.

Grep Wild-Card Characters

Character	Meaning
.	Any character.
#	Any digit 0–9.

Grep Modifiers

Character	Meaning
*	Any occurrences of a character (0 or more).
+	At least one (1 or more) occurrence.
?	A single occurrence or none (0 or 1).
^	No occurrences (0).
\	If a Grep special character needs to be read literally, precede it with the \backslash.

Creating Patterns with Grep

Character	Functionality
-	Denotes a range (for example, [0-9]).
[ ]	Patterns are enclosed in brackets. Use ^ inside brackets: [^abc]. Use *?+ outside brackets: [abc]+.
( )	Enclosing a pattern in parentheses saves it for reuse. Parentheses may go around entire patterns: ([^abc]+).

Thus, in the earlier example, combining . (any character) with * (any occurrences) finds just about anything. A few simple examples are shown in the following table.

Performing Specialized Searches

Search String	Result	Meaning
a*	Call AAA at 9!	Find any number of occurrences of the letter "a."

continues

Performing Specialized Searches (continued)

Search String	Result	Meaning
[^a]	C a l l AAA a t 9 !	Find any single character that is not an "a."
[a-z]	C a l l A A A a t 9!	Find any single letter in the alphabet.
[^a-z]	C a l l A A A a t 9!	Find any single character that is not a letter of the alphabet.
[a-z]+	Call AAA at 9!	Find any string of letters.
[^a-z]+	Call AAA at 9!	Find any string of characters that are not letters of the alphabet.

> **Note**
>
> One potentially confusing characteristic of Grep is that patterns inside brackets usually apply only to single characters. Thus, the Grep pattern [the] will find any single occurrences of either t, h, or e. It will not find the string "the", as in "theory." To make Grep identify strings, use the * or + modifiers. Thus, [abc]* will find the string "the" in "theory."

As you may already suspect, Grep enables the creation of very complex patterns using these basic building blocks. But even simple patterns can be useful. Say you want to remove all Bold and Italic tags in an HTML document. A normal search-and-replace would require a four-step process: one step each for <B>, </B>, <I>, and </I>.

Grep, however, enables a one-step search-and-replace with the following search criteria:

```
<[/?][BI]>
```

The < > tags form delimiters. Grep will find whatever is between occurrences of these two tags, as long as it matches the specified pattern. In the pattern above, the Grep search instructs BBEdit to look for a < followed by an optional / mark (remember that

? means 0 or 1 occurrences), followed by either a B or an I, followed by >. This search would thus find <B>, </B>, <I>, and </I> all in one pass. If you leave the replace line blank, all these tags will be deleted.

You should note that Grep uses a number of special characters in its search language, such as #, ?, (), and so on. Even so, you can search for these characters themselves by preceding them with \. For example, search for a period by using \. or search for parentheses by using \(or \).

Special Matching Situations

There are a few things to be aware of when you set up a search that includes special characters, such as tabs or spaces. The following points will help you with these types of searches.

Tabs or Spaces

White space in a text document may consist of a variable number of tabs or spaces. To find white space, use the Grep formula:

```
[ \t]+
```

This means match any string made up of one or more occurrences of either a space or a tab.

Delimited Strings

In many situations, you will want to find strings surrounded by delimiters. This can be a little tricky. For example, suppose you want to find text set off by two HTML tags, such as the following:

```
<H2>Here's some text</H2><EM>and here's some more</EM>
```

You could create the Grep search pattern:

```
Search for:      >(.*)<
```

With this pattern, Grep will actually find almost the entire line, because < and > are characters in the set (.*). Thus it would return:

```
<H2>Here's some text</H2><EM>and here's some more</EM>
```

Yes, it's the same. The solution is to tell Grep to exclude the delimiter characters (<>) in the matched pattern. Thus:

```
Search for:      >([^<>]*)<
```

This means find a string containing any characters except < or >, which is bounded by > and <. It would successfully find

```
Here's some text        and here's some more
```

Replacing with Wild-Card Characters

As discussed briefly in the preceding hyperlink example, Grep enables wild-card patterns to be used in the Replace function. At the simplest level, the "&" wild card will recreate the entire matched pattern. For example:

If the search string is: HTML

And the replace string is: & 3.0

The result will be: HTML 3.0

Parts of a matched pattern can also be reused during replaces in Grep. A pattern is defined by enclosing it in parentheses in the search string. The pattern can then be reused by indicating it with \n, where n is the number of the pattern. In the preceding hyperlink example, there was only one defined pattern (.*); thus, the pattern was referred to as \1.

Let's use a more complex example. Take a server-side image map file with 15 different rectangular "hot" areas. You'd like to convert the server-side map file into a client-side imagemap, which has a very different format from either the NCSA or CERN image maps. Converting the original map data by hand would be tedious and might introduce typographical errors. Grep automates the process. Here's how.

A single line in the original server-side file might read:

```
rect [tab] (0,0) [tab] (25,40) [tab] /graphics/eyeball.gif
➥[carriage return]
```

The Find pattern in Grep would be as follows:

```
Search for: rect\t\((.*)\)\t\((.*)\)\t(.*)\r
```

Figure 13.26 should help you break down the meaning of this.

There are two things to note. First, the backslash is used before each parenthesis to make Grep read the parenthesis as a literal character, rather than as a special character. Second, notice the three separate patterns defined through the use of the special-character parentheses.

Once the search string is ready, it's time to switch the server-side text into client-side format with the following string:

```
Replace with: <AREA SHAPE="rect" COORDS="\1,\2" HREF="\3">\r
```

The result is text suitable for a client-side image-map:

```
<AREA SHAPE="rect" COORDS="0,0,25,40" HREF="/graphics/
➥ eyeball.gif">[return]
```

Figure 13.26

*A Grep pattern
in BBEdit.*

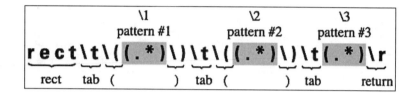

Common Grep Examples

If you're still confused by all of this, the following list of Grep examples should help
you set up searches commonly applicable to HTML documents.

Grep Examples

Search for	Replace with	Result
<[^<>]*>		Finds any HTML tag.
<(.?h[1-6])>		Finds any Heading tag (<H1>, </H3>, <H6>, and so on).
<(/?)B>(\r?)<(/?)B>	<\1B>	Finds duplicate bold tags, whether separated by a return or not (<B><B>, </B></B>, </B><B>, <B>\r<B>, and so on) and replaces them with a single <B> or </B>tag, as appropriate.
<(.?h[1-3])>(.*)<	<\1><A NAME="\2">\2</A><	Finds headings levels 1–3 and creates a NAME anchor using the text between the heading tags.

Thus:

```
<H1>The headline</H1>
```

becomes:

```
<H1><A NAME="The headline">The Headline</A></H1>
```

Search for	Replace with	Result
=([^<> "]+)	= "\1"	Finds tag attributes not surrounded by quote marks and adds quotes.

Thus:

```
<IMG SRC="graphic.gif" BORDER=0 ALT=(graphic) ALIGN=RIGHT>
```

becomes:

```
<IMG SRC="graphic.gif" BORDER="0" ALT="(graphic)" ALIGN="RIGHT">
```

Putting BBEdit to Work

This section has discussed a number of useful features in BBEdit, from the simply useful to the powerfully complex. What are some ways BBEdit is being used in the real world of Web production? Here are a few samples of how Web professionals are using BBEdit today. Some of them have been explained in detail earlier, while others should be easy to implement when you become familiar with the program.

- Use BBEdit to perform bulk clean-up on HTML files converted by other programs. Many designers use the search-and-replace functions to remove credit lines left by programs such as BBEdit or to remove superfluous or redundant code created by many HTML authoring tools.

- Make global changes to file and path names. This is a great way to help with Web site reorganization. If you move files into a new folder, for example, all the links need to be changed to reflect the new relative location. Grep searches are great for this kind of thing.

- Edit documents directly on a remote server. For quick fixes, this is a great way to make changes without having to download or upload a file. Be careful with this, however, as you are making live changes to a Web site by using this feature.

- Create HTML documents using a combination of BBEdit's HTML Tools and good old-fashioned typing. In addition to all its high-end features, BBEdit is a fine little HTML text editor.

● Sct up templates and glossary entries to maintain a consistent style across your Web site. This is a great way to handle navigational bars and other features you want on many or all of your Web pages.

● Check HTML syntax. Before you put your Web pages online, use BBEdit's HTML Checker to ensure you have not made mistakes in the HTML code.

BBEdit Wrap Up

BBEdit is a versatile text editor ideally suited for large Web sites. The HTML Tools palette can be used to create simple Web pages working directly in the HTML code. Color-coded tags make them easy to distinguish, and indenting helps you create clean, readable code. Image and file linking capabilities make this a great program for overall Web design.

More advanced features, such as multiple-page search functions and Grep search capabilities, provide powerful assistance when you need to make changes to many pages at once. You can use this program to automate many otherwise tedious and time-consuming tasks. If you work on a Macintosh, the search-and-replace functions alone make this program worth the purchase price.

Hot Dog Pro

Hot Dog Pro provides many of the features found in BBEdit, although no other program designed for HTML can handle the multiple-page or Grep-search functions that make BBEdit so popular. On the PC, however, Hot Dog Pro offers a great HTML text editor with support for most of the HTML tags you will ever need, the capability to add your own tags, the capability to customize the program, and many other useful features for Web design.

A friendly interface makes Hot Dog Pro an inviting tool for new Web designers. A long list of HTML tags, including Netscape and Microsoft extensions, provides a powerful tool for experienced HTML developers. Trial or demo versions of Hot Dog Pro (as well as other HTML text editors for Windows, such as HTML Assistant Pro II) are included on the CD-ROM that accompanies this book.

Hot Dog's Key Features

Hot Dog was selected because it provides many key features that make Web design easier. The following points describe the best options included in Hot Dog:

- Two rows of toolbars provide easy access HTML tags, Preview options, and more.

- FTP software is built in for putting your Web site online.

- A simple built-in conversion utility automatically adds HTML formatting to ASCII text files.

- A Preview option enables you to view your pages in Hot Dog's viewer (called Rover).

- The Browser Preview option enables you to preview your files in any Web browser.

- Background and Tiling tools enable you to view background images as they will be displayed on the Web, to ensure that colored text and other elements create a good design.

- An HTML Syntax checker verifies HTML code and alerts you to mistakes.

- Nearly 50 different preferences can be set.

- Image placement and link setting are accomplished with a drag-and-drop function.

- A spell checker is included.

- Multiple levels of Undo are available (up to 99 previous actions).

- The program includes good Help features for using Hot Dog, as well as a comprehensive HTML reference.

The Toolbars in Hot Dog

A colorful toolbar spans the top of the screen in Hot Dog, providing easy access to a range of program features. Figure 13.27 gives a view of the Hot Dog interface and toolbars.

The options in the top row are described here (from left to right).

1. **Preview.** This button launches any browser you have set in preferences and makes it easy to display your pages to see how they will look on the Web.

2. **Tags.** This button opens a Tags palette, providing easy access to a range of HTML tags. See figure 13.28 for a view of this palette.

3. **Charset.** This button opens a dialog box that lists all the special character tags, also known as entity tags. See figure 13.29 for a view of this palette.

Figure 13.27

The Hot Dog interface and toolbars.

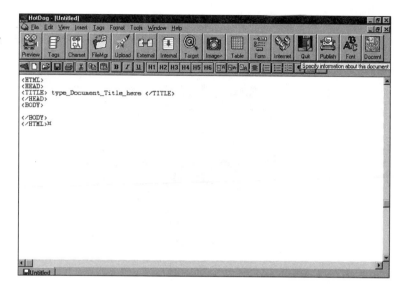

Figure 13.28

The Hot Dog Tags palette.

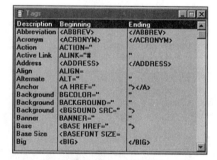

Figure 13.29

The Hot Dog Special Characters (Entities) palette.

4. **FileMgr.** This button launches the Hot Dog File Manager, where you can insert text files as preformatted text or create hypertext links by selecting any file or graphic (see fig. 13.30).

Figure 13.30

The Hot Dog File Manager.

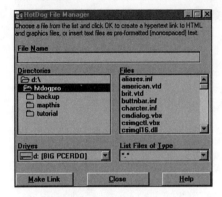

5. **Upload.** This button opens the FTP capabilities of this program, where you can set Hot Dog to transfer files directly to any server on the World Wide Web. The Launch HotFTP Standalone option enables you to use the file transfer capabilities on any files, even if you did not create them in Hot Dog (see fig. 13.31).

Figure 13.31

The Hot Dog upload dialog box for file transfer.

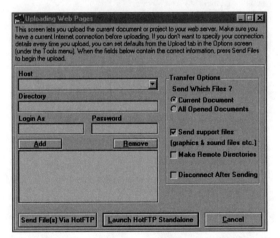

6. **External.** Enables you to create external links by typing any URL (see fig. 13.32).

7. **Internal.** This button lets you set internal links and requires a target to set a link to another place on the same page (see fig. 13.33).

Figure 13.32

The Hot Dog external link dialog box.

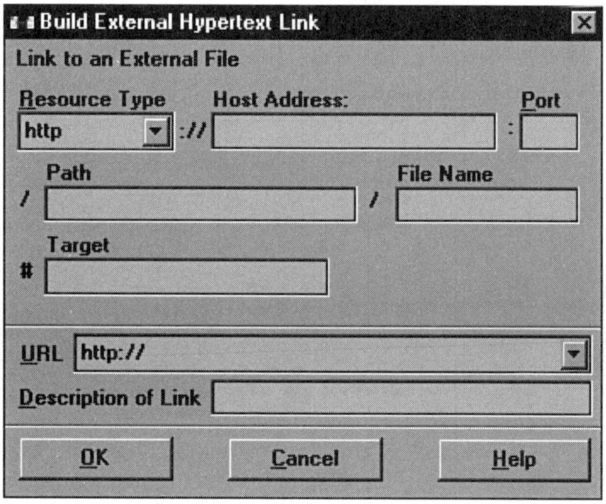

Figure 13.33

The Hot Dog internal link dialog box.

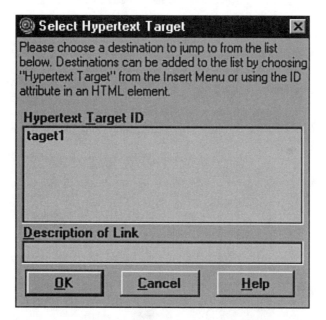

8. **Target.** Enables you to specify a target on the page to set internal links to a specific area of an HTML page. To do this, highlight the text or graphic you want to target, select the Target button, and name the target (see fig. 13.34).

Figure 13.34

The Hot Dog target dialog box.

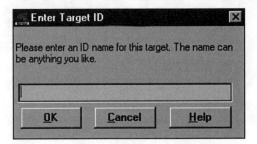

9. **Image.** This button is for linking images to the page. Simply select the image button and use the dialog box to locate the file you want to link. Hot Dog will automatically set the link, including the path and file name. The dialog box, as you can see in figure 13.35, enables you to set alternate text, alignment, border, and horizontal and vertical space. Height and Width are automatically calculated by Hot Dog and inserted in the HTML code.

10. **Table.** This option opens a dialog box for creating HTML tables. Features include the capability to set the number of rows and columns, height and width, alignment, cell padding and spacing, and headers. After these features are set,

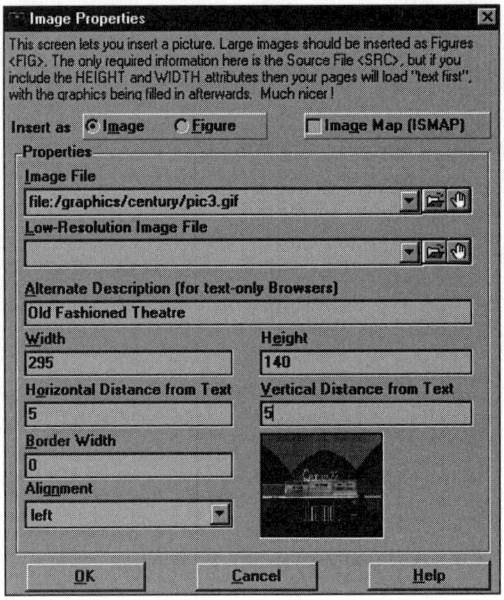

Figure 13.35

The Hot Dog Image Properties dialog box.

Hot Dog inserts the table in the HTML code at the location where you have placed the cursor. If you want to create table cells that span more than one column or row, you must do that manually in the HTML code (see fig. 13.36).

11. **Form.** Opens a dialog box where you can create basic HTML forms, using options such as text areas, radio buttons, and images (see fig. 13.37).

Figure 13.36

The Hot Dog Create Table dialog box.

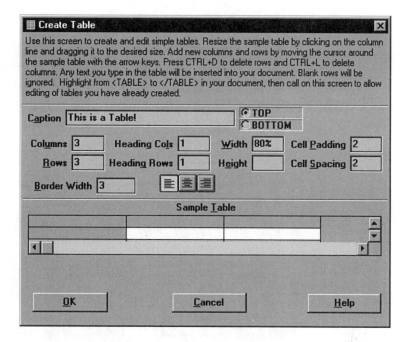

```
Create Table                                              [X]

Use this screen to create and edit simple tables. Resize the sample table by clicking on the column
line and dragging it to the desired size. Add new columns and rows by moving the cursor around
the sample table with the arrow keys. Press CTRL+D to delete rows and CTRL+L to delete
columns. Any text you type in the table will be inserted into your document. Blank rows will be
ignored. Highlight from <TABLE> to </TABLE> in your document, then call on this screen to allow
editing of tables you have already created.

Caption  [This is a Table!              ]        (•) TOP
                                                 ( ) BOTTOM

  Columns [3]    Heading Cols [1]    Width [80%]   Cell Padding [2]
     Rows [3]    Heading Rows [1]    Height [  ]   Cell Spacing [2]
  Border Width [3]        [≣][≣][≣]

                        Sample Table

    OK              Cancel              Help
```

12. **Internet.** Opens a dialog box where you can create hyperlinks to external resources. Use this option to set links to another Web site, to create an e-mail link, or to set links to many other Internet locations (see fig. 13.38).

13. **Quit.** Exit the program here.

14. **Publish.** A shortcut to save the file to the hard drive.

15. **Font.** Opens a dialog box where you can specify text-formatting tags such as bold, italic, and strong tags, as well as font size and text color.

16. **Docmnt.** This dialog box contains three option areas. You can set header information such as Meta tags and the document title. You can select a color in the color option area, and Hot Dog will calculate the hexadecimal code to set the background color. You can also specify a background image by using this dialog box (see fig. 13.40).

Figure 13.37

The Hot Dog Define Form Elements dialog box.

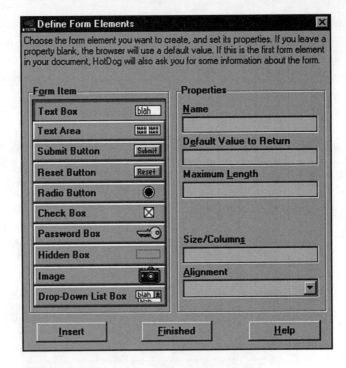

Figure 13.38

The Hot Dog Internet dialog box.

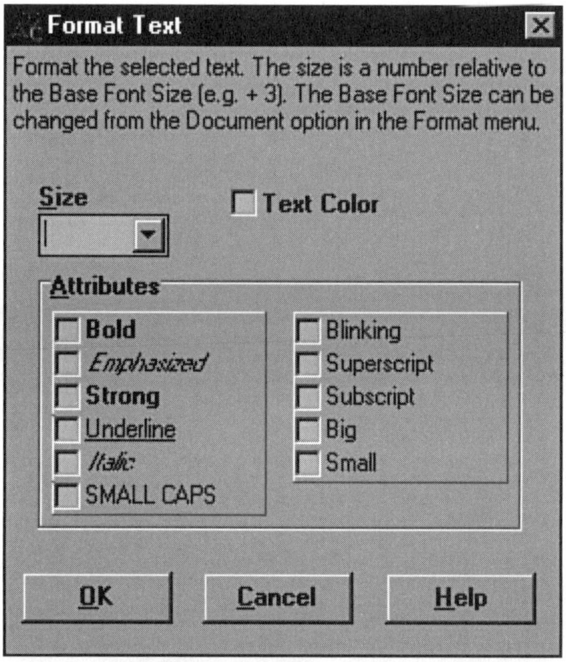

Figure 13.39

The Hot Dog Format Text dialog box.

Figure 13.40

The Hot Dog Format Document dialog box.

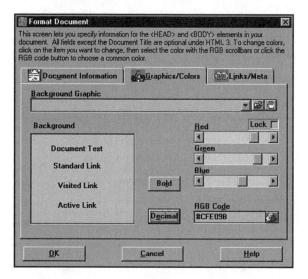

Hot Dog's Second Row Toolbar

This toolbar, visible in figure 13.27, includes some features familiar to anyone who uses word processing programs. The first image on the left is the Hot Dog mascot, essentially an ad for Hot Dog. The Blank Page icon next to it can be used to open a new file. Next is an Open Folder icon for opening files, a Disk icon for saving files, and a Printer icon for printing. Then come three very familiar buttons: scissors for Cut, two pages slightly offset for Copy, and a clipboard for Paste.

Starting with the button that has a B on it, the buttons become specific to HTML design.

1. The B, as you might guess, inserts <B> Bold tags around highlighted text.

2. The I is for italic <I>

3. The U is for underlined text.

4. The next six buttons represent header sizes 1 through 6.

5. The next three buttons are for image alignment options: top, middle, and bottom.

6. The next button can be used to center text or graphics.

7. Then there are buttons for numbered (ordered) lists, bulleted (unordered) lists, and definition lists.

8. The last three buttons in order from left to right are as follows:

   ● <P>, Paragraph tag

   ●
 Break tag

   ● <HR>, Horizontal Rule tag

Other Options Only Available Under the Menu

In addition to the options accessible through the toolbars, many other features are only available under the menu. These features are discussed in the following sections.

File Menu

The File menu contains the standard features you'd expect to find in a text editor, such as New, Open, Save, Save As, and Print.

Edit Menu

Under the Edit menu, you find the standard find-and-replace options common in most word processors. The Tag Information option shown in figure 13.41 is available under the Edit menu and is especially useful. It enables you to add HTML tags or any combinations of tags to the Tags palette, making the program highly expandable. This is a great way to create a shortcut to tag combinations you use frequently, such as an option that combines bold and center tags, but you must know HTML to do this. If you want to look up a tag, refer to Chapter 14.

Figure 13.41

The Hot Dog tag dialog box.

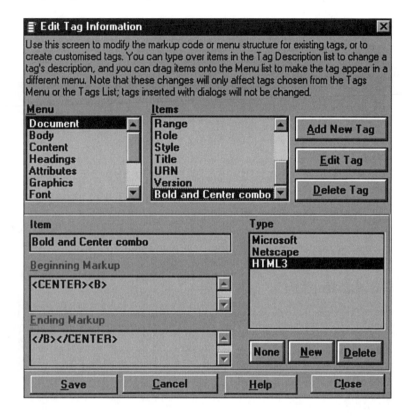

View Menu

The View menu enables you to tailor the interface by turning the toolbars on and off. This menu also provides access to the Tags palette, Special Characters palette, and the File Manager.

Insert Menu

The Insert Menu provides many HTML options not available from the toolbar. Most of these options are Netscape or Microsoft extensions.

- The Insert menu offers two options for image linking—a simple and a complex dialog box, also accessible through the image button in the toolbar. The simple dialog provides the basic HTML image tag; the complex dialog enables you to add image attributes such as alignment.

● The Embedded option can be used to link elements that require special viewers or plug-ins and use the Embed tag.

● The Marquee option creates a Microsoft extension that places a scrolling marquee on the page, only visible to viewers using Microsoft's Internet Explorer and ignored by browsers that don't support this Microsoft extension.

● The rest of the options under the Insert menu are also accessible from the toolbar and are described in the previous section.

Tags Menu

The Tags menu features many of the options in the toolbar and includes additional options, such as an Attributes dialog box that can be used to add attributes to any tag. A Miscellaneous option includes the <NOEMBED> and <NOFRAMES> tags you need for creating these options, and it includes alternative features for browsers that don't support them. For more information on these kinds of tags, see Chapter 14.

Format Menu

The Format menu provides access to options also available in the toolbar, such as the Format Text dialog box, bold, italics, underlining, and the center tag. This menu also includes the Blink tag, which makes text flash on and off on a Web page. Most good designers avoid this tag because it is considered distracting.

Tools Menu

The Tools menu includes a number of options that affect how Hot Dog works. The Options menu item lets you set preferences for a number of features in the program, such as how the toolbars are displayed and what dictionary is used. You can also use this to set the Preview browser and the options for uploading files in the FTP functions of this program. The Shortcut options enable you to associate key-command shortcuts to any program features you use frequently. The Make Template From Document and Create Template Field options enable you to create templates you can reuse to automate the creation of pages with similar designs. The Remove Hypertext Links and Remove HTML Tags options can be used to strip the code out of a file if you want a copy that does not include HTML formatting tags. Note that this will permanently remove the tags from your file, so it's a good idea to make a copy of the document first. The program's spell check feature is also available under the Tools menu.

Window Menu

The Window menu option is designed to help you organize multiple files you may have open at one time. Use the Cascade option to overlap all open documents from the top left to the bottom right of the screen so the title bars of all documents are visible. Use the Tile option to arrange open documents from top to bottom. (Note that the height of each document will be reduced to fit them all on the screen.) Arrange Icons reduces all open documents to small icons and lines them up across the bottom of the screen for easy access. When you double-click on any icon, that page returns to normal size. Close All quickly closes all open files. Windows List provides the same list of open files you find in the Documents Bar at the bottom of the page; however, the Documents Bar indicates if a file has been saved or not, and the Windows List shows the full path of the document.

Help Menu

The Help menu offers a full Contents list, Search function, HTML Reference, and memory information regarding how much RAM the program is using. This is particularly important to Windows 3.1 and Windows for Workgroups users who run the risk of crashing if they do not have enough RAM to handle all open files.

Using Hot Dog Pro

Overall, Hot Dog Pro is a user-friendly and intuitive program. You can open any HTML file with the program or use it to create new pages. The toolbars and menu options provide a wide range of HTML tags and other features that make this a good all-around tool.

The HTML Tags features in Hot Dog enable you to highlight any section of text, graphic, or other element and apply HTML tags or attributes by selecting button options or opening dialog boxes. Drag-and-drop image-linking and the capability to browse for files when setting hyperlinks makes setting paths and relative links much faster and helps ensure accuracy.

This program meets the needs of diehard HTML designers determined to work in the code directly. At the same time, it offers assistance that speeds the process of manual coding and helps ensure you don't have typos or other mistakes in your code. You can, of course, type the code in manually at any time, and you can also add your favorite tags or combinations of tags to the options available in the HTML Tags palette. This is a wonderfully versatile program capable of meeting the demands of almost any HTML developer on a PC.

When you're done with your pages, the HTML Syntax checker will verify that you don't have errors in your code. And finally, you can use the built-in FTP capabilities to put your files online on any remote Web server to which you have access.

Summary

The programs and concepts described in this chapter will help you tailor your HTML conversions and get them ready for final publication on the Web. The conversion programs covered in this book are great for moving information designed for print into a format that works on the Web, but most lack the formatting control you want for your final designs.

The goal of this book is to help you convert content quickly, so you can focus your time and energy on good design. This chapter introduces you to some of the best HTML editors available for tailoring your designs after conversion. Whether you are working on an intranet or the Internet, the programs in this chapter can help you speed up your work and create better Web pages. When used in combination with the HTML conversion programs described in other chapters in this book, these tools provide all the features necessary to create dynamic, interesting Web pages with high-end features and complex designs.

CHAPTER 14

HTML Tutorial and Reference

If you are new to the HyperText Markup Language (HTML), this tutorial will teach you the basics of HTML and how to design pages for the World Wide Web. If you are already familiar with HTML, this should serve as a refresher—a chance to correct any mistakes or misunderstandings you may have, and a reference for all the HTML tags in common use on the Web today.

HTML is not rocket science, as many teachers like to point out. It is not a programming language such as C or C++, used to create complex software applications. HTML does not take years to learn or master. And as HTML authoring tools evolve, it becomes less and less necessary to master the language at all. Nonetheless, to get the most out of HTML editors and converters, you will need a basic understanding of HTML, its features, and its limitations. This chapter is designed to arm you with the knowledge to understand the content of the rest of this book.

> **Note**
>
> **Don't Be Intimidated**
>
> For those who have never done any programming, HTML may be a bit intimidating at first, but don't despair. With just a little time and effort, you will know all it takes to create great Web pages and get the most out of the techniques and programs explained in the rest of the book.

HTML is a markup language used to design pages for the World Wide Web. If you have been using computers long enough to remember the old days of word processing, you'll immediately find some similarities to early word processors. As a markup language, HTML is used to indicate the display of words and images on a page. HTML is made up of a long list of *tags* (code set off in brackets such as these <>) that are inserted around the words and image descriptions on a page. If you want something to appear as bold type, for example, simply put the tags <B> and </B> on either side of the words you want bold. Most tags have an open tag followed by a similar close tag, distinguished by the forward slash "/" in the close tag. This tells the browser—programs such as Netscape Navigator that view the Web—where your formatting should begin and end.

The Volatile Nature of HTML

The biggest limitation of HTML is also one of its biggest advantages. It was designed to be universally viewable so that virtually every computer on the planet can display the pages you create for the Web. But not every computer has the same size monitor or the same fonts you may have at your disposal. This means that you are generally limited to relative descriptions. For example, instead of describing a headline as 24 point, Times, bold, use a tag that describes it as a header. Header 1—or <H1>, as the tag is written—is the largest heading size. You then have <H2>, <H3>, and so forth down to <H6>, which, somewhat counter-intuitively if you are accustomed to font sizes, is the smallest.

What this does is let the browser and user decide how to display pages on the Web, taking best advantage of their system. In Netscape Navigator, for example, the default font is the commonly used Times, but users have the option of using any font they prefer. So for one viewer, <H1> may be 24 point, Times, bold, yet on another computer, it may be 30 point, Helvetica. Your job is to organize the page design so that the information and layout will make sense at either setting, and then try to get over your frustration at not having more control.

Having introduced HTML this way, I have to warn you that things are changing. Netscape and Microsoft are both creating their own HTML tags that enable you to set the exact font and point size, at least for viewers that have them. That's a welcome and exciting part of the evolution of the language, but it's also something to be careful of. As I go through the various HTML tag options, I'll point out which ones are universally accepted and which ones are limited to specific browsers. You need to understand early on that not everyone is using Netscape Navigator or Microsoft's Internet Explorer, and that even those who are may not be using the latest versions of these programs. The enticing new options out there in HTML let you have greater control over the display, but use them with care or they can result in pages that are unreadable in older or more limited browsers.

Viewing HTML Document Source Code

Many people suggest that you can learn HTML by looking at the source code of pages on the Web. They are referring to an option in most browsers that enables you to bring up a display of the HTML code behind the page you are viewing. In Netscape Navigator, you do this by selecting Document Source, under the View menu option. While it's true that this is often a good way to learn new tricks, and you may be able to pick up the basics this way, be aware that it's also a way to learn bad habits.

It is surprising how many people make mistakes in their HTML code or use redundant HTML tags. Fortunately—or unfortunately, as the case may be—many browsers are forgiving about this and will provide a reasonable display even if you forget a close tag here or leave off a set of quotation marks there. The problem is that other browsers, and even other versions of the same browser, may have trouble displaying pages with these kinds of errors, distorting the intended view, or even crashing when they get confused by bad syntax. So be forewarned—just because a page looks okay in Netscape Navigator doesn't mean the code behind the page is without errors. As a general rule, you are much better off learning HTML from a carefully edited reference such as this one than from viewing random pages on the Internet. I've been amazed that even at large, well-respected sites such as HotWired, I've found errors in the code. Often it's just because the designer was in a hurry on the last update, and next week the page may be error-free again. But if you don't know what you are looking at, it's easy to pick up bad habits by viewing other people's code on the Web.

The History of HTML

The World Wide Web was created in 1991 by a group of physicists in Switzerland so that they could trade images of their scientific research, as well as the words they had been sending back and forth for years. Unfortunately for the graphic designers who jumped on their technology, those scientists didn't care much about fancy fonts or full-color images—they just wanted to get their research across the Net. Today, the more commercial and graphic side of the Web is still reeling from its almost accidental creation. Standards exist for HTML, but they have been so limited and slow in their development that many private companies, namely Netscape and Microsoft, have jumped in and added their own. This means that there are several levels of HTML, and not all the browsers and HTML authoring tools out there can display or create all the new features.

It's helpful to have a bit of the history and evolution of HTML to understand the differences among browsers and HTML authoring tools. Today, there are several versions of HTML in use. The first and most widely supported is called HTML 2.0. This set of tags was approved a couple of years ago by the World Wide Web Consortium (W3C), a group created to set standards on the Web. If you limit yourself to the HTML 2.0 tags, you can be assured that your display will be consistent in almost every browser in use, but many designers will be frustrated by the limitations. The 2.0 specification is so limited, it doesn't even include alignment—you can't center text or images and you can't wrap text around an image. It's okay if you want something quite basic, but it offers almost no design control.

For more than a year (eons in Web time), the W3C argued about a proposed 3.0 specification that includes alignment and other options to provide better design control. Only recently did they finally agree on what they now call the 3.2 specification. But while W3C members were arguing about what new tags would be appropriate, companies such as Netscape and Microsoft stepped in and started using the proposed tags anyway. Then, to make matters more confusing, and certainly more controversial, these private companies started adding their own HTML tags, generally called *extensions*. Netscape and Microsoft's competitiveness encourages them to keep up with one another's additions, but other companies who provide their own browsers, such as America Online and CompuServe, have fallen woefully behind. If you know that all your viewers are using a particular browser, you can safely do whatever you want with your code, but because most Web sites attract viewers with a variety of browsers, you'll want to use combinations of code carefully to ensure that the display works for everyone.

As the HTML tags are explained in the following pages, I'll point out what level of HTML they represent and what kind of support you can expect. I'll also refer to a few workarounds that will let you take advantage of the high-end options without excluding your low-end viewers.

Browser Differences

Designing for multiple browsers is a complex issue. If you are really into this, you should read my first book, *Hybrid HTML Design: A Multi-Browser HTML Reference*, co-authored with Kevin Ready and published by New Riders. This book goes into great detail about the differences among browsers and how to design HTML pages that work well in all of them. This chapter won't go into the depth covered in that book, but the differences among code will be pointed out. This will help you have an idea of which HTML tags you can expect to have consistent display among browsers and which tags will vary from browser to browser.

The saving grace of browser differences is that when a browser doesn't understand an HTML tag, it will ignore it. Thus, if you are considering using a feature that adds to your design, such as frames or background colors in a table, you should not hesitate just because not all browsers can view it. The majority of users on the Web are using Netscape Navigator and will be able to view the high-end features you want to include. If you are adding an option that enhances your view for some browsers, your only real loss in most cases is that lower-end browsers won't display it. Often this simply means that your high-end users enjoy the benefit of the feature and low-end browsers won't even miss it. In cases where features that are not displayed will radically change the display or distort some things so much they may be unreadable, I'll point out workarounds and teach you about alternative tags often provided for the browser-specific HTML extensions. For the most part, however, I'll simply indicate if the display is consistent and you can decide if you want to include the option.

The Browser Default for Text

Words in an HTML document not marked with any HTML tags will display in the browser's default HTML size. In Netscape Navigator, this is Times, 12 point, unless the user has changed it in Preferences. I prefer a bigger font, so I always set Netscape to display regular text as Times, 14 point. Each browser has its own Preferences settings, so you'll have to check how to make such changes in your own browser. The thing to be aware of is that your users can do anything they want with their preferences, including setting the default to something horrid such as Courier, 36 point. You can't possibly design with every font and size in mind, but you need to design in a logical fashion, using relative options so that the display will still work even if your user sets the default to the Vina Chan font at 24 point. You'll soon learn that HTML was designed with this potential problem in mind, but it's helpful to understand this so you can better understand the way HTML works.

HTML 2.0

The focus of this book is not to teach you how to do HTML, but this chapter will certainly give you the basics. The following sections will give you a reference to the tags available to you and include descriptions of what each of those tags do. You do not need to use all these tags in your documents, but you should know that they are all available to you. Part of the reason for breaking them out into categories is to help you understand the limitations of some of the HTML editors and converters discussed in this book. Many programs have intentionally limited their tag options to 2.0 with just a few 3.2 options to ensure consistent display in a variety of browsers. The goal of this book is to help you understand the trade-offs and teach you how to add more options as they seem appropriate to you. This is discussed in Chapter 13, "Tailoring Converted Files." You may be able to work more efficiently with a conversion program, even if it has limited options, but you will quite likely want to go back afterward and add more advanced features to make your pages more interesting.

HTML 2.0 is the standard that has long been approved by the W3C and is thus the most widely supported by the various browsers used to view the Web. If you want your page design to be identical, or nearly identical, in all browsers, stick to the tags in this section, but be aware you will be limiting your options considerably. You won't be able to control alignment (everything is left aligned), you cannot use background colors or tables, and images are the only nontext media type you can place in your Web pages by using HTML 2.0. Nonetheless, because all the rest of the HTML tags are based on the HTML 2.0 specification, we'll start here to give you an introduction. Just make sure you don't stop at HTML 2.0. Once you are familiar with these options, you'll want to progress to the more advanced features allowed by HTML 3.2 and the browser-specific extensions covered later in the Netscape and Microsoft sections.

My intention in this chapter is to teach you about the HTML tags that are most widely used, so I have intentionally restricted the tags I will teach you about to those that have been the most widely accepted and implemented. HTML 2.0 tags have now become a subset of the tags available to HTML 3.2 browsers, so in the rest of this chapter, you will be building on the knowledge and tags you learn about here.

As each of the HTML tags is described, their attributes will also be discussed. *Attributes* are "extra" features of the tag. For example, you have seen how the <BODY> tag designates the main area of the page. It can also include many attributes that you will learn about in the HTML 3.2 and other sections. Attributes include additions, such as background color, which are included in the <BODY> tag like this: <BODY BGCOLOR="ffffff">. Don't worry if this doesn't make much sense to you yet—it will soon. For now, understand that a tag such as the <BODY> tag may have additional features called attributes. At the end of each section, you'll find a sample HTML page that provides examples about how attributes may be used with the tags.

The Simplest HTML Document

All HTML documents start and end with the same basic code. At the top of the page, it's good form to put the open <HTML> tag to indicate to a browser that this is an HTML document (this is not a requirement, however). Similarly, at the very end of the page, you close with the HTML tag </HTML>. You follow the open HTML tag with the head information. This is where you put the <title>—the words that will display at the top of the browser window to identify the page to your viewers. After closing the title and the head, you open the body of the document with—surprise—the <BODY> tag. All the words, images, and other HTML code that make up the document go between the body tags. The spacing in the following document is included for clarity. To set spaces in a Web page that will display, you will have to use the paragraph <P> and break <BR> tags, but we'll talk more about that later. It's enough now to say that all the returns and spacing you put in your document won't make any difference in the display, but will make your code much more readable for you and any other designers that may work on your pages.

Thus, the simplest HTML document would look like this:

```
<HTML>
<HEAD><TITLE>A Simple HTML Page</TITLE></HEAD>
<BODY>
This is a simple HTML document.
</BODY></HTML>
```

In the image shown in figure 14.1, you see how that simple HTML document is displayed in Netscape Navigator. Notice the title at the top of the page appears after the word "Netscape."

Figure 14.1

The display in Netscape Navigator.

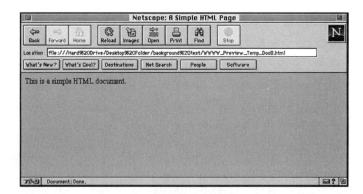

Document Elements

The following elements (which you saw previously in the simple HTML document) initiate and divide an HTML document. All other tags are contained between these tags and their corresponding closing tags.

- <HTML>: This tag indicates to a browser that the page was created by using HTML.

- <HEAD>: This is where you place general information about the page for the host computer. The only tag that will display in this section is the <TITLE> tag.

- <BODY>: This indicates the main viewing area of the page, where nearly all your information will be displayed.

● <! ..comment.>: Comment tags are generally used to make notes to yourself or to other people who may be working on your HTML pages. These are notes you would not want viewable to your users. It is a good idea to include comments close to the material you are commenting on. They can be placed anywhere in the document, but are often best located in the head element if they refer to the entire page. If your comment concerns a specific item in the page, place it near the specific item. The exclamation point tells the browser that this is a comment field. Comment fields can be used anywhere in the document and tell the browser to ignore all text between the "<!" and ">". There is no closing tag for comments and all your comment text should be included between the < >.

The document elements should always appear in the following order:

```
<HTML>
<HEAD></HEAD>
<!this is just to show you the order they appear in>
<BODY></BODY>
</HTML>
```

All head elements are contained within the opening and closing <HEAD> tags, and all body elements are contained within the opening and closing <BODY> tags.

Head Elements

The following elements can be placed between the <HEAD> and </HEAD> tags. Head elements are useful for organizing and indexing purposes. With the exception of the <TITLE> tag, the HTML tags in the head section are not visible to the browser.

> **Note**
>
> The inclusion of most <HEAD> tags is to aid search and index functions for host computers. For more information about how to set up a searchable index or other functions, you'll need to talk to your system administrator to find out the unique requirements of your server and the programming used for searching. This is a rather advanced HTML function, but you should understand that there are other uses for the <HEAD> section besides the <TITLE>.

● <BASE>: This feature provides a base URL for relative referencing within the HTML document. If you do not use this element, the default URL (or Web address) is the pathway to the folder or directory that contains the HTML document. The <BASE> tag is useful primarily for testing. If you are working on a document on your hard drive, but want to display images or other elements on the server not available on your hard drive, you can reference a base URL.

For example, if you view the document source on a page on the Web, save it to your hard drive, and then want to play around with the code without downloading all the graphics, you can insert a <BASE> tag so that you have access to the other elements on the page. Let's say you go to Microsoft's site and copy down the code from their main page. You could then set the <BASE> to Microsoft's URL, and while viewing the document on your hard drive, you would see the images or whatever is online. To do that, you would set the <BASE> to the following:

```
<BASE HREF="http://www.microsoft.com/">
```

- <LINK>: This tag, which is not commonly used on the Web, contains information linking the HTML document with other documents or entities. If you use this tag, you must include the HREF that calls the URL. The TITLE, REL, and REV attributes of the <LINK> tag are optional.

- <HREF>: The URL of the document that has a relationship with the document you are working on.

- <TITLE>: The title of the related document.

- <REL>: The nature of the relationship between the document you are working on and the URL specified by the HREF attribute. Possibilities are "next," "previous," "parent," and "made."

- <REV>: Same as REL, except generally in the reverse direction.

- <ISINDEX>: Indicates that a searchable index is available for the document on the server.

- <TITLE>: Contains the title of the HTML document. This is the only HEAD element you really have to worry about for basic HTML, and the only one that displays in a browser.

Body Elements

Body elements describe the display of the main browser window. These include text-formatting tags, list tags, spacing tags, image tags, anchor tags, horizontal rule tags, and form tags. The <BODY> tag, as you have seen, includes an open <BODY> and close </BODY> tag. There are no body attributes in HTML 2.0, but you'll learn about adding many new attributes for controlling backgrounds and text colors in the HTML 3.2 specification, detailed in a later section of the chapter.

Text Formats

Text formats are grouped into physical and logical styles. In HTML 2.0, the standard tags available to all browsers are the following:

- <H1, H2, H3...H6>: Heading styles 1 through 6. As explained earlier, these tags set relative sizes, with <H1> being the largest and <H6> the smallest (unless users choose to change this in their own browser settings). The actual size and font is determined by the browser.

- <STRONG>: The Strong tag. This tag is usually interpreted as bold. It is the preferred logical alternative to the <B> tag. Using <STRONG> instead of <B> gives your viewers greater control over the display because they can set <STRONG> to display in the format they prefer.

- <EM>: The Emphasis tag. This tag is usually interpreted as italic. It is the preferred logical alternative to the <I> tag for the same reasons <STRONG> is preferable to <B>.

- <B>: The Bold tag. This tag is the physical alternative to <STRONG> and makes the text bold.

- <I>: The Italic tag. This tag is the physical alternative to <EM> and makes the text italic.

- <PRE>: The Preformatted tag. This tag distributes all characters and punctuation evenly, using a fixed-width font that enables columnar page design in browsers that do not support tables. This is the only alternative for creating HTML tables (which will be explained in detail in the HTML 3.2 section), but it can be unpredictable. Even text that's well aligned in a text editor may not display well in your browser.

> **Tip**
>
> If you use Notepad for Windows to set the alignment of your ‹PRE› text, your display should be the most consistent. This may seem odd, but after testing this in many text editors (MS Word, SimpleText, and others), I found that Notepad provides the most consistent display.

Other Text-Formatting Options

Although not as commonly used as the tags just listed, the following tags are also text-formatting options in HTML 2.0:

- <U>: The Underline tag, as you probably could have guessed, underlines text. Although this tag is supported by many browsers that support the HTML 2.0 specification, it is not supported by Netscape Navigator and many designers discourage its use because links are generally underlined by the browser. Under-lined text that is not a link can be confusing to users.

● <ADDRESS>: Text within this tag is usually italicized and is almost always set off in its own paragraph. This tag is often used as a signature by the document creator or publisher at the end of a Web page.

● <BLOCKQUOTE>: This tag usually indents a section of text and was intended for material quoted from another source.

● <CITE>: This tag usually forces an italicized font and is sometimes fixed-width. It is intended for citations of others' works.

● <CODE>: This tag is usually set with a fixed-width font and is intended to designate computer code displayed on a page.

● <KBD>: This tag is usually set with a fixed-width font and is intended to indicate that the text is to be entered by the user.

● <PLAINTEXT>: Characters between the opening and closing tags will appear in the browser window as fixed-width text, and any other formatting placed between these tags will not be displayed.

● <SAMP>: The Sample tag. Another fixed-width font tag, <SAMP> is used to demarcate sample areas.

● <STRIKE>: The Strikeout tag. This tag puts a line through the middle of text, and is not widely supported.

● <TT>: Typewriter text. This tag can be fixed-width, bold, or other. It is one of the least predictable tags, and is rarely used.

● <VAR>: The Variable tag. This tag is usually italic. This tag is intended to indicate that the highlighted text is treated as a variable.

● <XMP>: The Example tag. This tag is usually rendered as a fixed-width font, and generally commands its own paragraph.

Selecting the Most Appropriate Text Format

It is often recommended that you use logical instead of physical styles. By using <EM> instead of <I>, for instance, you give your users the benefit of selecting the text formatting that they prefer. If users have had a problem distinguishing italicized text, they may want to set emphasized text to underline, or set it as a larger font size. Another suggestion is to identify and avoid tags that are dissimilar in various browsers. If you stick with the first set of text-formatting tags described in this chapter, you can be reasonably sure your page display will be consistent in most browsers. The formats in the second section are not supported equally in all browsers, even though they are part of the HTML 2.0 specification. Including them in your HTML design can have inconsistent results and is generally discouraged.

Using Tags in Combination

If you use more than one tag together (for example: <H1> and <EM>), you need to keep them in the proper order. If a tag is opened while another tag is still open, the second tag should be closed before the first tag is closed. For example: <H1><EM> This is my italicized headline</EM></H1>. Notice that the <H1> and close </H1> appear first and last and the <EM> and </EM> tags are completed in the middle. Although some tags may not be affected by being overlapped with other tags, this can cause problems in many browsers and is generally considered bad form.

Spacing Tags

Pressing the return key in your text editor will put space in your code, but is not the way to put a return in the page that will display in your browser. To create a line return in a Web page, you need to use the <P> or <BR> tags, as follows:

-
: The Line Break tag ends a line and puts a hard return at the end of it in the display.

- <P>: The Paragraph tag ends a line and adds a second blank line below it.

The tags <BR> and <P> will only provide one line return each. This means that you cannot place two <P> tags and hope to see two blank lines of space. Although some browsers may place more space between elements if you use these tags in repetition, most browsers will ignore them. This may seem frustrating at first if you want to have greater control of spacing on your pages, but we'll explore other ways to create white space later in this tutorial. For now, it's enough to know that you should not use multiple <P> tags to put in more space—it simply won't work in most browsers.

> **Note**
>
> You should also be aware that the space character is limited to one at a time in HTML. That means that even if you enter two spaces after a period, only one will appear in the browser's display. Similarly, the tab key in your text editor will have little or no effect in most browser displays.

Limitations on formatting white space with the <P> and <BR> tags stem from one of the original goals of the creators of the Web, which was to make things efficient. Thus, multiple spaces were seen as wasted space. As more designers take to the Web, you can expect to see more browsers supporting multiple spaces in HTML. Already, Netscape Navigator and a few other browsers do support multiple spaces.

On the other hand, placing physical, keyboard-entered spaces, tabs, and returns in your HTML code is a good habit because it makes the code much easier to read in a text editor. Inexperienced HTML designers (and, unfortunately, some of the WYSIWYG HTML editors on the market) often don't put enough space in their code, making it much more difficult to edit later. In the following HTML example, notice the use of spacing in the HTML document that does not appear in the browser display, which follows in figure 14.2. You'll also notice that some HTML tags include their own spacing. Header tags, for example, force a hard return after the close tag. This may also be frustrating to you if you want to control the font size within a line of text. Later sections in this chapter will look at some alternatives that, although limited to only certain browsers, will let you control the size of the text without forcing a line break. For now, however, we're sticking with the basic and most supported tags. Here's a sample HTML page that uses the tags we've discussed so far.

```
<HTML>
<HEAD>
<TITLE>Text and Spacing Tags</TITLE>
</HEAD>
<BODY>
<H1>Header 1</H1>
<H2>Header 2</H2>
<H3>Header 3</H3>
<H4>Header 4</H4>
<H5>Header 5</H5>
<H6>Header 6</H6>
<STRONG>Strong</STRONG><BR>
<EM>EM (Emphasis)</EM><BR>
<B>B (Bold)</B><BR>
<I>I (Italic)</I><P>
<PRE> PRE uses a fixed-width font
➥ and is the one tag that displays the text exactly as it's typed,
➥ showing line breaks even though I didn't use any spacing tags.
➥ PRE even displays    tabs and multiple        spaces</PRE><P>
<U>U (Underline)</U>, <CITE>CITE<CITE>, <CODE>CODE</CODE>,
<KBD>KBD</KBD>, <SAMP>SAMP</SAMP>, <TT>TT</TT> <STRIKE>STRIKE<
STRIKE>, <VAR>VAR</VAR>, <ADDRESS>Address is usually italicized.<
ADDRESS><P>
```

continues

continued

```
<BLOCKQUOTE>This is a BLOCKQUOTE section. There are usually indents
from the right- and left-hand margins, but this is not always true
in all browsers.</BLOCKQUOTE>
</BODY>
</HTML>
```

Figure 14.2

*How document text
and spacing tags
display in a browser.*

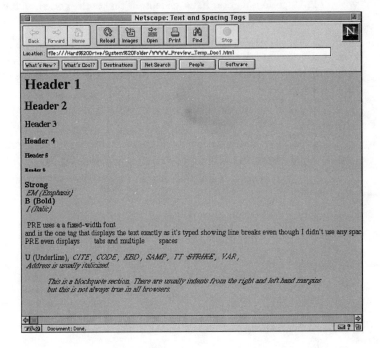

In figure 14.2, you see how Netscape Navigator displays the previous HTML document example. Notice that the spacing in the HTML text is not the same as the spacing in the browser display.

> **Note**
>
> **HTML Limitations**
>
> If you're starting to get frustrated by the limitations of HTML, don't worry too much yet. Although you don't get all the design options you may be accustomed to in print programs, you'll find many more features in the next sections as we get into HTML 3.2 and the Netscape and Microsoft extensions.

List Tags

There are several types of list tags in HTML 2.0. These are used to create lists with such features as indentation, bullets, and numbers. There are four categories of HTML lists: ordered lists, unordered lists, definition lists, and directory lists. Definition tags are unique here in that they do not allow for bullets or other distinguishers, but they are included in this section because they have a similar effect on the formatted text. First, though, the List Item tag is discussed.

The List Item Tag: <LI>

This tag is contained within the <OL>, <UL>, <MENU>, <DIRECTORY>, and <DIR> tags that follow. This is one of the few tags that does *not* have a closing tag. The <LI> tag indicates an individual list item and must be contained within one of the list tags.

Ordered Lists

The ordered list tag (<OL>) displays the <LI> tags as numbered list items in the browser. The first <LI> tag beneath the <OL> tag will be 1, the second <LI> tag will be 2, and so on.

Unordered Lists

The unordered list tag (<UL>) displays the <LI> tags that follow as bulleted list items in the browser. All the first level <LI> tags contained within the <UL> and </UL> tags will be bulleted. If you create a second level by nesting the <UL> tags inside one another, the <LI> tag display changes, usually to a small box, but different browsers treat this differently. An example of this is shown in the sample page that follows.

Both the ordered and unordered lists can include the COMPACT attribute, which indents the list a little less from the left margin. This can give you more control over spacing, but it is not supported by all browsers.

Definition Lists

Definition lists enable HTML designers to create hierarchical lists, such as glossaries and indices. These tags can be nested, which gives a tier-like structure to your Web page. Using a combination of embedded definition lists with other lists, such as the <UL> or <OL> tags, can give you greater control over the layout of your pages.

The definition tags are as follows:

- <DL>: The Definition List tag. This tag contains <DT> and <DD> tags.

- <DT>: The Definition Term tag. In the definition list hierarchy, this tag precedes the <DD> tag and is occasionally slightly indented from the left margin. It has no attributes and no closing tag.

- <DD>: The Definition Description tag. This tag places text slightly more indented on the page than the definition term. The <DD> tag, like the <DT> tag, generally does not have bullets preceding it. It has no attributes and no closing tag.

Directory Lists

Directory lists are intended for smaller, more compact lists. These are not supported in as many browsers as the other lists, nor are they rendered as more compact lists. It is usually the case that directory lists are treated like the unordered lists, with or without bullets.

The tags are as follows:

- <DIRECTORY>: The Directory tag is intended for very small names. The list is sometimes broken into two or more columns. The <LI> tags often have bullets and are slightly indented.

- <DIR>: This tag functions the same as the <DIRECTORY> tag.

- <MENU>: The menu option provides a more condensed display than the <UL> tag. The <LI> tags in a menu directory list usually appear with a smaller bullet.

Selecting an Appropriate List

Which list tags you choose is mostly a question of style, although the choice is strongly influenced by the nature and content of the information you want to organize.

Ordered lists work well for documents that have a linear nature to them, such as recipe steps or chapters.

If your list is of objects that have no hierarchical or ordinal relationship, such as a list of Web sites related to a topic but not to each other, an unordered list might be the most appropriate. The unordered list almost always has a bullet on the left side.

If you want to list a series of books and a brief description of their contents, you may find a definition list the best choice. Stylistically, using <DL>, <DT>, and <DD> tags in the place of other nested list formats is generally preferred.

The choice of <MENU>, <DIRECTORY>, and <DIR> is not as common in HTML as the ordered, unordered, and definition list tags. There may be several reasons for this. These tags are among the least predictable in the various browsers. Sometimes they are single column; sometimes multicolumn; sometimes fixed-width; sometimes indistinguishable. If you want to give a predictable list of items in a multicolumn format, you may want to consider the <PRE> tag. An even better option is the <TABLE> tag, which will be covered in the HTML 3.2 section.

One solution to unpredictable or undesired bullet formats is substituting your own bullet by using the <IMG> tag. This would be done by creating a bullet (or finding one somewhere), converting it to GIF or JPEG format, and including it as an inline image (you'll learn how to place images soon). To make an indented line with a custom bullet, place the inline image as the first character in a <DD> tag or in place of an <LI> tag, replacing the default bullet in the <UL> tag.

The following example will give you a better idea of how list tags appear in a browser (see fig. 14.3). Notice that spacing tags are not included between the lists and the headings, as the list tags force their own spacing.

```
<HTML>
<HEAD>
<TITLE>List tags</TITLE>
</HEAD>
<BODY>
<H1>List tags</H1>
<H2>The Ordered List.</H2>
<OL>
<LI> This is the first item in an ordered list.
<LI> This is the second item in an ordered list.
</OL>
<H2>The Unordered List.</H2>
<UL>
<LI> This is the first item in an unordered list.
<LI> This is the second item in an unordered list.
<UL>This is to show you how a nested list displays.
<LI> Notice that at the second level the bullet changes.
<LI> This is the second item at the second level.
<UL>Now we see the third level. Make sure you use close tags for
➥every open tag.
<LI> Notice that at the third level the bullet changes again.
<LI> This is the second item at the third level.
```

continues

continued

```
</UL>
        </UL>
                </UL>
<H2>The Definition List.</H2>
<DL>
<DT>This is a Definition Term tag within a Definition List.
<DD>This is the Definition Description tag within the same Defini
➥tion List.
<DT>This is another Definition Term tag.
<DD>This is the accompanying Definition Description tag again.
<DD>This is a second Definition Description tag beneath the second
➥Definition Term tag.
</DL>
</BODY>
</HTML>
```

Figure 14.3

A display of the list tags.

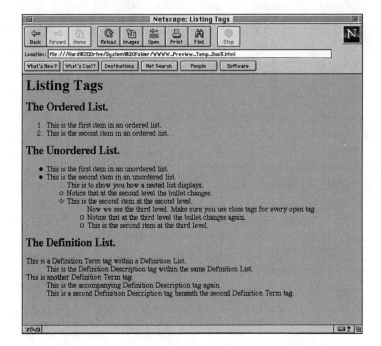

The most common and most predictable list tags are displayed here in Netscape Navigator. Notice the use of nested <UL> tags to provide variation. At each level a new kind of bullet is displayed. Make sure that you close each tag you nest. Thus, the three open <UL> tags require three close </UL> tags at the end of the list.

List Tag Displays

The following HTML example is provided to show you how list tags display. Given their unpredictability in other browsers, however, they are not generally recommended.

```
<HTML>
<HEAD><TITLE>List tags, continued</TITLE></HEAD>
<BODY>
<H1>List tags, Continued</H1>
<H3>The DIRECTORY tag is not always recognized. The format is not
➥very predictable.</H3>
<DIRECTORY>
<LI>Directory 1
<LI>Directory 2
<LI>Directory 3
<LI>Directory 4
</DIRECTORY>
<H3>The DIR tag is not always recognized. The format is not very
➥predictable.</H3>
<DIR>
<LI>Dir 1
<LI>Dir 2
<LI>Dir 3
<LI>Dir 4
</DIR>
<H3>The MENU tag is not always recognized. The format is not very
➥predictable.</H3>
<MENU>
<LI>Menu 1
<LI>Menu 2
<LI>Menu 3
<LI>Menu 4
</MENU>
</BODY>
</HTML>
```

HTML Tutorial and Reference

The rest of the list tags are included in the display in figure 14.4. These are the most unpredictable tags, because they vary from browser to browser in their display. Thus, they are not generally recommended unless you are certain of your browser audience.

Figure 14.4

Another display of the list tags.

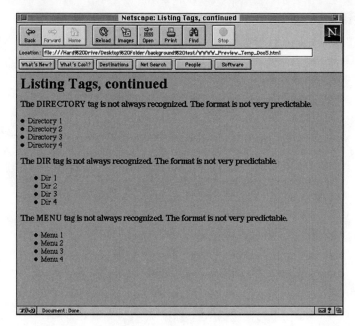

Using List Tags and Spacing Tags in Combination

The following example includes some spacing to demonstrate how you can make your Web pages more aesthetically appealing. Experiment with them in various combinations to see what works best for your designs. You may find, for instance, that the <DT> tags do not space their contents enough for you. Alternating <BR> and <P> tags can give the definition list more visual structure.

Here's an example:

```
<HTML>
<HEAD><TITLE>List tags and Spacing tags combined</TITLE></HEAD>
<BODY>
<H2>Using list tags and spacing tags in combination</H2>

<DL>
<DT>First Author Name<BR>
<DD>Description of first author's book<P>
<DT>Second Author Name<BR>
<DD>Description of second author's book<P>
</DL>
<P>
This example would force additional space between the author and
➥title definitions, making the grouped pairs more prominently asso
➥ciated on the page.
```

```
<H2>The Ordered List</H2>

<OL>
<LI>This is the first item in an ordered list.<P>

<LI>This is the second item in an ordered list.<P>
</OL>

Here you see how an ordered list can be spread out by using the
➥paragraph tag.

</BODY>
</HTML>
```

In figure 14.5, you see how adding spacing tags can spread out the design of a list when it is displayed in Netscape Navigator.

Figure 14.5

A display of list tags and spacing tags in combination.

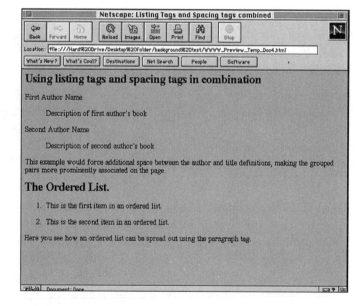

The Image Tag: <IMG>

Now we start getting to the fun stuff. You've learned the basics about building a Web page and formatting text. You undoubtedly are ready to add some images to make your page come alive. It's time to introduce the Image tag. Before we talk about the details, you'll need a general understanding of how this tag works. When you place an image in an HTML page, you are linking the image file into the HTML document.

Placing the image in relation to other elements in the HTML page is pretty straight-forward: wherever you put the Image tag, the image will appear. Therefore, if you want your image between two lines of text, put the Image tag between those lines of text. Aligning the image relative to the text is generally done within the <IMG> tag, and you'll soon learn the attributes needed to control alignment.

The complicated part for those who are new to all this is how to tell the browser where the actual image is in relationship to the HTML document. This gets into the issue of links, which will be discussed at length in the section on linking pages, but the concept is the same for images. For now, let's assume that your image and HTML files are in the same directory (for all you Mac and Windows 95 users, directory and folder mean the same thing). If your image is in the same directory as your HTML file, you can simply name the image in the Image tag and the browser will find it. For Web site organization, it is generally recommended that you keep images in a separate folder, but this will be discussed later in Chapter 12, "Web Site Organization and Manage-ment," which highlights the elements of Web site organization. The concept of relative links will also be discussed in the links section that follows in this chapter.

For now, familiarize yourself with the Image tag and its attributes. The <IMG> tag contains all the information it needs within the tag itself, and it has no closing tag. Its contents describe an image to be displayed in the browser. The image is referenced by the SRC attribute. This attribute and others are discussed as follows:

- SRC: This attribute represents the source, or URL address, (read location) of the image. If the image is in the same directory as the document, this can be described by simply naming the image. The source can be described as an absolute or relative link. If you don't understand this yet, don't worry; the <SRC> tag will be explained more in the links section and Chapter 12, and it works the same way for images and links.

- ALT: This is a great, and all too often overlooked, attribute that lets you specify text to appear in place of the image if you are surfing with images turned off or are using a text-only browser (yes, there really are still browsers out there that can't view images at all). The alternate text also appears in some browsers before the image loads on the page. If you want the viewer to navigate by clicking on an image, this attribute becomes even more important to include in the tag description.

- ALIGN: Some browsers support top, bottom, and center alignment; some support left, right, and middle; others support both. Experiment and see what works best, but be aware that this will not always display equally in all browsers.

● ISMAP: This attribute indicates that the image functions as an image map, and requires server programming. To use <ISMAP>, you'll need to include information that calls the map file, and you'll need to create a coordinates file that designates the area of the image to be linked.

The <IMG> tag can be used to insert any graphic and is a great way to add custom bullets, logos, or other graphic elements not described by HTML.

The following example demonstrates an <IMG> tag using most of the attributes just described. Once you realize that IMG SRC means Image Source, it's easier to remember. The attributes, such as ALIGN and ALT, can be placed between the IMG and SRC or after the image name, as was done here. The quotation marks are optional, but are considered good form—just make sure that you put them on both sides of the file name. Leaving off a start or end quote mark can lead to unpredictable results (for example, your image may not display at all), and a missing quote tag can be hard to find in your page.

```
<IMG SRC="name.gif" ALIGN=LEFT, ALT="Our Logo">
```

The following is an example of a simple HTML document using an <IMG> tag:

```
<HTML>
<HEAD><TITLE>The Image Tag</TITLE></HEAD>
<BODY>
<H2>Adding images is so easy...</H2>
<P>
<IMG SRC="littlecats.gif" ALT="This is a picture of two cats"
➡ALIGN=LEFT> When you align an image to the left as I have here,
➡you can expect the text that follows to appear to the right of the
➡image.<BR>
(Illustration by Tom McCain)
<P>
</BODY>
</HTML>
```

Figure 14.6 demonstrates how Netscape Navigator displays an image called in an HTML document by using the <IMG SRC> tag. Notice that this image has been aligned to the left, allowing the text to flow to the right. The space between the image and the words is created by a background area in the graphic which has been made transparent. You'll learn about other ways to control spacing around an image in the more advanced HTML sections.

Figure 14.6

The Image tag.

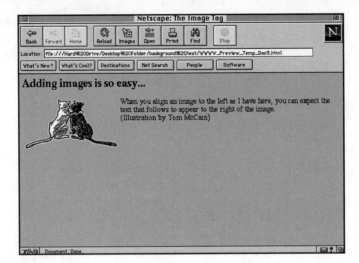

Anchor Tags

One of the most unique and exciting features the Web brings to content is the "hyperlink," made possible by the Anchor tag. A link is formatted to respond to a mouse click by opening another HTML page or element. This link can be another page in your Web site, or it can be a link to a page on another Web site anywhere else on the Internet. Links can be set by using graphics or text. When you create a hyperlink, you are telling the browser the location of the referenced item. Again, this example assumes that any page you are linking to in your Web site is in the same directory as the original HTML document. An additional example in the following text will show a link to another Web site.

The Anchor tag contains the text or graphic object referenced to or by another HTML Anchor tag or document. The Anchor tag must include the </A> tag. Anchor tag attributes include the following:

- HREF: In the basic link tag, the Anchor tag must include an HREF attribute that references the location to which the anchored text or graphic object takes you when selected.

- NAME: The NAME attribute of the Anchor tag is used to designate a specific location on a page to which you want to link. This attribute enables you to set links to another place on the same page or to a specific location on another page.

- REL: Similar to its use in the <LINK> tag in the <HEAD> section, the relationship attribute is not very common on the Web. It references another document with which it has a relationship. Possible values are "next," "previous," "parent," and "made."

● REV: This Attribute is the same as REL, except generally in the reverse direction. Again, this is not very common.

● TITLE: This is the title of the URL to which the HREF attribute links. This attribute, like REL and REV, is not commonly used.

Here's an example of a basic link tag that references another page in your Web site:

```
<A HREF="name.html">This is the text that will be linked</A>
```

Here's an example of a link tag that references another Web site:

```
<A HREF="http://www.domain_name.com">This is the text that will be
➥linked</A>
```

The following tag can also be used to set e-mail links:

```
<A HREF=MAILTO:"janine@well.com">
```

> **Note**
>
> **Relative vs. Absolute Links**
>
> You can set absolute links to pages within the same Web site by using the full URL, for example: <AHREF="http://www.domain_name.com/file-name.html">. Although this has the same overall effect of linking you to the new page, it has some drawbacks. It does work, but you are better off using a relative link, such as <A HREF="file_name.html">, rather than an absolute link that includes the full URL. First of all, if you use the longer absolute link, you will not be able to test your links on your hard drive. This is important, because you want to be able to see that everything works before you put it on a server where all your viewers can see it. In addition, you won't want to have to move everything online before you can test. Relative links are also faster. Forcing the browser to go though the entire URL to get to the page you want takes a little more time than simply having it find another file in a relative location in the same Web site.

Setting Links

You can set links anywhere within the body of an HTML page, and you can set as many links as you want on any page. Links are generally displayed as blue-underlined text or images surrounded by a blue border. After a link has been selected, its color changes to red. In many browsers, links are also indicated when the pointer changes to a hand. In later sections in this chapter, you'll learn how to change the colors of links, turn off the border on your images (a great trick because most images look bad with a blue or red border), and a few other additions that make links a more subtle and appealing part of your Web page design.

The example that follows shows an HTML page with both text and graphic links. Some link to local pages within the main Web site, using relative links, and some to external pages on another Web site. Here's what it looks like:

```
<HTML>
<HEAD><TITLE>The Anchor Tag</TITLE></HEAD>
<BODY>
<H2>Setting links...</H2>
<P>
<A HREF="cats.html"><IMG SRC="littlecats.gif" ALT="This is a pic-
➥ture of two cats" ALIGN=LEFT></A>
If you want to set a link in the text, simply <A HREF="dogs.html">
start the Anchor tag at the beginning of the text you want "hot"
and close it</A> where you want the linked text to end.<BR>
(Illustration by Tom McCain)
<P>
If you want to set a link to <A HREF="http://visiontec.com/">an-
➥other Web site</A> it would look like this.
</BODY>
</HTML>
```

Notice the underlined links in figure 14.7. This is an option in Netscape Navigator where viewers can turn off underlining in the Preferences section of the Options menu. Most graphic designers don't like underlined text, so it is recommended that you change this selection in your browser preferences. I left underlining on for now to demonstrate how the default option works in most browsers.

Figure 14.7

Underlined hypertext links.

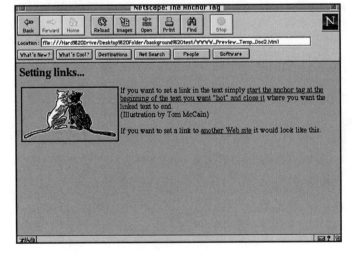

Setting Links to a Specific Part of a Page

Let's look now at the NAME attribute of the Anchor tag. This tag can be used to link to another part of the same page or to set links to a specific location on another page. An example follows to illustrate. If you set a standard link, the browser will open the page you reference, displaying the top of the page. By using the NAME attribute with the Anchor tag, you can mark a place anywhere on a page (at a particular heading in the middle of the page, for example), and then reference that in a link so that the browser display starts at the designated location.

To do this, first set an anchor at the desired location. You do this with the <A NAME="LinkName">Anything can go here</A> tag. You can wrap this around any text or graphic. Because the anchor is not a link itself, it won't change color or be underlined; the anchor is just a marker so the browser will have a target. You then indicate this kind of link by using the # sign in the link tag. If you are linking to a place on the same page, it looks like this:

```
<A HREF="#LinkName"> Anything can go here</A>
```

If you are linking from another page, it looks like this:

```
<A HREF="otherdoc.html#LinkName">Anything can go here</A>
```

Here's an example, using one document that has links to other areas of the same. The Netscape Navigator display that follows shows how the links appear in the first document and how that document would display when the link is used to go directly to the NAME set in the middle of the same document (see fig. 14.8).

```
<HTML>
<HEAD><TITLE>The Anchor Tag using the NAME attribute</TITLE></HEAD>
<BODY>
<H2><A NAME="top">The Anchor</A> Tag using the NAME attribute</H2>
<P>
Here's how you would <A HREF="#middle">link to the middle</A> of
the document where I have set the A NAME=middle. In figure 14.9,
you will see what Netscape Navigator displays if you select this
link.
<P>
The NAME attribute is generally used in long documents, but I kept
this one short so it is easy to see what is going on. Notice that
the A NAME tag does not affect the text.<P>
<H2><A NAME="middle">Let's</A> set a link so it shows up here</H2>
In addition to using this option to move around the same page, you
can also link to a specific part of another page. On the same page,
```

continues

continued

```
it is common to set a link that takes you back to the <A
HREF="top">top</A> of the page.
<P>
<A HREF="top">Back to the top</A> of the page
</BODY>
</HTML>
```

Figure 14.8

*Using the NAME
attribute.*

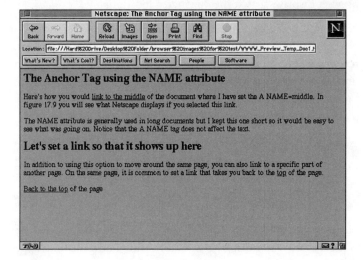

Notice that the <A NAME> reference does not affect the text the way a link tag does. The <A NAME> reference sets an invisible marker. The browser uses this marker to find the location to be displayed, but does not display the marker to the viewer (see fig. 14.9).

Here you see what is displayed when the link to the middle of the page is selected. Notice that the browser displays the headline marked with the <NAME> attribute at the very top of the window.

Figure 14.9

How the NAME attribute displays.

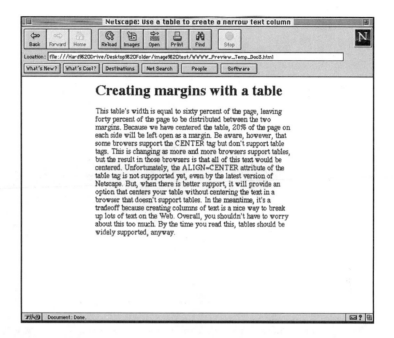

The Horizontal Rule Tag

The Horizontal Rule tag <HR> provides another way to add space and break up an HTML document. It has no closing tag and no attributes in HTML 2.0, but you will learn ways to provide greater variation later in the HTML 3.2 section. This tag inserts a horizontal line across the page. Unlike spacing tags, this tag can be used repetitively. In HTML 2, this tag has no attributes.

Here's what it looks like in use:

```
<HTML>
<HEAD><TITLE>The Horizontal Rule Tag</TITLE></HEAD>
<BODY>
<H2>The Horizontal Rule Tag</H2>
<P>
The Horizontal Rule tag puts a line across the browser display like
this:
<P>
<HR>
<P>
You can use it as much as you like, but I recommend you use it
sparingly.
<P>
<HR>
```

continues

continued

```
</BODY>
</HTML>
```

In figure 14.10, you see the line across the browser created by the <HR> tag.

Figure 14.10

The Horizontal Rule tag.

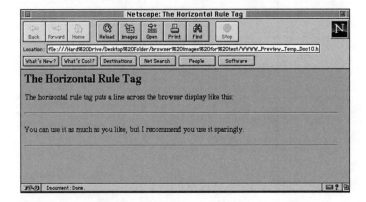

> **Note**
>
> **Don't Overuse the HR Tag**
>
> Many graphics "experts" recommend not using the ‹HR› tag because it puts such a dramatic break in a page. I would recommend using it sparingly. Consider alternatives to break up your page layout, such as small graphics and other features you'll learn about in the HTML 3.2 section.

Forms in HTML 2.0

Creating forms in your Web site is a great way to invite comments, feedback, orders, and other interaction from your viewers. Forms enable viewers to enter or access information. Be aware, however, that creating forms is more complicated than the other HTML options we've reviewed so far. And although forms are part of the HTML 2.0 specification, not all browsers support them. You also need to understand that there are two crucial parts to a form. The HTML designer provides the display side of the form by using HTML tags to create the design, but for the form to function, a programmer must create a program that enables the form to cause some action. For example, the form may collect data to be sent to a specific e-mail address or it may enter the information into a database. The programming side is called the Common Gateway Interface (CGI) script and is generally written in a language such as Perl or C++. The script processes the data from the fields returned by the user and interacts with the server containing the form document.

To help you understand this better, a diagram is included at the end of this section to demonstrate what a CGI script does and how it works. Many service providers offer simple form scripts to their Web site clients. You'll need to talk to your system administrator to find out how to refer to the CGI script and what it can do. If your server does not provide such scripts, refer to Appendix C for online resources for free CGI scripts and information on how to create them.

Form Tags

The <FORM> tag contains all the other form elements and must be closed with the </FORM> tag. The <FORM> tag can contain other HTML tags, and it's a good idea to use header tags, spacing tags, and other formatting options to make your forms more readable. Tables, which you'll learn about in the HTML 3.2 section, are also a good way to format forms, as they enable greater control of spacing between the captions and the fields in a form.

The <FORM> tag has the following attributes. Many of these relate to the CGI script used to process the form. Again, note that this information depends on the script:

- ACTION: This attribute targets the URL of the CGI script that processes the form field data.

- METHOD: This attribute describes the manner in which the form field data will be processed. Possible values are GET or POST.

- <INPUT>: This form field enables the user to enter data in a manner determined by the type attribute. In HTML 2.0, this tag has the following attributes:

  - TYPE: Determines how the form field is processed and appears in the browser. Possible values are TEXT, PASSWORD, HIDDEN, RADIO, CHECKBOX, SUBMIT, RESET, and IMAGE.

  - NAME: Names the input tag. In the case of radio buttons, NAME is shared by all input tags in a group. In other types of input files, the NAME may vary. This is used for processing by the host computer.

  - VALUE: Defines a value for the input tag entry.

  - SIZE: Sets the width of the TEXT or PASSWORD type and is measured in number of text characters.

  - MAXLENGTH: Sets the number of characters permitted in the TEXT- or PASSWORD-type INPUT field.

  - SRC: Sets the file source of an IMAGE type in the <INPUT> tag.

HTML Tutorial and Reference

Form Input Types

There are a number of TYPE definitions for the <INPUT> tag as defined in the bulleted list that follows. In particular, be aware of the difference between the RADIO button and CHECKBOX. RADIO enables only one selection at a time, usually of mutually exclusive categories. With CHECKBOX, you can list multiple options. Its selections are generally nonexclusive, and it is expected that more than one option will, at least on occasion, be chosen.

- <CHECKBOX>: The CHECKBOX selection allows multiple selections of options. This also uses the NAME and VALUE attributes, but requires each option to have a unique NAME. The VALUE is passed on to the computer only if the CHECKBOX is selected.

- <HIDDEN>: This field is not visible at browser level and is used for form processing by the computer serving the HTML documents. It uses the NAME and VALUE attributes.

- <IMAGE>: Sets an image type. This type supports selection by clicking on an image specified by the SRC attribute and uses the NAME, VALUE, and SRC attributes.

- <OPTION>: Defines a single selection within an option group. There is no closing Option tag. It has the following attributes:

  - NAME: This names the selection, but does not determine the value as read by the server.

  - VALUE: Associates each selection as a value for each variable named by the SELECT tag.

  - SELECTED: As the form page is first accessed, this attribute highlights the default option selection. This can only be used once in an option group, unless the MULTIPLE attribute is contained in the SELECT tag. Use this if you want to set a default option, such as United States in a list of countries when you know most of your users will select United States.

- <PASSWORD>: This is used for password entry and uses the NAME, VALUE, SIZE, and MAXLENGTH attributes. For security reasons, data entered into this field is usually obscured by asterisks or other characters in the browser display.

- <RADIO>: The RADIO button enables only one selection from the options and uses NAME and VALUE attributes. To limit the selection options, the same NAME is used for all options.

- <RESET>: The RESET button resets all the form field data entered to give users the chance to start over. Again, by using the VALUE attribute, you can put any text you want on this button—for example, <RESET VALUE=I changed my mind, let me try again>.

- <SELECT>: Defines an option group and contains Option tags. This looks like a pop-up menu or list in the browser display. Some browsers do not support all its attributes, which are the following:

  - NAME: This attribute names the SELECT option group and is used for processing by the host computer.

  - SIZE: This attribute sets the height of the SELECT entry box as measured in lines of text. The list will scroll as necessary.

  - MULTIPLE: This attribute enables you to select more than one option from a SELECT option group.

- <SUBMIT>: The SUBMIT button sends the form field data back to the computer that will process the information. The VALUE attribute is used here to change the visible name on the button to something other than SUBMIT. Using VALUE=, you can change this to anything you want—for example, <SUBMIT VALUE=Charge my credit card>.

- <TEXT>: This creates a text input area and uses the NAME, VALUE, SIZE, and MAXLENGTH attributes.

- <TEXTAREA>: Unlike the <INPUT> tag, this tag supports multiple lines of text. Although defined within the HTML 2.0 specifications, this tag is not supported by all browsers. It is useful, however, for comment areas and other places where users may want to enter multiple lines of text. You would expect that setting the width of a text area would force a return at the end of each line as it comes to the edge of the box. Unfortunately, that will only happen if you use the WRAP attribute, supported by even fewer browsers. Thus many of your viewers will have to enter a carriage return to move to the next line within the text area box. The <TEXTAREA> tag has the following attributes:

  - NAME: This attribute names the TEXTAREA and is used for processing by the host computer.

  - ROWS: Sets the height of the TEXTAREA, as measured by the number of lines of text displayed. This does not control the amount of text a user can enter.

- COLS: Width of the TEXTAREA, as measured by the number of text characters displayed. Again, this does not control the amount of text a user can enter and will not force a return at the end unless the WRAP attribute that follows is also included.

- WRAP: This attribute is not supported as widely as the other three, but it greatly improves the intuitive use of the text area, because it forces a return at the end of the line when a user types to the edge of the box.

Browser Support for Forms

Most browsers are able to recognize forms these days. In addition to wanting forms supported, many companies and individuals are demanding security in form processing. Netscape and Microsoft are both developing their own security protocols, which are optimized when both their server and client products are used. Security issues should not affect your HTML design too much, although Navigator 3.0 has added new HTML tags specifically for security issues. The differences between browser displays of forms are relatively minimal if you stick to the HTML 2.0 tags.

Here's an example:

```
<HTML>
<HEAD>
<TITLE>The Form Tags</TITLE>
</HEAD>
<BODY>
<H1>Form Elements</H1>
<FORM METHOD=POST ACTION="/cgi-bin/">
We will start with a simple text box: <BR>
Name: <INPUT TYPE="text" SIZE=45 MAXLENGTH=10><P>
Radio buttons:<BR>
Gender:
<INPUT TYPE="radio" NAME="Sex" VALUE="Male">Male
<INPUT TYPE="radio" NAME="Sex" VALUE="Female">Female
<P>
Checkboxes:<BR>
Music:
<INPUT TYPE="checkbox" NAME="Rock"> Rock
<INPUT TYPE="checkbox" NAME="Country"> Country
<P>
```

```
A pop-up menu. If you select this box, you will see options two and
➥three.<BR>
<SELECT name="list" width=300>
<OPTION VALUE="First">One
<OPTION VALUE="Second">Two
<OPTION SELECTED VALUE="Third">Three
</SELECT>
<P>
With this variation, all options are displayed.<BR>
<SELECT name="list" size="3" MULTIPLE width=300>
<OPTION VALUE="First">First
<OPTION VALUE="Second">Second
<OPTION SELECTED VALUE="Third">Third
</SELECT>
<P>\
A text area. (Note: If you insert text between the TEXTAREA tags,
➥it will be visible in the text box when the document is
➥loaded.)<BR>
<TEXTAREA ROWS=3 COLS=40 WRAP></TEXTAREA>
<P>
Submit and Reset buttons with send and cancel selection as
➥values.<BR>
<INPUT TYPE="SUBMIT" VALUE="Send Selection">
<INPUT TYPE="RESET" VALUE="Cancel Selection">
</FORM>
</BODY>
</HTML>
```

Figure 14.11 provides a view of an HTML form as it is displayed in the Netscape Navigator browser.

Note

CGI Scripts for Forms

The HTML for a form is only part of what is needed to create an interactive form. The HTML tags described here create the display of the form, but you will also need a CGI script to process the user input in a form. Most service providers offer a simple form script that will cause the form data to be sent to a specified e-mail address. To use this script, you will need to talk to your system administrator or service provider so that you can call the script properly, using the form tag attributes. Many forms scripts also require supplementary files, such as a CONF (confirmation) file that designates the e-mail address the data should be sent to.

HTML Tutorial and Reference

Figure 14.11

An HTML form.

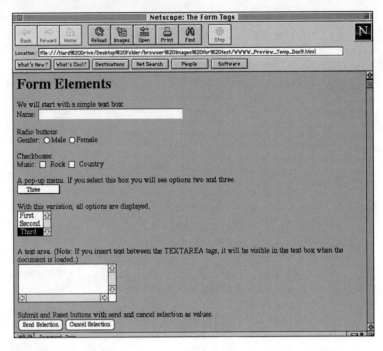

Form Design Considerations

To design great Web pages, you need a combination of HTML tags. Keep this in mind when designing forms and remember that you are not limited to only form tags within your forms. The following is an example of a form designed by using other HTML tags to add formatting control.

```
<HTML>
<HEAD><TITLE>Survey of Ice Cream Favorites</TITLE></HEAD>
<BODY>
<H1>Survey of Ice Cream Favorites</H1>
<FORM>
<DL>
<DL>
<DT><IMG ALIGN=TOP SRC="red_ball.gif"> <STRONG>What is your favor
ite ice cream?</STRONG>
<P>
<DD><INPUT TYPE="radio" NAME="Favorite">Rocky Road
<DD><INPUT TYPE="radio" NAME="Favorite">Strawberry Shortcake
<DD><INPUT TYPE="radio" NAME="Favorite">Vanilla
<DD><INPUT TYPE="radio" NAME="Favorite">Peach
<DD><INPUT TYPE="radio" NAME="Favorite">Mud Pie
</DL>
<P>
```

```
<DL>
<DT><IMG ALIGN=TOP SRC="red_ball.gif"> <STRONG>What are your favor
ite toppings?</STRONG> <EM>(Please select only one)</EM>
<P>
<DD><INPUT TYPE="checkbox" NAME="Hot Fudge"> Hot Fudge
<DD><INPUT TYPE="checkbox" NAME="Strawberry"> Strawberry
<DD><INPUT TYPE="checkbox" NAME="Blueberry"> Blueberry
<DD><INPUT TYPE="checkbox" NAME="Caramel"> Caramel
<DD><INPUT TYPE="checkbox" NAME="Whipped Cream"> Whipped Cream
</DL>
</DL>
</FORM>
</BODY>
</HTML>
```

In this example, the <DL> definition list tag has been used to give an indented layout to the form elements. Notice also that the <DL> tags have been nested to give greater indentation. A graphic element has also been integrated, in this case just a simple red bullet. Any image that can be used on a Web page can be integrated into a form (see fig. 14.12).

Figure 14.12

*Integrating form tags
with other HTML tags.*

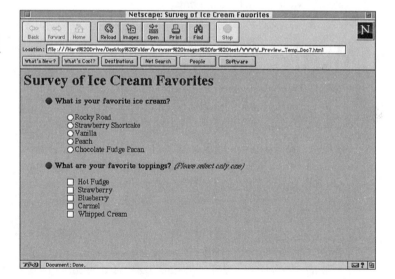

HTML 2.0 Wrap-Up

Experiment, experiment, experiment, and then test, test, test. That's the best advice I can offer for learning good Web design. One of the greatest advantages to HTML development is that you can immediately test your design in a browser and see how it looks. Some of the HTML authoring tools described in this book facilitate such testing by providing a preview option. Most browsers, however, will let you open a local file directly and, assuming you have set relative links, you can test all your pages and links on your hard drive as you create them.

In this section, you've learned the basics: HTML 2.0, the most widely supported of the HTML tags and the simplest to master in general. In the following sections, you'll learn about the more advanced options of HTML 3.2 and the browser-specific features added by Netscape and Microsoft extensions. You'll learn about tables, one of the greatest additions for format control in HTML, as well as such controversial features as Netscape Navigator frames, now supported by the latest versions of Microsoft's Internet Explorer, with support from other browsers promised soon.

The HTML versions have been broken into these sections for two reasons. First, starting with the HTML 2.0 specification gives you a basic introduction without overwhelming you with the other, more advanced features. Now that you have learned these tags, you should be well prepared to add the attributes and other tags that come next. These have also been broken down to help you understand the differences among browser support and, similarly, the kinds of features you will find in HTML authoring tools. After you understand that there is more than one variety of HTML, you will better understand the differences among the software programs designed to create and view HTML documents.

HTML 3.2

HTML 3.2 is the new specification for HTML, developed by the W3C after more than a year of debate and meetings with developers and companies such as IBM, Microsoft, Netscape, Novell, SoftQuad, Spyglass, and Sun Microsystems.

HTML 3.2 makes official many HTML tags and attributes that have already been supported on the Web for some time by such browsers as Netscape Navigator and Microsoft's Internet Explorer. Although it does make official some of the most popular features of the previously proposed HTML 3.0 specification, HTML 3.2 lacks many options HTML designers had hoped for. Specific font sizes and type, for example, are not recognized as official HTML, even though Microsoft and Netscape now enable their use. These and many other features already in use on the Web, such as frames, are still not "official" HTML and thus may never be supported by all the browsers and authoring tools on the Net.

What Happened to HTML 3.0?

You'll find this question on the W3C Web site, so you know I'm not the first to ask. Their answer goes like this:

> "HTML 3.0 was a proposal for extending HTML published in March 1995 ... However, the difference between HTML 2.0 and HTML 3.0 was so large that standardization and deployment of the whole proposal proved unwieldy. The HTML 3.0 draft has expired, and is not being maintained."

In other words, W3C couldn't agree on everything so they threw a bunch of it out, settled on the options everyone felt they had to have, and went home. This comes, mind you, after more than a year of debate and recommendations from developers all over the Web. The problem for HTML designers is that while the W3C was arguing about what would become "official" HTML, many browsers and development tools began to implement those "proposed" HTML 3.0 tags anyway.

Today, a mess exists on the Web because there are so many versions of HTML. This means that the next thing you should know is what's now considered "official" HTML 3.2, even though many software companies don't support these tags yet. (Bear in mind that Netscape and Microsoft have additional tags that are not part of 3.2, but even *they* don't support all the newly official 3.2 tags and attributes.) When finished looking at 3.2, you'll learn that the most controversial set of HTML tags are the ones Microsoft and Netscape created on their own because they weren't willing to wait for the W3C. (As much as standards are appreciated and the current Web chaos that makes the Web far less than accessible to all viewers is despised, most Web designers appreciate having the option of the HTML tags described in this chapter.) So, once again, you'll see which tags are widely supported and which ones to watch out for, and learn a couple of workarounds. This will help ensure your pages are presentable to everyone—even if some viewers are still using limited browsers such as AOL and Mosaic.

Third-Party HTML 3.2 Extensions

The W3C continues to "work with vendors," (read as argue and debate) on extensions that will support multimedia objects, scripting, style sheets, layout, and math. According to their Web site: "W3C plans on incorporating this work in further versions of HTML. See The W3C Activity Statement on HTML for details." You can find those statements on their Web site at http://www.w3c.org/. They make a point of requesting that you read about current debates and proposals before you add your own suggestions. Unless you think you have something really stellar to offer, however, you shouldn't bother. Learn about all the tags available on the Web, such as frames and the ability to insert multimedia features, even if they aren't official HTML and may never become sanctioned by the W3C. If you design your pages carefully, and test them in a

HTML Tutorial and Reference

low-end browser or two to make sure everything still works, you can get away with a lot more than the W3C has made possible and create much more interesting pages.

What's New in HTML 3.2

The main features added to the "official" set of HTML tags are tables, applets, text flow around images, superscripts, and subscripts. In addition, a host of new attributes add greater design control to the tags you learned about in HTML 2.0. Overall, however, not that much has changed.

HTML 3.2 builds on HTML 2.0, so in the following sections on new tags, you will see some repetition. This should serve as a review for the previous section and help you better understand how the new tags fit in. Greater explanation will be provided as completely new tags are introduced in the following pages.

The <!DOCTYPE> Tag

The first addition you'll find in HTML 3.2 is the <!DOCTYPE> declaration. This tag, set off as a comment line so it doesn't display on screen, is designed purely to distinguish HTML 3.2 from other versions of HTML and should be the first thing on the page, even before the <HTML> tag. This tag is optional. As the W3C readily admits, many documents don't contain a <!DOCTYPE> declaration. Inclusion of this new tag is not a bad idea because it helps browsers, validation tools, and other software determine the version of HTML used in your HTML pages. Here's how the code should look in a simple HTML page:

```
<!DOCTYPE HTML PUBLIC "-//W3C//DTD HTML 3.2//EN">
<HTML>
<HEAD>
<TITLE>HTML 3.2</TITLE>
</HEAD>
<BODY>
Aren't you glad they finally approved HTML 3.2?
</BODY>
</HTML>
```

The HEAD Element

The <HEAD> tag, as introduced in HTML 2.0, is where you put the TITLE, the only part of this section of the document that will display. The TITLE appears at the top of your browser window, not in the HTML page itself. Two new additions are described next, even though they have not been widely implemented into browsers.

The other HEAD tags introduced in HTML 2.0 are, of course, still valid, though not as common as the TITLE. The following new elements belong in the document head:

- STYLE: This looks promising for graphic designers, but don't get too excited. STYLE doesn't officially do anything yet. It's reserved for future use with style sheets.

- SCRIPT: Another promising addition that lets the browser know that a scripting language application is running. The scripting language is specified by the <LANGUAGE> attribute. This will probably be expanded for other scripting languages in the near future.

You should note that TITLE, STYLE, and SCRIPT require both open and close tags, while the other elements do not use close tags.

The BODY Element

All text and other elements on a Web page should be placed between the <BODY> tags. The 3.2 specification adds some great attributes to the <BODY> tag. Although they have been widely used because Netscape and Microsoft have supported them for some time, you can now officially add background color and images, and text and link colors. All the attributes described in the following list fall within the <BODY> tag, as they affect the entire HTML document.

- BACKGROUND: This is where you set a background image.

- BGCOLOR: This attribute is used with hexadecimal color codes to set a solid color background. You'll learn more about hexadecimal colors later, but for now understand they are rather cryptic six-digit codes that represent RGB colors. You can also use the 16 common color names, detailed later in this chapter, but they are not supported by as many browsers as hexadecimal codes.

- TEXT: This attribute is used with a hexadecimal color code to set the text color in a document. Again, you can also use the 16 color names. This will change all regular text from black to the color you specify.

- LINK: This attribute uses a hexadecimal color code or color name to set the color for hyperlinks.

- VLINK: This attribute distinguishes a visited link from the standard link so that you can have link colors that change when someone has selected them.

- ALINK: This attribute represents an activated link and displays the selected color as someone selects the link.

Changing Link Colors

The capability to change link colors is a welcome addition to HTML. The default colors are blue for an active link and red for a visited link—not very intuitive when you think that blue is hot and red is cold on the Web. Be aware, however, that you should always use different colors for visited links than for active links so that viewers have the navigational reference of what they have already seen. Also note that many monitors may display colors darker than your monitor does. Be careful not to set colors that are hard to see against your backgrounds.

Changing <BODY> Attribute Colors

If you change one or more of the BODY attributes, it is a good idea to change them all and make sure they will look good together. Consider this example of what could happen if you don't: you set the background color to white and take for granted the text will be black. A viewer who visits your page with the browser's default background set to black and default text to white will not be able to view your page. Thus, even if you set the text to black and most people don't even notice it (because their default text color is already black), it's a good idea because of the viewers who may have changed the colors in their browsers.

> **Note**
>
> Although most designers use either a background color or a background image, it is possible to use both in combination. Both will not display in the same browser. Some browsers still don't support background images, however, so adding a background color attribute means you will at least have a colored background if your lovely background image can't be seen.

When you set a background color, the browser fills the entire screen with that color. A background image is repeated horizontally and vertically to fill the entire screen. Note that images don't load as quickly as hexadecimal colors, so make sure any background image you use is small and fast. Don't leave viewers waiting just to see wallpaper on your page—they may leave before your page even arrives. For more information on how to create good background images, check out the image conversion section in Chapter 11. If you want to use a background image, the BODY tag should look like this:

```
<BODY BACKGROUND="image.gif" TEXT="#FF0000" LINK="#FFCC33"
 ➥VLINK="#9260FF" ALINK="#F212FF">
```

The following is an example of a simple HTML document using the BODY attributes with hexadecimal color codes:

```
<HTML>
<HEAD><TITLE>Background and Text colors</TITLE></HEAD>
<BODY BGCOLOR="#000000" TEXT="#FF0000" LINK="#FFCC33"
➥VLINK="#9260FF" ALINK="#F212FF">
<H1>Background and text colors</H1>
➥Notice that the background fills with a solid color, in this case
➥black because I've set the hexadecimal code to 000000, the code
➥for black. The code for white is FFFFFF.
<A HREF="link1.html">This is an example of a hyperlink that would
➥display in the LINK color set above.</A><P>
<A HREF="link2.html">Once the link has been selected, the color
➥changes to the visited link, or VLINK color.</A><P>
<A HREF="link3.html">The activated link, ALINK, color only displays
➥while it is being selected.</A><P>
</BODY>
</HTML>
```

Notice in figure 14.13 that the background is set to the hexadecimal color code for black; thus, I have used relatively light colors for the words that will display. The text in this image is red, hyperlinks are yellow, visited links are purple, and activated links are pink.

Figure 14.13

Background and text colors.

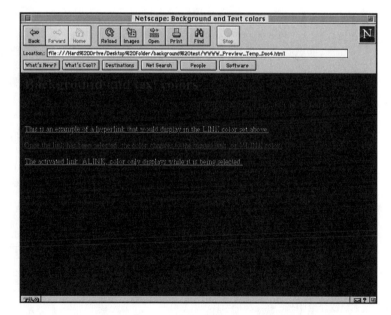

Hexadecimal Color Codes

Before we go on to the browser-specific extensions, let's take a minute to catch up on those cryptic hexadecimal color codes. Don't forget that in addition to hexadecimal colors, many browsers will now display named colors, using any of the 16 common colors: aqua, black, blue, fuchsia, gray, green, lime, maroon, navy, olive, purple, red, silver, teal, white, and yellow. This is, however, a very limited list of color options, and because hexadecimal colors are more widely supported by browsers than the color names, you are still generally better off with the hexadecimal color codes.

Before you start stressing about the hexadecimal system, you should know that there are lots of utilities out there that will calculate these codes for you, and many of the authoring tools included in this book include color utilities for this purpose. In Appendix B, you'll find a list of shareware and freeware utilities that can be used to calculate hexadecimal color codes by selecting any color from a color wheel. For those of you who still want to know how this works, move on to the following explanation.

The Hexadecimal Color Coding System

The hexadecimal color coding system uses a base 16 reference. Using base 16, there are 256 possible values for Red, Green, and Blue, using two digits for each color. Base 16 numbers and their corresponding base 10 equivalents are as follows:

0	1	2	3	4	5	6	7	8	9	A	B	C	D	E	F	10
0	1	2	3	4	5	6	7	8	9	10	11	12	13	14	15	16

11	12	13	14	15	16	17	18	19	1A	1B	1C	1D	1E	1F	20
17	18	19	20	21	22	23	24	25	26	27	28	29	30	31	32

As shown in the table, the A takes the place of 10; the B takes the place of 11; the C takes the place of 12; the D takes the place of 13; the E takes the place of the 14; and the F takes the place of the 15, with 16 represented by 10; 17 by 11; 18 by 12, and so on. To take command of the color in this new medium, you need to become familiar with both the hexadecimal numbering system and the RGB method of manipulating colors. If you have used Photoshop or another program that uses an RGB color-based system, you have probably had some experience in combining the Red, Green, and Blue colors to create blends. The hexadecimal color coding works in this same way. The six characters that describe the color are interpreted as follows:

RGB Values

Red	Green	Blue
XX	XX	XX

The first two digits give a value for Red, the second two for Green, and the third for Blue. The range in hexadecimal is 00 to FF, or 0 to 255. Cyan is the opposite of Red; Magenta is the opposite of Green; Yellow is the opposite of Blue. If you need more Yellow in a color, decrease the number given to the Blue component. Graphic designers will be using the colors in hexadecimal just as they would with Photoshop. The only problem might be in doing some of the math conversions. If you're still completely in the dark on this, don't fret—just check out one of those nifty utilities mentioned and they'll take care of it for you.

Text Formatting Tags

In the following sections, text-formatting tags will be broken down into what the W3C calls *Block-Level elements*, meaning those that cause paragraph breaks, and *Text-Level elements*, meaning those that don't add space to your document. Common Block-Level elements that cause breaks include the header discussed earlier, <H1> through <H6> in HTML 3.2, as well as <P> (paragraph) tags,
 (break) tags, <LI> (list items), and <HR> (horizontal rules). Contrast these with text elements that don't force space into the document, such as <EM> (emphasis), <I> (italics), and <B> (bold).

Block-Level Tags

As mentioned in the preceding paragraph, W3C defines Block-Level tags as those tags that are responsible for creating paragraph breaks within Web page text. The following sections will go into more detail about each of the individual tags that perform paragraph breaks.

Headings

The HTML 3.2 specification adds alignment options to the header tags. You still have the same headings (H1, H2, H3, H4, H5, and H6) and you will always need the open and close tags; however, now you can have alignment control by using the new ALIGN attribute.

Here's an example:

```
<HTML>
<HEAD><TITLE>Header tags with alignment</TITLE></HEAD>
<BODY BGCOLOR="#FFFFFF">
<H1 ALIGN=CENTER> This displays as the largest size heading,
➥aligned in the center, and would force a hard return at the end of
➥the close tag.</H2>
<H2 ALIGN=RIGHT> This displays as the second largest size, aligned
```

continues

continued

```
➥to the right, and would force a hard return at the end of the
➥close tag.</H2>
<H3 ALIGN=LEFT> This displays as the third largest size, aligned to
➥the left, and would force a hard return at the end of the close
➥tag.</H3>
<H4 ALIGN=CENTER> This displays as the fourth largest size heading,
➥aligned in the center, and would force a hard return at the end of
➥the close tag.</H4>
 <H5 ALIGN=RIGHT> This displays as the fifth largest size, aligned
➥to the right, and would force a hard return at the end of the
➥close tag.</H5>
<H6 ALIGN=LEFT> This displays as the sixth largest size, aligned to
➥the right, and would force a hard return at the end of the close
➥tag.</H6>
</BODY>
</HTML>
```

In figure 14.14, you see the display of all of the header tags, using varied alignment options.

Figure 14.14

Header tags with alignment.

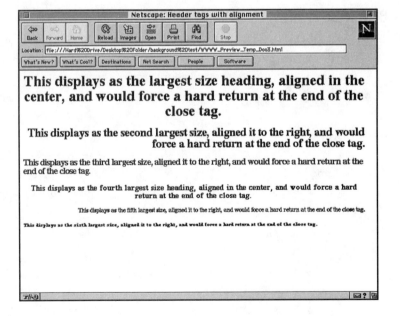

Other Block-Level Tags

Heading tags are not the only ones that initiate paragraph breaks. For design reasons, you may want to offset specific text to highlight their importance. This text may not always be appropriate as a heading. Luckily, you have several other formatting options available to you as described in the following list.

- ● **<P>**: The Paragraph tag still puts a return followed by a blank line in your document, but in HTML 3.2, the ALIGN attribute is also added to the Paragraph tag. Use this tag to control alignment of images, for example, or for text that is not formatted with a header tag. The paragraph requires an open tag, but the close tag is optional. If you are using the ALIGN attribute, however, you should always include the close tag to inform the browser of where your alignment formatting ends.

- ● **<UL>**: Unordered lists have not changed in HTML 3.2. They still require open and close tags and still contain the <LI> tag to create bullets before list items.

- ● **<OL>**: Ordered lists are also the same and use the <LI> tag to represent numbers.

- ● **<DL>**: Definition lists remain unchanged in HTML 3.2.

- ● **<PRE>**: Preformatted text is unchanged and displays in a monospaced font, with the layout as it is typed in the document.

- ● **<DIV>**: This tag is new and is used to help create divisions and align information in a document. Again, the ALIGN attribute can be used with LEFT, CENTER, or RIGHT. <DIV> requires both open and close tags and is used to group related elements together.

- ● **<CENTER>**: The Center tag was originally created by Netscape and is now official HTML. This is another text alignment tag that uses open <CENTER> and close </CENTER> tags around text, images, or other elements to provide alignment.

- ● **<BLOCKQUOTE>**: This tag is the same as it was in HTML 2.0. It is generally used for quotations and set off with indented margins on each side.

- ● **<ISINDEX>**: This tag is so old it was created before the FORM tag in HTML 2.0. When used in the body of a document, it can serve as a way to indicate a simple form, such as one that has only a single text input field. It has no close tag.

● <HR>: The Horizontal Rule tag now offers attributes to provide greater formatting control in your Web pages. You can now control the width, height, size, and shading. Here are the new attributes:

    ● WIDTH: This attribute enables you to control the width of the HR line using pixels or a percentage.

    ● SIZE: This attribute enables you to set the height of the HR line.

    ● NOSHADE: This attribute enables you to turn off the shading feature of the HR line that gives it the three-dimensional look. If you use NOSHADE, the HR link will appear as a solid, black line.

    ● ALIGN: This attribute controls alignment, using LEFT, RIGHT, and CENTER.

Here's some example HTML code for the new tags and the tags that have new attributes:

```
<HTML>
<HEAD><TITLE>Block elements with attributes</TITLE></HEAD>
<BODY>
<H1>Block elements with attributes</H1>
➥<P ALIGN=RIGHT> The paragraph tag can now include alignment op-
➥tions. This will be aligned to the right. Although the close P tag
➥is optional, if you use the alignment attribute you should include
➥the close tag to designate where the alignment formatting should
➥stop.</P>
<DIV ALIGN=CENTER> This tag can be used with any text or images, as
➥can the P and CENTER tags. In the following example, I've used the
➥DIV tag to align an image.</DIV>
<DIV ALIGN=CENTER><IMG WIDTH=184 HEIGHT=98 ALT="Friendly cats"
➥SRC="littlecats.gif"></DIV>
<CENTER> The center tag has the same effect as DIV ALIGN=CENTER
➥but, obviously, is used only for center alignment.</CENTER>
<P>
This is an HR tag using height and width attributes as well as
➥alignment and NOSHADE
<HR WIDTH=40% SIZE=5 ALIGN=CENTER NOSHADE>
<P>
Here's another example of an HR tag using different values for the
➥attributes without the NOSHADE attribute:
<HR WIDTH=80% SIZE=3 ALIGN=LEFT>
</BODY>
</HTML>
```

The addition of attributes to the block-formatting tags makes it possible to control the alignment and, as seen here in the <HR> example, the size and width of <HR> lines (see fig. 14.15).

Figure 14.15

Block-Level tags with attributes.

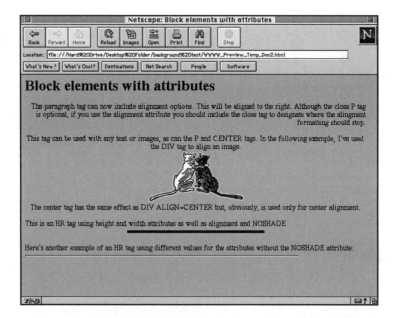

HTML Tutorial and Reference

Text-Level Tags

Text elements affect formatting without forcing paragraph breaks. These tags can be nested and can contain other text-level tags, but cannot contain Block-Level tags. All of these require open and close tags, and most of them are the same ones you learned in HTML 2.0. The tags that remain unchanged include <B> bold, <I> italic, <TT> teletype or monospaced text, <U> underlined text, and <STRIKE>, which puts a line through the text. The new Text-Level tags added in HTML 3.2 are as follows:

- <BIG>: This tag formats your text in a larger font size than the default and is handy because it does not force a line break in your text.

- <SMALL>: This tag formats your text in a smaller font size than the default and does not force a line break in your text.

- <SUB>: This tag can be used to create a subscript style.

- <SUP>: This tag can be used to create a superscript style.

Phrase Elements

The W3C breaks out the following tags as phrase elements. Again, all of these require open and close tags. They remain unchanged since HTML 2.0, but they will be explained briefly as a refresher:

- <EM>: Generally displays as italics.

- <STRONG>: Generally displays as bold.

- <CODE>: Used to display program code.

- <SAMP>: Another fixed-width tag usually used for sample output from programs and scripts.

- <KBD>: Used for text that is to be typed by the user.

- <VAR>: Used for variables or arguments to commands.

- <CITE>: Intended for use with citations or references to other sources.

Special Text-Level Elements: The <FONT> Tag

The <FONT> tag addition to HTML was first introduced and supported by Netscape. The FONT tag enables you to specify a size and a color for the text (see fig. 14.16). You still can't use specific point sizes, but this does give you more options for setting relative sizes and is especially useful because it does not force a line break in your text the way header tags do. Be aware, however, that FONT is still not supported by many browsers. Thus, when appropriate, you are better off using the header tags. Here are the attributes:

- SIZE: The FONT tag uses sizes 1 through 7. In contrast to the header tags, FONT SIZE 1 is the smallest, and SIZE 7 is the largest.

- COLOR: The color attribute can use a hexadecimal color code or any of the 16 widely understood color names: aqua, black, blue, fuchsia, gray, green, lime, maroon, navy, olive, purple, red, silver, teal, white, and yellow.

Figure 14.16

The FONT tag.

Here's an example of the FONT tag in use:

```
<HTML>
<HEAD><TITLE>The FONT tag</TITLE></HEAD>
<BODY BGCOLOR=#FFFFFF>
<CENTER><FONT SIZE=6 COLOR=#FF0000>The FONT tag</FONT><BR>
<FONT SIZE=6>T</FONT>he FONT tag is great if you only want <FONT
➥SIZE=5>part of a line</FONT> to be a larger size.
<P>
<FONT SIZE=1>This is FONT SIZE 1</FONT><P>
<FONT SIZE=2>This is FONT SIZE 2</FONT><P>
<FONT SIZE=3>This is FONT SIZE 3</FONT><P>
<FONT SIZE=4>This is FONT SIZE 4</FONT><P>
<FONT SIZE=5>This is FONT SIZE 5</FONT><P>
<FONT SIZE=6>This is FONT SIZE 6</FONT><P>
<FONT SIZE=7>This is FONT SIZE 7</FONT><P>
<FONT COLOR=BLUE>This text will display in blue at the browser's
➥default size</FONT><P>
<FONT SIZE=4 COLOR=#FF0000>This text will display in red, using the
➥hexidecimal color code at font size 4</FONT><P>
<FONT SIZE=5 COLOR=PURPLE>This text will display in purple at font
➥size 5</FONT><P>
</CENTER>
```

continues

continued

```
</BODY>
</HTML>
```

The Break Tag

The Break tag <BR>, as you saw in HTML 2.0, adds a line break, but the new CLEAR attribute provided by HTML 3.2 is very helpful.

The CLEAR attribute of the <BR> tag lets you force text to move down below an image on a page and can be set to LEFT or RIGHT. This is useful when you have an image you want to align so you can wrap text, but you want other text to appear below the image instead of beside it. There was no easy way to control the spacing until we got the CLEAR attribute.

Thus, <BR CLEAR=LEFT> and <BR CLEAR=RIGHT> will give you greater control of text in relation to images.

In the following HTML example, the <BR CLEAR=LEFT> tag is marked by bold, italic text so it stands out:

```
<HTML>
<HEAD><TITLE>Profile</TITLE></HEAD>
<BODY bgcolor="#000000" text="#ff0000" LINK="#7777ff"
➥ALINK="#7777ff" VLINK="#7777ff">
<CENTER>
<H2>Jett Film & Video Profile</H2>
<STRONG>Hands-on coordination from pre-production through post<
➥STRONG>
<P>
<HR width=80%>
<H3>Producer/Director Richard Jett</H3>
<STRONG>Send E-mail to <A HREF="MAILTO:rjett@connectmedia.com">Jett
➥Film</A></STRONG></CENTER>
<P>
<IMG ALIGN=LEFT ALT="Richard Jett" SRC="Graphics/richard.jpg">
<H2>References</H2>
Jim Brown, EvensGroup<BR>
415-398-2669<BR>
Lori Anderson, Varitel Video<BR>
415-495-3328<BR>
Tom Banducci, Bay Shore Studios<BR>
415-282-7250<BR>
Chuck Jessen, Jessen Advertising<BR>
415-391-5030
<BR CLEAR=LEFT>
```

HTML Tutorial and
Reference

```
<CENTER><hr width=80%></CENTER>
<H2 align="center">Education</H2>
A.A. Degree Electronic Engineering, Fullerton Jr. College<br>
B.A. Degree Radio and Television, Calif. State University, L.B.<BR>
M.A. Theater Arts and Filmmaking, Humbolt State University<br>
</BODY>
</HTML>
```

In this HTML page, the <BR CLEAR=LEFT> tag enables you to control the spacing around the image. Without the tag and attribute, the horizontal rule line that separates the references from the beginning of the Education section would be up next to the image. This tag is especially useful for handling the issues of browser window width settings, another option you have no control over. Often in a narrow browser window, a design like this works fine, but if the user widens the window, undesired spacing results. Using the <BR CLEAR=LEFT> tag can help you control this kind of display (see fig. 14.17).

Figure 14.17

The <BR> tag using the CLEAR attribute.

Image Tags in HTML 3.2

Linking images in HTML 3.2 is performed in the same manner as in HTML 2.0, but there are a few more attributes to work with now. Remember that there is no close tag for <IMG>. As you've already learned from the sections in HTML 2.0, the <IMG> tag must contain the SRC attribute to designate the image you want to display and its location. You've also learned about the ALT attribute for including alternative text to be displayed if a viewer has images turned off or is using a browser that does not support images. You've seen alignment for LEFT, RIGHT, and CENTER. You've also been introduced to the ISMAP attribute for image maps. Now with HTML 3.2, there are a few more attributes to add to Image tag. Here's a list of the new <IMG> tag attributes and what they offer:

- WIDTH: Use this attribute to include the width of your image in pixels.

- HEIGHT: Use this attribute to include the height of your image in pixels.

- BORDER: This can be used to create a border around an image. One of its best uses, however, is to turn off the border on an image that is hyperlinked. You saw in HTML 2.0 that when a link tag was set around an image, Netscape Navigator displayed an ugly blue border around the image. Now, you can add BOR-DER=0 to your Image tags and your linked images won't have those unwanted colored borders around them.

- HSPACE: This attribute enables you to put horizontal space around your image and is measured in pixels. This will place space at both the left and right sides of your image.

- VSPACE: This attribute enables you to put vertical space around your image, and is measured in pixels. This will place space at the top and bottom of your image.

Using the HEIGHT and WIDTH Attributes

You can set the height and width of your images to any pixel size by using the HEIGHT and WIDTH attributes. The primary use of the HEIGHT and WIDTH attributes is to provide information to the browser. A browser, such as Netscape Navigator, needs to know the size of an image before it can build the rest of the page, because it has to know how much space the image will require. By including the HEIGHT and WIDTH attributes, you let the browser know right away how big your image is so that it can draw the rest of the page while your image is still loading. This speeds the total load time in most browsers and is a useful addition to the IMG tag. Many HTML editors now automatically include the HEIGHT and WIDTH of images when they are imported, a handy feature because you would otherwise have to note the size in an image program such as Photoshop and then write the size in manually in whatever text editor you use to create HTML.

The HEIGHT and WIDTH can be set to any size; however, if you use this HTML feature to make your images smaller, you are defeating the purpose of small images on the Web. If you set the images to a smaller size than they actually are, the browser still has to load the larger image and then resize it to the smaller size. The only time this is an advantage is when an image has already been displayed and you want to show it in a smaller size on a subsequent page. In this case, you save a little time because the first image has been cached and the browser only has to resize it. If, however, you try to use HEIGHT and WIDTH make a small image bigger, you will find the image looks pretty distorted. Be aware of this tag. If you edit your images after you have inserted them into a page, don't forget to change the image size in the HTML.

Here's an example of the new image attributes in action:

```
<HTML>
<HEAD><TITLE>The Image Tag</TITLE></HEAD>
<BODY BGCOLOR="#FFFFFF">
<H2>The New image attributes</H2>
<P>
<A HREF="cats.html"><IMG WIDTH=184 HEIGHT=98 VSPACE=5 HSPACE=5
➥BORDER=0 ALT="This is a picture of two cats"ALIGN=LEFT
➥SRC="littlecats.gif"></A>
Remember that cute little cat image and how bad it looked with that
➥ugly border? Now I've set the BORDER to =0 so that the unwanted
➥blue border created by the link tag will disappear.<P>
I've also used the spacing tags to create more space around the
➥image, although this one has a transparent background that adds to
➥the spacing. Finally, I've included the HEIGHT and WIDTH tags so
➥the page should load faster.<P>
(Illustration still by Tom McCain)
</BODY>
</HTML>
```

In figure 14.18, you see the image attributes at work. Notice the unattractive border caused by the link tag is gone now that the BORDER=0 attribute has been added. Your viewers will still be able to tell this is a link by the hand that appears in most browsers when the cursor passes over a link. I've also used the spacing attributes here and included the HEIGHT and WIDTH so that the page will load faster.

HTML Tutorial and Reference

Figure 14.18

The new image attributes.

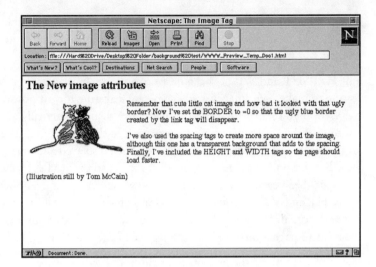

The <MAP> Tag

The addition of the <MAP> tag enables client-side image maps. These are image maps that do not require a server-side script to function; however, they only work in the latest versions of Netscape's and Microsoft's browsers (although other browsers promise to support them in the future). The advantage of this tag is that it enables HTML designers to create image maps more easily than by creating a script, which requires sophisticated programming. Client-side image maps also generally work faster than server-side image maps and do not put as much strain on server resources. To create an image map, you must specify areas on the image that are hot and then link them to URLs that they will call. For more on image maps, see Chapter 8 on image conversion issues.

The <APPLET> Tag

The new <APPLET> tag in HTML 3.2 requires both an open and close tag and is used to link Java applets into a Web site. It is only supported by Java-enabled browsers. The attributes are CODE, CODEBASE, NAME, ALT, ALIGN, WIDTH, HEIGHT, HSPACE, and VSPACE. <APPLET> uses associated PARAM elements to pass parameters to the applet.

Java is really beyond the scope of this book, but you can find out more about it by checking out the online Java resources in Appendix C. This tag is included here to let you know it is part of the HTML 3.2 specification.

Tables

The most useful new design feature in the HTML 3.2 specification is the <TABLE> tag. Tables in HTML can be used for far more than just aligning columnar text or numbers, as you would generally do in a word processor or spreadsheet table. Although tables do serve this function in HTML, they are used for many other design options on the Web, where they provide one of the only ways to divide a page into sections you can align independently. Tables can be compared to graphic and text boxes in a desktop publishing program. For example, if you want to align text in one area with two graphics to the right of it, you might create separate boxes in QuarkXPress and then move them to the desired locations on your page. In HTML, you'll have to create a table to have this kind of design control.

Before we get into the tags, be forewarned that tables are one of the more complicated design features to grasp. For this reason, several examples will be provided in the following section. More time will be spent on HTML table elements than almost any other HTML feature because they are essential for good design on the Web. One of the biggest problems with tables in the past was that they were not supported by all browsers. This is changing quickly now that they are "official" HTML. Expect <TABLE> tags to be universally supported soon.

Table Tags

Although they offer greater design control than other HTML tags, you still need to understand that tables have to be created by using square or rectangular areas. Essentially, you are creating a grid in which you can place text or graphic elements to control their placement. You build a table by creating rows and then placing cells inside those rows. You can also let the cells of a table span more than one row or column to create varied designs.

The following list contains the HTML table-related tags and their attributes. Once you are familiar with all the tags, a variety of examples will be shown.

- <TABLE>: All tables must begin and end with the open and close <TABLE> tags. All other table tags must be placed between them. Tables may also be nested, meaning you can place a TABLE within a TABLE for even greater design control. The attributes for the TABLE tags are as follows:

  - BORDER: This attribute sets the size of the border that will surround your table and data cells. It has a three-dimensional look to it and can be set as large as you want, using pixels as its measurement. The larger the number you use to set the border, the larger the border. If you do not use the border attribute, the default is 0; thus, if there is no border specified, your table edges will not be visible. Tables are often used without borders when they are used for alignment and positioning of text and graphic elements, where you wouldn't want a border displayed.

- CELLPADDING: This attribute specifies the distance between the text or graphic element within a table cell and the inner cell border. This attribute is also measured in pixels.

- CELLSPACING: This attribute sets the distance between the borders of the cell and borders of other cells or the outside edge of the table. This attribute is also measured in pixels.

- WIDTH: This attribute sets the width of the entire table. If specified in pixels, it sets a fixed width. Width can also be specified with a percentage, which enables the table to resize in accordance with the width your user has set for the browser window.

- ALIGN: This attribute sets the alignment of the entire table, using RIGHT, LEFT, or CENTER. Table alignment can also be controlled by using the alignment options described earlier for use with text, images, and other elements. This is important, because even Netscape Navigator 3.0 doesn't yet support the alignment attribute in tables. Just treat the table as another element on your page for which you can control alignment by placing other tags, such as <CENTER> </CENTER>, around the entire table.

- <CAPTION>: This tag is used to give a title to the table. It includes the ALIGN attribute with the values TOP and BOTTOM so you can control the position of the caption in relation to the top of the table. You may still choose to use header or other tags to create a title for your table, because this tag displays outside the table border.

- <TR>: The table row tag designates a single row of table cells. This tag contains the table data tag explained next and sets up the table one row at a time. At the end of each row, you should include a close </TR> tag, although it is not required. You can have as many table data sections as you want within a table row.

- <TD>: The Table Definition or Data tag creates the cell where you will place your text, graphic, or other elements. Again the closing </TD> tag is recommended, but not required. The default of this tag is aligned left, using plain text. You can change this default by using the following attributes:

  - ALIGN: This attribute can be set, using LEFT, RIGHT, and CENTER.

This affects the alignment of the contents within the table data cell and enables greater design control of each element in each cell of the table.

- VALIGN: This attribute sets the vertical alignment of the cell data, using TOP, BOTTOM, and MIDDLE. This is especially useful when you want to align elements so that they appear at the same level in relation to each other within a table row.

- WIDTH: Sets the width of a table cell and can be written in the exact number of pixels or a percentage of table width.

- COLSPAN: This attribute describes the number of columns that the table cell spans and is used to create tables with an uneven number of columns.

- ROWSPAN: This attribute describes the number of rows that the table cell spans and is used to create tables with an uneven number of rows.

- <TH>: The Table Header tag is similar to the table definition tag, but is specifically designed for headings within a table. Unlike the TD tag, the TH tag defaults to center alignment with bold text. This can be changed by using the following attributes:

  - ALIGN: As with the TD tag, the values are LEFT, RIGHT, and CENTER. The attribute affects the alignment of contents within the table cell.

  - VALIGN: Again, the values are TOP, BOTTOM, and MIDDLE.

  - WIDTH: This sets the width of a table cell and can be described in the exact number of pixels or as a percentage of the table width.

  - COLSPAN: This attribute describes the number of columns that the table cell spans and is used to create tables with an uneven number of columns.

  - ROWSPAN: This attribute describes the number of rows that the table cell spans and is used to create tables with an uneven number of rows.

Building a Simple Table

Now that you know all the tags and their attributes, it's time to start putting them together. The following example demonstrates a simple, gridlike table, using only the border attribute so you can see the table border in Netscape Navigator. Here's how it looks:

```
<HTML>
<HEAD><TITLE>A simple table</TITLE></HEAD>
```

continues

continued

```
<BODY>
<H1>A simple table</H1>
<TABLE BORDER=2>
<TR>
<TD>row 1, cell 1</TD><TD>row 1, cell 2</TD><TD>row 1, cell 3</TD>
</TR>
<TR>
<TD>row 2, cell 1</TD><TD>row 2, cell 2</TD><TD>row 2, cell 3</TD>
</TR>
<TR>
<TD>row 3, cell 1</TD><TD>row 3, cell 2</TD><TD>row 3, cell 3</TD>
</TR>
</TABLE>
</BODY>
</HTML>
```

The simple table shown in figure 14.19 forms the same type of grid you would see in a spreadsheet or word processing program. Although this use of the table tag has its place, it is only the beginning of what tables make possible on the Web.

Figure 14.19

A simple table.

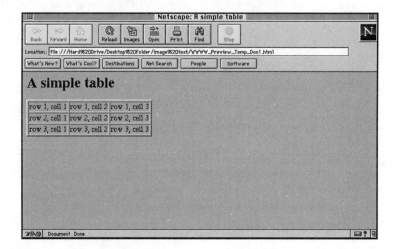

Using Tables to Create Columns

Another simple but very useful function of tables is to indent text to create the effect of a column. The trick is to set the width of the table to 60 percent and then center the entire table. This is an ideal way to create columns of text and makes long text documents less intimidating and easier to read on the Web. Unfortunately, the ALIGN=CENTER attribute of tables is not yet supported, even by the latest version of Netscape Navigator (at this writing, Navigator 3.0), so use the CENTER tag to center the table. This works well in browsers that support tables, but can cause problems in browsers that support the CENTER tag and don't support the TABLE tag. Here's an example of a table used to create an indented column:

HTML Tutorial and
Reference

```
<HTML>
<HEAD>
<TITLE>Use a table to create a narrow text column</TITLE>
</HEAD>
<BODY BGCOLOR=#FFFFFF TEXT=#000000>
<CENTER>
<TABLE WIDTH=60%>
<TR>
<TD>
<H1>Creating margins with a table</H1>
This table's width is equal to sixty percent of the page, leaving
➥forty percent of the page to be distributed between the two
➥margins. Because we have centered the table, 20 percent of the
➥page on each side will be left open as a margin.
Be aware, however, that some browsers support the CENTER tag, but
➥don't support table tags, which results in all this text being
➥centered. (This is changing as more and more browsers support
➥tables.) Unfortunately, the ALIGN=CENTER attribute of the table
➥tag is not supported yet, even by the latest version of Netscape
➥Navigator. When there is better support, it will provide an option
➥for centering your table without centering the text in a browser
➥that doesn't support tables. In the meantime, it's a trade-off,
➥because creating columns of text is a nice way to break up large
➥areas of text on the Web. Overall, you shouldn't have to worry
➥about this too much. By the time you read this, expect tables to
➥be widely supported.
</TD>
</TR>
</TABLE>
</CENTER>
</BODY>
</HTML>
```

In figure 14.20, you can see that the narrow width of the table combined with the use of the <CENTER> tag creates a column down the middle of the page. This is a great way to break up long text documents that can be difficult to read on a computer screen. This could be done without the <CENTER> tag, in which case the column would run down the left side of the page.

Figure 14.20

Using a table to create an indented column.

Table Design Concepts

Now that you've seen two of the simplest table designs, you're ready to take on some more complex table formatting. A basic rule to remember is to design tables from top to bottom and from left to right. Complete your rows one at a time across the page, regardless of whether or not a single cell stretches across multiple columns or rows.

Cells that Span Multiple Columns

The next example demonstrates how to build a table that does not have an equal number of cells in each row. Although more complex to create, these are some of the most useful tables for providing sophisticated design control on the Web. This table is three rows by three columns, but the first row has only one cell, the second row has two cells, and the third row has three cells. The border attribute is used here to illustrate what's happening, but this kind of table would often be created without a border just to have design control. You'll see another example of that soon, using images and other elements, but for now, you should be focusing on the COLSPAN attribute for creating cells that span more than one column. Here's what the code for this type of table looks like:

```
<HTML>
<HEAD><TITLE>Table cells that span columns</TITLE></HEAD>
<BODY>
<CENTER><H1>Table cells that span columns</H1>
```

```
<TABLE BORDER=2>
<TR>
<TD ALIGN=CENTER COLSPAN=3>This cell spans three columns and is
➥centered</TD>
</TR>
<TR>
<TD COLSPAN=2>This cell spans two columns and is centered<
➥TD><TD>This cell spans one column</TD>
</TR>
<TR>
<TD>This cell spans one column</TD><TD>This cell spans one column<
➥TD><TD>This cell spans one column</TD>
</TR>
</TABLE>
</CENTER>
</BODY>
</HTML>
```

To vary your designs, you'll need to use the COLSPAN attribute so that your table cells can span across more than one column, as seen in figure 14.21.

Figure 14.21

Table cells that span columns.

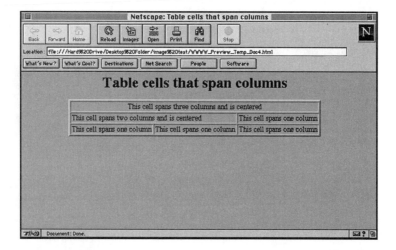

Cells that Span Multiple Rows

Now you'll want to learn about setting cells that span more than one row. This works in much the same way as the COLSPAN attribute. Here's an example:

```
<HTML>
<HEAD><TITLE>Table cells that span rows</TITLE></HEAD>
<BODY>
```

continues

HTML Tutorial and Reference

continued

```
<CENTER><H1>Table cells that span rows</H1>
<TABLE BORDER=2>
<TR>
<TD ROWSPAN=3>This cell spans three rows</TD><TD>This cell spans
➥one row</TD><TD>This cell spans one row</TD>
</TR>
<TR>
<TD>This cell spans one row</TD><TD ROWSPAN=2>This cell spans two
➥rows</TD>
</TR>
<TR>
<TD>This cell spans one row</TD>
</TR>
</TABLE>
</CENTER>
</BODY>
</HTML>
```

Use the ROWSPAN attribute to vary your designs by creating cells that span more than one row, as shown in figure 14.22.

Figure 14.22

Table cells that span more than one row.

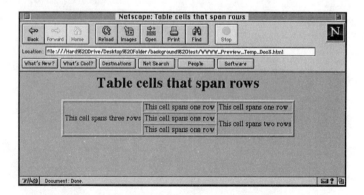

Tables with Cells that Span Rows and Columns

Now let's put those attributes together and set up a complex table that enables you to have cells that span more than one row, as well as cells that span more than one column. In the following example, you'll also see how one cell can use both attributes.

```
<HTML>
<HEAD><TITLE> Table cells that span rows and columns </TITLE><
➥HEAD>
<BODY>
<CENTER><H1>Table cells that span<BR>
```

```
rows and columns</H1>
<TABLE BORDER=2>
<TR>
<TD COLSPAN=2 ROWSPAN=2>This cell spans two rows<BR>
and two columns</TD>
<TD>This cell spans one row<BR>
and one column</TD>
</TR>
<TR>
<TD>This cell spans one row<BR>
and one column</TD>
</TR>
<TR>
<TD>This cell spans one row<BR>
and one column</TD>
<TD>This cell spans one row<BR>
and one column</TD>
<TD>This cell spans one row<BR>
and one column</TD>
</TR>
</TABLE>
</CENTER>
</BODY>
</HTML>
```

In figure 14.23, you see that a table cell can span more than one row and column to create an even more varied design. The next example includes images to demonstrate the usefulness of this kind of variation.

Figure 14.23

Table cells that span rows and columns.

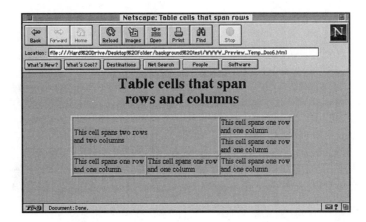

Aligning Graphics and Text with Tables

One of the greatest design uses of tables is to align graphics and text with alignment control not offered by other HTML options. In the next example, you'll see how images can be aligned with text, putting your new HTML talents to practical use. Here's the HTML for this example:

```
<HTML>
<HEAD><TITLE>Aligning images and text with a table</TITLE></HEAD>
<BODY BGCOLOR=#FFFFFF TEXT=#000000>
<CENTER>
<TABLE BORDER=2>
<TR>
<TD ALIGN=CENTER COLSPAN=2><IMG WIDTH=240 HEIGHT=72
➥ALT="ConnectMedia logo" SRC="logo.gif"></TD>
</TR>
<TR>
<TD VALIGN=TOP ROWSPAN=2><IMG WIDTH=122 HEIGHT=288 ALT="Camera"
➥SRC="camera.gif"></TD>
<TD VALIGN=TOP>ConnectMedia is a resource for the Northern Califor-
➥nia Film, Video, and Multimedia production community. This site is
➥built by professionals from the film/video production and computer
➥arena, who have come together specifically to provide creative
➥access to the World Wide Web. The site includes The Reel Directory
➥with more than 2,000 listings providing a wide range of resources
➥for the film and video community. To visit their Web site, point
➥your favorite browser at: <A HREF="http://www.connectmedia.com
➥">http://www.connectmedia.com</A>.</TD>
</TR>
</TABLE>
</CENTER>
</BODY>
</HTML>
```

In this example, in order to align these two images and have text placed to the right of the camera graphic and below the logo, table alignment attributes are implemented (see fig. 14.24). Notice that the first TD cell is centered so that the logo displays in the middle of the cell, and that VALIGN=TOP is used on the cells containing the camera and the text so they will line up with each other. In this example, a border is used to illustrate what's happening. The image that follows is the same page without the BORDER attribute. In most cases, you will not want a border in this kind of design, but will use the table only to control the alignment.

Figure 14.24

Using tables to align graphics and text

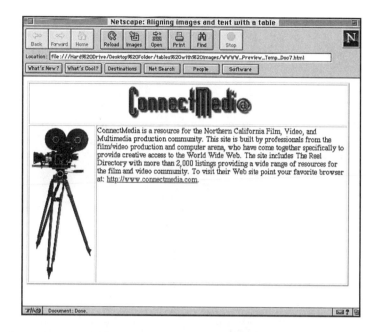

The HTML code for the same table without the BORDER attribute is shown in the following listing:

```
<HTML>
<HEAD><TITLE>Aligning images and text with a table</TITLE></HEAD>
<BODY BGCOLOR=#FFFFFF TEXT=#000000>
<TABLE>
<TR>
<TD ALIGN=CENTER COLSPAN=2><IMG WIDTH=240 HEIGHT=72
➥ALT="ConnectMedia logo" SRC="logo.gif"></TD>
</TR>
<TR>
<TD VALIGN=TOP ROWSPAN=2><IMG WIDTH=122 HEIGHT=288 ALT="Camera"
➥SRC="camera.gif"></TD>
➥<TD VALIGN=TOP>ConnectMedia is a resource for the Northern Cali-
➥fornia Film, Video, and Multimedia production community. This site
➥is built by professionals from the film/video production and
➥computer arena, who have come together specifically to provide
➥creative access to the World Wide Web. The site includes The Reel
➥Directory with more than 2,000 listings providing a wide range of
➥resources for the film and video community. To visit their Web
➥site, point your favorite browser at: <A HREF="http:/
➥www.connectmedia.com/">http://www.connectmedia.com</A>.</TD>
</TR>
```

continues

continued

```
</TABLE>
</CENTER>
</BODY>
</HTML>
```

The desired effect is shown in figure 14.25. You get the design control you want, but because the BORDER attribute is excluded, your viewers don't need to know you have used a table. Setting the BORDER=0 will also result in no border, but it's unnecessary.

Figure 14.25

The same table without the border.

Tip

Many times you will use tables such as these to control alignment and you will not want a border; however, as you are building the table, it is helpful to add a border just so you can see what you are doing. This will make it easier to find your mistakes and see where you may have extra columns or rows you did not intend to have. It's easy to make mistakes when you first start building tables, so turn on the border while you are building and testing, and then turn it off when you have your design the way you want it.

Nested Tables

If you want even more control, you may want to *nest* tables, which means creating a table inside another table. This provides even greater control because you can align elements within other elements. Here's an example using the previous design, but adding a second table in the text so that columnar information can be displayed. Here's what it looks like in HTML:

```
<HTML>
<HEAD><TITLE>Aligning images and text with a table</TITLE></HEAD>
<BODY BGCOLOR=#FFFFFF TEXT=#000000>
<TABLE>
<TR>
<TD ALIGN=CENTER COLSPAN=2><IMG WIDTH=240 HEIGHT=72
➥ALT="ConnectMedia logo" SRC="logo.gif"></TD>
</TR>
<TR>
<TD VALIGN=TOP ROWSPAN=2><IMG WIDTH=122 HEIGHT=288 ALT="Camera"
➥SRC="camera.gif"></TD>
<TD VALIGN=TOP>ConnectMedia is a resource for the Northern Califor-
➥nia Film, Video, and Multimedia production community. This site is
➥built by professionals from the film/video production and computer
➥arena, who have come together specifically to provide creative
➥access to the World Wide Web. The site includes The Reel Directory
➥with more than 2,000 listings providing a wide range of resources
➥for the film and video community. To visit their Web site, point
➥your favorite browser at: <A HREF="http://www.connectmedia.com
➥">http://www.connectmedia.com</A>
<P>
<BR>
<CENTER>
<!--This is where the nested table begins-->
<TABLE BORDER=3>
<TH COLSPAN=3>The Reel Directory Includes</TH>
<TR>
<TH>Talent</TH><TH>Technical Resources</TH><TH>Other Resources</TH>
</TR>
<TR>
<TD ALIGN=CENTER>Actors</TD><TD ALIGN=CENTER>Camera Techs</TD><TD
➥ALIGN=CENTER>Animals</TD>
</TR>
<TR>
<TD ALIGN=CENTER>Voice Overs</TD><TD ALIGN=CENTER>Sound Special
➥ists</TD><TD ALIGN=CENTER>Boat and Car Rentals</TD>
```

continues

continued

```
</TR>
<TR>
<TD ALIGN=CENTER>Models</TD><TD ALIGN=CENTER>Video Editors</TD><TD
➡ALIGN=CENTER>Location Specialists</TD>
</TR>
</TABLE>
<!--This is where the nested table ends-->
</CENTER>
</TD>
</TR>
</TABLE>
</CENTER>
</BODY>
</HTML>
```

In this case, the border for the second table is used to make the columns more readable, without using the border on the first table (see fig. 14.26). Nested tables can be used for many complex designs in HTML. Often you won't include any borders because you are using the tables purely for complex design control.

Figure 14.26

Nested tables.

Table Wrap-Up

As with any HTML tags, the best way to learn how to use tables is to experiment. Tables can be a little frustrating at first. Study the examples provided and then start creating them yourself, and you'll master table design, as well as any other tags you want in your pages. Keep in mind that you create tables one row at a time and that you can control the spacing of each cell, as well as its span across rows or columns, and you'll be able to create beautiful designs with just a little practice. Experiment. Create a page and test it in your favorite browser. and then keep trying until you like the way it looks. Also remember that even if your goal is to create a table with no border, adding the BORDER attribute while you are building the table can make it much easier to find your mistakes.

Netscape Extensions

If you're still not satisfied with the HTML options of 2.0 and 3.2, you may want to consider using Netscape extensions. Netscape has become notorious, and controversial, for pushing the limits of the HTML standards; however, graphic designers have appreciated their contributions and many of the newly approved 3.2 tags were originally Netscape extensions. Before you learn about these new features, you should be aware that these are browser-specific HTML tags and attributes and may only work in the latest versions of Netscape Navigator. Some of these tags will work in Navigator 2.0; others are so new they only display in the 3.0 version.

Microsoft and Netscape have been so competitive that many of these tags will also display in the latest versions of Internet Explorer. And, working hard not to be left out, even America Online and others are trying to incorporate some of these extensions. The best way to know for sure is to test your pages. It's a good idea to keep a variety of browsers on your hard drive to ensure your pages work for the broad audience of the Web. Don't throw away old versions of browser, either. Developers are always the first to upgrade, but just because Netscape 3.0 has been released doesn't mean that everyone has moved on. Many people don't know how, or don't want to bother downloading a new browser. Large institutions, such as universities and corporations, are especially slow to upgrade because it means changing the browser for many users at once.

The saving grace in all of this is that browsers that don't support these new extensions, such as background colors in tables, will simply ignore them. If you plan your designs with that in mind—using text colors that will work on a gray background if your table colors don't display, for example—you should have nothing to lose by incorporating these new design features into your pages. Another feature of the more dramatic browser-specific extensions, such as <FRAMES>, is that they generally include an option that will let you design pages that work in browsers that don't display them, such as <NOFRAMES>.

At the same time, things are slowly improving, and even low-end browsers are starting to support features, tables, and background colors. Browsers get updated almost weekly these days and display more tags with each new version. Thus, by the time you read this, many of these features may have become as common as the HTML 3.2 tags and enjoy support in a variety of browsers. The following Netscape tags are provided to give you a sense of the most common Netscape options available to you. It is not an exhaustive list, however, and there will undoubtedly be new tags in the coming months. If you're really into the latest of the latest, stay tuned to http:// home.netscape.com for a more comprehensive list and any new tags that may have been added since this book was published.

Netscape Tags and Attributes

Many of the Netscape extensions offer additional attributes to tags you have already learned about. As each new group of tags and attributes are described, you'll get a reminder of the main tag and then a list of the new tags. All the attributes you learned about in the previous sections of this chapter still apply to these tags.

The Body Tag: Netscape Attributes

The <BODY> tag continues to have the function of defining the main area of the page that will be displayed. In addition to all of the Body attributes you learned about in HTML 2.0 and 3.2, there are several new features you can incorporate into the <BODY> tag. These attributes can also be used with other tags, such as the Fig and Banner tags, that appear within the open and close <BODY> tags. Additional attributes for the <BODY> tag include the following:

- CLASS: The Class "type" identifies and further specifies the characteristics of an element, allowing the extension of HTML tags for new functions. This is especially useful in the construction of style sheets (which you'll learn more about in the Style Sheets section that follows). You can specify multiple classes (i.e., subclasses) for an element by separating class names with a period.

- ID: This "keyword" designates a location in the document as a destination for a link. This attribute replaces the <A NAME> tag.

- LANG: "ISO standard language abbreviation" indicates the language of the text element.

The Image Tag: Netscape Attributes

The basic <IMG> tag requires the SRC attribute to designate the file name and location and includes all of the attributes you learned about earlier. Netscape adds these attributes:

- ALIGN: In Netscape browsers, all of these additional alignment options are possible:

  - TEXTTOP: This aligns with the top of the tallest text in a line. The TOP attribute in 3.2 often has the same effect, but it aligns with the tallest item, which is not necessarily text.

  - ABSMIDDLE: This aligns the middle of the current line with the absolute middle of the image and often provides better control and slightly different effect than MIDDLE.

  - BASELINE: This aligns the bottom of the image with the baseline of the current line.

  - ABSBOTTOM: This aligns the bottom of the image with the absolute bottom of the current line.

- LOWSRC: This is a very cool Netscape attribute that enables you to do at least two new tricks because it loads the image linked with LOWSRC= before it loads the regular SRC image. You can use this to place a lower-resolution image that will load faster and give the appearance that the page is loading faster. This can be a black-and-white version of the same image, a version that has fewer colors, or a smaller version that will be stretched into the space by the Height and Width attributes. LOWSRC can also be used to create simple, two-frame animations by loading one image and then loading a second image on top of it. This only works once, however, and can't be set to loop or repeat. Browsers that don't support the LOWSRC attribute will only load the image linked with the SRC.

Here's an example of an HTML page using these image attributes.

```
<HTML>
<HEAD><TITLE>Image Example</TITLE></HEAD>
<BODY>
<IMG WIDTH=70 HEIGHT=74 ALIGN=TEXTTOP SRC="image3.gif">    TEXTTOP
➥aligns with the top of the tallest text in a line.
<P>
<IMG WIDTH=70 HEIGHT=74 ALIGN=ABSMIDDLE SRC="image3.gif"> ABSMIDDLE
➥aligns the middle of the current line with the absolute middle of
```

continues

continued

```
➡the image
<P>
<IMG WIDTH=70 HEIGHT=74 ALIGN=BASELINE SRC="image3.gif"> BASELINE
➡aligns the bottom of the image with the baseline of the current
➡line
<P>
<IMG WIDTH=70 HEIGHT=74 ALIGN=ABSBOTTOM SRC="image3.gif"> ABSBOTTOM
➡aligns the bottom of the image with the absolute bottom of the
➡current line.
<P>
<IMG WIDTH=70 HEIGHT=74 SRC="image1.gif" LOWSRC="image3.gif"> The
➡Low Source attribute can't be appreciated in a still image such as
➡the figure in this book, but it allows one image to be loaded
➡before another on the same page.
</BODY>
</HTML>
```

Netscape Attributes for the List Tags

The list tag attributes offer new options for bulleted lists and additional ways to identify the items in an ordered list.

- <UL>: This is the Unordered List tag. Now you can add a TYPE attribute to control the kind of bullet that displays. Your choices are: TYPE=disc, circle, square.

- <OL>: The Ordered List tag can now have more options than 1, 2, 3. Here they have added two new attributes.

  - TYPE: Use this to set: large letters (TYPE=A), small letters (TYPE=a), large Roman numerals (TYPE=I), small Roman numerals (TYPE=i), or the default numbers (TYPE=1).

  - START: Enables you to start a list with a value other than 1. This attribute always uses numbers to specify where to begin a series and follows the type set with the TYPE attribute. For example: START=2 would result in: B, e, II, ii, or 2 depending on the TYPE.

- <LI>: The List Item tag can also include a TYPE attribute and uses the same values as OL and UL. In Ordered Lists, you can also add a VALUE attribute to change the count for that list item and all subsequent items.

The following HTML page provides example lists using the Netscape attributes:

```
<HTML>
<HEAD><TITLE>Netscape List attributes</TITLE></HEAD>
<BODY BGCOLOR=#FFFFFF TYPE=#000000>
<CENTER><H2>Netscape List attributes</H2></CENTER>
<UL>
<LI> This is the default provided by HTML 2.0. Browsers that do not
➡support Netscape attributes will display this kind of bullet.
<LI TYPE=disc> TYPE=disc
<LI TYPE=circle> TYPE=circle
<LI TYPE=square> TYPE=square
</UL>

<OL TYPE=A>
<LI> An ordered list
<LI> Using capital letters
</OL>
<OL TYPE=a>
<LI> An ordered list
<LI> Using lower case letters
</OL>
<OL TYPE=I>
<LI> An ordered list
<LI> Using large roman numerals
</OL>
<OL TYPE=i>
<LI> An ordered list
<LI> Using small roman numerals
</OL>
```

You can also create a list and use the LI tag to designate the type. By adding the VALUE attribute, you can start at any letter or Roman numeral. In this case, I've set VALUE to equal 4 so the fourth character of each TYPE displays.

```
<UL>
<LI TYPE=A VALUE=4>  TYPE=A VALUE=4
<LI TYPE=a  VALUE=4> TYPE=a  VALUE=4
<LI TYPE=a  VALUE=4> TYPE=a  VALUE=4
<LI TYPE=i  VALUE=4> TYPE=i  VALUE=4
</UL>
```

HTML Tutorial and
Reference

Font Control

There are also a number of Netscape attributes for the <FONT> tag that enable you to alter and customize the font appearance on your Web pages. They are as follows:

- <FONT SIZE>: In addition to sizes 1 through 7 provided by HTML 3.2, Netscape offers + and - options that set a font size relative to the default size. The default in Netscape is FONT SIZE=3.

- <FONT FACE>: Using this tag, you can now specify a particular font, such as Courier or Helvetica. Netscape will then check the user's computer for the font and, if available, use the expressed font in place of the default. You can even list more than one font, and if the browser can't find the first font on the user's hard drive, it will look for the second. A good option here is to use a special font, even if it's not common, and then list a more common, similar font that is more likely to be installed on most users' hard drives. If the browser can't find any of the fonts you have specified, it will use the default font set in the browser (usually Times). This tag also uses the close </FONT> tag.

  The following is an example of what the Font Face tag would look like:

  <FONT FACE=Papyrus,Tekton> This text would display in the Papyrus font if available on the hard drive. If not, the browser would look for David Siegel's famous Tekton font, and if it couldn't find that either, the text would display in the browser's default font, usually Times.</FONT>

  If used in combination, the Font Size and Font Face tags can be combined like this:

  <FONT FACE=Papyrus,Tekton FONT SIZE=7>This would display in the largest possible font size.</FONT>

- <BASEFONT SIZE=value>: This is placed at the top of the page and sets the default font for the entire document. It is overridden by any other Font tags that appear later in the document. Again, the default is 3 and the range is from 1 to 7.

Other Netscape Additions

In addition to enhancing existing HTML tags with its own attributes, Netscape has also added some useful tags of its own, as described in the following list.

- <BLINK>: As the name implies, this tag makes text blink, alternating from visible to invisible. Most designers strongly argue against the use of this tag because it can be distracting to viewers.

- <NOBR>: This forces the text within the opening and closing tags to remain unbroken and can make the text extend beyond the view of the page, requiring the viewer to scroll to see all of your text. Use it sparingly—viewers get frustrated if they have to scroll left and right and some of them are on 14" monitors.

- <WBR>: If you still want some breaks within your NoBreak tag, this tag enables you to insert a line break within the <NOBR> tags.

- <BANNER>: The Banner tag enables you to include a banner in your document. A *banner* is a non-scrolling, separate region in the document that is often used for toolbars, corporate logos, and disclaimers. You can also use the Link tag, with the banner attribute. The close tag is </BANNER>. The attributes for the Banner tag are the same as the new attributes, Class, ID, and Lang, as previously described for the Body tag previously.

- <FN>: The Footnote tag creates a footnote in your HTML document that is generally displayed in a pop-up window. The close tag is </FN>. The attributes for the Footnote tag are the same as the new attributes, Class, ID, and Lang, as previously described for the Body tag previously.

- <ISINDEX>: Netscape added a PROMPT attribute to ISINDEX tag so you can specify the message you want before the text input field of the index. The default is: This is a searchable index. Now you can make it something more interesting. For example: <ISINDEX PROMPT>="This index will let you search for your favorite ice cream">.

Client-Side Image Maps

Image maps enable you to use one image to point to more than one URL. But, until Netscape added this new feature, they required a CGI script on the server and a supplementary coordinates file to function. With the addition of client-side image maps, you can now embed all of the information you need right into your HTML document. You also get the added advantage that Netscape will display the URL when the user passes the cursor over the linked area. With server-side image maps, your viewer only sees the image map coordinates in the URL display.

Another advantage of client-side image maps is that they do not tax your server and thus often work faster than server-side image maps. If you are concerned about browsers that do not support image maps, you can use both in combination. If you do, Netscape will use the client-side image map and ignore the server-side information. Thus, low-end browsers will still be able to access the server-side image map. This is, of course, optional and takes more time and effort to set up.

As an HTML designer, you should also appreciate that client-side image maps work on your hard drive as well as your server. This is useful for testing and local demonstrations. It is also great for projects such as a CD-ROM/Web site combination where the image map may reside on the CD and for new, back-end browsers that download pages in the background so that users may view them offline.

Creating Client-Side Image Maps

To indicate that an image will be used as an image map, you add the USEMAP attribute to the IMG tag. As noted earlier, you can simultaneously call a server-side image map by also including the ISMAP attribute. Image maps are indicated with attributes to the Image tag such as USEMAP, which specifies the map file in much the same way the SRC tag specifies the image. If the argument to USEMAP starts with a "#", it is assumed to be in the same document as the IMG tag. The following is an example:

```
<IMG HEIGHT=24 WIDTH=45 SRC="../images/picturemap.gif"
➥USEMAP="my_map.html#map1">
```

Designating Hot Spots on an Image

Image maps are created by designating certain distinct sections of the image and then linking them to different URLs. Thus, you must create a set of coordinates that the browser can use to control the effect when a user clicks on a certain part of the image.

The hot areas of the image are described in the MAP tag. The MAP includes both the coordinates of each region of the map and the URLs they correspond to. Hot spots must be created in geometric shapes indicated by the SHAPE attribute. Your choices are: rectangles (RECT), polygons (POLY), and circles (CIRCLE). The default is a rectangle.

- COORDS: Provides the coordinates of the shape in the image.

- RECT: For a rectangle, you must provide four coordinates corresponding with each of the four corners.

- CIRCLE: Circles are defined as a center point and a radius, indicated by two coordinate numbers, one for each end of the radius.

- POLY: The polygon is defined using the six outsize points and requires two coordinate numbers for each point.

You can designate as many "hot" areas as you want, but be aware that if they are too small, it will be harder for your user to select the intended hot spot. If two areas intersect, the one that appears first in the map definition will be given precedence.

You can also create areas of an image map that are not linked by using the NOHREF attribute. Any region of the image that is not defined by an AREA tag is assumed to be NOHREF.

An HREF tag specifies where a click in that area should link. Note that a relative anchor specification will be expanded using the URL of the map description as a base, rather than using the URL of the document from which the map description is referenced. If a BASE tag is present in the document containing the map description, that URL will be used as the base. The following is an example of a client-side image map:

```
<HTML>
<HEAD><TITLE>A Client Side Image Map</TITLE></HEAD>
<BODY bgcolor="#FFFFFF">
<IMG SRC="images/navmap.gif" USEMAP="#navmap" BORDER=0 ALIGN=RIGHT>
<MAP NAME="navmap">
<AREA SHAPE=rect COORDS="137,7,178,41" HREF="news.html">
<AREA SHAPE=rect COORDS="63,20,120,53" HREF="network.html">
<AREA SHAPE=rect COORDS="2,9,47,40" HREF="design.html">
</MAP>
</BODY>
</HTML>
```

Netscape Additions to the Form Tag

The HTML 2.0 and 3.2 specifications only allow forms that users can type into or mark using check boxes and radio buttons. Netscape wants users to be able to submit an entire file in a form field. The new attribute for this is ENCTYPE. Here's an example of it in action:

```
<FORM ENCTYPE="multipart/form-data" ACTION="_URL_" METHOD=POST>
Please include your file: <INPUT NAME="userfile" TYPE="file">
<INPUT TYPE="submit" VALUE="Send My File In Now!">
</FORM>
```

The Most Dramatic Addition: The Frames Tag

Frames provide one of the most innovate navigational options in HTML. They are also the most controversial. The benefit is that you can create separate, scrollable windows in the same browser screen; then you can set links in one window that affect another window on the same screen. A simple example would be a list of menu items that appear on the left and a window on the right where they display. When a user selects one of the menu options on the left, the window on the right displays the linked page.

Building HTML Pages with Frames

When you use Frame tags in HTML, it's important to understand that each framed section of the screen represents a different HTML page. The example in figure 14.30 is created by displaying three different HTML pages, each in a separate frame. There is also a fourth HTML document that calls those three pages into place. This is what makes creating frames so complex, but it will make more sense as we go along. For now, you need to get familiar with the HTML tags used to create frames; then we'll get into examples to show you how this works. Here are the tags and attributes:

- <FRAMESET>: This tag replaces the Body tag in an HTML page and is used to define the framed document. The close tag is </FRAMESET> that replaces the </BODY> tag at the end of the page. The Frameset tag has the following attributes:

  - ROWS: This determines the size and number of rectangular rows within a <FRAMESET>. You can set the height using an absolute number of pixels or a percentage of screen height. You can also use an asterisk (*) character to set a relative size that will be determined by the size of the browser window. This is used when you want to create more than one row. You can then set a specific height for one row and let the other frame row fit the remainder of the window in the browser. This enables you to compensate for the differences between screen sizes and browser window sizes that may be set by your users. All frame values should be placed within quotation marks and separated by commas.

  - COLS: This determines the size and number of rectangular columns within a Frameset. Again you can use absolute pixel units, a percentage of screen width, or relative values using the asterisk (*) character. In this case, the asterisk enables the developer to allocate horizontal space proportionately in the browser window. Values should be written within quotation marks and separated by commas.

● <NOFRAMES>: The Noframes tag was created by Netscape for browsers that do not support frames. This HTML tag enables you to create a second page that does not use frames and will be viewable to lower-end browsers. All HTML within this tag is ignored by Netscape Navigator and other frames-capable browsers, such as Microsoft Internet Explorer. Other browsers will ignore all Frame tags, and interpret the Noframes content, beginning with the Body tag. Although the Frameset tag replaces the Body tag in the frame section of the page, you will need a Body tag in the Noframes section. You can use all of the attributes of the Body tag in this case the same way you would in a page that does not use frames.

● <FRAME>: This tag defines a single frame within a Frameset. All frames and nested Framesets must be accounted for in the Cols and Rows attributes of the Frameset tag. The Frame tag has the following attributes:

  ● SRC: Provides the URL reference for the source of the frame.

  ● NAME: Names the frame to enable targeting by other HTML documents. This works in conjunction with the TARGET attribute of the <A>, <AREA>, <BASE>, and <FORM> tags. All names must begin with an alphanumeric value and not the underscore character. The exception is the special target names later in this chapter.

  ● MARGINWIDTH: This attribute is optional and must be specified in pixels. Marginwidth determines the horizontal space between the frame contents and the frame's borders.

  ● MARGINHEIGHT: Another optional attribute specified in pixels. The Marginheight determines vertical space between the frame contents and the frame's borders.

  ● SCROLLING: This enables you to control whether a framed window on the page will be scrollable. If left with the default option, the window will scroll only if necessary. Other values are "yes," to always create a scrollbar and "no," to never create a scrollbar.

  ● NORESIZE: This attribute enables you to set a specified width and height of a frame and then prevent viewers from resizing the frame's borders. Without this tag, viewers can stretch or shrink the frame's display by selecting the frame's border and moving it up, down, left, or right.

● TARGET: The Target attribute is used to specify where linked information should be displayed. You use the Target with the <A>, <AREA>, <BASE>, and <FORM> tags with the following in reference to the Name attribute specified in the target location. For example: if you create three frames and want the contents in the frame on the left to link so that when selected the information that they link to will appear in the frame on the right, then you might set the frame on the right with NAME="right_frame" and the link from the left frame section would look like this:

```
<A HREF="destination.html" TARGET="right_frame">;
```

In an image map, the link would look like this:

```
<AREA SHAPE="RECT" COORDS="5,15,25,40"
➥HREF="framedoc.htm" TARGET="right_frame">
```

If you wanted to set that target for all of the links, you could use a base target at the top of the page, such as:

```
<BASE TARGET="right_frame">
```

In a form, the target would be set like this:

```
<FORM ACTION="cgi_bin/script" TARGET="right_frame">
```

Reserved Target Names

The target attribute has several special names that cannot be used in the Name attribute of the Frame tag simply to designate another page as the target. Each of these reserved names serves a special function for framed documents. These special names and functions are as follows:

● TARGET="_top": This reloads the full main viewing area of the browser with the URL specified by the HREF attribute. This is particularly useful for navigating to other Web sites or to other pages that include frames.

● TARGET="_blank": Opens a new browser window.

● TARGET="_self": Loads the document in the same window where the anchor was clicked. This is the default setting. This attribute would generally only be used to override the TARGET attribute of the Base tag.

● TARGET="_parent": If the frame where this target is called from has a parent frame on the page (i.e., a frame that targeted and opened the frame), then the document will be loaded in the parent frame. If there is no parent frame, the attribute is ignored.

Creating a Frame Document

When you create a frame document, you have one HTML page that calls the other HTML pages into each of the frame areas. You create this page much as you would any other HTML page, but in place of the Body tag you place a Frameset tag. Then, each of the comma-separated values in the ROWS and COLS attributes of the <FRAMESET> tag represent a single frame, or window, of the page. As you saw in the preceding introduction, you can set the spacing of these areas using absolute pixel values, relative heights and widths, and/or the asterisk (*) character to have the frame fill all unused browser space. Absolute values are often used together with the asterisk in the ROWS or COLS definitions. The following HTML defines a page with two frames: the left one 90 pixels wide; the other as wide as possible:

```
<FRAMESET COLS="90,*">
```

It is also possible for more than one frame or frameset to share the unused browser display, as in the following example:

```
<FRAMESET COLS="100,*,2*">
```

In this case, there are three frames: the first 90 pixels wide; the second taking up one third of the remaining browser display; and the third frame taking up the two remaining thirds of the browser display.

The following is the HTML page that calls the three frames into place:

```
<HTML>
<HEAD><TITLE>Frames</TITLE></HEAD>
<FRAMESET COLS="100,*,2*">
<FRAME SRC="frame1.html" NAME="dsnlft" SCROLLING="auto">
<FRAME SRC="frame2.html" NAME="dsnwin" SCROLLING="auto">
<FRAME SRC="frame3.html" NAME="dsnwin" SCROLLING="auto">
</FRAMESET>
</BODY>
</HTML>
```

The HTML code for the first frame:

```
<HTML>
<HEAD><TITLE>Frame 1</TITLE></HEAD>
<BODY BGCOLOR="#FFFFFF">
<H1>Frame 1</H1>
This HTML page will appear in the first frame.
```

continues

continued

```
</BODY>
</HTML>
```

The HTML code for the second frame:

```
<HTML>
<HEAD><TITLE>Frame 2</TITLE></HEAD>
<BODY BGCOLOR="#FFFFFF">
<H1>Frame 2</H1>
This HTML page will appear in the second frame.
</BODY>
</HTML>
```

The HTML code for the third frame:

```
<HTML>
<HEAD><TITLE>Frame 3</TITLE></HEAD>
<BODY BGCOLOR="#FFFFFF">
<H1>Frame 3</H1>
This HTML page will appear in the third frame.
</BODY>
</HTML>
```

Adding Rows to the Frame Page

Combining columns and rows enables you to further break up the page. In this way you can create a frame document. The following is the HTML code needed to create a similar frame page. Notice that the frameset for the rows is opened, then the frameset for the columns is opened, and then both require close </FRAMESET> tags at the end of the document.

```
<HTML>
<HEAD><TITLE>Frames</TITLE></HEAD>
    <FRAMESET ROWS="120, *">
<FRAME SRC="frame1.html">
<FRAMESET COLS="100,*">
    <FRAME SRC="frame2.html">
                        <FRAME SRC="frame3.html">
    </FRAMESET>
</FRAMESET>
</HTML>
```

Using the same HTML pages for frames 1, 2, and 3, you can implement a frame main page that uses both rows and columns, as defined in the preceding HTML. You can use any combination of columns and rows to create very complex frame pages on the Web.

The ‹NOFRAMES› Tag

The <NOFRAMES> tag was created so that browser that cannot read frames will still display an HTML page. Be aware that if you do not use the Noframes tag, your viewers with browsers such as America Online that don't support frames will see a blank page. You read that right. They won't see anything. Using the <NOFRAMES> tag, you must re-create the HTML page without using the navigational features of frames and you must create supplementary pages that link from it without frames. That means you have to create two Web sites that parallel each other—one with frames and one without. The following is an example of the HTML page previously described with the addition of the <NOFRAMES> tag and text as it would display in a browser such as America Online. Notice that the text within the <NOFRAMES> tag is created just as if there were no Frame tags on the rest of the page. This means that the <BODY> tag is included and that background colors can be set. Any browser that supports frames will ignore everything that is placed within the <NOFRAMES> tag.

The following is an HTML page using the <FRAME> and <NOFRAMES> tags:

```
<HTML>
<HEAD><TITLE>Frames</TITLE></HEAD>
     <FRAMESET ROWS="120, *">
<FRAME SRC="frame1.html">
<FRAMESET COLS="100,*">
     <FRAME SRC="frame2.html">
                    <FRAME SRC="frame3.html">
     </FRAMESET>
</FRAMESET>
<NOFRAMES>
<BODY BGCOLOR="#FFFFFF">
<H1>Using the NoFrames Tag</H1>
This is a page for browsers that don't support frames.
</BODY>
</NOFRAMES>
</HTML>
```

Note

Testing in America Online's Browser

A great trick for testing your HTML pages in the America Online browser on the Macintosh without going online. Using Macintosh drag and drop, you can simply drag the HTML file icon you want to test over the AOL browser icon and it will open the page in AOL's browser, even if you are not online. This is the only way to test with AOL without loading the page on a server and going online to see the results. Unfortunately, this doesn't work in the Windows operating system.

New Frame Features

Spurred on by new attributes to the <FRAME> tag created by Microsoft, Netscape recently added a few new tricks to the frame options. Most notably, you can now create frames with no borders, much like tables with no borders, and color the borders and sections of a framed page. Additional <FRAMESET> attributes include the following:

- FRAMEBORDER: This enables you to create borders the size that you prefer or to make them invisible by setting the value to 0. Other border sizes are set in pixels.

- BORDERCOLOR: This enables you to set the color of the border using hexadecimal color codes or the 16 common colors described in the hexadecimal section earlier in this chapter.

Multiple Columns

To create the kind of page layout common in newspapers and magazines, Netscape created the <MULTICOL> tag to enable you to display text in multiple columns. The <MULTICOL> tag works with the following attributes:

- COLS: This attribute designates the number of columns across the page.

- GUTTER: Lets you set the amount of space between columns in pixels.

- WIDTH: Sets the individual width of respective columns.

The ‹EMBED› Tag

The <EMBED> tag is used in conjunction with helper applications and plug-ins, and enables you to place elements on a page that can only be displayed with these special viewers (although the most common ones are built into Netscape 3). If you want to insert a Macromedia Director Shockwave file, for example, you use the <EMBED> tag to link the file and call the Shockwave plug-in to display the Director document. The file type is determined by the suffix of the file name and each file type has its own suffix. The <EMBED> tag has no closing tag, but does feature the <NOEMBED> tag, which can be used to display an alternative file, such as a GIF, for a browser that does not support the Embed tag. This works in much the same way the Noframes tag works, enabling you to design a page with the more advanced feature while providing an alternative for viewers using lower-end browsers.

> **Note**
>
> **Ensure Your Viewers Have Plug-Ins**
>
> If you are going to use file types that require plug-ins to display, it's a good idea to include a link on your HTML page to a page where the viewer can download the plug-in necessary to view your animation, PDF file, and so on. Many designers recommend sticking to the most widely supported plug-ins to help ensure that a majority of your users will already have the software needed to view your pages. You never want to make a viewer leave your site, go and download a special plug-in, and then come back only to find a simple animation of your logo. Many won't bother, and the ones who do are likely to feel it was a waste of their time. To help with this problem, Netscape now builds several plug-in technologies directly into Navigator 3.0. You'll find a list of the latest plug-ins supported on Netscape's Web site at the following:
>
> ```
> http://home.netscape.com/
> ```

- <EMBED>: The Embed tag enables you to link to file formats not supported by the HTML 3.2 specification such as Shockwave files, PDF files, and more. There is no close tag.

- <NOEMBED>: Similar to the <NOFRAMES> tag, the Noembed tag enables you to provide an option for browsers that do not yet support plug-in options. The <NOEMBED> tag requires a close </NOEMBED> tag.

Here's an example of the two tags used together:

```
<EMBED SRC="cool_animation.dcr" HEIGHT=130 WIDTH=180>
<NOEMBED>
<IMG SRC="boring.gif" HEIGHT=130 WIDTH=180>
</NOEMBED>
```

Viewed in Netscape Navigator, the previous code displays a Director file, while browsers that do not recognize the <EMBED> tag display the "boring" GIF described in the Image tag.

Both the <EMBED> and the <NOEMBED> tags can contain the following attributes:

- ALIGN: Determines the alignment of embedded element, using left, right, and center.

- BORDER: Similar to the Image tag, the Border attribute in the Embed tag can be set in pixels to control the width of a border and can be set to zero so that there is no border around the element.

- HEIGHT: Height of the embedded object in pixels.

- WIDTH: Width of the embedded object in pixels.

- PLUGINSPAGE: This attribute lets you direct users to an URL for a page where they can download the plug-in. This requires the SRC attribute.

Plug-Ins

The <EMBED> tag enables Netscape Navigator to handle additional features provided by third-party plug-ins or helper applications. Plug-ins are software extensions that work in conjunction with the browser and allow the display of media in formats not otherwise available in HTML. In addition to the attributes described in the previous section, many plug-ins require their own attributes. To learn more about specific plug-ins, check Netscape's home page or the Web site of the manufacturer of the plug-in.

JavaScript

Working with Sun, the creators of Java, Netscape created JavaScript, which can be embedded directly into an HTML page. JavaScript provides an excellent way to add simple animation and interactive features to your Web pages, but the intricacies of the language are beyond the scope of this HTML tutorial. A great reference is a book called *Plug-n-Play JavaScript*, by Kevin Ready and Paul Vachier (New Riders, 1996). The beauty of *Plug-n-Play JavaScript* is that you don't have to know JavaScript to use it. The book is packed with scripts you can build right into your pages with only minor customization, and all of the scripts are included on a CD-ROM so you don't even have to retype them. For more information on JavaScript, check out the references on the Web listed in Appendix C of this book.

Netscape Wrap-Up

Netscape offers many tantalizing new HTML features, such as frames, greater alignment control, and the capability to specify fonts. Many of the new HTML 3.2 tags were proposed by Netscape before they became part of the W3C, and it can be assumed that many of the tags that are still "unofficial" will follow and be incorporated into HTML 3.5 or 4.0 in the future.

In the meantime, these tags should be used with care, and options such as the Noframes and Noembed tags should be included to ensure that your pages are presentable to all of your viewers. If you are on an intranet, you may not have to worry about this because you can be assured that all of your viewers are using a current version of Netscape. If you are trying to reach the general audience, however, you will want to create pages that are designed for a variety of browsers.

In the next section, you'll get an overview of the Microsoft Extensions. Similar to Netscape, these extensions are generally not supported by other browsers. However, Netscape and Microsoft have been so competitive that they generally support each other's tags and extensions.

HTML Tutorial and
Reference

Microsoft Extensions

In addition to the HTML tags and attributes created by Netscape, you may want to add some of the special features created by Microsoft. Microsoft and Netscape have been extremely competitive in their development of HTML new tags and both of their browsers support many of the same features. This section is designed to highlight the additions that Microsoft's Internet Explorer supports, with a focus on features created by Microsoft. This is not intended to be a complete reference, but it covers most of the Microsoft-specific tags currently available.

Keep in mind that things are changing quickly and that many of the tags described here may be supported by Netscape Navigator by the time you read this. Also note that earlier versions of Netscape Navigator and Microsoft Internet Explorer, as well as most other browsers, do not support these new features. For an up-to-date look at HTML tag support, visit each company's Web site. You can find new Microsoft information at the following:

```
http://www.microsoft.com/
```

Microsoft is leading the way with style sheets, one of its most dramatic additions to the HTML tag set. A design concept borrowed from desktop publishing programs such as QuarkXPress and PageMaker, style sheets enable you to specify a variety of formatting options that can be applied to many sections of a page and even to many pages within a Web site.

Style Sheets

HTML style sheets are a giant step in the right direction for those with a graphics design background. Similar to style sheets desktop publishing programs, this feature enables you to define a style at the beginning of the document and then refer to it later to apply all of the formatting specified in the style sheet to a section of text. This also enables you to change the formatting anywhere the style sheet is used, simply by changing the style sheet at the top of the page. Style sheets are designed for applying styles to many places in a document with the advantage that you can make global changes to them later if necessary. If all you want to do is apply one or two HTML tags to one section of an HTML page, it's probably not worth the time to set them up. However, if you use consistent formatting, such as every headline is aligned center, bold, and in the same font and point size, style sheets will save you lots of time. Building on other extensions and HTML tags, style sheets enable you to specify any font, set font sizes in points, set margins, indentation, change link colors, as well as nearly any other text-formatting option available in HTML.

> **Note**
>
> Style sheets were quickly adopted by Netscape and are being incorporated into the HTML 3.2 specification by the W3C. They are listed in this section because they are still so new on the Web that no other browsers support them, and Microsoft has been the clear leader in developing and supporting style sheets on the Web.

Creating Style Sheets

<STYLE> is the HTML tag used to specify style sheets. It is paired with its close tag: </STYLE>.

To create a style sheet, you assign styles to common HTML tags. Then, each time that HTML tag is used in the document, the styles you've assigned will also be applied to the formatted section. Be aware that browsers that do not support style sheets will ignore style settings and display the contents of HTML tags as they are traditionally supported. The following is an example of a style sheet that could be placed at the top of an HTML document (if you don't understand the styles yet, they are listed in the following section):

```
<STYLE>
BODY {background: blue; color: red}
H1 {font: 18pt Helvetica bold}
P {font: 10pt Helvetica ; text-indent: 0.5in}
A {text-decoration: italic; color: blue}
</STYLE>
```

Formatting Options for Style Sheets

A range of style information options can be used in style sheets. Notice that they are generally created with common terms, such as the word "bold" instead of HTML codes, such as <B>. The following are the text-formatting features supported by Internet Explorer 3.0.

Font Styles Options

The font specification can be used to set many formatting options at once. Some of the options you see in the following list can be set using the font option alone. Others must be set using specific font style options, as described in the following. (In addition to the examples provided in this section, other examples are included in the section "What Kind of Style Sheet to Use" to help you understand the implementation of these options.)

The following is an example of the font option used alone to specify several formatting options at once: font: bold 12pt/14pt "Arial, Helvetica".

Explanation: This would set the text to display as bold, 12 point with 14 point leading and would use the Arial font if available and Helvetica as the second option. (More detailed descriptions of these options are included in the other font features described in the following section.)

Text-Formatting Options

Some of the text-formatting options are included in the following list:

- Font-size: Specifies an exact font size using point sizes.

- Font-weight: Specifies the weight of the type. Currently only normal and bold are supported.

- Font-style: Currently only italic is supported.

- Text-decoration: Options are: none, underline, italic, or line-through. None is an especially useful feature because it can be used to turn off underlining in linked text.

- Line-height: This feature is roughly equivalent to leading because it sets the height of each line of text. This is also specified in point sizes. Currently the extra spacing is added before lines of text, not after, but Microsoft states that this may be changed to match the standards set by desktop publishing applications.

● Font-family: In the case of font family, you can specify a list of font names separated by commas. The browser will then search the user's hard drive for the font and, if the first font listed is not available, it will search for the second. If none of the specified fonts are found on the user's hard drive, the browser's default font is displayed.

● Background: Specifies a background color using a hexadecimal color code or common color name. This can also be used to link a background image.

Layout Formatting Options

In addition to the text-formatting options described, style sheets support layout formatting options. All measurements can be set in inches, centimeters, or pixels. Layout options are:

● Margin-left and margin-right: Specify the right and left margins.

● Text-indent: Sets the indentation for each paragraph.

● Text-align: Can be set to left, right, or center to specify text alignment.

What Kind of Style Sheet to Use

There are three ways to set and use styles sheets. Each serves a different purpose.

● External style sheets: The most powerful of style sheets enable you to specify styles for an entire Web site.

● Page style sheets: Specify the styles for an entire HTML document.

● Inline styles sheets: Specify the style of a specific section of a page.

External Style Sheets

External style sheets enable you to create a style that can be applied to all of the pages in your Web site. Using this HTML feature, you can make global changes to a document or series of documents and automate much of the HTML coding that is applied to your pages. But, Microsoft warns, "This method does cause a very slight decrease in performance, roughly equivalent to placing a small image on each page, because often an extra connection must be opened to download the style sheet."

> **Note**
>
> External style sheets require that you create a new page with the extension .css. This is a new MIME type that requires that your server is configured to handle text/css files. If you are unsure about this, you will need to talk to your system administrator or Internet Service Provider. If you use page style sheets or inline styles, this will not be necessary.

To create an external style sheet, create a new text document in any text editor or HTML editor. This file will serve as a master style guide for the entire site. Style sheets essentially add formatting features to other, more common, HTML tags. Thus, if you assign font: 24 pt to the <H1> tag, every use of the <H1> tag in the document will be formatted as point size 24. To assign more than one style option to an HTML tag, simply separate the options with colons. The following is an example of an external style sheet:

```
BODY {background: black; color: white}
H1 {font: 24pt Helvetica bold}
P {font: 10pt Helvetica ; text-indent: 0.5in}
A {text-decoration: none}
```

A style sheet, such as the one described in the preceding, must be saved on your server and referenced in the Head section of each HTML page. If you saved the example as "style.css," then you would reference it in your HTML pages like this:

```
<HTML><HEAD><LINK REL=STYLE TYPE="text/css"
SRC="style.css"><TITLE>My Cool Page that uses Style Sheets<
➥TITLE></HEAD>
<BODY>
<H1>This headline would display as Helvetica, bold, 24 point</H1>
<P>This paragraph would display as Helvetica, 10 point, and would
➥be indented half an inch from the left margin</P>
<A HREF=http://www.microsoft.com>This link would not be under
➥lined</A>
</BODY>
</HTML>
```

Page Style Sheets

Page style sheets are created and placed at the top of an HTML document and are applied only to that page. After you have created such a page, you can copy that style to the top of other pages to avoid the download delay of external style sheets, while still maintaining consistent styles and automating the mark-up process. If you use an HTML or text editor that allows for the creation of templates, style sheets can be built into templates, making it easier to use the same styles on each page. The following is an example:

```
<HTML>
<HEAD>
<STYLE>
BODY {background: /images/bground.gif}
H1 {font: 24pt Helvetica bold}
P {font: 10pt Helvetica; text-indent: 0.5in}
A {text-decoration: none; color: red}
</STYLE>
<TITLE>My Cool Page</TITLE></HEAD>
<BODY>
<H1>This headline would display as Helvetica, bold, 24 point.</H1>
<P>This paragraph would display as Helvetica, 10 point, and would
➥be indented half an inch from the left margin.</P>
<A HREF="http://www.microsoft.com">This link would not be under
➥lined and would display in blue.</A>
</BODY>
</HTML>
```

Inline Style Sheets

Inline style sheets enable you to apply a style to only one specific location on a page. This does, in some ways, defeat the purpose of style sheets and you may find it just as easy to apply the regular HTML formatting tags directly. It does, however, provide a way to override page or external style sheets in specific sections of a page.

There are two ways to use inline style sheets. The first is to assign a style within the brackets of an HTML tag. For example:

```
<P STYLE="font: 10pt Helvetica; text-indent: 0.5in">
```

This paragraph would display in 10-point text, Helvetica and would be indented half an inch from the left margin.</P>

The second way to create an inline style sheet is to use a new tag called SPAN. The following is an example:

```
<SPAN STYLE="font: 10pt Helvetica; text-indent: 0.5in">
```

This would apply the same formatting as you saw in the previous example, but could be used to set a style to a much larger area of the page.</SPAN>

> **Note**
>
> Internet Explorer 3.0 beta 1 had a bug that made it impossible to override external style sheets with page or inline styles. That bug was fixed in later versions.

Using Style Sheets

As you see, style sheets can be used to globally assign many new HTML style features at once, eliminating much of the tedium of coding text in your Web pages. Again, remember that very few browsers support these options yet, so you should make sure that you create designs that will still look good even if the styles are not applied to the display.

Microsoft Table Attributes

In addition to all of the HTML Table tags and attributes you learned about in the HTML 3.2 and Netscape sections, Microsoft has added a few new attributes to let you set background images in a table and even within table cells, as well as a few other new features described here:

- BACKGROUND: Adding the BACKGROUND attribute to <TABLE>, <TD>, or <TR> tags enables you to place a background image in a table or table cell and then overlay text or images. This attribute is used with the same options as you learned when it was introduced for the <BODY> tag. Example: <TD BACKGROUND="bground.gif"> This text would display on top of the background images></TD>.

- BGCOLOR: Enables you to set a hexadecimal or common color code as the background color attribute to <TABLE>, <TD>, or <TR> tags.

- BORDERCOLOR: Sets border color and must be used with the BORDER attribute. Can be used with the <TABLE>, <TD>, or <TR> tags.

- BORDERCOLORLIGHT: Sets independent border color control over one of the two colors used to draw a 3D border, opposite the border color set with BORDERCOLORDARK. This attribute is also used with the BORDER attribute. Can be used with the <TABLE>, <TD>, or <TR> tags.

- BORDERCOLORDARK: Sets independent border color control over one of the two colors used to draw a 3D border, opposite of BORDERCOLORLIGHT. It must be used with the BORDER attribute. Can be used with the <TABLE>, <TD>, or <TR> tags.

● TABLE RULES: This new attribute enables you to turn off part of a table border while maintaining the rest. Thus, you can create a table with the rules between rows or columns without maintaining the outside border, or a table with an outside border and now rules between columns and rows. To create a table that only has rules between rows, use the following:

```
<TABLE RULES=ROWS>
```

For a table with rules only between columns, use:

```
<TABLE RULES=COLS>
```

For a table with an outside border, but no rules between columns or rows, use:

```
<TABLE RULES=NONE>
```

● BASELINE: This attribute enables you to align text of varying sizes to the bottom of a table data cell by adding VALIGN=BASELINE to any TD tag. For example: <TD VALIGN=BASELINE><Font Size=24pt>This is large text </Font></TD><TD VALIGN=BASELINE><Font Size=12pt>This is much smaller text that would not align properly without the VALIGN attribute. </TD>.

● TBODY: Defines the table body. Use this element to distinguish the rows in the table header or footer from those in the main body of the table. If a table does not have a header or footer (does not have a THEAD or TFOOT element), the TBODY element is optional. The end-tag is always optional. You can use the TBODY element more than once in a table. This is useful for dividing lengthy tables into smaller units and for controlling the placement of horizontal rules.

● TFOOT: The table footer distinguishes the rows in a table as footers distinct from the header or main body of the table. Only one footer is allowed.

● THEAD:The table header distinguishes the rows in the table header from those in the footer or main body of the table. Only one header is allowed.

New Image Formats

Internet Explorer 3.0 adds support for BMP files and animated GIFs. Animated GIFs are also supported by Netscape (refer to Chapter 11 for more information on how to create animated GIFs).

BMP files can be created using Microsoft Paint and were added by Microsoft for users who do not have a graphics program such as Photoshop capable of creating GIF or

JPEG images. BMP files are linked to a Web page just as you would any other image. Example:

```
<IMG SRC="/images/mypic.bmp">
```

The problem with BMP files is that they are not supported by any other browser, nor are they likely to be supported by other browsers very soon. Microsoft adds support for BMP files because its program Microsoft Paint does not yet support GIF or JPEG image creation or conversion. If you have the option, always use GIFs or JPEGs instead. BMP files are safest on an intranet where you can better assess if users will be able to view them.

Creating Columns

The <COL> and <COLGROUP> tags enable you to create columns of text on a page and control their span and alignment, but it must be used within an HTML table. The close tag is not required and not recommended.

Example:

```
<TABLE>
<COLGROUP>
    <COL ALIGN=RIGHT>
    <COL ALIGN=LEFT>
<COLGROUP>
    <COL ALIGN=CENTER>
<TBODY>
    <TR>
    <TD>This is the first column and is right-aligned.</TD>
    <TD>This is the second column and is left-aligned.</TD>
    <TD>This column is in a new group and is centered.</TD>
    </TR>
</TABLE>
```

Iframes

Following Netscape's lead, Microsoft implemented frame support in the 2.0 version of Internet Explorer. Their biggest addition is the capability to create floating frames. Many designers have disliked the thick lines created by frames because of the harsh division they created in a page layout and the inability to control the spacing and alignment of the contents of a frame. With the addition of floating frames, Microsoft gives designers greater control of the display of their pages. The <IFRAME> tag defines a floating frame and requires the end-tag </IFRAME>. <IFRAME> includes the attributes in the following list:

● ALIGN: Sets the alignment of the frame or of the surrounding text. Values are set as TOP, surrounding text is aligned with the top of the frame; MIDDLE, surrounding text is aligned with the middle of the frame; BOTTOM, surrounding text is aligned with the bottom of the frame; LEFT, the frame is drawn as a left-flush "floating frame," and text flows around it; RIGHT, the frame is drawn as a right-flush "floating frame," and text flows around it.

● FRAMEBORDER: This attribute enables you to set the border to 0 so that there is no border displayed around a frame area.

● HEIGHT: Controls the height (in pixels) of the floating frame.

● MARGINHEIGHT: Controls the margin height for the frame and is specified in pixels.

● MARGINWIDTH: Controls the margin width for the frame and is specified in pixels.

● NAME: Provides a target name for the frame.

● NORESIZE: Prevents the user from resizing the frame.

● SCROLLING: Controls scrolling of a frame. Values are yes or no. The default creates a scrollbar if the contents of the frame extend beyond the display area on the screen.

● SRC: Displays the source file for the frame.

● WIDTH: Controls the width of the floating frame and is specified in pixels. Example: <IFRAME FRAMEBORDER=0 ALIGN=RIGHT SRC="frame1.htm"></IFRAME>.

The Embed and Object Tags

The <EMBED> tag has long been used to place objects on a Web page that require helper applications or plug-ins to be displayed. Microsoft Internet Explorer prefers the <OBJECT> tag, but supports the <EMBED> tag for backward compatibility with earlier HTML documents. The <EMBED> tag is also supported by other browsers. Thus, unless you are designing pages only for Internet Explorer, you are better off using the <EMBED> tag instead of the <OBJECT> tag.

The ‹EMBED› Tag

The <EMBED> tag is used to link embedded objects such as sound or video files. The attributes of this tag are described in the following list:

- HEIGHT: Specifies the height of an object on a page in pixels. Unlike most tags that support height as an optional attribute, the Embed tag requires it.

- NAME: The name used by other objects or elements to refer to this object.

- OPTIONAL PARAM: Specifies any parameters that are specific to the object.

- PALETTE: Sets the color palette to the foreground or background color.

- SRC: As in the Anchor tag, this specifies the name and location of the file.

- WIDTH: Specifies the width of an object on a page in pixels. Unlike most tags that support width as an optional attribute, the Embed tag requires it.

The ‹OBJECT› Tag

The <OBJECT> tag inserts an object, such as an image, document, applet, or control, into the HTML document. The end tag is required. An object can contain any elements ordinarily used within the body of an HTML document, including section headings, paragraphs, lists, forms, and even nested objects. The attributes for this tag are described in the following list.

- ALIGN: Specifies the alignment for the object using: BASELINE to align the object to the bottom of surrounding text; CENTER, centers the object between left and right margins and forces subsequent text to start on the next line after the object; LEFT, aligns with the left margin and subsequent text wraps along the right side of the object; MIDDLE, aligns with the baseline of surrounding text; RIGHT, aligns with the right margin, and subsequent text wraps along the left side of the object; TEXTBOTTOM, aligns with the bottom of surrounding text; TEXTMIDDLE, aligns with the midpoint between the baseline and the height of the surrounding text; TEXTTOP, aligns with the top of surrounding text.

- BORDER: Specifies the width of the border if the object is linked. This should generally be set to 0 to prevent the ugly colored borders created by linking.

- CLASSID: Identifies the object implementation or URL. The syntax of the URL depends on the object type. For example, for registered ActiveX controls, the syntax is: CLSID:class-identifier.

- CODEBASE: Identifies the code base or URL for the object. The syntax of the URL depends on the object.

- CODETYPE: Specifies the Internet media type for code.

- DATA: Identifies data for the object. The syntax of the URL depends on the object.

● DECLARE: Declares the object without instantiating it. Use this when creating cross-references to the object later in the document or when using the object as a parameter in another object.

● HEIGHT: Specifies the height for the object.

● HSPACE: Specifies horizontal space on either side of an object and is specified in pixels.

● NAME: Sets the name of the object when submitted as part of a form.

● SHAPES: Specifies that the object has shaped hyperlinks.

● STANDBY: Enables you to specify the message that displays while the browser loads the object.

● TYPE: Specifies the Internet media type for data.

● USEMAP: Specifies the image map to use with the object.

● VSPACE: Specifies vertical space at the top and bottom of an object and is specified in pixels.

● WIDTH: Specifies the width for the object.

The ‹SCRIPT› Tag

Scripts execute and instantiate objects in the order in which they appear in the HTML document. Named objects can be referenced only in the order in which they appear. The attributes for the <SCRIPT> tag are described in the following list:

● SCRIPT: Specifies the use of a script.

● LANGUAGE: Indicates the ActiveX scripting language in which the enclosed script was written. Examples of an ActiveX scripting language are "VBScript" and "JScript."

The ‹MARQUEE› Tag

The <MARQUEE> tag creates a scrolling text marquee. A similar feature can be created with JavaScript, but the <MARQUEE> tag is much easier to set up. The attributes of this tag are described in the following list:

● ALIGN: Specifies how the surrounding text should align with the marquee. Uses LEFT, RIGHT, CENTER, TOP, MIDDLE, and BOTTOM.

- BEHAVIOR: Specifies how the text should behave. The SCROLL value starts off one side and scrolls across and completely off the page before starting again. (This is the default.) The SLIDE value starts completely off one side, scrolls in, and stops as soon as the text touches the other margin. The ALTERNATE value causes the text to bounce back and forth within the marquee.

- BGCOLOR: Specifies a background color for the marquee.

- DIRECTION: Specifies the direction the text should scroll. Values are LEFT or RIGHT (LEFT, which means scrolling to the left from the right, is the default).

- HEIGHT: Specifies the height of the marquee, in pixels or as a percentage of the displayed screen.

- HSPACE: Specifies left and right margins for the outside of the marquee, in pixels.

- LOOP: Specifies how many times a marquee will loop when activated. (If n=-1, or if LOOP=INFINITE is specified, it will loop indefinitely.)

- SCROLLAMOUNT: Specifies the number of pixels between each successive draw of the marquee text.

- SCROLLDELAY: Specifies the number of milliseconds between each successive draw of the marquee text.

- VSPACE: Specifies top and bottom margins for the outside of the marquee, in pixels.

- WIDTH: Sets the width of the marquee, either in pixels or as a percentage of the screen width. Example: <MARQUEE BGCOLOR-"FFFFFF" HSPACE=5 VSPACE= 5 BEHAVIOR=SCROLL SCROLLAMOUNT=15 SCROLLDELAY=400>Watch me scroll across your screen.</MARQUEE>

Background Sound

One of the more dramatic Microsoft extensions is background sound that adds sound files to a page that begin to play as soon as a viewer loads the document. Sound files can be samples using .wav or .au format, or can be in MIDI format. Unfortunately, this feature only works on Windows 95 or NT operating systems using Internet Explorer. The <BGSOUND> tag adds background sound to a page. The attributes for this tag are as follows:

- SRC: Specifies the name and location of the sound file.

- LOOP: Specifies how many times a sound will be repeated. If LOOP=INFINITE, it will play indefinitely.

Microsoft Wrap-Up

Microsoft adds some exciting new features to the HTML specification, but keep in mind that if your users are not using Internet Explorer 3.0, they will not be able to view these options. In fact, some of these features even require that users are on a Windows 95 or NT system to function. Thus, unless you are on an intranet and can be assured that all of your viewers meet these requirements, it's important to create designs that will work without these new features. Style sheets, for example, are an enticing and potentially time-saving addition to HTML. But if you have assigned a style to an <H1> tag, for example, make sure that the page will still work if the only formatting applied to the text is the <H1> tag by itself.

Many of the new tags and attributes described in this section are likely to be incorporated into other browsers and some are already being adopted by Netscape and the W3C. If you use them carefully, you should be able to create pages that will work in all browsers and include these advanced design elements for an increasingly broad audience.

Summary

This chapter was designed to provide a basic HTML tutorial for those who are new to the HyperText Markup Language, and a convenient reference to those who have worked with HTML but may not know all of the tags by heart. The sections are intentionally divided into HTML 2.0, 3.2, and then Netscape and Microsoft extensions to help you better understand the differences among HTML tags and the support you can expect among various browsers.

If you limit your pages to HTML 2.0, your Web site should have a consistent display in all browsers, but it will be boring. If you add HTML 3.2 or browser-specific tags and attributes, make sure that you test your pages in a variety of browsers to ensure they will work for all of your viewers. If you are on an intranet, you should enjoy the advantage of knowing what browser your target audience is using so that you can create pages designed with its features and limitation in mind.

Fortunately, you don't need to understand all the HTML tags and their attributes to build good Web sites. In fact, when using many of the programs described in this book, you don't *need* to know much HTML at all. But having a general knowledge of the language, recognizing that there is more than one form of HTML, and understanding the basic features and limitations of the HyperText Markup Language will make learning the programs described in the book much easier.

HTML has changed so dramatically and quickly, it has been difficult for HTML authoring-tool developers to keep up. Thus, even the latest HTML editors and converters may not support all the HTML features you want to use in your designs. The best programs make it possible to add your own HTML tags to their list of options, but that, of course, requires that you know the HTML tags you want to add. The goal of this chapter has been to prepare you to create HTML pages, as well as to tailor the results of the programs described in this book. Now that you're informed, you should be able to focus on the creative part of Web design to create beautiful and intuitive HTML pages.

If you want to stay up on the latest features of HTML, visit the Netscape and Microsoft Web sites frequently, as well as the W3C site.

```
Netscape: http://home.netscape.com/
Microsoft: http://www.micosoft.com/
The World Wide Web Consortium (W3C): http://www.w3.org/
```

Special Character Tags

Special characters require a unique set of HTML code equivalents. In the table that follows, you learn how to create characters on a Web page such as copyright symbols, ©; accent marks, á, or other foreign characters; and typographers' marks, such as smart quotes (you know, the curly ones graphic designers love so much). Although you can create most of these characters with special commands or fonts in a text editor, browsers won't display them unless you use the special character tags described in the following table. Instead, most browsers will display characters such as smart quotes as strange symbols on the page. To get the desired special character, use the special codes that follow.

Unlike most other HTML tags, special characters are case-sensitive. For example, if you want a capital "A" with an accent, you'll use Á if you want a lowercase "a" with an accent, use &aacute. These tags are inserted in place of the character you want to represent, and spacing should be maintained as it would be in a text editor. Thus, if you were writing the Spanish word "dónde," you would represent it in HTML as "dónde." This may look strange to you in the text, but a browser will display the word with the accent mark over the "o" and create "dónde" on the Web page.

Numbered HTML	Intended Display	HTML Entities
&#34;	"	&quot;
&#35;	#	
&#36;	$	
&#37;	%	
&#38;	&	&amp;
&#39;	'	
&#40;	(	
&#41;	)	
&#42;	*	
&#43;	+	
&#44;	,	

continues

continued

Numbered HTML	Intended Display	HTML Entities
-	-	
.	.	
/	/	
0	0	
1	1	
2	2	
3	3	
4	4	
5	5	
6	6	
7	7	
8	8	
9	9	
:	:	
;	;	
<	<	<
=	=	
>	>	>
?	?	
@	@	
A	A	
B	B	
C	C	
D	D	
E	E	
F	F	
G	G	

Numbered HTML	Intended Display	HTML Entities
&#72;	H	
&#73;	I	
&#74;	J	
&#75;	K	
&#76;	L	
&#77;	M	
&#78;	N	
&#79;	O	
&#80;	P	
&#81;	Q	
&#82;	R	
&#83;	S	
&#84;	T	
&#85;	U	
&#86;	V	
&#87;	W	
&#88;	X	
&#89;	Y	
&#90;	Z	
&#91;	[	
&#92;	\	
&#93;	]	
&#94;	^	
&#95;	_	
&#96;	'	
&#97;	a	
&#98;	b	

Special Character Tags

continues

continued

Numbered HTML	Intended Display	HTML Entities
&#99;	c	
&#100;	d	
&#101;	e	
&#102;	f	
&#103;	g	
&#104;	h	
&#105;	i	
&#106;	j	
&#107;	k	
&#108;	l	
&#109;	m	
&#110;	n	
&#111;	o	
&#112;	p	
&#113;	q	
&#114;	r	
&#115;	s	
&#116;	t	
&#117;	u	
&#118;	v	
&#119;	w	
&#120;	x	
&#121;	y	
&#122;	z	
&#123;	{	
|			
&#125;	}	

Numbered HTML	Intended Display	HTML Entities
&#126;	~	
&#127;	none	
&#128;	•	
&#129;	™	
&#130;	,	
&#131;	*f*	
&#132;	„	
&#133;	…	
&#134;	†	
&#135;	‡	
&#136;	^	
&#137;	‰	
&#138;	…	
&#139;	‹	
&#140;	Œ	
&#141;	Ÿ	
&#142;	/	
&#143;	–	
&#144;	Æ	
&#145;	'	
&#146;	'	
&#147;	"	
&#148;	"\	
&#149;	•	
&#150;	–	
&#151;	—	
&#152;	~	

continues

continued

Numbered HTML	Intended	Display	HTML	Entities
&#153;	™			
&#154;	–			
&#155;	›			
&#156;	œ			
&#157;	ÿ			
&#158;				
&#159;	Ÿ			
	non-breaking space			
&#161;	¡		&iexcl;	
&#162;	¢		&cent;	
&#163;	£		&pound;	
&#164;	¤		&curren;	
&#165;	¥		&yen;	
&#166;	|		&brvbar;	
&#167;	§		&sect;	
&#168;	¨		&uml;	
&#169;	©		&copy;	
&#170;	ª		&ordf;	
&#171;	«		&laquo;	
&#172;	¬		&not;	
&#173;	–		&shy;	
&#174;	®		&reg;	
&#175;	¯		&macr;	
&#176;	°		&deg;	
&#177;	±		&plusmn;	
&#178;	^{2}		&sup2;	
&#179;	^{3}		&sup3;	

Numbered HTML	Intended Display	HTML Entities
&#180;	´	&acute;
&#181;	μ	&micro;
&#182;	¶	&para;
&#183;	·	&middot;
&#184;	¸	&cedil;
&#185;	¹	&sup1;
&#186;	º	&ordm;
&#187;	»	&raquo;
&#188;	¹/₄	&frac14;
&#189;	¹/₂	&frac12;
&#190;	³/₄	&frac34;
&#191;	¿	&iquest;
&#192;	À	&Agrave;
&#193;	Á	&Aacute;
&#194;	Â	&Acirc;
&#195;	Ã	&Atilde;
&#196;	Ä	&Auml;
&#197;	Å	&Aring;
&#198;	Æ	&AElig;
&#199;	Ç	&Ccedil;
&#200;	È	&Egrave;
&#201;	É	&Eacute;
&#202;	Ê	&Ecirc;
&#203;	Ë	&Euml;
&#204;	Ì	&Igrave;
&#205;	Í	&Iacute;
&#206;	Î	&Icirc;

continues

Special Character Tags

continued

Numbered HTML	Intended Display	HTML Entities
&#207;	Ï	&Iuml;
&#208;	‹	&ETH;
&#209;	Ñ	&Ntilde;
&#210;	Ò	&Ograve;
&#211;	Ó	&Oacute;
&#212;	Ô	&Ocirc;
&#213;	Õ	&Otilde;
&#214;	Ö	&Ouml;
&#215;	×	&times;
&#216;	Ø	&Oslash;
&#217;	Ù	&Ugrave;
&#218;	Ú	&Uacute;
&#219;	Û	&Ucirc;
&#220;	Ü	&Uuml;
&#221;	Ý	&Yacute;
&#222;	Þ	&THORN;
&#223;	ß	&szlig;
&#224;	à	&agrave;
&#225;	á	&aacute;
&#233;	é	&eacute;
&#234;	ê	&ecirc;
&#235;	ë	&euml;
&#236;	ì	&igrave;
&#237;	í	&iacute;
&#238;	î	&icirc;
&#239;	ï	&iuml;
&#240;	›	&eth;

Numbered HTML	Intended Display	HTML Entities
&#241;	ñ	&ntilde;
&#242;	ò	&ograve;
&#243;	ó	&oacute;
&#244;	ô	&ocirc;
&#245;	õ	&otilde;
&#246;	ö	&ouml;
&#247;	÷	&divide;
&#248;	ø	&oslash;
&#249;	ù	&ugrave;
&#250;	ú	&uacute;
&#251;	û	&ucirc;
&#252;	ü	&uuml;
&#253;	ȳ	&yacute;
&#254;	-	&thorn;
&#255;	ÿ	&yuml;

APPENDIX B

Software Reference

A wide range of software is covered in this book—from graphics programs, such as Adobe Photoshop, to shareware conversion utilities for spreadsheet to HTML conversion. The software covered in this book should include everything you could need to create great Web sites from content in just about any format you could ever receive it in. Many of these programs are included in demo or trial form on the CD ROM that accompanies this book.

This appendix is included to provide a quick reference to every program covered in this book (and a few that deserve honorable mention). In the following pages, you'll find a brief description of each program, what programs it converts or works as an add-on to, and where you can find out more about it. Programs are divided into categories based on their use.

Word Processing Conversion Programs

The list of programs that follow will help you convert word processing documents.

HTML Transit 2, InfoAccess (Windows)

    http://www.infoaccess.com

HTML Transit is a multiple file conversion utility that features customizable templates and a sizable gallery of graphical art to use on your Web pages. HTML Transit converts word processing, RTF, and FrameMaker files.

Internet Assistants, Microsoft (Windows, Macintosh)

    http://www.microsoft.com/msdownload/

For: Microsoft Word (also available for Excel and PowerPoint)

Internet Assistants are no-charge add-ons to the Office Suite applications that convert Office formats for the Web.

WordPerfect Suite 7, Corel (Windows)

```
http://www.corel.com
```

Corel's latest version of WordPerfect Suite (an Office Suite of applications) has HTML conversion capability built into the applications.

ClarisWorks 4.0, Claris Corp. (Windows, Macintosh)

```
http://www.claris.com
```

Like Corel WordPerfect Suite, ClarisWorks 4.0 has conversion capability built into its word processing application.

XTML+ (Macintosh)

```
http://www.hotfiles.com/swbrowse/mc14/4/4/mac-MC14445.html
```

For: ClarisWorks

XTML+ is an XTND filter. It converts the formatting of any document created with a word processor that supports XTND exports (which ClarisWorks does). It then assigns HTML tags based on that formatting. It also works with the freeware program clip2gif to translate graphics into GIF images, creating the necessary links to these images as it converts the document.

WordPerfect HTML Macros (Macintosh)

```
http://www.tiac.net/users/mdw/imap/wpmacro.html
```

For: WordPerfect

WordPerfect HTML Macros adds several HTML macros to your Macro menu. When you select one of these macros, you are prompted to enter information. After you enter this information, the macro runs, replacing the regular formatting of your document with HTML code. Some of the HTML macros available from this pull-down menu are HTML Forms, HTML Headers, HTML Image, HTML Links, and HTML Lists. Using this macro program does require some knowledge of HTML tags.

WPTOHTML (Windows)

```
http://www.lib.ox.ac.uk/~hunter
```

For: WordPerfect

WPTOHTML 2.0 converts WordPerfect files to HTML and also provides a set of
HTML editing tools. The conversion tools make it easy for someone who knows very
little HTML to convert a document successfully. It also provides a nice set of HTML
authoring and editing tools for users who do know HTML. In this sense,
WPTOHTML 2.0 scales to the ability of its users. If your WordPerfect document
contains cross-references, indexes, endnotes, or a table of contents, they will not
convert when you use WPTOHTML 2.0.

RTFtoHTML (Macintosh or Windows)

```
http://www.sunpack.com/RTF/
```

For: ClarisWorks, WordPerfect, Microsoft Word, and all major word processing
programs

RTFtoHTML is a fantastic utility that converts documents saved in RTF (Rich Text
Format) to HTML. *RTF* is a file format developed by Microsoft and now widely used
by most major word processing programs on the MacOS, Windows, and Unix
platforms. In addition to being a superior utility, the documentation and guidelines
for its use are also very good. You can check out the RTFtoHTML manual at the
following:

```
http://www.sunpack.com/RTF/guide.htm
```

Software Reference

Web Publisher Pro, Skisoft (Windows)

```
URL: http://www.skisoft.com
```

Web Publisher Pro is a multiple file conversion utility that features customizable
templates and a Long Document utility that can convert long HTML files into
smaller, more manageable files. It works well with RTF files and creates excellent
tables.

WebAuthor 2.0, Quarterdeck Corporation (Windows)

`http://www.quarterdeck.com`

WebAuthor 2.0 converts Word 6.0 and 7.0 files and doubles as an HTML editor; this utility also supports tables and forms.

2HTML, Group Cortex (Macintosh)

`http://www.cortex.net/`

This program is a Microsoft Word 6.0 macro for the Macintosh designed to strip out smart quotes and other special characters, and convert basic formatting such as bold and center to HTML. Point sizes can be mapped to HTML header sizes, and ordered lists can be automatically converted.

Adobe File Utilities 1.0

`http://www.adobe.com`

Adobe File Utilities 1.0 converts word processing and spreadsheet files from platform-to-platform and from file type to file type between more than 200 programs and formats. This program also converts simple files to HTML, and converts many different graphics files (but doesn't convert to GIF89a or progressive JPEG).

Spreadsheet Conversion Programs

Internet Assistant for Excel (Windows, Macintosh)

`http://www.microsoft.com/msdownload/`

The Internet Assistant for Excel is a no-charge add-on that converts Excel spreadsheets into HTML tables for the Web. Note: the Microsoft Word Internet Assistant may be a better alternative for Table conversion, especially if you have a table with empty cells. (See Chapter 3, "Microsoft Office Document Conversion," for more details.)

TableCloth Pro (Macintosh)

```
http://pinky.istore.com/tc/index.html
```

For: ClarisWorks, Quattro Pro, Excel, Lotus 1-2-3, FileMaker Pro, and any spreadsheet or database program that can output tab-delimited, ASCII text

TableCloth is an AppleScript applet that converts tab-delimited text to HTML table format. Because it converts simple ASCII text, it can convert files from a multitude of spreadsheet and database applications. Users of Microsoft Excel, ClarisWorks, Lotus 1-2-3, and Claris FileMaker Pro can all benefit from the easy table generation provided in TableCloth.

TwoClicks Tables (Windows, Macintosh)

```
URL: http://www.twoclicks.com/cgi-bin/tabdemo.pl
```

For: All spreadsheet data

This online application enables you to paste your spreadsheet data into a window in a browser, select your formatting preferences, and press a button to generate an HTML table. You can then download the source code and use the table yourself. This application is described in this chapter in the section called "Converted ClarisWorks Spreadsheets."

QuarkXPress Conversion Programs

BeyondPress 2.0, Astrobyte

```
http://www.astrobyte.com
```

BeyondPress is a QuarkXPress XTension that converts XPress files into HTML and graphics into JPEGs and GIFs. BeyondPress adds a Document Content palette under the View menu and lists all the elements of an XPress document so you can specify what is exported, and turn large XPress files into multiple HTML pages. One of the most useful features of this program is the capability to map XPress styles to HTML styles. This can be set globally and can be overridden, enabling you to alter the style of any individual element while leaving the rest set with the global style. Image conversion capabilities include the capability to scale, set transparency, create image maps, and convert images into GIFs or JPEGs. Using the XTension's Preferences, you can customize each article you export. In addition to a list of HTML options included in BeyondPress 2.0, you can create and add your own HTML styles.

HexWeb XT, HexMac International (Macintosh)

http://www.hexmac.de/

HexWeb XT is similar to BeyondPress in that it is a Mac-only XTension for XPress conversion. Unlike BeyondPress, however, HexWeb XT does not map style sheets to HTML code and lacks many of the other more sophisticated features of BeyondPress. The program is limited to matching point sizes to header tags and converting basic formatting such as bold and italics. HexWeb XT provides basic image conversion and can be used to set links by specifying elements in the original document. Header and footer elements that are repeated on every page can be defined in settings. One feature BeyondPress lacks is the HexWeb Index, which automatically generates a table of contents file after all HTML articles have been exported.

e-Gate, Rosebud Technologies (Macintosh)

http://www.rosebud.fr/

Rosebud Technologies, a consulting company in Paris that services the European publishing market, offers a custom XPress conversion tool for high-end users. The program is a bit beyond the scope of this book, partially because it has to be customized and partially because it costs a minimum of $950 (that's 4,800 francs). According to Rosebud Technologies, the goal of e-Gate is to export Quark articles using "meta-information" such as publication name, section name, date of publication, page number, source file name, and so on. The program was designed to enable publishers to build editorial or document databases (in structured ASCII or HTML) as part of the conversion process. In order to do this, the company requires at least one day to customize the system for each publication.

CyberPress, Extensis (Macintosh)

http://www.extensis.com/

CyberPress, by Extensis, is scheduled to ship by the fall of 1996. Developed in cooperation with Astrobyte, CyberPress is a "lite" version of BeyondPress that will be bundled with Adobe PageMill. The package will retail for $149.95. Registered CyberPress users may upgrade to BeyondPress from Astrobyte for $449.95.

FrameMaker Conversion Programs

WebWorks Publisher 3.0, Quadralay Corporation

`http://www.quadralay.com`

WebWorks Publisher is a conversion-to-HTML program designed specifically to handle conversion of FrameMaker documents. The program is highly configurable and provides for arbitrary file splitting, TOC conversion, and table conversion. It is the user's option to handle graphics internally or to export them for individual handling.

Harlequin WebMaker, Harlequin Incorporated

`http://www.harlequin.com`

Harlequin WebMaker is a conversion-to-HTML program dedicated to conversion of FrameMaker documents. WebMaker translates text to Web format by converting FrameMaker tags (layout styles) to HTML. This program can convert FrameMaker tables (including table straddles). Graphics are automatically transferred as inline GIF images; equations are converted into either HTML or graphics, at your option. You can customize the conversion template with WebMaker's library of pre-defined layout styles to optimize the positioning of your content for the Web.

HTML Transit 2, InfoAccess (Windows)

`URL: http://www.infoaccess.com`

HTML Transit is a multiple file conversion utility that features customizable templates and a sizable gallery of graphical art to use on your Web pages. HTML Transit converts word processing, RTF, and FrameMaker files.

PageMaker Conversion Programs

HTML Author, Adobe Systems, Inc. (Macintosh, Windows)

`http://www.adobe.com`

Software Reference

This plug-in is bundled with PageMaker 6.0 to convert documents into HTML. Although Adobe shows great foresight in packaging this program with PageMaker, HTML Author is a very limited conversion program capable of handling the simplest designs into HTML code. The plug-in does not convert graphics. Check Adobe's Web site for upgrades that may be better in the future.

WebSucker 2.8, Mitchell S. Cohen (Macintosh)

http://www.iii.net/users/mcohen.html/.

WebSucker 2.8 is a hypercard stack for the Macintosh designed for the Clark University Scarlet Student Newspaper. The best part about this program is that it's free. But even at that price, it may not be worth the download time. As the program's creator, Mitchell S. Cohen, readily admits, "This really is a hack. The programming is an absolute mess, really to the point of embarrassment." Although the 2.8 upgrade is supposed to support PageMaker 6.0 as well as 5.0, it's buggy and even more limited than HTML Author. But again, it is free, so if you want to try it out on your projects, all you have to lose is the download time (the program is about 1.3 MB).

Dave, Jeff Boulter (Macintosh)

http://www.bucknell.edu/bucknellian/dave/

If you query most online search engines with the words "PageMaker to HTML," the first program that appears on the list is *Dave*, another Macintosh program created for a student newspaper. Unfortunately Dave's not first on the list because it's one of the best—it's first because it seems to have been the first program ever developed for PageMaker conversion. Unfortunately, it hasn't changed since then. According to the program's creator, Jeff Boulter, the program hasn't been updated since Sept. 11, 1995. Boulter recommends WebSucker (described previously) and states that he hopes the upgrade to PageMaker 6.0 will make it unnecessary to improve his program Dave. Unfortunately, PageMaker 6.0 hasn't proven much more helpful.

pmtohtml (Windows)

http://www.w3.org/pub/WWW/Tools/PM2html.html/

pmtohmtl is yet another limited HTML converter for PageMaker, but this one works on Windows.

Portable Document Format (PDF) Programs

Programs from Adobe Systems, Inc.

`http://www.adobe.com`

Adobe is the leader in PDF software. Two versions of Adobe's Acrobat are included here as the 3.0 version is still too new to be widely used.

Acrobat Pro 2.1 (Windows and Macintosh)

The leading tool for making computer-generated documents portable for reading on any computer platform (DOS, Window, Mac, Unix) almost exactly as it appeared (including all type characteristics, photos, illustrations, and layout) on the originating platform. Works for both PostScript and TrueType fonts. Acrobat now lets you add hypertext navigation, multimedia, and live Internet links to its PDF documents. Adobe furnishes a free plug-in viewer for Acrobat files that can be used with Netscape Navigator and other browsers.

Acrobat 3.0 (Windows and Macintosh)

The upgrade to Acrobat 2.1, this program lets you create PDF files that can be easily viewed, navigated, and browsed seamlessly within the leading Web browsers such as Netscape Navigator, and even fill in visually rich, interactive PDF forms. With the Capture plug-in, you can scan and OCR any printed document or TIFF image to PDF. And when CD-ROMs created with Acrobat software are uploaded to your Web site, all the links work automatically—no re-authoring is required. Note: Acrobat 3.0 support for Microsoft Internet Explorer 3.0 is currently under development, but not yet available.

ENVOY, Corel (Windows and Macintosh)

This is a portable document generator and viewer that can be bought separately and is bundled with Windows versions of WordPerfect Office Suite. This program works with all WordPerfect Office documents. Corel distributes a free plug-in that works with Netscape Navigator for viewing Envoy portable documents.

Software Reference

Common Ground 2.0, Common Ground Software (Windows and Macintosh)

http://www.commonground.com

Common Ground is a program for creating portable electronic documents. These documents are called Digital Paper and have the advantage that the viewer can be embedded into the document so that anyone who opens the document can view it instantly. Common Ground has a separate Web publishing utility and does not have inline viewing support from major browsers. Instead, the browser runs the Common Ground Viewer as a helper app in a separate window. The Web publishing utility does have the capability to optimize portable documents for the Web so that they upload one page at a time.

Graphics Programs

Programs from Adobe Systems, Inc.

http://www.adobe.com

Adobe makes a range of graphics software programs. The following are useful for Web design work.

Photoshop 4.0 (Windows, Macintosh, Sun)

This professional-level image editor is the most widely used product of its kind. In Chapter 10, you'll find specific step-by-step examples of how to use Photoshop to modify and create graphics for use on the Web.

Illustrator 6.0 (Windows, Macintosh, Sun)

This professional-level drawing tool for creating illustrations is the most widely-used product of its kind. In Chapter 10, you'll find specific step-by-step examples of how to modify and create graphics for use on the Web. The current version of Illustrator has been enhanced for Web graphics.

Freehand to Illustrator Plug-In (Macintosh, Windows)

This add-on for Illustrator makes it easier to convert Freehand files.

Adobe TextureMaker (Macintosh)

TextureMaker is a resolution-independent texture design program that lets you create sophisticated textures—marble, wood, and stone, as well as clouds, fire, and other environmental elements. Ideal for making background tiles, frame borders, and textured buttons and horizontal bars. This is the only texture maker that supports Adobe Photoshop plug-ins (excepting, of course, texture makers that are plug-ins).

Programs from Macromedia (http://www. macromedia.com)

Freehand 5.5 (Windows, Macintosh)

Freehand 5.5 is a powerful cross-platform illustration program that is the arch competitor to Adobe Illustrator. This program has 100 levels of Undo, including special effects drawing tools such as Fisheye Lens, 3D Rotation tool, Calligraphy Pen, Dragging Knife, and Starburst tool. Freehand is also compatible with many special effects plug-ins for Adobe Illustrator. This program can save files as bitmaps at your choice of resolutions.

xRes 2.0 (Windows, Macintosh)

xRes 2.0 is a cross-platform image compositing, acquisition, editing, and natural media tool all rolled into one. Very powerful features make this an excellent choice if you're only going to buy one image editing program—although you really should also have industry-standard Photoshop in your arsenal. This program is unique in being the only cross-platform program that enables you to edit and compose print-publication quality files in minimal RAM, making it a serious alternative consideration to Live Picture. xRes also provides built-in support for Web- and Internet-friendly formats such as Gif89a, progressive JPEG, and PNG.

Programs from Corel (http://www.corel.com)

Corel Xara (Windows)

Corel Xara is a vector image maker that saves directly to GIF89a, progressive JPEG, and PNG.

Corel WEB.GALLERY CD (Macintosh, Windows)

This program includes more than 7,500 Internet-ready images, featuring 240+ arrows, 480+ bullets, 400 buttons, 135+ dividers, 390+ dropcaps, 100+ objects, 215+ photos, 4,350+ clip art images, 340+ backgrounds, and 120 pre-designed matching sets of banners, dividers, and buttons.

Corel Gallery I & II (Macintosh, Windows)

Corel Gallery I & II includes 10K clip art images in vector format bundled with an image browser. The program is also OLE-compatible and works with all popular drawing programs.

Corel Professional Photos CD-ROM (Macintosh, Windows)

These collections comprise the largest library of photos on CD-ROM. They are in Kodak PhotoCD format and are readable on all platforms. The images are not as slick as in PhotoDisc or ColorBytes collections, but represent very good value for the money. The images can be especially useful in image compositing, as backgrounds, and as "atmosphere" shots for illustrating publications and sites.

CorelDRAW™ 6 (Power Macintosh)

CorelDRAW 6 is a fully featured software application for illustration, photo-editing, bitmap and texture creation, 3D rendering, and multimedia file management. This program features an intuitive Macintosh interface, workspace of up to 150 feet by 150 feet, enhanced speed, and precision to 0.1 micron. In addition, Drag & Drop, AppleScript, and Apple Guide are included, ensuring professional-looking projects.

Programs from Fractal Designs Corporation (http://www.fractal.com)

The Fractal Designs Corporation site now includes products originally from Ray Dream, Inc.

Painter (Macintosh, Windows)

Painter is the first, most versatile, and still-leading "natural media" paint program. "Natural media" is the buzzword for brush strokes that imitate analog artists' tools such as oil paints, watercolors, canvas, and watercolor paper.

Ray Dream Designer/Studio (Macintosh, Windows)

These are three-dimensional modeling and ray-traced rendering programs intended for artists (rather than engineers). Studio adds numerous enhancements and animation capabilities.

JAG (Macintosh, Windows)

"Jaggies Are Gone" is a program for getting rid of "jaggies" when you enlarge a bitmap that's too small or forget to leave antialiasing on when you import a drawing to Photoshop.

Other Useful Fractal Products

Expressions, Poser, Add Depth, Detailer, and Dabbler.

Programs from ULead Systems (http://www.ulead.com)

PhotoImpact V1 (Windows 95)

Combination Image Editor, Imaga Catalogue, and Batch File converter (BMP, CGM, CLP, CUR, DCS, DCX, DRW, EPS, FAX, GIF, HGL, ICO, IFF, IMG, JPG, MAC, MSP, PCD, PCT, PCX, PIC, PLT, PNG, PSD, PXR, RAS, RLE, SCI ,SCT, SHG, TGA, TIF, UFO, UPI, WMF, WPG, 001). This program supports all OLE, Office, Windows 95, and also includes a library of 3K images and textures. Image Editor is PS plug-in compatible, and can save files in GIF, progressive JPEG, and PNG.

PhotoImpact GIF/JPEG SmartSaver (Windows 95)

This is a utility for adding more control over Internet graphics; it can operate as a stand-alone or Photoshop-compatible plug-in. You can select multiple files in Windows Explorer for batch processing. When used as plug-in, this utility has real time before and after preview; it can also use the smoothing function to reduce artifacts during compression. Multiple GIF files can be made to share Explorer or Netscape palettes. This utility can also batch save to several parameters, enabling you to experiment on all files at once. PhotoImpact can also compress to a target file size and create progressive JPEGs.

ImagePals/2 (Windows 95)

This program is similar to PhotoImpact without the more sophisticated image editing features and with less power. This is a good solution for simple office work involving storing, managing, and retrieving graphics with some built-in scanning, retouching, and image-creating capabilities. This program is a direct competitor of HiJaak.

HiJaak Graphics Suite 95, Quarterdeck Corporation (Windows)

```
http://www.quarterdeck.com
```

This is a multiple-purpose batch graphics file converter, image editor, paint, draw, and cataloging program. HiJaak converts to and from the largest number of file formats of any of the general-purpose converters: 19 vector formats, 35 raster formats, and 24 fax formats. The program makes image icons for Windows Explorer (which makes a PC more Mac-like), auto-traces bitmaps into vector files, and has a built-in hand-sketching program from FutureWave Software (makers of Smart Sketch). HiJaak even comes with a library of 10,000 stock photos on CD-ROM.

Live Picture, Live Picture, Inc. (Macintosh)

```
http://www.livepicture.com/
```

This is the premier image composition tool. Live Picture permits the composition of files consisting of hundreds of megabytes of data in less than 32 MB of RAM, and even lets you work in real time. It's especially worth considering this tool if you'll be creating an image for the Web that you'll want to use in print as well. LP renders re-scaled files with uncanny accuracy. Note: this software is mainly used as a high-end print photo illustration and compositing tool. However, it does save to GIF89a and support transparency.

Programs by Specular International (http://www.specular.com)

Specular 3D Web Workshop (Macintosh)

This is a very cool tool. It lets you drag 3D clip art directly on to a Web page, automatically converts selected standard text to high-styled 3D, and can drag and drop in backgrounds. This tool can also drop in QuickTime animations made in Specular LogoMotion.

Collage (Macintosh)

Collage is excellent for multi-layered compositing of high-resolution photos in low-memory computers.

Texturescape (Macintosh)

Texturescape is a vector-based tool for creating very complex scalable and tileable textures. The reasonable price of this tool makes it a must have for the graphic designer's toolkit.

Programs from MetaTools (http://www.metatools.com)

Kai's Power Tools (Macintosh, Windows)

If you only get one third-party Photoshop-compatible filter, this is it. This program is invaluable for making textures, seamless background tiles, neon, and gradient text. KPT works with almost all image-editing programs (but don't take it for granted).

KPT Convolver (Macintosh)

KPT Convolver gives ultimate control over image qualities, and is the best way to customize such things as embossing, color-reduction, blur, sharpen, emboss, tint, color contrast, Gaussian blur, and unsharp masking. Because unsharp masking isn't the proprietary Adobe algorithm, you can use it in a Debabelizer script to correct the blurring that results when images are reduced.

KPT Goo (Macintosh, Windows 95 and NT)

KPT Goo makes it possible to distort images to make them appear as though they're warping, melting, and dripping—a good way to turn portraits into caricatures in order to emphasize a point or convey a message. According to its site, "Goo turns pictures into images that feel like liquid on your screen as you stretch, grow, animate, and fuse images or apply a host of other special effects in real time."

KPT Vector Effects (Macintosh)

This program includes plug-ins compatible with Illustrator and Freehand, and makes it possible to warp and twist text, add distortion, and do 3D extrusion.

KPT Power Photos (Macintosh)

KPT Power Photos are very worthwhile and reasonably-priced collections of royalty-free stock photos. They include numerous pre-masked retro objects, toys, traffic signs, and other images useful for communicating ideas quickly or acting as navigational signs on your Web site. Masking makes it easy to isolate objects from transparent background, but you will still need to use something like the GIF89a export filter for Photoshop in order to save the files as transparent GIFs.

Programs by Asymetrix Corporation (http://www.asymetrix.com)

3D F/X 2.0 (Windows)

3D F/X is a simple modeling program that enables you to create a three-dimensional scene the first time you use the program. Simply drag-and-drop a 3D model from the catalog, add an interesting surface effect, lighting, shadows, and a backdrop, and you have created a 3D scene. This program is also an excellent vehicle for manipulating and rendering prepared "clip art" models produced in other programs, and for building 3D text for headlines and logo art.

Web 3D (Windows)

Web 3D is essentially the same program as 3D F/X, but with a Netscape-compatible plug-in for viewing 3D images on the Web with functionality similar to Apple's QuickTime VR objects. This program also enables you to save 3D objects in GIF89a format, and creates sequential GIF animations for use in server-push/client-pull applications. It enables you to generate true reflections, shadows, and dramatic optical effects using ray tracing. Select from a variety of preset lights, then modify their direction, intensity, shadows, and colors in seconds to create your own unique scenes. Extend Asymetrix Web 3D with OLE 2.0 support and Microsoft Office compatibility.

FutureSplash Animator, Future Wave Software (Macintosh, Windows)

```
http://www.futurewave.com
```

This program is a very versatile general-purpose animation program that has the capability to create vector-based 2D animations for the Web. The result loads faster than you can blink, and even enables you to incorporate interactive mouse-down events. Animation sequences created with FutureSplash Animator are streamed onto the Web pages, which means the animations play as they are downloaded. Sequences using the new FutureSplash vector-based format can be played at any color depth, and are scaleable to any size. FutureSplash Animator supports a variety of other Import/ Export file formats for drawings and animations. Although the native FutureSplash animations require a plug-in, the program imports from and exports to most other popular vector graphics in still and animation formats, including FutureSplash Player, Animated GIF, EPS 3.0 Sequence, Adobe Illustrator Sequence, DXF Sequence, JPEG Sequence, GIF Sequence, QuickTime Movie (Macintosh), PICT Sequence (Macintosh), Windows AVI (Windows), EMF Sequence (Windows), WMF Sequence (Windows), and Bitmap Sequence (Windows). Still image formats include FutureSplash Player SPL (Export), Adobe Illustrator (88, 3.0, 5.0, 6.0), EPS 3.0 (Export), AutoCAD DXF, JPEG Image, GIF Image, PICT Bitmap & Vector-based (Macintosh), Enhanced Metafile EMF (Windows), Windows Metafile WMF (Windows), and Bitmap BMP (Windows).

Pantone ColorWeb, Pantone, Inc. (Macintosh, Windows)

```
http://www.pantone.com/
```

Pantone is the leading company for setting color standards in the computer and print industries. It could be argued that this company knows more about color than anyone. Their newest product, ColorWeb, includes the Pantone Internet Color System, a library of 216 "Internet-safe" colors that appear accurately across computer platforms. With ColorWeb, Web authors can design with confidence, knowing that their pages will appear correctly to all Internet users.

Graphics Conversion Programs

Debabelizer, Equilibrium (Macintosh)

This is the must-have tool for converting graphics files for Internet use. The program's powerful image processing, color-reduction, and dithering capabilities are often said to be unmatched by other utilities. The newest version supports PNG (all attributes), GIF89a with selectable transparency and interlacing, and progressive JPEG.

Conversion Artist, North Coast Software (Windows)

(603) 664-6000 / Fax (603) 664-7872

Batch file conversion enables simultaneous automation of conversion, color reduction, and compression (this may be the Windows product closest to Debabelizer). So far, this program still has no scripting for running filters, Photoshop-compatible plug-in capability, GIF89a, PNG, or progressive JPEG.

GraphicsTools!, Delta Point (Windows)

```
http://www.deltapoint.com
```

This program includes graphics file conversion and cataloging.

HTML Editors

HTML Text Editors

The first two programs described in the following section are covered in Chapter 13, "Tailoring Converted Files," and are considered by the authors of this book to be the best HTML text editors on the market. Other programs are included here (as well as on the CD-ROM) for comparison. Many of these programs are similar, and the editor you choose should depend on subject choices such as interface and ease of use.

BBEdit 4.0, Bare Bones Software (Macintosh)

```
http://www.barebones.com/
```

One of the useful HTML authoring tools available, BBEdit is both simple and extremely powerful. It's also fast, especially when dealing with large numbers of documents. Featuring a Tools palette with a host of HTML tags, this program can be tailored to add any HTML options. Sophisticated search and replace functions are the most powerful feature this program offers for working on Web sites or batches of converted HTML files. BBEdit can do multiple-file searches to change text in every document in a directory, and even within sub-directories all at once—for example, if you want to change one of the items in a navigational bar that appears at the bottom of every page on your 500-page Web site. In minutes BBEdit can do automatically what would have taken you hours to do manually.

Hot Dog V2.0, Sausage Software (Windows)

```
http://www.sausage.com/
```

Hot Dog is a great program for working directly in the HTML code. This program is one of the few editors to support Microsoft extensions such as DYNSRC and MAR-QUEE. Any tags can be added and the toolbar can be customized to support your favorite options. Large, colorful buttons give this program a user-friendly interface, and handy pull-down menus clearly explain options. An extensive help menu includes a comparison of the differences between HTML 2.0 and the Microsoft and Netscape extensions, a rare feature in an editor. Drag-and-drop link and image setting is also supported. For more information on Hot Dog, see Chapter 13.

World Wide Web Weaver, Miracle Software

```
http://www.miracleinc.com/
```

Providing a menu bar, toolbar, and three floating palettes, Web Weaver offers many options for selecting and inserting HTML tags. The palettes can be placed anywhere on the screen and easily edited to host any tag or combination. A Preview button lets you view your work in any browser and can be set to handle more than one browser.

A table builder assists in creating simple HTML tables and supports cellspacing and cellpadding. Data can be added to each cell independently. A link option lets you set links to local files and also facilitates external links. The program automatically determines the height and width of GIFs when you set image links, and features border, alignment, and hyperlink options.

HTML Assistant Pro 2, Brooklyn North Software Works

```
http://fox.nstn.ca/~harawitz/
```

HTML Assistant Pro 2 features a toolbar with HTML 2 and HTML 3.2 tags, and can be tailored to include your own tags and combinations. Advanced HTML Table options include colspan, rowspan, and cellpadding. A template can also be created by simply setting the total number of rows and columns. Many of the features offered in HTML Assistant Pro 2 are split into two levels. The first level handles basic HTML tags; selecting Advanced options reveals a list of attributes that can be added to a tag. A preview option lets you view documents in any browser without leaving the editor.

Software Reference

WYSIWYG HTML Editors

WYSIWYG editors shelter you from the HTML code, making it possible to create Web pages in a graphic environment similar to a word processing or desktop publishing program. The best ones include a text editor so you can work in the code directly without leaving the program. An ever-growing number of WYSIWYG HTML editors make it difficult to determine which is best. And, even more than with the text editors, interface design and other subjective factors will be part of your final decision. Many of the programs listed here are included in demo or trial form on the CD-ROM so that you can try them out for yourself. Most are available for download from the Web sites listed with each company.

Claris Home Page 1.0 (Macintosh, Windows 95, NT)

```
http://www.claris.com
```

Claris Home Page, discussed in Chapter 13, features a WYSIWYG editor that supports high-end features such as frames, complex tables, and image maps. You can also edit the HTML code in a text editor built into the application. Home Page includes most of the HTML 2.0 and 3.2 tags you'd want, as well as Netscape and Microsoft extensions. Best of all, you can add your own HTML tags. In addition to the preview option to view your work in Home Page, a Browser Preview lets you check your designs in any Web browsers. Images can be linked with drag-and-drop ease, and the program supports basic image conversion. Advanced users can quickly integrate applets and other elements using the embed tag. Because it's cross-platform, this is a great tool for working on Web sites with a team that includes developers on more than one operating system.

FrontPage 1.0, Microsoft

```
http://www.microsoft.com
```

FrontPage provides a WYSIWYG interface, making it easy to create simple pages. Bundling an HTML editor with software to run a personal Web server, CGI scripts, and a site manager for organizing links makes this a powerful tool. The HTML editor provides a graphic interface, but no preview option to check your work in other browsers. The program provides a decent list of HTML tags, but you can't add your own.

A "view generated source" option lets you see the HTML code, but it's not a text editor, so you can't change anything in the code. Graphics can be imported into the WYSIWYG environment, but it cannot convert images.

SiteMill 2.0 and PageMill 2.0, Adobe

`http://www.adobe.com`

SiteMill is a powerful Web site management tool that displays an entire site in a graphic environment where you can change and correct links with drag-and-drop ease. This program is covered in detail in Chapter 12, "Web Site Organization and Management." SiteMill is bundled with PageMill (although PageMill can also be purchased separately). Version 2.0 eliminates many critics' complaints, such as poorly spaced HTML code, and adds features to make it one of the easy-to-use WYSIWYG HTML editors. A built-in text editor makes it possible to now edit HTML code without leaving the program, and spaces code more evenly so that it's easier to read. High-end HTML features, such as tables and client-side image maps, have also been added.

HotMetal Pro 2.0, SoftQuad Corporation

`http://www.sq.com/`

HotMetal Pro supports HTML 2, as well as many HTML 3.2, Microsoft, and Netscape extensions. The biggest criticism of this program is its interface. It lets you switch between a WYSIWYG environment and an option that enables you to see the tags, but won't let you change them. The tags can be deleted individually if they are on, but they can't be typed in directly and you can't manually add attributes once they are in place.

Backstage Designer Plus, Macromedia (Windows)

`http://www.macromedia.com`

Although this program is so new it lacks some of the high-end HTML features supported by other HTML editors, it does have an intuitive interface and a number of Macromedia's other programs bundled with it. Backstage features Macromedia PowerApplets, a collection of customizable Shockwave for Director and Java applications that add multimedia to Web pages without programming. Backstage Designer Plus also includes Macromedia xRes SE, a powerful image editor for creating Web graphics. You'll also find a collection of Web page templates, and a library of clip art to help get a Web site up and running quickly.

Software Reference

Miscellaneous Software

Adobe File Utilities 1.0

```
http://www.adobe.com
```

This program converts word processing and spreadsheet files from platform to platform and from file type to file type between more than 200 programs and formats. It also converts many different graphics files (but doesn't convert to GIF89a or progressive JPEG).

Corel Visual CADD Plug-in (Windows)

```
http://www.corel.com
```

This software supports all Corel and Autodesk CADD formats (VCD, DWG, DXF, GCD), supports URL links within drawings, full layers management while viewing files over the Web, and lets you save files to a local drive. This plug-in is free, and will be available shortly for download from the Corel Web page or the Numera Web page (www.numera.com).

Programs from Macromedia (http://www.macromedia.com)

Director 4.0 and 5.0 (Windows, Macintosh)

Director is considered the most popular multimedia authoring tool. Using special plug-ins and a compression program called Afterburner, Director files can now be displayed on Web sites in a format called Shockwave.

Afterburner (Macintosh, Windows)

Afterburner is a tool for compressing Director movies so that they can be transmitted efficiently over the Web. Director Shockwave Developer's Guide, available at the Macromedia Web site, is an online guide with essential information about developing Director movies for the Web. Visit Macromedia's Shockwave Support Area, where you'll find Shockwave TechNotes and assistance for installing and troubleshooting Shockwave for Director.

Shockwave for Director (Windows, Macintosh)

Shockwave for Director makes it possible to view interactive and URL-linked Director movies inline on a Web page. Competes (to some degree) with Java, animated GIFs, and a plethora of private-label animation plug-ins.

Shockwave for Freehand (Windows, Macintosh)

Shockwave for Freehand competes head-to-head with several other plug-ins for reading EPS vector files over the Web.

Shockwave for Authorware (Windows, Macintosh)

Shockwave for Authorware is not yet available, but will allow full multimedia titles to play over the Web. Now, all you need is a cable modem or a T3 line.

TRMoov, San Francisco Canyon Company (Windows)

`http://www.www.sfcanyon.com`

TRMoov is an AVI-to-QuickTime video conversion utility that is robust, user-friendly, and very useful for video conversion.

Software Reference

Online Resources for Web Developers

Often the best place to learn about the Web is the Web, but you have to know where to look. The following is a comprehensive collection of online resources for Web developers.

ActiveX Resources

Microsoft ActiveX Development Kit

Download the ActiveX Development Kit and Explorer 3.0 from this site. Also links to gallery and related sites.

```
http://www.microsoft.com/intdev/sdk/
```

Internet Explorer—ActiveX Gallery

This site showcases the ActiveX objects in Explorer 3.0.

```
http://www.microsoft.com/ie/
```

Internet Control Pack

This page describes the ActiveX controls.

```
http://www.microsoft.com/icp/
```

Animations

Everything You Need

This Web site offers how-to tips on creating animated GIFs and links to all the software you'll need to create them.

```
http://webreference.com/dev/gifanim.html/
```

Clip2Gif and GifBuilder

These programs, contained on the CD-ROM, are two excellent programs by Yves Piguet.

```
http://iawww.epfl.ch/Staff/Yves.Piguet/
```

Cool Animations

This page has lots of very cool animated GIFs. Interestingly, they are being used to simulate QuickTime movies.

```
http://www.specular.com/products/workshop/After_animation.html
```

Royal Frazier's INTERcoNnEcTions

This site has links to all sorts of animated GIF resources.

```
http://www.reiworld.com/royalef/royal.htm
```

Keeping Animations Small

A page that shows you how to keep those anims slim n' trim with just a weeee bit of trickery.

```
http://www.webmonkey.com/geektalk/
```

Audio

MAZ Sound Tools Page

This page features links to all kinds of audio software, including sample editors, converters, and recorders.

```
http://www.th-zwickau.de/~maz/index.html
```

midiSource QuickHelp

This site gives descriptions for commonly used MIDI terms.

```
http://netris1.corpcomm.net/~jjorgensen/mshlp-lg.html
```

GoldWave Digital Audio Editor

Chris Craig has designed an excellent audio editor available from this site, hosted by the Computer Science Department of Memorial University in Newfoundland, Canada.

```
http://web.cs.mun.ca/~chris3/goldwave/
```

Digital Music Zone

Jack Orman put together this list of links to pages related to electronic music creation.

```
http://users.aol.com/jorman/
```

Browsers

Netscape Navigator

```
http://home.netscape.com/
```

Microsoft Internet Explorer

```
http://www.microsoft.com/
```

Sun HotJava

```
http://java.sun.com/
➡HotJava/index.html
```

NCSA Mosaic

```
http://www.ncsa.uiuc.edu/
➡SDG/Software/Mosaic/Docs/
➡help-about.html
```

Spry Mosaic

```
http://www.spry.com/
```

CompuServe Mosaic

```
http://www.compuserve.com/
```

America Online

```
http://www.aol.com/
```

Prodigy

```
http://www.prodigy.com/
```

Apple Cyberdog

```
http://cyberdog.apple.com/
```

PointCast PCN Browser

```
http://www.pointcast.com/
```

Online Resources
for Web Developers

GNN

```
http://www.gnn.com/gnn/
```

NetManage WebSurfer

```
http://www.netmanage.com/
```

Netcom

```
http://www.netcom.com/
```

Cello

```
http://www.law.cornell.edu/
➥cello/cellotop.html
```

Accent Multilingual Mosaic

```
http://www.accentsoft.com/
```

Browser Comparisons and Other Browser Resources

Browser by Design

This site is the online companion to *Hybrid HTML Design: A Multibrowser HTML Reference* by Kevin Ready and Janine Warner (New Riders, 1996). It contains pages for testing your browser and links to hundreds of sites.

```
http://www.browserbydesign.com/
```

BrowserWatch

This page contains browser information and links to other online browser resources; includes "plug-in plaza" with one of the most up-to-date lists of plug-ins on the Net.

```
http://www.browserwatch.com/
```

Yahoo—Browser Usage Statistics

This site can help you plan for your demographic audience. The number of people still using Navigator 1.1 and other questions can be answered here.

```
http://www.yahoo.com/Computers_and_Internet/Internet/
➥World_Wide_Web/
```

Cyberatlas

A good site that has all kinds of up-to-the-minute statistics on users, browsers, Internet news, forecasts, and so on.

```
http://www.cyberatlas.com/Browsers/Browser_Usage_Statistics/
```

The Browser Tuneup

This page enables you to test browsers to compare HTML support.

```
http://www.eit.com/goodies/tuneup/
```

CNET Browser Review

CNET provides ongoing reviews of computer hardware and software products.

```
http://www.cnet.com/Content/Reviews/Compare/Browsers/
```

BrowserCaps

This site has links to many browser resources.

```
http://www.objarts.com/bc/
```

Domain Names

InterNIC

Responsible for registering all domain names.

```
http://rs.internic.net/
```

Domain Check

A great site to look up any domain name. Responds with availability and registration information if a name is already taken.

```
http://www.primopasta.com/whois.htm
```

Online Resources for Web Developers

General Resources

Art & the Zen of Web Sites

(much more about philosophy, really)

```
http://www.tlc-systems.com/webtips.shtml
```

The Internet Help Desk

References for beginner and advanced users on just about anything that has to do with using the Internet.

```
http://w3.one.net/~alward/
```

Graphics Sites

Lynda's Homegurrl Page

The Web page of Lynda Weinman, author of *Designing Web Graphics* (New Riders, 1996). There are some excellent links to graphics resources from her site, as well as information on her book.

```
http://www.lynda.com/
```

David Siegel's Web Wonk

One of the most popular collections of design tips and tricks for writers and HTML designers.

```
http://www.dsiegel.com/tips/
```

Web Reference Graphics Resources

A great collection of graphics resources all in one place.

```
http://www.webreference.com/graphics/
```

Digital Directory

Graphics and Web design resources.

```
http://www.DigitalDirectory.com/
```

The Netscape Palette

This site is the original "magic palette." The 216 colors that are supported cross-platform by Netscape are provided.

```
http://help.netscape.com/
```

Communication Arts

Tons of stuff—exhibits of graphic art, columns on design and design technology issues, info on hardware and software, job listings, links to other graphics-related Web sites, and so on.

```
http://www.commarts.com/
```

No Dither Netscape Color Palette

```
http://the-light.com/netcol.html
```

Clip Art

DTP Internet Jumplist list of clip art resources on the Internet.

```
http://www.teleport.com/~eidos/dtpij/clipart.html
```

Computer Graphics

This is an international collection of computer graphics college programs maintained by the Perceptual Science Laboratory at the University of California, Santa Cruz. This site is an excellent resource for those who want to study computer graphics.

```
http://mambo.ucsc.edu/psl/cg.html
```

Online Resources for Web Developers

INFO-MAC HyperArchive ROOT

This site has a large volume of Macintosh freeware, shareware, demos, updates, and more.

```
http://hyperarchive.lcs.mit.edu/HyperArchive.html
```

The Graphics File Format Page

Martin Reddy provides an excellent resource for describing image file formats. Links to pages describing 2D and 3D image formats and downloadable utility programs are listed.

```
http://www.dcs.ed.ac.uk/~mxr/gfx/
```

OAK Repository—SimTel Windows Mirror Index

This is a repository for every type of Windows application, including a big list with all sorts of categories.

```
http://www.acs.oakland.edu/oak/SimTel/SimTel-win3.html
```

Aaron's Graphic Archive

This site has links to graphics on the Web. There is a copyright disclaimer (the small print) that instructs visitors on the use of graphics.

```
http://hoohoo.ncsa.uiuc.edu/Public/AGA/
```

Clear GIFs

Sean Kerney created this site dedicated to providing free transparent gifs and other graphics resources that users can apply to their own personal pages.

```
http://www.inforamp.net/~dredge
```

WebImage Information

WebImage is a suite of applications that is designed for creating Web graphics.

```
http://www.group42.com/webimage.htm
```

PNG (Portable Network Graphics) Home Page

The home pages of the PNG file format are maintained by Greg Roelofs. There are links to all things PNG from this page.

```
http://quest.jpl.nasa.gov/PNG/
```

HTML Tutorials and References

Creating Net Sites

Netscape provides these pages that describe traditional HTML, as well as the Netscape-specific tags, like <FRAME> and <EMBED>.

```
http://home.netscape.com/assist/net_sites/
```

Yale HTML Style Manual

This site gives some good design guides. It is administered by Patrick Lynch at the Yale Center for Advanced Instructional Media.

```
http://info.med.yale.edu/caim/StyleManual_Top.HTML
```

Web Reference

This site is designed to have everything a Web designer needs—from beginner to advanced.

```
http://www.webreference.com/
```

WebMonkey

Includes sections on HTML, browsers, plug-ins, geek talk, demos, and an extensive tutorial section. Very well laid out.

```
http://www.webmonkey.com/html/
```

Online Resources for Web Developers

Style Guide for Online Hypertext

A nuts and bolts digestion of what makes a good Web site, with sections on structure, organization, and etiquette.

```
http://www.w3.org/pub/WWW/Provider/Style/Overview.html
```

Cascading Style Sheets, Level 1

This is the World Wide Web Consortium draft on style sheets.

```
http://www.w3.org/pub/WWW/TR/WD-css1.html
```

Inserting Objects into HTML

This describes how the <OBJECT> tag is treated in HTML. Microsoft refers developers to this page for tag usage.

```
http://www.w3.org/pub/WWW/TR/WD-object.html
```

HTML DTDs (and other public text)

This page discusses the many HTML dialects that are appearing. It provides and has links to Document Type Definitions, including HTML 2, HTML 3, Netscape, and Explorer extensions.

```
http://www.w3.org/pub/WWW/MarkUp/html-pubtext/
```

HTML Reference Manual

This site is maintained by the Sandia National Laboratories. It has links to HTML tutorials and many online resources.

```
http://www.sandia.gov/sci_compute/html_ref.html
```

HyperText Markup Language Specification 3.0

This site is generally considered to be the official HTML 3.0 specifications. The site is maintained by Dave Raggett of Hewlett-Packard Laboratories.

```
http://www.hpl.hp.co.uk/people/dsr/html/Contents.html
```

W3C Tech Reports

This site has a list of working drafts for the proposed HTML specifications.

```
http://www.w3.org/pub/WWW/TR/
```

HyperText Markup Language (HTML): Working and Background Materials

This is one of the W3 Consortium's principal sites. There are links to historic documents, proposed specs, and other W3C documents.

```
http://www.w3.org/pub/WWW/MarkUp/
```

HTML Verification and Testing

Weblint

An online HTML verification and syntax tester. Checks the code on any page on the Web in seconds.

```
http://198.59.155.54/staff/neilb/weblint.html
```

Dr. HTML

Retrieves a Web page and performs several tests to see if your document is in tip-top shape.

```
http://www2.imagiware.com/RxHTML/
```

Image Maps

Client-Side Image Maps

A comprehensive tutorial on client-side image maps.

```
http://www.spyglass.com/techspec/tutorial/img_maps.html
```

MapServe Home Page

An image mapping CGI program for use with MacHTTP or WebSTAR.

```
http://www.spub.ksu.edu/other/machttp_tools/mapserve/mapserve.html
```

Mac-ImageMap Home Page

A CGI script for image maps on a Macintosh WWW server, which runs with the software WebSTAR or MacHTTP.

```
http://weyl.zib-berlin.de/imagemap/Mac-ImageMap.html
```

NSCA Image Map Tutorial

A no-nonsense guide to everything you always wanted to know about NCSA server-side image maps.

```
http://hoohoo.ncsa.uiuc.edu/docs/tutorials/imagemapping.html
```

MapMaker

An online image map editor.

```
http://www.tns.lcs.mit.edu/cgi-bin/mapmaker
```

Web Hotspots

An image map editor that supports client- and server-side image maps for Windows 3.1 and Windows 95.

```
http://www.cris.com/~automata/
http://www.ecaetc.ohio-state.edu/tc/mt/
```

Mapmaker v1.1 Home Page

An image map editor for Unix.

```
http://icg.resnet.upenn.edu/mapmaker.html
```

glorglox Advanced Image Mapper

An NCSA server-specific image map editor that lets you map each pixel to a distinct URL.

```
http://www.uunet.ca/~tomr/glorglox/
```

Internet Service Providers

Internet Services Group

A service provider offering mirrored sites in 26 countries and 64 U.S. cities.

```
http://www.thehost.com/
```

Internet Services (General Products and Services)

ISPs and other Internet-related resources.

```
http://www.einet.net/galaxy/Business-and-Commerce/General-Products-
➥and-Services/Internet-Services.html
```

Yahoo: Web Presence Providers

Yahoo's list of Web service providers.

```
http://www.yahoo.com/Business_and_Economy/Companies/
➥Internet_Services/Web_Presence_Providers/
```

World Wide Web Servers

A list of registered Web servers listed alphabetically by continent, country, and state.

```
http://www.uni-kl.de/Weitere-WWW-Server/Geographical.html
```

Internet Services

A comprehensive list of ISPs in Wisconsin.

```
http://www.inmarket.com/wisconsin/internet.htm
```

Online Resources
for Web Developers

California Internet Services WWW Servers

A comprehensive list of ISPs in California.

```
http://www.calif.com/ca/internet.services.html
```

Web Developer's Virtual Library: Providers

Service providers in the U.S. that offer Web servers.

```
http://www.stars.com/Vlib/Misc/Providers.html
```

Providers of Commercial Internet Access (POCIA)

More than 850 ISPs from the U.S., Canada, and 46 other countries.

```
http://www.celestin.com/pocia/index.html
```

NetAccess WorldWide

ISPs from Africa, America—Central and South, Asia, Europe—Central, Europe—Eastern, Europe—Western, and the Middle East.

```
http://www.best.be/iap.html
```

Sharing Knowledge Worldwide

A list of ISPs from throughout the U.S.

```
http://www.primus.com/staff/peggy/provider.html
```

Java

Java: Programming for the Internet

This is Java's home page. The site is maintained by Sun and has links to documentation and other resources.

```
http://java.sun.com/
```

FutureTense, Inc.

This is a Java-based Web authoring tool. The company also provides a viewer.

```
http://www.futuretense.com/
```

Concurrent Programming in Java

This page links to many sites dealing with designing multithreaded code.

```
http://g.oswego.edu/dl/pats/aopintro.html
```

Making Sense of Java

This site is a down-to-earth look at Java, and answers a lot of often-asked questions.

```
http://reality.sgi.com/employees/shiffman_engr/Java-QA.html
```

Borland's Internet Tools

This is Borland's Java products page. They have introduced several GUI Java development tools.

```
http://www.borland.com
```

Symantec Java Central

This is Symantec's main Java products page. There are links to Symantec information, as well as general Java.

```
http://cafe.symantec.com/javacentral/index.html
```

GUI Programming Using Java

This tutorial was put together by Jan Newmarch of the University of Canberra.

```
http://pandonia.canberra.edu.au/java/tut/tut.html
```

The Java Developers Kit

This page enables you to download the Java Developers Kit for designing applets.

```
http://java.sun.com/JDK-1.0/index.html
```

Hyperwire, Java Authoring Program

Hyperwire by Kinetix is a Java editor for Windows 95 and NT that enables the creation of applets in a graphics environment.

```
http://www.ktx.com
```

Gamelan

This has to be the greatest collection of things Java on the Internet.

```
http://www.gamelan.com
```

JavaWorld

This online 'zine is maintained by IDG.

```
http://www.javaworld.com/cgi-bin/w3com/start?JW+main
```

JavaScript

Gamelan's JavaScript

This page has a large number of links to JavaScript sites.

```
http://www.gamelan.com/frame/Gamelan.javascript.html
```

JavaScript

Netscape provides this list of JavaScript resources.

```
http://home.netscape.com/comprod/products/navigator/version_2.0/
➥script/ script_info/index.html
```

JavaScript Index

This site is an excellent resource for JavaScript links.

```
http://www.c2.org/~andreww/javascript/
```

JavaScript Authoring Guide

This is Netscape's own JavaScript authoring guide. Links are available to describe all the syntax in the language.

```
http://home.netscape.com/eng/mozilla/Gold/handbook/javascript/
➥index.html
```

White Paper: Verifying Form Input with JavaScript

This site is maintained by Gordon McComb, author of *The JavaScript Sourcebook*. It has some good examples for form input checking.

```
http://gmccomb.com/javascript/valid.htm
```

Organizations for Web Designers and Developers

HTML Writers Guild

The HTML Writers Guild is the premiere international organization of World Wide Web page authors and Internet publishing professionals.

```
http://www.hwg.org/
```

The World Wide Web Artists' Consortium (WWWAC)

Sponsors regular meetings and events in the New York City area and sponsors an active e-mail list with more than 1,500 members.

```
http://www.wwwac.org/
```

Noend

The Noend Group in San Francisco is a smaller, but very active group of developers in the Bay area.

```
http://www.noend.org
```

Plug-Ins

WebMonkey

Tune up your browser and get all the latest plug-ins.

```
http://www.webmonkey.com/html/
```

PC Magazine InternetUser—Plug-In Central

This is *PC Magazine*'s list of plug-ins.

```
http://www.pcmag.com/iu/
```

Plug-Ins

This is Netscape's list of plug-ins.

```
http://home.netscape.com/comprod/products/navigator/version_2.0/
➥plugins/ index.html
```

Movie Viewers

Site for Movie Viewer Software with dozens of links to file downloads.

```
http://www.netaxs.com/people/dmorgen/video.html
```

Promotional Services

Submit It!

Submit It! helps you publicize your Web site.

```
http://www.submit-it.com/
```

WebPromote

WebPromote also helps publicize Web sites.

```
http://www.webpromote.com/
```

How Search Engines Work

This address provides information on how search engines work so you can best advertise your Web sites on them.

```
http://www.webreference.com/search.html
```

Web Robots and Spiders

A technical reference to how Web robots, crawlers, and spiders work.

```
http://info.webcrawler.com/mak/projects/robots/norobots.html
```

Cybernautics

A Web development and promotion company that has become well known for its promotional services.

```
http://www.cybernautics.com
```

Search Engines

Alta Vista

Alta Vista is an extremely powerful search engine that claims to search every word on every page on the World Wide Web, searching billions of words in millions of Web pages.

```
http://www.altavista.digital.com/
```

Online Resources for Web Developers

Yahoo

Yahoo is one of the most well-known search engines.

    http://www.yahoo.com/

Search.com

Founded by CNET, this site searches more than 15 other search engines.

    http://www.search.com/

Switchboard

Switchboard helps you locate individuals.

    http://www.switchboard.com/

WhoWhere

A comprehensive listing of e-mail addresses, personal home pages, and other resources similar to yellow and white pages in a phonebook.

    http://www.whowhere.com/

Lycos

This is one of the original search engines. A good way to find an old friend.

    http://www.lycos.com/

Metasearch

Metasearch uses other search engines to conduct searches.

    http://metasearch.com/

The Electric Library

This engine uses newspapers, periodicals, books, and other printed sources for its searches.

```
http://www.elibrary.com/id/2525/
```

Software Resources

Shareware.com

This site, maintained by CNET, provides a searchable database with the most comprehensive list of shareware you'll find.

```
http://www.shareware.com/
```

FTP and Software Search Engines

Internic's searchable database to help you find anonymous FTP files and software.

```
http://www.internic.net/tools/soft.html
```

Tools for Aspiring Web Authors

Extensive compilation of hyperlinks to shareware, freeware, and other HTML authoring tools.

```
http://www.nas.nasa.gov/NAS/WebWeavers/
```

VBScript

VBScript: Working Description

Visual Basic and VBScript are presented here.

```
http://www.microsoft.com/INTDEV/vbs/vbscript.htm
```

Online Resources
for Web Developers

Video

Cross-Platform QuickTime

This site is managed by Robert Lentz at Northwestern University. It has links to QuickTime viewers and other utilities.

```
http://www.astro.nwu.edu/lentz/mac/qt/
```

MPEGe Lib

This MPEG library is maintained by Alex Knowles. There are links to an MPEG editor, as well as MPEG resources.

```
http://www.tardis.ed.ac.uk/~ark/mpegelib/
```

Yahoo—Computers and Internet: Multimedia:Video:Collections

This is Yahoo's catalog of online digital video collections.

```
http://www.yahoo.com/Computers_and_Internet/Multimedia/
➥Video/Collections/
```

Watch Videos

Here are some videos that can be watched using the VDOlive plug-in.

```
http://www.vdo.net/enhanced.html
```

Virtual Reality Modeling Language (VRML)

Virtual Reality Modeling Language (VRML) Forum

Mark Pesce and Brian Behlendorf put together this site. Links to historic VRML documents, bios of key VRML participants, and the VRML mailing list are available. The mailing list also has a rule of etiquette to which you can link.

```
http://vrml.wired.com/
```

VRML World

This site, submitted by Dave Blackburn, is on the Mecklermedia iworld pages. There are links to new VRML sites, VRML Architecture Group sites, sites using VRML since its inception, and some odd links to Java and HotJava resources.

```
http://netday.iworld.com/devforum/
```

QuickTime VR

Apple offers its own 3D, photorealistic standard with the QuickTime VR player. The player is available cross-platform, and requires that QuickTime is already installed.

```
http://quicktime.apple.com/
```

Caligari Home World

Caligari is a company specializing in VRML design. They make a browser and development product. Lots of links on their site.

```
http://www.caligari.com/
```

WebSpace Navigator

WebSpace was one of the first VRML browsers, and is available in several platforms.

```
http://www.sd.tgs.com/~template/WebSpace/monday.html
```

VRML Library Archive: "History of VRML"

This page gives a history of VRML as notated by one of its founders, Mark Pesce. The discussion is rather broad and traces the history of the Web, as well as VRML. Relatively short, concise, easily readable.

```
http://webspace.sgi.com/Archive/VRML-history/index.html
```

VRML Design Notes

This page describes the Moving Worlds Proposal for VRML 2.0. This standard is being supported by Silicon Graphics, Netscape, Sun Microsystems, Apple, and others.

```
http://webspace.sgi.com/moving-worlds/Design.html
```

Online Resources
for Web Developers

VRML Repository

This site is maintained by the San Diego Supercomputer Center. Of all the sites listed here, this could be the most complete. A large number of browsers, software libraries, texture libraries, geometry converters, and other links are available.

```
http://sdsc.edu/vrml/
```

CGI Scripts

Use of CGI Forms and Scripts Tutorial

How to write and use basic scripts in C.

```
http://huckleberry.sfsu.edu/%7Ehodges/FormsScriptUse.html
```

CGI Scripts

A comprehensive tutorial on how to write scripts in Perl.

```
http://oscar.teclink.net/~noumen/cgi.html
```

Using and Writing Shell Scripts

How to use and write shell scripts.

```
http://www.tc.cornell.edu/Edu/Tutor/Basics/shell/
```

Introduction to CGI Programming

Introduction to CGI programming in Unix Bourne Shell language (sh) and Perl.

```
http://www.usi.utah.edu:80/cgi-programming/
```

CGI Scripts and Perl

Basic information about Perl and links to many other CGI references.

```
http://www.msg.net/tutorial/cgi/perl.html
```

Perl

The Perl programmer's handbook (a comprehensive guide).

```
http://www.atmos.washington.edu/perl/perl.html
```

Perl Handbook

Another great guide to writing Perl.

```
http://www.metronet.com/0/perlinfo/perl5/manual/perl.html
```

More on Perl

```
http://www.eecs.nwu.edu/perl/perl.html
```

And if you still want to know more about Perl...

```
http://www.perl.hip.com/
```

Death's Gate Scripts

Scripts tutorial for C with a focus on creating games.

```
http://www.cypronet.com/~dg/bresource/scripts/
```

An Introduction to Shell Scripts

A short course on shell scripts from Rice University.

```
http://riceinfo.rice.edu/Computer/Documents/Classes/Unix/
➥script/script.html
```

Computer Science

Resources for C++ programming and scripts.

```
http://gnofn.org/whs1/education/subjects/compsci.html
```

Online Resources for Web Developers

The Common Gateway Interface Specification

The NCSA Common Gateway Interface Specification.

http://hoohoo.ncsa.uiuc.edu/cgi/interface.html

CGI/Perl

How to write Common Gateway Interface with Perl.

http://media.it.kth.se/mms/cgi/

Overview of CGI

The World Wide Web Consortium (W3C) overview on CGI scripts.

http://www.w3.org/hypertext/WWW/CGI/

Thanks!

Thanks to all who contributed to this list, especially Sheila Castelli, Kevin Ready, Kim Ladin, Malinda McCain, Jessica Burdman, Eric Wolfram, George Harris, Vicki Jean Beauchamp, and Ken Milburn.

Putting a Web Site Online: FTP Software

Most Web sites are created on a desktop computer and then transferred to a Web server with File Transfer Protocol (FTP) software. Even if you run your own server, you may use FTP software to send and retrieve files between computers. Many Internet users are familiar with FTP programs because they have downloaded software, often using anonymous FTP to retrieve programs from public sites. Sending files to a Web site, however, requires a unique user ID and password. If you use a commercial server, you should be assigned a password when you set up your account so that you can control who has access to your directory. If you are at a university or other organization with its own server, you'll need to get this access information from the system administrator.

FTP Software

There are a number of FTP programs available on the Web for Macintosh and Windows. On Unix machines, FTP functions are generally built into the system software. If you don't have an FTP program, you can download one using a browser such as Netscape. Most of these programs are small (as little as a 300 KB), and simple to install and use. They are easily configured to work with almost any server, and most can store logon information for more than one host computer.

Uploading Files with FTP

When using FTP software, keep in mind that as you send files to a server, you are making live changes to your Web site. As soon as the new files are loaded, they will be accessible to your viewers. This means that it is best to make changes during off hours, when you know fewer people will be viewing your site. Assuming you haven't made any mistakes, the FTP process shouldn't disrupt your site much because as soon as each file loads, it becomes available to your viewers. Loading time depends on the speed of your connection and the size of the file. Graphics are usually larger and take longer to load, so it's a good practice to load graphic files before you load the HTML pages on which they will appear. This way, you avoid the risk that someone will view an HTML page before the graphics get to the server. Some developers create a special directory where they can test files online before linking them to the rest of the site. If you don't do this, it's a good idea to at least test your site with a browser immediately after loading new files. Because FTP programs use very little RAM, most computers can run a browser simultaneously. If you keep your FTP program open while you test with your browser, it will be easier to make corrections quickly. This is one place where a small text editor such as SimpleText or Notepad can be handy for quick changes. Many HTML Editors—such as BBEdit and Hot Dog, described in Chapter 13, "Tailoring Converted Files"—provide built-in FTP capabilities.

Directory Control with FTP

FTP programs can be used to upload, download, or delete entire directory trees, sub-directories, and individual files. You must, however, send files to the proper directory on the server. Your home directory will be assigned by your service provider or system administrator, and all your files and sub-directories should reside in that directory. Within your directory, you can organize files and sub-directories in any combination as long as you maintain relative links. Be aware, however, that all files must stay in the same relative locations on the server. This means that the "index.html" file and directories will be sent to the top level of the home directory on the server. If, as an example, you keep all your images in a folder called "graphics," then to send a graphic as an individual file, you would first need to open the "graphics" directory on the server, and then send the graphic into that directory. Within most FTP programs, you can easily move from one directory level to another to ensure that your files are sent to the right location and maintain their relative links. Although many FTP programs will enable you to rename or delete a file on a server, most will not let you move the file once it has been uploaded. In the next few pages, you'll learn the basics of the most common FTP programs for Windows and Macintosh and where to find them online.

> **Note**
>
> **HTML Editors Bundled with Service Providers**
>
> A new category of commercial Web server has emerged. Designed for those who know little or nothing about HTML, these companies bundle a WYSIWYG HTML editor or form-based development system with FTP software preset for their server. These systems take much of the hassle—and control—out of Web site development. Although some offer high-end services such as secure servers and custom programming, most of these all-in-one development packages are limited to the most basic HTML design, with little or no room for customization. And many of the service providers that come packaged this way charge higher rates than you may find elsewhere.

Fetch 3.0 for Macintosh

Fetch was created in 1989 at Dartmouth to enable Macintosh computers to take advantage of the University's newly acquired Internet connection. Since then, it has grown to be one of the most popular FTP programs for the Macintosh. Fetch allows point-and-click, drag-and-drop file transfers, and works with any FTP server over a TCP/IP network.

Features include support for multiple connections, bookmark lists, AppleScript, Internet Config, and Open Transport. Fetch also provides Apple Event Object Model support for easier scripting with languages such as AppleScript, Frontier, and others. Fetch is recordable, so writing a script can be as simple as hitting the Record button in your script editor, and then creating a sequence of actions.

Files can be uploaded in AppleSingle, BinHex, and MacBinary II format, as well as the common Text and Raw Data formats. This gives you many options as you send files, but make sure you use the appropriate format for your server and browser audience. Most Web browsers cannot display files encoded in a format such as MacBinary. You can set the default format and suffix options in preferences. To ensure that your files will work, use the "Raw Data" format for graphics and other binary files and the common "Text" option for HTML files. You may use the "Wrapped Text" option, which forces a line break after a specific number of characters. This is usually set to 80 characters, but it can be changed in preferences. This option is offered to prevent text files from loading as one very long line on a Unix machine.

Fetch comes with a list of suffix mappings that relate file-name extensions, such as .html and .gif. You can also add your own. Suffixes are automatically added to all files, unless you change the preferences in the default mappings. Because you should have added suffixes to your files as you created them, you will probably want to turn this feature off. Otherwise, Fetch will add a second suffix as it loads your files on the server.

Fetch can display text files, directory listings, and server messages in its own windows. Fetch only supports simple (userid@host style) proxy servers. In addition, Fetch is free to users affiliated with educational institutions or non-profit organizations and may be downloaded as shareware. A single user license costs $25. For more information on Fetch, check out their online users manual, complete with a tutorial and reference topics, at the following URL:

```
http://www.dartmouth.edu/
```

A commercial version is also available from Adobe through the following:

```
http://www.adobe.com/
```

WS_FTP for Windows

WS_FTP is an FTP application for Windows that offers a point-and-click interface and features such as saving site profile information and facilitating multi-file transfers. As a WinSock-compliant application, this program works on Windows 3.x and Windows 95 operating systems.

When you log onto a site, WS_FTP displays the local directories and files in the left half of the screen and the remote server in the right. Two lists are displayed—one on each half of the main window. The top half lists your directories, and the lower half lists files. To transfer multiple files, use the standard window methods of selecting multiple files or directories with the Shift or Control keys. You can also select multiple files by clicking on the first file that you want and dragging the mouse down to the last file in the group. After selecting the desired files, press the transfer button for the function you want to use.

WS_FTP enables you to save logon information for a remote host so that you can return to the server by simply choosing the host from the list and clicking on the OK button. With this program, as with any FTP program, you must be careful to use the proper File Transfer Modes. For text files, use the ASCII option; for all other files, use Binary. If your server's computer and development machines use the same operating system, you can always use Binary mode.

The simplest way to upload or download files with WS_FTP is to double-click on a file name. If you double-click on the local file, it will transfer, or upload, to the server. If you double-click on a remote file, it will transfer, or download, to your hard drive. If you double-click on a remote file, it will be transferred in binary mode to the Windows temporary directory. You can execute a file locally in WS_FTP by clicking on a file name and then selecting Execute.

If the file name has an extension other than .EXE, .COM, .BAT, or .PIF, then the file associations from the file manager are used. If the extension has no association, you will be allowed to specify the association at runtime. This association is saved in the WIN.INI file in the Extensions section and will also be valid for the File Manager. You can set associations by selecting Options and then selecting Associations.

You can also click on a directory or file to change the name. You can drag one or more files from the Windows file manager anywhere on the main computer to transfer them to the current directory of the remote host. You cannot drag and drop directories on the remote computer, however, nor can you drag or drop from the remote host to another application. If you can connect to a remote host, but don't get a directory listing, try changing the host type in the connect or options dialog boxes. "Auto detect" and host types work on about 90 percent of all servers, but may have to be set manually for some systems.

WS_FTP is available for download from many Windows FTP directories. For more information, direct your browser to the following:

```
http://csra1.csra.net/junodj/ws_ftp.htm
```

Glossary

32-bit structure

A program or computer that processes 4 bytes of information at a time.

8.3 rule

In DOS and Windows, file names should not have more than eight characters and extensions not more than three.

absolute link (URL)

An HTML hyperlink set by using the complete URL in the path. Example: `<A HREF="http://www.domain_name.com/name.html>`. See *relative link*.

Acrobat 3.0

Adobe System's software suite for creating a publishing portable electronic document that will look the same on any computer. The suite gives you everything you need: Acrobat Exchange (TM), Acrobat Distiller, Acrobat Catalog, and the new Capture plug-in.

```
http://www.adobe.com/acrobat/overview.html
```

ActiveX

A set of technologies created by Microsoft that enables software components to interact with one another in a networked environment, regardless of the language in which they were created. ActiveX is essentially OLE (Object Linking and Embedding) repackaged for use on the Internet.

```
http://www.microsoft.com/activex/activex-contents1.htm
```

add-on

An accessory or utility program that extends the capabilities of an application program. See *plug-in*.

algorithm

A specific set of procedures for solving a problem in a finite number of steps. Computer programs are based on algorithms.

alignment

The horizontal arrangement of lines of text, graphics, or other elements on a page with respect to the left and right margins.

analog

A form of representation in which the indicator is varied continuously (for example, analog sound files on a computer). Contrast with *digital.* Colloquial definition: the real-life version of something that is often represented digitally.

anchor

The start or destination of a hyperlink.

animated GIFs

Part of the GIF89a specification that allows multiple still frames to be stored in the same file and (upon loading) to be shown in a specified sequence, duration, and location. Created by programs such as GIFBuilder (included on the CD-ROM that accompanies this book). See *animation.*

For more on animated GIFs, check out:

```
http://webreference.com/dev/gifanim.html/
```

animation

A series of images created in successive positions to create the effect of movement by the characters or other elements.

antialiasing

The smoothing of pixelated (jagged) edges in a graphic image. Actually, the illusion of smoothing the edges of graphic objects by intermixing pixels of the adjoining colors along that edge.

applet

A small application created with the Java programming language that can be embedded in an HTML page to execute animations or interactive applications. For more on applets, check out:

```
http://www.sun.com/950523/appletdef.html
```

application programs

Programs that perform functions directly for a user. Includes word processors, spreadsheets, databases, presentation programs, and desktop publishing programs. Are often referred to as either "application" or "program," but mean the same thing.

ASCII (American Standard Code for Information Interchange)

Pronounced *ask-ee.* The original 128-character set, or a file containing only those characters and no special formatting.

attribute

HTML code included in an opening tag to provide extra information about the behavior of the tag and the text, graphic, or other element it describes.

AVI (Audio/Video/Interactive)

The Microsoft file format for Video for Windows movies.

audio

Relating to electrical frequencies relating to normally audible sound waves. See *sound; video.*

background

The solid color, image, or textured pattern behind the text and graphics on a Web page.

bandwidth

A measure of the carrying capacity of the Internet. Some kinds of information, such as graphics, take up much more bandwidth; other kinds, such as text, take up much less.

banner

An advertisement on a Web page. Usually a commercial advertisement that links to the advertiser's site or to another page dedicated to the advertised product. Banners are almost always composed of bitmapped GIF graphics, sometimes with animated GIFs.

batch processing

Performing the same function on many files or documents at the same time.

baud

A measure of the speed at which data is transmitted. Baud rate indicates the number of bits of data transmitted in one second. One baud is one bit per second. Common modems today have baud rates of 14,400 or 28,800.

beta version

The last stages of development for a computer program. In this stage, the program is released to a select group of users for testing.

binary numbers

The number system having a base of 2. Preferred for computers for precision and economy. See *bit.*

bit

A binary digit, the smallest piece of information used by a computer. Bits can be turned on or off and used in various combinations to represent different kinds of information. Eight bits form a byte.

bitmap

A "paint" or "photo" file. Graphic image formed by an array of screen dots (pixels).

bookmark

Means of saving the URL of a Web site in the browser for easy access later.

broadcast

Sending information that can be received by all nodes on a network such as the Internet. See also *multicast; narrowcast.*

browse

To look over a collection of information casually, especially in an effort to find something of interest, as in browsing through directories (folders) to find a specific file. See also *browser.*

browser

A program, such as Netscape Navigator or Mosaic, used through an Internet connection to search (browse) the World Wide Web.

bullets

Simple graphics that call attention to something. Usually, they look like tiny buttons without words and are used to set items apart in an unnumbered list.

bundled

Software included with hardware or with other software at the same price.

byte

A measurement of computer storage. Usually 8 bits.

C, C++

Programming languages preferred by many professional programmers.

cache

Pronounced "cash." Special section of RAM or disk memory set aside to store frequently accessed information.

CGI (Common Gateway Interface) script

A format and syntax for passing information from browsers to servers via forms or queries in HTML. Generally written in Perl, C, or C++.

clear GIF

A completely invisible GIF. It can be any size, but is usually only a single pixel. Used to create white space on a Web page for better placement of text by changing the Height and Width attributes of the image tag.

```
http://www.dsiegel.com/tips/wonk5/single.html
```

client

The Internet is a client/server arrangement. The *client* is the end-user side, which resides on a personal computer and communicates with the *server* on a remote computer.

client-side image map

An image map that is interpreted by the browser. See *server-side image map.*

compressed file

A data file that has been modified to consume less space than it did before modification. Prior to use, it must be decompressed.

computereze

Also written as "computerese." Slang to describe the jargon and special terminology related to computers.

contact links

Information to make it easy for visitors to a Web site to contact people "behind" the Web site. It could link to the site developer's e-mail address, to a mail form, or to a page with a directory of e-mail addresses for key company contacts.

cross-platform

A computer program with versions for more than one operating system, such as Unix, Macintosh, and Windows. Can also mean applications, such as those created in Java, which run across multiple incompatible computers systems with little or no modification.

cyberspace

Refers to the entire world of online information and services. Coined by William Gibson is his fictional novel *Neuromancer.*

database program

Enables collection of data in an organized format, permitting manipulation of the data in a variety of ways (examples: Foxpro, dBase).

default

The condition set automatically in a program when no selection has been made explicitly. In HTML, the value assigned to an attribute when none is supplied.

desktop

In a graphical environment, a representation of your day-to-day work as though you are looking at an actual desk littered with folders full of work to do.

desktop publishing program

Application programs, such as PageMaker and QuarkXPress, used for typeset publications, such as newsletters and magazines.

dialog box

An on-screen message box that conveys or requests information.

digital format

The form of something, such as an image or sound, when stored as computer data.

dingbats

Ornamental characters, such as bullets, stars, and flowers, used to decorate a page.

Director movie

An animation, presentation, or interactive title created in Macromedia Director, the most widely-used program for creating multimedia titles.

```
http://www.macromedia.com/software/director/index.html
```

directory (subdirectory)

A list of computer files contained on a disk or drive. May be nested to facilitate organization of data on the disk or drive. Called *folders* on Macintosh or Windows 95 systems.

dithering

A method employed to simulate natural shading in images with a limited color range. Shades are represented with combinations of different colored dots (pixels) on-screen in various patterns. Often used to give appearance of smoother transitions between shades of color.

document source

The HTML code behind a page displayed on the Web. This information can be viewed for almost every page on the Web.

domain name

A unique identifier that assigns a name to a specific IP address. Translates computer names (IP addresses) into physical addresses. Domain names in the U.S. are read from right to left. The rightmost part is the zone and tells what type of institution the name is related to: .COM (commercial), .EDU (educational), .NET (network operations), .GOV (U.S. government), or .MIL (U.S. military). Most countries also have a domain; for example, .US (United States), .UK (United Kingdom), and .AU (Australia).

DOS (Disk Operating System)

The underlying control system for many personal computers. Usually refers to MS-DOS, the operating system for IBM-compatible computers.

download

The process of moving information from a remote computer to your computer.

dpi (dots per inch)

A measure of image resolution that counts the dots in a linear inch.

drag and drop

A method for moving text or graphics to other locations. Point to the item with the cursor, hold down the mouse button, and then drag the item to its new location. Release the mouse button, and the item has now moved. This process can also be used to launch applications. Many HTML editors also set links to images and graphics using drag and drop.

dynamic (adj.)

Marked by continuous activity or change. See *static.*

element

A component of a hierarchical structure (for example, in a Web site). Also used to mean any individually manipulable shape in a graphic. In this usage, the term "element" is synonymous with the term "object."

e-mail address

A domain-based address used for sending electronic mail (e-mail) to a specified destination. Must include an @ sign and extension, such as .com or .org; for example, president@whitehouse.com.

embedded

A command placed directly in a program. Also an HTML tag used to link objects and elements that require plug-ins for viewing.

end tag

In HTML programming, identifies the end of an element, also called the close tag.

end user

A person who uses a computer program or device to perform a function such as word processing.

environment

The hardware and/or operating system for application programs (DOS, Macintosh, Windows).

event

A user-initiated happening, such as clicking a mouse. Programs are often designed to respond to such events.

extension, file name extension

(1) Tags or attributes introduced by a browser company, such as Netscape or Microsoft, which are not part of the current HTML specification and are usually only supported by that browser. (2) The latter portion of a file name on a DOS or Unix machine, such as .doc for document or .gif for Graphic File Format. Macintosh file names don't require extensions; however, all files that are to be displayed by a browser must include an extension.

FAQs (Frequently Asked Questions)

A list of questions and answers with basic information about a Web site or other Internet resource.

Fetch

The most popular Macintosh program for file transfer between client and server.

```
http://www.adobe.com/
```

first-generation browsers

Early versions of browsers that pre-date the capability to recognize plug-ins, tables, animated GIFs, background colors, or background images.

folder

A list of computer files contained on a disk or drive. May be nested to facilitate organization of data on the disk or drive. Called *directories* on DOS or Unix systems; *subdirectories* when nested.

font

One complete collection of letters, punctuation marks, numbers, and special characters with a consistent and identifiable typeface, weight, posture, and font size. Sometimes used to refer to typefaces or font families.

font family

A set of fonts in several sizes and weights that share the same typeface.

frames

A Netscape HTML extension, now also supported by Microsoft Internet Explorer, which enables more than one HTML document to be displayed on a Web page. Creates distinct sections on a page that can be individually scrollable and contain links that alter the contents of other sections, or frames, on the same Web page.

```
http://home.netscape.com/
```

FTP (File Transfer Protocol)

Used for copying files to and from servers elsewhere on a network, such as the Internet.

gamma curve controls

A dialog box that permits the user to control smooth transitions in contrast over limited areas of tonal range in an image. For example, you may want to lower the contrast in the image's brightest highlights.

GIF (Graphics Interchange Format)

A bitmapped, LZW-compressed format pioneered by CompuServe for storing and transmitting graphics over remote networks. It is currently the most universally accepted graphics file format on the World Wide Web.

GIF87a and GIF89a

GIF87a is the original specification for this standard. GIF89a is a much enhanced specification that gives this format the capability to display any specific color as transparent and the capability to store and display multiple files as an animation. See *animated GIF*.

```
http://www.web.co.za/WebCo/royalef/gifabout.htm
```

global

Of, relating to, or applying to a whole (as a computer program or Web site).

Gopher

A system that enables you to find information across the Internet by using a series of nested menus.

graphic

A representation of an object on a two-dimensional surface.

graphical environment

An environment that includes the use of graphics rather than only text.

grep (General Regular Expression Parser)

Simple, Unix-based language that enables you to specify complex search-and-replace strings by using wild card characters.

halo

A word usually used to describe the off-color ring surrounding a transparent GIF image resulting from stray-edge pixels that don't quite match the color specified as transparent. Also known as UHS (Ugly Halo Syndrome).

hexadecimal color codes

Numbered and lettered codes used to represent colors in HTML. The hexadecimal color coding system uses a base 16 reference; 256 values for Red, Green, and Blue are possible, using two digits for each.

hits

Visits to a Web site. Hits can be very misleading because they are counted in varying ways. The most traditional systems for counting hits on a Web page count all the graphics and external links as hits when one user views a page. For example, a page with three graphics and two external links would count as five hits when one user viewed the page.

home page

The first page seen when someone accesses a Web site—the "title page." On a small site (for example, a personal site), this may be the only page. On a larger site (business or organization, for example), it is the central page and includes links to other pages within the site.

host

A computer that enables users to communicate with other hosts by using application programs such as e-mail, Telnet, and FTP. Any computer capable of connecting to others on the Internet is a host. When used, this term generally refers to Web servers, but hosts are not always servers.

HTML (HyperText Markup Language)

A hypertext-based, distributed information system created in 1991 by a group of physicists in Switzerland to trade images of their scientific research, as well as the words they had been sending back and forth for years. Later adopted by graphic designers for use on the World Wide Web. HTML is a subset of the SGML standard.

HTML authoring tools

Programs designed to edit or convert HTML documents.

HTML converters

Programs that convert (change) documents from various programs into HTML documents.

HTML editors

Programs that can be used to alter or create HTML pages. HTML editors can be text or WYSIWYG editors.

HTTP (HyperText Transfer Protocol)

A fixed set of messages and replies between a World Wide Web browser and a World Wide Web server.

hyperlink (link)

A programmed connection between locations in the same file (Web site) or between different files. See *hypertext*.

hypermedia

Links between pictures, sounds, and text in the same or related files or Web sites.

hypertext

A word or series of words with related HTML programming linking the words to other locations. Users who click on these words can skip from one document to the next, or from one area of a document to another area in the same document.

icon

Small, "high-concept" image meant to give the reader a message that takes less time to read and is more universally understood than if the same message were spelled out in words.

image maps

GIF or JPEG images that have a corresponding set of coordinates to designate distinct areas of the image using square, circular, or polygon shapes. Those areas can be linked to any URLs so a user reaches different destinations by selecting different sections of the image. See *client-side image map; server-side image map.*

inline images

Images that can be given a specific location on a Web page, in context with text and other multimedia elements. Inline images can be viewed by the browser and don't require a plug-in or separate window for viewing.

interaction

Mutual or reciprocal action or influence.

interface

The place where independent and often unrelated systems meet and act on or communicate with one another. Also, the design of the computer screen's graphical command layout in reference to the clarity and convenient placement of such application control elements as menu bars, toolbars, status bars, and so on. This type of interface is most often referred to as the "user interface" or GUI (Graphical User Interface).

interlacing

Enables an image to load in several stages of resolution. Creates the illusion that graphics (and, therefore, whole pages) load more quickly and gives the reader a chance to see a "fuzzy" recognizable image quickly enough to know whether to wait or move on.

Internet

Note the capital I. While an internet is a network, the term "Internet" refers to an international collection of networks interconnected with routers. The Internet is the largest internet in the world.

Internet Assistants

Microsoft Office add-ons that convert existing Word, Excel, and PowerPoint documents into HTML.

```
http://www.microsoft.com/
```

InterNIC Information Services

A nonprofit organization in Reston, Virginia, that registers domain names and addresses so no two sites use the same name or number.

```
http://www.internic.org/
```

intranet

The term used for Web site and other Internet communications set up and maintained within a corporation.

IP (Internet Protocol)

Allows information to be passed from one network (set of computers) to another by using a unique string of numbers (address) for each network.

ISDN (Integrated Services Digital Network) connections, ISDN lines

Digital technology for Internet connections and other telecommunications that offers higher bandwidth and better signal quality than telephone lines.

ISP (Internet Service Provider)

A national or local company that sells access to the Internet. Well-known examples include CompuServe, America Online, Prodigy, and The Well.

```
http://www.well.com/
```

Java

A programming language invented at Sun Computer that executes on any computer platform. This makes it possible to place applications on remote computers that will run on any computer connected to that remote computer. Small Java applications, called "applets," are used on many Web pages to perform operations that can't normally be accomplished in HTML code.

```
http://www.sun.com/
```

JPEG (JPG)

A file format in which to save graphics for use on the Web if they are full-color, continuous-tone images (such as photographs) larger than approximately 150 pixels square. Gets its name from the committee that originated it, the Joint Photographic Experts Group.

Kbps (Kilobits per second)

A measurement of communication speed (of modems, for example).

kerning

The space between two characters in a text program.

kilobyte (KB)

1,024 bytes of data.

landscape view

A page of text or graphics that is wider than it is tall.

LED (Light Emitting Diode)

A small electronic device made from semiconductor materials; emits light when current flows through it. Sometimes used for computer displays.

ligature

In typography, two or more characters designed and cast as a distinct unit for aesthetic reasons (commonly fi, ff, fl, ffi, ffl, ae, and oe).

link (hyperlink)

A connection between locations in the same file (Web site) or between different files created by the HTML Anchor or Link tag. See *hypertext*.

load, loading

To transfer program instructions or data from a disk or drive into the computer's random access memory (RAM).

local links

Links that go to HTML documents or other files within your Web site.

logical styles

HTML markup tags that provide emphasis or indicate a particular kind of device or action. See *physical styles*.

loop, looping

A set of program instructions that execute repeatedly until a condition is satisfied.

lossy compression

So called because not all original image detail is preserved when the file is compressed (there is some "loss").

Lynx

A character-mode World Wide Web browser that displays only text.

macro

A stored list of commands to perform tedious and often-repeated tasks.

markup language

Special characters embedded within a text file to instruct a computer program how to handle or display the contents of the file itself. HTML is a markup language.

megabyte (MB)

1,024 kilobytes, or 1,048,576 bytes.

menu, menu bar

A list of options presented to a user by a program or Web site. In graphical programs, the menu may appear as a bar that is actually an image map of the site, enabling the user to click on a menu item and jump to the linked page automatically.

metacharacter

A specific character within a text file that signals the need for special handling. In HTML, angle brackets (< >), ampersand (&), pound sign (#), and semicolon (;).

Microsoft Internet Explorer

One of the two most widely used graphical World Wide Web browsers.

Microsoft Office Viewers

Enable users to view Word, Excel, and PowerPoint documents over the Internet in their native form without converting them to HTML. Can be used in conjunction with a browser. Especially useful on intranets.

MIDI (Musical Instrument Device Interface)

Pronounced "middy." Protocol for the exchange of information between computers and musical synthesizers. After being placed into computer-represented form, all the aspects of the digitized sound can be edited and altered.

MIME (Multipurpose Internet Mail Extensions)

An extension to Internet e-mail that enables the transfer of nontextual data, such as graphics, audio, and video.

```
http://www.dnai.com/~thomst/@inet029.html
```

modem

A device that converts (modulates) electrical pulses from a computer to signals suitable for transmission over a telephone line. Acronym for MODulator-DEModulator.

Moiré

Pronounced "mwah-ray." Optical illusion perceived as flickering that sometimes occurs when high-contrast line patterns are placed too close together.

Mosaic

The first graphical World Wide Web browser created for the Internet.

Mozilla

An early name coined for Netscape products that derives from "Mosaic meets Godzilla." The word and associated image often appear in Netscape products or in references to them.

multicast

Sending information that can be received by multiple nodes on a network such as the Internet. See also *broadcast; narrowcast.*

multimedia

The presentation of information on a computer by using video sequences, animation, sound (either as background or synchronized to a video or animation), and vector illustrations.

nanosecond

One-billionth of a second.

narrowcast

Information aimed at specific viewers assumed to have identical browser and hardware configurations and high-speed connections. See also *broadcast, multicast.*

navigation bar

A set of links to key pages in a Web site placed on every page in the Web site.

navigational icons

In this case, Navigation refers to the use of hyperlinks to move through a Web site. Navigational icons show the user where to find information. These icons often move viewers through sequential pages and back again.

NCSA (National Center for Supercomputing Applications)

Department at the University of Illinois where the Mosaic Web browser, the first browser ever created, was developed.

nested, nesting

When one structure occurs within another, it is said to be nested. HTML tags are often nested.

netiquette

"Internet etiquette." Written and unwritten rules for behavior on the Internet. When in doubt, ask.

```
http://www2.pbs.org/uti/guide/netiquette.html
```

Netscape Navigator

One of the two most widely used graphical World Wide Web browsers.

```
http://home.netscape.com
```

newbie

Slang for newcomer or neophyte.

node

An individual connection point in a network.

palette

An array showing each color in an indexed image. Netscape and Microsoft have created palettes that best utilize colors for cross-platform display. Copies of both palettes are included on the CD-ROM included with this book.

pan, panning

Rotating a camera to keep an object in view or to give a wider view of the object. Computer programs simulate panning for the same purpose.

PDF (Portable Document Format)

A file that carries all font and layout specifications with it, regardless of the platform on which it is viewed. The best solution for putting print documents on the Web when those print documents must be as close as possible to their paper counterparts. Generally requires a viewer such as Adobe Acrobat.

```
http://www.adobe.com
```

Perl (Practical Extraction and Reporting Language)

First developed by Larry Wall for Unix systems, this language is frequently used for writing CGI scripts.

phosphor

Electrofluorescent material used to coat the inside face of a cathode ray tube. This determines the color temperature of an image displayed on a monitor.

physical styles

HTML markup tags that specifically control character styles, such as Bold <B> or Italic <I>. Contrast with *logical styles.*

PICT

A metafile that can contain both raster and vector images. Probably the most common Macintosh graphics format. Enables use of JPEG compression when saving a file on a Macintosh. However, neither a Web browser nor any other program will recognize a PICT file as a JPEG file.

pixel

Pronounced "picks-L" (short for picture element). Smallest element (dot) a computer can display on-screen. Images created for the Web are most commonly measured in pixels. Spacing attributes in HTML tags are also commonly measured in pixels. A pixel measured on a screen is the equivalent of a dot (as in dots per inch) on a printed page.

plaintext

Text format that does not include formatting codes that maintain layout and appearance of text.

platform

Computer hardware standard, such as IBM PC-compatible or Macintosh personal computers.

plug-in

An accessory or utility program that extends the capabilities of an application program, such as the RealAudio player. See *add-on.*

PNG

Pronounced "ping." Bitmapped file format, designed especially for network graphics. PNG is a new format meant to be a patent-free replacement for GIF, but it is not yet widely readable by browsers.

portrait view

A page of text or graphics that is taller than it is wide.

progress-thermometer windows

Animated windows that "fill up" to monitor a progressive computer function such as saving or installing a file.

progressive JPEG

Like interlaced GIF, progressive JPEG enables an image to load in stages of increasingly higher resolution.

properties

The characteristics of an object defining its state, appearance, or value.

protocol

A set of rules for how programs on a network interact. These rules generally include requirements for formatting data and error checking.

QuickTime

Created by Apple Computer, QuickTime is the industry standard multimedia architecture used by software tool vendors and content creators to store, edit, and play synchronized graphics, sound, video, text, and music. QuickTime is the most pervasive container and playback engine for multimedia content delivered on CD-ROM and the Internet. Includes QuickTime Movies and QuickTime VR.

```
http://www.quicktime.apple.com
```

RAM (Random Access Memory)

Computer memory that stores ongoing work or any operating systems and applications actually running at the moment.

raster image

See *bitmap*.

raw code

Refers to the HTML code behind a Web page.

RealAudio

A sound technology developed by Progressive Networks to enable streaming sound play on Web pages.

```
http://www.realaudio.com/
```

relative link (URL)

Link set using the path within a Web site directory structure that does not include the domain name. For example: `<a HREF=file_name.html>` or `<a HREF=/resources/file_name.html>`. Contrast with *absolute links*.

resolution

The number of picture elements per unit in an image. For example, the resolution of a full-screen image on a 15-inch, 640 by 480 monitor is 72 dpi.

ROM (Read-Only Memory)

Non-volatile computer memory, programmed with a specific set of system instructions.

router

A device that reads the destination address on information sent over a network and sends the information to the next step in its route.

RTF (Rich Text Format)

Special plaintext format that retains formatting code and can be interpreted by a variety of text editors.

scrolling

Moving the window horizontally or vertically to make information that extends beyond the viewing area visible.

search engine

(1) Web sites that contain searchable databases or search programs capable of retrieving other Web pages based on user queries. (2) A program created to search the contents of a particular Web site for information related to a specific topic or keyword supplied by a user.

serif, sans serif

Serif fonts have cross-strokes across the ends of the main strokes of characters. Sans serif fonts have no cross-strokes.

server (Web server)

A computer connected to the Internet that "serves" files. The Internet is a client/server arrangement. The *server* is on a remote computer and responds to requests from the *client*.

server-side image map

An image map that requires a CGI script on the server. See *image map*.

SGML (Standard Generalized Markup Language)

A sequence of characters organized physically as a set of entities and logically into a hierarchy of elements. Document definition, specification, and creation mechanism that makes platform and display differences across multiple computers irrelevant to the delivery and rendering of documents. HTML is a subset of SGML.

```
http://www.sgmlopen.org/
```

shareware

Copyrighted software that can be freely shared with others provided certain restrictions regarding distribution are followed, as specified by the author. Often involves payment of a fee to the author for continued use.

```
http://www.shareware.com
```

Shockwave

Macromedia Director files that are compressed with a program called Afterburner for use on Web pages. There are Shockwave plug-ins for both Director 4.0 and 5.0 and for both Mac and PC.

```
http://www.macromedia.com
```

special characters

(1) Typed characters such as ~ or &. On Web pages, these characters must be created as HTML entities, or using special character tags. (See Appendix A for a list of special characters for HTML.) (2) With the exception of the underline (or underscore) character, these characters should not be used in file names.

spell checker

A program that checks text against a file of correctly spelled words and indicates when words don't match (that is, when they are presumably misspelled).

splash screen

The opening screen that appears when you start a program. Usually includes information about the manufacturer.

spreadsheet

A program that simulates an accountant's worksheet on-screen and enables the embedding of hidden formulas to perform calculations on data (examples: dBase, Excel, and Paradox).

start tag

In HTML programming, identifies the start of an HTML element; can include attributes.

static

Characterized by lack of movement, animation, or progression. See *dynamic*.

still graphics

Representations of objects without animation.

streaming

"Streaming" technology starts playing sound, video, or other data as soon as enough material has downloaded so that the rest will download before the movie or sound file finishes playing.

string

A series of related text or formatting characters.

structural element

An element that determines how your document looks; for example, a heading is a structural element, but paragraph text is not.

surf, surfing

Used to describe the action of moving from one place to another on the Web with no apparent plan or pattern—following any "wave" that looks like a good one.

synchronize

To arrange events so that they happen at the same time.

syntax

A connected or orderly system; rules that govern the use of HTML code.

system administrator

Also known as network administrator. The person or group responsible for configuring and maintaining a network or Web server.

T1 line

A high-speed, dedicated connection to the Internet. Transmits a digital signal at 1.544 megabits per second.

T3 line

A high-speed, dedicated connection to the Internet. Transmits a digital signal at 44.746 megabits per second.

tables

HTML table tags organize text and/or graphics in relation to one another on a Web page.

tags

The formal name for an element of HTML markup, usually enclosed in angle brackets (< >).

TCP/IP (Transmission Control Protocol/Internet Protocol)

A suite of protocols and services used to manage network communications and applications over the Internet.

third-party (programs, plug-ins)

Developed by a company other than the company who developed the program they function with.

tools

(1) Icons or palette items in a graphical program that perform specific functions when selected. (2) Useful software programs.

transparent GIF (tGIF)

Generally means a GIF that appears as a graphic that "floats" over the background because the image's background is transparent. Transparency can be set to any single color section.

typeface

The distinctive design of a set of type. Grouped into two categories, serif and sans serif.

Unix operating system

Pronounced "U-nicks." Operating system written in C programming language for a variety of computers from PCs to mainframes.

upload

The process of moving information from your computer to a remote computer, as in uploading Web site files to a server.

URL (Uniform Resource Locator)

Pronounced as either "earl" or "U-R-L." Server and path information that locates a document on the Internet; for example, `http://www.domain_name.com`.

user

A person who visits a Web site. See *viewer*.

utility software

Software used in maintaining and improving the efficiency of a computer system.

vector graphics

Images whose shapes are described by geometric formulae. Vector files are resolution-independent, meaning that they are always drawn at the best possible resolution of the device generating them. Because even a fairly complex geometric shape can be described in a few lines of text as a formula, vector images tend to be much smaller than a typical equivalent bitmap image, which has to be described using several bits of data for each per pixel in the image.

video

Information displayed on a TV screen or computer terminal. See *audio*.

viewer

(1) Special program launched by a browser to display elements such as sound files or video that cannot be displayed by the browser. (2) Person who visits a Web site. See *user*.

viewing window

A defined area of the screen through which portions of text or other information can be seen.

virtual memory

A method of extending the apparent size of a computer's random access memory (RAM) by using part of the hard disk as an extension of RAM.

virtual reality

An artificial environment experienced through sensory stimuli (sights and sounds) provided by a computer, and in which one's actions partially determine what happens in the environment.

VRML (Virtual Reality Modeling Language)

Enables the creation of three-dimensional models and walk-through spaces that provide a more real-life experience. Graphics can be mapped to the surfaces of 3D models, and links can be attached to surfaces. Links can display a media type, take users to another model or another part of the current model, or perform any of the functions of any Web hyperlink.

```
http://www.vrml.org/
```

Web designer

Anyone, professional or hobbyist, who creates Web pages. Also called Web developers.

Web page

One file in a collection of files that make up a Web site. Usually used to describe the first page that appears in a Web site.

Web site

A specific location on the Internet, housed on a Web server and accessible through an URL. Consists of one or more Web pages.

wizard

A program sequence within software products that leads you step-by-step through a task.

World Wide Web

All Web servers available on the Internet.

World Wide Web Consortium (W3C)

An industry consortium that seeks to promote standards for the evolution of the Web and interoperability between WWW products by producing specifications and reference software. The international group is jointly hosted by the MIT Laboratory for Computer Science in the United States and by INRIA in Europe.

```
http://www.w3.org
```

WYSIWYG (What You See Is What You Get)

Pronounced "wizzy-wig." Describes HTML authoring tools and other programs that attempt to show on-screen what the final document will look like.

zip

A compression method used on Windows and DOS computers. Uses the .zip file extension.

zipped archive

A file that consists of many compressed files.

zoom, zooming

Enlarging a document view so it fills the screen, or making it smaller so more overall detail can be seen.

Index

Symbols

<! ..comment.> HTML tag, 536
<!DOCTYPE> HTML tag, 570-571
2HTML conversion utility, 646
32-bit structures, 699
3D F/X, 658
8.3 rule, 699

A

<A HREF=...> HTML tag, 66
<A HREF="#...> HTML tag, 66
<A> HTML tag, 552-556
Aaron's Graphic Archive Web site, 674
About Preference (BeyondPress), 206
absolute hyperlinks, 445, 699
Accent Multilingual Mosaic, 670
Acrobat 3.0, 50, 651, 699
Acrobat Exchange 3.0, 292, 312
Acrobat Pro, 651
Acrobat Reader 3.0, 295-296
ACTION attribute, <FORM> HTML
  tag, 559
Actions Palette (Photoshop 4.0), 359-360
ActiveMovie animations, 354-355
ActiveX, 667, 699
add-ons, 699
    Alien Skin Software, 376
    GIF89a Export, 379
    Photo/Graphic Edges, 374
    PowerPoint presentations, 104
    QTVR Player, 354
    see also extensions
adding
    Master Elements to QuarkXPress docu-
      ments, 195-196
    Web pages to Web sites with HomePage, 491
<ADDRESS> HTML tag, 539
Adjustment Layer (Photoshop 4.0), 360
Adobe Web site, 379, 651
Adobe Acrobat 3.0, 288

PDF Writer printer driver, 291
performance, 289-290
suite utilities, 292-296
Adobe File Utilities, 173-179, 646, 664
    file format compatibility, 173
    HTML element compatibility, 174
Adobe File Utilities 1.0 conversion
  utility, 646
Afterburner, 664
AimTech Web site, 356
alerts (Web page graphics), 359, 405
algorithms, 699
Alien Skin Software add-ons, 376
ALIGN attribute
    <IMG> HTML tag, 340, 550
    <TABLE> HTML tag, 586
Align Text icon, Basic toolbar (HomePage),
  472
alignment, 699
    graphics
        in FrameMaker documents, 243, 260
        in QuarkXPress documents, 200
        in Web pages, 550, 575
        in Web pages with tables, 594-596
        troubleshooting in Web pages with
          HomePage, 482-483
    headers in Web pages, 573-574
    paragraphs in Web pages with HomePage,
      467
    tables in QuarkXPress documents, 204
    text
        in converted ClarisWorks docu-
          ments, 112
        in Web pages, customizing with
          HomePage, 486
        in Web pages, customizing with tables,
          594-596
    Web page content, 27, 35-38
    Web pages, troubleshooting with HomePage,
      480-481

C

I

T

V

X–Y–Z